41: *Afro-American Poets Since 1955,* edited by Trudier Harris and Thadious M. Davis (1985)

42: *American Writers for Children Before 1900,* edited by Glenn E. Estes (1985)

43: *American Newspaper Journalists, 1690-1872,* edited by Perry J. Ashley (1986)

44: *American Screenwriters,* Second Series, edited by Randall Clark, Robert E. Morsberger, and Stephen O. Lesser (1986)

45: *American Poets, 1880-1945,* First Series, edited by Peter Quartermain (1986)

46: *American Literary Publishing Houses, 1900-1980: Trade and Paperback,* edited by Peter Dzwonkoski (1986)

47: *American Historians, 1866-1912,* edited by Clyde N. Wilson (1986)

48: *American Poets, 1880-1945,* Second Series, edited by Peter Quartermain (1986)

49: *American Literary Publishing Houses, 1638-1899,* 2 parts, edited by Peter Dzwonkoski (1986)

50: *Afro-American Writers Before the Harlem Renaissance,* edited by Trudier Harris (1986)

51: *Afro-American Writers from the Harlem Renaissance to 1940,* edited by Trudier Harris (1987)

52: *American Writers for Children Since 1960: Fiction,* edited by Glenn E. Estes (1986)

53: *Canadian Writers Since 1960,* First Series, edited by W. H. New (1986)

54: *American Poets, 1880-1945,* Third Series, 2 parts, edited by Peter Quartermain (1987)

55: *Victorian Prose Writers Before 1867,* edited by William B. Thesing (1987)

56: *German Fiction Writers, 1914-1945,* edited by James Hardin (1987)

57: *Victorian Prose Writers After 1867,* edited by William B. Thesing (1987)

58: *Jacobean and Caroline Dramatists,* edited by Fredson Bowers (1987)

59: *American Literary Critics and Scholars, 1800-1850,* edited by John W. Rathbun and Monica M. Grecu (1987)

60: *Canadian Writers Since 1960,* Second Series, edited by W. H. New (1987)

61: *American Writers for Children Since 1960: Poets, Illustrators, and Nonfiction Authors,* edited by Glenn E. Estes (1987)

62: *Elizabethan Dramatists,* edited by Fredson Bowers (1987)

63: *Modern American Critics, 1920-1955,* edited by Gregory S. Jay (1988)

64: *American Literary Critics and Scholars, 1850-1880,* edited by John W. Rathbun and Monica M. Grecu (1988)

65: *French Novelists, 1900-1930,* edited by Catharine Savage Brosman (1988)

66: *German Fiction Writers, 1885-1913,* 2 parts, edited by James Hardin (1988)

67: *Modern American Critics Since 1955,* edited by Gregory S. Jay (1988)

68: *Canadian Writers, 1920-1959,* First Series, edited by W. H. New (1988)

69: *Contemporary German Fiction Writers,* First Series, edited by Wolfgang D. Elfe and James Hardin (1988)

70: *British Mystery Writers, 1860-1919,* edited by Bernard Benstock and Thomas F. Staley (1988)

71: *American Literary Critics and Scholars, 1880-1900,* edited by John W. Rathbun and Monica M. Grecu (1988)

72: *French Novelists, 1930-1960,* edited by Catharine Savage Brosman (1988)

73: *American Magazine Journalists, 1741-1850,* edited by Sam G. Riley (1988)

74: *American Short-Story Writers Before 1880,* edited by Bobby Ellen Kimbel, with the assistance of William E. Grant (1988)

75: *Contemporary German Fiction Writers,* Second Series, edited by Wolfgang D. Elfe and James Hardin (1988)

76: *Afro-American Writers, 1940-1955,* edited by Trudier Harris (1988)

77: *British Mystery Writers, 1920-1939,* edited by Bernard Benstock and Thomas F. Staley (1988)

78: *American Short-Story Writers, 1880-1910,* edited by Bobby Ellen Kimbel, with the assistance of William E. Grant (1988)

79: *American Magazine Journalists, 1850-1900,* edited by Sam G. Riley (1988)

**(Continued on back endsheets)**

Dictionary of Literary Biography • Volume One Hundred Six

# British Literary Publishing Houses, 1820-1880

Dictionary of Literary Biography • Volume One Hundred Six

# British Literary Publishing Houses, 1820-1880

Edited by
Patricia J. Anderson
*Simon Fraser University*
and
Jonathan Rose
*Drew University*

A Bruccoli Clark Layman Book
Gale Research Inc.
Detroit, London

Printed in the United States of America

Published simultaneously in the United Kingdom
by Gale Research International Limited
(An affiliated company of Gale Research Inc.)

ISBN 0-8103-4586-2
91-13358 CIP

# Contents

# Plan of the Series

*. . . Almost the most prodigious asset of a country, and perhaps its most precious possession, is its native literary product—when that product is fine and noble and enduring.*

Mark Twain*

The advisory board, the editors, and the publisher of the *Dictionary of Literary Biography* are joined in endorsing Mark Twain's declaration. The literature of a nation provides an inexhaustible resource of permanent worth. We intend to make literature and its creators better understood and more accessible to students and the reading public, while satisfying the standards of teachers and scholars.

To meet these requirements, *literary biography* has been construed in terms of the author's achievement. The most important thing about a writer is his writing. Accordingly, the entries in *DLB* are career biographies, tracing the development of the author's canon and the evolution of his reputation.

The purpose of *DLB* is not only to provide reliable information in a convenient format but also to place the figures in the larger perspective of literary history and to offer appraisals of their accomplishments by qualified scholars.

The publication plan for *DLB* resulted from two years of preparation. The project was proposed to Bruccoli Clark by Frederick G. Ruffner, president of the Gale Research Company, in November 1975. After specimen entries were prepared and typeset, an advisory board was formed to refine the entry format and develop the series rationale. In meetings held during 1976, the publisher, series editors, and advisory board approved the scheme for a comprehensive biographical dictionary of persons who contributed to North American literature. Editorial work on the first volume began in January 1977, and it was published in 1978. In order to make *DLB* more than a reference tool and to compile volumes that individually have claim to status as literary history, it was decided to organize volumes by topic, period, or genre. Each of these freestanding volumes provides a biographical-bibliographical guide and overview for a particular area of literature. We are convinced that this organization—as opposed to a single alphabet method—constitutes a valuable innovation in the presentation of reference material. The volume plan necessarily requires many decisions for the placement and treatment of authors who might properly be included in two or three volumes. In some instances a major figure will be included in separate volumes, but with different entries emphasizing the aspect of his career appropriate to each volume. Ernest Hemingway, for example, is represented in *American Writers in Paris, 1920-1939* by an entry focusing on his expatriate apprenticeship; he is also in *American Novelists, 1910-1945* with an entry surveying his entire career. Each volume includes a cumulative index of subject authors and articles. Comprehensive indexes to the entire series are planned.

With volume ten in 1982 it was decided to enlarge the scope of *DLB*. By the end of 1986 twenty-one volumes treating British literature had been published, and volumes for Commonwealth and Modern European literature were in progress. The series has been further augmented by the *DLB Yearbooks* (since 1981) which update published entries and add new entries to keep the *DLB* current with contemporary activity. There have also been *DLB Documentary Series* volumes which provide biographical and critical source materials for figures whose work is judged to have particular interest for students. One of these companion volumes is entirely devoted to Tennessee Williams.

We define literature as the *intellectual commerce of a nation:* not merely as belles lettres but as that ample and complex process by which ideas are generated, shaped, and transmitted. *DLB* entries are not limited to "creative writers" but extend to other figures who in their time and in their way influenced the mind of a people. Thus the series encompasses historians, journalists, publishers, and screenwriters. By this means readers of *DLB* may be aided to perceive litera-

*From an unpublished section of Mark Twain's autobiography, copyright © by the Mark Twain Company.

ture not as cult scripture in the keeping of intellectual high priests but firmly positioned at the center of a nation's life.

*DLB* includes the major writers appropriate to each volume and those standing in the ranks immediately behind them. Scholarly and critical counsel has been sought in deciding which minor figures to include and how full their entries should be. Wherever possible, useful references are made to figures who do not warrant separate entries.

Each *DLB* volume has a volume editor responsible for planning the volume, selecting the figures for inclusion, and assigning the entries. Volume editors are also responsible for preparing, where appropriate, appendices surveying the major periodicals and literary and intellectual movements for their volumes, as well as lists of further readings. Work on the series as a whole is coordinated at the Bruccoli Clark Layman editorial center in Columbia, South Carolina, where the editorial staff is responsible for accuracy of the published volumes.

One feature that distinguishes *DLB* is the illustration policy–its concern with the iconography of literature. Just as an author is influenced by his surroundings, so is the reader's understanding of the author enhanced by a knowledge of his environment. Therefore *DLB* volumes include not only drawings, paintings, and photographs of authors, often depicting them at various stages in their careers, but also illustrations of their families and places where they lived. Title pages are regularly reproduced in facsimile along with dust jackets for modern authors. The dust jackets are a special feature of *DLB* because they often document better than anything else the way in which an author's work was perceived in its own time. Specimens of the writers' manuscripts are included when feasible.

Samuel Johnson rightly decreed that "The chief glory of every people arises from its authors." The purpose of the *Dictionary of Literary Biography* is to compile literary history in the surest way available to us–by accurate and comprehensive treatment of the lives and work of those who contributed to it.

The *DLB* Advisory Board

# Foreword

In his biographical account of the early modern book trade, *Shadows of the Old Booksellers* (1865), the Victorian publisher Charles Knight remarks that among British publishers, printers, and booksellers there had been "scarcely any division" of labor "until very modern times." Common practice had long been for the publisher not only to commission and finance his publications but also to print them and to sell them directly to the public. When specialization did begin it was, as Knight notes, "of very slow growth."

Indeed, it was some two decades into the nineteenth century before publishing emerged in any significant way as a distinct trade, increasingly separate from printing and bookselling. Around 1820 some businesses founded earlier in the century, or in the 1700s, began to assume, in Knight's words, "less of a retail and even a peddling character" as they gradually turned from printing and direct selling to publishing; firms founded in or after 1820 were apt to establish themselves principally as publishers. Thus, 1820 marks the approximate time that specialization in the book trade becomes readily discernible from today's perspective.

As the century progressed, the railway and telegraph facilitated distribution of books and communication within the trade. There was a decreasing need for any single business to perform more than one function, and specialization became still more common. One sign of this trend was the appearance of trade publications, each representative of a particular branch—for example, the *Publishers' Circular* in 1837 and the *Bookseller* in 1858. In the early 1860s the distinction among trade functions had developed almost as fully as it ever would, and only a minority of firms continued in more than one capacity. By the early years of the twentieth century the process of separation would be virtually complete.

From about the mid 1800s one sees increasing regulation of the trade. The Copyright Act of 1842 protected authors for a longer period than had any previous legislation: forty-two years from first publication or seven years after the author's death, whichever was longer. The year 1846 saw the earliest use of the International Copyright Act of 1838, which allowed for the sale of the foreign rights and reduced the incidence of piracy. In 1848 booksellers attempted to develop a general system of fixed prices for books, but such regulation would not come into effect until the 1900 Net Book Agreement among authors, publishers, and booksellers.

Other important trends also marked the years between 1820 and 1880. In *Shadows of the Old Booksellers* Knight observes that "this modern era is remarkable for an extended commerce in books." Reading societies and circulating libraries such as Mudie's played a central role in "rendering the demand [for reading material] to a considerable degree certain." Rising literacy—the result of widespread working-class self-instruction and the 1870 act providing general access to elementary education—further increased the demand for books. Additionally, the introduction of the steam-powered press early in the century and later advances in the mechanization of printing so encouraged the low-cost dissemination of printed matter that by 1850 many publishers were catering to what was even by today's standards a mass market—one that would continue to grow in the twentieth century.

Meanwhile, people's preferences in reading material changed dramatically. In 1820 poetry had long enjoyed the greatest favor; forty years later the novel was the predominant popular form. The latter's rise to popularity was much facilitated by the common practice of serial publication in widely affordable parts. When it was not serialized the novel was for the most part marketed in a three-volume format designed mainly to cater to the requirements of the influential Mudie's and other major circulating libraries. By the mid 1890s these establishments no longer favored the "three-decker," and it gave way to the single-volume novel.

The character and structure of the individual publishing business also underwent modification. During the early 1800s publishers most often operated as sole proprietorships or as partnerships of family members or friends. By the third quarter of the century the family partnership was still common, but so were formal partnerships established for primarily commercial motives. Partnerships of the latter kind were regularly entered into and dissolved, but rarely were there large mergers or takeovers. At this time only a few publishing houses took advantage of the limited liability allowed for in legislation of 1862.

These broad developments are reflected and elaborated on in this volume's individual entries. In selecting the publishing houses to be included we have adopted a wide definition of *literary*. Entries thus treat not only publishers of literature in the restricted sense of high-culture fiction, fine poetry, and the literary essay, but also take in publishers of light fiction for a mass market, general nonfiction, criticism, specialized academic studies, art books, and limited editions which might themselves be regarded as visual art. Coverage ranges from major publishing houses in existence for a century or more to small, short-lived private presses; from general trade publishers to those catering to a specialist market; from producers of popular romance to university presses. The majority of the houses discussed here are, or were, based in London, which has been the center of the British book trade since the early nineteenth century; but other publishers of note throughout the United Kingdom are also represented. Vanity presses and imprints controlled by political or religious sects are not included, nor are those houses whose main output falls beyond the sphere of what we have defined as literary—for instance, publishers of timetables; technical manuals; legal, medical, and other professional casebooks; and textbooks. We have also excluded newspaper and magazine presses and printing firms that were not substantially publishers of books. Where pertinent, entries trace their subjects' eighteenth-century antecedents and pursue their history to the present day, if they still survive, or to the point at which they ceased operations.

The heading of each entry lists the name by which a given publisher is best known, the location of its headquarters, and the years during which the firm bore that name. Many publishing houses underwent multiple name changes, and these changes and their dates are noted in subordinate headings. Some houses began as printer/publishers or booksellers; others did not operate continuously as publishers in their early years. Such matters are explained in the texts of the entries. Where applicable and when the information is available, each entry also discusses major changes in the firm's ownership, organizational structure, and management; mergers with other publishers and the acquisition of imprints; bankruptcies and lawsuits; influential editors and major authors; areas of specialization and noteworthy sidelines; and important and representative titles published by the firm. The primary focus is the publication of books, but part-issue fiction, magazines, newspapers, and academic and trade journals are usually noted as well. Each entry concludes with a list of references to aid further research on the particular firm; additionally, a general bibliography on modern British publishing is appended to the volume.

In a majority of cases a substantial amount of the information presented is the product of archival and other primary source research—much of which is published here for the first time. Our contributors have endeavored to augment and bring up to date material contained in previous general surveys and studies of British publishing history. Because of their comprehensiveness a few such studies have proven particularly helpful: Robin Myers's *The British Book Trade* (1973), Frank Mumby and Ian Norrie's *Publishing and Bookselling* (1974), and John Feather's *A History of British Publishing* (1988) provide invaluable historical and bibliographical information. At present, wide-ranging histories of British publishing are comparatively scarce. There is, however, a good deal of research under way on both sides of the Atlantic, and our efforts here are part of a vigorous and growing branch of historical scholarship. It is our hope that this project will facilitate the endeavors of others in the field and thus provide a useful link between pioneering works like Mumby's and studies yet to follow.

*—Patricia J. Anderson and Jonathan Rose*

# Acknowledgments

This book was produced by Bruccoli Clark Layman, Inc. Karen L. Rood is senior editor for the *Dictionary of Literary Biography* series. Philip B. Dematteis was the in-house editor.

Production coordinator is James W. Hipp. Systems manager is Charles D. Brower. Photography editors are Edward Scott and Timothy D. Lundy. Permissions editor is Jean W. Ross. Layout and graphics supervisor is Penney L. Haughton. Copyediting supervisor is Bill Adams. Typesetting supervisor is Kathleen M. Flanagan. Information systems analyst is George F. Dodge. Charles Lee Egleston is editorial associate. The production staff includes Rowena Betts, Polly Brown, Teresa Chaney, Patricia Coate, Sarah A. Estes, Robert Fowler, Mary L. Goodwin, Ellen McCracken, Kathy Lawler Merlette, Laura Garren Moore, John Myrick, Pamela D. Norton, Cathy J. Reese, Laurrè Sinckler-Reeder, Maxine K. Smalls, and Betsy L. Weinberg.

Walter W. Ross and Timothy D. Tebalt did library research. They were assisted by the following librarians at the Thomas Cooper Library of the University of South Carolina: Jens Holley and the interlibrary-loan staff; Roger Mortimer and the staff of the Department of Rare Books and Special Collections; reference librarians Gwen Baxter, Daniel Boice, Faye Chadwell, Jo Cottingham, Cathy Eckman, Rhonda Felder, Gary Geer, Jackie Kinder, Laurie Preston, Jean Rhyne, Carol Tobin, Virginia Weathers, and Connie Widney; circulation-department head Thomas Marcil; and acquisitions-searching supervisor David Haggard.

The editors are, above all, grateful to our contributors for their expertise, diligent efforts, and support throughout this project. We would additionally like to thank the following individuals for their generous advice and help: Robin Alston, Richard D. Altick, Diana Athill, William R. Blackmore, Thomas F. Burns, Simon Cobley, Robert A. Colby, D. Steven Corey, Penny Cornwall, Sally Davison, Robin de Beaumont, Charlotte de la Bedoyere, Andre Deutsch, Charmazel Dudt, Tim Farmlicoe, John Feather, Sally Floyer, Norman Franklin, Paul F. Gehl, Vicky Groot, John Handford, Michael Harris, Louis James, Catherine Johnston, Roger Lubbock, E. J. W. McCann, Bill McCullen, Liz Newlands, Robert L. Patten, William S. Peterson, Martin Redfern, Max Reinhardt, Briar Silich, Reinhard S. Speck, Peter Stansky, Philip Sturrock, James D. Startt, Gillian Watson, Tony Whittome, and Ian Willison.

The author of the William Milner entry, Victor Neuburg, wishes to express his deepest thanks to Mr. C. R. Eastwood of Bridgwater, whose unpublished manuscript, "William Milner of Halifax," was invaluable in the writing of the entry. He is also grateful to Miss M. B. Halstead of Enfield for drawing his attention to a series of articles on Milner by D. Bridge in the *Courier* of Halifax.

# British Literary Publishing Houses, 1820-1880

# Dictionary of Literary Biography

## Aberdeen University Press Limited
*(Aberdeen, Scotland: 1900-   )*
## G. and R. King
*(Aberdeen: 1840-1850)*
## Arthur King and Company
*(Aberdeen: 1850-1900)*

Aberdeen University Press has never had any formal relationship with Aberdeen University; it did not effectively become a publisher until it was taken over by Robert Maxwell in 1978; and there was no firm named Aberdeen University Press until 1900. There is, however, a clear line of descent from the publishing firm which the brothers George and Robert King established in Aberdeen in 1840. George King had opened a bookshop in one of the new thoroughfares of a bustling and prosperous Aberdeen in 1826. This shop provided a more stable living than his previous occupation as "bagman," a hawker of books around the towns, villages, and farm settlements of Buchan. Robert King had begun in bookselling in nearby Peterhead but had expanded into printing and publishing. George's increasing success in the larger town brought Robert to Aberdeen and into a partnership with his brother in 1840. Robert died in 1845, his immortality guaranteed in a limited sort of way by his book *The Covenanters in the North* (1846), published by G. and R. King. The firm withdrew from its printing activities in 1850 and from publishing in 1866 but continued trading as booksellers. George King, however, retained some personal interest in publishing. He had been cofounder of a weekly newspaper, the *North of Scotland Gazette*, in 1847, and this paper had been succeeded in 1853 by the *Aberdeen Free Press*. He was a bibliophile who had collected more than four thousand pamphlets dating back to the seventeenth century. The pamphlets were

bound in 405 half-calf volumes and, after his death in 1872, were donated to Aberdeen University Library.

A third brother, Arthur King, had set up a separate printing business in the city and seems to have taken over George and Robert King's business in 1850. *The Phaedo of Plato* by W. D. "Homer" Geddes, published by Williams and Norgate in 1863, and Alexander Bain's *English Composition and Rhetoric*, published by Longmans, Green, Reader and Dyer in 1866, were printed by Arthur King and Company. George King also sent much of the printing work of the *Aberdeen Free Press* his brother's way. After Arthur's death in 1870 Arthur King and Company was managed for a while by his son; the son took little interest in the business, preferring to pursue a career in journalism.

Arthur King and Company was taken over by John Thomson and two partners in 1872, but Thomson rapidly emerged as the driving force behind the firm and became sole owner in 1887. This dynamic figure increased the turnover, acquiring much of Aberdeen University's printing and successfully seeking work from several London publishers. By 1887 the work force had quadrupled, and it continued to expand. Thomson introduced female compositors into the case room, despite the hostility of the printers' union; this victory for women's emancipation also lowered the wage bill and increased management control over the tightly knit male printers. In 1900 male apprentices earned six shillings a week while

*John Thomson, the "driving force" in Aberdeen printing and publishing from 1872, when he became part owner of Arthur King and Company until his death in 1911 (portrait by Robert Brough; from Alexander Keith,* Aberdeen University Press, *1963)*

trained case-room girls, outside the formalized career ladder of apprentice/journeyman/master, earned five shillings and sixpence. Alexander Keith gives a striking illustration of Thomson's management style: "the then very limited and primitive toilet accommodation was kept locked, and the key lay on the master's desk." By 1905 the company, by then under new management, had 199 employees. Until his death in 1911 Thomson dominated printing in Aberdeen. Indeed, his influence was felt and his reputation known throughout the United Kingdom.

The Aberdeen University Press Limited, registered as a public company in late 1900, was formed under the convenership of Sir William Ramsay, Professor of Humanity (Latin) at King's College, to take over the business of Arthur King and Company. Thomson remained as a director and seems to have mitigated the authoritarian na-

ture of his industrial relations by distributing one thousand of his personal shares in the new enterprise among the oldest members of his staff. In its first year Aberdeen University Press made a gross profit of £4,823, a net profit of £1,755, and paid out an ordinary dividend of 6 percent. The press had no formal connection with Aberdeen University, although informal links existed through the presence of various university worthies at various times on its board of directors. It was purely a printing company, attempting to compensate for its geographical peripherality by undertaking specialist typesetting, such as mathematical works and foreign scripts. The most significant printing task executed by Aberdeen University Press was the *Bibliotheca Lindesiana* (1910), the catalogue of the library at Haigh Hall of the earl of Crawford and Balcarres. The earl wrote in the introduction "For many years the University Press of Aberdeen has undertaken all my work, and the printing was entrusted to the establishment. It is right that I should here express my warm thanks to Mr. Thomson for the constant care and attention which have been given to the work. He has allowed the galleys to remain standing since the commencement, for convenience of arrangement, and at one time there were very nearly five tons of type set up ready for printing. Another feature which should be noted is the fact that almost every language is represented in its own character (of course with a transcription or translation)." Aberdeen University Press also undertook the catalogues of the Mingana Collections of Middle Eastern manuscripts in the John Rylands Library in Manchester. Aberdeen University Press and its forerunners have been associated with the production of several notable periodicals, for example, *Mind* (since 1887), the *Annual Register* (since 1892), and the *English Historical Review* (since 1934). Its work also formed one of the key early influences on many past generations of British schoolchildren in the form of the Janet and John Primary Readers.

Aberdeen University Press has expanded by buying out a great deal of the local competition: the Rosemount Press fell in 1932; William Jackson, a bookbinder, lost its independence in 1949 after nearly a century; John Avery and Company, with a pedigree almost as long as that of Aberdeen University Press itself, was taken over in 1953; and Edmond and Spark, founded in 1807 and therefore the oldest vintage of all, was absorbed in 1966. The press did not do any publishing, apart from a limited number of one-shot books of specialist or local interest. By 1970 perhaps half of its business came from the printing of books and journals, chiefly educational in nature, and the other half from general, or jobbing, printing and bookbinding. In that year Aberdeen University Press was itself taken over by the British Bank of Commerce. Under the new ownership Aberdeen University Press absorbed the Central Press and G. Cornwall and Sons with its subsidiary, the White Heather Publishing Company.

In 1978 Aberdeen University Press became a wholly owned subsidiary of Robert Maxwell's Pergamon Press. That year the press became a publisher again for the first time since 1850. Aberdeen University Press built up an impressive list in the fields of Scottish literature, history, and politics and through its publications has contributed to the revival of interest in national and local matters. Its publication in 1985 of the *Concise Scots Dictionary*, edited by Mairi Robinson, achieved critical and popular acclaim; it also published the

*Scottish National Dictionary* (1931-1976) and publishes the *Dictionary of the Older Scottish Tongue* (beginning with volume three in 1983). A compact list in the fields of medicine, health care, and mental health has been expanded. In 1989 the printing and publishing divisions were divorced. The former became part of BPCC (British Printing and Communications Corporation); the latter, as Aberdeen University Press Limited (Publishers), remains a constituent part of the Maxwell Macmillan Pergamon Publishing Corporation, which is itself part of the Maxwell Communications Corporation.

**Reference:**

Alexander Keith, *Aberdeen University Press: An Account of the Press from Its Foundation in 1840 until Its Occupation of New Premises in 1963* (Aberdeen: Aberdeen University Press, 1963).

*—Alistair McCleery*

# George Allen
*(Orpington, Kent & London: 1871-1911)*
## George Allen and Company Limited
*(London: 1911-1913)*

Although the firm's name is now better known through its later incorporation into the Allen and Unwin imprints, between 1871 and 1913 George Allen ran one of the most important British publishing houses. The firm's significance lay not in its bringing out especially important books or developing a specialist list of outstanding quality but in its persistent attacks on conventional bookselling and publishing practices. These attacks resulted from the firm's role not just as John Ruskin's publisher but as a public manifestation—in the early years of its existence, at least—of Ruskin's social, economic, and commercial theories. In its later years the firm established a reputation for the publication of reprinted literary classics in gift-book formats, designed and illustrated by many of the outstanding book artists of the 1890s. The main significance of the later history of the firm up to its bankruptcy in 1913 lies in the modifications made to the Ruskinian critique of book production and bookselling formulated in the 1870s. The radicalism of Ruskin's original attack was slackened and diffused under Allen's cautious stewardship, as Ruskin himself withdrew more and more from public life due to illness and insanity. Even so, George Allen and Company's role in influencing some of the major legislative reforms of late Victorian publishing was widely acknowledged and celebrated by contemporaries.

Born in 1832, George Allen came to London in 1849 to serve an apprenticeship as a carpenter in his uncle's building firm. He became a highly skilled joiner, worked on the interiors of Dorchester House, and, as a student of drawing at the Working Men's College in the early 1850s, met Ruskin. Allen quickly became assistant drawing master at the college, while continuing to study engraving under Ruskin and other printmaking techniques under Thomas Goff Lupton. (The high quality of his work can be seen from his engravings for Ruskin's books, most notably the 1879 one-volume edition of the first six parts of *Prosperpina*.) Allen's skills as a joiner brought him an offer to become craftsman in charge of furniture for Morris and Company, and another to be superintendent of the furnishings of the royal palace. But Allen's personal devotion to Ruskin caused him to enter Ruskin's service as engraver, copyist, fellow geologist, and general assistant. Allen's capabilities and probity made him an obvious choice to run Ruskin's experimental publishing business. As Frank Arthur Mumby and Frances H. S. Stallybrass put it, sentimentally but not inaccurately: "Thus it was, at a week's notice, and with no previous experience of the trade, that Allen was set up as Ruskin's publisher in 1871, 'in the middle of a country field,' as one of Ruskin's trade critics expressed it at the time." Certainly a cottage in Keston, Kent, was an odd place to establish a major publishing house, and Allen, for all his Victorian virtues, an odd man to run it.

The George Allen firm was established in 1871 to distribute Ruskin's *Fors Clavigera*, a monthly publication aimed at "the workmen and labourers of Great Britain." Allen was charged additionally with launching the "Revised and Enlarged" edition of Ruskin's works, a long-contemplated project of Ruskin's to focus attention on his social, cultural, and economic theories rather than on his writings on art and architecture. Initially Allen was to be a distributor of books rather than a publisher, and this function was carried on well into the 1880s. The firm of Smith, Elder remained Ruskin's printers for several years after 1871, and in the original scheme was to act jointly with Allen in publishing the "Revised and Enlarged" volumes. Ruskin's increasing sense of his role as a social conscience for the age meant, however, that his relatively small-scale plans rapidly evolved into a polemical gesture in which he used George Allen to attack what he saw as the three great evils of the bookselling trade: the discount system, underselling, and the monopoly of London-based publishers and booksellers over the trade.

Ruskin's attack on the discount system was based on his belief that middlemen—booksellers and publishers—were exploiting the labor and therefore the "worth" of authors by making profits from their works. The value of literary productions, he believed, ought to be established by the unmediated response of the readers rather than by the commercial interests which controlled book production. Ruskin's contempt for underselling was based on similar arguments: the cost of a book under this system was falsely determined in the marketplace by a form of haggling. Ruskin was interested in value, not cost, and believed that value was established by readers' recognition of the amount of labor and intellectual 'worth' that went into the making of a book. The London-based monopoly of publishing and bookselling, which was largely controlled by the gentlemanly entrepreneurs who were his father's friends, further infuriated Ruskin and led him to seek a rural base for the production and distribution of his books. Ruskin insisted on extremely high standards of book production for his works: the books were to be simple, substantial, long-lasting, and (in a sophisticatedly restrained way) elegant, thus exemplifying the ideas of functional craftsmanship which had informed all of his anti-industrial, anti-Victorian writings on work. One consequence was that the price of the "Revised and Enlarged" volumes was extremely high; the high price, coupled with Ruskin's policy of not advertising his works (because advertisement would pervert the direct dialogue over value established

*George Allen*

between author, text, and reader) and his refusal to use booksellers (so that his works were available only by mail from Allen's home in Kent), meant that Allen began his business with a substantial, perhaps even crippling, burden.

Whatever the commercial consequences of his publishing policies, Ruskin's grasp of their polemical potential was brilliant. Through *Fors Clavigera*, through letters to the press, and through his personal correspondence Ruskin succeeded in the 1870s in constructing a running debate with his public in which practice was continually referred back to theory. The combination of hostile vested interests (publishers and booksellers), anxious friends and well-wishers, and the workingmen and women whom he had sought to legitimate as serious readers through *Fors Clavigera*, provided Ruskin with a wonderfully diverse audience to harangue, irritate, and cajole.

Allen, as a faithful retainer and convinced Ruskinian, was left to try to develop the firm in commercially sound directions without destroying the ideological force of Ruskin's attack on commercial practices in the 1870s. He achieved this goal by gradually making concessions to conventional business practice. In 1882 Allen, with Ruskin's support, entered into an agreement with the booksellers which established fixed discounts and consistent prices for Ruskin's works. The booksellers had approached Ruskin in the matter, and both Ruskin himself and later critics have seen this agreement as a triumph for Ruskinian principle. The truth is that the booksellers, whom Ruskin had wanted to abolish, made some concessions, but from 1882 on Allen used the very discounting and net pricing arrangements which Ruskin's earlier writing had sought to destroy altogether.

The key change for the firm in the 1880s was Ruskin's withdrawal from much practical engagement with the business due to illness, overwork, and other interests. In many ways Ruskin's absence was helpful to Allen in that it allowed him to develop the business as he wished without continual reference to the "Master" (as Ruskin's position in the Guild of St. George entitled him to be called). But Ruskin's illness also meant that many of the ideas which had seemed radical and urgent while they were being formulated in the 1870s came to seem fossilized and even absurd as they were overtaken by events. Allen had to tread a thin line between betraying Ruskin's publicly argued and ferociously defended views on commercial practice, on the one hand, and acknowledging the commercial and practical needs of what was becoming a substantial publishing concern, on the other. His problems were complicated by Ruskin's increasing dependence on income from his books as his inherited fortune was spent on large-scale projects, and by Allen's not altogether happy relationships with Ruskin's guardians and nurses at Brantwood. If the development of the George Allen firm in the 1880s seems largely one of consolidation through cautious development, there were underlying tensions between dependence and self-reliance, between old ideas and new contexts, between Orpington and Brantwood, which Allen never fully resolved.

In one respect, however, even in these years of increasing conventionality George Allen did offer a progressive attitude to publishing. Ruskin's cult of honest worth in commodities had led him to deplore foreign pirated editions of his work, a view shared by most major Victorian authors. Allen's devotion to Ruskin's opinions led him to be particularly fierce in his opposition to unauthorized editions, and he used his increasingly prominent position in the publishing world to campaign for copyright protection. When the Chace Act was passed in 1891, Allen was one of the first publishers to try to use its provisions to obtain some returns from America. Although the act caused almost as many difficulties as it solved for British publishers in trying to protect their literary property, Allen's Ruskin-inspired activities doubtless helped to formulate international copyright legislation.

The rural setting for Allen's activities was finally overtaken by commercial and practical imperatives, and in 1893 Allen moved to 156 Charing Cross Road in London. Allen continued to produce lavish editions of Ruskin's works with many plates, wide margins, handmade papers, and fine bindings: the two-volume *Poems* (1891), the revised edition of *The Oxford Museum* (1893), and *Verona and Other Lectures* (1894). He also published some lavish critical and biographical works on Ruskin. In these publications Allen was pursuing the interest in luxury-book production shown by some of his 1880s projects—notably *Wren's City Churches* (1883) and such uncharacteristically austere Ruskin volumes as *The Art of England* (1884) and *The Storm-Cloud of the Nineteenth Century* (1884), which look forward to the chaste simplicity of the Doves and Nonesuch private press books. Allen's major publications in the 1890s, however, look away from these experimental 1880s books back to more stolid mid-Victorian conceptions of the "book beautiful." Allen also continued and extended the reprints of small-format editions of Ruskin's works which he had begun in the late 1880s. The constant production and distribution of these green cloth octavo reprints formed the basis of Allen's business and kept the firm commercially viable during its major shifts in business practice. In both financial and historical terms the three most important books of the decade for Allen were the small octavo editions of *Fors Clavigera* (1896), *Modern Painters* (1897), and *The Stones of Venice* (1898). Given the limited circulation of these famous books in their expensive early editions, their sales figures in their new small format are important: 1,802 volumes of *Fors Clavigera* were sold in the first six months of 1896 and 2,459 in the second. By the beginning of 1898 Allen was able to claim of *Modern Painters* that "the public appreciate this new small edition. I am at the very tail end of the 3,000 copies and have already ordered a reprint." Even the absent Ruskin was at last forced to recognize the demands of the popular market, which his idealism had frustrated for so long. By the late 1890s Allen was able to begin to exploit the enormous popular market for Ruskin which he had long known to exist, but which Ruskin's intellectual legacy had forced him to deny.

The non-Ruskin books Allen published in the 1890s reflect his training in engraving and book illustration thirty years earlier. He brought out mainly expensive books with copious illustrations; most of these books were memoirs, biographies, or reprints of literary classics with new plates. The biographies included a lavish work on Lord Horatio Nelson; Augustus Hare's *The Story of Two Noble Lives* (1893), *The Gurneys of Earlham* (1895), and *The Story of My Life* (1896-1900); Helen Pelham Dale's *The Life and Letters of Thomas Pelham Dale* (1894); and a few other forgettable if well-produced works. The reprints Allen brought out were also attractive, if predictable—Jane Austen's *Pride and Prejudice* (1894) and Samuel Richardson's *Sir Charles Grandison* (1895) illustrated by Chris Hammond; Oliver Goldsmith's *Comedies* (1896); the "Pensees," a series of selected aphorisms from established writers; and—most ambitious of all and in conscious homage to the Kelmscott Press *Works of Geoffrey Chaucer* (1896)—Edmund Spenser's *Faerie Queene* (1897), lavishly illustrated by Walter Crane. Allen chose artists with some flair, within the conventional limits of his taste. His reprints were excellently produced but rather dull. Allen's other specialties included fairy tales, folktales, and legends, an interest undoubtedly fostered by the presence of Joseph Jacobs as his literary adviser. Yet even with Jacobs's influence, Allen produced nothing as successful as Jacobs's series of tales illustrated by J. D. Batten and published by David Nutt. Here as in so much else Allen was a follower rather than an innovator. Another field of interest was genteel travel books, especially those by Hare, which sold steadily for many years. Before 1898 Allen published no novels, although he was sent many manuscripts, nor any original poetry, although again he often had opportunities to do so. He deliberately limited his interests, and even within these limits he was a cautious and stolid publisher.

When Ruskin's books began to come out of copyright early in the new century, Allen had no real answer to the flood of cheap editions which followed, and his subsequent bankruptcy was assured—especially as none of Allen's children had the same determination or ability as their fa-

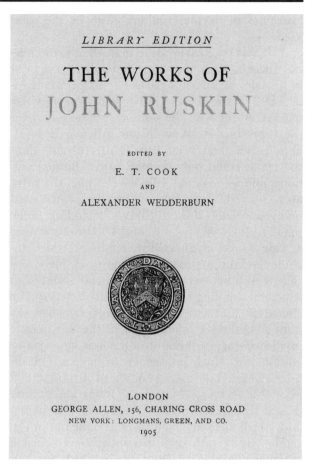

*Title page for volume 17 of the thirty-nine-volume Library Edition of Ruskin's works. Although Allen died before the edition was completed, it was the crowning achievement of his career.*

ther. The firm had never been hugely successful, and it had never extended its list far beyond Ruskin's works. The narrow if idealistic policy of producing mainly "fine" books was entirely the result of Allen's tastes and interests. As he revealingly put it in a letter, "I am always interested in works where the illustrations constitute an important part," and the firm's correspondence contains an enormous number of letters to artists. Allen's illustrators form a distinguished list: Hugh Thompson, C. E. Brock, Walter Crane, Chris Hammond, Arthur Gaskin, T. H. Robinson, Heywood Sumner, Linley Samborne, and Phil May. Allen was a perfectionist when it came to the reproduction of plates; his constant attention to detail and to quality had undoubtedly been learned in his apprenticeship with Ruskin. As an engraver Allen had an interest in literature. In his 1896 list, for example, out of a total of twenty-four titles by authors other than Ruskin and Hare, fifteen could be classed as illustrated books; and great emphasis is laid on the illustrators in the descriptions given by the catalogue.

It was on Ruskin alone that Allen's commercial success, such as it was, depended; and even in his sales of Ruskin's books he was primarily interested in the luxury rather than the popular market. Along with the infinite care he took over the reproduction of his plates, Allen gave bindings, paper, and print equally careful attention; the result could only be high prices, limited editions, and large-paper editions in which the print area covered hardly any of the page. Allen used many specially chosen papers, including some made to his own specification; he also advertised a wide range of alternative bindings, which included vellum, morocco, half-morocco, roan, and calf in addition to cloth. He frequently offered to supervise bindings personally even down to the choice of color and the style of tooling. Allen seldom published a major work in the last decade of the century without an attendant large-paper edition, for which he seemed to have a guaranteed market. The special edition of Ruskin's 1873 essay *The Poetry of Architecture* (1893) was a fairly typical example, with large margins, fine plates, and, needless to say, high costs. It came out in December 1892 with only two subscribers refusing to pay the ten shillings, sixpence by which the published price exceeded the subscription. The demand for these expensive books was strong, but it showed signs of faltering in the last five years of the century. The three-decker novel was giving way to the cheap single-volume edition as readership expanded even below the class of relatively well-off artisans. The days when *The Poetry of Architecture* could make the *Bookman* best-seller list even with a price of one pound, one shilling had gone. Yet Allen, in spite of the evidence of his accounts, could not bear to compromise the standards he had learned from Ruskin.

Allen succeeded as a publisher in the 1890s neither through the literary quality of his books (Ruskin excepted) nor through wide sales but through catering for a small but constant market in luxury goods which allowed him to express an unwavering attention to detail. Letters in Allen's hand range from requests to his office boy's parents to get their son up earlier to an order for a new coal scuttle for the Charing Cross Road premises. Even though Allen's sons William and Hugh and his daughter Grace took much of the day-to-day business off their father's hands, including most of the work of seeing the small reprints of Ruskin's work through the sometimes unwilling

press of Ballantyne and Hanson in Edinburgh, Allen continued to dominate the firm. His letters suggest that he was a hard but not unfair businessman constantly pressed for time and, on occasion, money. He demanded prompt, precise, and accurate work and had little sympathy with inefficiency, and his letters suggest that he saw his work as a constant struggle against incompetence and bad workmanship. His complaints are often petty, but they stem from the perfectionist's intolerance and from overwork rather than from any unpleasantness of disposition. Perhaps as a result of his artisan origins, Allen's business manner was autocratic, demanding, seldom generous, and brusque to a fault. The burden he had inherited from Ruskin brought him, it seems, more responsibility than pleasure. He remained an old-style genteel Victorian publisher for whom taste was more important than profit, and whose contempt for mass-circulation cheap literature, learned from Ruskin, never abated. Such radicalism as his firm expressed in the 1890s was more the product of Allen's reverence for and sense of duty toward Ruskin than of any temperamental or ideological inclination toward the progressive or controversial.

The seeds of the failure of George Allen had been sown by Allen's failure to expand his list beyond his own limited tastes in the 1890s, but the immediate cause of the firm's demise was the expiration of the Ruskin copyrights seven years after the author's death in 1900. Allen had tried to prepare cheap popular editions of the works, but a combination of his own meticulousness, Ruskin's still pervasive influence, and major developments in the cheap-book market made the firm's survival difficult. Allen died in 1907, with the great thirty-nine-volume Library Edition of Ruskin's *Works* (1903-1912), edited by E. T. Cook and Alexander Wedderburn, still half-finished. He was succeeded by his children, who bought out the publishing business of the Derby-based printers and publishers Bemrose and Son in 1909. In 1911 Swan Sonnenschein and Company was added to the business, which was reformulated under the name George Allen and Company Limited. Despite the relinquishing of the expensive Charing Cross Road premises in 1909 for new premises in Rathbone Place, Oxford Street, the firm soon found itself in difficulties, and it entered into receivership in 1913. In 1914 the firm's assets were sold to Stanley Unwin, and a new company, George Allen and Unwin Limited, was formed.

**References:**

H. J. Keefe, *A Century in Print: The Story of Hazell's, 1839-1939* (London: Hazell, Watson & Viney, 1939);

Brian E. Maidment, "Author and Publisher—John Ruskin and George Allen 1890-1900," *Business Archives*, no. 36 ( June 1972): 21-32;

Maidment, "John Ruskin and George Allen," Ph.D. thesis, University of Leicester, 1973;

Maidment, "John Ruskin, George Allen, and American Pirated Books," *Publishing History*, 9 (1981): 5-20;

Maidment, ed., *Archives of British Publishers—George Allen & Co.* (Bishops Stortford: Chadwyck-Healey, 1973);

Frank Arthur Mumby and Frances H. S. Stallybrass, *From Swan Sonnenschein to George Allen & Unwin* (London: Allen & Unwin, 1935).

—*Brian E. Maidment*

---

# J. W. Arrowsmith
*(Bristol: 1871-1911)*

# Evans and Arrowsmith
*(Bristol: 1854-1857)*

# Isaac Arrowsmith
*(Bristol: 1857-1871)*

# J. W. Arrowsmith Limited
*(London: 1911-   )*

The Bristol bookselling firm of H. C. Evans in Clare Street took Isaac Arrowsmith into partnership in 1854 when he arrived in the city from Worcester. Arrowsmith had previously been employed in the printing trade and had been a publisher of a newspaper, the *Worcester Chronicle*. In Bristol he quickly developed his interest in printing and his new business soon established a reputation in that field.

At this time provincial printers often became provincial publishers, particularly if a title of local interest was involved. Indeed, Arrowsmith had already published such an item in Worcester: *The Consecration of St. Mary's Church, Abberley, Worcestershire* (1852), by John Noake. In

July 1854 Evans and Arrowsmith began to publish *Time Tables and General Advertiser for Bristol, Bath, the Western Counties, and South Wales: Steam Packets and Railway Trains*. Other publications followed, the most notable being the second edition of John Addington Symonds's *Sleep and Dreams: Two Lectures Delivered at the Bristol Literary and Philosophical Institution* (1857), but publishing was only a sideline and the basis of the business was bookselling and job printing. (The title-page imprint of *Sleep and Dreams* is Longmans, Brown; but the name Arrowsmith appears in the printer's colophon, and Symonds says in the preface: "I had no thought of putting so slight a work again before the public, until Mr. Arrowsmith in-

*11 Quay Street, Bristol, the home of Arrowsmith from 1857 until 1954. Printing presses occupied the basement.*

formed me that there was a demand for it, sufficient to make him desirous of printing it at his own risk.")

In 1857 a dispute arose between Evans and Arrowsmith, the details of which remain vague; as a result the partnership was dissolved, and Arrowsmith set up in business on his own. He moved to 11 Quay Street and began trading purely as a printer.

In 1862 Isaac's son James Williams Arrowsmith abandoned his career as a builder and joined his father's firm. Printing remained an important part of the business, but under the guidance of J. W. Arrowsmith publishing rose to prominence. Father and son continued to work together at printing and publishing until Isaac Arrowsmith died in 1871. During these years the publications were still limited to items of local interest, such as the Bristol and Exeter Railway's *General Regulations for the Traffic Department* (1869) and J. S. Handcock's *Bristol and Clifton Street Directory for 1870*. There were also at least two works by Mary Carpenter, a well-known philanthropist who had founded several schools for poor children in Bristol. After his father's death J. W.

Arrowsmith carried on with the printing business and with similar publications: for example, James F. Nicholls and J. Taylor's *Bristol Past and Present* (1881-1882), published in fortnightly parts and then in three volumes; and more works by Carpenter. Books of more general interest also appeared: Frank Desprez's *Readings and Gossip about Rings* (1877), John Lewellin's *Bells and Bell-founding: A Practical Treatise on Church Bells* (1879), and Helen Blackburn's *A Handbook for Women Engaged in Social and Political Work* (1881).

In 1881 Arrowsmith seems to have made up his mind to widen the scope of his publications, and he persevered despite two initial setbacks. His first attempt began when he invited twelve friends to dinner and suggested that each of them write a piece for the first number of a new Christmas annual he planned to publish. The result was *Thirteen at Dinner and What Came of It: Being Arrowsmith's Christmas Annual 1881*. The public showed no interest in the book. Arrowsmith's second Christmas annual was *Brown Eyes* (1882), by May Crommelin. As before, the book went unnoticed and unsold. Arrowsmith still did not lose faith in his project, and the third Christmas annual, Hugh Conway's *Called Back*, appeared in 1883.

In early 1884 sales of *Called Back* looked just as hopeless as those for the previous annuals; but then the book was reviewed by Henry Labouchere, the outspoken radical politician and journalist, in his popular and influential magazine *Truth*: "Who Arrowsmith is and who Hugh Conway is I do not know, but . . . Wilkie Collins never penned a more enthralling story. I am in despair at thinking that I have read it. Those who have not, have a pleasure to look forward to." Arrowsmith's fortunes were changed immediately. For the next eighteen months, one of Arrowsmith's presses, and sometimes more than one, was continually at work on reprints of the book. In the first ten years more than 365,000 copies were sold. Copyright expired on the title in 1933, and up to that time the book was never out of print.

The profits from *Called Back* obviously gave Arrowsmith stability and confidence, but they do not explain his ability, previously not at all apparent, to go on discovering successful authors and books in almost constant succession. Labouchere's review would account for the remarkable sales of *Called Back* but not for the sequence of best-sellers which followed it. Many titles were published from the mid 1880s onwards. Authors who had first editions published by Arrowsmith include G. K. Chesterton, George and Weedon Grossmith, Anthony Hope, Jerome K. Jerome, Andrew Lang, Eden Phillpotts, Arthur Quiller-Couch, and Edgar Wallace; titles include Jerome's *Three Men in a Boat* (1889) and *Three Men on the Bummel* (1900), the Grossmiths' *Diary of a Nobody* (1892), Hope's *The Prisoner of Zenda* (1894) and *Rupert of Hentzau* (1898), Lang's *My Own Fairy Book* (1895), and Chesterton's *The Man Who Was Thursday* (1908). The correspondence between Jerome and Arrowsmith concerning the publication of *Three Men in a Boat* reveals the respect Jerome felt for the publisher. In a letter discussing royalties, dated 19 March 1889, Jerome writes, "I am anxious to bring it out through you [rather than a London publisher] as I know yours is for energy and push—I suppose the leading firm now." *Three Men in a Boat*, of course, is one of the outstanding success stories in all publishing history; an immense number of copies have been sold worldwide. In Britain alone more than three million copies had been sold by 1956, and the book was still selling at a rate of about fifteen thousand copies a year. Translations have ap-

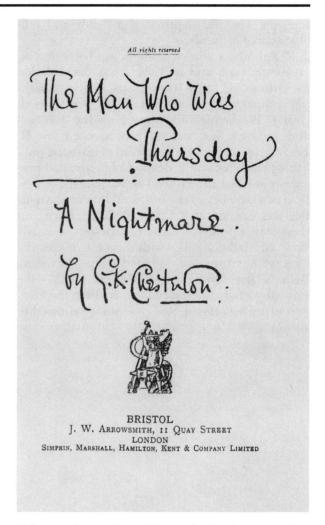

The Man Who Was Thursday

A Nightmare.

by G. K. Chesterton.

BRISTOL
J. W. ARROWSMITH, 11 QUAY STREET
LONDON
SIMPKIN, MARSHALL, HAMILTON, KENT & COMPANY LIMITED

*Title page for the first edition of G. K. Chesterton's third novel, published by Arrowsmith in 1908*

peared in many languages, and the story has been filmed three times. A few years after publication Arrowsmith is reported as saying, "I can't imagine what becomes of all the copies of that book I issue. I often think the public must eat them."

Arrowsmith died in 1913 and was succeeded as head of the firm by his nephew, J. A. Arrowsmith-Brown. Arrowsmith's death, followed so closely by World War I, slowed down the publishing program to such an extent that it became difficult to start up again. Another obstacle at this time was the declining sales of the *Time Tables*, which had continued to be published regularly since 1854. The income from such a title would seem to be insignificant beside that from Arrowsmith's famous books, but until World War I and the subsequent changes in the transport system, the *Time Tables* provided a steady and reliable source of funds.

Publishing outside London was becoming increasingly rare, and in 1924 it was decided that the firm would move from Bristol. A new publishing company, Arrowsmith: London, was formed, with J. W. Arrowsmith putting up the goodwill and its back list; capital was invested by H. Bravington, a jeweler who wanted to learn the publishing business; and J. Belton Cobb, who had previously worked for Fisher Unwin, joined the new firm as a member of the board of directors. An office was opened at 6 Upper Bedford Place, but the venture was not a success. Despite a steady flow of publications, with several books by Cherry Kearton and Hilaire Belloc—including Belloc's *But Soft—We Are Observed* (1928)—the company gradually lost money. In 1938 the London office was closed, and publishing returned to Bristol.

World War II also caused difficulties for the publishing department. Paper was strictly rationed, and the allowance to Arrowsmith was not sufficient to supply the demand for reprints even for *Three Men in a Boat*. Finally, in 1949 the rights to titles published up to that date were sold to J. M. Dent. Although there have been occasional publications since then, the company has mainly concentrated on printing. It has been located since 1954 on Winterstoke Road in Bristol. The managing director is Miss V. E. Arrowsmith-Brown.

### References:

J. H. Arrowsmith-Brown, *Arrowsmith 1854-1954, 1954-1979* (Bristol: Arrowsmith, 1979);

R. H. Brown, *Arrowsmith 1854-1954* (Bristol: Arrowsmith, 1955).

—*John R. Turner*

# B. T. Batsford

*(London: 1874-    )*

The character of B. T. Batsford as a publisher of quality architecture books was molded by the firm's origins in bookselling. Bradley Thomas Batsford opened his bookshop in 1843 at 30 High Holborn; he soon moved down the street to No. 52. At first he was a medical and general bookseller, but in the 1860s his son Bradley Batsford expanded into architecture, the arts, and engineering. It was the son who took the firm into publishing, the first known title being J. K. Colling's *Examples of English Medieval Foliage and Coloured Decoration* (1874). The firm moved to 94 High Holborn in 1893.

Colling's book set the tone for the Batsford list. The firm would specialize in publishing beautiful volumes, including fine engravings, on the decorative arts and architectural history. There were also handbooks for builders, most notably Charles F. Mitchell's *Building Construction and Drawing*: first published in 1888, it has gone through many editions, and its latest incarnations still sell well. In the early 1890s the firm became the first English publisher to use photographs in architecture books. The Batsfords closely supervised the enormously complex job of reproducing masses of illustrations—a total of 1,254 for Francis Bond's *Gothic Architecture in England* (1905). Bradley Thomas Batsford died in 1904.

*Bradley Thomas Batsford in the 1880s*

The firm developed unusually lasting and loyal relationships with its authors. J. Alfred Gotch, for example, remained with B. T. Batsford for fifty-six years, beginning with *The Buildings of Sir Thomas Tresham* (1883) and continuing through his magnificent *Architecture of the Renaissance in England* (1891-1894) and *Early Renaissance Architecture in England* (1901). At first B. T. Batsford published mainly for professional architects, until Bradley's youngest son, Herbert, tapped a more general audience with finely illustrated and expertly researched books on English villages, churches, and country houses. In 1910 he purchased Newnes' Collectors' Library for two hundred pounds and went on to reprint it.

Staff shortages during World War I brought in the first female workers. One of them was Bradley Thomas Batsford's youngest daughter, Florence, who may have been the first traveling saleswoman in the English book trade; she found the work demoralizingly déclassé.

Harry Batsford, grandson of the founder, had come into the business in 1897. He became chairman and managing director on the death of his uncle Herbert in 1917, and held those posts for the rest of his life. In 1918 the company published a pioneering work in the field of popular social history, *A History of Everyday Things in England* by Marjorie and C. H. B. Quennell. This was the first of many volumes in the Quennells' Everyday Life series, which ultimately sold more than a million copies.

Harry Batsford hired Charles Fry as his personal assistant in 1924 and his nephew Brian Cook in 1928. The three invented what the reading public would come to recognize as the distinctive "Batsford book." Cook designed dust jackets, and he produced something quite novel and striking for A. K. Wickham's *The Villages of England* (1932), a volume in the English Life series. It had the look of an Art Deco travel poster, employing vivid and unexpected colors, with a panoramic design wrapped completely around the book.

With such books B. T. Batsford was able to reach a broader audience, and their success sustained the company through the Great Depression. Forced to cut back on staff, Harry Batsford and Fry became authors themselves, writing books on rural Britain that Cook illustrated. In 1933 the trio explored Scotland in an old car and produced *The Face of Scotland*, the first of the British Heritage series: it sold well at seven shillings, sixpence. A companion series, The Face of Brit-

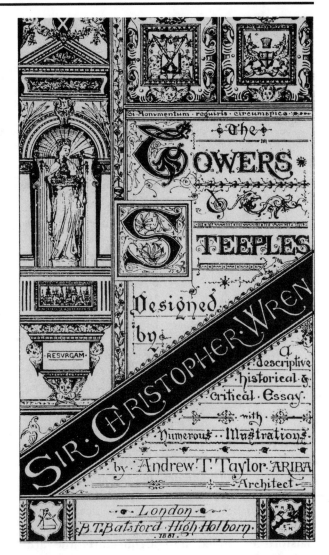

*Title page representative of the elegant Victorian volumes on architectural history for which B. T. Batsford was known*

ain, was published from 1936 to 1950. Both series maintained sales through the paper shortages of World War II, as Harry Batsford had built up a large inventory of back stock. Together with The Pilgrim's Library, they would sell nearly half a million copies by 1943.

"From the nature of their list Batsford never has brought out a literary masterpiece," observed Sam Carr, who came to the firm in 1937. All the same, Fry did manage to acquire some fairly stellar authors. The company published Sacheverell Sitwell's *British Architects and Craftsmen* (1945; fourth edition, 1948), as well as his guides to travel and art: *Roumanian Journey* (1938), *The Netherlands* (1948), *Spain* (1950), *Portugal and Madeira* (1954), and *Denmark* (1956). Cecil Beaton contributed several volumes of photographs: *Cecil*

*Beaton's Scrapbook* (1937), *Cecil Beaton's New York* (1938), *Time Exposure* (1941), *Near East* (1943), *Far East* (1945), *Chinese Album* (1946), *Indian Album* (1946), and *Ashcombe* (1949). After Gertrude Stein's *Picasso* appeared in October 1938, she rejoiced (in her inimitable syntax) that it "is about sold out 7500 not so bad in 3 months." B. T. Batsford went on to put out her children's story *The World Is Round* (1939), her *Paris France* (1940), and her *Wars I Have Seen* (1945). The firm acquired James Pope-Hennessy's first book, *London Fabric* (1939), which won the Hawthornden Prize. Paul Richey's anonymous *Fighter Pilot* (1941) sold 75,000 copies and could have sold more but for wartime paper rationing.

In 1930 the company had moved to an elegant eighteenth-century townhouse at 15 North Audley Street in Mayfair. During the war Harry Batsford and some staff people were relocated to Malvern Wells; the stock was scattered to several storage sites to insure that it could not all be wiped out by one German bomb. Cook left the firm to serve in the Royal Air Force; he returned at the end of the war. In 1946, at his uncle Harry's request, he adopted the surname Batsford.

In 1947 Fry attempted to set up an American branch of B. T. Batsford at 122 East 55th Street in New York. The first two floors were a retail shop for new and used books, while Batsford books were marketed from offices on the upper floors. Sales, however, could never cover the high overhead: by 1949 the enterprise had lost £21,807. The offices were then converted into the British Book Centre, to serve as an American distribution point for several English publishers who invested in the project. That strategy only multiplied the losses, which after another year totaled £49,254. In 1951 the firm of Simpkin, Marshall bought out the operation for £10,000. Harry Batsford died that year, and Brian Batsford became chairman of B. T. Batsford.

The Irish poet Monk Gibbon spoke for many Batsford authors when he eulogized Harry as "vital, impulsive, a character that might have walked straight out of Dickens rather than out of our so often dull 'scientific age.'" In the mid twentieth century, however, the business of publishing could no longer be conducted on a Pickwickian basis. Under Brian Batsford, a cheerfully unmethodical family firm was transformed into a modern, organized corporation. For the first time there were regular board meetings, sales meetings, and editorial conferences. Art, publicity,

*Building at 94 High Holborn where B. T. Batsford moved in 1894*

and sales departments came into being. After more than a century the firm got out of new-book retailing, which was no longer very profitable and which planning regulations did not permit at No. 4 Fitzhardinge Street, where the firm moved in 1952. The used-book business continued, conducted mainly through catalogues.

Brian Batsford was elected to Parliament as a Conservative in 1958. Carr then became joint managing director; from 1961 to 1974 he was sole managing director. The used-book business began to lose money and was sold to Basil Blackwell in 1962.

Via its parliamentary connections, Batsford published three volumes of speeches by the Conservative politician Enoch Powell; unlike most such collections, they sold fairly well. The poet John Betjeman edited *Victorian and Edwardian London from Old Photographs* (1969); it has remained in print ever since, the first in a series of more than seventy similar books. Desmond Morris and Barbara Woodhouse published with Batsford before they became best-selling celebrities.

After entering the field in 1969, Batsford rapidly became the world's largest publisher of chess books, acquiring such eminent grandmasters as Anatoly Karpov, Gary Kasparov, and Raymond Keene. An equally successful investment was made in crafts books, covering lacework, woodwork, pottery, needlework, kite-making, flower arrangement, and weaving. B. T. Batsford continued to specialize in architecture, art, English heritage, and costume and fashion, and branched out into travel, film, music, and military history. The educational list was dominated by history textbooks.

Brian Batsford was knighted in 1974, when he retired from both politics and publishing. There were no Batsford heirs, so he sold a controlling interest in the company to the directors and to his friends. Carr became chairman, with Peter Kemmis Betty, who had come to the firm in 1959, as managing director. In place of the old rule-of-thumb methods, computers were introduced to manage stock control, marketing strategies, budgeting, and sales projections. The firm launched an Australian affiliate in 1974, but it failed after a year.

As of 1990 Batsford was still a private company, owned by eighty-two shareholders, with ten editors and about sixty other employees. It had a yearly turnover of nearly five million pounds on about 130 titles, with roughly thirty percent of sales coming from foreign markets.

**References:**

Hector Bolitho, *A Batsford Century* (London: Batsford, 1943);

Jean Richardson, "Batsford: A Tradition of Arts and Crafts Publishing," *British Book News* (February 1990): 80-83.

*—Jonathan Rose*

# S. O. Beeton
*(London: 1855-1866; 1875-1876)*
## Clarke, Beeton and Company
*(London: 1852-1855)*

Samuel Orchart Beeton began his publishing career in 1852 in the publishing house of Charles Henry Clarke; in the same year he became a partner, and the firm became known as Clarke, Beeton and Company. This was a time of considerable expansion in publishing, particularly for the newly educated lower classes, and Beeton was influential in producing many educational but entertaining works for the new market.

Like many successful publishers, he began with a best-seller. Harriet Beecher Stowe's *Uncle Tom's Cabin; or, Life among the Lowly* was published by John Jewett in Boston on 20 March 1852. A young man who worked for G. P. Putnam bought a copy and boarded a ship for London. When he arrived he sent the copy to David Bogue, suggesting that he might want to reprint it. Bogue thought it unsuitable for his list, but suggested that his friend Henry Vizetelly might be interested. Vizetelly, who had been publishing in association with Charles Clarke, offered to put up one-third of the cost of a printing of seven thou-

*Samuel Orchart Beeton and Isabella Beeton in 1860*

19

sand copies to sell at two shillings, sixpence each, if Clarke's firm would publish it. The subtitle was changed to *Negro Life in the Slave States of America*, and a preface by Frederick Greenwood, explaining the background of the book for British readers, was added. Twenty-five hundred of the seven thousand copies were bound in cloth. Although the advertising was extensive, sales were slow at first; only after Richard Bentley brought out an edition at one shilling and Clarke, Beeton bound the rest of the sheets in paperboards for sale at a shilling per copy did the book really take off. By the autumn of 1852 Clarke, Beeton and Company had printed one hundred fifty thousand copies of the book. Although the book was not under copyright in Great Britain, several rival publishers reprinted from Clarke's edition, with the British preface, and were held up for breach of the British copyright. Clarke, Beeton bought the whole of their rival Frederick Warne's edition at less than the cost of printing and changed the title page.

Beeton visited America, and the firm offered Mrs. Stowe a royalty. She would only accept £750 as a gift, but it enabled Clarke, Beeton to share in the publication of *The Key to Uncle Tom's Cabin*. During this visit Beeton met Robert Lowell, Henry Wadsworth Longfellow, and Oliver Wendell Holmes and published many of their books as well as works by Mark Twain and Artemus Ward; but none had as great a success as *Uncle Tom's Cabin*, which is said to have sold a million copies from a dozen publishers in Great Britain within a year of its first publication.

Like that of many Victorian publishers, Beeton's success was based on the growth of the magazine-reading public. In 1852 he began a series of books and magazines to which he attached his name as editor, author, publisher, or all three. The first of the magazines, the *Englishwoman's Domestic Magazine*, aimed at "the improvement of the intellect, the cultivation of the morals, and the cherishing of domestic virtues," was selling twenty-five thousand copies by the end of its second year and fifty thousand by 1860. In 1855 Beeton started the *Boy's Own Magazine*, an illustrated journal of fact, fiction, history, and adventure. It continued, with various changes in title, until 1874 (and is not to be confused with the more famous *Boy's Own Paper*, which did not start until 1879).

In early 1855 Clarke and Beeton ended their partnership. Beeton acquired the copyright in the two magazines, and set up in business on

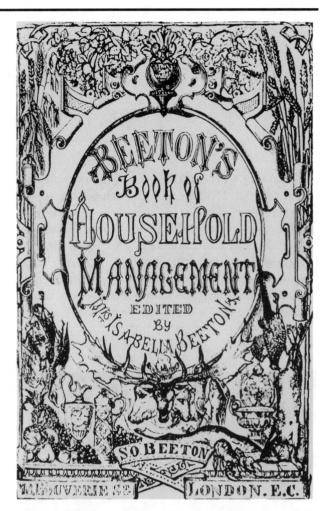

*Title page for the 1861 first book edition of Isabella Beeton's guide for the Victorian middle class, previously published in monthly parts in 1859*

his own at 18 Bouverie Street. He remained there until he moved to larger premises at 248 Strand in 1860. On 10 July 1856 Beeton married Isabella Mayson, and until her death in 1865 she contributed many stories and recipes to his magazines and books. *The Book of Household Management* was published in 1859 as a series of monthly parts and as a single volume in 1861. Eleven hundred seventy-two pages long with five hundred wood engravings and fifty color plates, it sold for seven shillings, sixpence. Sixty thousand copies were sold the first year, and a second edition appeared in 1863.

The repeal of the paper duty in 1861 encouraged the cheap press, and in particular the magazines. In 1861 Beeton brought out the *Queen* magazine in a large folio format at sixpence, with news of the week and many topical pictures specially engraved for the magazine. The *Young Englishwoman* appeared in 1864, to balance out the market he had created with his boys' magazines and books with a magazine for young ladies. He produced many popular titles covering such subjects as biography, pets, hobbies, poetry, chemistry, wild animals, and gardening, and he reprinted many of the classics in series. Many of the larger books were published in parts sold at monthly intervals, and much of the information was repackaged (as were Mrs. Beeton's cookery books) over and over again. In 1860 appeared the first number of *Beeton's Christmas Annual*, "100 large pages, beautifully printed and illustrated, with a most handsome Eidographic Almanac in gold and colours." It sold for one shilling, threepence.

The collapse of the banking firm of Overend, Gurney and Company in 1866 brought Beeton to the verge of bankruptcy, from which he was saved only by agreeing to sell his copyrights to Ward, Lock and Tyler and to work as their literary adviser for a salary and a percentage of the profits. He continued to edit the many books and magazines with his name on them, but they were published by Ward, Lock and Tyler. In 1871 he decided to give *Beeton's Christmas Annual* a radical political and satirical slant. The next

year's issue was even more radically critical, and in 1874 Ward, Lock (Tyler had retired in 1873) refused to publish it. Beeton tried to sell it to another publisher, but he had agreed to use his name only on Ward, Lock publications. Ward, Lock obtained an injunction to prevent Beeton from publishing his annual elsewhere. The relationship was thereby dissolved, and Beeton was free to resume publishing on his own. Ward, Lock refused to allow him to publish under his own name, however, and he lost when he sued for the right to do so.

Beeton established himself at 39-40 Bedford Street in the autumn of 1875. *Edward VII*, the last of his Christmas annuals, was published in 1876. Beeton died in a sanatorium in Richmond on 6 June 1877 and was buried in Norwood Cemetery beside his wife.

**References:**

H. Montgomery Hyde, *Mr. & Mrs. Beeton* (London: Harrap, 1951);
Nancy Spain, *Mrs. Beeton and Her Husband* (London: Collins, 1948).

*—Peter Stockham*

# George Bell and Sons
### (London: 1873-1910)
# George Bell
### (London: 1839-1856)
# Bell and Daldy
### (London: 1856-1873)
# George Bell and Sons Ltd.
### (London: 1910-1977)
# Bell and Hyman Ltd.
### (London: 1977-1989)

In 1839 George Bell founded a publishing firm that endured, in its modest way, for a century and a half. In his memoir of his father, *George Bell Publisher* (1924), Edward Bell remarked that the family firm was of "moderate size, of no great antiquity, and with no pretensions to any phenomenal successes in the book-world." Yet, at George Bell's death in 1890, the *Athenaeum* referred to him as "one of the most successful publishers of the latter half of this century." Bell specialized in the educational book trade and his sons carried on the tradition. The firm was not glamorous or innovative, although on occasion it became entwined with some of the more sensational characters in the London publishing world. Bell's inclinations tended toward the more solid side of the literary marketplace: school and university textbooks, theological works, and reprints of European classics. By following his instincts Bell established the foundation that would ensure the firm's longevity.

Born in 1814, Bell was the eldest son of Matthew Bell, a bookseller, stationer, bookbinder, and printer who now and then published manuscripts that came his way in the Yorkshire town of Richmond. It was in his father's shop that George Bell gained his first professional experi-ence. There he might have stayed had he not been exposed to wider horizons at the local grammar school. The Reverend James Tate, the headmaster, was a classics scholar of wide reputation who tutored Bell's literary tastes. When Bell left school at age sixteen, he cherished scholarly aspirations and an ambition to do more than run the local bookshop. After a couple of years assisting his father, Bell left Richmond to test his mettle in the London publishing world.

As an assistant at the wholesale booksellers Whittaker and Company of Ave Maria Lane, Bell made some of the connections that would determine the course of his own career as an independent bookseller/publisher. Whittaker specialized in the schoolbook trade; during the six years Bell spent with the firm he learned a great deal about the educational book market and decided to base his future on his contemporaries' passion for formal and informal education. Bell's first ventures into publishing took the form of writing shilling guides to subjects such as chess, cricket, angling, and architecture. They appeared under the imprint either of his employer's firm or that of Simpkin, another wholesale book dealer.

In 1839, having made a little profit on his handbooks and having some prosperous relatives who were willing to finance his first enterprise, he set up shop at 1 Bouverie Street as an educational book supplier. Armed with a letter of recommendation from Tate, who by then was canon of St. Paul's, Bell canvassed the academic publishers of England's two major university towns. He persuaded the firms of Deighton, Grant, Hall, Stevenson, and Johnson of Cambridge and Parker, Vincent, and Slatter of Oxford to use him as their London agent. In his first catalogue in 1840 Bell announced that his premises would henceforth be the London depot for supplying university books to serious readers in the general public.

In establishing a secure source of income from the retail trade as he took his first steps into the more turbulent world of publishing, Bell followed a practice widespread among his peers. His first independent publications, which appeared in 1840, also displayed his cautious inclinations. An edition of Cicero's *De Senectute* with explanatory notes and translations and a gardening handbook were the first to carry the imprint "George Bell, 1 Bouverie Street." Classical texts and practical guidebooks were to dominate the Bell lists in years to come. Bell also had a keen eye for up-and-coming public enthusiasms: in 1840, for instance, he published a series of railway guides to take advantage of the first burst of railway tourism. His "Railway Companions" combined practical information about timetables and fares with descriptions of towns and historic sites along the route.

Within his first year as a bookseller and publisher Bell outgrew his original premises and rented more expansive quarters at 186 Fleet Street. He had a personal reason for moving as well: he wanted to secure suitable accommodations for his bride, Hannah Simpson Bell, a neighbor from his hometown whom he married in 1840. His son Edward, who was to lead the firm into the twentieth century, was born in 1844 and spent the first five years of his life in the Fleet Street house.

During the 1840s Bell's literary circle widened and his business connections became more complex. After a heartening success with Mrs. Jane Loudon's *The First Book of Botany* (1841), which sold nearly nine hundred copies, Bell went into partnership with Henry Wood, another neighbor from the Richmond days, in 1842. Wood had a talent for writing humorous handbooks on card games; he also had a penchant for playing those games, and frequently lost. The partnership lasted only a few months; Bell was left to face

Wood's creditors, who took all the capital Wood had brought in, plus a share of the profit and interest—£895 all told.

More satisfactory was Bell's friendship with the brothers Alexander and Daniel Macmillan, who launched their bookselling business in London just as Bell began his. Bell published Alexander Macmillan's anonymous biography of Percy Bysshe Shelley, which included a selection of Shelley's poems; Macmillan bore part of the expense of publication. Through Macmillan, Bell made his first connections with the Scottish educational milieu, resulting in a series of six schoolbooks by Scottish schoolmasters. After the Macmillan brothers moved to Cambridge in 1843, the close relationship between the firms persisted. Bell became Macmillan's representative in London, and the firms jointly published a theological book by Hugh Miller in 1844. Alexander Macmillan signaled the depth of his regard when he invited Bell to accompany the family at Daniel Macmillan's funeral in 1857. In the next generation, Edward Bell and Daniel Macmillan's eldest son, Frederick, were friends.

Another early friend whose association widened Bell's list was Henry Cole. A man of diverse interests, Cole was the savior of Britain's official documents, which he organized in the first Public Record Office. He was also a founder of the South Kensington Museum and an adviser on cultural matters to Prince Albert. Cole's interest in the practical application of art led him to project a series of illustrated handbooks intended to direct attention to Britain's architectural heritage. He chose the pseudonym "Felix Summerly" for his works, the first of which was a guide to the art treasures and grounds of Hampton Court, published by Hugh Cunningham in 1841. It was a great success, and the second edition came out in 1843 under the George Bell imprint. Bell also published Cole's *A Handbook for Holidays* (1842) and *The National Gallery* (1843), illustrated handsomely by artists such as J. B. Pyne and David Cox and, for the more modest pictures, by Cole himself. Cole cultivated another of his pet projects, his interest in skilled trades for women, in these productions: the illustrations were engraved by a group of women he had encouraged to learn woodcutting. Through his friendship with Cole, Bell began to gain a reputation for books on art, architecture, and archaeology—particularly those he produced in collaboration with Joseph Cundall, another of Cole's protégés, who was among the first to use photography in published books. *Examples of Ornament*, which Cundall produced for Bell in 1855, was illustrated by twenty-four plates depicting ornaments from the Crystal Palace and museums in London. (Later Cundall applied his interest in photographic reproduction to *The Great Works of Raphael Sanzio of Urbino*, which Bell and Daldy published in 1866.)

All the time he was expanding the publishing side of his business, Bell was still carrying on the retail side from his Fleet Street premises. He was a member of the Booksellers' Association, which aimed to limit the business to licensed booksellers who would agree to sell books at the published prices; the publishers would in turn protect the licensed booksellers by boycotting unlicensed ones. Their efforts to mitigate the precariousness of the publishing and bookselling business led to a collision with the champions of free trade in literature. At a time when liberalism was ascendant and laissez-faire the watchword of economic orthodoxy, any attempt to regulate the marketplace was bound to set up a public outcry. The question of free access to literature and knowledge became an emotional issue, and was inflamed by the well-publicized and spirited objections of authors and intellectuals such as Charles Dickens, John Stuart Mill, and Thomas Carlyle. The opposition overcame the ability of the Booksellers' Association to enforce its licensing regulations, and the society disbanded in 1852. Four decades later, Edward Bell was to lead a similar, and more successful, effort with the Net Book Agreement.

Although Bell was dabbling in many issues and a variety of publishing enterprises, educational books for schools or private self-improvement were his main interest. Beginning with his friendship with his old schoolmaster, Tate, and Tate's son James, who had succeeded his father as headmaster of Bell's old school in Richmond, Bell cultivated a wide network of headmasters and solicited their advice about gaps in the textbook supply. An early and ultimately profitable project was a series of school classics that would have sufficient English notes to explain references yet not do the pupil's translation work for him. Schoolmasters welcomed the idea, but the difficulty of finding well-established scholars who had sufficient leisure to do the work delayed the series. When the first volume, an edition of Xenophon's *Anabasis* by the Reverend J. F. Mac-Michael, came out in 1847, its eager reception in almost all the schools teaching Greek encouraged

*George Bell, age thirty-seven*

Bell to persist with his scheme. To advance the pace of publication he sought out his old employers, Whittaker and Company, to join him in the venture. The Grammar School Classics appeared in rapid succession throughout the 1850s. His ambition and confidence increasing, Bell expanded his project to include more sophisticated classics texts for university and upper-form students, the Biblioteca Classica. Both series were edited by A. J. Macleane and George Long. The sales from the most popular books in the series, F. A. Paley's edition of the works of Aeschylus (1855) and J. Conington's edition of the works of Virgil (1866), fully justified Bell's enthusiasm.

Two periodicals reinforced the educational character of the firm. Bell published the *Journal of Education* for professional teachers from 1847 until 1854, when it became independent. Intended for laymen, *Notes and Queries* was initially edited in 1850 by W. J. Thoms, librarian to the House of Lords. Its weekly issues sold well, and there was great demand for the half-yearly volumes as well. In 1863 it expanded into its own quarters.

Through his classics series and periodicals Bell formed lasting friendships with some of the most important scholars and educators of the time, and his reputation as a publisher of reputable educational works solidified. Bell's ideas for textbook innovation endeared him to many of the generation of reforming headmasters, such as William Haig Brown of Charterhouse, B. H. Kennedy of Shrewsbury, and E. W. Benson, future archbishop of Canterbury. Through these men and their clerical colleagues Bell expanded his catalogue of published sermons, which he had begun to publish in the mid 1840s. Among the most successful of her theological books were those of the popular preacher W. Farquhar Hook, dean of Chichester. One of the most often reprinted of Hook's works, *The Christian Taught by the Church Services* (1847-1848), was actually written by his wife and edited by the clergyman.

The Reverend Alfred Gatty, vicar of Ecclesfield, also offered his sermons for publication by Bell in 1847. What recommended Bell's firm to the vicar was, once again, the Richmond connection: Gatty's wife, Margaret, had been a childhood friend of Bell. Her father, the Reverend Dr. Alexander John Scott, was famous as the chaplain who was present when Nelson died at Trafalgar. Dr. Scott was also a bibliophile who had haunted William Bell's bookshop when George Bell was growing up. The association between the Bell and Gatty families, which was to extend over two more generations, brought Bell into the expanding realm of children's literature. Margaret Gatty proved to be a writer whose delicate fancies enchanted children from the time Bell published her first book, *The Fairy Godmother*, in 1851. She was Bell's most prominent children's author until her daughter, Juliana Horatia Ewing, outshone her in this department.

The series that established Gatty's reputation was *Parables from Nature*, which began in 1855. In these little stories she adorned her impressive knowledge of botany with imaginative embroidery and infused the whole with the Christian spirit that was never absent from her work. Mrs. Gatty illustrated the first few volumes, but for subsequent volumes and later editions Bell commissioned illustrations from Holman Hunt, Edward Burne-Jones, and John Millais. *Parables from Nature* was a perennially popular series into the 1920s. It was translated into French, Italian, German, Russian, Danish, and Swedish. Fittingly, since Mrs. Gatty took her first inspiration from Hans Christian Andersen, the Danes were particularly enthusiastic about her "parables."

With children's literature, art, and architecture added to his basic interest in educational and theological publishing, Bell's business was diversifying. By the mid 1850s it was expanding geographically as well. In 1850 he had opened a bookshop for Brighton College, chiefly to provide an occupation for his brother, John; but it was not profitable, and he had soon given it up. In 1854 the publishing firm of J. and J. J. Deighton of Cambridge came on the market. Bell had acted as the London agent for Deighton since his earliest days as an independent businessman. Acquiring this old, established concern made Bell one of the major educational publishers in Britain. He made W. Wright Smith resident partner in the Cambridge firm, which was renamed Deighton, Bell and Company. Even so, Bell was obliged to make frequent journeys to Cambridge. He was becoming personally overextended and therefore entered into partnership with Frederick R. Daldy in 1856. Bell and Daldy cemented their union with a new title-page symbol, the bell and anchor. The anchor derived from the anchor symbol used by the Venetian printer Aldus Manutius, whom Daldy fancied as an ancestor. Bell's acquisition in 1854 of the Aldine Edition of British Poets series from the firm of William Pickering, which also used Aldus's symbol, further justified the logic of Bell and Daldy's logo. As it began to republish the Aldine editions, poetry became another of Bell and Daldy's subspecialties. One of the most noteworthy volumes in the series was William Morris's early epic, *The Defence of Guenevere* (1858).

In addition to the Aldine Poets series, Bell and Daldy published the scholarly and humorous verses of the academics C. S. Calverley and George Otto Trevelyan. In the late 1850s Bell and Daldy began to publish the popular didactic lyrics of Adelaide Anne Procter, a protégée of Dickens. Her first two volumes of poetry sold very well: *Legends and Lyrics* (1858-1861) was still being republished by the firm in 1913. Even so, because of his professional and personal connections to theologians and his own fervent commitment to the Church of England, Bell refused to publish the verses that reflected Procter's conversion to Roman Catholicism just before her death in 1864. An even more popular poet of the domestic virtues, Coventry Patmore, entrusted his work to Bell and Daldy, though by his own choice he published it at his own expense. Two other popular Victorian poets whose work Bell and Daldy published from time to time were Andrew Lang and the future poet laureate Robert Bridges. Giftbook anthologies usually brought sure sales: Bell and Daldy reaped large profits from its poetry books for children, which soon saturated the elementary school market.

Bell and David Bogue had formed an agreement in their early days to act as each other's executors, and when Bogue died in 1860 Bell was able to acquire the British rights to *Webster's Dictionary* from Bogue's estate. Henceforth, English and foreign-language dictionaries would become prominent features of Bell and Daldy's catalogues.

Bell and his partner Daldy were casting about for further investment opportunities when the extensive properties of Henry Bohn came on the market in 1864. Bohn's "Libraries" of more than six hundred works, including copyrights, plates, and stock, represented a more ambitious expansion than the partners had originally envisaged. Daldy was apparently more sanguine about investing than was the cautious Bell. In this case, Daldy's flair for financial juggling proved itself as he persuaded the Clowes printing company and the stationers Spalding and Hodge to lend part of the thirty-five thousand pounds the acquisitions entailed. Soon Bell and Daldy presided over a much larger company with an expanded staff, which included Spalding's son, Howard, as an apprentice. To accommodate their expanding business Bell and Daldy took over Bohn's two houses in York Street, Covent Garden, plus a third house in the neighborhood. Bohn, however, was reluctant to accept the fact of his retirement: although he had sold his business, he still occupied the main office in York Street until, exasperated, Bell broke into the office one morning in 1867 and took possession of the desk. Bohn then retired with reasonably good grace. With sales of the Bohn Libraries standing at over one hundred thousand volumes a year, Bell and Daldy no longer needed the retail side of the business. In 1867 they abandoned the Fleet Street address and henceforth concentrated on publishing from York Street.

The year 1867 also brought Edward Bell's graduation from Cambridge and entry into the family firm. During his first few years in the publishing business Edward indulged his literary penchants, spending most of his time developing the Bohn Libraries and the Aldine Poets series and reading in the British Museum. These congenial pursuits ended abruptly when the death of the cashier obliged Edward to take a more practical involvement in the firm's affairs. His initiation into the financial side of the business coincided with one of the most perilous episodes of its history.

Though prospering, Bell and Daldy were indebted to their stationers Spalding and Hodge. Indebted to the same firm, but on a much greater scale, was the flamboyant impresario of publishing, Alexander Strahan. Perhaps because Spalding had a stake in the prosperity of both firms, he persuaded Bell and Daldy to make Strahan their retail distributor after they gave up the Fleet Street outlet. The result was to add Bell and Daldy to Strahan's string of nervous creditors. In addition to what he owed Spalding and Hodge, Strahan began to accrue debts to Bell and Daldy as he sold their books but failed to pass on the profits. Because they relied on Strahan to sell their books, Bell and Daldy had to keep on supplying him with them; their chances of recovering the money he already owed them hinged on Strahan's future success. This predicament came to a head in 1869, at a time when George Bell was ill and frequently absent from the office. Without the cautious Bell to act as a brake on his impetuousness, Daldy bound the firm's financial future even more tightly to that of Strahan: anxious to disentangle themselves from Strahan's financial snare, Spalding and Hodge persuaded Daldy to take over the management of much of Strahan's empire and to underwrite ten thousand pounds of Strahan's debt to themselves. Bell and Daldy purchased eight thousand pounds worth of Strahan stock and copyrights and took over some of Strahan's most popular productions, including the *Contemporary Review* and the *Sunday Magazine*. For another six thousand pounds they were to have rights to the much vaunted "pocket" Tennyson series that Strahan had scheduled to come out in 1870. When Alfred Tennyson objected to a change of publisher the Strahan imprint remained, but Bell and Daldy published the series and was supposed to profit from the sale. The whole gambit was designed to simplify the network of debts connecting the three firms and to steady Strahan's course by reducing his responsibility within his firm. In reality Strahan's debts continued to outdistance the profits his creditors were able to glean from his publications. When Edward Bell reflected on this episode in *George Bell Publisher*, he described Strahan's ideals of publishing in charitable terms as "laudable, even grand, but not tempered with prudence"; but, he ruefully admitted, Bell and Daldy's connection with Strahan was "a rash adventure."

The Strahan affair overshadowed all other concerns at Bell and Daldy for the three years the two firms' fates were entwined. It was during this period, 1869 to 1872, that George Bell decided to end his partnership with Daldy. The presence of his sons, Edward and Arthur, in the family business was his ostensible reason for not renewing the partnership, but the Strahan affair undoubtedly strained the relationship. In the spring of 1872 Strahan was obliged to withdraw from his company; an ally of Spalding's, James Virtue, managed the firm so as to retrieve some eleven thousand pounds to put toward the Bell and Daldy / Spalding and Hodge debt. But the final resolution derived from a high-minded gesture by Thomas Spalding, who took back the Strahan copyrights and stocks and relieved Bell and Daldy of the debt. Spalding then endowed his son Howard with the Strahan line and engaged him to work with Virtue. It was to this firm that Daldy retreated with his share of the Bell and Daldy assets and goodwill. In 1873 the new firm Virtue, Spalding and Daldy took up headquarters in Ivy Lane; Bell's firm was renamed George Bell and Sons.

It was ironic that while Bell was grappling with the Strahan labyrinth he was being pressured by his friends, the Gatty family, to wage a more vigorous war against the Strahan competition. The Gattys' concern centered on their interest in children's periodicals. In 1866 Bell and Daldy had introduced a high-quality children's magazine which Margaret Gatty edited and named *Aunt Judy's Magazine* after her most popular book, *Aunt Judy's Tales*. A year later Strahan launched *Good Words for the Young*, a junior version of his popular *Good Words*. With Norman McLeod and then the fairy-tale writer George MacDonald as editors and a string of well-known writers, Strahan aimed to capture the juvenile market. He advertised his magazine flamboyantly. Both *Good Words for the Young* and *Aunt Judy's Magazine* were aiming at the same comparatively small readership of well-to-do and well-educated boys and girls. Competition between them was keen, and the Gatty family was eager to expand the market share of *Aunt Judy's Magazine*. The Reverend Alfred Gatty repeatedly goaded George and Edward Bell to "cram a little powder and shot" into their promotion of *Aunt Judy's Magazine* and edge out Strahan's magazine. His nagging was in vain: George Bell was not in the frame of mind to light fireworks, especially given his intimate and sobering knowledge of how Strahan's pyrotechnics really worked. Moreover, although Bell had published two religious periodicals, *Mission* *Field* and *Gospel*, for the Society for the Propagation of the Gospel in Foreign Parts, *Aunt Judy's Magazine* represented his only venture into secular children's magazine publishing. He did not have as much experience as Strahan did with magazine advertising, and he was reluctant to employ the huckstering techniques necessary to secure popularity. He was also less generous than Strahan in his terms with his editors and authors. Mrs. Gatty received ten pounds per month for every ten thousand readers, which was approximately the average circulation of *Aunt Judy's Magazine*. In contrast, Strahan paid MacDonald six hundred pounds per year. Bell's rather low rates of pay for authors also limited Gatty's ability to attract popular names. Ten shillings a page was too little for the rising young humorist W. S. Gilbert, who demanded two guineas for his contribution. Gatty did manage to lure submissions from Lewis Carroll and Ascott R. Hope; she also offered translations of Hans Christian Andersen stories to her young subscribers. But the mainstay of the magazine came from the pen of her daughter, Juliana Horatia Ewing. Ewing's enduringly popular stories, such as "A Flat Iron for a Farthing" and "Six to Sixteen," were first published in *Aunt Judy's Magazine* for the meager return of seven shillings, sixpence a page. It was galling to the Gatty family when a critic suggested that Ewing would reach a larger audience if she contributed to *Good Words for the Young*. Even John Ruskin, a loyal patron of *Aunt Judy's Magazine*, urged Ewing to seek a wider public and to join him in a revolt against publishers. Out of loyalty to Bell, she declined.

Moreover, Ewing paid a tribute to Bell's generosity in other spheres when she modeled a character in the serialized novel "The Miller's Thumb," which appeared in *Aunt Judy's Magazine* in 1873, after Bell and his philanthropic efforts on behalf of homeless boys. In Ewing's novel, the hapless Jan is rescued from life in the street by a robustly Christian businessman who takes him to a cheerful home where boys learn practical trades. She describes in some detail the workings of an institution very much like the Regent's Park Boys' Home which Bell and other Broad Churchmen such as F. D. Maurice, Thomas Hughes, and William and George Spottiswoode founded in 1858.

"The Miller's Thumb" was published in book form by George Bell and Sons as *Jan of the Windmill* in 1876. Although Ewing's last books were published by the Society for the Promotion of Christian Knowledge, she left most of her popular books in the hands of Bell. She might well have found more fame and fortune with a more adventurous publisher, but she preferred to stay with the family friend. Her books remained on the lists of George Bell and Sons well into the twentieth century.

The Gatty family's loyalty to and admiration for the Bells were reciprocated. George Bell continued to publish *Aunt Judy's Magazine* even though it turned a profit in only one year of its twenty-year run. In 1881 Bell reluctantly decided that the *Aunt Judy's* connection had to end, despite the pleas of Ewing's sister, Horatia Gatty, that she would continue to edit the magazine for only three pounds per issue if only it could survive. The magazine went through three more publishers and a one-hundred-pound subsidy from Ruskin before it finally ended in 1885, the year of Ewing's death.

The last two decades of the nineteenth century were years of consolidation and modest expansion for the Bell firm. Unencumbered by partners, Bell followed his own shrewd and cautious instincts and prospered. Among fellow publishers he acquired a reputation as an assessor of publication stock and copyright and was frequently called on to evaluate assets. For instance, George Smith, during a financial dispute with Ruskin, cited Bell's expertise on the value of copyright. The Bohn Libraries continued to sell so well that Bell was encouraged to expand the series with new editions of well-known classics of English, American, and European authors. American readers were especially enthusiastic about the series: in New York the firm of Scribner and Welford acted as Bell's agents until Edward Bell shifted the business to Macmillan in 1871.

Bell's extension into art and architectural publications because of his early friendship with Henry Cole had led him into a close association with the Chiswick Press. The press had a reputation for meticulous work and old-style type. It was at the Chiswick Press that William Morris conducted his first experiments in reviving the old typography, experiments he later elaborated at his own Kelmscott Press. When the Chiswick Press came on the market in 1880 Bell bought it to provide a berth for his brother John, who managed the press until his death in 1885. The Chiswick Press continued to be associated with the Bell firm until 1919 and enhanced the company's prestige in art and architectural publications.

Another temporary expansion of George Bell and Sons derived from George Bell's continued association with the employer of his youth, Whittaker and Company. Whittaker had cooperated with him in the early classics series, and Bell's part in these two series had remained separate from the Bell and Daldy lists. The series continued to sell well, but by the 1880s Whittaker and Company was not as prosperous as it had been. In April 1884 Bell eventually acquired the firm that had taught him his first lessons in publishing. He was motivated in part by benevolence and paid an annuity to its last owner, William Hood, who died a few years later. Hoping to sell most of the business to a young German, Bell nursed the firm along until the new owner was ready to assume responsibility. But just as the transfer was completed, the German drowned. Edward Bell was then diverted for several years to straightening out the financial and editorial commitments that Whittaker and Company had incurred. Ultimately, Henry Rayment, who had been helping Edward Bell with the work, purchased the firm. That Rayment was the son of the first master and matron of the Regent's Park Boys' Home made the resolution of this affair doubly satisfying to George Bell.

By this time Edward was at the helm of George Bell and Sons. In 1888 Bell settled the firm on his sons Edward and Ernest, and charged them with compensating the other four surviving children. Arthur had left the firm and established himself as an artist. But George Bell never retired, continuing to come into the York Street office until he died of bronchitis in November 1890.

Edward Bell shared his father's academic aspirations and, as a graduate of Trinity College, Cambridge, had had a greater opportunity to develop his aptitude for scholarship than his father, who had left school at sixteen. The publishing business gave Edward further chance to pursue his interests, which were impressively broad. His list of publications includes editions of works by Johann Wolfgang von Goethe, Miguel de Cervantes, and Thomas Chatterton and other English poets. He wrote biographical essays about Edmund Burke, Demosthenes, and Goethe, and works on classical and English historical architecture.

For all his scholarly pursuits, Edward Bell did not neglect the firm's business affairs. George Bell and Sons continued to expand under his leadership. One of its more lucrative ac-

*Advertisement in the 1884* North British Railway Tourist Guide. *Twenty years earlier Bell and Daldy had purchased the stock of Bohn's Libraries, a venture that allowed the firm to abandon retail bookselling.*

quisitions was the English rights to the works of the American author Ralph Waldo Trine, whose *In Tune with the Infinite* (1900) was a best-seller on both sides of the Atlantic. George Bell and Sons further indulged the contemporary interest in philosophical and spiritual speculation when it published the work of Henry Salt, whose humanitarian socialism gained him many prominent converts. Salt's book *Animals' Rights* (1892) was a far more penetrating critique of the treatment of animals than anything else undertaken to that date.

During this period George Bell and Sons' overseas connections expanded through its Colonial Libraries. The firm bought unbound editions of British novels whose publishers did not want to be bothered with distribution to the dominions. George Bell and Sons would then have them bound plainly and sell them overseas. Ironically, because George Bell and Sons was able to acquire the originals for a low price, these Colonial Libraries editions made popular British novels cheaper in the colonies than they were for British readers. The profit margin was slight, but the sales volume was sufficiently vast that George Bell and Sons and its rival in this field, Thomas Fisher Unwin, engaged in spirited competition for new titles.

Even though the publishing industry was relatively buoyant in this period, both publishers and booksellers felt themselves to be continuously plagued by the unscrupulous "undersellers." In the 1890s Frederick Macmillan led other publishers resolved to set limits on the damage undersellers could do to the stability and prosperity of the trade. The Publishers' Association of Great Britain and Ireland was formed in 1896. In 1899 the publishers put into practice a plan Macmillan had first proposed in 1890: the Net Book Agreement, which would secure the publishers' price of some books, called "net books," and leave the free trade system open for others. But just as the publishers were beginning to feel secure about their achievement, the *Times*, anxious to boost circulation, launched a book club in 1905. The club ostensibly offered subscribers privileges in an elaborate lending library organized by the newspaper. But since the Times Book Club also promised members attractive prices for books that had only to be borrowed once or twice to render them "second hand," the *Times* was to all intents and purposes entering the bookselling business. The operators of the book club, however, refused to cooperate with the Net Book Agreement or to recognize any limitations on how they might dispose of the books in their possession. Thus, the Times Book Club undermined the net book system and set off the "book war" which ravaged the trade from 1906 to 1908. As president of the Publishers' Association in this period, Edward Bell was responsible for upholding the Net Book Agreement, which he prized as much as his friend Macmillan.

In his account of the opening shots of the book war, Edward Bell charged Moberly Bell, business manager of the *Times*, and Horace E. Hooper, the American speculator who initiated the Times Book Club, with deviousness and ungentlemanly behavior which he attributed obliquely to their un-English origins (Moberly Bell seems to have been born in Egypt). The way they presented their case to the public showed, according to Bell, an unscrupulous disregard for the civilized discussions which had taken place between the Publishers' Association and the *Times*. In his opinion, the behavior of Moberly Bell and Hooper made inevitable a war that might otherwise have easily been averted. The *Times* was a formidable foe, with far easier access to the public ear than the Publishers' Association could muster. In sensational advertisements for its book club, the newspaper tried to prove that publishers were making exorbitant profits on books that cost them a pittance to produce and were attempting to establish a monopoly. The Publishers' Association responded by resolving not to supply any net books at wholesale prices to the Times Book Club until the *Times* signed the Net Book Agreement. The *Times* found its access to books for its subscribers substantially reduced and resorted to bribery of booksellers' employees to get around the boycott. The Times Book Club also organized its own proscription campaign: *Times Literary Supplement* reviews in this period commonly ended with a plea to readers not to purchase the books reviewed until the dispute with the publishers was resolved. Arthur Walters, the chief proprietor of the *Times*, sent out a missive to subscribers urging them to avoid all the publications of five firms; his list included George Bell and Sons.

The *Evening News* willingly voiced the Publishers' Association side of the dispute, and, indeed, almost the whole press world allied itself with the publishers against the mighty *Times*. Moreover, in contrast to the earlier attempt by George Bell and other publisher/booksellers to regulate their trade in 1852, this time writers, represented by the Society of Authors, sided with the Publishers' Association; a few renegades, including George Bernard Shaw, came out against the Society of Authors and the Publishers' Association. The book war wound down in 1908 when the original proprietors of the *Times* parted company, mainly as a result of dwindling dividends which the expenses of waging the book war only exacerbated. Ownership of the *Times* passed to Lord Northcliffe, whose views on the book war were rather different from those of Moberly Bell. Northcliffe decided that the book club should continue but that it must come to an agreement with the Publishers' Association. The press baron was anxious that no side pronounce itself the winner; thus, to allow the Times Book Club to save face, the publishers agreed to modify the Net Book agreement slightly. Privately, Edward Bell and his allies judged that the publishers had won the day. Edward Bell and his adversary, Moberly Bell, signed the concord on 18 September 1908.

A concrete manifestation of the permanent stature of the company George Bell had founded more than half a century before came with the erection of its own building, York House in Portugal Street, in 1910. George Bell and Sons became a limited liability company that same year.

Bell's participation in the book war was the last sensational episode in the firm's history. Quiet prosperity was in keeping with Edward Bell's scholarly and literary tastes. More adventurous was the career of his only son, Arthur, who fought in the Boer War and World War I and served in India and Ireland before he retired in 1928 as Colonel Bell, D.S.O., O.B.E. Edward Bell had died in 1926; his son was the last Bell to serve in the family firm. Arthur Bell was chairman of George Bell and Sons Ltd. until his own death in 1968. But management of the company had long since fallen to men more experienced in publishing—such as Guy Bickers, who took an active part in the Publishers' Association. During World War II Bickers, acting under the auspices of the Publishers' Association, negotiated an agreement with the government to enable publishers to produce the greatest number of books possible given the stringencies of paper rationing. His achievement was considered a triumph for the industry though some felt that the poor quality of the books produced in such circumstances handicapped British products in overseas markets. After the war George Bell and Sons Ltd. specialized in educational books. The firm became Bell and Hyman Limited when R. P. Hyman became chairman and managing director in 1977. It moved out of the Portugal Street headquarters to Denmark House, Queen Elizabeth Street, where it remained until the firm went out of business in 1989.

**References:**

James J. Barnes, *Free Trade in Books: A Study of the London Book Trade since 1800* (Oxford: Clarendon Press, 1964);

Edward Bell, *George Bell Publisher: A Brief Memoir* (London: Privately printed at the Chiswick Press, 1924);

Sir Frederick Macmillan, *The Net Book Agreement 1899 and The Book War 1906-1908: Two Chapters in the History of the Book Trade, including a Narrative of the Dispute between The Times Book Club and The Publishers' Association by Edward Bell, M.A., President of the Association 1906-1908* (Glasgow: Privately printed by Robert Maclehose and Co. University Press, 1924);

Patricia Srebrnik, *Alexander Strahan, Victorian Publisher* (Ann Arbor: University of Michigan Press, 1986).

*—Marjory Lang*

# William Bemrose
*(Wirksworth; Derby; Derby and London: 1826-1858)*
## Bemrose and Sons
*(Derby: 1858-1978)*
## Bemrose UK Limited
*(Derby: 1978-    )*

William Bemrose began in business in October 1826 as a bookseller, printer, and bookbinder when he bought the bookshop in which he was employed as manager. This was the foundation of a company which still exists as the Bemrose Corporation and which was important as a provincial publisher in the second half of the nineteenth century and as a publisher of bibliographies and scholarly facsimiles in the twentieth century.

Bemrose's shop was in the small town of Wirksworth; the following year he moved about thirteen miles to the southeast to Derby, a more prosperous town with much greater business potential. He formed two short-lived partnerships in the early years, but from 1830 he was on his own. The business seems to have been quite typical for a British provincial town at that time in that printing was the mainstay with only secondary support from bookselling and bookbinding. Publishing was of even less importance. If the opportunity arose, Bemrose would issue a publication of local interest, but he could not be de-

scribed as a publisher with a regular, planned program. Throughout the firm's history printing has been the most important aspect of the business, although there have been periods when publishing has made a significant contribution.

The fortunes of the firm were indirectly secured in 1839 when the railway arrived in Derby. The town soon became an important railway junction, and in 1841 Bemrose began to print train timetables and railway stationery. Printing for British Rail and the London Underground remains a profitable part of the business today. The railways also influenced Bemrose publications; in July 1847 the first issue of *Bemrose's Traveller's Guide* appeared, followed by several similar items, such as *Midland Railway: Scenery, Industries, History* (1902).

Bemrose's sons, Henry and William Junior, entered the business in the 1840s, and in 1858 their father allowed them to take control. From this time publishing was organized on much clearer lines. Although the publications were at first still strongly influenced by local considera-

*William Bemrose*

tions, other patterns of interest began to emerge. An important early success was *The Derbyshire Red Book* (1862-1915), an annual almanac of local information.

The brothers themselves became authors. Henry, who was something of a musician, edited *The Chorale Book* (1862), which contained about two hundred psalm and hymn tunes, many of which he composed himself. William Junior was more prolific. He wrote *A Manual of Wood-Carving* (1862; twenty-third edition, 1906), *Fret-Cutting and Perforated Carving* (1868; fourteenth edition, 1891), *Manual of Buhlwork and Marquetry* (1872; third edition, 1891), *Paper Rosette Work* (1873), *Mosaicon; or Paper Mosaic and How to Make It* (1875), *Bow, Chelsea and Derby Porcelain* (1898), *The Life and Works of Joseph Wright, ARA, Commonly Called "Wright of Derby"* (1885), and *Longton Hall Porcelain* (1906). In addition to the applied art books represented by William Junior's works, archaeology and theology became the firm's principal subject areas. In archaeology there was

Thomas Bateman's *Ten Years' Diggings in Celtic and Saxon Grave Hills in the Counties of Derby, Stafford and York* (1861); in theology, Arthur E. B. Lawrence's *The Holy Communion: Its Institution, Purpose and Privilege* (1905). The most common theological publications were sermons and collections of hymns.

William Senior was not always in agreement with his sons about the publications; in particular he objected to a satirical political periodical, the *Derby Ram*, which ran from 1865 to 1868. Letters to his sons survive in which he claims that the publications are not making a profit. This divergence of views within the firm about the advisability of engaging in publishing was often lurking under the surface.

Despite William Senior's misgivings, publishing was successful under his sons. In 1865 an office was opened in London at 21 Paternoster Row, in the heart of the publishing district. In 1875 the office moved to Paternoster Buildings. William Senior died in 1880. In 1881 the firm moved to 23 Old Bailey, where a London printing office opened at the same time. In 1901 the London publishing office moved to 4 Snow Hill.

The firm's decision to begin educational publishing was due to external stimulus rather than internal planning. A greatly increased market suddenly opened up to British publishers as a result of the 1870 Education Act, and the Bemroses had this market pointed out to them by a local headmaster, J. Chadwick. Textbooks were soon appearing in their lists, such as the Jubilee series: *Jubilee Readers, Jubilee Arithmetic, Jubilee Algebra, Jubilee Grammar*, and so on, each title available in graded parts to suit the various age groups. Nevertheless, the more mundane, less risky, and annually renewable printing for education ran side by side with publishing and probably provided as much income. The firm printed a series of copybooks for teaching handwriting; the series had very large sales, so much so that in 1876 the lithography department had to be enlarged. The company also printed school registers and record cards and all kinds of school stationery.

William Junior died in 1908. He was succeeded by his brother, Henry Howe Bemrose, who died in 1911. William Wright Bemrose then became chairman.

William Junior appears to have been the force behind the publishing business, because within a year of his death the publication stock and goodwill were sold to George Allen. Bemrose had decided, according to the company history (1926), "to devote their energies and plant to the further development of their printing contracts." From the earliest days the printing business had gone from strength to strength, and it continued to do so after the sale of the publishing business. There were 35 employees in 1849; 57 in 1855; 228 in 1870; 872 in 1922, after mergers with Alf Cooke of Leeds and Norbury Natzio of Manchester; and about 3,000 in 1976.

The year 1909, however, did not see the final demise of publishing. The printing firm of Balding and Mansell was acquired in 1961, when it was about halfway through printing the 263 volumes of the *British Museum* (now the *British Library*) *Catalog*. This enormous undertaking provided Balding and Mansell with experience unobtainable from everyday printing work, and as a result a new company, Mansell Information/Publishing Limited, was established in 1967 within the Bemrose Corporation. The *British Museum Catalog* was printed by photolithography directly from the original library catalogue cards.

The Library of Congress had a similar, but immensely larger, catalogue, and Mansell Information/Publishing undertook to print and also to publish this catalogue over twelve years. The publication of the *National Union Catalog: Pre-1956 Imprints* was completed in 1979; a series of supplementary volumes completed in 1981 brought the total to 754 volumes.

When it was obvious that the *National Union Catalog* was going to be successful, Mansell Information/Publishing also began to publish normal-sized books. The firm specialized in bibliographies and works on librarianship, such as *Theses on Africa 1963-1975 Accepted by Universities in the United Kingdom and Ireland* (1978), *Reports of the European Communities, 1952-1977: An Index of Authors and Chairmen* (1981), and Peter Beal's *Index of English Literary Manuscripts 1450-1625* (1980-  ), the first volume of a series planned to include all manuscripts written before 1900.

In 1972 the Bemrose Corporation acquired a second publisher, the Scolar Press, which had been founded in 1966 and which published a large range of facsimiles of original texts in English literature, history, music, and linguistics. In the field of English literature Scolar Press published at least three hundred facsimiles covering the period from the beginning of printing to about 1800. All the major writers were represented. Whenever possible an attempt was made to reproduce the most textually significant edition and to include extra items to illustrate the textual history of that particular work. For example, the facsimile of Milton's *Poems* (1645), published in 1970, also includes the text of "Lycidas" from its first appearance in print in *Justa Eduardo King Naufrago* (1638) and a fragment of a proof copy for this edition with Milton's own corrections.

As had happened previously, the commitment to publishing did not last. In 1981 both Mansell Information/Publishing and Scolar Press were sold, and the Bemrose Corporation once again concentrated its interests on printing.

**References:**

Henry Howe Bemrose, *The House of Bemrose, 1826-1926* (Derby: Bemrose Press, 1926);

Dennis Hackett, *The History of the Future: The Bemrose Corporation, 1826-1976* (London: Scolar Press, 1976).

—*John R. Turner*

# Benn Brothers Limited
*(London: 1897-1981; Tonbridge, Kent: 1981-1991)*
# J. W. Benn
*(London: 1880-1885)*
# J. W. Benn and Brothers
*(London: 1885-1897)*
# Benn Business Publishing
*(Tonbridge, Kent and London: 1991-    )*

The origin of the house of Benn was as a trade journal publisher, and despite its later historical significance as a book publisher, its core strength remains in providing specialized services to a wide range of trades. Although many others have contributed, four generations of the Benn family have set their own highly individual stamp on a concern where paternalism was married to considerable business acumen.

It was in 1880 that the thirty-year-old John Williams Benn, a junior partner in a London furniture business, decided to set up on his own to harness two complementary qualifications: draftsmanship and wide contacts in the trade. Thus was born *Cabinet Maker*—the first of the long line of Benn journals, and one that survives to this day. Benn's risky venture was supported by income from his illustrated lectures on a variety of subjects.

The business originally occupied a single room at 5 Finsbury Square, but within five years it moved a short distance to 42 City Road, with a sign that read The Cabinet Maker's Exchange and Sample Rooms. The company name was J. W. Benn and Brothers, the founder having been joined by Julius, Henry, and Robert Davis Benn. (Robert Davis Benn wrote a standard work, *Style in Furniture* [1904], published by Longman.) In 1897 the company was registered as Benn Brothers Limited. Nine years later it moved to much larger premises at Christopher Street, Finsbury.

Meanwhile, the next generation was entering the business, headed by the founder's eldest son, Ernest John Pickstone Benn. Born in 1875, he joined as junior office boy at the age of sixteen—destined, it seemed, for the editorship of *Cabinet Maker*. There were then no electric lights, no telephone, and of course no women in the office. Ernest Benn later recalled that when a telephone *was* installed, no one was allowed to touch it except the senior partners. He traveled to work, wearing a top hat, in a three-horse omnibus; like all the staff, he put in a sixty-hour week, including Saturday mornings. Ernest soon became secretary of Benn Brothers as well as advertisement manager of *Cabinet Maker*. He was already set to justify his father's tribute as the one who "collected the bricks to build the house of Benn."

With Ernest Benn in charge, John Williams Benn had more time to devote to his other abiding interest, active politics, and stood successfully as a Progressive in the first elections for the London County Council (LCC) in 1889. Although he also became a leading Liberal member of Parliament, it was mainly due to his services to the LCC, of which he was chairman in 1904, that he was knighted in 1906 and created a baronet on the eve of the outbreak of World War I. The honors were in recognition of his efforts to improve the lot of the poor, particularly in the East End of London. (The name Benn continues to be prominent in British politics: John Williams Benn's second son, William Wedgwood Benn, gave up publishing quite early for a political career, becoming a notable Liberal M.P. and later Viscount Stansgate. That is the title which *his* elder surviving son was to disclaim to become plain Tony Benn, M.P.)

Books were not part of the Benn output in the early years. But in 1917 *Gas World* magazine came under the company banner, and with it its annuals and technical books. The *Electrician* was acquired in the same year, along with the long-established *Electrical Trades Directory* (the "Blue Book"); there were also other technical works at this time with the Benn imprint. By then, Benn Brothers was based at 6-8 Bouverie Street, off Fleet Street, and the first director from outside the family had been appointed: H. P. Shapland, editor of *Cabinet Maker*. In 1922 came the death of the founder. Ernest Benn, whose busy wartime career had included stints at the ministries of munitions and reconstruction and weekend shifts at Woolwich Arsenal, succeeded to the chairmanship—and to the baronetcy, being henceforth known in the firm as "the Bart." He paid tribute to his father: "Our hope and belief is that the 40 years which he devoted to establishing the spirit of this business, to giving it a character and a purpose of its own, to making the name of Benn a synonym for the best in technical publishing, will have so moulded our habits and aspirations as to enable us worthily to maintain those great traditions." Sir Ernest was a pioneer of the five-day workweek, participated in the Whitley Councils to establish wage levels, instituted staff shareholding, and established the company's responsibility for providing secure employment.

The early 1920s were especially significant on two fronts. First, Benn Brothers set up a separate book department in 1921 which developed into an associate company, Ernest Benn Limited, two years later. It became a direct subsidiary of Benn Brothers in the mid 1930s. Sir Ernest was its first chairman, and Victor Gollancz, manager of technical books, was appointed managing director of the new company. Gollancz quickly made his mark both creatively and in the marketplace. Another director was Cecil Hughes, Sir Ernest's brother-in-law, whose professional skill as an artist and business interest in that field led to a succession of books on fine and applied art in which high literary standards were allied to splendid production values. An early example was *The Catalogue of the George Eumorfopoulos Collection* (1925), a limited-edition, multivolume folio work. A series of classics from the master typographer Stanley Morison was launched with *Four Centuries of Fine Printing* (1924), incorporating more than six hundred collotype plates; this series culminated

with *The Typographic Book, 1450-1935* (1963), in which Kenneth Day, Ernest Benn's post-World War II production director, collaborated with Morison. Sir Francis Meynell's *Typography of Newspaper Advertisements* (1929) was the forerunner of Day's *Typography of Press Advertisement* (1956)—a textbook that remained in print for more than twenty years. Another landmark in Benn production was the English translation of Elie Halévy's masterpiece *History of the English People in the 19th Century* (1949-1952). Some twelve years after the manuscript for the last of the six volumes was delivered to Benn by Halévy's widow, a massive paperback edition was printed. Among the early series, The Players' Shakespeare (circa 1923) was a most ambitious project; it was never completed. In a more popular vein, The Mermaid Dramatists series (circa 1926-1927) was highly regarded. With some of these prestigious titles already to its name, Benn was the first book publisher to advertise on the front page of the *Times* and with a full page in the *Daily Mail*. The emphasis on Middle and Far Eastern art, for example in *The Catalogue of the George Eumorfopoulos Collection*, led to the adoption of the slogan "Published at the Sign of the T'ang Horse." The familiar Ernest Benn logo, adopted circa 1924-1925, was based on the T'ang Horse.

The other principal legacy of the era was the emergence of Sir Ernest Benn as an advocate of right-wing capitalism. Despite—perhaps because of—his wartime service, any form of centralized state control became anathema for him; individualism was all. He wrote a stream of books—twenty-one in all, mostly published under the Ernest Benn imprint—and pamphlets. Sir Ernest founded the Individualist Bookshop in 1926, and in 1942 he would cofound the Society of Individualists. Despite its postwar preoccupations, the public took notice when, as a gesture, he tore up his census form. Not surprisingly, this unyielding standpoint led to friction with the very left-inclined and equally independent-minded Gollancz, and in 1927 the latter broke away and founded his own firm. Sir Ernest's generous comment was: "The clash of opposing philosophies made it wise to arrange a separation."

But in the meantime this unlikely partnership had masterminded both a dramatic acquisition and a publishing revolution. The acquisition, which transformed company fortunes almost overnight, was the imprint of T. Fisher Unwin in 1926. This purchase allowed Ernest Benn to reprint the works of such authors as H. G. Wells, Jo-

*Ernest Benn, eldest son of company founder John Williams Benn. He entered the firm in 1881 at sixteen and became chairman in 1922.*

seph Conrad, Ethel M. Dell, Olive Schreiner, Robert W. Service, and E. Nesbit. Wells was a special case in that Benn Brothers was the publisher of several original works, notably the massive "three-deck" *The World of William Clissold* (1926), as well as the notable twenty-four-volume Essex Thin Paper Edition (1926-1927) of all his work to date and *The Short Stories of H. G. Wells* (1927). Sales of the short stories eventually totaled around half a million. An unusual tour de force was the publication in 1927 of Arnold Bennett's classic 1908 novel, *The Old Wives' Tale*, in two volumes of facsimile manuscript. All five hundred copies were signed by the author.

Dorothy L. Sayers was a promising name on T. Fisher Unwin's "hand-over" list. She had three crime stories published by Benn before throwing in her lot with Gollancz, with whom she had struck a close working relationship. The Yorkshire novelist Phyllis Bentley also came from Unwin to Benn and then left with Gollancz.

The revolution the company instigated in

the 1920s was mass publishing in paperback. The Augustan Poets series—later known as The Sixpenny Poets—and The Contemporary Dramatists series were followed by the 150-volume Benn's Sixpenny Library, with its vivid orange covers. Marketed as "a complete reference library to modern thought," the Sixpenny Library sold in the millions. Many years later, the series was collated into twenty-five hardback volumes as The Modern Knowledge Library, selling at three shillings, sixpence each.

With a parallel growth in trade-oriented journals, Benn Brothers needed larger, centralized offices. In 1926 the firm moved into the highly prestigious seven-story Bouverie House at 154-160 Fleet Street. The move was approved by Sir Ernest as "bringing the business where it rightly belonged, alongside the national press."

Shortly afterwards, representatives of the next generation of the family were elected to the boards of both the parent company and Ernest Benn Limited. These were John Andrews Benn and Edward Glanvill Benn, sons of Sir Ernest, and Keon Eldred Hughes, the son of Cecil and a grandson of the founder. Hughes was to be a director of Ernest Benn for fifty-two years.

One of the most successful—certainly the longest-running—series in Ernest Benn's lists was Muirhead's Blue Guides. L. Russell Muirhead had begun editing the guides for Macmillan, but Benn acquired them in 1931, and they continued in ever-growing profusion and reputation under the Benn imprint for more than half a century.

In 1932 another major paperback series was launched. The Benn Ninepenny Novels eventually totaled thirty-two original works by leading authors; but they proved to be ahead of their time, and never achieved the success of their "sixpenny" predecessors.

The company had long cherished international ambitions in publishing as well as marketing, and the first of its many journals concerned with export trade had appeared in London as early as 1907. Benn Brothers Overseas had been registered the following year, and in 1909 a publishing office had been opened in Buenos Aires to service the South American market, supported by a Spanish-language monthly. This connection was renewed by John Benn in 1931, when the magazine *Industria Britanica* was launched in London. An editorial office was also opened in Vienna from 1922 to 1924. Glanvill Benn took charge of production of all Ernest Benn books but switched to journal editorship when the company purchased the weekly *Newspaper World* in 1933.

Sir Ernest recruited Gordon Robbins, day editor of the *Times*, as his deputy in 1926. When war came in 1939, there were four managing directors of the parent company: Robbins, Crole-Rees, John Benn, and Glanvill Benn. Crole-Rees retired, and the two Benns left to join the forces. Sir Ernest had ceased to be managing director in 1937; when he relinquished the chairmanship in September 1941, Robbins took over. With paper controls rigidly enforced, the thirteen Benn journals were severely restricted in size and format. But demand from trade and industry was as keen as ever, and Bouverie House survived the blitz undamaged. Robbins died in 1944, and Glanvill Benn was elected chairman while still serving abroad.

After the war John Benn returned as chairman of Ernest Benn, which announced six new titles and fifteen reprints in its first postwar list. The most immediately successful was Winston Churchill's *Painting as a Pastime* (1948), published jointly with Odhams Press.

But John Benn gave up his role in the firm in 1950 to take up a City appointment. Glanvill Benn succeeded him as chairman of Ernest Benn, and Keon Hughes returned from military service to become deputy chairman of both the parent company and Ernest Benn.

Sir Ernest Benn died in January 1954. His fellow directors recorded "their great sense of irreparable loss" and said that "his forthright and sound judgment, his wise counsel and guidance contributed beyond all calculation to the development and expansion of the company's business over the past 60 years."

As chairman, Glanvill Benn was responsible in the 1950s for two major innovations: first, to meet a demand from the advertising industry, the firm was the first "trade and technical" publisher to join the Audit Bureau of Circulations; second, the firm began to produce and market a series of specialized directories for sale in place of the yearbooks that had previously been included in journal subscriptions. The first of the new annuals directly associated with, but sold separately from, a Benn journal was, appropriately, *The Cabinet Maker Directory to the Furnishing Trade* (1957); but six years before, the first *Newspaper Press Directory* under the Benn banner had appeared. Founded by Charles Mitchell in 1846, and thus with a strong claim to be the oldest surviving trade guide in the world, this noted reference work was transformed into the two-volume *Benn's*

*Media Directory* in 1986. The new-style *Benn's Hardware Directory* (1963) signaled the end of the free-issue yearbooks.

It was decided in the 1960s that the firm would move out of London in stages. The first premises in Tonbridge, Kent, included a warehouse for the current output of some 850,000 Ernest Benn books a year.

Children's books such as Tove Jansson's Moomins series and Elisabeth Beresford's *Wombles* (1970) were a particular success. The children's list was the particular province of John Denton, who was appointed general manager of Ernest Benn in 1966, remaining so until 1973. Quality Press, Williams and Norgate, and Lindsay Drummond were among the imprints acquired by the parent company, and Benn Brothers Incorporated was registered in the United States.

Benn House in Tonbridge was opened in July 1981. Most remaining group operations—administration, journals, and directories—were concentrated in that area, where Benn is among the principal employers. But Tolley Publishing Company, specializing in tax law and accountancy, and its subsidiary, the old, established firm Charles Knight, acquired from Brown, Knight and Truscott and specializing in the local government field, are based in Croydon.

In June 1983, control of Benn Brothers passed to the Extel Group. In 1984 Ernest Benn Limited was sold to A. and C. Black. Muirhead's Blue Guides, The New Mermaids drama texts, Susanna Gretz's Teddybears series, and Frank Muir's *What-a-Mess* (1977) were among the few major titles extant when the deal went through.

Richard Woolley succeeded Glanvill Benn as chairman when Benn was appointed life president of Benn Brothers in 1976. John Benn's younger son, Timothy, was the last member of the family to be chairman. He left in 1983 and formed his own company, Timothy Benn Publishing, also mainly in the magazine field.

The Extel Group was acquired by United Newspapers in 1987. In March 1991 the name Benn Brothers disappeared after ninety-four years, to be replaced by Benn Business Publishing Limited, an operating company within Morgan-Grampian plc, based in London. Production of the Benn journals and directories continues from the Tonbridge offices.

**References:**
Deryck Abel, *Ernest Benn: Counsel for Liberty* (Lon-

don: Benn, 1959);

Ernest Benn, *The Confessions of a Capitalist* (London: Benn, 1925);

Benn, *Happier Days: Recollections and Reflections* (London: Benn, 1949);

Benn, *The Letters of an Individualist to The Times, 1921-26* (London: Benn, 1927);

Benn, *The Murmurings of an Individualist*, 2 volumes (London: Individualist Bookshop, 1941-1942);

Benn, *Why Freedom Works: Passages from Sir Ernest Benn's Books, 1924-1953*, edited by Glanvill Benn (London: Benn, 1964);

Ruth Dudley Edwards, *Victor Gollancz: A Biography* (London: Gollancz, 1987);

A. G. Gardiner, *John Benn and the Progressive Movement* (London: Benn, 1925);

Victor Gollancz, *Reminiscences of Affection* (London: Gollancz, 1968);

Sydney Higgins, *The Benn Inheritance: The Story of a Radical Family* (London: Weidenfeld & Nicolson, 1984);

Sheila Hodges, *Gollancz: The Story of a Publishing House, 1928-1978* (London: Gollancz, 1978);

Douglas Jerrold, *Georgian Adventure* (London: Collins, 1937);

Gordon Robbins, *Fleet Street Blitzkrieg Diary* (London: Benn, 1944);

Richard Woolley, *The House of Benn: The First 100 Years* (London: Benn, 1980).

**Papers:**

Most of the archives of Benn Brothers were deposited in 1984 in the Modern Records Centre, University of Warwick Library, Coventry. Material relevant to Ernest Benn and Sir Ernest Benn as a publisher was passed to A. and C. Black after the latter acquired the company, also in 1984.

　　　　　　　　　　　　　　　　　　*—David Linton*

# Richard Bentley
*(London: 1832-1871)*
## Henry Colburn and Richard Bentley
*(London: 1829-1832)*
## Henry Colburn
*(London: circa 1806-1820; 1824-1829; 1832-1851)*
## Henry Colburn and Company
*(London: 1820-1824; 1851-1852)*
## Richard Bentley and Son
*(London: 1871-1898)*

Henry Colburn and Richard Bentley were partners for only three years; for most of their careers they ran separate and even rival publishing firms. Nevertheless, they tended to arouse similar emotions—generally negative ones—among writers and other publishers. Their methods frequently caused them to be attacked; puffery and sharp dealing were not beneath their dignity, and some of their colleagues questioned whether they had any dignity at all. Yet Colburn and Bentley were ahead of their time in their advertising methods; and they were—even if only by accident—partly responsible for the advancement of literature and literacy in the nineteenth century. It is not entirely fair, moreover, to tar Bentley with Colburn's brush. Bentley may not have been more sinned against than sinning, but his actions indicate a greater integrity than those of his sometime partner.

Colburn's birthdate is unknown, but rumors about his origin had him as the illegitimate son of either Lord Lansdowne or the duke of York. Given Colburn's ability throughout his career to manipulate the media, and his adoration of nobility, one might suspect that Colburn had a hand in fashioning such genealogies.

As early as 1806 Colburn published at least three works of minor fiction in London. In 1807-1808 he published seven titles, including Frederic Shoberl's translation of Christoph Mei-

ners's *History of the Female Sex* in four volumes. Until 1808 Colburn also served as assistant to William Earle, a bookseller at 47 Albemarle Street; then he became an assistant at Morgan's Circulating Library, known also as the British and Foreign Library, at 50 Conduit Street. In 1816 he became proprietor of the library. As a publisher he became well known for his trade in fiction and other light literature. From 1806 until his retirement at the end of 1852 Colburn published at least 996 new titles, not including several series of reprints. Of these, 527 were novels, 394 of them three-deckers (three volumes); 141 were travel books; 207 were memoirs; only 29 were poetry. It was with the three-deckers that his fortunes rose and fell.

They rose for much of his first decade in business. Colburn showed a propensity for gauging public taste—if not for having literary taste—by publishing ten works by Mme de Genlis and seven by Mme de Staël between 1806 and 1817, and the complete works in fourteen volumes of Mme Sophie Cottin in 1811. His first major success, however, came when he paid Lady Sydney Morgan £550 for *O'Donnel* (1814), which quickly sold two thousand copies. Even this early in Colburn's career, his list of publications filled nine pages of advertisements at the end of the novel's third volume.

In the same year Colburn founded the *New Monthly Magazine and Universal Register* with Shoberl, to compete with Richard Phillips's *Monthly Magazine*. Shoberl became its first editor as well as a reader for the firm. For as long as he owned it, Colburn used the magazine to puff his own publications list, frequently in the guise of leading articles extolling the virtues of the book reviewed. Colburn also bought advertisements in other periodicals and newspapers, partly to induce the reviewers to write favorably about his publications. In 1819 he informed Lady Morgan that his advertisements in the *Examiner*, the *New Times*, and *John Bull* insured positive reviews of her books. By then he had also published her novel *France* (1817), for which he had originally offered £750; she had refused that amount and had approached Archibald Constable, who had rejected the work, and Colburn had increased his offer to £1,000. The novel quickly went into four English and two French editions. For her next novel, *Florence McCarthy* (1818), Colburn had paid £1,200, and it had quickly gone through five editions. Throughout his career Colburn was generous to those authors whose works were profitable. Thus he increased his payment to Lady Morgan to £2,000 for her next novel, *Italy* (1821).

In 1817 Colburn founded the *Literary Gazette*, a one-shilling weekly review. It immediately reflected his personality by its obsequious attitude toward the nobility and its puffing of the owner's publications. Within six months the *Gazette* achieved a circulation of three thousand. At that point Longman's bought a one-third share, as did William Jerdan, formerly editor of the *Sun*, who replaced H. E. Lloyd and a Miss Rose as *Gazette* editor. Selling off a majority interest in the new venture so soon may indicate that Colburn was suffering a financial crisis.

At the same time that he was establishing the *Gazette*, Colburn took a significant step in publishing history. At the suggestion of the antiquarian William Upcott, he purchased the rights to John Evelyn's diary, which had lain virtually unread for more than 150 years. Richard, Lord Braybrooke edited it for Colburn, who published it in 1818 in two volumes for six guineas. For the next two editions he lowered the price to five guineas.

Evelyn's *Diary* brought Colburn into initial contact with the man who was to become first his business associate, a decade later his partner, and finally his antagonist. Richard Bentley was born in 1794 in Paternoster Row in London, where his father, Edward Bentley, and his uncle, John Nichols, published the *General Evening Post*. Educated for a time at St. Paul's School, he joined his uncle's printing firm to learn the business that had been in the family for three generations. There he met Colburn in 1818 in connection with the publication of Evelyn's *Diary*. In 1819 Richard and his older brother Samuel became partners in their own printing firm in Dorset Street. The brothers achieved a reputation for the excellent quality of their work, and in 1820 Colburn employed them to print the *New Monthly Magazine*.

In 1819 Colburn published only four new titles, and in 1820 he put the library on Conduit Street, with its fifty thousand volumes, up for sale; he also changed the name of his firm to Henry Colburn and Company. By this time the *Literary Gazette*'s editors were adopting a more independent stance, at least to the extent of occasionally actually criticizing a Colburn-published novel. In 1821 Colburn temporarily suspended advertising in its pages after the *Gazette* reviewed Lady Morgan's *Italy* unfavorably. Throughout his publishing career Colburn would supply periodicals in which he advertised with articles in praise of his list; when the articles appeared, he would send copies to country newspapers to create a demand beyond London. Such puffery infuriated Colburn's competitors and also offended the editors of the selected journals.

Colburn's financial problems, evident as early as 1817, plagued him for more than a decade. His *New Monthly*, struggling with competition from the *London Magazine*, needed bold action to reverse its fortunes. Just as he offered large payments to authors whose books he believed would be profitable, in 1820 he offered Horace Smith, then writing for the *London Magazine*, twenty guineas a sheet (sixteen pages) for prose or verse to be published in the *New Monthly*. By the end of 1821 Colburn had hired Smith; William Hazlitt, who brought his "Table Talk" series with him; and others away from the *London Magazine*. In 1820 Colburn offered the popular poet Thomas Campbell five hundred pounds per year for an initial three-year contract, beginning in January 1821, to be the editor of the magazine, which was renamed the *New Monthly Magazine and Literary Journal*. Campbell served as an inactive editor but an active writer for the magazine; the subeditor, Edward Dubois, did the bulk of the editorial work for the January issue, and Cyrus Redding took over the real editorial duties beginning with the February issue. The *New Monthly* became a miscellany, modeled on the *Gentleman's Magazine*, containing original poems and Campbell's "Lectures on Poetry." Circulation soon doubled to five thousand copies.

In 1820 Colburn had offered Theodore Hook £600 for a novel; Colburn viewed the payment as an investment not so much in a work of fiction as in the individual who was editor of *John Bull* and thus controlled its contents. Hook accepted the offer, and Colburn proudly and profitably published the thirty-shilling, three-volume *Sayings and Doings* (1824). Six thousand copies sold quickly; Colburn paid Hook an extra £350 and offered £1,000 for each of the next two series, published in 1825 and 1828.

In 1824 Colburn sold the British and Foreign Library to the new firm of Saunders and Otley, moved his publishing business to 8 New Burlington Street, and changed the firm's name back to Henry Colburn. His major coup in 1825, for posterity if not for his own immediate profit, was his decision to purchase for £2,200 the rights to Samuel Pepys's diary, which he quickly published as *Memoirs of Samuel Pepys, Esq., F.R.S., Secretary to the Admiralty in the Reigns of Charles II. and James II., Comprising His Diary from 1659 to 1669*. The firm made little money but gained respect and prestige, at least for a short time.

From 1825 to 1829 Colburn was particularly successful in gauging the public's taste and in developing popular authors: he published 197 books, of which 107 were fiction, 80 of them the particularly profitable three-deckers. His income from publishing novels during this period has been estimated at twenty thousand pounds per year. In the financial crisis of 1826 Constable's firm failed, banks closed, and other publishers went out of business or at least reduced their publication lists; but not Colburn. He continued publishing fiction and helped develop the "Silver Fork" school with such three-deckers as Robert Plumer Ward's *Tremaine; or, The Man of Refinement* (1825), Thomas Henry Lister's *Granby* (1826), and the marquis of Normanby's *Yes and No: A Tale of the Day* (1828). At the same time Colburn was negotiating with a young man who, although he had not experienced fashionable society, had aspirations to do so and had a vivid imagination. Shoberl, Colburn's chief reader, recommended against publishing the young man's manuscript, but another assistant, Charles Ollier, suggested that Colburn read it himself. Colburn did,

and offered the young author two hundred pounds. *Vivian Grey* appeared in five volumes in 1826-1827, and Benjamin Disraeli became one of Henry Colburn's popular authors. Colburn subsequently published all of Disraeli's early fashionable fiction. Edward Bulwer's *Pelham* appeared in 1828 and was to become one of the pillars of the firm's fortunes. In 1829 the young G. P. R. James became one of Colburn's successful authors with his first novel, *Richelieu*. Also popular for Colburn in the late 1820s were Anna Jameson, Lady Charlotte Bury, and Mrs. Gore, and he expanded his business at the very time other publishers were retreating in financial fear. By 1829, in fact, Colburn was the largest publisher of books for general trade in England, publishing more than 10 percent of all new titles. It is estimated that his firm published 90 percent of the Silver Fork novels.

The second half of the decade was significant for the firm for both its successes and its failures. Beginning in 1826 Colburn published John Burke's dictionaries and genealogies of the British peerage, works whose valuable copyrights he kept to the end of his life. Late in 1827 the eighteen-year-old William Gladstone approached Colburn with an idea to republish the *Eton Miscellany*, which Gladstone had edited, but Colburn rejected the idea in February 1828. Colburn was angry at the *Literary Gazette* again, this time over its treatment of Lady Morgan's *The O'Briens and the O'Flahertys* (1827). Still part owner of the magazine, Colburn had been advertising extensively in its pages again. He felt betrayed by Jerdan, who seemed to be part of a growing chorus of reviewers attacking the quality of the firm's publications and the integrity of Colburn's advertisements. Colburn wrote to Jerdan on 31 December 1827 that he and James Silk Buckingham were about to begin a new literary and critical journal because of the unfair and politically motivated criticism of his authors by the *Gazette*. Jerdan responded that most of the reviews of the firm's publications were positive, and the evidence supports Jerdan's position. Nonetheless, Colburn's mind was set, and the first issue of the *Athenaeum* appeared in January 1828. Colburn owned a one-half interest, as did Buckingham, who became editor. By April 1828, however, Buckingham was attacking virtually the entire Colburn publications list. Colburn sold his share in the *Athenaeum* on 21 May 1828. Thereafter, especially under the editorial guidance of Charles Wentworth Dilke, the

*Athenaeum* led the attacks against Colburn's puffing.

In May 1829 Colburn founded the *Court Journal*, a weekly whose reports on fashionable events and news catered to the same audience that was reading Silver Fork fiction. It was an obvious mechanism by which Colburn could puff his three-deckers. He also founded the *United Service Journal*, appealing to the same readers who were buying the newly published military and nautical fiction, as represented by Captain Frederick Marryat's *The Naval Officer; or, Scenes and Adventures in the Life of Frank Mildmay* (1829). Colburn owned an interest in the *Sunday Times* newspaper as well, and thus, including the *New Monthly* and the *Literary Gazette*, was involved to a significant degree in five periodicals by the end of the decade.

The successes Colburn had during the second half of the decade apparently did not compensate for the failures. His firm, which was doing between three thousand and thirty-five hundred pounds in annual business with Samuel and Richard Bentley, was unable to pay all of its bills. Edward Morgan, chief clerk for Colburn since 1825, eventually determined that Colburn owed eighteen thousand pounds to his creditors at this time. To protect his interests, Richard Bentley proposed that he and Colburn form a partnership. Samuel Bentley bought out his younger brother's share of the printing business, thus providing Richard with the funds to buy into Colburn's firm.

The partnership agreement, signed on 3 June 1829, included more than thirty articles and favored Colburn. For the three-year trial partnership, Bentley was to bring twenty-five hundred pounds to the firm, be the active partner in seeking manuscripts and keeping the books, and receive two-fifths of the profit; Colburn was to provide three-fifths of the capital and receive three-fifths of the profit. Publishing decisions were to be made jointly. In the event that the partnership failed before the three years were up, Bentley was to buy out Colburn for ten thousand pounds—less if the firm's profits proved to be less than that amount—and Colburn was to agree to cease publishing except for his periodicals and the copyrights he had held before the partnership was formed. The new firm, Henry Colburn and Richard Bentley, remained at 8 New Burlington Street.

The partnership lasted slightly more than three years. Like Colburn's business in the 1820s it achieved resounding successes and deafening failures. Most noteworthy among their failures were three series of inexpensive books announced in the spring of 1830: the National Library of General Knowledge, the Juvenile Library, and the Library of Modern Travels and Discoveries. The National Library, under the editorship of G. R. Gleig, was a disaster from its inception. Announced at five shillings a volume, the price was soon raised to six shillings, but Gleig was unable to hire the contributors he wanted, such as Scott and Robert Southey. Instead, the first volume, published on 25 August 1830, was Bentley's choice, John Galt's *The Life of Lord Byron*. The first volume of Gleig's *History of the Bible* (1830-1831) appeared a month later. Both were attacked, the latter for inaccuracies and disorganization, the former for being simplistic and poorly written. The firm's preliminary puffs for these volumes also were strongly criticized, but those early advertisements did result in Galt's book selling nearly its complete initial edition. Gleig's book fared less well, and sales of subsequent volumes were failures. In all, thirteen volumes of the National Library appeared; of the 55,750 copies printed, 21,829 were sold to Thomas Tegg as remainders at one shilling, sixpence per volume. The Juvenile Library was an even greater failure. On 30 April 1830 the firm signed Jerdan, Colburn's antagonistic partner and editor of the *Literary Gazette*, to edit the series at an annual salary of three hundred pounds plus bonuses. Only three volumes of the Juvenile Library ever appeared, and they were widely attacked as being hastily conceived and poorly written. The firm lost nine hundred pounds on the venture. Given these results, it is not surprising that the Travels and Discoveries library never appeared. Another failure occurred in 1831, when the partners decided not to publish a manuscript submitted by a little-known reviewer and translator named Thomas Carlyle; *Sartor Resartus* was published by *Fraser's* beginning in 1833.

Overall, however, Colburn and Bentley were successful. Their success resulted in part from their spending twenty-seven thousand pounds advertising their publications during their three years together. In addition, they were not above attempts at intimidation: at one point they served legal notice on the *Athenaeum* to preclude its reviewing a book before the official publication date; the delay enabled them to place early positive reviews in the *Literary Gazette* and the *Court Journal*.

*Richard (left) and George Bentley*

The most important reason Colburn and Bentley succeeded was because they catered to the public taste. Bulwer's *Paul Clifford* (1830) aroused interest in the "Newgate" or criminal novel, and was succeeded by his *Eugene Aram* (1832). The firm published Hook's *Maxwell* (1830) and Disraeli's *The Young Duke* (1831), and Mrs. Gore added four Silver Fork titles in 1831 to her growing list. Most of the Colburn and Bentley novels were three-deckers, the correct length for the circulating libraries that were large-quantity purchasers. The publishers felt justified in asking T. C. Grattan to shorten *The Heiress of Bruges* (1830) to fit into three volumes; Grattan refused to do so, and, when it appeared in four volumes for forty-two shillings, the critics attacked the last two volumes for their length.

As Bentley and Colburn looked to see what was successful for other publishers, their attention had to be attracted by two recent series that were selling well. John Murray's Family Library, originally priced at five shillings, consisted of biographies, histories, and travel narratives, but no fiction. Even more successful was Thomas Caddell's Author's Edition of the Waverley Novels, also published at five shillings per volume. But these inexpensive editions frequently contained two or more volumes for each title, and Bentley and

Colburn recognized a potentially profitable alternative. In February 1831 they began publishing one-volume reprints of three-decker novels whose copyrights they had owned previously or had recently bought. Colburn and Bentley's Standard Novels series was a landmark in nineteenth-century publishing. At six shillings per volume, the Standard Novels immediately expanded the market for fiction to include the mass of people who could not afford a guinea and a half for the original three-decker and were willing to wait a year or two for the low-cost reprint. Moreover, since Colburn and Bentley owned the copyrights to the works they reprinted, all of the profit was theirs. They had no contractual obligations to the authors, who had received their one-time payment for the three-decker format and did not share in the continuing income from subsequent publication in one volume.

James Fenimore Cooper's *The Pilot* (25 February 1831) was the first novel in the series; Cooper's *The Spy* (2 May 1831) was the third volume; and his *The Last of the Mohicans* (30 July 1831) was the sixth. In all, twenty-one of Cooper's novels appeared in the series. Jane Austen's novels appeared in five volumes; eleven of Marryat's novels, three of Bulwer's, five of James's, and two of Frances Trollope's were also included. Colburn and Bentley had secured revisions, where possible, from living authors whose works they reprinted; thus, they could with some accuracy claim that their reprints were the most authoritative texts available. Sometimes, however, changes were imposed on authors by the publishers, who wanted a three-decker condensed to fit the one-volume format. Together, Colburn and Bentley published the first 19 volumes in a series that would extend to 126 volumes in twenty-four years.

The success of the Standard Novels was astounding: in its first year it provided the firm with a profit of £1,160. Even before those results were known, Colburn began another series of cheap reprints, Colburn's Modern Novelists. The early volumes, however, at six shillings each, consisted of little more than unsold sheets of fiction that he had published before the partnership.

By 1831 the partnership was showing signs of failure. Costs of purchasing copyrights of fiction to be reprinted were mounting: although five Austen novels cost only £210, and *Pride and Prejudice* (1833) an additional £40, Colburn and Bentley paid Longman's £700 for the novels of Jane and Marie Porter and lost £230 on the first six published. Bentley learned from Morgan just how precarious their financial condition was, and the firm averted bankruptcy in September only by Colburn's selling his share in the *Sunday Times* and at least part of his ownership of the *Court Journal*.

By early 1832 Bentley realized that the partnership was a disaster. He and Colburn had stopped working together, or even speaking to each other. Morgan, who as chief clerk had organized Colburn's incoherent account books, served as mediator between Bentley's and Colburn's lawyers. After months of mutual threats and recriminations a settlement was reached on 1 September 1832. Bentley agreed to purchase the firm for £1,500, in addition to the £2,500 he had paid in 1829 to establish the partnership. He kept the premises on New Burlington Street and renamed the firm Richard Bentley. He also agreed to pay Colburn £5,580 2s. for books and manuscripts owned by the partnership, including the Standard Novels series. Colburn retained his journals but agreed not to publish any new books and not to publish within twenty miles of London reprints of the works whose copyrights he still owned; if he violated these provisions, he would pay Bentley a penalty of £5,000.

Almost from the day the partnership was dissolved Colburn violated the spirit, if not the letter, of the agreement. He published a new book at the end of the year, claiming that it was merely a reprint of material that had appeared in one of his journals. He began a reprint series, Colburn's Irish National Tales and Romances, at four shillings a volume, including three novels by John and Michael Banim and a four-volume reprint of Lady Morgan's *The O'Briens and the O'Flahertys*. From 1833 through 1835 Colburn published thirteen new titles. In accordance with a provision of the partnership's termination agreement, these works were published by Bentley's firm. Most of Colburn's authors, however, went with Bentley or to Saunders and Otley.

At this time Colburn became involved in legal problems apart from the agreement with Bentley. The duke of Richmond claimed that Colburn was responsible for a libel printed in the *Court Journal*. Colburn denied the allegation and sued the editor, whom he blamed for the libelous statement. On 13 February 1834 Colburn won his case and was awarded £193 in damages.

In August 1834 Colburn advertised the Naval and Military Library of Entertainment, a monthly library of "the Choicest Modern Works from the pens of Distinguished Officers" in twenty volumes. It was actually a series of reprints of the earlier military and nautical novels whose popularity had waned. Colburn was trying to find some way to profit from the copyrights he had owned before the partnership.

He was doing well elsewhere, however. Campbell left the editorship of the *New Monthly* at the end of 1830, angered both because Colburn was expecting him actually to perform some editorial duties and because he felt his artistic integrity was being sacrificed at the altar of Colburn's puffery. Bulwer then became a working editor of the magazine. By 1834 the *New Monthly* was strong, with a circulation of five thousand, and Hook's "Gilbert Gurney" appearing in its pages; Samuel Carter Hall, who had become subeditor in 1830, served as editor briefly in 1831 and again from 1833 through 1836; in 1837 Hook became editor and served until his death in 1841.

In January 1835 Colburn announced a "New and Improved Edition" of his Modern Novelists series at five shillings a volume, beginning with the ever-popular *Pelham* in two volumes. Even this series was being published by Bentley's firm, but the battle between the former partners was joined. In February 1835 Bentley advertised the continuation of his Standard Novels series at six shillings a volume but emphasized that, unlike Colburn's series, most of Bentley's novels would appear in one volume. In April Colburn retaliated by publishing two novels—*Pelham* and *Tremaine*—in one volume, still at five shillings. He soon realized, however, that he could not make a profit under these circumstances, and in 1836 he raised the price to six shillings.

To strike another blow at his former partner, who had become a hated rival, Colburn changed the title of his series from Colburn's Modern Novelists to Colburn's Modern Standard Novelists. The move was clearly calculated to confuse his series with Bentley's. To keep his costs down Colburn required several authors to shorten their novels, but he nowhere indicated that these reprints were abridged versions of the original three-deckers. Under this new title Colburn published from 1836 to 1842 twenty volumes that included thirteen novels and the three series of Hook's *Sayings and Doings*. From October 1835 well into 1836 he also published these works in one-shilling weekly numbers, of which numbers one through six contained Bulwer's *Pelham*. (The idea of a part-issue was to be used most successfully by Charles Dickens for *The Pickwick Papers*, published by Chapman and Hall in 1836-1837.)

Colburn could not retreat from the business that was so much a part of him. In 1835 he set up as a publisher in Windsor, just beyond the twenty-mile limit to which he had agreed in dissolving the partnership. Competition with Bentley was now in the open, particularly when Colburn advertised in London newspapers and sold his volumes in London shops. In April 1836 Morgan again mediated between the two publishers and, with the help of the antiquarian and bibliographer William Upcott, arranged for Colburn to buy his release from the 1832 agreement. On 11 June 1836 Bentley and Colburn, still not speaking, signed the release by which Colburn paid his former partner thirty-five hundred pounds and once again was to be permitted to publish new books in London. Colburn immediately set up his new firm, Henry Colburn, at 13 Great Marlborough Street, where he remained for the rest of his career.

Bentley emerged from the partnership in 1832 in a considerably stronger position than did Colburn. He owned the business; he had bought the copyrights of works published by the defunct partnership; and there were no constraints on his publishing as there were on Colburn's. Nonetheless, extricating himself from Colburn had been costly, and Bentley approached his new independence cautiously. He was aided by the personnel who came with him upon the partnership's termination. In many ways the most important individual for Bentley was not one of his authors: Morgan, Colburn's clerk since 1825, remained with Bentley's firm until 1858. While Colburn and Bentley were partners Morgan had suffered a breakdown but had recovered. He became one of Bentley's most trusted advisers and was to be instrumental in the firm's success later in the decade. William Shoberl and Charles Ollier, both of whom had worked for Colburn before the partnership, stayed with Bentley's firm as well. Shoberl, whose father had cofounded and co-owned the *New Monthly* with Colburn, returned to Colburn in the early 1840s. Ollier remained with Bentley until the publisher released him in 1839 and replaced him with Richard Harris Barham, a former classmate of Bentley's at St. Paul's School. Barham served until 1843, when Bentley, to save the ten pounds a month he had been paid, let him go. Considering that Barham's *The Ingoldsby Legends*, whose first two series (1840 and 1842), reprinted from *Bentley's Miscellany*, were slow sellers but still among the firm's profitable early publications, Bentley cannot be accused of sentimentality, or perhaps even gratitude. Bentley's treatment of Barham looks even worse when later results are examined. A third series was published in 1846, and reprints of the three series appeared for much of the rest of the century. Between 1862 and 1877 profit from the series was at least £14,345; between 1847 and 1894 there were seventy-seven printings totaling close to 450,000 copies of *The Ingoldsby Legends*. For his efforts, Barham was paid one guinea a page as the work appeared in *Bentley's Miscellany*; he received some payment when they were printed in series form; and on 16 January 1840 he sold the copyright for the first series to his publisher for £100. There is no record that he received any additional payment for the profit the reprints brought to the firm.

Through the influence of a friend, Bentley was appointed Publisher in Ordinary to His Majesty in 1833. It was a hollow title, since neither William IV nor Victoria ever had anything published by his firm. Although it set Bentley up as an object of ridicule, at the time the newly independent publisher may have viewed it as a valuable prop.

Throughout his career Bentley was well served by his authors. In 1833 Bulwer wrote to Bentley offering the copyright to an as yet unwritten novel for twelve hundred pounds. Negotiations reduced the amount to eleven hundred pounds, and *The Last Days of Pompeii* appeared in three volumes in 1834. The novel sold strongly for more than twenty years. Bulwer, however, was unhappy with the appearance of the novel, protesting to Bentley that many of his emendations had been ignored. Bulwer eventually stopped having his novels published by Bentley, who nonetheless continued to profit from the copyrights he already owned. In May 1834 Bentley published William Harrison Ainsworth's three-volume *Rookwood*. A historical romance, it was the biggest hit of the season; a second edition appeared in August 1834 and a third in 1835.

Bentley's early publications list included volumes by Leigh Hunt, Hazlitt, Maria Edgeworth, and Mrs. Trollope. Hook remained on good terms with, and wrote for, both Bentley and Colburn. Except for *The Last Days of Pompeii*, Bentley's firm was achieving a reputation for quality that Colburn's had never achieved, and indeed that Colburn had not particularly sought. Bentley capitalized further on these early successes by publishing collected editions of the works of some authors whose books had appeared in the Standard Novels: in October 1833, for example, Austen's novels were published separately; they became the standard edition for more than half a century.

In October 1836 Bentley was considering the purchase of the *Monthly Magazine*, in part possibly as a challenge to Colburn's *New Monthly*. Morgan proposed a new periodical instead, and wrote a prospectus that appealed to Bentley. Originally to be called "The Wits' Miscellany," its title was changed by Bentley to *Bentley's Miscellany*. Barham is alleged to have asked in jest, "Why go to the other extreme?" The first issue appeared in January 1837.

Dickens was a rising literary star who had attracted Bentley's attention because of the success of *The Pickwick Papers*. Just before the appearance of the sixth monthly number of *The Pickwick Papers* in September 1836, Dickens agreed to edit Bentley's new periodical, to contribute a novel to be serialized beginning in the second issue, and to write two more novels for Bentley's firm. Initially, Bentley was to pay him forty pounds per

month for his duties; by 1838 that figure was one thousand pounds per annum, with additional amounts for the second and third novels. *Bentley's Miscellany* was an immediate success, selling eleven thousand copies of its early numbers in 1837. The appearance of *Oliver Twist*, with plates by George Cruikshank, beginning in February, was a major reason; and William Makepeace Thackeray's first published fiction, "The Professor," appeared in the July 1837 issue. Dickens, however, began almost immediately to chafe at what he believed to be inadequate compensation for his increasing popularity, and he demanded and received changes in the original agreement; his and Bentley's lawyers and advisers hammered out nine different contracts between November 1836 and July 1840. In his desire to capitalize on his developing reputation Dickens overextended himself: writing *The Pickwick Papers* for Chapman and Hall; writing *Oliver Twist* for *Bentley's*, which he was also editing; preparing another novel for Bentley, eventually to become *Barnaby Rudge* (1841) and to be published not by Bentley but by Chapman and Hall; agreeing to edit a work for Colburn; and contracting to write two more books for Chapman and Hall.

Through the nearly four years of negotiations Bentley remained calm in public; privately, he railed against Dickens's constant complaints but then backed down, delayed deadlines, and provided his author with more money as it was demanded. Bentley recognized that an unhappy author was an unproductive author, though he did occasionally behave in a niggling manner: more than once he docked Dickens's monthly pay for falling short of a full sixteen pages of contributions, even though the shortfall may have been mandated by lack of space. To buy out his contract Dickens had to pay Bentley £2,250, which was advanced to him by Chapman and Hall. For this amount he received the copyright and stock of *Oliver Twist*, and he was released from having to write any other novels for Bentley. In retrospect it was inexpensive for Dickens, though it galled him at the time. In retrospect, it was terribly expensive for Bentley: he lost the age's most popular author and the profits from Dickens's subsequent work.

Ainsworth became editor of *Bentley's Miscellany* but lasted less than three years. Circulation decreased dramatically by 1843, and costs increased: Bentley could no longer pay cash for supplies and lost the 10 percent discount he had received for doing so. The quality of fiction in

*Bentley's* declined, while the quantity of reviews increased. Bentley, apparently having learned the technique from Colburn, used the pages more and more in the 1840s and 1850s to puff his own publications, including extensive quotations as part of the reviews and short positive comments in regular features such as "Literature of the Month." While Bentley owned the magazine, American literature figured prominently in its pages: Edgar Allan Poe's "The Fall of the House of Usher" appeared anonymously in August 1840; Cooper's works appeared frequently in the 1840s; and Herman Melville's novels were regularly reviewed in the early 1850s. Cooper and Melville were also making regular appearances among Bentley's Standard Novels at the time, so such exposure was not surprising.

Despite the difficulties with Dickens, the firm of Richard Bentley did well during the first four years of *Bentley's Miscellany*. Ainsworth's *Jack Sheppard* was a particular success: it appeared in *Bentley's* from January 1839 to February 1840, as a three-decker in October 1839, then as a one-volume reprint in 1840 and simultaneously as a serialization in fifteen weekly parts. After all of the exposure, the novel still had value: Ainsworth bought the copyright back in 1847 for two hundred pounds. Another lucrative deal was Bentley's purchase in late 1837 or early 1838 of seven of Marryat's copyrights from Saunders and Otley for approximately fifteen hundred pounds. These novels cleared at least six thousand pounds profit until Bentley was forced to sell them twenty years later to reduce the firm's debt.

Colburn was finding Bentley, whom he disliked personally, to be a formidable rival. Leaning heavily on the fashionable novels that had been the cornerstone of his earlier success, Colburn published a slim list in 1836, his first year in Great Marlborough Street. Late in the year, hearing that Bentley was contemplating a journal of literature and humor to rival the *New Monthly*, Colburn initially proposed a new humorous journal but decided instead to remodel his current monthly, which he renamed the *New Monthly Magazine and Humourist* in 1837; Hook replaced Hall as editor. Among the contributors he hired, Thackeray was most welcome, for Colburn lured him away from *Bentley's Miscellany*. Thackeray began a series for the *New Monthly* in 1838 and contributed occasionally for several years, but he had stopped well before he satirized his two former publishers as "Bacon [Bentley] and Bungay

[Colburn]" in *The History of Pendennis* (1848-1850).

In 1837 and 1838 Colburn published novels by Disraeli and Marryat, three Silver Forks by Mrs. Gore, and two by Lady Bury. In 1839-1840, capitalizing on Dickens's triumph with *The Pickwick Papers*, Colburn published Mrs. Trollope's *The Life and Adventures of Michael Armstrong, the Factory Boy* in one-shilling monthly parts. In a jarring note among the "factory" and Silver Fork novels he published Charles Darwin's journal of the voyage of the *Beagle* (1839). Capitalizing on Hook's popularity, he published *Precepts and Practice*, a collection of Hook's short stories and sketches, all of which had previously appeared in the *New Monthly*. In 1840 he began publishing Agnes and Elizabeth Strickland's *Lives of the Queens of England* (1840-1848), which he had purchased for £2,000; fifteen years later, the copyright was valued at £6,900.

But financial success for the firm did not change the character of its proprietor. Colburn exercised strong editorial control over contributions to his publications: when Dickens was editing *The Pic-Nic Papers* (1841), to be published by Colburn as a fund-raiser for John Macrone's widow, Colburn removed one contribution which Dickens had already approved. In retaliation, the novelist refused for a while to include his own contribution. Dickens finally relented, but only so that Mrs. Macrone could benefit.

In 1842 Colburn sold his remaining interest in his early periodical, the *Literary Gazette*, to William Jerdan. Colburn also continued puffing his novels in his periodicals, and hence continued to enrage both his enemies and his editors. Thomas Hood, who had become editor of the *New Monthly* after Hook's death in 1841, believed that the puffs—inserted by Shoberl and Patmore without consulting him—would reflect adversely on his integrity. Hood was also upset that Colburn or his assistants would frequently accept or reject contributions without telling him. One of the puffs that particularly offended Hood involved *The Tuft-Hunter* (1843), a three-decker allegedly written by Lord William Pitt Lennox. When Colburn demanded that it be reviewed favorably in the *New Monthly* Hood refused, but a positive review appeared in February 1843 nonetheless. Ironically, it was Colburn's former possession, the *Athenaeum* (25 February 1843), that exposed the novel as a plagiarism of several of Scott's novels, one by Henry Chorley, and even Hood's own *Tylney Hall* (1834). Hood resigned shortly thereafter. The

*Frontispiece and title page for a book published by Henry Colburn in 1843, eleven years after he and Richard Bentley dissolved their partnership*

break between Hood and Colburn was so acrimonious that in January 1844 Colburn refused mail arriving at Great Marlborough Street addressed to Hood by writing on the letters, "Not known to Mr. Colburn."

On Hood's departure Colburn himself took the reins, assisted by P. G. Patmore, D. E. Williams, and William Shoberl. During their association with Colburn these three were most often entrusted with writing the reviews, for the *New Monthly* and elsewhere, puffing Colburn's products.

Colburn's actions may be explained in part by economic conditions at the time. The book trade was in a depression in 1843, and he may have been trying to publish his way out of it as he had the 1826 crisis. He was not above using trickery to do so, as when Charles J. C. Davidson sent him a manuscript for consideration. There

is some disagreement whether what happened subsequently was planned by the two men or manipulated by Colburn, but Davidson took the publisher to court to retrieve his manuscript. The *Morning Chronicle* (26 October 1843) featured this story, as Colburn apparently hoped some newspaper would; three days later, amid all the publicity, Colburn published the book.

Yet Colburn had some legitimate successes during the 1840s. The firm published *Windsor Castle* (1843), a strong historical romance by Ainsworth; Disraeli's *Coningsby* (1844), *Sybil* (1845), and *Tancred* (1847); Eliot Warburton's *The Crescent and the Cross* (1845); and an enlarged version of Pepys's *Diary* (1848-1849). In addition, the firm of Henry Colburn had the distinction of publishing Anthony Trollope's early novels, although *The Kellys and the O'Kellys* (1848) sold only 150 copies, and *La Vendée* (1850) 350 copies. As the sales did not cover the costs Trollope, who had agreed to accept half the profits in lieu of a fee, received no money for either.

Colburn missed some opportunities as well. Early in 1845 Thackeray sent two manuscripts, for which Colburn had paid a small advance, for possible inclusion in the *New Monthly*. One manuscript was part of a short story; the other, the opening pages of a novel. On 18 May Thackeray requested their return, assuming that, having heard nothing further from Colburn, the publisher was not interested in either. In June Colburn sold the *New Monthly* to Ainsworth for twenty-five hundred pounds and refused to return the manuscripts until Thackeray returned the advance. Thackeray did so and received his material. The novel, published by Bradbury and Evans, was *Vanity Fair* (1847-1848). Colburn also faced increasing competition at this time from other series, particularly George Routledge's Railway Library, which began in 1849, forcing him to lower the prices of his reprint series to three shillings, sixpence and then to two shillings, sixpence.

Colburn added "and Company" to the firm's name in 1851, as he had done in 1820. In 1852 he published fifteen titles of fiction—mainly domestic fiction, a new style that had replaced his earlier favorite, the fashionable novel. He retired at the end of 1852 and sold the firm to Daniel Hurst, one of his assistants, who entered into partnership with Henry Blackett. The new firm of Hurst and Blackett opened for business at 13 Great Marlborough Street in January 1853.

Colburn kept some of his more valuable copyrights—Warburton's *The Crescent and the Cross*, Evelyn's and Pepys's diaries, Burke's *Peerage*, the Stricklands' *Lives of the Queens of England*—and the manuscript correspondence of David Garrick. On 16 August 1855 he died in his house in Bryanston Square, leaving these possessions and some thirty-five thousand pounds to his second wife, Eliza, whom he had married in 1841. He had no children by either marriage. On 24 September 1856 Eliza married John Forster, who had revised Evelyn's *Diary* for Colburn. On 26 May 1857 Colburn's copyrights and stock were auctioned off for fourteen thousand pounds. Despite the several depressions in the book trade during his career as a publisher, then, Colburn had made a considerable sum of money.

For Bentley, however, the 1843 depression in books was the beginning of nearly twenty years of financial struggle. The situation seemed sufficiently desperate in 1849 that Bentley's closest assistant, Edward Morgan, asked that his own salary be reduced from £450 annually to £300. Throughout these years, Bentley suffered from increased competition, legal machinations, and his own failed ventures. On 4 January 1845 he began a sixpenny weekly newspaper, *Young England*. Intended to reflect the ideals of the political group of that name, the paper failed after fourteen issues. In 1846 the Belfast publishing firm of Simms and M'Intyre introduced the Popular Novelist, a two-shilling reprint series—the first direct competition other than Colburn's series to Bentley's Standard Novels. In 1847 Simms and M'Intyre reduced the price and renamed the series the Parlour Library. When Routledge introduced the one-shilling Railway Library in 1849, Bentley responded by reducing the price on his Standard Novels to two shillings, sixpence and three shillings, sixpence. In 1853, using copyrights he already owned, he published his own Railway Library series—known also as Bentley's Shilling Series—and the Parlour Bookcase series. The two series were only moderately successful: the Shilling Series consisted of eleven volumes in 1853 and 1854, and the Parlour Bookcase series contained twenty-one volumes in the same period. In contrast, Simms and M'Intyre's Parlour Library included 279 volumes from 1847 to 1863. In 1853 Bentley also attempted to increase sales by reducing the price of other reprints to three shillings, sixpence a volume and the price of three-deckers to ten shillings, sixpence. Within a couple of months, however, he had returned to the original prices.

During these troubled years Bentley was forced to sell remainders and copyrights in an effort to pay his creditors. In 1843 he sold 14,500 volumes to Thomas Tegg for £725. In 1852 he sold the Prince Rupert memoirs and the Fairfax correspondence, both of which he had recently acquired and published and on which he had suffered a £2,000 loss. With the Crimean War deepening the depression in the book trade in 1854, Bentley found it necessary to part with one of his prized possessions: in October he sold *Bentley's Miscellany* to Ainsworth for £1,700. Bentley had to agree not to begin a competing periodical, but Ainsworth had little to fear: desperate for money, the firm of Richard Bentley continued publishing the Ainsworth-owned *Bentley's Miscellany* into the next decade. In 1855 Bentley sold 15,730 volumes of remainders for only £525. In 1856 he sold another of his prizes, the Marryat copyrights, to Routledge, though he did receive approximately twice what he had paid for them in 1837.

Bentley and Colburn were both capable of maximizing profits at the expense of an author. For her *Confessions of a Pretty Woman* (1846), Julia Pardoe had received £150 from Colburn and a promise of an additional £50 if sales reached 750 copies. When sales seemed to stick at 744, she suspected Colburn of not being entirely truthful and offered her next novel to Bentley. She received £200 for *The Rival Beauties* (1848) and £400 for another novel; but the amounts decreased thereafter, Bentley claiming that trade was distressed—as indeed it was. In the late 1850s he stopped buying her novels altogether but kept reprinting those whose copyrights he owned. The firm profited significantly as late as 1890 from its ownership of her copyrights.

In addition to distressed trade, Bentley also suffered from changes in copyright law. He had accumulated English copyrights for many American novels and had profited handsomely by publishing them both in three-volume and reprint editions. When all rights to foreign copyrights were withdrawn in 1849, Routledge and Henry Bohn immediately began publishing cheap reprint editions of American works. By the time the 1849 decision was reversed in 1851, Bentley estimated he had lost seventeen thousand pounds in profits. Bentley's solicitor, G. N. Devey, threatened legal action against the other two publishers over the copyrights of Washington Irving and James Fenimore Cooper. Routledge settled with Bentley out of court in June 1851, and Bohn settled in December.

In 1855 Bentley's fortunes hit bottom. By 1 April the firm was in danger of being declared bankrupt; its creditors demanded that action be taken to keep the business going. Bentley agreed that an inspectorate be set up to oversee the firm's operations and reduce its debt. William Clowes and G. A. Spottiswoode, well-known and trusted printers, became the inspectors. In 1857 Bentley was taken to court by Charles Reade, who had agreed that the firm should publish his *Peg Woffington* (1853) under a half-profits contract; the initial edition of five hundred copies provided Reade with a total payment of ten pounds, twelve shillings, eightpence. The agreement, however, covered every edition that Bentley might publish. By 1857 Reade was a well-known author whose copyrights were worth more than a half-

profits agreement would pay. Reade took Bentley to court, claiming that the agreement was for one edition only, and that his objection invalidated the contract. Reade lost and had to pay costs.

In 1859 Bentley, just beginning to emerge from the long years of financial hardship, wanted to establish his own quarterly to rival the *Edinburgh Review* and *Quarterly Review*. He hired John Douglas Cook of the *Saturday Review* as general editor; William Scott, also of the *Saturday Review*, as literary editor; and the young Lord Robert Cecil, later to become prime minister, as political editor. The first issue of *Bentley's Quarterly Review*, for March 1859, appeared on 28 February to critical acclaim for the topics covered and the excellent writing. But sales were poor, Bentley quickly lost six hundred pounds, and *Bentley's Quarterly Review* survived for only four numbers. The review was behind the times: quarterlies were declining in popularity, and monthlies—such as *Macmillan's*, beginning in 1859, and the *Cornhill*, in 1860—were gaining.

Yet even as *Bentley's Quarterly Review* was dying, the firm of Richard Bentley was showing renewed signs of life. From 29 June 1859 to 28 May 1860 Bentley imitated the success of Tales from Blackwood's with his own series, Tales from Bentley. The four volumes of reprints from *Bentley's Miscellany* were an indication that the publisher, approaching his mid sixties, was becoming more conservative in his business affairs. Indeed, when Bentley published Mrs. Henry Wood's *East Lynne* (1861) after two other publishers had turned it down, he did so on half-profits to minimize his risk. *East Lynne* sold out four editions in six months and had even more success as a reprint in 1862. In twenty years the book sold 110,250 copies. Geraldine Jewsbury, a novelist and Bentley's most trusted reader at this time, had recommended that he publish *East Lynne*. By weeding out the mediocre or worse manuscripts, she and Bentley's other readers played a significant role in the firm's recovery.

In January 1866 Bentley bought *Temple Bar* from George Augustus Sala for £2,750. A one-shilling monthly magazine founded in 1860, it was a direct competitor with the Ainsworth-owned *Bentley's Miscellany*. Edmund Yates, the editor since December 1863, stayed on for nearly two years. Bentley's son, George, became editor of *Temple Bar* in late 1867, and remained in that position until his death in 1895. George had joined the firm in 1845 at the age of seventeen but had not been particularly active until 1859. He assumed greater control in 1867 when his father was injured in an accident at the Chepstow railway station. Richard Bentley never regained the energy with which he had directed the business for thirty-five years.

In June 1868 Ainsworth's financial misfortunes enabled the Bentleys to repurchase *Bentley's Miscellany* for £250. At the end of the year they merged it into *Temple Bar*, bringing together perhaps the finest roster of contributors to any periodical at the time: Anthony Trollope, his brother Thomas Adolphus Trollope, Rhoda Broughton, Wilkie Collins, Marie Corelli, Henry Kingsley, Reade, and Mrs. Wood, to be joined later by Arthur Conan Doyle, George Gissing, Edmund Gosse, and Robert Louis Stevenson.

While Richard and George Bentley were consolidating their gains in the periodicals, they were advancing strongly in the fiction market. On Mrs. Jewsbury's advice George rejected Broughton's *Not Wisely but Too Well* (1867), which was published by Tinsley, but published *Cometh Up as a Flower* (1867) in two volumes. George Bentley urged Broughton to expand her novels, both to fit the standard three-decker format and to be serialized in *Temple Bar*. Her value to the firm steadily increased as her novels, short though some were, maintained their popularity. George Bentley paid her £800 for *Good-bye, Sweetheart!* (1872) and £1000 for *Nancy* (1873). In 1875, recognizing his error in not publishing *Not Wisely but Too Well*, he paid £250 for its copyright and stock. As late as 1880 George was still trying to convince Broughton to write only three-deckers: he offered her £1,200 for her eighth novel, *Second Thoughts* (1880), in three volumes, or £750 in two. She accepted the £750. It seemed to matter little; the firm profited handsomely from all of the Broughton novels it published.

These business arrangements had been made by George Bentley because Richard Bentley had died on 10 September 1871 at seventy-seven. The firm, renamed Richard Bentley and Son at the time of Richard Bentley's death, was as strong in the early 1870s as it had ever been. George Bentley was a careful and conscientious owner: he had learned the trade from his father, who late in life had adopted a conservative approach to his business.

George Bentley certainly understood the value of a series of cheap reprints. In 1879 he established Bentley's Empire Library, each of the sixteen volumes costing half a crown. The price was certainly right, and Bentley provided a mix of fic-

tion, including Collins's *A Rogue's Life* (1879), Broughton's *Twilight Stories* (1879), and Dickens's *The Mudfog Papers* (1880).

Yet profit margins were being squeezed in a changing marketplace, as exemplified by an increasingly recalcitrant Mudie's Circulating Library. The libraries had long bargained for special low rates based on their large-quantity purchases, but in January 1881 Mudie's offered a particularly low twelve shillings for an order of only twenty-five copies of Mrs. Charlotte E. L. Riddell's *The Mystery of Palace Gardens* (1880), and in February wanted to return fifty unused copies of *A Political Diary* (1881), by the earl of Ellenborough. To make matters worse, on 25 September 1884 Charles Edward Mudie complained to Bentley that he was losing money on two-thirds of the three-deckers he carried in his library. Over the next decade, trade in the three-volume novel deteriorated. On 13 July 1894 Arthur Mudie, having succeeded to his father's business, virtually demanded an end to the three-decker. For 1895 Richard Bentley and Son published only fifteen novels, just two of them in three volumes.

In 1895 George Bentley died, leaving an estate of £85,846 to his wife and son. Forty-one years old when he inherited Richard Bentley and Son, Richard Bentley II was less interested in business than his father and grandfather had been. He began negotiations in 1897 to sell the stock and copyrights of Richard Bentley and Son to the firm of Smith, Elder for £20,000, but no agreement was reached. In 1898 Frederick Macmillan, chairman of Macmillan's since 1896, purchased all of the possessions of Richard Bentley and Son for £8,000.

**References:**

Nigel Cross, *The Common Writer: Life in Nineteenth-Century Grub Street* (Cambridge: Cambridge University Press, 1985);

Henry Curwen, *A History of Booksellers* (London: Chatto & Windus, 1873);

Royal A. Gettmann, *A Victorian Publisher: A Study of the Bentley Papers* (Cambridge: Cambridge University Press, 1960);

Thomas Hood, *The Letters of Thomas Hood*, edited by Peter Morgan (Toronto: University of Toronto Press, 1973);

Edgar Johnson, *Charles Dickens: His Tragedy and Triumph*, 2 volumes (New York: Simon & Schuster, 1952);

Leslie Marchand, *The Athenaeum: A Mirror of Victorian Culture* (Chapel Hill: University of North Carolina Press, 1941);

Robert L. Patten, *Charles Dickens and His Publishers* (Oxford: Clarendon Press, 1978);

Matthew Rosa, *The Silver Fork School* (New York: Columbia University Press, 1936);

Michael Sadleir, *XIX Century Fiction: A Bibliographical Record*, 2 volumes (London: Constable/ Berkeley & Los Angeles: University of California Press, 1951);

John Sutherland, "Henry Colburn Publisher," *Publishing History*, 19 (1986): 59-84;

Sutherland, *Victorian Novelists and Publishers*, (London: Athlone Press, 1976).

—*Roger P. Wallins*

# Basil Blackwell Publisher
*(Oxford: 1978-  )*
## B. H. Blackwell
*(Oxford: 1879-1922)*
## Basil Blackwell and Mott, Limited
*(Oxford: 1922-1978)*

Benjamin Harris Blackwell sold second-hand books in Oxford from 1845 until his death in 1855. His widow, Nancy Stirling Lambert Blackwell, worked as a seamstress to raise her three children, Benjamin Henry, Mathilda, and Frederick. Benjamin Henry Blackwell worked in several bookshops as an apprentice. In 1879 he opened a bookshop in rented quarters at 50 Broad Street, Oxford. Fulfilling a pledge he had made to his mother, he gave the business the same name his father had used: B. H. Blackwell. In its first year the shop had gross sales of £1,267; by the end of the next year sales were at £1,841 with a profit of £226. Blackwell's first catalogue indicates that his list, which included classics as well as grammars and dictionaries in use at Oxford university, was confined to used books. The university expanded its enrollments after the University Tests Act of 1871 opened both Oxford and Cambridge to non-Anglicans. During the same period the number of public schools grew, and educational opportunities for women expanded. Consequently, the book business prospered. There was a shift in literary interests; in 1875 religion had been the leader in sales, but during the next decade history, economics, and science came to dominate the nonfiction market. Poetry was in decline, but enthusiasm for the novel continued to grow. The principal problem confronting the book trade during this period was the practice of "underselling"; no one expected to pay the retail cost of new books, and used books were sold at deflated prices.

Nonetheless, Blackwell prospered, and in 1883 the shop at 50 Broad Street was purchased. During the 1880s sales averaged three thousand pounds; by 1900, gross sales were fifteen thousand pounds, and Blackwell had a standing stock of a hundred thousand volumes. Between 1879 and 1900 Blackwell issued seventy-two catalogues, including its first catalogue of foreign books in 1895; made special arrangements with the university to publish lectures and expanded its holdings to support some courses; and enlarged its mail-order business significantly.

The first book to carry the Blackwell imprint was *Mensae Secundae: Verses Written in Balliol College* (1879); it consisted of poetry by Oxford students and faculty. In 1880 Blackwell began to publish the short-lived magazine *Waifs and Strays*, which printed the poetry of James Rennell Rodd, J. St. Loe Strachey, H. C. Beeching, J. W. Mackail, and A. E. Housman. Perhaps the most significant work published by Benjamin Henry Blackwell was *Hymns: The Yattendon Hymnal* (1895-1899), which was edited by Robert Bridges and H. Ellis Wooldridge for a local parish church; it was well received and had an impact on the development of Ralph Vaughan Williams's *English Hymnal*. Blackwell published many prize compositions by Oxford students, including Gilbert Murray, Laurence Binyon, and John Buchan. He also published a wide range of lectures and pamphlets for the faculty, including John Cook Wilson's inaugural lecture, *On an Evolutionist Theory of Axioms* (1889). In 1901 Blackwell published *The Book of the Horace Club* upon the demise of that poetry organization. By 1913 the Blackwell list contained more than four hundred titles published by the firm.

Book sales expanded rapidly after the practice of underselling was controlled by the Net Book Agreement of 1 January 1900. Blackwell's gross sales were twenty-seven thousand pounds in 1913, with profits at eleven percent of sales. During this period books on science, medicine, economics, and technology, along with fiction, sold very well; overseas sales increased steadily.

Blackwell had married Lydia Taylor in 1886; they had two children, Dorothy, born in 1887, and Basil Henry, born on 29 May 1889. At the age of twelve Basil Blackwell matriculated at Magdalen College School; from there he proceeded to Merton College, Oxford. On leaving the university he served an apprenticeship at Oxford University Press in London for sixteen months in 1911-1912. In January 1913 he joined his father in managing the firm. In September 1913 a separate publications department was established in the company. Also in 1913 Basil Blackwell initiated the annual *Oxford Poetry*, which, during the next three decades, published the works of Robert Graves, W. H. Auden, Cecil Day Lewis, Louis MacNeice, and Stephen Spender. In 1916 two additional poetry annuals were launched: *Adventurers All*, which endured for eight years but

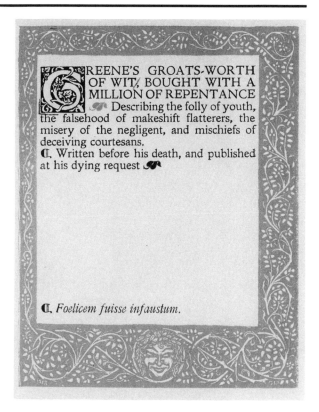

*Title page for the fourth in the Sheldonian series of "short masterpieces in all languages." This volume was published in 1919.*

had to be abandoned because of the financial drain it placed on the firm, published the works of Aldous Huxley, Dorothy L. Sayers, and Sacheverell Sitwell; *Wheels* was dropped after four issues. Basil Blackwell published Edith Sitwell's first three volumes of poetry: *The Mother and Other Poems* (1915), *Twentieth-Century Harlequinade and Other Poems* (1916), and *Clowns' Houses* (1918). By 1923 the Blackwell list announced more than fifty volumes of poetry, including the work of the American Amy Lowell. From 1919 to 1939 Basil Blackwell published *Oxford Outlook*, a magazine that appeared once each term and consisted primarily of short stories, essays, reviews, and poetry by students. Among the contributors to and editors of this journal were Sayers, Julian Huxley, John Betjeman, Graham Greene, Stephen Spender, Isaiah Berlin, Vera Brittain, and A. L. Rowse.

Other early publishing efforts included a Virgilian Studies series and the Percy Imprints. Blackwell published three studies of the *Aeneid* by W. Warde Fowler of Lincoln College between 1915 and 1919; by the mid 1920s the Virgilian Studies list comprised more than a dozen titles. The Percy Reprints series, begun in 1920 under the ed-

*New buildings erected in 1938 at Nos. 48-50 Broad Street, Oxford. Blackwell's bookshop has been located at this site since the company was founded in 1879.*

itorship of H. F. B. Brett-Smith of Corpus Christi College, reprinted rare English masterpieces, including a two-volume edition of Sir George Etherege's plays and poems in 1927. The Sheldonian series comprised reprints of small books or sections from classics, such as the *Funeral Oration Spoken by Pericles* (1917) from Thomas Hobbes's translation of Thucydides' *The Peloponnesian War*.

Dorothy L. Sayers served as Basil Blackwell's first editorial assistant, beginning in 1916; she was replaced in 1920 by Blackwell's friend Adrian Mott. In 1922 Blackwell and Mott formed the firm of Basil Blackwell and Mott, Limited, and the imprint was changed from Blackwell to Basil Blackwell. That year the firm acquired the Davenant Bookshop and the Ovenall and Fowles Bindery. Also in 1922 Blackwell and Mott hired Ernest Wilfred Parker to serve as managing director of its education department. Parker supervised the publication of a series of histories for elementary schools by C. H. K. Marten and E. H. Carter. This series first appeared in 1925; by 1927 it was selling at the rate of one thou-

sand volumes per week and assured the profitability of the firm. Subsequent school titles included *A Short Bible* (1930); *Introduction to Science* (1932-1935), by Edward Neville Da Costa Andrade and Julian Huxley; and *Man the World Over* (1938-1941), by Clement C. Carter and Harold C. Brentnall. The Andrade and Huxley text never realized its projected profit level because of the consequences of the depression and the costly delays in publishing the book. Parker died in 1935.

The Shakespeare Head Press of Stratford-upon-Avon, established by A. H. Bullen and Frank Sidgwick in 1904, had published the acclaimed *Stratford Town Shakespeare* (1904-1907). Sidgwick had left in 1908 to found Sidgwick and Jackson, and when Bullen died in 1919 the Shakespeare Head Press was near bankruptcy because of poor management; two years later Basil Blackwell purchased it for fifteen hundred pounds and made Bernard Henry Newdigate managing director. Newdigate published a series of quality editions of the works of Jean Froissart (eight volumes, 1927-1928), Geoffrey Chaucer (eight vol-

*Sir Basil Blackwell in 1979*

umes, 1928-1929), Edmund Spenser (eight volumes, 1930), Homer (five volumes, 1930-1931), and Michael Drayton (five volumes, 1941), as well as low-cost editions of works by Henry Fielding, Daniel Defoe, Jonathan Swift, Anthony Trollope, and the Brontës. The Shakespeare Head Press moved to Oxford in 1930. Newdigate's design of Sir Thomas Malory's *Le Morte d'Arthur* (1935) in attractive two-column pages led Basil Blackwell to develop a one-volume collected works of Shakespeare that was published in 1935; by 1937 it had sold fifty thousand copies. The Shakespeare Head Press became a subsidiary of Blackwell and Mott in 1942. The firm initiated a series of juvenile publications in 1923. The centerpiece of this effort was an annual, *Joy Street*, which continued to be published until 1935; Hilaire Belloc, G. K. Chesterton, and A. A. Milne were frequent contributors.

After his father's death on 24 October 1924 Basil Blackwell supervised all aspects of the business, including the book sales and publications. In 1928 Blackwell acquired the Coverley Bookshop. During the next thirteen years, the Morley Brothers, Hayes, and W. T. Brown binderies were

purchased and placed under the management of Geoffrey Barfoot. Blackwell and Mott's sales for 1939 were £118,000.

Immediately prior to the outbreak of World War II in 1939 Blackwell Scientific Publications became a new component of the firm, specializing in medical publications. With John Grant as managing director, Blackwell Scientific Publications produced its first book, *The Essentials of Anaesthesia* by R. R. Macintosh and Freda Pratt Bannister, in November 1940. This department would develop rapidly after the war. The anticipated negative impact of the war on Basil Blackwell and Mott was never realized. Many London firms were devastated by air raids, but Oxford was not attacked. Demand for books expanded during the war, and in spite of rationing of paper to forty percent of prewar usage, Basil Blackwell and Mott was able to publish twenty new books and thirty-one reprints.

In 1946 Richard Blackwell, Basil's oldest son, returned from serving in the Royal Navy and began a process of modernization that would increase sales from £165,000 in 1946 to £27 million in 1979. Richard Blackwell recognized the need for expanded mail-order sales and the general development of education throughout the world. Within Basil Blackwell and Mott he promoted specialization in the management of the business, and after some reluctance the managing board accepted the concept. Each employee was to develop expertise in a specialized area, and each area would be evaluated on its records and prospects.

A notable postwar achievement was the publication in 1950 of Fred Hoyle's *The Nature of the Universe*; designed for the general reader, the book sold more than one hundred thousand copies. In 1952 Richard Blackwell's brother Julian joined the firm.

After 1945 the sales of children's books and school texts declined, and the publication of juvenile titles was abandoned. In 1951 John Cutforth was hired as educational editor. Interested mainly in elementary education, Cutforth launched the successful Learning Library series in 1954; it was soon followed by texts for secondary schools, including the much lauded *The Twentieth Century* (1964), by M. N. Duffy. During the same period Henry Schollick, a director of the company, was determined to establish Basil Blackwell and Mott as a leading academic publisher; success was realized when the firm published the works of Ludwig Wittgenstein.

In 1955 Basil Blackwell and Mott sales reached a hundred thousand pounds. Basil Blackwell was knighted in 1956. The bindery business was reorganized into a single unit in 1962, with Julian Blackwell serving as chairman and Geoffrey Barfoot as managing director.

Blackwell Scientific Publications has expanded since the 1950s under the leadership of Per Saugman, a Dane, who became managing director of the division in 1954. Saugman expanded the list to include undergraduate and graduate texts; the medical orientation of the unit was broadened to include other fields of science—the introduction of the Botanical Monographs series in 1962 is representative of this diversification. In 1955 the *British Journal of Haematology* was launched; since then fifty additional periodicals have emerged through Blackwell Scientific Publications. Editorial offices were opened in London and Edinburgh, and existing firms in Europe were acquired. In 1963 Blackwell purchased the Danish publisher Ejnar Musksgaard; the later acquisition of C. Kooyder of Leiden led to the establishment of Kooyker Scientific Publications in Rotterdam. Blackwell Scientific Publications entered a partnership in 1979 with the American firm C. V. Mosby to sustain its position in North America.

Mott died in 1964. A new bindery plant at Osney Mead became operational in 1965. In 1969 Sir Basil Blackwell relinquished the chairmanship of the board to his son Richard. Basil Blackwell and Mott sales reached £400,000 in 1971. In 1975 the firm acquired some assets of the dissolving Richard Abel Company of Oregon and established Blackwell North America. The publishing component of the firm became Basil Blackwell Publisher in 1978; sales in 1979 were £2 million of the £27 million recorded by the Blackwell organization. Richard Blackwell served as chair until his death in 1980, when he was succeeded by his brother Julian. Sir Basil Blackwell died in 1984 at the age of ninety-five. In 1988 B. H. Blackwell Ltd., still a family business under the direction of Julian Blackwell, recorded sales in excess of £100 million.

**Reference:**

A. L. P. Norrington, *Blackwell's 1879-1979: The History of a Family Firm* (Oxford: Blackwell, 1983).

—*William T. Walker*

# David Bogue
*(London: 1842-1856)*
# Tilt and Bogue
*(London: 1840-1842)*

In 1840 Charles Tilt made David Bogue, one of his employees, his partner in his publishing business at 86 Fleet Street, London. During their brief partnership Tilt and Bogue published children's books, including *Robin Hood and His Merry Forresters* (1841) by Stephen Percy (pseudonym of Joseph Cundall). Tilt sold the firm to Bogue in 1842 for approximately fifty thousand pounds, which he generously allowed Bogue to pay over an extended period.

Bogue introduced to England the American practice of publishing inexpensive copies of classic books. William Roscoe's *Life of Lorenzo de Medici Called the Magnificent* (1845) was the first of twenty volumes in Bogue's European Library. The series also included Alexandre Dumas's *Marguerite de Valois* (1846), François Guizot's *History of the English Revolution of 1640* (1846), and John Galt's *Life of Cardinal Wolsey* (1846), as well as books by François Mignet, William Hazlitt, Augustin Thierry, Jules Michelet, and Joseph Berington. Bogue set the price of the series at three shillings, sixpence per volume, far lower than was then standard.

Other English publishers quickly imitated Bogue in publishing low-priced books. Henry Bohn, in particular, established several series of inexpensive books and soon dominated the market. Competition between the two firms resulted in litigation when Bohn sued Bogue for pirating illustrations: Bohn had purchased some remainders containing copyrighted illustrations, and Bogue had reprinted the illustrations in Roscoe's *Life of Lorenzo de Medici Called the Magnificent*. The Court of Chancery issued an injunction against Bogue. The lawsuit and subsequent competition seriously weakened Bogue, and within a few years Bohn bought Bogue's European Library and incorporated it into his own Standard Library series.

Despite his problems with Bohn, Bogue continued to publish. His list included Gerald Massey's *Voices of Freedom and Lyrics of Love* (1850) and an English-French traveler's dictionary (1853). Several series also came from his press, in-

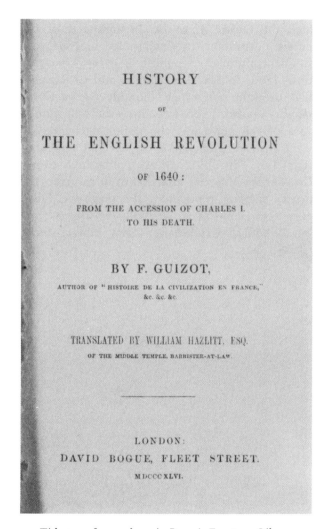

*Title page for a volume in Bogue's European Library*

cluding Comic Natural History (seventeen volumes, 1847), which satirized Victorian England; Manuals of Utility (eight volumes, 1847); and Bogue's Traveller's Guides (1853), which included guides to the Low Countries, Switzerland, and Paris. Bogue also published humor and children's books by August and Henry Mayhew. Bogue and Joseph Cundall copublished several children's books, including *The Playmate Second Series* (1847-1848), the Little Mary's Books series (1847-1850), *The Boy's Almanac for 1849* (1849),

*Harry's Ladder to Learning* (1849-1850), and *Maja's Alphabet* (1852). William Makepeace Thackeray wrote the text for *Sketches after English Landscape Painters* (1850), which contained engravings by Louis Marvy. Thackeray refused, however, to write a series of short volumes for a "Social Zoologies" series that Bogue proposed.

Bogue collaborated on several projects with the illustrator George Cruikshank. Tilt had initiated the *Comick Almanack*, an annual that contained illustrations by Cruikshank, in 1834, and Bogue continued to publish it every Christmas until 1852. In May 1841 Bogue and Cruikshank had brought out a new monthly *George Cruikshank's Omnibus*. There were, however, only nine issues of the magazine; the popular imagination went instead with *Punch*, which first appeared that July. In 1852 Bogue published *George Cruikshank's Magazine* in an effort to resurrect the artist's sagging reputation; the magazine failed after the second issue. Nevertheless, Bogue went on to publish Cruikshank's Fairy Library series (1853-1854).

Following Bogue's death in November 1856, Tilt returned to settle Bogue's affairs. Bogue's imprint was succeeded by that of W. Kent and Company, but most of his business had been absorbed by Bohn.

**References:**

John Buchanan-Brown, *The Book Illustrations of George Cruikshank* (London: David & Charles, 1980);

Michael Wynn Jones, *George Cruikshank: His Life and London* (London: Macmillan, 1978);

Ruari McLean, *Joseph Cundall: A Victorian Publisher. Notes on His Life and a Check-list of His Books* (Pinner, U.K.: Private Libraries Association, 1976);

Lewis Melville (pseudonym of Lewis Saul Benjamin), *William Makepeace Thackeray* (London: Lane, 1910);

Henry Vizetelly, *Glances Back through Seventy Years: Autobiographical and Other Reminiscences*, 2 volumes (London: Kegan Paul, Trench, Trübner, 1893), I: 102-118.

—*David B. Mock*

# H. G. Bohn
### (London: 1831-1864)

Born in London to German parents, Henry George Bohn entered the book trade in 1812, when, at the age of sixteen, he toured Europe purchasing books for his father's bookstore. He often found bargains among the nobles who wished to dispose of their libraries before they were confiscated by Napoleon's armies. In 1831 he left his father's business when he was denied a partnership in the firm. He established his own bookshop at 4 York Street, Covent Garden, London, with two thousand pounds, half of which he borrowed from his father-in-law, William Simpkin. Multilingual and experienced in finding and purchasing rare books, he quickly came to dominate the used-book trade in the 1830s. In 1841 Bohn established his reputation when he published his "guinea catalog," a 1,936-page listing of the 23,208 rare books he had for sale. Bohn noted in the catalogue that his prices were considerably cheaper than those of his competitors. At this time Bohn also began to purchase the copyrights of remainders and to republish the books at lower prices than they had originally carried. It was here that he found his niche in the market.

In 1846 Bohn published the first of a series of reprinted classics. Similar to David Bogue's European Library, which had begun to come out in 1845, Bohn's 150-volume Standard Library offered the public classic works at relatively low prices. Bohn went on to publish many other series: Extra Volumes Uniform with Standard Library (7 volumes, begun in 1846), Scientific Library (63 volumes, begun in 1847), Antiquarian Library (40 volumes, begun in 1847), Classical Library including an Atlas (89 volumes, begun in 1848), Illustrated Library (76 volumes, begun in 1849), Shilling Series (begun in 1850), Philosophical (sometimes referred to as the Philological and Philosophical) Library (19 volumes, begun in 1852), British Classics (29 volumes, begun in 1853), Collegiate Series (10 volumes, begun in 1859), Library of French Memoirs (6 volumes, 1855-1856), Cheap Series (76 volumes), Historical Library (13 volumes, begun in 1857), Ecclesiastical Library (18 volumes, begun in 1859), School and Collegiate Series (1 volume, 1853), English

*Henry George Bohn*

Gentleman's Library (8 volumes, begun in 1849), and the Royal Illustrated Series (21 volumes). Bohn had more than 600 volumes in print when he retired.

Although Bohn is best known for these series of inexpensive books, he published other books as well. His list covered a great diversity of fields: fine arts, architecture, heraldry, topography, theology, natural history, mathematics, medicine, music, agriculture, history, and literature. Nor were all of Bohn's publications low-priced. *The Works of James Gillray* (1851), with 588 drawings by Gillray, sold for ten pounds. Bohn himself wrote several of the books he published, including *Handbook of Proverbs* (1855). He also revised and enlarged William Thomas Lowndes's *Bibliographer's Manual of English Literature*, which had appeared in four volumes in 1834; Bohn's edition, in eleven volumes, was published from 1857 to 1864. Other titles from Bohn's press included *Polyglot of Foreign Proverbs* (1857), *Dictionary of Latin and Greek Quotations* (eight volumes, 1860), *Index Verborum to the Dictionary of Quotations* (1860), and *Pictorial Handbook of Modern Geography* (1862). He also collaborated with Joseph Cundall on publication projects, including the fourth edition of Cundall's *Tales of the Kings of England* (1846).

One significant consequence of Bohn's Standard Library and his subsequent series was the reduction in the average cost of all titles published in England. Between 1828 and 1853 the average price of a book declined from sixteen shillings to eight shillings, four and half pence. The initial price of Bohn's Standard Library was three shillings, sixpence per volume; subsequent volumes and later series were priced at five shillings per volume. Bohn's prices became the standard for the market for twenty years.

In 1845 David Bogue published William Roscoe's *Life of Lorenzo de Medici Called the Magnificent* and included illustrations that had been copyrighted by Bohn. Bohn sued his competitor for breach of copyright; the Court of Chancery ruled in his favor and issued an injunction against Bogue. Bohn also had difficulty with another competitor, George Routledge. Soon after Bohn reprinted Ralph Waldo Emerson's *Representative Men* (1850), he found that the work had also been included in Routledge's Popular Library. In retaliation Bohn reprinted books by Washington Irving, whose works were included in Routledge's series. Two other British publishers, John Murray and Richard Bentley, had bought the rights to publish the works of several American authors, including Irving. When Bohn and Routledge republished Irving's works, they were sued by Murray and Bentley for copyright violation. During the proceedings Bohn and Routledge raised several key points of law concerning the actual dates and locations of publication of Irving's works. As these were common-law issues, in 1850 Chancery advised Murray and Bentley to take their cases to a common-law court. Murray took his suit to Queen's Bench the following year; but Murray settled out of court with Routledge in May 1851 and with Bohn three months later. In his settlement Bohn agreed to purchase Murray's copyrights to Irving's works for two thousand pounds on the condition that Murray discontinue the litigation. In October

Bohn reached an out-of-court settlement with Bentley, who received four hundred pounds for his copyright to three of Irving's works.

Bohn's decision to settle with Murray and Bentley was due in large part to another case involving copyright protection for foreign authors. This case, *Boosey* v. *Jefferys*, had several similarities to Murray's suit against Bohn. When *Boosey* v. *Jefferys* was about to be appealed to the House of Lords, Bohn and other publishers who were reprinting the works of foreign authors and musicians decided to help defray Jefferys's expenses by forming the Society for Obtaining an Adjustment to the Law of Copyright. Following a preliminary inquiry in March 1852, the House of Lords heard the case in August 1854. The Lords ruled that for an author to have a claim to copyright protection he must live in England or one of its colonies. The effect of the ruling was to force American authors to travel to Great Britain or some part of the British Empire and reside there long enough to witness publication of their works. The ruling remained in force until it was superseded by the U.S. International Copyright Law in 1891. Bohn's interest in the copyright issue led him to write and publish *The Question of Unreciprocated Foreign Copyright in Great Britain* (1851).

Bohn retired in 1864. As his sons were not interested in publishing careers, he sold his stock of new books to Bell and Daldy for forty thousand pounds; Chatto and Windus purchased his copyrights for twenty thousand pounds. Bell and Daldy moved into Bohn's York Street offices; during the next three years Bohn moved his stock of used books to a warehouse at 18 Henrietta Street, where he retained an office until 1881. Bohn eventually sold his used books, earning about thirteen thousand pounds. During his active retirement Bohn catalogued his holdings, translated foreign classics, and helped aristocrats such as the duke of Hamilton develop their libraries. He died in 1884.

## References:

James J. Barnes, *Authors, Publishers and Politicians: The Quest for an Anglo-American Copyright Agreement* (Columbus: Ohio State University Press, 1974; London: Routledge & Kegan Paul, 1974), pp. 92, 154-157, 159-165, 168, 285-287;

Edward Bell, *George Bell Publisher: A Brief Memoir* (London: Chiswick Press, 1924);

# BOHN'S CLASSICAL LIBRARY.

### A SERIES OF LITERAL PROSE TRANSLATIONS OF THE GREEK AND LATIN CLASSICS WITH NOTES AND INDEXES.

*Uniform with the* STANDARD LIBRARY, *5s. each (except Thucydides, Æschylus, Virgil, Horace, Cicero's Offices, Demosthenes, Appendix to Æschylus, Aristotle's Organon, all of which are 3s. 6d. each volume).*

1. HERODOTUS. By the REV. HENRY CARY, M.A. *Frontispiece.*

2 & 3. THUCYDIDES. By the REV. H. DALE. In 2 Vols. (3s. 6d. each). *Frontispiece.*

4. PLATO. Vol. I. By CARY. [The Apology of Socrates, Crito Phædo, Gorgias, Protagoras, Phædrus, Theætetus, Euthyphron, Lysis.] *Frontis.*

5. LIVY'S HISTORY OF ROME, literally translated. Vol. I., Books 1 to 8.

6. PLATO. Vol. II. By DAVIS. [The Republic, Timæus, and Critias.]

7. LIVY'S HISTORY OF ROME. Vol. II., Books 9 to 26.

8. SOPHOCLES. The Oxford Translation, revised.

9. ÆSCHYLUS, literally translated. By an OXONIAN. (Price 3s. 6d.)

9* ————— Appendix to, containing the new readings given in Hermann's posthumous edition of Æschylus, translated and edited by G. BURGES, M.A. (3s. 6d.)

10. ARISTOTLE'S RHETORIC AND POETIC. With Examination Questions.

11. LIVY'S HISTORY OF ROME. Vol. III., Books 27 to 36.

12 & 14. EURIPIDES, literally translated. From the Text of Dindorf. In 2 Vols.

13. VIRGIL. By DAVIDSON. New Edition, Revised. (Price 3s. 6d.) *Frontispiece.*

15. HORACE. By SMART. New Edition, Revised. (Price 3s. 6d.) *Frontispiece.*

16. ARISTOTLE'S ETHICS. By PROF. R. W. BROWNE, of King's College.

17. CICERO'S OFFICES. [Old Age, Friendship, Scipio's Dream, Paradoxes, &c.]

18. PLATO. Vol. III. By G. BURGES, M.A. [Euthydemus, Symposium, Sophistes, Politicus, Laches, Parmenides, Cratylus, and Meno ]

19. LIVY'S HISTORY OF ROME. Vol. IV. (which completes the work).

20. CÆSAR AND HIRTIUS. With Index.

21. HOMER'S ILIAD, in prose, literally translated. *Frontispiece.*

22. HOMER'S ODYSSEY, HYMNS, EPIGRAMS, AND BATTLE OF THE FROGS AND MICE.

23. PLATO. Vol. IV. By G. BURGES, M.A. [Philebus, Charmides, Laches, The Two Alcibiades, and Ten other Dialogues.]

24, 25, & 32. OVID. By H. T. RILEY, B.A. Complete in 3 Vols. *Frontispieces.*

26. LUCRETIUS. By the REV. J. S. WATSON. With the Metrical Version of J. M. GOOD.

27, 30, 31, & 34. CICERO'S ORATIONS. By C. D. YONGE. Complete in 4 Vols. (Vol. 4 contains also the Rhetorical Pieces.)

28. PINDAR. By DAWSON W. TURNER. With the Metrical Version of MOORE. *Front.*

29. PLATO. Vol. V. By G. BURGES, M.A. [The Laws.]

33 & 36. THE COMEDIES OF PLAUTUS, By H. T. RILEY, B.A. In 2 Vols.

35. JUVENAL, PERSIUS, &c. By the REV. L. EVANS, M.A. With the Metrical Version of GIFFORD. *Frontispiece.*

37. THE GREEK ANTHOLOGY, translated chiefly by G. BURGES, A.M., with Metrical Versions by various Authors.

38. DEMOSTHENES. The Olynthiac, Philippic, and other Public Orations, with Notes, Appendices, &c., by C. RANN KENNEDY. (3s. 6d.)

    1 c

*Advertisement for Bohn's Classical Library, printed on the endpaper of one of his volumes in 1848*

Victor Bonham-Carter, *Authors by Profession*, 2 volumes (London: Society of Authors, 1978), I: 77, 226;

George Watson Cole, "Do You Know Your Lowndes?," *Papers of the Bibliographic Society of America*, 33 (March 1939): 1-22;

Francesco Cordasco, *The Bohn Libraries: A History and a Checklist* (New York: Franklin, 1951);

William Hazlitt, *Confessions of a Collector* (London: Ward & Downey, 1897), p. 16;

Wilmarth Lewis, *Collector's Progress* (New York: Knopf, 1951), pp. 124-125;

Anthony Lister, "Henry George Bohn (1796-1884): Bookseller, Publisher and Controversialist," *Antiquarian Book Monthly Review*, 15 (February 1988): 54-61;

Ruari McLean, *Joseph Cundall: A Victorian Publisher. Notes on His Life and a Check-list of His Books* (Pinner, U.K.: Private Libraries Association, 1976).

—*David B. Mock*

# Bradbury and Evans
### (London: 1830-1865)
## Bradbury, Evans and Company
### (London: 1865-1872)
## Bradbury, Agnew and Company
### (London: 1872-1969)

Bradbury and Evans, printer and proprietor of *Punch*, became one of the foremost publishers of fiction in the 1840s. The firm is particularly noted for publishing works by Charles Dickens and William Makepeace Thackeray.

William Bradbury came to London from Derbyshire. In 1830 he became associated with Frederick Mullet Evans, who had been a printer in Southampton. For the first ten years they were exclusively jobbing printers. The first book they printed was a law book by Alexander Maxwell. Printing law books became an early specialty; additionally, the firm gained a reputation for fine art printing.

In July 1833 Bradbury and Evans moved to 11 Bouverie Street and Lombard Street, Whitefriars, where they installed "a machine of the largest size and best construction" which was well suited to printing newspapers and periodicals. The firm was advanced and competent. So efficient was Bradbury and Evans that it could help other firms that were in difficulty; it sometimes printed the *London Journal* and, on one occasion, an issue of the *Illustrated London News*. Among the firm's clients were the publishers Chapman and Hall and Edward Moxon.

One of the firm's earliest publishing ventures came about almost by chance. In 1841 Bradbury and Evans became printers of a new humorous journal, *Punch; or, The London Charivari*, which had been started by the engraver Ebenezer Landells and Joseph Last. Bradbury and Evans gradually established a financial interest in the periodical, and in December 1842 they entered into a partnership with Mark Lemon, the editor of *Punch*, and Douglas Jerrold.

Much of the early success of *Punch* seems to have been due to the way in which its affairs were organized at weekly dinners, which became legendary for their sociable atmosphere. *Punch* was noted for its generosity; its maxim was "Go to any expense, and the office will pay." *Punch* soon gained a reputation for its topicality and daring. It attracted many of the major authors of the day, and published illustrations by such leading artists as John Leech, Hablôt K. Browne, John Tenniel, and Richard Doyle. Thackeray was on its staff. *Punch* was the great success story of the 1840s, and it did much to enhance the reputa-

*The founders of Bradbury and Evans (top and bottom) and two of the sons who took over their fathers' business in 1865 ( from M. H. Spielmann,* The History of "Punch," *1895)*

tion of Bradbury and Evans. In the 1850s Shirley Brooks and Charles Keen became regular contributors.

It is the firm's relationship with Dickens, however, that did the most to establish its reputation. Following a dispute with Chapman and Hall, Dickens was in search of a new publisher. On 1 June 1844 he signed an agreement with Bradbury and Evans whereby he received an advance of £2,800 and assigned to the firm a quarter share of the profits from whatever he might write during the ensuing eight years. The first book, a successor to *A Christmas Carol* (1843), was to be ready for Christmas 1844. *The Chimes* proved difficult for Bradbury and Evans to distribute, and the firm had to enlist the help of Chapman and Hall; the

book carries the Chapman and Hall imprint and an 1845 publication date. Despite the problems, the book was a success, making a profit of £1,420. Dickens was delighted with the profits and the appearance of his book and wrote enthusiastically about his new publisher. For the next fourteen years Bradbury and Evans published all of Dickens's literary output; the majority of his novels were published as green-covered monthly serials. Great security was enforced whenever a new novel was being published because of the high risk of piracy; it is said that *David Copperfield* (1849-1850) was printed by the sons of the firm's owners—Henry Bradbury, W. H. Bradbury, and Frederick Evans—in a separate room to prevent any employee's leaking information.

Dickens's contract with the firm was renegotiated in 1850; under the new terms Bradbury and Evans continued to receive a quarter of the profits from his works but ceased to levy the publisher's 10 percent commission on gross sales.

Their appetites whetted by the success of *Punch*, Bradbury and Evans were anxious to start another periodical. In 1845 the architect and editor Joseph Paxton broached to William Bradbury the idea of starting a daily newspaper that would be liberal in outlook and would be financed by the advertising of the new railway companies. Bradbury and Evans decided to go ahead with the newspaper, to be called the *Daily News*, and asked Dickens to be its editor. Dickens was not enthusiastic; but he was hard-pressed for funds, and on 3 December 1845 he accepted on the condition that there would be a reliable subeditor. W. H. Wills was appointed as subeditor and Thomas Hodgkinson as assistant subeditor. The paper commanded an impressive range of editorial writers, including Lemon, Jerrold, John Forster, and Richard Henry Horne. Dudley Costello was responsible for foreign news, Frederick Knight Hunt for provincial intelligence, and a Mr. West for naval and military news. For a time Dickens's father, John Dickens, reported for the paper from the House of Commons gallery. Dickens was to receive a salary of two thousand pounds per year.

The first advertisement for the *Daily News* appeared in *Punch* on 27 December 1845: "NEW MORNING PAPER to commence at the opening of Parliament. Price 5d.... A Morning Newspaper of Liberal Politics and thorough Independence.... the literary editorship of the *Daily News* will be under the direction of Charles Dickens." The paper's offices were at 90 Fleet Street.

Management of a newspaper was not one of Dickens's talents, and after only seventeen issues he relinquished his control; he finally resigned from the editorship in March 1846. Some of the problems may not have been Dickens's fault; from the first issue there was a series of blunders at the printing office in Whitefriars. The paper also had an inauspicious start financially; its capital of fifty thousand pounds was insufficient. Bradbury and Evans called on Charles Wentworth Dilke, editor of the *Athenaeum*, for advice. In April 1846 Dilke assumed financial management of the paper for three years. In 1847 the *Daily News* ceased to be published by Bradbury and Evans, appearing instead under the imprint of William King Hales of 8 Lombard Street. It was

*Title page for the first book edition of Thackeray's first novel, which Bradbury and Evans had previously published in installments*

said that Bradbury could not bear to walk past its office without grieving at the losses of more than two hundred thousand pounds that he and Evans had incurred.

Unlike Dickens, Thackeray was not an established author when he went to see Bradbury and Evans, carrying "a small brown paper parcel with him"; he was, of course, known to the proprietors as a member of the *Punch* staff. To Thackeray's delight, Bradbury and Evans accepted *Vanity Fair* (1847-1848) for sixty pounds a month plus half the profits. Bradbury and Evans cautiously did not specify the number of installments, in case the work was a disaster and publication had to cease. But *Vanity Fair* was extremely successful, and some 10,500 copies were sold. Bradbury and Evans also published Thackeray's *The History of Pendennis* (1848-1849) and *The History of Samuel Titmarsh and the Great Hoggarty Diamond* (1849). Feeling that he was not receiving sufficient remuneration from Bradbury and Evans for his novels, Thackeray resigned from the permanent staff of *Punch* in 1851, ostensibly over the attitude of the magazine toward the French emperor; he continued, however, to supply occasional articles for the magazine until 1856, and Bradbury and Evans published his novels *The Newcomes* (1853-1855) and *The Virginians* (1857-1859).

Apparently unchastened by his unsatisfactory editorship of the *Daily News*, a few years after its demise Dickens was prompting Bradbury and Evans to think of establishing a weekly periodical, with serious rather than humorous entertainment, to complement *Punch*. *Household Words* first appeared on 1 March 1850; it became enormously successful, selling some forty thousand copies a week over the next nine years. Dickens had negotiated a hard bargain with Bradbury and Evans: in addition to an annual salary of five hundred pounds, he received half the profits.

Besides the association with Dickens, which clearly contributed to its success, *Household Words* also attracted many other leading authors. Elizabeth Cleghorn Gaskell was a frequent contributor; her *Lizzie Leigh* was serialized in the first three issues in 1850. Dickens serialized his own *A Child's History of England* between January 1851 and December 1853 and *Hard Times* in 1854, but generally he only provided one weekly article and relied on the efforts of his many talented contributors.

In November 1858, following his separation from his wife, Catherine, Dickens inserted a personal announcement in *Household Words*. He expected the announcement to appear also in *Punch*; when it did not, Dickens summoned the proprietors of *Household Words* to a meeting at which he moved a resolution to dissolve the partnership and discontinue the journal. Bradbury and Evans refused to recognize the meeting or the resolution, and an embittered correspondence ensued. In December Bradbury and Evans declined an offer of one thousand pounds for their share of the copyright of *Household Words*; Dickens thereupon announced that the partnership was dissolved and that *Household Words* would cease publication. The matter came to a head in March 1859 when Dickens issued an advertisement for a new periodical, *All the Year Round*, to be published by Chapman and Hall. Bradbury and Evans responded by filing an affidavit in Chancery to restrain him. The publishers insisted that Dickens had never requested Bradbury and Evans or the editor of *Punch* to insert his personal apologies in the magazine. Dickens did not contradict the affidavit. The result was that the copyright of *Household Words* was auctioned, and

the final issue appeared in May 1859.

Bradbury and Evans were determined to counter Dickens by launching their own new periodical, *Once a Week*, from the ashes of *Household Words*. A four-page prospectus in May 1859 announced that the new journal was to contain "a considerable amount of fiction by celebrated novelists." Its editor was Samuel Lucas; among its regular contributors were Harriet Martineau, Shirley Brooks, and George Henry Lewes, and it was illustrated by Leech, Tenniel, and Charles Keene. Charles Reade's "A Good Fight" (1859) and George Meredith's *Evan Harrington* (1861) were serialized in *Once a Week*. Although the magazine was artistically brilliant, as a commercial venture it was not successful; its sales dropped steadily from an initial fifty-seven thousand copies to thirty-five thousand in the mid 1860s. Bradbury and Evans sold *Once a Week* in 1869. Other periodicals with which the firm was associated were an early journal by Paxton, the *Horticultural Register* (1831-1836); a newspaper, the *Gardener's Chronicle and Agricultural Gazette*, which was started by Dilke in 1841 and remained under Bradbury and Evans's ownership until the 1860s; and the *Field*, a sporting weekly edited by Lemon that first appeared on 1 January 1853 and was sold the following November.

Important novels published by Bradbury and Evans include Wilkie Collins's *The Dead Secret* (1857) and Robert Smith Surtees's *Mr. Facey Romford's Hounds* (1865). Charles Reade's *The Cloister and the Hearth*, published by Trübner in 1861, was originally serialized in *Once a Week* as "The Good Fight."

The firm's correspondence files reveal that Bradbury and Evans were generally on good terms with their authors. Many wrote requesting advances, and these appear to have been provided. Despite his reputation for keen business acumen, Evans earned praise for his cordiality from Harriet Martineau. In a letter written in September 1860 (now in the Bodleian Library) she wrote: "Mr. Evans had some business with me which turned out to be a great pleasure. We propose to publish certain series of papers of mine and a book which he does me the honour to think will be useful."

In 1865 the founding partners retired. Their sons took over the firm, which became Bradbury, Evans and Company. W. H. Bradbury married the daughter of the art dealer Thomas Agnew; and following the departure of F. M.

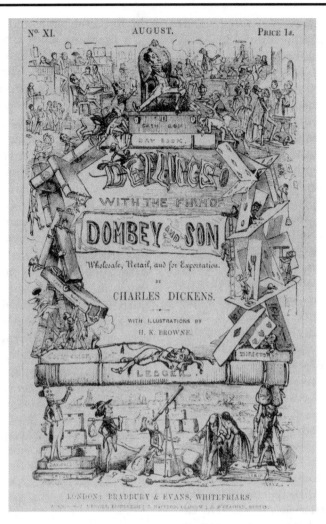

*Cover for one of the monthly parts of the second book by Dickens to bear the Bradbury and Evans imprint*

Evans, the son of Frederick Evans, in 1872, the firm became Bradbury, Agnew and Company.

W. H. Bradbury, who remained as chairman, felt that he could not maintain the publishing interests of the firm, and apart from publishing *Punch* and a few associated books, the firm reverted to being a printer. *The Real Adventures of Robinson Crusoe* (1893) and various other writings by Francis Burnand carried the Bradbury, Agnew and Company imprint; but on the whole, the firm's days as a book publisher were over. Under Bradbury, Agnew and Company *Punch* had eight editors: Tom Taylor from 1874 to 1880, Burnand from 1880 to 1906, Sir Owen Seaman from 1906 to 1932, E. V. Knox from 1932 to 1949, Kenneth Bird from 1949 to 1952, Malcolm Muggeridge from 1953 to 1957, Bernard Hollowood from 1957 to 1968, and William Davis in 1968 and 1969.

Laurence Bradbury succeeded his father,

W. H. Bradbury, in 1892, remaining as joint managing director until his retirement in 1920. On the Agnew side, Sir William Agnew was succeeded as joint managing director by his son Philip; he was succeeded by Alan Agnew, who remained in office until his son Peter took over in 1953. The company acquired various printing works, including in 1951 the Leagrave Press of Luton which was known for its fine letterpress and modern color work. The firm also owned a stationery business, Pulmans of Bletchley, and published such periodicals as the *Countryman, Arable Farming, Farmer's Guardian, Sportsworld*, and *Dairy Farmer and Pig World*. In the late 1960s Bradbury, Agnew and Company ran into financial difficulties; United Newspapers was anxious to acquire *Punch* and made a bid of eighty-six thousand pounds for the firm. The offer was accepted by the board of Bradbury, Agnew and Company in April 1969.

**References:**

William E. Buckler, "Dickens the Paymaster," *PMLA*, 66 (December 1951): 1177-1180;

Buckler, "Edward Walford: A Distressed Editor," *Notes and Queries*, 198 (December 1953): 536-538;

Buckler, "E. S. Dallas's Appointment as Editor of 'Once A Week,'" *Notes and Queries*, 195 (24 June 1950): 303;

Buckler, "*Once A Week* under Samuel Lucas 1859-65," *PMLA*, 67 (December 1952): 924-941;

Robert J. Cruikshank, *Roaring Century 1846-1946* (London: Hamish Hamilton, 1946);

Gerald G. Grubb, "Dickens' Pattern of Weekly Serialization," *English Literary History*, 4 (1942): 141-156;

Grubb, "Dickens and the *Daily News*: Preliminaries to Publication," *Nineteenth Century Fiction*, 6 (December 1951): 174-194;

Anne Lohrli, *Household Words, a weekly journal 1850-59* (Toronto: Toronto University Press, 1973);

Robert L. Patten, *Charles Dickens and His Publishers* (Oxford: Oxford University Press, 1978);

R. G. G. Price, *A History of Punch* (London: Collins, 1957).

**Papers:**

Bradbury and Evans's correspondence is in the Bodleian Library, Oxford.

*—Diana Dixon*

# Browne and Nolan
### (Dublin: 1870-1967)

The Irish publishing firm Browne and Nolan was started in Dublin in 1870 when the printer John Browne went into partnership with William Nolan. When other Scottish and Irish publishing firms began to fail at the turn of the century, Browne and Nolan survived. In the 1960s it had offices in Dublin, Cork, and Belfast. From 1879 until 1967 Browne and Nolan was the publisher of the *Cambridge Review*. Among the many famous authors associated with this periodical were Sir Arthur Quiller-Couch, G. E. Moore, William Morris, Roger Fry, J. B. Priestley, T. S. Eliot, and Raymond Williams. In 1967 Browne and Nolan was bought by Longmans and ceased to operate as an independent publishing house. The Browne and Nolan imprint exists today only on an educational line published by Longmans.

**References:**

Eric Homberger, William Janeway, and Simon Schama, eds., *The Cambridge Mind: Ninety Years of the Cambridge Review 1879-1969* (Boston: Little, Brown, 1970);

Frank A. Mumby, *Publishing and Bookselling*, fourth edition (London: Cape, 1974), p. 534.

*—Beverly Schneller*

# Burns and Oates
*(London: 1867-1919, 1948-1970, 1974-   )*
## James Burns
*(London: 1835-1849)*
## Burns and Lambert
*(London: 1850-1864)*
## Burns, Lambert and Oates
*(London: 1864-1867)*
## Burns, Oates and Washbourne
*(London: 1920-1947)*

James Burns, who was born in 1808, came to London in 1832 to work for the publishing firm of Whitaker and Company. He opened his own business as a bookseller and stationer around the beginning of 1835 at 1 Duke Street, Manchester Square, moving to 27 Portman Street in 1836 and to 17 Portman Street in 1838. Originally a Scottish Presbyterian, Burns not only conformed to the Church of England but soon became an ardent High Churchman; he was writing to John Henry Newman as early as 1836. He quickly established himself as publisher for the younger High Churchmen (Rivington had the older ones) and also published two distinguished general series, the Englishman's Library and the Fireside Library. In 1847 Burns followed the example of the radical High Churchmen and converted to Roman Catholicism. He thereby sacrificed the position he had built up as a High Anglican publisher, a position significant enough that his conversion was reported in the *Times*. Burns sold off his old list and, in effect, started over as a Roman Catholic publisher.

Newman took pity on Burns and gave him *Loss and Gain* (1848) to publish. This work began a connection that became a mainstay of the firm, continuing with Newman's other novel, *Callista* (1856), the very successful *Dream of Gerontius* (1865), and *An Essay in Aid of a Grammar of Assent* (1870). All of these works were intended for a specifically Catholic audience; Newman's *Apologia pro Vita Sua* (1864) was published by Longman, Green, Longman, Roberts and Green. Other converts, such as F. W. Faber, published with Burns, and in 1848 the firm began publishing a convert-founded magazine, the *Rambler*. The bookselling side of the business had a steady market among Catholics for its devotional books and prints and

church music. There had been Catholic bookseller-publishers in London since the early 1700s; Burns was fortunate in that several old firms left the business at about the time he entered it. His firm had become the leading Catholic publisher in England by the early 1860s.

By then the firm had begun its changes of name, becoming Burns and Lambert at the beginning of 1850. Lambert is a shadowy figure; the name is an old Catholic one, and perhaps he was added to develop that connection. The firm did well enough that it added the next-door premises at 18 Portman Street and a branch at the center of the book trade, 63 Paternoster Row. In 1861 the firm lost the *Rambler*, which had become too liberal; but it was rewarded for its orthodoxy in 1863 by being made publisher of the *Dublin Review*, the organ of Cardinals Nicholas Wiseman and Henry Edward Manning, and later it was intermittently publisher or copublisher of the Jesuit *Month*. It also took over the publishing of serials founded in the 1830s, the *Annals of the Propagation of the Faith* and the *Catholic Directory*.

William Wilfred Oates, also a convert, had originally been a schoolmaster; since 1857 he had had his own publishing house, Austin and Oates, in Bristol. In 1864 he sold that business and joined the London firm, which became Burns, Lambert and Oates. In 1867 Lambert departed the scene, and the name Burns and Oates was adopted. When Burns died in 1871 Oates took over the firm but kept the name. In 1876 Oates himself died, and his son Wilfred took over. In 1882 the firm moved from Portman Street to larger premises nearby at 28 Orchard Street. It developed an American connection, copublishing with Benziger of New York and using the Catholic Publication Society as agent.

*Wilfrid Meynell at about the time he became associated with Burns and Oates*

Wilfred Oates carried on the business vigorously until, in the words of a terse note, "his withdrawal in 1885." It was presumably at that time that the firm was acquired by J. G. Snead-Cox—a relative of Cardinal Herbert Vaughan and editor of a weekly Catholic newspaper, the *Tablet*, from 1884 to 1920—and E. F. Riddell (later Riddell-Blount).

Burns and Oates's "Classified Catalogue of Standard Catholic Publications" for 1897-1898 has large sections headed Meditations, Spiritual Reading and Devotion; Biography and Hagiology; and Tale Books. The covers advertise the works of Cardinal Manning and a Burns and Oates edition of Alban Butler's *Lives of the Saints*. The catalogue contains an announcement that the firm handles the sales of publications of the Jesuit Fathers, including Manresa Press. Separate catalogues were offered for prayer books, liturgical works, schoolbooks (a big item since the ad-

vent of mass education), school and church furniture, and vestments.

A new era for Burns and Oates began at the turn of the century. Wilfrid Meynell, an extraordinary editor and publisher, had earlier collaborated with Snead-Cox at the Westminster Press. Having sold the *Weekly Register* in 1899, Meynell joined the staff of Burns and Oates as a reader about 1900, becoming general manager and receiving a one-third share of the firm in 1903. Meynell brought to Burns and Oates many of the writers he had earlier enlisted for the monthly *Merry England*, which he had edited from 1883 to 1895 (Burns and Oates had been part owners of the magazine during the first year). His wife, Alice Meynell, was one of these writers. Burns and Oates published her later work, notably *Poems* (1913), *The Last Poems of Alice Meynell* (1923), and a complete edition, *The Poems of Alice Meynell* (1923). Another poet of this second Catholic Revival was Meynell's protégé Francis Thompson, whose posthumous works were great successes: *Selected Poems* (1908) sold some eighteen thousand copies, the separately published *Hound of Heaven* (1908) fifty thousand. With Alice Meynell and Thompson Catholic publishing became major literary publishing. A younger generation was represented by G. K. Chesterton's *Poems* (1915). Katharine Tynan and R. H. Benson were also Burns and Oates authors.

Meynell's other great contribution to Burns and Oates was in book design and typography. In 1903 he began to entrust the design of the most important works to Bernard Newdigate of the Arden Press. In 1911 Meynell's younger son, Francis, joined the firm, learning from Newdigate and a year later taking charge of design and production. Francis Meynell and Stanley Morison, who joined the firm in 1913, were to be the leading figures in the revival of fine printing and typography in the next half century, and by giving them their first opportunity Burns and Oates played an innovative role in the history of the craft of printing. Their principal work for the firm was a program of liturgical publishing, the finest product being an *Ordo Administrandi Sacramenta* (1915) printed in the original Fell types by Oxford University Press. The Burns and Oates device—the arms of St. Thomas Becket—first appeared on the title page of this work; it was designed by Eric Gill. In 1916 Francis Meynell left the firm to avoid causing it embarrassment on account of his pacifism; Morison, imprisoned for the same cause for a few months in 1917 or 1918, continued to work for Burns and Oates intermittently until 1921.

Wilfrid Meynell's share of the firm's growing profits allowed him to withdraw from active management after 1919, and William Andrews Mackenzie took over the daily running of the firm. In 1920 the name was changed to Burns, Oates and Washbourne after the acquisition of R. and T. Washbourne, a London Catholic house that had been publishing since at least the 1870s. New competition was supplied by the founding of Sheed and Ward in 1926. In 1929 a large shareholding was acquired by Walter Hutchinson, whose publishing and printing empire included dozens of firms; but his imprints retained their distinct identities, and the Catholic character of Burns, Oates and Washbourne was not impaired.

By 1930 the firm had moved from the West End to 43 Newgate Street in the City, a good business move to the heart of the book trade but unfortunate in its consequences during the blitz a decade later. In 1932 the chairman was Percival Deeley, and the managing director was Percy Briggs. The 1932 catalogue is especially strong in devotional works and hagiography, with even the novels and "General Literature" catering to the Catholic market. The firm imported many foreign—especially American—works. It had a second London branch at 129 Victoria Street, Westminster, and branches in Birmingham, Manchester, and Glasgow. Carrying on the Meynell tradition, the firm did bookbinding and printing; its motto was "Our printing is good because it is Designed."

In the late 1930s Lt. Col. P. A. Meldon was both chairman and managing director. In 1939 Burns, Oates and Washbourne was acquired by Eyre and Spottiswoode, the King's Printers. At the time, this traditionally Church of England firm, whose mainstays were the Authorized Bible and the Book of Common Prayer, had a Catholic chairman in Col. Oliver Crosthwaite-Eyre. Eyre and Spottiswoode was expanding its interests under the inspiration of Douglas Jerrold, who became chairman of Burns, Oates and Washbourne and the recently founded Hollis and Carter. Christopher Hollis and Crosthwaite-Eyre represented the Catholic interest on the board of Burns, Oates and Washbourne, which was dominated by Eyre and Spottiswoode representatives. The new ownership made no change in the Catholic character of Burns, Oates and Washbourne and its associ-

*Francis Thompson in 1878 or 1879. Burns and Oates became his publisher after his mentor, Meynell, joined the firm.*

ated firms and periodicals. At the end of 1940 the Newgate Street premises were destroyed in an air raid; among the losses were the records of the firm. The firm moved to temporary offices at 6 Great New Street, still in the City of London. By 1942 the administrative offices had been moved to the relative safety of Birmingham, at 5 Norfolk Road, Edgbaston, near the Birmingham Oratory, but a London office was maintained at the Victoria Street branch. In 1945 Jerrold became chairman of Eyre and Spottiswoode and was succeeded at the Burns firms by Oliver Crosthwaite-Eyre. In 1946 the firm moved its offices back to London; its new quarters were at the eminently Catholic address of 28 Ashley Place, in the shadow of Westminster Cathedral and backing on the Victoria Street premises. It would be several years before the Burns enterprises resumed the prewar scale of business.

In 1946 Thomas Ferrier Burns, a great-nephew of James Burns, was invited to join the staff of Eyre and Spottiswoode and became managing director of Burns, Oates and Washbourne.

In 1948 he acquired a majority shareholding, and he eventually gained complete control of the firm. A holding company, BOW Holdings, was organized to include Burns, Oates and Washbourne; Hollis and Carter; the *Dublin Review* and other magazines; and the *Tablet*, which had been acquired from the Archdiocese of Westminster by Burns and two friends in 1935. The name of the original firm was changed back to Burns and Oates. By 1950 the board of directors was entirely Roman Catholic, with Douglas Woodruff, editor of the *Tablet*, as deputy chairman; David James was managing director. Burns edited the *Dublin Review* from 1947 to 1956. Under his leadership Burns and Oates revived to share with Sheed and Ward the position of leading Catholic publishers in the 1950s. The firm's most distinguished publication of this period was perhaps Frederick Copleston's nine-volume *History of Philosophy*, which began in 1946. Hollis and Carter, which was used to publish works not specifically Catholic in character, was sold to Max Reinhardt in 1962.

The situation for Catholic publishing houses became less favorable in the 1960s. The post-Vatican II style of faith rendered unfashionable many of the devotional aids, particularly missals, which had been mainstays of the bookselling side of the business. In 1967 Burns gave up publishing to edit the *Tablet*. He sold Burns and Oates to the international firm Verlag Herder of Freiburg. Burns and Oates's most distinguished periodical, the *Dublin Review*, one of the last of the dying breed of quarterly reviews, was renamed the *Wiseman Review* shortly before ceasing publication in 1968. In 1970 Herder decided to cease publishing and doing business under the name of Burns and Oates. The firm's list of books was disposed of, many being remaindered and some sold to other houses; a core list of 238 titles was sold to Search Press, a subsidiary of Herder's New York subsidiary, Herder and Herder. Burns and Oates was not liquidated, but remained a shell company for four years. In 1974 Search Press—which its founder, Countess Charlotte de la Bedoyère, had separated from Herder and Herder—bought the majority shareholding of Burns and Oates and resumed publication of religious works under that imprint. (Under its own name, Search Press publishes a line of craft books.) The final volume of Copleston's *History of Philosophy* was published under the Burns and Oates imprint in 1975.

**References:**

*Early Chapters in the History of Burns and Oates* (London: Burns & Oates, 1949);

Francis Meynell, *My Lives* (London: Bodley Head, 1971);

Viola Meynell, *Francis Thompson and Wilfrid Meynell* (London: Hollis & Carter, 1952).

                                   —*Josef L. Altholz*

# Cassell and Company Limited
*(London: 1883-1969)*
## John Cassell
*(London: 1848-1858)*
## Cassell, Petter and Galpin
*(London: 1858-1878)*
## Cassell, Petter, Galpin and Company
*(London: 1878-1883)*
## Cassell and Collier Macmillan
*(London: 1969-1978)*
## Cassell Limited
*(London: 1978-1986)*
## Cassell plc
*(London: 1986-   )*

Cassell and Company was the inspiration of the tea and coffee merchant-turned-publisher John Cassell. What he initiated in the late 1840s as a one-man publishing business would become "a household word" less than five decades later. By the final quarter of the twentieth century the company would rank among the United Kingdom's one hundred largest publishers.

The son of Manchester working people, Cassell was born on 23 January 1817. He began his own working life first as a mill and factory operative and later became a carpenter's apprentice. In the mid 1830s he became an itinerant missionary for the National Temperance Society. In 1841, with the help of his wife's money, he established a wholesale tea and coffee business to purvey an alternative to intoxicating beverages. His first venture into the world of publishing also reflected his commitment to temperance: the *Teeto-*

*tal Times; or, Monthly Temperance Messenger* was published on Cassell's behalf by the temperance publisher William Brittain of Paternoster Row from March 1846 until it was absorbed into the National Temperance Society publishing enterprise in 1851.

Although not strictly speaking his own publication, the *Teetotal Times* must have whetted Cassell's enthusiasm for the publishing trade. He continued to sell tea and coffee, but from 1848 until his death publishing would be his most absorbing business interest. The foundation of his publishing firm can be dated to 1 July 1848 and the initial appearance of a weekly newspaper, the *Standard of Freedom*—the first publication to bear the imprint "published by John Cassell."

Cassell conducted his infant publishing business from premises at 335 Strand which he shared with the printer William Cathrall. From

1848 to 1850 there appeared a series of tracts and almanacs bearing the Cassell imprint; but his major publication of this early period was the *Standard of Freedom*, which continued into 1851. As Cassell himself expressed it in the first number, this new radical paper undertook "to supply an interesting series of comments on passing events, tending to rectify the public judgment of men and measures and promote a rational and beneficial management of public affairs."

This concern both to interest and to educate the public became the hallmark of what Cassell would shortly come to regard as his specialty: the publication of periodicals. Beginning in 1850, when he bought the entirety of the Strand premises and printing plant from Cathrall, Cassell's growing business sought and captured the new working-class market for entertaining and informative periodical literature. Indeed, in January 1850, just before buying out Cathrall, he had already begun his first notable magazine, the *Working Man's Friend, and Family Instructor*. Offering a compelling range of general-knowledge material—history, literature, travel, biography, politics, gardening, and more—this penny weekly achieved what Cassell claimed to be a circulation of one hundred thousand in twelve months.

Despite its fair popular success, the *Working Man's Friend* was not long-lived, lasting only until early 1852. By then Cassell had turned his attention to other ventures in serial publishing. He had become particularly intrigued by the commercial possibilities of illustration, an interest which coincided with the widespread enthusiasm for the Great Exhibition at the Crystal Palace in 1851. That year he brought out the *Illustrated Exhibitor, a Tribute to the World's Industrial Jubilee* in weekly numbers at twopence each and monthly parts at eightpence, with the latter regularly selling in the range of forty thousand per issue. Other illustrated serial publications by Cassell included the *Popular Educator*, begun in 1852, and the successor to the *Exhibitor*, the *Illustrated Magazine of Art*, begun in April 1853. The latter covered both the practical and the fine arts and was in large part responsible for Cassell's contemporary reputation as a popularizer of art.

Of the illustrated magazines that bore his company's imprint at midcentury the best selling and longest lived was *Cassell's Illustrated Family Paper*, which first appeared in December 1853 and, with varying titles, ran continuously until, as *Cassell's Magazine of Fiction*, it ceased publication in 1932. (From 1926 it was under new owner-

*John Cassell*

ship, although it retained the name *Cassell's* in its title.) In the 1850s *Cassell's Illustrated Family Paper* built up a wide following of perhaps a million regular readers with its winning mix of well-illustrated general knowledge, humor, needlework patterns, chess problems, and—the biggest attraction of all—melodramatic fiction. Chief among the authors of the latter was J. F. Smith, one of the most popular writers of his day, whose serialized novels—for example, "The Soldier of Fortune" (1855) and "Smiles and Tears" (1858)—secured *Cassell's Illustrated Family Paper* its place as the second most widely circulating magazine of the mid 1850s after the *London Journal*.

In the early part of the decade Cassell began publishing books as well as periodicals. This new aspect of his enterprise can be traced back to 1850 and one of his periodical publications, a sixpenny monthly, *John Cassell's Library*. Each issue contained serializations of such works as a biographical dictionary, a treatise on the steam engine, and a history of England. By May

1851 Cassell had published six such works in cloth-bound editions. So began what his biographer, G. Holden Pike, would characterize as a "new epoch in cheap literature." In 1852 Cassell published an edition of the new best-seller, Harriet Beecher Stowe's *Uncle Tom's Cabin*, in book form as well as twopenny parts. In 1854 yet another kind of book bore the Cassell imprint: the first of many such publications which the firm would produce to the present day, *Cassell's Latin Dictionary* was compiled by one of the firm's regular authors, a Unitarian minister from Manchester named John Beard.

In the spring of 1852 Cassell moved his plant and offices from the Strand to 9 La Belle Sauvage Yard, Ludgate Hill. The first few years in this location were difficult ones for the firm. The building was in need of extensive renovation, an expense which the business could by no means support; for despite the popular success of many of its publications, and for all its growing reputation in the trade, the firm was in financial trouble. Cassell purportedly had a poor head for business, preferring to devote the greater part of his attention to temperance and other social causes. In 1855, to meet credit obligations, he sold his plant and name to the printing firm of Petter and Galpin. He remained with the firm as a salaried editor until 1858, when he became a partner.

Between 1855 and 1858 the new owners, Thomas Dixon Galpin and George William Petter, added only a few publications to Cassell's existing list. The most notable of these was *Cassell's Illustrated History of England*, written by Smith and published in penny parts from 1856 to 1864. For the most part, during their first three years of ownership Petter and Galpin prudently relied on established and profitable endeavors such as *Cassell's Illustrated Family Paper*.

By 1859 the partnership of Cassell, Petter and Galpin had begun to prosper under its careful new management. Operating from the recently renovated and expanded Belle Sauvage premises, the business enjoyed modest growth and in 1860 established a branch office in New York. From 1859 until Cassell's death in 1865 the firm steadily increased its publication list. Among the most ambitious ventures of this period was *Cassell's Illustrated Family Bible* (1859); costing about one hundred thousand pounds to produce, its sales exceeded 350,000 copies at the end of six years; from 1861 its original appeal would be further enhanced by the inclusion of illustra-

Advertisement for a printing press manufactured by Cassell's partners, Petter and Galpin

tions by Gustave Doré. Other religious and religious literary publications made their appearance in the wake of the *Illustrated Family Bible*: for example, John Bunyan's *Pilgrim's Progress* (in weekly parts), *Cassell's Family Prayer Book*, and *The Bible Dictionary, Illustrated*, all published in 1863; *Foxe's Book of Martyrs* (1865-1866); John Milton's *Paradise Lost*, illustrated by Doré (circa 1866); and the *Quiver* (1861-1926), a weekly periodical "Designed for the Defence and Promotion of Biblical Truth." In 1861 and 1862 the latter publication included serialized versions of *The Channings* (1862), *Mrs. Halliburton's Troubles* (1862), and other novels by Mrs. Henry Wood, author of *East Lynne* (1861).

At the same time that it was producing religious reading, the partnership of Cassell, Petter and Galpin also introduced a series of secular classics. These pictorial versions of familiar stories— Daniel Defoe's *Robinson Crusoe*, the works of Shakespeare, Oliver Goldsmith's *The Vicar of Wakefield*, and Jonathan Swift's *Gulliver's Travels*—were published at widely affordable prices in weekly or monthly parts in 1863 and 1864. With illustrations by Doré—whose English reputation owed largely to his extensive employment by Cassell— the showpiece of the series was Miguel de Cervantes's *Don Quixote*, of which the first number appeared in November 1864. In May of the same year a more prosaic publication had begun: *Cassell's Time Tables of the Metropolitan Railways and Through-Route Glance Guide*, which would survive under various titles until 1922. By the time Cassell succumbed to cancer on 2 April 1865 the business he had founded had grown to include five hundred employees, and its output was such that it required 855,000 sheets or 1,310 reams of paper weekly.

The next two decades or so were a time of even more pronounced expansion. The number of employees had grown to twelve hundred by 1888; half of these were housed in the firm's new printing works, built in the early 1870s at the back of the La Belle Sauvage Yard location. Covering 13,000 square feet, with a frontage of 230 feet along Fleet Lane and Seacoal Lane, the expanded premises held thirty-six presses in 1875. By then, in addition to its New York office, the firm also boasted a branch in Paris, established in 1871; in 1884 a third office was opened in Melbourne. Between 1895 and the early 1950s Cassell would also found branches in Sydney, Toronto, Wellington, Calcutta, Johannesburg, Karachi, and Auckland. In 1865 three magazines bore the Cassell imprint; in 1888 there were seven. In the former year the firm published fewer than a dozen part-issues in any one month; in the latter year the monthly output in this category never fell below forty.

Between 1868 and 1878 Petter and Galpin took in three new partners: Henry Jeffery, head of the countinghouse; Petter's brother Arthur; and Robert Turner, a onetime Islington printer and bookseller. This expanded partnership became Cassell, Petter, Galpin and Company in 1878. Five years later it was incorporated as Cassell and Company Limited, with a nominal capital of five hundred thousand pounds. Galpin became chairman and managing director; Turner was made general manager. Petter retired from active participation in the business; he died in

1888. In the same year Turner, who had been replaced as general manager in 1885 by Edward Whymper, succeeded Galpin as chairman. By this time the firm's printing plant was "the largest concern of the kind anywhere in the world"—or so it was reported in a press interview given by Wemyss Reid, the new general manager, who had replaced Whymper in 1887. Cassell and Company further distinguished itself in the 1880s as the first British printing and publishing firm to initiate a rudimentary employee benefits plan, which included bonuses, loans, and a provident and emergency fund.

When Petter and Galpin were active in the company, the former managed the editorial end while the latter looked after the business side of the firm. Both men came from Nonconformist families; Petter's background in particular was strongly evangelical and influenced his editorial policy. Like Cassell, he dedicated himself to the popularization both of religion and of general knowledge. His editorial staff included John Willis Clark as chief editor in the early 1860s and Thomas Teignmouth Shore from 1865 to 1888. Among the many religious works the company brought out in the 1870s and 1880s were the illustrated *Bible Educator* (1873-1875), edited by E. H. Plumptre, professor of New Testament exegesis at King's College, London; *Life of Christ* (1874), by F. W. Farrar, with frontispieces by Holman Hunt; *History of Protestantism* (1874-1877), by J. A. Wylie; and *Martin Luther: His Life and Work* (1887), by Peter Bayne. Contemporary educational publications in such fields as topography, architecture, and science included Walter Thornbury and Edward Walford's *Old and New London* (1873-1878); T. G. Bonney's *Cathedral Churches of England and Wales* (1884) and *Abbeys and Churches of England and Wales* (1887); *Cassell's Natural History* (1876-1882), edited by Martin Duncan, president of the Geological Society; and *The Story of the Heavens* (1885), by Sir Robert Stawell Ball, who was also one of the many professorial editors of the *Technical Educator* (first series, 1870-1872). The 1870s and 1880s also brought the publication of several works of history: *Cassell's History of the War between France and Germany* (1871-1872), by Edmund Ollier, who would turn out to be Cassell's most prolific historian; Ollier's *Cassell's History of the United States* (1874-1877); James Grant's *Cassell's History of India* (1876-1877); and yet another ambitious work by the productive and versatile Ollier, *Cassell's Illustrated Universal History* (1882-1885), with illustrations by Alma Tadema and other eminent artists of the day.

In addition to educational works aimed at a primarily adult readership, from the late 1860s the firm published textbooks that anticipated and then continued to serve needs attendant on W. E. Forster's 1870 Education Act, which introduced universal elementary education into England and Wales. In 1869 the company brought out Cassell's Primary Series, which it advertised as "specially prepared with a view to meeting the want indicated by Her Majesty's Commissioners of Education in National and other Schools." Among the many publications for schools that would follow the Primary Series were *The Marlborough French Grammar* (circa 1870) and Hugh O. Arnold-Forster's *Citizen Reader* (1886), a widely used political education textbook that would sell a quarter of a million copies by 1891 and as many more by 1906.

Apart from educational publications for both the student and the serious self-educator, the company provided its public with a range of practical information in the form of railway timetables, maps, and travel guidebooks published throughout the 1870s and 1880s. In the same period the firm also produced several publications of specifically domestic interest: for instance, *The Family Physician* (1880-1882); *Cassell's Dictionary of Cookery* (1875, with many reprints thereafter); and *Cassell's Book of Indoor Amusements, Cardgames and Fireside Fun* (1881). For youthful readers and others whose taste was for entertaining fantasy and fiction rather than household hints or serious learning, Cassell's list included an 1882 edition of *The Arabian Nights*; H. Rider Haggard's *King Solomon's Mines* (1885); and Robert Louis Stevenson's *Treasure Island*, published initially as a serial from October 1881 to January 1882 in the magazine *Young Folks*.

Most of the firm's fiction and nonfiction works were originally published as part-issues: weekly, monthly, or sometimes both. While the part-issue was Cassell's staple and most profitable format in the 1860s, 1870s, and 1880s, during this period the firm also produced many works as bound volumes. These included the book version of *Treasure Island* (1883) and such other adventure books by Stevenson as *Kidnapped* (1886), *The Black Arrow* (1888), and *The Master of Ballantrae* (1889). By this time Cassell's list additionally boasted the many volumes that made up the Red Library of English and American Classics. This series, renamed Cassell's Red Library

in 1884, reprinted the works of such popular writers on both sides of the Atlantic as Charles Dickens, Harrison Ainsworth, James Fenimore Cooper, Nathaniel Hawthorne, and Edgar Allan Poe. In the same period an assortment of other bound volumes also bore the Cassell imprint: among the notable examples are *The Rule of the Monk; or, Rome in the Nineteenth Century* (1870), a romance by Giuseppe Garibaldi; a two-volume biography of William Gladstone by George Barnett Smith (1879); a volume of autobiography by Louis Kossuth, *Memories of My Exile* (1880); a luxury limited edition of Henry Wadsworth Longfellow's *Evangeline* (1882), illustrated by Royal Academy artist Frank Dicksee; C. A. Fyffe's *History of Modern Europe* (1880-1889); Sir Henry Lucy's *Diary of Two Parliaments* (1885-1886); and Edwin Hodder's *The Life and Work of the Seventh Earl of Shaftesbury* (1886).

The part-issue and the bound volume formats were both represented in a publication that also brought together entertainment and education. This was the series Cassell's Library of English Literature, a wide-ranging compilation of summaries and excerpts from the classics accompanied by editorial commentary. Published first in sevenpenny parts between 1875 and 1881, the series was reprinted at a lower price and subsequently republished as five bound volumes, each covering a particular literary field: shorter English poems, English religion, English plays, shorter works of English prose, and abstracts of longer works in English prose and verse. The editor of this ambitious project, which spanned pre-Beowulf poetry to the works of Robert Browning and George Eliot, was Henry Morley, Professor of English Literature at University College, London. Morley was a dedicated popularizer of literature and general knowledge, and, in addition to his Library of English Literature for Cassell, he edited Morley's Universal Library (1883-1888) for Routledge. He scored yet another success for Cassell with Cassell's National Library, published from 1886 to 1890 in weekly parts selling at three- or sixpence each, depending on the quality of binding. Like most of Morley's endeavors, the National Library cast its net widely, taking in "Standard Works in every Branch of literature, including travel, biography, history, religion, science, art, adventure, fiction, drama, belles lettres, and whatever else may be worth lasting remembrance." The influence and breadth of readership of the National Library were such that a com-

*Henry Morley, who edited two popular series for Cassell and Company between 1875 and 1890*

mentator for *Punch* was moved to remark: "The old proverb was 'Every man's house is his castle'; in the future this will be 'Every Englishman's house has his Cassell.'"

Rivaling, if not surpassing, the popularity of Cassell's two Library series was that category of publication around which John Cassell had initially developed his business: the periodical. During the firm's era of expansion from 1865 to 1888 it continued successfully to market magazines that had been launched in prior years—for example, the *Magazine of Art*; the *Quiver*; the *Paper*, retitled *Cassell's Magazine*; and the *Photographic News*, begun around 1858, one of the first serial publications to cater to the growing popular enthusiasm for the camera. The mid 1860s to the end of the 1880s also brought the debut, and sometimes the demise, of diverse other magazines, yearbooks, and papers. Among the specialist publications were the monthly *Scientific Review and Journal of the Inventor's Institute*, begun in 1865; the weekly *Live Stock Journal*, started in 1875; the *Stock Exchange Year-Book* (1874-1890); and yearbooks, quarterlies, and monthlies treating business, religion, real estate, medicine, sport,

and education. The interests of a wider reading public found expression in the *Working Man*, begun and discontinued in 1866; *Little Folks*, published weekly and monthly from 1871 to 1874, monthly from 1874 to 1926; the *Boy's Newspaper*, begun in 1880 and sold in 1881; *Cassell's Saturday Journal*, published weekly and monthly from 1883 to 1921; the monthly *Lady's World*, started in 1886 and renamed the *Woman's World* in 1887; and Cassell's only venture into daily journalism, the *Echo*, begun in 1868 and sold in 1875.

A few of the company's periodical publications brought some notable literary figures into its sphere. In the 1860s and 1870s *Cassell's Magazine* ran such serials as Sheridan Le Fanu's "A Strange Adventure in the Life of Laura Mildmay" (1869) and *Checkmate* (1870-1871), Wilkie Collins's *Man and Wife* (1869-1870) and *Poor Miss Finch* (1871-1872), and Charles Reade's *A Terrible Temptation* (1871), a daring tale of upper-class depravity. In the following decade the *Saturday Journal* included the adventure stories of John Berwick Harwood, Arthur Conan Doyle's mysteries, tales of the sea by W. Clark Russell and Arthur Quiller-Couch, and the thrilling serial fiction of Frank Barrett and Richard Dowling. From 1881 to 1886 the *Magazine of Art* was edited by William Ernest Henley, poet, journalist, editor of the *National Observer*, and collaborator with Stevenson on several plays in the mid 1880s.

Prominent among those whose literary talents from time to time graced Cassell periodicals was Oscar Wilde. He assumed the editorship of the *Lady's World* toward the end of 1887, and it was he who insisted on changing the title to the *Woman's World*. As he explained in a September 1887 letter to Reid, the earlier name had "a certain taint of vulgarity about it" which reconciled poorly with an editorial policy whose aim was to produce a magazine for "women of intellect, culture, and position." But for all his initial enthusiasm for the project Wilde's restless brilliance was ill-suited to the discipline that effective editing demanded. His visits to the Belle Sauvage offices, at first twice weekly and punctual, became increasingly sporadic and of ever shorter duration. Ultimately he failed to turn up at all, and in the autumn of 1889 an anonymous editor took over for the remaining year of the magazine's life. Fleeting though it was, Wilde's editorship brought the *Woman's World* a degree of literary distinction that it might otherwise have lacked: among the contributors he enlisted were E. Nesbit, Ouida, and Olive Schreiner.

During the time Wilde was pursuing his erratic editorial course, the company was riding the crest of prosperity. But in 1888 there began what the house historian, Simon Nowell-Smith, would later describe as "twenty years of descent": decreasing profits were reflected in falling dividends, until between 1905 and 1908 no dividend at all was declared. According to Nowell-Smith, the cause of the decline was twofold. The managers who followed Galpin—the chairman, Henry Fowler; the general manager, Reid; and the company secretary, Arnold-Forster (author of Cassell's best-selling textbook *Citizen Reader*)—divided their attention between the publishing business and other interests, notably politics. (Both Fowler and Arnold-Forster were members of Parliament.) The corollary of the upper management's outside preoccupations was the failure of Cassell and Company to cater effectively to an ever-growing market: what was by the 1890s a full generation of newly literate beneficiaries of the 1870 Education Act. Other publishers outdistanced the firm that had once been the pacesetter in promoting the popular taste for reading. Added to the company's difficulties at this time was the lack of the kind of assured and continuous editorial leadership that Shore had long provided. His resignation in 1888 was followed by a succession of short-term chief editors whose various editorial departments were also in constant flux.

Not surprisingly under such circumstances, the history of the business in the 1890s and first five years of the twentieth century is punctuated by a series of failed ventures and costly misjudgments. After passing up the chance in 1889 to publish W. T. Stead's *Review of Reviews* (which George Newnes profitably took on), Cassell proceeded instead to launch a succession of periodicals, five of which failed within a year or two of commencing. Of the survivors, two were for children: *Chums* (1892-1926) and *Tiny Tots* (1899-1926). Just one aimed to attract a large general market: the *New Penny Magazine* (1899-1925), a deliberate attempt to evoke and profit from the onetime popularity of Charles Knight's pioneering pictorial weekly, the *Penny Magazine* (1832-1845). Although the later version would run for a quarter of a century, in its early years it lagged well behind such livelier and more up-to-date competitors as Alfred Harmsworth's *Penny Pictorial Magazine*. Even old mainstays such as *Cassell's Magazine* and the *Saturday Journal* trailed in the wake of Newnes's *Strand Magazine* and

Harmsworth's *Answers*. The latter publisher also led the way in part-issue publications, bringing out serialized works with intriguing titles, new material, and modern illustrations while Cassell produced mainly reprints illustrated from stock woodblocks of a half century earlier.

Meanwhile, the company's efforts to capture the ever more lucrative market for entertaining novels were also failing to pay. The central cause was corporate blindness to the popular taste and trends of the day. One notable error was the decision by the chief editor, John Williams, and the publishing manager, John Hamer, to reject on the grounds of its gloominess Hall Caine's *The Bondsman*. Published by the new firm of William Heinemann in 1890, the novel proved highly profitable. More disastrous still, in a time when the single-volume edition had recently become the preference of both the writers and readers of novels, Cassell chose to promote the old three-decker format. This decision limited its ability to attract leading authors. Thus, from 1888 until it largely abandoned the three-decker in 1895, the firm was forced to rely largely on either the obscure and pseudonymous—"Leslie Keith," "Mrs. Alexander," "Florence Warden"—or the hopelessly out of date, such as James Payn with his *A Modern Dick Whittington* (1892). Having admitted defeat with the three-decker series, Cassell immediately ventured in the opposite direction and in 1895 brought out the Pocket Library—short novels whose small format imitated Fisher Unwin's Pseudonym and Autonym libraries. The series lasted only a year, and, apart from Gertrude Atherton's *A Whirl Asunder* and George Gissing's *The Paying Guest*, its six volumes were undistinguished.

The 1890s and early 1900s were not, however, entirely calamitous. One of the three-decker series, J. M. Barrie's *The Little Minister*, had enjoyed a modest success in 1891 and did even better as a one-volume reprint the following year. Cassell's five-shilling novels also consistently kept pace with the competition, and in the early 1890s this list included the works of Barrie, Conan Doyle, Anthony Hope, and E. W. Hornung, creator of Raffles, the gentleman cracksman. Three specialized weekly magazines started during the period would also prove to be reliable if not spectacular sellers: *Work* (1889-1924), *Cottage Gardening* (1892-1926, with several name changes), and the *Building World* (1895-1920). The *Magazine of Art* continued to hold its own and in one area— the technology of color reproduction—consistently outdid its rivals. In the field of general-interest periodicals, the fortunes of *Cassell's Magazine* took an upturn through the efforts of Max Pemberton, editor from 1896 to 1905. Pemberton brought new life to the magazine with a liberal dose of fiction from such writers as Hope, Haggard, Ouida, Austin Freeman, Stephen Crane, and Rudyard Kipling, whose *Kim* ran as a serial in 1901.

If fairly constant output is any indication, the guidebook, reference, and educational branch of the business also successfully weathered the turn-of-the-century doldrums. The company continued to publish an assortment of its guidebooks and reference works, the latter category including Cassell's first English dictionary (1891). School textbooks also remained a staple, the most notable example being Arnold-Forster's lively *History of England from the Landing of Julius Caesar to the Present Day* (1897), which sold fifty thousand copies. Nowell-Smith quotes Sir Philip Gibbs, who was employed in the educational department at the time, as saying that Arnold-Forster dictated the entire book "with hardly a note" while a no doubt harried subordinate transcribed this feat of memory on what was in 1897 the only typewriter at the Belle Sauvage Yard offices.

The death of Reid in 1905 marked the end of a particularly lackluster period in the history of Cassell and Company. The new general manager was Arthur Spurgeon, who had been the literary manager of the National Press Agency. Although he lacked book publishing experience, Spurgeon had energy and business sense, as well as the necessary detachment—"ruthlessness," as Nowell-Smith calls it—to cut costs by dismissing thirty staff members in 1906. But this was merely a short-term measure; in Spurgeon's judgment the way to restore lasting fiscal health was to strengthen Cassell's traditional backbone, the periodical publication. To head up this endeavor he hired W. Newman Flower, a young man who had trained under Lord Northcliffe at the Harmsworth Press.

Under Flower's vigorous direction the magazine side soon revived the fortunes of the business as a whole. In only a few weeks Flower's improvements to the *Penny Magazine* tipped its circulation over the one hundred thousand mark, and in 1907 he launched a new periodical, the *Story-Teller*, with comparable success. With contributing authors including W. Somerset Maugham, E. Phillips Oppenheim, G. K. Chesterton, and Kipling, the *Story-Teller* achieved and maintained grati-

fying sales and by the late 1920s had earned well over a quarter of a million pounds. *Cassell's Magazine*, however, had not been faring well under the editors who had succeeded Pemberton, and in 1912 Flower turned his hand to rejuvenating this struggling survivor from the company's earliest days. He improved the magazine's appearance, added new features, and secured stories from well-known writers, all of which resulted in an increased circulation and, before long, a yearly profit of twenty thousand pounds. Other successes in the periodical line in the early years of the twentieth century were the *Girl's Realm*, purchased from another firm around 1908, and the *New Magazine*, begun in 1909.

In addition to the revitalized *Penny Magazine* and the flourishing *Story-Teller*, Cassell also showed a profit with a series of uniform editions of the classics, the People's Library, which sold half a million copies of its first fifty titles. In 1908 the business was sufficiently recovered to permit the resumption of dividends. According to Nowell-Smith, the turnaround was due not only to Spurgeon's management and Flower's editorship but also to the acumen of the advertising manager, Thomas Young.

In 1909 the firm established a subsidiary, the Waverley Book Company, under the management of A. Bain Irvine. Set up to market high-priced illustrated books on the installment plan, Waverley was an instant success. Meanwhile, its parent company's book-publishing side was doing poorly. Haggard had returned after a lengthy hiatus, and Cassell would publish thirteen of his books beginning with *The Brethren* (1904) and ending with *The Virgin of the Sun* (1922). The firm could also boast one or two additional authors of contemporary repute—most notably Chesterton, who gave Cassell the rights to his first collection of Father Brown stories, *The Innocence of Father Brown* (1911). Generally speaking, though, the book list in the first decade or so of the new century was neither impressive nor lucrative.

In the beginning of 1913, when Flower took over the book side of the business, this situation started to change. Through his work on Cassell's magazines he had developed connections with many talented writers, from each of whom he had secured the promise of at least one book. In this way he gradually built up a trade book list of considerable distinction. This list, along with the continuing success of the periodicals, helped the firm to weather the hardships—fiscal and otherwise—imposed by World War I and contributed to its profitability in the years immediately following. Among the many noteworthy titles and authors associated with Cassell from 1913 to 1925 were *The Country of "The Ring and the Book"* (1913), a pictorial appreciation of Robert Browning's Italy by Sir Frederick Treves, who would later bring Cassell *The Elephant Man* (1923); Katherine O'Shea's firsthand account *Charles Stewart Parnell: His Love Story and Political Life* (1914); *Mr. Britling Sees It Through* (1916), by H. G. Wells; and *The Lion's Share* (1916), by Arnold Bennett, who would stay with the firm until his death in 1931 and would allow it to publish, among other distinguished titles, *Riceyman Steps* (1923). Beginning with her *Towards Morning* (1918), I. A. R. Wylie would have several books published by Cassell, as would Sheila Kay-Smith, Rosita Forbes, Ernest Raymond, and Warwick Deeping, whose *Sorrel and Son* (1925) enjoyed wide and continuing popularity. In addition, during this period the company published several histories of the war and continued to bring out such house staples as textbooks, dictionaries, and travel guides; it also published children's books and such works of domestic interest as *Cassell's Book of Fancy Needlework* (1913).

In 1920, when Cassell's share prices were on a downward trend, the company's shareholders accepted a lucrative offer from the newspaper magnates William and Gomer Berry (later Viscounts Camrose and Kemsley). Under its new ownership the firm became a private company, retaining its prior directorship of Spurgeon, Young, and Flower. Young succeeded Spurgeon as chairman in 1922, and Irvine became general manager. The following year the company went public again, with 500,000 one-pound ordinary shares (of which the Berry Brothers held 397,740) and 350,000 one-pound 7 percent cumulative preference shares, fully subscribed. The labor unrest of the mid 1920s, culminating in the 1926 General Strike, led to the closing of the printing department by a management who had had enough of constant agitation and stoppages.

The next major change, decided on around the end of 1926 or the beginning of the next year, was the elimination of the periodical publishing side of the business: by 1927 the Berry brothers had absorbed the firm's periodicals—including the prior year's new venture, the *Argosy*—into another of their concerns, the Amalgamated Press. In May the literary director, Flower, raised sufficient capital to become the new proprietor of the book-publishing business; shares were is-

*La Belle Sauvage Yard in 1921*

sued soon after, and once again Cassell became a private company. Its directorship at that time consisted of Flower as literary and managing director; Young as chairman; and H. Aubrey Gentry, newly promoted from editor, as business director. Flower's son Desmond joined the firm in 1930 and a year later was elected to the board to assist his father with the literary end of the business; additionally, he took over supervision of the design department.

The next ten years or so were a time of brilliant literary achievement for Cassell. The decade began with the acquisition of the English translations of the works of André Gide and Guy de Maupassant, as well as works by such renowned authors as Willa Cather and Dashiell Hammett, all of which had come from the New York publisher Alfred Knopf when he discontinued his London office. In the following years Cassell's list also boasted such outstanding works as Louis Bromfield's *Twenty-Four Hours* (1930) and *The Rains Came* (1937); Wyndham Lewis's *Snooty Baronet* (1932) and *The Revenge for Love* (1937); Stefan Zweig's *Marie Antoinette* (1933), *The Queen of Scots*

(1935), and his one novel, *Beware of Pity* (1939); Ernest Raymond's *We, the Accused* (1935); and Ayn Rand's *We the Living* (1936). In 1938 Newman Flower retired from active participation in the day-to-day operation of the company, although he retained his seat on the board; Desmond Flower became literary director in his place. That year was among the most significant of the decade for the company: there appeared Robert Graves's *Count Belisarius*, the first of many of his books the firm would publish, and Eric Knight's novel *You Play the Black and the Red Comes Up*, which would be followed during the war years by such memorable others as *This Above All* (1941) and *Lassie Come-Home* (1941). In 1939 came Nicholas Monsarrat's first book to be published by Cassell, *This Is the Schoolroom*, as well as Marco Pallis's study of Tibet, *Peaks and Lamas*, and the first volume of Sir Charles Petrie's *Life and Letters of the Right Honourable Sir Austen Chamberlain*.

In 1940 Desmond Flower joined the army, and his father resumed his active role in the firm. In May 1941 Cassell's premises were struck by incendiary bombs; La Belle Sauvage Yard and most of the firm's records were destroyed in the fire that ensued. Throughout the following decade and a half Cassell operated from a series of temporary premises.

For all the hardship and disruption of the war and postwar years, Cassell maintained the quality of its list. With Newman Flower as chairman (replacing Young, who had resigned), and Desmond back to take charge of the literary end, by 1945 the company was equal to the task of meeting the period's growing demand for books. Despite the difficulties imposed by postwar paper rationing and the firm's lack of permanent premises, it nonetheless brought out such noteworthy books as the duke of Windsor's *A King's Story* and Monsarrat's *The Cruel Sea*, both of which appeared in 1951. By 1957 Cassell had published one million copies of the latter work. Another notable best-seller of the postwar period was Winston Churchill's six-volume history of World War II, which began with *The Gathering Storm* in 1948 and concluded with *Triumph and Tragedy* in 1954; Cassell also did well with Churchill's four-volume *A History of the English-Speaking Peoples* (1956-1958). Proceeds from the two Churchill works contributed significantly to the financing of the firm's new premises in Red Lion Square, Holborn, into which it moved in January 1958.

Other successful works were published during the 1950s in history, reference, autobiography, sport, literature, and general fiction. They included *Splendid Occasions in English History, 1520-1947* (1951), edited by Ifan Kyrle Fletcher; *Cassell's Encyclopedia of Literature* (1953), under the editorship of H. S. Steinberg; the memoirs of the Aga Khan (1954); Stirling Moss's *Book of Motor Sport* (1955); F. L. Lucas's *Style* (1955); *The Letters of Edward Gibbon*, edited by J. E. Norton (1956); Sloan Wilson's *The Man in the Grey Flannel Suit* (1956); and Alec Waugh's *Island in the Sun* (1956). Cassell's history of outstanding publishing persisted into the 1960s with Graves's poetry and a deluxe illustrated one-volume version of Churchill's *A History of the English-Speaking Peoples*, retitled *The Island Race* (1968).

It is on grounds other than literary achievement that the last year of the 1960s and the years following have been memorable. This has been a period characterized by significant changes in ownership, new acquisitions, and shifts in the focus of the company's list. In 1969 Desmond Flower became chairman after a period as deputy chairman. In the same year the majority shareholders—mainly members of the Flower family—sold their controlling interest to the New York firm Macmillan Inc., then operating in the United Kingdom as Crowell, Collier-Macmillan Ltd. The new group, called Cassell and Collier Macmillan, included a library supply company and Macmillan's British distribution arm; in 1978 the business was reorganized and Cassell Limited became strictly a publisher once more. Four years later the firm was absorbed into another American corporation, CBS Publishing Europe. Cassell regained its independence in 1986 when a City of London consortium bought it from CBS. Since then it has been a public company, Cassell plc.

The decade or so preceding this latest change in ownership had not been notably successful; the company had actually run at a loss between 1976 and 1979. Even so, in the latter year it stood fifty-fifth among the United Kingdom's one hundred largest publishers, according to the number of new books published annually. The titles which had placed Cassell among the most prolific United Kingdom book producers in 1979 were primarily, if not exclusively, nonfiction. By the time it was purchased by CBS, the company could no longer boast a substantial fiction list. During the 1970s and 1980s the mainstay of the business was a category of publication with which the

Cassell imprint has long been associated: the reference work. Among the new publications, updated editions, and reprints that have been carrying on the house tradition of providing general knowledge and basic information are *Cassell's New Spelling Dictionary* (1976); *Cassell's Compact French-English English-French Dictionary* (1977); *Cassell's Businessman's Travel Guide* (1978); and *Cassell's Concise English Dictionary* (1985), first published in 1949. The firm has also produced self-instruction textbooks on English grammar, typing, and mathematics, and from time to time it has brought out such recollections of the past as a facsimile edition of the 1882 *Cassell's Book of Indoor Amusements, Cardgames and Fireside Fun* (1973) and *Cassell's Compendium of Victorian Crafts*, the 1978 version of a nineteenth-century edition of *Cassell's Household Guide*. Additionally, since 1960 the company has published annually *Cassell's Directory of Publishing, in Great Britain, the Commonwealth, and Ireland*, which has been enlarged to include South Africa and Pakistan and has become a standard reference work.

In December 1986, after a period in which its staff was scattered—some in London, some in Eastbourne—the company moved to a building in Artillery Row in southwest London. Recently it moved into offices in Villiers House, 41-47 Strand—not far from where John Cassell first shared a printer's premises well over a century ago.

In its latest incarnation as an independent public company, Cassell has been experiencing a period of growth. The 120 new titles of 1986 increased to 300 by 1988; the firm continues to publish about 300 new books a year, along with a back list of about 2,800 titles. Under the leadership of its chairman and managing director, Philip Sturrock (organizer of the purchasing consortium), the company has two divisions, academic and trade, each with its own set of imprints. The academic division takes in religious books with either the Geoffrey Chapman or Mowbray imprints; textbooks and professional reference works bearing the Cassell name; and directories, indexes, and bibliographies carrying the Mansell imprint. Trade books include Studio Vista publications on art and design; works on natural history and horticulture displaying the Blandford imprint; and dictionaries and general-interest books (including art, cookery, and gardening) with the Cassell imprint. Also associated with Cassell plc are Wisley Handbooks, New Orchard Editions, the Arms and Armour Press, Javelin,

Robert Royce, and Tycooly Publishing. The firm's latest acquisition, made around 1989, is Ward Lock, among whose best-known publications is Mrs. Beeton's *Cookery Book*, which, under various titles, has been in print continuously from the middle of the nineteenth century.

Endeavoring to redefine and enhance a corporate identity for the 1990s, Cassell's development strategy involves the promotion of established areas of strength—in particular the reference and educational lists, which include a new edition of *Cassell's English Dictionary* and texts for English-language teaching. In directing a major portion of its resources toward the marketing of basic information to students and the general public, the present-day company evokes something of the spirit of its founder. For, as his nineteenth-century biographer, G. Holden Pike, explained it, John Cassell's unwavering mission was the advancement of "a wider and unfettered diffusion of knowledge."

**References:**

"Cheap Literature," *British Quarterly Review*, 29 (April 1859): 337-339;

Henry Curwen, *A History of Booksellers* (London: Chatto & Windus, 1873), pp. 267-274;

Peter J. Curwen, *The UK Publishing Industry* (Oxford: Pergamon Press, 1981), pp. 20, 29;

Newman Flower, *Just as It Happened* (London: Cassell, 1950);

Thomas Frost, "John Cassell and His Literary Staff," in his *Forty Years Recollections* (London: Low, 1880), pp. 226-228;

Vivienne Menkes, "Cassell," *British Book News* (June 1988): 408-412;

V. E. Neuburg, *Popular Literature* (Harmondsworth, U.K.: Penguin, 1977), pp. 205-210;

Simon Nowell-Smith, *The House of Cassell 1848-1958* (London: Cassell, 1958);

"An Old Printer" [John Forbes Wilson], "John Cassell," in his *A Few Personal Recollections* (London: Privately printed, 1896), pp. 66-72;

G. Holden Pike, *John Cassell* (London: Cassell, 1894).

**Papers:**

Records of Cassell and Company's history during the nineteenth century and first four decades of the twentieth century were destroyed in the fire of 1941. Other archival material is housed with the Macmillan Publishing Company, New York.

*—Patricia J. Anderson*

# W. and R. Chambers

*(Edinburgh: 1832-1853; Edinburgh and London: 1853-1973; Edinburgh: 1973-    )*

Founded in May 1832 in Edinburgh by the brothers William and Robert Chambers, the firm of W. and R. Chambers played a leading role in the cheap literature movement of the nineteenth century. Pioneers in supplying inexpensive, wholesome books and periodicals to the growing number of readers in the middle and working classes, the brothers exerted a powerful influence on the popular culture of their time. Unlike most other nineteenth-century publishing firms, W. and R. Chambers is notable for the comprehensive nature of its undertakings. As William Chambers proudly says in his *Memoir of Robert Chambers* (1872), the business in its prime might have been described as "a great book factory, or perhaps more properly, a literary organisation, somewhat original in character. Under one roof were combined the operations of editors, compositors, stereotypers, wood-engravers, printers, bookbinders, and other labourers—all engaged in the preparation and dispersal of books and periodicals." The brothers themselves wrote a large proportion of the works they published.

The Chambers brothers were born in Peebles, on the river Tweed south of Edinburgh, William on 16 April 1800 and Robert on 10 July 1802. Sons of James Chambers, a cotton manufacturer who at one time employed as many as one hundred hand-loom weavers, and Jean Gibson Chambers, the daughter of a local landowner, the boys attended the local schools in Peebles but were largely self-educated. Robert attributed much of his learning to wide reading, at the age of ten or eleven, in the fourth edition of the *Encyclopaedia Britannica*, a copy of which his father had stored in a chest in the attic. "It was a new world to me," Robert recalled. "I felt a profound thankfulness that such a convenient collection of human knowledge existed, and that here it was

spread out like a well-plenished table before me. What the gift of a whole toy-shop would have been to most children, this book was to me. . . ." The circulating library of Alexander Elder, a local bookseller, introduced the boys to the works of Jonathan Swift, Miguel de Cervantes, Tobias Smollett, Alexander Pope, and Oliver Goldsmith.

Following the collapse of the father's business, the Chamberses moved to Edinburgh in 1813. On 8 May 1814 William was apprenticed for five years to John Sutherland, a bookseller in Calton Street, at four shillings a week. While learning the book trade, in his spare time he read the works of Adam Smith, William Paley, John Locke, and Hugh Blair; along with his brother, he also developed an interest in astronomy and chemistry. An anecdote suggests William's desire to read as well as his straitened circumstances: during the winter of 1815-1816 he was daily rewarded by a baker in Canal Street with "a penny roll newly drawn from the oven" for reading aloud to the baker and his sons from 5:00 to 7:30 each morning from the novels of Smollett and Henry Fielding.

Robert Chambers received more formal schooling than his brother, gaining some proficiency in Latin; for a time following the move to Edinburgh he was enrolled in a classical academy, with the expectation that he would subsequently attend the university and then enter the ministry, but these hopes were abandoned when his father's finances worsened. After leaving school in 1816 he did some private teaching in Portobello and then worked for several months as a junior clerk in commercial houses before being fired "for no other reason that I can think of but that my employer thought me too stupid to be likely ever to do him any good." At the age of sixteen, in 1818, Robert followed his brother's advice and opened a bookstall in Leith Walk, a road that led from Edinburgh to the seaport of Leith. The family's miscellaneous collection of books and his own schoolbooks provided his initial stock.

On completing his apprenticeship in May 1819 William Chambers decided to open his own bookstall near his brother's. Like Robert, William was influenced by the example of James Lackington, the shoemaker's son who had made his fortune in London between 1774 and 1792 selling remaindered books at low prices. In return for some help offered to an agent of Thomas Tegg, the London publisher who was among the first to profit from cheap editions of standard works, William was granted ten pounds' worth of books on credit. Having arranged this stock on a handful of shelves he built himself, he began his career as a bookseller in June 1819, "elated, it may be supposed, in no ordinary degree at this fortunate incident, and not the least afraid of turning the penny long before the day of payment came round." From the start he chose to sell new books inexpensively bound in boards, rather than old leatherbound volumes. Always seeking ways of saving money, he soon decided to buy books in sheets and fold, sew, and bind them in boards himself, "thereby saving on an average threepence to fourpence a volume, my only outlay being on the material employed; for my labour was reckoned as nothing." The next step was the purchase for three pounds of an old handpress and "thirty pounds-weight of brevier [types], dreadfully old and worn, having been employed for years in the printing of a newspaper, and, in point of fact, only worth its value as metal"; with this apparatus he performed odd printing jobs, such as lottery tickets and handbills. More ambitiously, he "managed to execute an edition [of 750 copies], small size, of the Songs of Robert Burns, with my own hands bound the copies in boards with a coloured wrapper, sold the whole off, and cleared eight pounds by the transaction." After having purchased "a tolerably good fount of longprimer" types, he wrote, printed, and published several chapbooks, including *Exploits and Anecdotes of Scottish Gipsies* (1821), a six-penny pamphlet.

In the fall of 1821 the two brothers determined to collaborate in a fortnightly journal. With William as printed, publisher, and occasional writer, and Robert as editor and chief writer, the *Kaleidoscope, or Edinburgh Literary Amuse-*ment ran from 6 October 1821 until 12 January 1822. Each number was sixteen pages octavo and sold for threepence. The satirical journal sold well but produced little profit because of the high price of paper. An interest in calligraphy and a suggestion by Archibald Constable led Robert to handwrite an anthology of songs from Sir Walter Scott's *The Lady of the Lake* (1810); by presenting the finished book to Scott, Robert made a friend and powerful ally. In 1822 Robert wrote, and William printed and published, *Illustrations of the Author of Waverley*, which described the actual persons on whom many of Scott's characters were based. Robert followed this moderate success by writing *Traditions of Edinburgh* (1825), a book, as William later described it, of "amusing particulars concerning old houses, distinguished characters, and curious incidents, such as could be picked up from individuals then still living." The work was a great success and further cemented the connection with Scott, who wondered in astonishment "where the boy got all the information."

By this time the brothers' stock had increased to a worth of about two hundred pounds each. In 1823 they moved into Edinburgh proper, Robert to a shop in India Place, William to one in Broughton Street. Robert followed his success with *Traditions of Edinburgh* with a series of other books on Scottish subjects, including *Popular Rhymes of Scotland* (1826), *Picture of Scotland* (1827), and, as part of Constable's Miscellany, *History of the Rebellion of 1745-6* (1828), *History of the Rebellions in Scotland from 1638 till 1660* (1828), and *History of the Rebellions in Scotland in 1689 and 1715* (1829). He also wrote *Life of King James I* (1830). William wrote *Book of Scotland* (1830), which described the secular and ecclesiastical institutions of the country. Jointly, the brothers wrote *Gazetteer of Scotland* (1832), with William doing most of the research and writing; the project earned the brothers one hundred pounds. As William later noted of his writings at this time, "though these and some other literary exercises were of no pecuniary advantage adequate to the time and trouble spent upon them, they were immensely serviceable as a training preparatory to the part which it was my destiny to take in the cheap literature movement of modern times."

For some years William had been aware of the relative lack of good reading material at a price that the lower-middle and working classes could afford, at a time when the movement for extension of the franchise made apparent the need for mass education. He watched with interest the success of Constable's Miscellany, a series of inexpensive new works launched in 1827, as well as John Limbird's *Mirror*, a cheap weekly begun in London in 1822, and George Mudie's *Cornucopia*, an Edinburgh serial of the same period that consisted of four folio pages and sold for three-halfpence. William was also influenced by the efforts of the Society for the Diffusion of Useful Knowledge (S.D.U.K.) to reach—in part to create—a mass reading public through a series of cheap publications. In late 1831 he decided to edit and publish a low-priced periodical of original writing that was instructive and entertaining; Robert agreed to write for the journal but refused a larger role in such an uncertain undertaking. William sent out notices of the new weekly journal in January 1832, and on 4 February the first number of *Chambers's Edinburgh Journal*, consisting of eight folio pages, printed in three columns, was published at a cost of three-halfpence. In the "Address to His Readers" that headed the first number, William announced that *Chambers's Edinburgh Journal* would offer essays and articles on literature, science, government, trade and commerce, education, agriculture, and industry. In addition, each number would feature a weekly tale, "no ordinary trash about Italian castles, and daggers, and ghosts in the blue chamber, and similar nonsense, but something really good." The inclusion of fiction and the decision to avoid political and religious controversy allowed William to distinguish his new journal from the publications of the S.D.U.K., including the *Penny Magazine*, which began its run on 31 March 1832. In later years William vigorously defended his claim to have pioneered the idea of a cheap, high-quality popular journal, attributing the collapse of the *Penny Magazine* in the mid 1840s to several causes: "the treatises of the Society were on the whole too technical and abstruse for the mass of operatives; they made no provision for the culture of the imaginative faculties; and, in point of fact, were purchased and read chiefly by persons considerably raised above the obligation of toiling with their hands for their daily bread. In a word, they may be supposed to have been distasteful to the popular fancy."

The Chamberses had reason to be pleased with the success of their journal. By the fourteenth number, dated 5 May 1832, Robert had reconsidered his decision not to involve himself other than as a contributor of articles; from that time the two brothers jointly edited the journal.

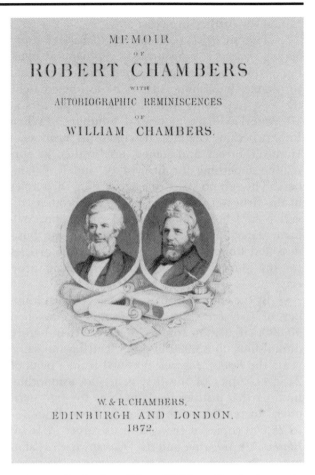

*Title page for the first edition of William Chambers's popular memoir of his brother and business partner. The book went through fifteen editions in twenty-five years.*

Of the first twelve numbers, thirty-one thousand copies were printed for distribution in Scotland. The journal's fame spread quickly: starting with the thirteenth number, William entered into an agreement with the publisher W. S. Orr to print a second edition in London; this expensive plan was made less costly beginning with the twenty-first number, when two sets of stereotype plates were cast in Edinburgh for each issue, thus eliminating the need for two typesettings and for printing in advance sufficient stock for back orders, as was then the practice of most journals. Since stereotype plates could be stored easily, copies of back issues could be printed as needed; before the advent of stereotype plates, publishers were forced to print more copies than could be sold immediately, since resetting type was prohibitively expensive. Given the low price of *Chambers's Edinburgh Journal*, and consequently the small margin of profit per copy, printing only as many copies as could be sold—especially in an era of a high tax on paper—was a financial boon that freed capital for further projects.

The surprising success of *Chambers's Edinburgh Journal* transformed William Chambers's small bookselling business into a large and profitable publishing firm almost immediately, the first step being a move to larger quarters at 19 Waterloo Place in central Edinburgh. When Robert became coeditor, he closed his business in Hanover Street and joined his brother in formally establishing the firm of W. and R. Chambers. Though no strict rules governing their roles in the firm were ever laid down, the brothers divided the labor to their mutual satisfaction: William managed the commercial side of the business and Robert wrote essays and leading articles for the journal and pursued other literary projects.

By the end of the first year sales of each number of *Chambers's Edinburgh Journal* approached 50,000; circulation rose to 70,000 in 1840 before diminishing to 53,000 in 1843. During the same years the *Penny Magazine* declined from a peak of 213,241 copies of the first issue—an astounding number that justifies its claim to be the first periodical to reach a mass market in Great Britain—to 25,000 copies at the end of its career in 1846; *Blackwood's Magazine* and the *Quarterly Review*, aiming at a more prosperous audience, averaged sales of less than 10,000 copies during the same period. To boost flagging sales in the mid 1840s, and in response to complaints from their readers about the cumbersome size of the journal, the brothers reduced the format from folio to royal octavo but continued to provide the same amount of reading material per issue at the familiar price of three-halfpence. The change in size proved a wise business decision, as circulation soared from 53,000 to nearly 87,000 copies within a year. Though sales did not remain at this level, *Chambers's Edinburgh Journal*—renamed *Chambers's Journal* in 1853—continued its profitable hold on the reading public until it was discontinued in 1956.

As Richard Altick has noted, *Chambers's Journal*, along with the *Penny Magazine*, powerfully influenced the course of popular journalism in the nineteenth century, introducing a wide public to new cultural interests while observing high standards of moral and social respectability. In accomplishing this goal, William Chambers later asserted, "the object never lost sight of was not merely to enlighten, by presenting information on matters of interest, and to harmlessly amuse, but to touch the heart—to purify the affections;

thus, if possible, imparting to the work a character which would render it universally acceptable to families." The weekly essays of Robert Chambers, "alternately gay, grave, sentimental, philosophical," contributed largely to the journal's success, especially as he refused to condescend to his audience: "it was my design from the first to be the essayist of the middle class—that in which I was born, and to which I continued to belong. I therefore do not treat their manners and habits as one looking *de haut en bas*, which is the usual style of essayists, but as one looking round among the firesides of my friends." Over the years Robert wrote between four hundred and five hundred essays; collected, they fill three volumes of the seven-volume *Select Writings of Robert Chambers* (1847).

Many other professional writers contributed poetry, fiction, and nonfiction to the journal between 1832 and 1850, including Selina Bunbury, Robert Carruthers, Maria Edgeworth, John Galt, Basil Hall, Thomas Hood, Mary Howitt, Harriet Martineau, David Masson, Hugh Miller, Mary Russell Mitford, Dinah Maria Mulock, Agnes Strickland, and Anna Maria Hall, the most prolific contributor of fiction during the period. Later in the century contributors included Grant Allen, Walter Besant, John Buchan, C. S. Calverley, Anthony Hope, E. W. Hornung, Margaret Oliphant, James Payn, and Leslie Stephen. George Meredith's first published work, the poem "Chillianwallah," appeared in the 7 July 1849 issue of *Chambers's Edinburgh Journal*; Thomas Hardy, with "How I Built Myself a House" in 1865, and Arthur Conan Doyle, with "The Mystery of Sasassa Valley" in 1879 (while he was still a medical student at Edinburgh University), also made their first published appearances in the journal. In addition to a high quality of writing, the journal enjoyed stable editorial and business management throughout the century. William Chambers realized from the start that dependability—of quality, cost, and appearance—was crucial to the success of a periodical. The poet Thomas Hood was surprised, on visiting the printing office of W. and R. Chambers in 1843, to find the presses printing sheets of the journal dated nearly three weeks in advance; but William was determined that no issue should ever be distributed to local booksellers throughout the United Kingdom later than its announced day of publication.

William Chambers delighted in anecdotes supporting his claim that the journal "pervades the whole of society," reaching members of all classes, from upland shepherds to Glasgow mill-workers to Cambridgeshire schoolboys. One man who wrote to Chambers remembered "how eagerly the *Journal* was read, in its early days, by all classes. At a country town seventeen miles from Edinburgh, a little band of young men used to walk out two or three miles on the road to intercept the carrier, and bring in the parcel of *Journals* consigned to the local bookseller for more immediate distribution. It was too slow work for these impatient spirits to wait delivery of the parcel in the usual course of carrier-work. Going home on Saturdays, dozens of young men might be seen reading their copy of *Chambers's* by the way." The 13 April 1901 issue of *Chambers's Journal* included a laudatory reminiscence by Jessie M. E. Saxby, who fondly remembered her father calling the journal "the pioneer of a free press," among the first to provide "a literature freed from the prejudices of sect as well as the trammels of party; a literature giving to all sorts and conditions of men reading on every subject which interests humanity; a literature not cumbered by technical details, but within the comprehension of general readers; a literature so cheap that the poorest can procure it—a free press indeed!" Despite such glowing anecdotal accounts of wide readership among the working classes, the majority of the journal's readers came from the middle classes—not surprising given the editorial emphasis on family and the avowedly neutral tone of the contents during a time when the working classes were developing a powerful political consciousness. William Chambers admitted as much, noting in the issue of 25 January 1840 that "this paper is read, we believe, by a class who may be called the *élite* of the labouring community; those who think, conduct themselves respectably, and are anxious to improve their circumstances by judicious means. But below this worthy order of men, our work, except in a few particular cases, does not go. A fatal mistake is committed in the notion that the lower classes read. There is, unfortunately, a vast substratum in society where the printing-press has not yet unfolded her treasures." In an age which afforded little formal education to the majority of citizens, according to Altick, *Chambers's Journal* and the *Penny Magazine* "were responsible, perhaps more than any other single factor, for whatever smattering of culture the class of shopkeepers and skilled artisans possessed during the early Victorian age."

Buoyed by the popularity of *Chambers's Edinburgh Journal*, the brothers launched in the next several years several informative nonfiction serials aimed at the mass reading market. The folio *Information for the People* (1833-1835), issued in one hundred fortnightly parts priced at three-halfpence, then published as a volume in 1835, was designed, as the preface to the 1842 edition noted, "to place a work of the character of an encyclopaedia *really* within the reach of the working-classes and those next above them.... The plan on which the work is formed is to select only the subjects on which it is important that the classes in question should be informed." The work was unburdened by technical details, presenting in accessible language "a series of articles on the most important branches of science, physical, mathematical, and moral, natural history, political history, geography, and literature, together with a few miscellaneous papers.... Thus all is given which, if studied and received into the mind, would make an individual of those classes a *well-informed man*." The popularity of *Information for the People* proved the potency of the ideology of self-help as well as the firm's ability to compete successfully with the S.D.U.K.'s *Penny Cyclopaedia*, also published in parts beginning in 1833. W. and R. Chambers sold an average of 70,000 copies of each number during the first year; by 1874-1875 the work had gone through five editions, with more than 170,000 copies sold. A translation appeared in Paris, and in 1851 Ebenezer Thomas translated parts of the work into Welsh.

The brothers followed the success of *Information for the People* by announcing in 1835 a still larger project, *Chambers's Educational Course*, a series of treatises and schoolbooks which ultimately included 306 parts, issued variously in sixteen<sup>mo</sup>, octavo, and quarto at intervals until 1896. Based at the outset on the phrenological theories of George Combe, *Chambers's Educational Course* came to reflect Scottish educational practice, as many of the volumes were written by teachers in Scottish schools; this series of schoolbooks was among the first to include the physical sciences. It also offered maps, allowing William and Robert to redress the insufficiencies of their own schooling. As Henry Curwen noted admiringly in 1873, "this series begins with a three-halfpenny infant primer, and goes onward through a whole library of grammars, dictionaries, histories, scientific, and all primary class books, and cheap editions of standard foreign and classical authors, till it culminates in a popular 'Encyclopaedia in

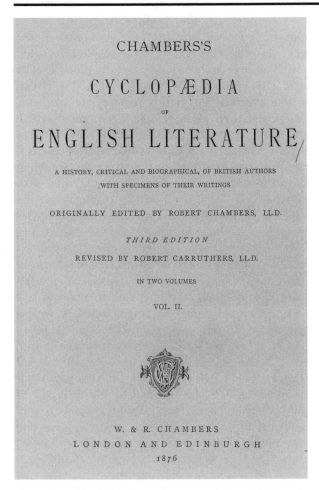

CHAMBERS'S

CYCLOPÆDIA

OF

ENGLISH LITERATURE

A HISTORY, CRITICAL AND BIOGRAPHICAL, OF BRITISH AUTHORS
WITH SPECIMENS OF THEIR WRITINGS

ORIGINALLY EDITED BY ROBERT CHAMBERS, LL.D.

THIRD EDITION

REVISED BY ROBERT CARRUTHERS, LL.D.

IN TWO VOLUMES

VOL. II.

W. & R. CHAMBERS
LONDON AND EDINBURGH
1876

*Title page for the third edition of the book that owed much of its success to the addition of questions on English literature to the British civil-service examinations*

ten thick volumes.'" Robert Chambers wrote several of the schoolbooks, including *History of the English Language and Literature* (1836) and *History of the British Empire* (1873). William contributed to the undertaking by traveling to the Netherlands in 1838, there finding support for the nonsectarian approach to education that was to characterize the Chambers series.

In 1838 W. and R. Chambers began to publish its People's Editions of standard authors; by 1840 the series of cheap reprints numbered thirty-two volumes, including works by Locke, Smollett, Burns, Paley, Scott, George Crabbe, Mungo Park, Francis Bacon, Joseph Addison, William Godwin, and Daniel Defoe. The next major project of the firm in this vein was largely the work of Robert Chambers, in conjunction with Robert Carruthers of Inverness: *A Cyclopaedia of English Literature: A History, Critical and Biographical, of British Authors, in All Departments of Literature, Illustrated by Specimens of Their Writings*, published in eighty-six

weekly parts in 1842-1843 at the by-then expected price of three-halfpence and published in two volumes, royal octavo, in 1844. Building on the example of Vicesimus Knox's *Elegant Extracts: or, Useful and Entertaining Pieces of Poetry, Selected for the Improvement of Young Persons* (1770), a standard schoolbook, Chambers wove "a systemized series of extracts from our national authors"—a total of 832 writers—into a biographical and critical history of British literature. Once again the Chamberses accurately judged the temper of the times, setting themselves in opposition to the dry informativeness of the S.D.U.K: within a few years some 130,000 copies of the *Cyclopaedia* were sold. In the second half of the century, after the civil-service examinations began to include a section on English literature, the book became valued by applicants seeking to cram for the tests. It went through four editions by the end of the century; in 1910 a fifth edition was published under the editorship of David Patrick, who undertook a substantial revision and expansion with the aid of such well-known writers as George Saintsbury, Andrew Lang, and Austin Dobson. Further editions were published until 1938.

On the first anniversary of the founding of *Chambers's Edinburgh Journal*, William reported with pride that the firm was printing 2,600,000 sheets annually on its steam presses, a total of 5,416 reams of paper on which had been paid a duty of sixteen thousand pounds. In the 4 January 1845 issue of the journal he reported on a decade of further growth: "we write at present in a huge building of four storeys, flanked by a powerful steam-engine, and with the noise of ten printing machines continually sounding in our ears. Several of these are engaged in working off impressions, the production of which at a common hand-press, would have required nearly the time then requisite for a voyage to India and back. A hundred and twenty persons are required for all the duties which proceed in this large structure, though these have exclusively a regard for works edited by ourselves. Upwards of a quarter of a million of printed sheets leave the house each week, being as many as the whole newspaper press of Scotland issued in a month about the year 1833." Despite its growth, the organization of the firm remained the same until 1853. At that time the brothers ended their association with W. S. Orr, the London publisher who handled printing and distribution of the Chambers publications in England. For years there had been complaints about the quality of paper Orr used in *Chambers's Edinburgh Journal* as well as about the quality of printing. William Chambers also doubted that Orr was reporting accurately the number of copies sold (their agreement required Orr to pay the Chamberses sixteen shillings per thousand copies). By 1853 Orr owed W. and R. Chambers a substantial amount of money and left them with debts of approximately twelve thousand pounds. To avoid similar troubles in the future, the firm opened a branch office in London under the direction of David Chambers, youngest brother of the founders. From 1853 until 1973 the publications of the firm bore the imprint "W. & R. Chambers, Edinburgh and London."

One series followed another in the 1840s and 1850s. Chambers's Miscellany of Useful and Entertaining Tracts, published in 177 parts (1844-1847) before being bound in twenty volumes priced one shilling each, was intended for "parish, school, regimental, prison, and similar libraries"; eighty thousand were sold. Despite the popularity of the series, William Chambers claimed that it returned no profit, "absolutely choked to death by the tax" on paper. A second edition was not published until 1869-1872, after the repeal of the paper duty in 1861. In the 1870s and 1880s the firm published selections from this popular series, including *Famous Men* in sixteen parts and *Lives of Eminent Women and Tales for Girls* in thirteen parts, both in 1886. The duty on paper did not prevent the Chamberses from publishing the twelve-volume *Papers for the People* (1850-1851), a series of articles on diverse subjects "mainly addressed to that numerous class whose minds have been educated by the improved schooling and the popular lectures and publications of the last twenty years, and who may now be presumed to crave a higher kind of Literature than can be obtained through the existing cheap periodicals," according to an advertisement. The titles of articles in the first volume suggest the eclectic breadth of the work as a whole: "The Bonaparte Family," "The Sepulchres of Etruria," "Valerie Duclos—A Tale," "Education of the Citizen," "The Myth," "The Sunken Rock—A Tale," "Popular Cultivation of Music," and "Ebenezer Elliott." During this same period the firm also published Chambers's Repository of Instructive and Amusing Tracts (1852-1854) and Chambers's Pocket Miscellany (1852-1853), for both of which the brothers contributed a significant amount of the writing, as well as Chambers's Library for Young People (nineteen volumes,

1848-1851) and Chambers's Instructive and Entertaining Library (twenty-six volumes, 1848-1852).

From 1860 to 1868 the brothers published what they termed their "crowning effort in cheap and instructive literature," *Chambers's Encyclopaedia: A Dictionary of Universal Knowledge*, edited by Andrew Findlater but under the direction of William and Robert Chambers. Published in 520 weekly numbers, priced at three-halfpence, and subsequently collected in ten volumes, the *Encyclopaedia* was based on the *Konversations-Lexikon* (1838-1841) published by F. A. Brockhaus of Leipzig; the firm entered into an agreement with Brockhaus permitting the transformation, not the simple translation, of the German work into English. As William Chambers explains in his *Story of a Long and Busy Life* (1882), he and his brother were moved to publish the work by the difficulty of locating information in other encyclopedias, where it was frequently presented "not under a variety of specific heads, as they commonly occur to our minds when information is required, but aggregated in large and formal treatises, such as in themselves form books of considerable bulk. Our object was to give a comprehensive yet handy and cheap Dictionary of Universal Knowledge; no subject being treated at greater length than was absolutely necessary." In other words, the work was accomplished, with the help of one hundred contributors, according to the same guidelines that governed most of the firm's publications: articles were to be short, accessible, and unburdened by technical information not needed by a general audience. The *Encyclopaedia* proved popular and, following the repeal of the paper tax, profitable. A revised edition, under the direction of David Patrick, was published in 1888 to 1892; a third, edited by William Feddie, was published from 1923 to 1927 and in 1935. Following World War II the firm of George Newnes, Ltd., arranged with W. and R. Chambers to revise the encyclopedia, which was republished in fifteen volumes in 1955 under the same name but with a new owner. From its appearance to the present, *Chambers's Encyclopaedia*, international in scope but with an emphasis on Great Britain, has had a reputation for sound, literate treatment of subjects in the humanities, geography, and biography.

The great success of W. and R. Chambers made wealthy men of its founders, but their wealth did not seduce them from working hard throughout their lives. In addition to the vast amount of writing he did for *Chambers's Journal* and other of the firm's series, Robert Chambers found time to write or edit many other books, among them *Life and Works of Robert Burns* (1851), *Songs of Scotland Prior to Burns* (1862), and *Smollett: His Life and a Selection from His Writings* (1867); reflecting his geological interests and expertise were *Ancient Sea Margins* (1848), *Tracings of the North of Europe* (1850), and *Tracings of Iceland and the Faröe Islands* (1856). The best-known of his scientific works was *Vestiges of the Natural History of Creation* (1844), published anonymously through the agency of Alexander Ireland of Manchester. Chambers feared that a negative response to his evolutionary ideas might damage his and the firm's reputation, so his authorship was not acknowledged publicly until 1884, after his and his brother's deaths. The book for which Robert Chambers is best remembered, it was praised by Charles Darwin as having performed "excellent service in this country in calling attention to the subject, in removing prejudice, and in thus preparing the ground for the reception of analogous views." Robert's last substantial book, the writing of which ruined his health during a lengthy stay in London, was *Book of Days* (1862-1864), "a miscellany of popular antiquities in connection with the calendar, including anecdotes, biographies, curiosities of literature, and oddities of human life and character." Robert Chambers died at his home at St. Andrews on 17 March 1871. His brother David, head of the London branch of the firm, died four days later.

William continued throughout his long life as head of the firm; in addition, he wrote a wide array of books, including *Glenormiston* (1849), about the estate he purchased for his home; *Fiddy, an Autobiography of a Dog* (1851), a volume printed in colors for the National Exhibition in Hyde Park; *Things as They Are in America* (1854) and *American Slavery and Colour* (1857), which detailed his journey to America; and *History of Peeblesshire* (1864). His fondness for his native Peebles had been demonstrated in 1859, when he gave the town a library, art gallery, museum, and lecture hall. In 1865 he was elected lord provost of Edinburgh; during his term in office he promoted the Edinburgh City Improvement Act of 1867, which authorized the demolition of cramped and crowded sections of the city. His last major contribution to Edinburgh was a plan to restore St. Giles's Church, along with nearly thirty thousand pounds to bring the plan to fruition. William Chambers died on 20 May 1883, just three days before the ceremony to mark the

reopening of the restored church. His *Memoir of Robert Chambers* (1872) had proved popular, going through eleven editions during its author's lifetime; following his death a supplemental chapter was added to the book, and it was retitled *Memoir of William and Robert Chambers* (1883). A fifteenth edition of the book was published in 1897, suggesting the public's continuing fascination with the two Scotsmen whose rags-to-riches careers had produced the powerful publishing firm of W. and R. Chambers.

Following William's death, directorship of the firm passed to Robert Chambers, son of the elder Robert, until his death in 1888. The family connection with the firm continued unbroken for a century longer.

Throughout the twentieth century W. and R. Chambers continued to be a major force in the publication of reference and educational books, building on its strengths in the nineteenth century. The first dictionary the firm published was A. J. Cooley's *Dictionary of the English Language* (1861); *Chambers's Etymological Dictionary* (1867) and *Chambers's English Dictionary* (1872), both edited by James Donald, established the firm as a leader in the field. *Chambers's English Dictionary*, renamed *Chambers's Twentieth Century Dictionary* in 1901, passed through many revisions before reverting to the original name in the 1988 edition. Other important reference books include *Chambers's Biographical Dictionary* (1897), *Chambers's World Gazeteer and Geographical Dictionary* (1954), and *Chambers's Science and Technology Dictionary* (1988), each of which has gone through many editions. The company also developed in the twentieth century a comprehensive list of mathematical tables.

In the field of education, W. and R. Chambers has continued the aims of its original Educational Course with the Radiant Way and Radiant Reading series, which have helped millions of children in the United Kingdom as well as in India and Australia learn to read. (Margaret Drabble invoked, with ironic intent, the title of the reading series in her 1987 novel *The Radiant Way*.) In the 1930s W. and R. Chambers offered its No Lumber educational series in several subjects in response to a call in the Hadow Report of 1931 to rid the curriculum of useless "lumber." In the 1960s the company published jointly with the firm of Blackie and Son Modern Mathematics for Schools, by the Scottish Mathematics Group; the series was an international success, with editions produced by publishers in Germany, Holland, Norway, Spain, and Sweden. In 1967 the firm published for the Nuffield Foundation the Nuffield Mathematics Project, an educational series that has had a great influence on the teaching of mathematics at the primary level. Rights for this series were sold to publishers in Denmark, France, Germany, Holland, Italy, Norway, Spain, and the United States. The London office closed in September 1973 on the expiration of the lease on a building in Dean Street; high rents made renewal of the lease uneconomical. In 1989 A. S. Chambers, great-great-grandson of Robert Chambers, retired as chairman and the firm was sold to Group de la Cité PLC, a British subsidiary of the large French publishing group of the same name that includes Larousse, Le Robert, Nathan, Bordas, and Presses de la Cité. The company continues as W. and R. Chambers Limited, with offices at 43-45 Annandale Street in Edinburgh. W. G. Henderson, long the managing director of the firm, is now chairman.

Though the primary emphasis of the firm is educational and reference works, W. and R. Chambers continues to publish works that treat Scottish subjects—poetry, geography, crafts, food, nursery rhymes, language, and social and economic history; the company even lists a 1980 edition of Robert Chambers's *Traditions of Edinburgh*. The range of the firm's current offerings and its business vitality (fifty-six titles published in 1987, forty-one in 1988, fifty-three in 1989, and thirty-five in 1990) attest to its continuing role as "publishers for the people."

**References:**

Richard D. Altick, *The English Common Reader: A Social History of the Mass Reading Public 1800-1900* (Chicago: University of Chicago Press, 1957);

Scott Bennett, "Revolutions in Thought: Serial Publication and the Mass Market for Reading," in *The Victorian Periodical Press: Samplings and Soundings*, edited by Joanne Shattock and Michael Wolff (Toronto: University of Toronto Press, 1982), pp. 225-257;

William Chambers, *Memoir of William and Robert Chambers*, twelfth edition (Edinburgh & London: Chambers, 1883);

Chambers, *Story of a Long and Busy Life* (Edinburgh & London: Chambers, 1882);

Sondra Miley Cooney, "Publishers for the People: W & R Chambers—The Early Years, 1832-1850," Ph.D. dissertation, Ohio State University, 1970;

Henry Curwen, *A History of Booksellers: The Old and the New* (London: Chatto & Windus, 1873);

James Payn, *Some Literary Recollections* (New York: Harper, 1884).

*—Lowell T. Frye*

# John Chapman
*(London: 1844-1845; 1847-1860)*
## Chapman Brothers
*(London: 1845-1846)*

In business only from 1844 until 1860, John Chapman had an impact which far outweighed his publishing longevity. He introduced the English reading public to three of the most significant writers of their day in philosophy and religion: David Friedrich Strauss, Ludwig Feuerbach, and Auguste Comte.

Chapman was born on 16 June 1821 in Warser Gate, Nottinghamshire, the third son of William Chapman. The father was the proprietor of a drugstore, and from him the children acquired an abiding interest in science and medicine. Apprenticed to a watchmaker in Worksop, Chapman ran away from his master and sought refuge with his brother, a medical student in Edinburgh. The latter not only helped him accumulate a stock of watches and chronometers to begin a business of his own, but also paid for his younger brother's passage to Australia.

Chapman was an able salesman "down under" but longed to return to Europe, which he did in 1842. Emulating his brother, he studied medicine first in Paris and then at St. Bartholomew's Hospital in London. Finding himself perpetually impecunious, he sought to marry a woman of means, a plan enhanced by his Byronesque looks and lively personality. On 27 June 1843 he wed Susanna Brewitt, fourteen years his senior and heiress to a fortune left by her father.

Chapman also had literary aspirations. He wrote a semiphilosophical work titled *Human Nature* and approached John Green, a bookseller and publisher at 121 Newgate Street, about publishing it. Green hesitated to accept the book because he was planning to sell his business, and Chapman, intrigued by the possibility of becoming a book merchant, purchased Green's stock with Susanna's money. The Chapmans moved into rooms above the shop. Not surprisingly, one of the firm's first publications was Chapman's own book. For a short time during 1845-1846 the business carried the name Chapman Brothers because Chapman's brother Thomas was involved; but in 1847 it reverted to John Chapman. That

*John Chapman*

year the family and the business moved to a large house at 142 Strand. The ground floor was devoted to bookselling and publishing; to supplement Chapman's modest income, lodgers filled the many rooms upstairs. Since his predecessor had specialized in the sale and reprinting of American books, Chapman followed suit. As a result, Yankee authors and publishers such as Horace Greeley, George Palmer Putnam, Noah Porter, and William Cullen Bryant frequented the premises; Ralph Waldo Emerson boarded with the Chapmans for three months.

Also inherited as a legacy from Green was a periodical, the *Christian Teacher*, with a predilection to publish material written by Unitarians. Chapman changed the title of the magazine to *Prospective Review* but continued to solicit contributions from, and seek editorial assistance of, prominent church members such as James Martineau, John James Taylor, and Charles Wicksteed. He also published books by American Unitarians, including Emerson's *Poems* (1847) and Theodore Parker's *Theism, Atheism, and Popular Theology* (1853).

Chapman's willingness to encourage debate and controversy about religious matters was not lost on the radical politician Joseph Parkes, who commissioned a translation of Strauss's monumental *Das Leban Jesu* (1835). Marian Evans, the future novelist George Eliot, agreed to translate it, and the task was formidable indeed. Not only was the German text fifteen hundred pages long; it also had extensive passages in Latin, Greek, and Hebrew which had to be rendered into English. Parkes subsidized the translation and publication in the amount of three hundred pounds, and *The Life of Jesus Critically Examined* appeared in 1846. Albert Schweitzer would describe the book as "one of the most perfect works of scholarly literature," and modern theologians agree that nineteenth-century Christian understanding of the Gospels was profoundly influenced by its contents. No longer could the role of historical myth in comparative religion be ignored.

Chapman challenged Christian orthodoxy with works of fiction as well. In 1849 he published James Anthony Froude's novel *The Nemesis of Faith*, in which a young man enters holy orders against his better judgment and painfully loses his belief in divine revelation. Shortly after its publication it was burned ceremoniously in the dining hall of Exeter College, Oxford, where Froude was a teaching fellow. As a result, he tendered his resignation.

One of Chapman's most prolific authors was Francis W. Newman, professor of Latin and classical literature at University College, London, and brother of the future cardinal, John Henry Newman. The brothers differed markedly in matters of religious dogma. In 1847 Chapman published F. W. Newman's *History of the Hebrew Monarchy*, followed two years later by *The Soul: Her Sorrows and Her Aspirations*. *Phases of Faith*, a highly controversial autobiography of Newman's odyssey into skepticism, appeared in 1850, and the next year his *Lectures on Political Economy* was re-

leased. After a lapse of nearly of a decade, Chapman published Newman's *Theism, Doctrinal and Practical*, in 1858.

Financed by a subsidy from the eccentric philanthropist Edward Lombe, Harriet Martineau abridged and translated Comte's *Cours de philosophie positiv* (1830-1842) for Chapman as *The Positive Philosophy of Auguste Comte Freely Translated and Condensed* (1853). Martineau and others recognized Comte's important role in introducing a more scientific approach to the study of social institutions. He coined the term *sociology* to describe his new science, and called his methodology *positivism*.

Marian Evans translated an even more profoundly influential work, Feuerbach's *Das Wesen des Christentums*, for Chapman. After appearing on the Continent in 1841, the book quickly became the most widely read work on philosophy since the death of Georg Wilhelm Friedrich Hegel. Feuerbach supplanted Hegel's idealism with materialism, and in so doing attracted the young Karl Marx and Friedrich Engels as ardent disciples. Evans's translation, published by Chapman in 1854 as *The Essence of Christianity*, contained Feuerbach's revolutionary challenge to established religion: "we will not find happiness on earth until we put man in the place of God, and reason in the place of faith."

Chapman introduced Herbert Spencer to the British public in 1851 with his first major work, *Social Statics*, and published James Martineau's *The Rationale of Religious Inquiry* (1845), *Endeavours after the Christian Life* (1847), and *Miscellanies: A Selection of Essays* (1852). These intellectual publications contributed to Chapman's perpetual accounting difficulties. He always hovered on the verge of bankruptcy and was rescued only by timely subventions from admirers and friends. It was ironic that ventures which enhanced Chapman's reputation as a publisher also drained his financial resources. As an example, Chapman purchased the *Westminster Review* with Lombe's assistance for three hundred pounds in October 1851, hired Evans as its editor, and rushed the next issue into print in January 1852. Well launched, it was seriously jeopardized when its benefactor died suddenly in March of that year, leaving Chapman heavily in debt.

Further complicating his business affairs was the so-called Bookselling Question of 1852. Beginning in late 1851 Chapman tried to improve the retail side of his trade by offering a substantial discount from the selling prices of new British and American works. This practice brought the collective wrath of the London trade down upon him, and his publications were boycotted and denied special trade terms. Through the efforts of Charles Dickens and others, restrictive practices in the London book trade were abolished in May 1852; but the controversy further isolated Chapman from his business associates.

A loan of six hundred pounds from silk-textile manufacturer Samuel Courtauld in 1852 staved off insolvency for a couple of years. The *Westminster Review* continued to appear, although a printing of 650 copies was too small to generate much profit. To attract good writers Chapman paid more than the ordinary rate, further contributing to his financial difficulties. The popularity of the *Westminster Review* warranted an increase to 1,600 copies per edition, but even this did not remedy Chapman's indebtedness. Others came to his rescue during the next few years, and Lord Stanley of the Colonial Office repaid the Courtauld loan in 1858.

Anticipating his eventual departure from the publishing business, Chapman devoted his spare time to attending lectures at several of the London medical colleges and hospitals. Lax criteria enabled him to secure a degree in medicine from St. Andrew's University in Scotland in 1857, and later that year to obtain a license to practice in London.

In March 1860 he sold his firm as well as the *Westminster Review* to George Manwaring. He remained as publisher of the magazine; but this arrangement suited neither man, and by the end of 1861 Manwaring had sold the *Westminster Review* back to Chapman. He, in turn, disposed of it to Nicholas Trübner, yet remained as editor even after moving to Paris with his family in 1874.

Since the early 1860s Chapman had supplemented his medical practice by writing books on topics such as chloroform, disorders of the stomach, diarrhea and cholera, neuralgia, seasickness, and prostitution. He died on 25 November 1894 after being struck by a cab.

Summarizing Chapman's career, Gordon S. Haight said that while the publisher's mode of raising funds was dubious, he undeniably introduced "important books that no one else would publish." Chapman himself said of his contribution to publishing, written in the third person for the April 1860 issue of the *Westminster Review*: "In commencing and continuing his Publishing Business, Mr. Chapman designedly offered in his establishment a platform from which opinions and doctrines, however diverse or opposed to each other, might be placed before the public, and during the last sixteen years he has issued numerous Theological and Philosophical works which have exerted a great and growing influence over English thought."

**References:**

*An Analytical Catalogue of Mr. Chapman's Publications* (London: Chapman, 1852);

Philip A. H. Brown, *London Publishers and Printers, c. 1800-1870* (London: British Library, 1982);

*A General Catalogue of American Books* (London: Chapman, 1850);

Gordon S. Haight, *George Eliot: A Biography* (New York: Oxford University Press, 1968);

Haight, *George Eliot and John Chapman*, second edition (New York: Archon, 1969).

*—James J. Barnes and Patience P. Barnes*

# Chapman and Hall

*(London: 1830-    )*

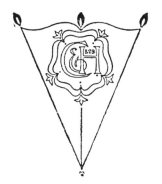

CHAPMAN & HALL'S
CENTENARY YEAR

Edward Chapman and William Hall established themselves as booksellers at 186 Strand in London early in 1830. Seeing the largest share of the proceeds from their sales going to publishers, they gradually moved into publishing. The first announcement of a publication of the firm, dated 5 June 1830, was for the first number of *Chat of the Week*, priced at sixpence and subtitled *Compendium of All Topics of Public Interest, Original and Select*. Shortly thereafter the firm announced the *Christian Register*, the "Annual Record of the Several Religious Metropolitan Meetings Held for the Promotion of Christianity and the Diffusion of Knowledge." The two men seemed to have understood the lure of advertising, for the announcement said that the *Christian Register* was to be printed on "sixty-four large plates, on one sheet, embracing a surface of Forty Square Feet, equal to the contents of the *New Magna Charta*, which was the largest sheet ever issued from the press." They then entered a cooperative venture with other booksellers to publish *A New Topographical Dictionary of Great Britain and Ireland* in forty-two monthly parts at one shilling each. The advertisement, on a broadsheet, said that the dictionary would contain "Every City, Town, Village, and Hamlet, in the Three Kingdoms." The two titles in Chapman and Hall's first advertisement in the *Athenaeum* (29 March 1834) are representative of the books published by the firm during its first few years: *Scenes and Recollections of Flyfishing, in Northumberland, Cumberland, and Westmoreland* (1834) by Stephen Oliver, the Younger, and *The Book of Science: A Familiar Introduction to the Principles of Natural Philosophy, Adapted to the Comprehension of Young People* (1833).

In 1835 Chapman and Hall published *The Squib Annual*, a comic work aimed at the Christmas trade, with illustrations by the well-known artist Robert Seymour. Encouraged by the book's success, Seymour suggested that he produce a series of comic plates showing a group of Cockney sportsmen, "The Nimrod Club," getting into difficulties because of their ineptness. Chapman saw merit in the idea but felt that it would sell better if the plates were accompanied by text. He turned to Charles Whitehead, who was beginning the job of editing Chapman and Hall's new monthly, the *Library of Fiction; or, Family Story-Teller; Consisting of Original Tales, Essays and Sketches of Character* (April 1836 - July 1837). Unwilling to take on the job of writing for Seymour's project, Whitehead recommended a young writer he recalled from his association with the *Monthly Magazine*. The writer used the pseudonym "Boz" and had contributed comic sketches to the *Monthly Magazine*, the *Morning Chronicle*, the *Evening Chronicle*, and *Bell's Life in London;* his real name was Charles Dickens. On 8 February 1836 a collection of his writings, *Sketches by Boz*, was published by John Macrone. On 12 February Hall called on Dickens in his chambers at Furnival's Inn; Dickens recognized Hall as the bookseller from whom he had purchased the December 1833 issue of the *Monthly Magazine* containing his first published piece of writing, "A Dinner at Poplar Walk." Hall presented Seymour's idea; Dickens objected that he knew little about hunting and fishing and that he could not write to order; he suggested that he be given a free "range of English scenes and people," and that Seymour's sketches arise from his text. Hall agreed. It was decided that the work should be published in monthly parts, each installment to consist of sixteen and one-half pages of text, for which Dickens would be paid fourteen guineas. Each number was to contain four plates by Seymour, with publication to begin as soon as Dickens had sufficient text. One of the first things Dickens did was to reject the name Nimrod and substitute Pickwick, a name he recalled from a coach at Bath.

The writing was well under way before Dickens thought to ask for a written agreement. Chapman and Hall sent him a letter outlining the terms and stipulating that if the publication should prove a success, the payment would be increased proportionally. On 31 March 1836 the first installment of *The Posthumous Papers of the Pickwick Club*—generally known as *The Pickwick Papers*—appeared. Only about four hundred copies were sold.

Dickens insisted that Seymour redraw one of the plates for the second installment. Seymour, who had never quite recovered from a nervous breakdown the year before, completed the work on the plate, went to a shed behind his house, and put a bullet through his head. The second installment appeared with only three plates; sales did not increase. A new illustrator, R. W. Buss, did the plates for the third part; he was replaced by "Phiz," Hablôt Knight Browne, who would continue to illustrate Dickens's novels for many years.

The drawing card for *The Pickwick Papers* had been the well-known artist, Seymour; but with Seymour dead and sales not covering expenses, the publishers were considering canceling the project before their losses increased. Dickens convinced them to continue for a few more installments. The number of plates was reduced to two; the text was increased to thirty-two pages; Dickens's payment was cut to ten pounds, ten shillings. In the fourth part Sam Weller was introduced. Whether it was the appearance of this character or merely that the readers finally discovered *The Pickwick Papers*, sales began to pick up after the fifth number. Fourteen thousand copies of the February 1837 installment were sold; the sales increased to twenty thousand copies for the May installment, twenty-nine thousand for September, and forty thousand for November. Dickens's payment was increased to twenty-five pounds for each installment.

Various publishers began to recognize Dickens's potential, and the author, thrilled by

*Edward Chapman, one of the founders of Chapman and Hall (portrait from Arthur Waugh,* A Hundred Years of Publishing, *1930)*

the attention, readily signed contracts. His first publisher, Macrone, brought out a second series of *Sketches by Boz* (1837), and Dickens signed a contract with Macrone for a novel to be called "Gabriel Vardon." When it became clear that the young novelist would not be able to produce the book within the specified time, Macrone began talking of a lawsuit. Just as *The Pickwick Papers* began to gain a large audience, Dickens entered an agreement with another publisher, Richard Bentley, to edit a new magazine, *Bentley's Miscellany*, for which he would write a serial novel, *Oliver Twist* (1838). In spite of these ties with competing publishing firms, Dickens expressed his devotion to Chapman and Hall in a November 1836 letter, declaring that if he should ever entertain "the most remote idea of dissolving the most pleasant and friendly connection," he would be the "most insensible, and at the same time the most jolter-headed scribe alive." He went so far as to nominate Chapman and Hall as his "periodical publishers, until he should be advertised in the daily press as having been compressed into his last edition—one volume, boards with brass plates."

It was at this time that John Forster became associated with Chapman and Hall as literary adviser. Forster had come to London from Newcastle in 1828 to study law, had become a prosperous lawyer, and had established himself as a highly respected drama and literary critic. With a genius for mediating disputes between writers and publishers, Forster stepped into the fray to help straighten out the complications the young, inexperienced Dickens had created. First, there was the matter of Macrone, who had purchased the entire copyright of *Sketches by Boz* for one hundred pounds and was threatening to publish the work in parts as a rival of *The Pickwick Papers*. Forster tried to buy back the copyright but found Macrone's price—two thousand pounds—exorbitant. He did, however, arrange a meeting between Macrone and Chapman and Hall. Macrone refused to budge from his price for the copyright. Chapman and Hall had the publication facilities and distribution network ready, so that a serial publication of *Sketches by Boz* would be an easy matter; feeling certain that they would recoup the investment, they met Macrone's price.

Chapman and Hall were also instrumental in solving a problem Dickens had with Bentley. *Bentley's Miscellany* had begun publication in January 1837 with the agreement that Dickens would receive a salary of £20 per month and £500 for *Oliver Twist*. Bentley also had a contract for Dickens to write two additional novels for £500 each, with the amount to increase to £750 when sales reached three thousand copies. The first of these novels was to be *Barnaby Rudge* (1841), the work originally contracted to Macrone as "Gabriel Vardon." By summer of 1837 Dickens realized that he could not fulfill these commitments by the time promised and also felt considerably underpaid. Forster negotiated with Bentley, arranging for the third of the novels to be dropped if Dickens were to begin *Barnaby Rudge* by November 1838. Even these terms became uncomfortable for Dickens, so at Forster's urging Chapman and Hall stepped in and purchased the remaining stock and the copyright of *Oliver Twist* for £2,250. Also, Dickens would receive £3,000 for the rights to *Barnaby Rudge* during serialization and for six months after the completion of the serial, at which time the rights would revert to Dickens. At last, Chapman and Hall had Dickens comfortably ensconced within their publishing house.

In November 1837 Chapman and Hall celebrated the conclusion of *The Pickwick Papers*. They then set about what was to be the main task of the house for a generation—looking after their literary property. One immediate annoyance was dealing with authors who wrote plagiarisms or continuations or who, at best, traded on the Pickwick name. The market was hit by a barrage of works: *Pickwick Abroad* (1838) by G. W. M. Reynolds; *The Post-humourous Notes of the Pickwickian Club* (1837-1839), by "Bos"; the *Pickwick Comic Almanac* (1837); and *Sam Weller's Pickwick Jest Book*. The Pickwick name was used on a vast array of products. There were many dramatic adaptations, including *Sam Weller* (1837), by William Moncrieff, produced at the Strand Theatre, in which Mr. Jingle was married to Mrs. Bardell.

Another annoyance was John Dickens, the novelist's father, who imprudently continued to sign promissory notes and found himself unable to pay them when they came due. On many occasions he came to the Chapman and Hall office to receive cash advances that were never repaid. Arthur Waugh says in his history of the company that "it was doubtless a pleasure to [Charles Dickens's] publishers to be able to save him from such petty vexations at so little cost." From April 1838 to October 1839 the publishers watched anxiously as Dickens worked up to the deadline on most of the monthly installments of *The Life and Adventures of Nicholas Nickleby* (1837-1839). With this novel he proved that he was going to last.

Exhausted from pushing himself to produce *Nicholas Nickleby* and wondering whether his readers would stick with him through another monthly serial, Dickens thought that the ideal vehicle would be a weekly periodical on the order of the eighteenth-century *Spectator*, with himself as editor and main contributor. In July 1838 he wrote Forster that he was besieged by publishers offering to take anything he wrote on extremely generous terms. He was, however, unwilling to leave Chapman and Hall, provided that they "behave with liberality to me." Dickens put his proposal in a letter: the magazine would be built around a fictional club, with the reappearance of Mr. Pickwick and Sam Weller. Dickens would undertake to write "the quantity of each number," and "in order to give fresh novelty and interest" he would travel—at the publisher's expense—to such places as Ireland and America, where he would produce a series of papers describing the people and places he saw. He would be a proprie-

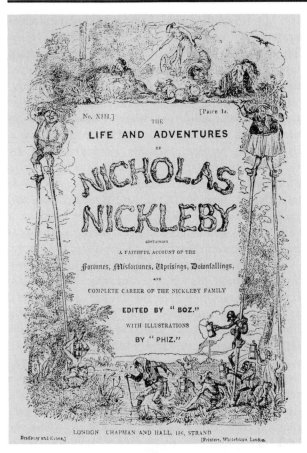

*Cover for an installment of the Charles Dickens novel that Chapman and Hall published in monthly parts from April 1838 to October 1839*

tor of the magazine and share in the profits. The publisher would take all of the risks in the venture, and Dickens was to receive fifty pounds for each monthly number regardless of how well the magazine sold. When a profit was made, he was to receive half. He considered two titles, "Old Humphrey's Clock" and "Master Humphrey's Clock," finally settling on the latter.

The first number of the new periodical appeared on 4 April 1840. Sales were spectacular: seventy thousand copies were sold at threepence the first day. But sales slumped the second week and fell disastrously the third. Chapman and Hall met with Dickens and Forster. The readers could be lured back, they reasoned, if a serial by Dickens were included. He had in mind a plot for a short story about an orphan girl and her grandfather that could be worked into a novel. Thus, in the fourth issue of *Master Humphrey's Clock* the first installment of *The Old Curiosity Shop* made its appearance. The appearance of the novel saved the magazine as the intense interest in the fate of Nell Trent captured the atten-

tion of the English-speaking world. When *The Old Curiosity Shop* completed its serialization in 1841, Dickens followed it with *Barnaby Rudge*, the novel originally promised to Bentley. Chapman and Hall took every opportunity to market *Master Humphrey's Clock:* in addition to the eighty-eight weekly parts at threepence, they sold the weekly installments gathered into monthly parts at one shilling or one shilling, threepence, according to whether there were four or five installments for the month. Then each six months the parts were sold in volumes at eight shillings for volumes 1 and 2, ten shillings, sixpence for volume 3. The work of keeping the magazine going eventually exhausted Dickens, and it was concluded in November 1841. He then signed an agreement for a new novel to commence in November 1842, for which he would receive £150 a month until its publication was begun, £200 a month during its serialization, and three-quarters of the profit for the six months after its serialization.

In the one-year interval during which Dickens had no obligations to produce any writing, he decided to take the opportunity to go to America. In spite of his intention to be free from work, he kept a notebook of his observations on the trip. The publishers had the responsibility of making all the arrangements for the journey. Traveling in America from January to June 1842, the novelist found enormous audiences eager to see the man whose works they revered. The fact that he had received no payment for the publication of his work in America rankled Dickens, and he angered his hosts by speaking out on the need for an international copyright law. Returning to England, Dickens set to work on converting his acerbic notes on America into book form. On Forster's advice he omitted the conciliatory introductory chapter that would have taken some of the bite out of his criticism of America. On 18 October 1842 Chapman and Hall published *American Notes for General Circulation*. It was such an immediate success that by year's end it had run through four editions and earned its author a thousand pounds.

In January 1843 *The Life and Adventures of Martin Chuzzlewit* began monthly serialization. The sales were at first disappointing, coming to only about one-third of what *Master Humphrey's Clock* had achieved at its height. When Hall casually mentioned a clause in the contract which would require the author to pay back advances if sales were insufficient, Dickens was infuriated. He wrote to Forster, "I am bent on paying the money back." He favored the firm of Bradbury and Evans as the successor to his present publisher, but "whoever it is, or whatever, I am bent on paying Chapman and Hall down. And when I have done that, Mr. Hall shall have a piece of my mind." William Bradbury and Frederick Evans were only lukewarm when approached, and Forster persuaded Dickens to do nothing about switching publishers for a year.

Dickens was in Manchester in October 1843 when the idea for *A Christmas Carol* came to him. Returning home, he worked feverishly on it, and it was published a few days before Christmas. On the day of publication it sold six thousand copies. Dickens had insisted on a new arrangement whereby he was responsible for the entire cost of publication and would receive all of the profit, except for the publisher's commission. Wanting the book to achieve the widest possible circulation, he had set the price at five shillings. He had chosen gilt edges, a two-color title page, and hand-colored illustrations. This last item comprised £120 of the £805 cost of the first edition. The result of the care Dickens lavished on *A Christmas Carol* was that his profit on the first six thousand copies amounted to only £230.

Dickens felt that the small profit was a final insult from Chapman and Hall. He approached Bradbury and Evans and agreed to their offer of twenty-eight hundred pounds for a quarter share in everything he might write for the next eight years. Thus on 1 June 1844 Dickens left Chapman and Hall.

In his history of the firm Waugh says that through the 1840s and 1850s the publishing list of Chapman and Hall "divides into two channels, one directed towards the goal of building up a tradition of sound literary taste," the other "towards that sort of popular success which would fill the coffers." One of the prizes of "sound literary taste" was William Makepeace Thackeray, who brought his work to the firm just as Dickens was leaving. Thackeray went to Ireland in the summer of 1842 and returned with *The Irish Sketch Book*, which Chapman and Hall published the next year. Next he traveled to Cairo, which resulted in *Notes of a Journey from Cornhill to Grand Cairo, by Way of Lisbon, Athens, Constantinople, and Jerusalem, Performed in the Steamers of the Peninsular and Orient Company* (1846). The firm also published his early Christmas books—*Mrs. Perkins's Ball* (1847), *Our Street* (1848), *Dr. Birch and His Young Friends* (1849), and *Rebecca and Rowena* (1850). Unfortunately for Chapman and Hall,

however, Thackeray took his major novels elsewhere for publication.

In 1843 Forster brought Thomas Carlyle to Chapman and Hall. Carlyle was pessimistic about his chances of being a successful author, for *Sartor Resartus* (1836) had been a failure, and he had made very little from *The French Revolution* (1837). He was not, in the beginning, profitable to his new publisher. Early on, he insisted on a collected edition, a demand to which Chapman and Hall did not accede until 1857-1858, although the firm did republish *Chartism* (1839), *On Heroes, Hero-Worship and the Heroic in History* (1841), and *The French Revolution* in 1842. As the years passed, Carlyle found his reading audience and became a valuable asset to the firm. Among his publications with Chapman and Hall were *Latter-Day Pamphlets* (1850), *The Life of John Sterling* (1851), *History of Friedrich II of Prussia, Called Frederick the Great* (1858-1865), *Shooting Niagara: And After?* (1867), *Critical and Miscellaneous Essays* (1872), and *The Early Kings of Norway* (1875).

Forster brought Robert Browning to Chapman and Hall in 1848. Browning's former publisher, Edward Moxon, had refused to take any risk in publishing the poet, insisting that Browning pay all publication costs. Chapman welcomed Browning and agreed to cover all costs himself. The two-volume *Poems: A New Edition* (1849) was followed by *Christmas-Eve and Easter-Day* (1850), *Men and Women* (1855), *Poems* (1863), *Selections from the Poetical Works of Robert Browning* (1863), and *Dramatis Personae* (1864). During the years Browning was with Chapman and Hall the firm also published the works of Elizabeth Barrett Browning, including *Poems: New Edition* (1850), *Casa Guidi Windows* (1851), *Aurora Leigh* (1857), *Poems before Congress* (1860), and, after her death, the five-volume *Elizabeth Barrett Browning's Poetical Works* (1866).

Chapman and Hall's list during the middle of the nineteenth century included works by Arthur Hugh Clough, William Allingham, Sir Henry Taylor, Bryan Waller Procter (Barry Cornwall), and Edward Bulwer-Lytton. The firm also published an edition of Philip James Bailey's immensely popular forty-thousand-line poem *Festus* (1854), as well as his *The Mystic and Other Poems* (1855) and *The Age* (1858).

In late 1845 William Harrison Ainsworth brought *Ainsworth's Magazine* to Chapman and Hall, which published it until December 1854. In December 1845 Ainsworth brought the firm another periodical, the *New Monthly Magazine*,

*Inscription from Dickens to Edward Chapman in Chapman and Hall's one-volume edition of* Nicholas Nickleby *( from Arthur Waugh* A Hundred Years of Publishing, *1930)*

which it continued to publish until 1869. In 1849 the firm began to publish a cheap edition of Ainsworth's novels, a highly successful and profitable venture. A problem arose, however, in that another publisher, Henry G. Bohn, who had paid two hundred pounds for the copyright and plates of *The Tower of London* (1840), threatened a Chancery suit if that book were included in the collected edition. In a move reminiscent of their dealings with the copyrights of Dickens's early work, Chapman paid three hundred pounds for the copyright, stereos, and plates. The company then had another best-selling author and went on to publish many subsequent novels by Ainsworth, including *The Constable of the Tower* (1861), *The Lord Mayor of London* (1862), *Cardinal Pole* (1863), *John Law the Projector* (1864), *The Spanish Match* (1865), *The Constable de Bourbon* (1866), *Old Court* (1867), *Myddleton Pomfret* (1868), and *Hilary St. Ives* (1870), each in three volumes.

In March 1847 Hall died; in spite of having left with hard feelings, Dickens attended the funeral in Highgate cemetery. The following year Elizabeth Gaskell was added to Chapman and Hall's list of authors. The wife of a Unitarian minister, she had found herself despondent over the death of her only son from scarlet fever. At her husband's suggestion, she had written a novel to distract her thoughts from her loss. The result was *Mary Barton*. The manuscript was rejected by several publishers before it came to Chapman and Hall. After lengthy deliberation, the firm gave her one hundred pounds for the copyright and published the novel in 1848. It was an instant success. Mrs. Gaskell chose the firm for some of her other works, including *The Moorland Cottage* (1850), *Ruth* (1853), *Cranford* (1853), and *North and South* (1855).

In 1852 the bookseller W. H. Smith and Son at 136 Strand needed to expand and purchased Chapman and Hall's building. Chapman and Hall moved to 193 Piccadilly.

In 1858 Anthony Trollope offered his novel *Doctor Thorne* to Bentley for four hundred pounds; Bentley at first agreed, then said that he could give only three hundred. Trollope immediately called at 193 Piccadilly "and said what I had to say to Mr. Edward Chapman in a quick torrent of words. They were the first of a great many words which have since been spoken by me in that backshop. Looking at me as he might have done at a highway robber who had stopped him on Hounslow Heath, he said that he supposed he might as well do as I desired. I considered this to be a sale, and it was a sale. I remember that he held the poker in his hand all the time that I was with him;—but in truth, even though he had declined to buy the book, there would have been no danger." Chapman paid four hundred pounds for Trollope's next book, *The Bertrams* (1859), and accepted the proposal that Trollope write a travel book while on an official trip for the post office to the West Indies. Trollope returned with the manuscript of *The West Indies and the Spanish Main* (1859), for which he received £250. Because of large sales, resulting from three laudatory notices in the *Times*, he asked for and received £600 for his next novel, *Castle Richmond* (1860). Before it was ready, Trollope received from George Smith of Smith, Elder an offer of £1,000 for a three-volume novel to be serialized in the new *Cornhill* magazine. Chapman readily agreed to the novelist's request to give up his right to *Castle Richmond*, but when Smith read it he feared that, as an Irish novel, it might not hold readers' interest. Consequently, the novel went back to Chapman, and the *Cornhill* got another novel, *Framley Parsonage* (1861), one of the best of the Barsetshire series. Trollope later wrote that "Mr. Edward Chapman always acceded to every suggestion [I] made to him. He never refused a book, and never haggled at a price." His connection with the *Cornhill* raised Trollope's price for his novels. For *North America* (1862) he requested and received £1,250; for *Orley Farm* (1861-1862), published in shilling part

issues, he received £3,135. Over the years Chapman and Hall published thirty-two works by Trollope, including *The Belton Estate* (1866), *Clergymen of the Church of England* (1866), *The Eustace Diamonds* (1873), *Phineas Redux* (1874), *The Way We Live Now* (1874-1875), *The Prime Minister* (1875-1876), *John Caldigate* (1879), *The Duke's Children* (1880), *Dr. Wortle's School* (1881), and *Marion Fay* (1882).

In May 1858 Dickens and his wife separated. Amid many rumors, Dickens published a public statement about his marital difficulties in the 12 June 1858 issue of his magazine, *Household Words*. He circulated the statement to newspapers and magazines, but Mark Lemon, the editor of *Punch*, declined to print it on the grounds that it was inappropriate for a humor magazine. Bradbury and Evans, the publishers of *Punch*, supported Lemon's decision. In a fury, Dickens decided to break his ties with Bradbury and Evans and return to Chapman and Hall. When Bradbury and Evans refused to sell their share of *Household Words* to him, he proceeded to make the property worthless by withdrawing from it and establishing a magazine of almost identical nature with Chapman and Hall. He abandoned his first choice for a name for the new periodical, "Household Harmony," when Forster pointed out that obvious jokes would be made about the lack of harmony in the Dickens household. On 26 March 1859 Dickens bought *Household Words* at auction for a fraction of its value and incorporated it into the new periodical, which he named *All the Year Round*. In retaliation, Bradbury and Evans established a competing magazine, *Once a Week*, but Dickens carried all the best contributors to *Household Words* with him to *All the Year Round*. It was an instant success and ultimately reached a circulation of three hundred thousand, eight times that of its predecessor. Selling for twopence, each issue contained an installment of a novel, one or two poems, an occasional short story, and several articles, usually on history, anthropology, geography, science, and natural history. The first installment of *A Tale of Two Cities* appeared in the first issue on 30 April 1859. When the novel finished its serialization late in the year, it was followed by Wilkie Collins's *The Woman in White*. The magazine also published fiction by Bulwer-Lytton, Gaskell, Trollope, and Charles Reade. Upon his death in 1870, Dickens was succeeded as editor by his son, Charles Dickens, Jr. Chapman and Hall continued to publish *All the Year Round* until it ceased publication in 1895.

In the 1850s Chapman and Hall received a windfall as a result of the development of the circulating libraries. In 1820 W. H. Smith and Son had opened a reading room in Duke Street where, for an annual subscription of one and one-half guineas, a reader could have access to all of the latest magazines as well as 150 newspapers each week. The idea of paying to read, rather than purchasing, gradually developed into the circulating library. In 1842 the most famous of the libraries, Mudie's, was established by Charles Edward Mudie. As the libraries expanded, they became important purchasers of books: a Mudie's advertisement said that in ten years the firm's purchases increased from 5,000 to 120,000 volumes. Publishers could be assured of covering the cost of producing a book by the prepublication orders placed by the circulating libraries.

In 1858 W. H. Smith, who had bookstalls in stations of all the important railways, decided to place circulating libraries in these establishments. He asked Mudie's to supply the books from its stock, but Mudie's rejected the offer. Smith then set up his own libraries, further increasing the sales of firms such as Chapman and Hall. At first Smith experienced some difficulty in procuring enough light fiction for his railway bookstalls. The solution was to publish what he needed, and he set about buying up copyrights to works by Charles Lever and other popular novelists. These volumes were bound in paper boards and referred to as "yellowbacks." Almost immediately he encountered vigorous protests from the publishers from whom he bought much of his stock, because he was now in competition with them. Smith approached Chapman and Hall and asked that the firm put its name on the books. Chapman and Hall was then able to get new titles from many novelists while reprinting their previous works. In this way the firm acquired for its list the works of Reade, Ouida, Hawley Smart, Edmund Yates, and R. D. Blackmore.

George Meredith became associated with the firm when it published his *The Shaving of Shagpat* in 1856. With the publication of *The Ordeal of Richard Feverel* in 1859 Meredith established himself as Chapman and Hall's most promising young author. Mudie ordered three hundred copies, telling Chapman that the novel would certainly be successful; but then it disappeared from Mudie's list. Chapman inquired and was told that the reason for its withdrawal was "urgent remonstrances of several respectable families who objected to it as dangerous and wicked and damnable." Concerning this matter, Meredith said, "I would rather have Mudie and the British Matron with me than the whole army of the press."

When Forster resigned as Chapman and Hall's literary adviser in August 1860, he was replaced by Meredith. The publisher's literary adviser in the mid-nineteenth century was, according to Waugh, "a sort of mysterious soothsayer, imprisoned in some secret back room, and referred to cryptically as 'our reader.'" Meredith's procedure was to have a half dozen or more manuscripts sent to his home, along with a book in which he recorded his decisions. The first manuscript he evaluated was "The Two Damsels: A Spanish Tale," by C. M. O'Hara. His first entry in the publisher's record book was "Childish: return without comment." His judgment on whether to publish was final. Waugh gives a sampling of Meredith's comments on other novels:

> "An infernal romance."
> "Apparently by a muddle-headed beginner, bothered by the expression of his views and ideas."
> "According to the dates given, this was done in a month. It has no other merit."
> "Elaborately done, with index to contents of chapters. After going through some, and running over the others, I found the index to be preferable."

Meredith believed that his principal task was to choose for publication books with literary merit and to pass over the trite and trivial, even though it would sell. During his first year as reader the manuscript for Mrs. Henry Wood's *East Lynne* arrived. Meredith rejected the book with the comment: "Opinion emphatically against it." Ainsworth, who had serialized the novel in *Ainsworth's Magazine* and had recommended it to the publisher, pressured Chapman to have the reader consider it again. Meredith held his ground and was supported by Chapman. The novel was published in 1861 by Bentley, who made a fortune on it. Another best-seller the firm missed because Meredith objected to the low literary quality of the manuscript was *The Heavenly Twins*, by Madame Sarah Grand. Meredith said that the author "has ability enough, and a glimpse of humour here and there promises well for the future," but that she should put the work aside until she had a better grasp of her art. William Heinemann published the book which became a smash hit in 1893. Meredith took seriously the firm's policy of avoiding materials which might shock readers. A writer too far ahead of the times or too far behind had to go elsewhere: Meredith at first declined the work of Ouida because of its frankness, and rejected Mrs. Lynn Linton on the basis of "her abhorrence of the emancipation of young females from their ancient rules."

In 1860 Dickens was planning for Chapman and Hall to publish his next novel, *Great Expectations*, in the old manner of monthly part issue. But because Lever's *A Day's Ride*, being serialized in *All the Year Round*, failed to attract a sufficient reading audience, the sales of the magazine dropped. Dickens saw no solution but to use his own popularity to restore the magazine's circulation. *Great Expectations* began serialization on 1 December 1860, and sales of the magazine increased.

In 1864 Chapman retired. His cousin Frederic Chapman, who had joined the firm in 1841, arranged to buy the publishing house with the backing of wealthy friends. Edward Chapman traveled in Europe with his family until failing health forced him to return to England in 1874. He lived quietly in Tunbridge Wells until his death at the age of seventy-six on 20 February 1880.

Frederic Chapman was described by Percy Fitzgerald as "an excellent fellow, somewhat blunt and bluff, but straightforward and good-natured." Having spent his youth in the country, he was an ardent sportsman. He kept a well-stocked wine cellar in the Piccadilly office and on one occasion hung a haunch of venison there until the employees objected to the aroma. Waugh says that Chapman "dearly loved a sporting tale, and a sporting novel, and it was during the first years of his rule that the firm became associated with a long line of vigorous and open-air stories, such as G. J. Whyte-Melville's, Edmund Yates's, Hawley Smart's, Charles Reade's, and Ouida's." Ouida was a particularly fascinating writer, whose books were considered indecent in her day. Waugh describes her as contentious and, in her later years, distrustful of everyone with whom she associated. She sent one manuscript to a typist with the pages misnumbered, insisting that the pages of typed copy correspond exactly to the handwritten pages. When it was completed, she put the pages in their correct order. In her mind, she had frustrated the typist's plan to purloin her work.

Of the periodicals published by Chapman and Hall, the *Fortnightly Review* was the most illus-

*Frederic Chapman*

trious. It differed from its contemporaries in that it espoused the views of no political party. The contributors were to be free to say what they thought and, in a departure from the common practice of the time, were to be identified. Trollope, one of the principal investors and the chairman of the board, insisted on George Henry Lewes as editor. The first issue appeared on 15 May 1865, carrying articles on art, finance, literature, philosophy, politics, and science. Trollope's novel *The Belton Estate* was serialized in its pages in 1865-1866. The magazine switched to monthly publication in November 1866. It did not immediately achieve financial success; it may be that the public needed time to become comfortable with a periodical with a variety of editorial views rather than one. The founders became discouraged; according to Trollope, "We carried out our principles till our money was all gone, and then we sold the copyright to Chapman and Hall for a trifle."

Lewes was succeeded as editor by John Morley in January 1867. Morley abandoned the eclectic editorial policy and made the *Fortnightly Review* into what he called "the organ of Positivists in the wider sense of that designation." By the time he retired in 1882 Morley had made the magazine a strong voice of social reform and had published works by Matthew Arnold, Robert Browning, Edmund Gosse, William Morris, Dante Gabriel Rossetti, and Algernon Charles Swinburne.

The *Fortnightly Review* declined under Thomas Escott's editorship from 1882 to 1884, but improved with Frank Harris in the editor's chair. He turned it in a more liberal direction and attracted some outstanding contributors, including Rudyard Kipling, Henry James, Thomas Hardy, George Moore, Walter Pater, H. G. Wells, and Oscar Wilde. Harris left in October 1894 after a row with the publisher over Charles Malato's article supporting anarchy. When the next editor, William Leonard Courtney, was appointed, his contract specified that at least four days before the publication of each issue the table of contents should be submitted to the managing director of Chapman and Hall, who could reject any article, poem, or short story he found unsatisfactory.

Courtney served as editor until 1928. Abandoning a career as an Oxford don, he had gone to London and become an editorial writer for the *Daily Telegraph* in 1890. He retained the position at the *Telegraph* when he became editor of the *Fortnightly Review*. By drawing on the outstanding group of correspondents of the *Telegraph* for the *Fortnightly Review*, he gave the magazine a fine reputation in foreign reporting. Among the eminent men and women of letters he attracted as contributors were John Galsworthy, James Joyce, Edith Sitwell, and William Butler Yeats. The *Fortnightly Review* enjoyed its peak of prosperity under Courtney, particularly during World War I. In the summer of 1929 Chapman and Hall sold the magazine.

In the early 1860s Dickens had gone through his works, making minor corrections. These were incorporated in the last collected edition in his lifetime, the Charles Dickens Edition, with a facsimile of the novelist's signature on the covers. Dickens also wrote new prefaces and provided descriptive headlines for his works. The volumes were issued monthly, starting in June 1867, at three shillings or three shillings, sixpence, depending on the length of the volume.

Through the late 1860s it became apparent that Dickens was a man rushing toward destruction. No one, not even his closest friend, Forster, could do anything to deter the novelist from driving himself so relentlessly that he was destroying his health. Consequently, the contract for *The Mystery of Edwin Drood* specified that Chapman would receive compensation if Dickens died or was otherwise incapacitated before completing the manuscript. Dickens got a good start on the novel during the last half of 1869, but he seemed to have lost his knack of estimating text: when the first two parts were set in type they were twelve pages short, so that a chapter had to be shifted from the second part to the first. When the first number went on sale on 1 April 1870, it sold fifty thousand copies. Dickens went to his home at Gad's Hill, Rochester, to complete the novel. He suffered a stroke on 8 June at dinner, remained unconscious all night, and died the next evening.

Forster was Dickens's literary executor. He had met the novelist while *The Pickwick Papers* was being serialized and had been a lifelong friend and adviser. As no one was better qualified to write a biography of Dickens, Forster took on the task, in spite of his own failing health. The first volume of *The Life of Charles Dickens* was published by Chapman and Hall in 1872, with two additional volumes appearing in the next two years. Although there was considerable criticism of the prominence Forster gave himself in the work, information might have been lost had he not written the book. Forster died in 1876.

Following the directions in Dickens's will, Forster had sold the copyright of the novels to Chapman and Hall. In 1872 Chapman began an ambitious project, the Household Edition, a complete edition of Dickens's works to appear over a period of six years. The reader had a choice of three formats: monthly parts for one shilling, penny numbers, or bound volumes. Fred Barnard was hired to make illustrations somewhat similar to those of "Phiz." In the 1870s and 1880s, Waugh says, "Dickens was selling in such profusion as to be strong enough to carry the burden of a business upon his own unaided shoulders." The first two volumes of the *Letters of Charles Dickens* appeared in 1880, the third in 1882; they had been edited by Dickens's sister-in-law Georgina Hogarth, with the help of Mamie Dickens. During the 1870s and 1880s the Chapman and Hall literature list was expanded considerably as John Morley's *Critical Miscellanies* (1871-1877) and *On Compromise* (1874) were published, along with his biographies of Voltaire, (1872), Jean-Jacques Rousseau (1873), Denis Diderot (1878), and Richard Cobden (1881). The novel list was augmented with works by Reade, Blackmore, Robert Buchanan, and Mrs. Brookfield.

Chapman and Hall had sensational good luck with an anonymously published work, *An Englishman in Paris* (1892). It was a best-seller, as everyone tried to guess the author's identity. Most of the well-known diplomats and politicians of the time were discussed as possibilities, while the book went through edition after edition. The secret was finally discovered by Archibald Grove, editor of the *New Review*, who was told by his barber that the mysterious author of *An Englishman in Paris* was in another chair in the shop. Grove cleverly asked the man to write an article for the *New Review*. When Albert D. Vandam signed his name to the article, the secret was out, and sales of the novel immediately ceased as the public lost interest.

In 1880, as the copyrights on Dickens's novels were beginning to run out, Chapman realized that he had to raise capital for expansion. He formed a limited liability company and sold seventy-five hundred shares at twenty pounds each. The first directors were H. B. Sandford (chairman), James Bird, A. K. Corfield, R. P. Harding, A. Taylor, and Trollope, with Chapman as managing director. The company moved from the Piccadilly office to 11 Henrietta Street. With the new capital Chapman was able to buy additional copyrights, including those of Thomas Carlyle, who died in 1881. The company published the seventeen-volume Ashburton Edition of Carlyle's works between 1885 and 1888.

The newly reorganized company favored books on travel and sport. Among the titles published were William Bromley Davenport's *Sport: Fox-Hunting, Salmon-Fishing, Covert-Shooting, Deer-Stalking* (1885); Charles Dixon's *Annals of Bird Life* (1890), *The Birds of Our Rambles* (1891), *The Migration of Birds* (1892), and *The Game Birds and Wild Fowl of the British Isles* (1893); R. C. Leslie's *A Sea-Painter's Log* (1886), *Old Sea Wings, Ways, and Words* (1890), *The Sea Boat: How to Build, Rig, and Sail Her* (1892), and *A Water Biography* (1894); Francis Trevelyn Buckland's *Log Book of a Fisherman and Zoologist* (1875); and W. H. Hudson's *The Naturalist in La Plata* (1892), *Idle Days in Patagonia* (1893), and *Birds in a Village* (1893). In the mid 1890s Chapman and Hall also became sole agents in Britain, the dominions, and Europe for John Wiley and Sons, the leading American publisher of engineering and scientific books.

From the time Meredith became Chapman and Hall's literary adviser, most of his books were published by the firm. Eventually, however, a break occurred. The first event leading up to

the rupture was Meredith's having to testify in 1890 in a libel suit over Alfred Burdon Ellis's *West African Stories* (1890), published by Chapman and Hall. The publisher had carefully protected the reader's anonymity, but Meredith's appearance in the witness box was required. Having his identity known was uncomfortable to Meredith, and already being weary of reading manuscripts, he left the firm. Shortly afterward he submitted his novel, *The Amazing Marriage*, and found Chapman unwilling to meet his terms. The book was published in 1895 by Archibald Constable and Company, where Meredith's son was employed. Thus ended Meredith's thirty-year association with Chapman and Hall both as literary adviser and as author.

In the early 1890s the board realized that the Chapman and Hall list was not competitive and that extreme measures needed to be taken. Their first move was to appoint a new chairman in 1894. The choice fell on Oswald Crawfurd, who had had several books published by the company, including *The World We Live In* (1884), *A Woman's Reputation* (1885), *Beyond the Seas* (1887), and *Round the Calendar in Portugal* (1890). He had also been editor of *Black and White*, an illustrated paper founded in 1891 which had been losing £150 a week but had, with Crawfurd as editor, been made to yield a profit of £70. The minutes of the board meetings show that Crawfurd and Chapman frequently disagreed, but that Crawfurd had the support of a majority. Chapman fell ill with influenza in February 1895 and died on 1 March, leaving Crawfurd in undisputed control of the company. Crawfurd decided to combine the positions of chairman and managing director.

One of Crawfurd's first projects was to launch a new monthly, *Chapman's Magazine of Fiction*. He wanted the periodical to carry only fiction and to attain the stature that the *Fortnightly Review* had achieved. For his sixpence the reader would get two serials and several short stories each month. Publication began in May 1895. The market, however, was saturated with similar periodicals—*Longman's, Macmillan's, Pearson's,* the *Strand*—and *Chapman's Magazine of Fiction* succumbed to the competition in October 1898.

Crawfurd published important editions of the works of two of Chapman and Hall's proven sellers—Dickens and Carlyle. The Gadshill Edition of *The Works of Charles Dickens* in thirty-six volumes, at six shillings per volume, featured new introductions by Andrew Lang and illustrations from the original steel plates. It began publication in 1897 and was completed in 1908. The Centenary Edition of *The Works of Thomas Carlyle* (1896-1899) was also produced under Crawfurd's direction. On the whole, however, Crawfurd's legacy was not a grand one, for when he stepped down the company was seriously overstocked with books for which there was no market.

For several years the board attempted to perform the duties of managing director. The results were not satisfactory. Courtney joined the board and gave some good direction, but his duties both at the *Daily Telegraph* and as editor of the *Fortnightly Review* severely limited him. A new, vigorous managing director was needed. Just after the turn of the century Courtney suggested Arthur Waugh, who for the past six years had been literary adviser and assistant manager for Kegan Paul, Trench, Trubner, and Company.

Waugh, like others before him, took advantage of the drawing power of the two most famous authors connected with the house. B. W. Matz, one of the most eminent Dickens scholars of the day, founded the *Dickensian* magazine in 1905; it was published by Chapman and Hall until 1926. In a joint venture with the Oxford University Press the firm published the seventeen-volume Oxford India Paper Edition (1901-1902) of Dickens's works. Chapman and Hall also published the nineteen-volume Biographical Edition (1902), which sold at the remarkably low price of three shillings, sixpence per volume; and a deluxe version of the Gadshill Edition (1903) with the illustrations on vellum. In 1902 Waugh produced a pocket edition of Carlyle's works selling for a mere two shillings in cloth, two shillings, sixpence in leather.

One of the first things the company accountant told Waugh was, "If it wasn't for Dickens, we might as well put up the shutters tomorrow." Waugh had to add new authors to the list. One of them was H. G. Wells, whose *Anticipations of the Reaction of Mechanical and Scientific Progress upon Human Life and Thought* was serialized in the *Fortnightly Review*. When it was published as a book in 1901, it sold so well that Chapman and Hall could not reprint it fast enough to supply the demand. Wells bombarded the firm with letters complaining about "old men sitting in gold mines and spoiling them for life within twenty-four hours." In person the writer was most genial; it was simply his policy to goad his publisher into doing the best possible job. Wells advised other authors to seek large advances because "it

makes the publisher sweat for his money." Other Wells books published by the firm included *Mankind in the Making* (1903), *A Modern Utopia* (1905), and *The Future in America* (1906). Waugh also published Arnold Bennett's *The Old Wives' Tale* (1908), "even if it has to be confessed," Waugh recalled, "that nobody in the firm realised that we were attending the birth of a masterpiece." Other Bennett works published by Chapman and Hall were *The Grim Smile of the Five Towns* (1907), *Buried Alive* (1908), *The Glimpse* (1909), and *Helen with the High Hand* (1910).

Some novelists, according to Waugh, regarded themselves "as allies of the house, and each of them could be relied upon for a fresh book, and a good seller, every year." One of these was W. P. Drury, a major in the marines, who wrote tales of military life. When he came to Chapman and Hall, the company bought up the copyrights of all his previous books and published them in a uniform edition. Another best-selling author was Ridgwell Cullum, who had lived in the American West and was among the earliest writers to exploit it in novels.

With the retirement of Meredith, the dawning of a new century, and the end of the Victorian Age, Chapman and Hall became more daring in its literary offerings. The manuscript of E. Temple Thurston's *The Apple of Eden* (1905) had been rejected by several publishers. The novel opens with a young man in the confessional, excusing his indiscretion because, he explains, he could not resist red hair; the priest violates his vow of celibacy when he sees the young lady with the red hair. Another Thurston novel, *The City of Beautiful Nonsense* (1910), proved to be popular year after year. Desmond Coke, who addressed his letters to the firm "Pickwick, London," would have no other publisher for his writings, starting with *The Bending of a Twig* (1906). Chapman and Hall also found best-sellers in Violet Hunt's *The Celebrity at Home* (1904) and *Sooner or Later* (1904).

Waugh had to deal with some eccentric novelists, including Harry Furniss, who frequently came into the office railing at various staff members because his *Poverty Bay* (1905) was not selling as well as George du Maurier's *Trilby* (1894) had. He would turn up the next morning, apparently having forgotten that he had created a terrible scene the previous day. Another author, Keble Howard, wanted to write his own publicity. In 1906 he offered a press release which said, "Messrs. Clowes telegraphed from Beccles this morning that they have just CLEARED THREE MACHINES to print the sixth edition of MR. KEBLE HOWARD'S 'SMITH'S OF SURBITON.' " Howard explained to the dismayed publisher that "Nobody will know what it means, but it sounds awfully important, anyway." William Hope Hodgson, whose *The Boats of the "Glen Carrig"* (1907) was not selling, wanted to have an enormous boat built on the back of a truck. The name of the novel would be on the mainsail, and a dozen men dressed as sailors would sell copies of the book as the truck was driven along the Strand. When Waugh objected that the firm would be charged with obstructing traffic, Hodgson charged out of the office, swearing vigorously.

Chapman and Hall also published works by Eden Phillpotts, Frederic Harrison, Ethel Colburn Mayne, Ernest Bramah, Ella MacMahon, and Vincent Brown. Philosophical and theological works included Alfred Russel Wallace's *Man's Place in the Universe* (1903), *My Life* (1905), and *The World of Life* (1910); L. T. Hobhouse's *Morals in Evolution* (1906), which sold well for three decades; and R. J. Campbell's *The New Theology* (1907), a book on comparative religion that sold twenty-five thousand copies. An inspirational book, *Letter to My Son* (1910), written by Winifred James but published anonymously, contains the bright hopes of a young woman addressed to her unborn child. The work proved such a favorite that it had to be reprinted yearly.

James Johnston Abraham's *The Surgeon's Log* (1911) was rejected, under a different title, by half a dozen other publishing houses before Chapman and Hall took it. The author, a medical doctor, had been ordered to travel to regain his health. Unable to afford to do so, he had signed on as a ship's doctor and kept a record of his experiences during the voyage. Waugh claimed that the new title was his own idea and that it made the book a steady seller for twenty years. Another Abraham manuscript, "Concerning Fitzgerald," which like its predecessor received a new name—*The Night Nurse* (1913)—also became a best-seller.

Chapman and Hall had a special affinity for books on cricket, for, as Waugh said, "We were all of us cricket mad." The first in a long line of such works was *How We Recovered the Ashes* (1904), by Pelham F. Warner. It was followed by P. G. H. Fender's *Defending the Ashes* (1921) and *Kissing the Rod: The Story of the Tests of 1934* (1934) and Montague Alfred Noble's *Gilligan's Men* (1925). So

"cricket mad" were the men of Chapman and Hall that they formed their own team, with Waugh as captain, to play on Saturdays against other publishing houses such as George Bell and Sons and Kegan Paul and Company.

Publication of yet another edition of the works of Dickens, the National Edition in forty volumes, began in October 1906 and was completed in April 1908. Priced at ten shillings, sixpence per volume, the edition was limited to 750 sets. Originally the plan was to call it the King's Edition and to dedicate it to Edward VII, but on application to the king's advisers the publisher was told that the monarch could not lend his name to a commercial enterprise. At about this time Chapman and Hall was approached by Arthur Bullen with a proposal to publish the collected works of Yeats. Bullen was an excellent editor but felt he needed the expertise of the publisher to see the work through the press and take care of distribution. It was in this manner that Chapman and Hall became connected with the Shakespeare Head Press edition of *The Collected Works in Verse and Prose of William Butler Yeats* (1908).

Some publishers felt that their trade organization, the Publishers' Association, was not doing all it could to facilitate communication among publishers and allow them to work out common problems. Consequently, in 1907, during what Frederick Macmillan in his book *The Net Book Agreement, 1899, and the Book War, 1906-1908* (1924) would call the "Book War," a group of publishers met at the instigation of A. D. Power, London manager for Pitman, and formed the Publishers' Circle. One problem which concerned them was that none of their number had ever served on the council of the Publishers' Association. To remedy this situation, they agreed to put up candidates from their group and to vote only for them. In this way they gained seats on the council for Chapman and Hall, Hodder and Stoughton, Hutchinson, Wells Gardner, and John Lane. Waugh served as a member of the council and also as president of the Publishers' Circle.

In 1913 Chapman and Hall noticed that the firm's books were not being reviewed in the newspapers owned by Lord Northcliffe. Soon the books were not even included in the "New Books" lists of the papers. Finally, even advertisements of the firm were rejected. On making inquiry through their advertising agents, they learned that all newspapers belonging to Lord Northcliffe had received instructions to make no mention whatsoever of Chapman and Hall. After

Waugh brought the matter up at the Publishers' Circle, William Heinemann spoke to Northcliffe and learned that he was offended by a book published by the firm, Keble Howard's *Lord London* (1913). Northcliffe said, "There is a description of my father in this book, which holds him up to ridicule, as a rather foolish old man, who spends his time playing a violin in an upstairs room . . . and, as long as that book is in circulation, its publishers' name will not appear in any of my papers." The firm withdrew the book from circulation but was threatened with court proceedings by Howard. In the end the company settled with the author by paying him damages of £150.

In the second decade of the century Chapman and Hall published two new editions of the works of Dickens, the thirty-six-volume Centenary (1910-1911) and the twenty-one-volume Universal (1913-1914). The Waverley Book Club bought thousands of sets, and the *Encyclopaedia Britannica* gave away a set with each order for the encyclopedia. Important art books such as R. G. Hatton's *Figure Drawing* (1913) and *Principles of Decoration* (1925) and James Ward's *Colour Decoration of Architecture* (1913) and *History and Methods of Ancient and Modern Painting* (1913) were added to the list.

World War I brought many changes to Chapman and Hall. For one thing, women were introduced to the staff to replace men who were called for military service. Before the war there had been only one woman in the office—the secretary of the managing director; by the end of hostilities the staff was more nearly balanced. Also, the cost of materials increased: paper went from two and a half pence per pound to one shilling, one pence; compositors' wages climbed from thirty-two shillings, sixpence a week to seventy-four shillings; binders' pay increased from thirty-five shillings for a forty-eight-hour week to five pounds. In the same period the price the publisher got from the bookseller for a novel only went from four shillings, twopence to five shillings, eightpence. Consequently, the publisher had to sell twice as many novels to meet its costs. Some publishing houses argued that the war canceled contracts between publishers and authors, but Chapman and Hall honored all agreements with its authors. Although sales declined drastically, the firm continued to make a profit and was able to retain all its staff.

A sensational book published by Chapman and Hall during the war was the anonymous *What I Found Out in the House of a German Prince*

(1915), purportedly the memoirs of an English governess. A literary agent had taken the manuscript to Heinemann, who wanted to publish it but insisted on knowing the identity of the author. When the author refused, the agent took the work to Chapman and Hall, which ran a portion of it in the *Fortnightly Review*, then published the whole work in book form. It was instantly successful, with the first edition of nine thousand copies and a subsequent edition of sixty-five hundred both selling out. No one knew the author's identity until 1931, when Alice M. Williamson revealed in her memoirs, *The Inky Way*, that she had written *What I Found Out in the House of a German Prince*, drawing largely on her imagination.

Chapman and Hall did well as agent for Wiley's technical and scientific books but was determined to develop its own line by English authors. The firm sought the advice of Wilfrid J. Lineham, head of engineering at Goldsmiths' College, New Cross, and author of *Textbook of Mechanical Engineering* (1894). Lineham recommended John Leslie Bale, who was later joined on the board by another engineer, R. E. Neale, a highly successful author of technical works. Together they increased the scientific and technical list to fourteen hundred works—as many as all of Chapman and Hall's other publications—giving the firm preeminence in the field.

In 1919 Alec Waugh, the managing director's son, joined the firm: that year Chapman and Hall published his *The Prisoners of Mainz*. He later became a member of the board. His other books published by the company included *Love in These Days* (1926), *The Last Chukka* (1928), *Three Score and Ten* (1929), and *The Coloured Countries* (1930). With his extensive connections among the writers of the day, he brought in many new names: Norman Davey, author of *Pilgrim of a Smile* (1921), *Good Hunting* (1923), *Babylon and Candlelight* (1927), and *Cats in the Coffee* (1939); Ralph Straus with *The Unseemly Adventure* (1924), *Our Wiser Sons* (1926), and *The Unspeakable Curll* (1927)—a biography of the bookseller Edmund Curll; Norman Douglas, who wrote *They Went* (1920), *Alone* (1921), and *Experiments* (1925); Charles Scott Moncrieff, with translations of *Song of Roland* (1919) and *Beowulf* (1921); Hilaire Belloc, who translated Marshal Ferdinand Foch's *The Principles of War* (1918) and *Precepts and Judgments* (1919); and, from America, Lothrop Stoddard, with *Revolt against Civilisation* (1922). The best-selling novels of W. L. George, a member of the board, were also published by Chapman and

Hall, as were the works of Oliver Onions. Arnold Lunn edited the annual *Georgian Stories* from 1922 to 1927.

In the 1920s Chapman and Hall established the Universal Art Series, a group of illustrated monographs printed by the Westminster Press. Some of the titles were *Modern Movement in Painting* (1920) and *Modern English Architecture* (1924), by Charles Marriott; *The Art of Illustration* (1921) and *Line: An Art Study* (1922), by Edmund J. Sullivan; and *Landscape Painting from Giotto to the Present Day* (1923-1924), by Lewis Hind. Other works in the series were by Walter Bayes, R. P. Gossop, E. B. Lintott, Herbert Furst, H. V. Lanchester, C. R. Ashbee, Percy Buckman, G. C. Williamson, and Amor Fenn.

Arthur Waugh's other son, Evelyn Waugh, had his novel *Decline and Fall* published by Chapman and Hall in 1928. The firm also published his *Vile Bodies* (1930), *Black Mischief* (1932), *A Handful of Dust* (1934), and *Mr. Loveday's Little Outing and Other Sad Stories* (1936).

In 1938 Chapman and Hall merged with Methuen. Methuen joined with other companies, including Eyre and Spottiswoode and E. and F. Spon, to organize Associated Book Publishers in 1955.

**References:**

S. M. Ellis, *William Harrison Ainsworth and His Times* (London: Lane, 1911);

John Forster, *The Life of Charles Dickens*, 3 volumes (London: Chapman & Hall, 1872-1874);

Fred Kaplan, *Thomas Carlyle: A Biography* (Ithaca, N.Y.: Cornell University Press, 1983);

Betty B. Miller, *Robert Browning: A Portrait* (London: Murray, 1952; New York: Scribners, 1952);

Robert L. Patten, *Charles Dickens and His Publishers* (Oxford: Oxford University Press, 1978);

Lionel Stevenson, *The Ordeal of George Meredith: A Biography* (New York: Scribners, 1953);

J. A. Sutherland, *Victorian Novelists and Publishers* (Chicago: University of Chicago Press, 1976);

Anthony Trollope, *An Autobiography* (2 volumes, Edinburgh & London: Blackwood, 1883; 1 volume, New York: Harper, 1883);

Arthur Waugh, *A Hundred Years of Publishing: Being the Story of Chapman & Hall, Ltd.* (London: Chapman & Hall, 1930).

**Papers:**

The Chapman and Hall archives are included in the Associated Book Publishers archives at Andover, Hampshire. Additional materials may be found at the Methuen office, 11 New Fetter Lane, London.

*—J. Don Vann*

# Chatto and Windus
*(London: 1873-1987)*
# John Camden Hotten
*(London: 1855-1873)*

The founder of the publishing house which became Chatto and Windus was John Camden Hotten from Cornwall. In 1846 Hotten was apprenticed to John Petheram, a bookseller in Chancery Lane, London. Hotten left with his brother for America in 1848; in 1855 he returned to London to establish his own bookshop at 151b Piccadilly. In the United States Hotten had become acquainted with the works of such American authors as Bret Harte, Oliver Wendell Holmes, and Ambrose Bierce, whose books Hotten introduced into the English market. In the early 1860s Hotten moved to 74-75 Piccadilly. In 1860 he turned his hand to authorship, writing and publishing *Macaulay the Historian*, followed in 1863 by *A Handbook to the Topography and Family History of England and Wales: Being a Descriptive Account of Twenty Thousand Most Curious and Rare Books*. In 1864 he published his biography of William Makepeace Thackeray, followed by biographies of Charles Dickens in 1870 and 1873.

Hotten's decision to publish the poetry of Algernon Charles Swinburne in 1866 was a controversial move which gave his firm a reputation that enabled it to survive past his death. Through what were to become characteristically devious business transactions, Hotten acquired permission to print *Poems and Ballads* (1866) from Edward Moxon, who withdrew his intention to publish it. Hotten paid Swinburne little if any of the profits from *Poems and Ballads*, which was a strong seller. Further, Hotten is believed to have forced Swinburne to pay blackmail to conceal the poet's authorship of two earlier poems, "Flagellation" and "Romance of the Rod." Between 1870 and 1872 Hotten tried unsuccessfully to assert copyright claims to all of Swinburne's publications from 1866 to 1872. When Hotten

*Andrew Chatto*

died on 14 June 1873, Swinburne summarized what many other authors and publishers who knew or who knew of Hotten must have felt: "Mr. Hotten was—I was about very inaccurately to say,—ambiguous. He was a serviceable sort of fellow in his own way, but decidedly what Dr. Johnson would have called a 'shady lot' and Lord Chesterfield 'a rum customer.' When I heard that he had died of a surfeit of porkchops, I observed that this was a serious argument against my friend (Sir) Richard Burton's views on cannibalism as a wholesome and natural method of diet." It was reported that Bierce's rage at receiving a bad check provoked the publisher's final, fatal collapse when Bierce, who was living in London at the time, confronted Hotten on his deathbed.

Andrew Chatto, a member of Hotten's firm since 1856 and publications manager at Hotten's death, purchased the firm from Hotten's widow for twenty-five thousand pounds. Chatto, about whom little is known, was the son of William A. Chatto, a writer who had flourished in the 1840s with books on wood engraving, card playing, and fishing. W. E. Windus, a minor poet whose first book, *Under Dead Leaves*, had been published by Hotten in 1871, became Chatto's partner in the business. Windus, an Oxford graduate and classmate of John Ruskin, was also a watercolorist, a dramatist, and an ardent yachtsman who was a member of the Royal Thames Yacht Club. In 1875 Chatto and Windus published Windus's *Broadstone Hall and Other Poems*, but his two plays, *Illiam Dhône* (1886) and *Fenella* (1890), were handled by other firms. Andrew Chatto, Jr., assisted in his father's business while Chatto's other son, Thomas, was a member of the firm of Pickering and Chatto, rare book dealers.

It seems that for Chatto the publication of the books was the most important aspect of his business, and he was willing to work with authors to get the literature he wanted to publish. He was careful to make clear sales contracts with his authors, to pay them their share of profits from their works, and to protect them to the extent that he could from piracies. In nearly every respect, Chatto was a much different man from Hotten. He repaired relations with Swinburne, who had been driven away by the fight with Hotten over copyrights; Chatto wooed him back by sending him a check for fifty pounds on 23 July 1873 with a formal request to publish his works. In January 1874 Chatto sent a check for one hundred seventy-three pounds, ten shillings, tenpence in payment of past profits. In May Swinburne agreed to let Chatto publish *Bothwell* (1874). In October he submitted to Chatto *George Chapman: A Critical Essay* (1875), the proofs of which were returned in six days—another feature of the Chatto business method. Chatto performed many services for his authors, such as getting books and magazines for their research, providing clippings of reviews of their publications, and sending complimentary copies of books to their friends and patrons. In Swinburne's case, these activities took on the character-

istics of a full-time job. For example, when Swinburne was writing *A Study of Shakespeare* (1880), Chatto provided him with copies of François Rabelais's plays and a list of the Macmillan student editions of the plays with the names of the editors and assistant editors; Chatto also checked references and quotations for Swinburne both in books Chatto published and those he did not. In January 1884 Chatto received what had become a standard type of letter from Swinburne: "Can you send me by tomorrow evening a copy bound in parchment of the edition de luxe of Lorna Doone—published by Sampson Low price 35sh? If I cannot have it at once, I shall not want it. If it came later than tomorrow evening—or Saturday morning at the latest—it would be of no use to me. There are two other books which I want, but am not in such special need of till next week— The Boats of the World 3s.6d. same publisher: and The Blue Veil by Florence Montgomery— published by Bentley and Son." In June 1887 Chatto was asked to provide seats for three of Swinburne's friends at one of the publisher's windows for the Jubilee Procession; Chatto obliged.

In addition to providing poetry for the magazine *Belgravia*, which Hotten had acquired in March 1866 and Chatto and Windus published through 1899, and poetry and essays for the *Gentleman's Magazine* (acquired in 1873 and published until 1907), Swinburne produced a steady stream of books bearing the Chatto and Windus imprint, including *Erechtheus* (1876), *Poems and Ballads, Second Series* (1878), *Studies in Song* (1880), *Mary Stuart* (1881), *Tristram of Lyonesse and Other Poems* (1882), *Marino Faliero* (1885), and the posthumously published *Charles Dickens* (1913). Swinburne introduced Chatto to Charles and Mary Lamb's *Poetry for Children, Entirely Original* (1809), which Chatto republished in July 1877. To the end, Swinburne complained about the quality of Chatto's printing jobs and to the end, Chatto staunchly refused to change printers—even in 1889, when Swinburne was so upset that he threatened to change publishers.

In 1875 Samuel Clemens (Mark Twain) was looking for an English publisher for *The Adventures of Tom Sawyer*. On the advice of his agent, Moncure Conway, he offered it to Chatto instead of to George Routledge, who was not receptive to Clemens's idea of publishing the book on consignment and at his own expense. In January 1876 Chatto and Clemens agreed that Chatto and Windus would receive a 25 percent commission instead of the 10 percent Clemens had originally proposed. In June Conway and Chatto arranged to distribute a fancy illustrated edition first, followed by a less expensive plain one. The illustrations, which it was Clemens's responsibility to procure and ship, did not arrive in London in time for the first edition's August publication. In early November Belford Brothers, which represented Chatto and Windus in Canada, published a pirated edition of *The Adventures of Tom Sawyer* despite Chatto's notice that the book bore an English copyright; thus Clemens's profits from both Canadian and American sales were lost as the Canadian publication preceded the American publication. In a letter to Conway, Clemens wrote: "Belford Brothers, Canadian thieves, are flooding with a pirated edition of Tom Sawyer. I have just telegraphed Chatto to assign Canadian copyright to me, but I suppose it is too late to do any good. We cannot issue for six weeks yet, and by that time Belford will have sold 10,000 over the frontier and killed my book dead. This piracy cost me $10,000. . . ."

While Clemens said he liked "Chatto exceedingly and shall continue to like him," the two had difficulties over their different manners of doing business. In April 1880 Clemens wrote Chatto in a state of agitation concerning illustrations for *A Tramp Abroad* (1880). Clemens was frustrated by Chatto's desire to deal directly with him when Clemens wanted Chatto to contact Conway or Frank Bliss, his American publisher: "I have nothing to do with publishing my books and I won't have anything to do with it either here or in England. With Mr. Conway right at your elbow, you keep writing to me. When you want electros, you write me.—I have no electros and never have had any electros. Why do you not write Bliss, who has electros? When things go wrong you complain to me. My dear Sirs, through Mr. Conway I send you advance-sheets (looking to it myself and seeing that it is done) for a royalty—it is all I have ever agreed to do—it is all that I have ever had the slightest intention of making myself responsible for." The following month, it was discovered that Bliss had left *A Tramp Abroad* open to piracy by not sending Chatto a complete text until the piece had already been published in America. Nevertheless, in December Chatto sent Clemens a check for £1,245.17.6 (approximately $6,053.50), despite the Canadian piracy.

In 1894 Clemens's own publishing house, Charles L. Webster and Company, declared bankruptcy; Clemens lost $170,000. Doubly in need of money when the Mount Morris bank nearly

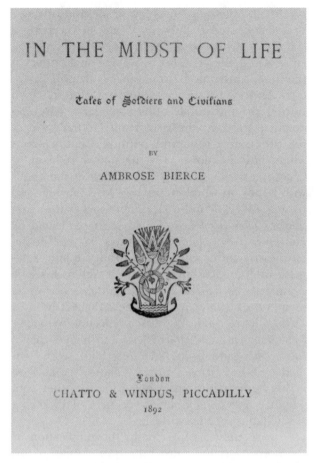

*Title page for the British edition of a book that was published in the United States under Bierce's title,* Tales of Soldiers and Civilians. *Andrew Chatto took the title of his edition from a sentence in the burial service in the* Book of Common Prayer: *"In the midst of life we are in death."*

failed, he wrote his London agent, Fred J. Hall: "I wish Brer Chatto would send along his little yearly contribution. I dropped him a line about another matter a week ago—asked him to subscribe for the Daily News for me—you see I wanted to remind him in a covert way that it was pay-up time—but doubtless I directed the letter to you or some one else, for don't hear from him and don't get any Daily News either."

In 1876 Percy Spalding, the son of the paper merchant H. B. Spalding of Spalding and Hodges, bought into the firm. In the same year Chatto and Windus acquired stocks and copyrights of the firm of Henry Bohn for twenty thousand pounds.

In the period 1876 to 1889 Chatto and Windus published *The Complete Poems of Sir John Davies* (1876), edited by Alexander Grosart; *The School of Shakespeare* (1878), by Richard Simpson; *Curiosities of Criticism* (1881), by Henry James Jennings; *Single Heart and Double Face* (1884), by Charles Reade; and *The Evil Genius* (1889), by Wilkie Collins. From 1882 to 1911 the firm published the *Idler*, which was a vehicle for the essays of Jerome K. Jerome.

In 1882 Chatto and Windus published a collection of Robert Louis Stevenson's essays, *Familiar Studies of Men and Books*. The firm went on to publish *Prince Otto* (1885), *Memoirs and Portraits* (1887), and *Ballads* (1890). When Chatto and Windus published Stevenson's *Father Damien* (1890), the story of the missionary priest to the lepers, Chatto sent Stevenson's share of the profits to the Leper Fund; Stevenson was so moved by Chatto's action that he sent him his travel letters, *Across the Plains with Other Memories and Essays*, (1892), although another firm had offered a higher fee. Perhaps the Stevenson-Chatto business transactions are best reflected in an October 1884 letter from Stevenson to Chatto: "I have an offer of £25 for Otto in America. I do not know if you mean to have the American rights; from the nature of the contract I think not; . . . You see, I leave this quite in your hands. To parody an old Scotch story of servant and master: if you don't know that you have a good author, I know that I have a good publisher. Your fair, open and handsome dealings are a good point in my life, and do more for my crazy health than has yet been done by any doctor."

M. E. Grenander has shown that Chatto's decision to change the title of Bierce's *Tales of Soldiers and Civilians* (1891) to *In the Midst of Life: Tales of Soldiers and Civilians* (1892) not only enhanced the book's appeal in English markets but also created a subtle unified theme for the collection—"that for the civilian as for the soldier, death was always at the heart of life"; the theme had been overlooked by Bierce, who objected at first to Chatto's tampering with his fiction. By changing the title, moving the story "The Suitable Surroundings" to serve as the keynote piece to the collection, and paying Bierce fifty pounds for the copyright, Chatto had created an English edition of the same stories without infringing on American copyrights. In 1898 G. P. Putnam, one of the publishers who had initially rejected the book, published the second edition in New York at the same time as Chatto and Windus did so in England. When the third edition was published in 1909 the book had expanded from nineteen to twenty-two stories; the American and English editions remained distinct

as Bierce, while he adopted the title, never accepted Chatto's arrangement of the stories.

In 1892 Chatto was approached by Tauchnitz of Leipzig about publishing a European edition of *In the Midst of Life*. Under the Bern copyright convention Chatto was allowed to sell the rights, which he did for twenty-five pounds. Bierce was angered because he was not consulted about the sale and because Chatto sent him only half of the twenty-five pounds. Bierce may not have realized that Chatto did not have to buy Bierce's copyright in the first place, nor did he have to share the profits of the German sale, as American authors' works were not protected by international copyright laws. Chatto, however, did not allow his authors to be abused because of the American government's unwillingness to support international copyright protections.

From 1902 through 1907 Arnold Bennett provided Chatto and Windus with a novel or two every year: *The Grand Babylon Hotel* (1902), *Anna of the Five Towns* (1902), *The Gates of Wrath* (1903), *Leonora* (1903), *A Great Man: A Frolic* (1904), *Teresa of Watling Street: A Fantasia on Modern Themes* (1904), *Tales of the Five Towns* (1905), *Sacred and Profane Love* (1905), *Hugo: A Fantasia on Modern Themes* (1906), *The City of Pleasure: A Fantasia on Modern Themes* (1907), and *The Ghost: A Fantasia on Modern Themes* (1907). Bennett was still a little-known writer, and these works were largely of the experimental sort which attracted Chatto and Windus.

In 1905 Philip Lee-Warner joined the firm as a partner. Among his accomplishments were bringing in Sir Israel Gollancz to supervise two Chatto and Windus series, The King's Classics and The Medieval Library; establishing a line of expensively produced art books; setting the standards for book production; and bringing into the business two people who were to influence the future of Chatto and Windus: Geoffrey Whitworth as art editor and Frank Swinnerton, a novelist and critic, as literary adviser.

In 1909 Windus retired; he died in June 1910. In 1911 Lee-Warner left the firm. The same year Andrew Chatto, Sr., retired; he died on 15 March 1913 at his home outside London at the age of seventy-three. During the 1920s and 1930s Chatto and Windus was headed by Charles Prentice, a renowned book designer; Harold Raymond; and Ian Parsons, who replaced Whitworth as art editor. When Prentice retired in 1934, Raymond and Parsons were joined by J. W. McDougall. That year the firm began publishing periodicals again, with *World Review of Reviews*—a merger of the *World* and the *Review of Reviews*—and Michael Bartlett's *Geographical Magazine*. In 1935 Chatto and Windus moved to 40-42 William IV Street.

In January 1920 Swinnerton read and accepted Aldous Huxley's *Limbo*, a collection of six short stories and a play. The book sold sixteen hundred copies, and a second book, *Leda*, was published in May 1920. In 1923 Chatto and Windus and Huxley drew up the first of their many triennial contracts which specified that Huxley would provide the publisher with two works per year, one of these to be a novel. In return, Huxley would receive an advance of five hundred pounds a year and a 15 percent royalty, which would increase to 20 percent when two thousand copies were sold and to 25 percent after eight thousand. These sales figures were often achieved. Among the many Huxley works published by the firm in the 1920s and 1930s were *Antic Hay* (1923), *Two or Three Graces and Other Stories* (1926), *Point Counter Point* (1928), *Brief Candles* (1930), *Brave New World* (1932), *Eyeless in Gaza* (1936), and *After Many a Summer* (1939). Because of the restrictions the government placed on the payment of royalties to authors living outside of England during World War II (Huxley had immigrated to California in October 1937), the usual contracts were first modified, then suspended. Huxley was plagued by insomnia and depression during the late 1930s and early 1940s; to counteract the periods of sleeplessness, Raymond's wife, Vera, asked Huxley to join her in her library work at St. Bartholomew's Hospital. The author did so for a brief period of time, until he found even the delivery of books to patients too strenuous. Sybille Bedford comments in *Aldous Huxley: A Biography* (1973) that "The Raymonds' kindness and affectionate concern were a great help to Aldous and Maria [Nys Huxley, Huxley's first wife] (it went well beyond, and it was different in kind, from a publisher's looking after an—in the long run—extremely profitable author)." In 1941 Huxley returned to the three-year contract, with the important changes that there was not a set number of books to be written and that the yearly advance would be twenty percent of whatever was sold during that year. This contract was renewed until Huxley's death in 1963. Among the works by Huxley the firm published in the 1940s and 1950s were *Time Must Have a Stop* (1945), *Ape and Essence* (1949), *Adonis and the Alphabet, and Other Essays* (1956), and *Brave New World*

*Revisited* (1958). In 1969 Chatto and Windus published *Letters of Aldous Huxley*, edited by Grover Smith.

Huxley's publications, because they spanned nearly forty years, overlapped with those of other writers, such as Wyndham Lewis, who achieved notoriety in 1931 with his encomium *Hitler*. Previously the firm had published Lewis's *The Art of Being Ruled* (1926), which argues against fascism; *Time and Western Man* (1927), his best-known philosophical work; *The Childermass* (1928), part of a projected political-fantasy trilogy; and *Paleface* (1929), an attack on D. H. Lawrence. In addition to *Hitler*, in 1931 the firm also published Lewis's *The Diabolical Principle and The Dithyrambic Spectator*, an attack on Gertrude Stein. In 1932 Chatto and Windus published the last of Lewis's works for the firm, *The Doom of Youth*, a diatribe on the childish attitudes of the modern citizen. Manifesting a slight interest in politics, the firm published Norman Douglas's *How about Europe? Some Footnotes on East and West* (1930) and the revised edition (1952) of *Norman Douglas* (1931), a work by Henry Tomlinson critiquing Douglas's political views. Chatto and Windus also published *An Almanac* (1945), a collection of quotations from Douglas's works, and *Norman Douglas: A Selection from His Works* (1955), edited by D. M. Low.

Richard Aldington was a writer whose novels reflected an antiwar theme. The husband of the poet Hilda Doolittle, he was best known as an imagist poet; the editor of the *Egoist*, the imagist organ; and later as the author of *Lawrence of Arabia* (1955). Before moving to America in 1940, Aldington had several novels published by Chatto and Windus: *Death of a Hero* (1929), which is largely drawn from his experiences as a soldier in World War I; *The Colonel's Daughter* (1931); *All Men Are Enemies* (1933); and *Women Must Work* (1934), an antifeminist novel. Chatto and Windus also published two collections of Aldington's short stories: *Roads to Glory* (1930) and *Soft Answers* (1932). Nonfiction works by Aldington published by Chatto and Windus were *D. H. Lawrence* (1930) and *Artifex: Sketches and Ideas* (1935).

For twenty years H. G. Wells was occasionally counted among the Chatto and Windus authors, beginning with *In the Fourth Year: Anticipations of a World Peace* (1918). In 1928 he edited an anthology of his wife's poetry and stories, *The Book of Catherine Wells*; three fictional works of his own followed: *The Croquet Player* (1936), *Star Begot-*

*ten: A Biological Fantasia* (1937), and *The Brothers* (1938). Wells used many publishers in his long career, and Chatto and Windus served him for a brief period.

Although Rosamund Lehmann's first novel was published by Holt, in 1932 Chatto published her *Invitation to a Waltz* which was followed much later by the successful *Echoing Grove* (1953). Her fiction, like that of William Faulkner and Elspeth Huxley, is of a psychological experimental mode.

The firm published most of the novels, short fiction, and criticism of T. F. Powys, beginning with *The Left Leg* (1923), a collection of three stories. His novels and short-story collections included *Innocent Birds* (1926) *The House with the Echo* (1928), *Fables* (1929), *The White Paternoster* (1930), *Kindness in a Corner* (1930), *Unclay* (1931), *Captain Patch* (1935), and *Bottle's Path* (1946). In 1929 Chatto and Windus republished Powys's only work of nonfiction, *An Interpretation of Genesis*, which had been privately printed in 1907. In 1966 a collection of eighteen previously unpublished stories was released as *Rosie Plum*.

British publishing houses suffered during World War II because of paper shortages. Chatto and Windus, however, was not badly affected and found that whatever it had in back stock rapidly sold. During the war Norah Smallwood, who had joined the firm in 1928, served as head of typography, and in 1945 she became a partner when McDougall left to head Chapman and Hall. In 1946 C. Day Lewis, later Poet Laureate, joined the firm as a literary adviser; but the major event of the year was the purchase of the Hogarth Press. Established in 1917 by Leonard and Virginia Woolf, the Hogarth Press was a small firm which produced only ten to twelve titles per year by such writers as Virginia Woolf, Vita Sackville-West, Bertrand Russell, and Sigmund Freud. During the 1930s, under the leadership of John Lehmann, the Hogarth Press had discovered W. H. Auden and Stephen Spender and had purchased the popular anthology *New Writing* from Lawrence and Wishart. The periodical featured the works of Auden, Spender, Day Lewis, Christopher Isherwood, Bertolt Brecht, and Jean-Paul Sartre. The war had affected the Hogarth Press seriously; from 1939 to 1941, only two books had been published. After Virginia Woolf died in 1941, management of the firm was shared by Leonard Woolf and Lehmann. When Lehmann left in 1946 to start his own firm, Woolf decided to merge with Chatto and Windus. Woolf retained all rights as manager of Hogarth Press, and although he died in 1969, books continue to be published with the Hogarth imprint. In his autobiography Woolf wrote: "Chatto was a moderate-sized publishing firm, but was large-scale compared to the Hogarth Press. It was one of the few remaining big publishing businesses in which the directors seemed to have a policy with regard to books and their publication similar to my own, and there were few, if any, books in our list which Chatto would not have been glad to publish and vice versa."

Chatto and Windus became a limited company in 1953, and a formal board of directors was created. Raymond was named chairman of the board and managing director; other members of the board included Parsons, Smallwood, Piers Raymond, Day Lewis, P. J. A. Calvocoressi, and Woolf.

Chatto and Windus was the British publisher of all of William Faulkner's major novels, which were attractive to the firm because of their experimental quality and because of his American reputation. According to Faulkner's biographer, Joseph Blotner, "Raymond was the sort of Englishman Faulkner admired. He was an Oxford honors graduate decorated with the Military Cross . . . and O. B. E. . . ." In 1956, on his way to receive the Nobel Prize, Faulkner stopped to call on Raymond and urged the publisher to provide him with a list of new English authors whose works he could promote in America. Other important authors from the period after 1950 include Jacquetta Hawkes, who popularized writing about archeology in 1951 with *Guide to the Prehistoric and Roman Monuments in England and Wales*.

Pamela Hill began contributing historical romances to Chatto and Windus in 1954 with *Flaming Janet: A Lady of Galloway*, followed by *Shadow of Palaces* (1955), *Marjorie of Scotland* (1956), and *Here Lies Margot* (1957). All of her novels were copublished with American firms, as was Chatto and Windus's practice with fiction. After finding success, Hill switched to the firm of Hodder and Stoughton, one of several British firms specializing in romances and historical novels (among the others are Mills and Boon, Ward Lock, Collins, and Hale). Ann Bridge, another romance novelist, created the character of Julia Probyn for a series of three novels published by Chatto and Windus—*Lighthearted Quest* (1956), *The Portuguese Escape* (1958), and *The Numbered Account* (1960), the latter coauthored with Susan Marques. Bridge, who was really Lady Mary Dolling

O'Malley, produced a steady stream of Gothic novels for the firm from 1926 through 1962. She also wrote three nonfiction works: *Portrait of My Mother* (1955); *The Selective Traveller in Portugal* (1958), with Marques; and *Facts and Fictions: Some Literary Recollections* (1968).

The first works of Frederick William Rolfe (who also used the names Fr. Rolfe and Baron Corvo) to be published by Chatto and Windus were *Hadrian the Seventh* (1904) and *Don Tarquinio* (1905). His autobiographical novel *Nicholas Crabbe* was suppressed until 1958—long after his death in 1913—because of its perceived libelous nature. Chatto and Windus published many novels by David Garnett, beginning with *Lady into Fox* (1922) and including *A Man in the Zoo* (1924), *The Sailor's Return* (1925), and *No Love* (1929). The firm published Garnett's autobiography in three volumes: *The Golden Echo* (1953), *Flowers of the Forest* (1955), and *The Familiar Faces* (1962).

The novelist Iris Murdoch, who is also an essayist, playwright, and lecturer, began publishing with Chatto and Windus in 1954 with *Under the Net*, followed by *The Flight from the Enchanter* (1955), *The Sandcastle* (1957), and *The Bell* (1958). In the 1960s she had eight novels published by Chatto and Windus, including *A Severed Head* (1961), which she also dramatized in 1964. In the 1970s the firm published her novels *A Fairly Honourable Defeat* (1970), *An Accidental Man* (1971), *The Black Prince* (1973), *The Sacred and Profane Love Machine* (1974), and *A Word Child* (1975). In 1965 Chatto and Windus published a critical work about Murdoch, Antonia Byatt's *Degrees of Freedom: The Novels of Iris Murdoch*.

To mark one hundred years of publishing, in 1955 Chatto and Windus published *A Century of Writers 1855-1955*, edited by David Low and with an introduction by Oliver Warner giving a detailed history of the firm until the early 1950s. This 736-page anthology contains works by major authors, as well as those who have become obscure. There is a representative cross section of all the types of literature Chatto published, including poetry, fiction and nonfiction. The entire text of *The Adventures of Huckleberry Finn* (1884) is reprinted within its pages.

The 1960s were a decade of growth and expansion for Chatto and Windus. In 1961 Parsons founded the Zodiac Library of reprinted British and American popular and classic novels. His Landmark Library of reprinted twentieth-century novels proved to be an additional success. In 1968 Chatto and Windus purchased Oliver and

Boyd's juvenile list. In 1969 Chatto and Windus merged with Jonathan Cape, both firms keeping their separate identities and editorial offices. In the same year Chatto and Windus became associated with the Scottish Academies Press, a publishing group formed from the presses of the University of St. Andrews and the University of Dundee. In 1970 Parsons and Graham C. Greene became joint chairmen of the newly formed holding company Chatto and Jonathan Cape, Limited. Other directors included Smallwood; Day Lewis; Geoffrey Trevelyan, who had joined Chatto and Windus in 1962 to supervise educational and technical publishing; Thomas Maschler from Jonathan Cape; and W. Robert Carr, who represented Granada, which had an interest in Jonathan Cape. In May 1970 G. Wren Howard, son of the cofounder of Jonathan Cape, retired and was succeeded as cochairman of Chatto and Jonathan Cape, Limited and as a managing director of Jonathan Cape by Greene, with Maschler taking Howard's place as chairman of Jonathan Cape. In 1971 Chatto and Jonathan Cape, Limited began publishing and distributing for Sussex University Press.

In August 1973 Chatto and Jonathan Cape, Limited purchased another major firm, The Bodley Head, forming the holding company Cape, Chatto and Bodley Head, with all three firms retaining their own offices and imprints. Max Reinhardt, the chairman of The Bodley Head, joined Greene and Parsons as cochairman of Cape, Chatto and Bodley Head. The unification of the three large publishing houses offered each of them protection from American or other takeover bids. All three firms were equally strong in publishing high-quality literature.

With The Bodley Head came the Nonesuch imprint, Putnam's, and Hollis and Carter. Bodley Head authors included Georgette Heyer, Graham Greene, Maurice Sendak, William Trevor, Vladimir Nabokov, J. P. Donleavy, Alistair Cooke, Charles Chaplin, and Pope John Paul II.

In 1980 Parsons died. When Smallwood retired in 1982, Hugo Brenner moved from managing director to chairman of Cape, Chatto and Bodley Head. The final purchase the group made was Virago, in 1982, started by Carmen Callil to reprint books by women writers. The new company was knows as Chatto and Windus, Virago, Bodley Head, and Cape (CVBC). In 1982 Callil joined Brenner as managing director. In 1987 Virago bought itself back for approximately eight hundred thousand pounds to avoid being sold to Random House, and the firm became Chatto, Bodley Head and Jonathan Cape, Limited.

In May 1987 the American publisher Random House purchased Chatto, Bodley Head and Jonathan Cape, Limited in a deal negotiated by Graham C. Greene with Robert L. Bernstein, representing Random House. At the time of the sale Chatto and Windus was producing around one hundred titles per year. The *New York Times*, in announcing the sale, noted that the consortium represented many of the best-known authors of the twentieth century: Graham Greene, Iris Murdoch, Virginia Woolf, Aleksandr Solzhenitsyn, Ernest Hemingway, Herman Hesse, T. E. Lawrence, and Doris Lessing. Chatto and Windus retains its imprint and exists as part of Random House.

Throughout its history Chatto and Windus maintained a commitment to its authors and to the publication of quality literature. Andrew Chatto and his successors did not hesitate to publish new and lesser-known authors and experimental fiction and verse. Another contribution to the English reading public was the publication of the works of leading American authors. The simultaneous publication method Chatto preferred benefited not only the publishing house but the authors and their readers.

**References:**
Sybille Bedford, *Aldous Huxley: A Biography*, 2 volumes (London: Chatto & Windus, 1973);
Joseph Blotner, *Faulkner: A Biography*, 2 volumes (New York: Random House, 1982);

Samuel L. Clemens, *Mark Twain's Letters to Publishers*, edited by Hamlin Hill (Berkeley: University of California Press, 1967);
M. E. Grenander, "Ambrose Bierce and *In the Midst of Life*," *Book Collector*, 20 (Autumn 1971): 321-333;
Michael S. Howard, *Jonathan Cape, Publisher* (London: Cape, 1971);
J. W. Lambert and Michael Ratcliffe, *The Bodley Head 1887-1987* (London: Bodley Head, 1987);
David M. Low, ed., *A Century of Writers 1855-1955* (Oxford University Press, 1957);
George Sims, *My Life: Sixty Years Recollection of Bohemian London* (London: Chatto & Windus, 1917);
Robert Louis Stevenson, *Letters*, 3 volumes, edited by Sidney Colvin (New York: Scribners, 1911);
George R. Stewart, Jr., *Bret Harte: Argonaut and Exile* (Boston: Houghton Mifflin, 1931);
Algernon Charles Swinburne, *The Swinburne Letters*, 6 volumes, edited by Cecil Y. Lang, (New Haven: Yale University Press, 1959);
Oliver Warner, *Chatto and Windus: A Brief Account of the Firm's Origin, History and Development* (London: Chatto & Windus, 1973);
Leonard Woolf, *The Journey Not the Arrival Matters: An Autobiography of the Years 1939-1969* (London: Hogarth, 1969; New York: Harcourt, Brace & World, 1970).

*—Beverly Schneller*

# E. Churton and Company

## (London: 1834-1852)

In 1834 Edward Churton, junior partner in the firm of Bull and Churton, succeeded to the entire business and began publishing under his own imprint from 26 Holles Street, Cavendish Square, London.

Churton's early lists were miscellaneous in character, with some emphasis on travel accounts, biographies of Continental politicians, and descriptions of foreign countries. Publishing peaked in 1835 with twenty-eight new books; subsequent annual lists were considerably smaller, usually averaging around fifteen new titles. At the same address Churton conducted the British and Foreign Public Library until at least the mid 1840s. The titles carried by the library reflect Churton's interest in works by Continental writers.

Novels published by the firm to 1840 include the popular American writer Catharine Maria Sedgwick's *The Linwoods; or, "Sixty Years Since" in America* (1835), which achieved considerable success. *The Coquette and Other Tales*, a collection of stories by Caroline Norton, who was better known as a poet and as an agitator for woman's rights, was also on the 1835 list; the firm published her *Tales and Sketches* in 1850. She also edited one of the firm's periodicals, the *Court Magazine and la Belle Assemblée* (1832-1848), which featured fashionable fiction, biographies of titled women, and colored fashion plates. She also edited the *English Annual* (1834-1838), which was composed largely of selections from the magazine; contributors included Mary Shelley, Mary Russell Mitford, H. F. Chorley, Jane Porter, Mrs. Hemans, and T. Haynes Bayley. Another early success for the firm was Charles Whitehead's renowned and immensely popular *Autobiography of a Notorious Legal Functionary* (1834)—usually known as *The Autobiography of Jack Ketch*—illustrated by Kenny Meadows. In this burlesque biography of the public hangman is interpolated a remarkable tale of serious intent, "The Confession of James Wilson." Bull and Churton had published Whitehead's *Lives and Exploits of English Highwaymen, Pirates, and Robbers* (1834).

E. Churton and Company published several books by John Hobart Caunter, including his best-known work, *The Romance of History: India* (1836). Much of his 1836 novel, *The Fellow Commoner*, was originally published in a slightly different form in the *English Annual*. Caunter produced much of the contents of the handsome *Oriental Annual*, which Churton took over from his predecessor and continued until 1840.

In the 1840s E. Churton and Company published several books dealing with publishing, the craft of writing, and related matters, whose authorship is generally attributed to Churton himself. These include *The Author's Handbook* (1844), *The Book Collector's Handbook: A Modern Library Companion* (1845), and *The Handbook of Taste in Book-Binding* (1847). In 1851 Churton compiled *The Railroad Book of England*, a gazetteer describing all the towns through which the railroads passed, which was glowingly reviewed in *Bell's Messenger*.

After 1840 heraldic and genealogical works, mostly by John and John Bernard Burke, were an increasingly important part of E. Churton and Company's lists. Ranging in price from three to eighty-four shillings, the more expensive books were handsome and imposing volumes. Such a specialty proved to be prestigious rather than profitable, however, and the burden of producing these magnificently engraved and ornamented books contributed to the collapse of the business. In the last two years of its existence, the company suffered a loss of more than twelve hundred pounds on its book ventures alone.

About one-fifth of E. Churton and Company's output was published anonymously; many of these works were quickly produced pamphlets on topics of the day, including one on Louis Napoleon in 1848 (reprinted in 1851), one on the Great Exhibition in 1851, and one providing advice on avoiding cholera during the epidemic of 1848. Churton himself had a low opinion of such productions, despite their profitability, contemptuously referring to them as "scissors and paste" compilations of newspaper accounts.

In 1848 David Wemyss Jobson, an obscure writer who had produced the pamphlet on Louis Napoleon, accused the company of withholding a small payment due him. E. Churton and Company denied the charge, and the case went to

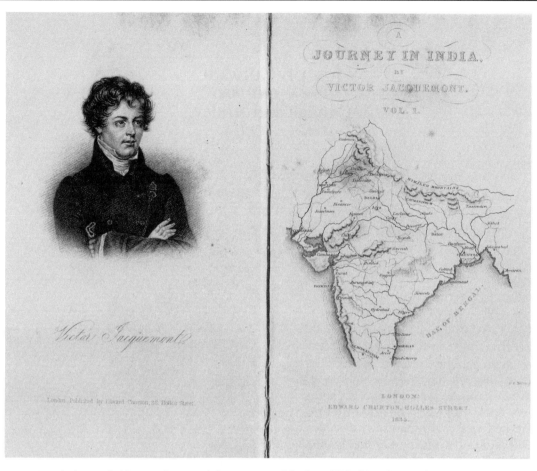

*Frontispiece and title page for one of the many travel books published by Churton during the 1830s*

court. There Jobson alleged that the proprietor was in league with John Bernard Burke in fabricating royal pedigrees, which were then sold at five guineas per lineage. There is no evidence that there was any basis for this charge. But since Churton and Company had published the Burkes' genealogical works and because the Burkes had edited a periodical, the *Patrician* (1846-1848), for the firm, the rumor gained some credence in the book trade and hurt the company's credibility at a time when any loss of confidence would produce material damage.

Neither Churton nor the firm ever fully recovered from the loss of reputation suffered in 1848. E. Churton and Company had long been known in the trade as a solid although old-fashioned establishment, and it was especially known for dealing straightforwardly and honorably with its authors. The company's respectability was its greatest asset, and the events of 1848, by distracting and dispiriting the proprietor at a cru-

cial juncture in the firm's fortunes, contributed to its bankruptcy three years later.

In 1851 the firm declared itself insolvent, due in part to large debts to its printer. With debts of twenty-one thousand pounds and assets, including property, of thirteen thousand pounds, the firm as it had been constituted was wound up in February 1852, although a few books were published under the Churton imprint from 15 Hanover Street in the early 1850s. As part of the bankruptcy proceedings, one hundred thousand volumes were sold at auction. Churton emigrated to New Zealand, and he died at Wanganui (the firm had published a book about this locality in 1845) at age seventy-five in 1885.

**Reference:**

Edward Marston, *After Work: Fragments From the Workshop of An Old Publisher* (London: Sampson Low, Marston, 1907).

*—S. D. Mumm*

# Joseph Cundall
*(London: 1841-1852)*
## Cundall and Addey
*(London: 1849-1852)*

Joseph Cundall was a commercial publisher in London from 1841 until he went bankrupt in 1849. He then became what in modern terms would be called a free-lance editor and book designer; in addition, he was a pioneer photographer. Every book with which he is known to have been associated was of distinguished design, at a time when that kind of quality was highly uncommon.

Cundall may have been a descendant of Henry Condell or Cundell, the actor and friend of Shakespeare who coedited the First Folio of Shakespeare's plays in 1623. Born in Norwich on 22 September 1818, he had some training as a printer and came to London at the age of sixteen to work for the well-known publisher and bookseller Charles Tilt. By the time Cundall was twenty-three he had written two books, under the pseudonym Stephen Percy, which Tilt published: *Tales of the Kings of England* (1840) and *Robin Hood and His Merry Foresters* (1841). In 1841 Cundall became the successor to N. Hailes at the Juvenile Library, a publisher of children's books at 12 Old Bond Street. Soon after that he met Henry Cole, a civil servant who had ambitious ideas for the improvement of books for children and who later was one of the creators of the Great Exhibition of 1851. Cole's publishing ideas were realized in the Home Treasury series of booklets, which he edited under the name Felix Summerly. The booklets were published by Cundall and printed by Charles Whittingham, who was at that time the most typographically skillful printer in England and probably in the world. These Home Treasury booklets have some claim to be called the

*Joseph Cundall*

most finely designed children's booklets ever produced. Their page size was about 6 1/2 by 4 3/4 inches. The covers displayed elegant nonpictorial designs, sometimes derived from Hans Holbein or Albrecht Dürer, printed in gold and silver on blue, orange, or emerald-green paper. The illustrations inside were by distinguished artists, at first hand-colored and then, as the series progressed, color-printed, at that time an important innovation. The series included some toys of an educational nature: *Tessellated Pastime* (1843), a box of variously colored tesserae with a book of patterns "purposed to cultivate correct taste in Ornament"; *Box of Terra-Cotta Bricks* (1845), each brick being one-eighth the size of the Common Brick, with a booklet, *Architectural Pastime*; and *Colour Box for Little Painters* (date unknown).

In 1844-1845 Cundall published Hazlitt's Holiday Library, three illustrated, cloth-bound books for children edited by William Hazlitt; the Myrtle Story Books, written by Mrs. Harriet Myrtle; Standard Story Books, which included a fine edition of Daniel Defoe's *The Life and Adventures of Robinson Crusoe of York, Mariner* (1845) with six hand-colored illustrations after T. Stothard and printed by Whittingham; and Oliver Goldsmith's *The Diverting History of John Gilpin* (1845), a landscape book with what are probably the first published illustrations by John Leighton, who was then in his early twenties.

All of Cundall's books had a strong visual component; he was not a plain "literary" publisher. In 1844 he published *The Passion of Our Lord Jesus Christ*, edited by Cole and illustrated with stereotypes made from Dürer's original woodblocks, thirty-five of which had been bought by the British Museum in 1839. Austin Dobson says in his *Little Passion of Albert Dürer* (1894) that to the stereotype copies (with permission from the trustees of the museum) "new borders were added, the worm-holes were cleverly stopped, and the injured portions were reengraved with great care by that accomplished xylographer, Mr. Charles Thurston Thompson." Thompson also reengraved the two missing subjects—number 8, "Christ parting from His Mother," and the vignette on the title page. It was altogether a remarkable publishing achievement.

This work was followed by three "illuminated" books, religious texts illustrated in chromolithography by contemporary artists: *A Booke of Christmas Carols* (1845), *The Creed, The Lord's Prayer and the Ten Commandments* (1848), and *Words of Truth and Wisdom* (1848). A feature of these books was that Cundall experimented with

highly elaborate and decorative styles of binding, using color-printed paper, flock papers with gold thread, and crimson leather blocked in gold and blind (that is, blocked without ink). Probably not unconnected with this lavishness is the fact that around 1849 Cundall went bankrupt. He was a brilliant producer of books but not equally successful at selling them.

In 1849 appeared *Songs, Madrigals and Sonnets*, the first book produced by Cundall with another publisher's imprint, that of Longman, Brown, Green and Company. It is an anthology of poems selected by Cundall, with sixty-four pages printed in color from wood. The color printing was shared by two firms of printers, Whittingham and Gregory, Collins and Reynolds. Longman's ledgers for this book have survived (most were destroyed during World War II) and show that by June 1850 only 250 copies had been sold: the rest were remaindered to H. G. Bohn. This commercial flop is now regarded as one of the treasures of Victorian art publishing.

In 1849 Cundall entered into partnership with H. M. Addey, a mysterious figure about whom nothing is known beyond the few books which appeared with the imprint of either Cundall and Addey or Addey and Company. The Cundall-Addey partnership seems to have ended in 1852.

After 1852, then, Cundall was no longer a publisher in his own right. He continued as editor, art editor, and producer for other publishers, at least eighteen of whom can be identified. One of his most important associations was with the firm of Sampson Low, for whom he produced Sampson Low's Illustrated Present Books. This was an elegant series of at least eleven titles, some with the imprint "Published for Joseph Cundall by Sampson Low & Son." Others carry Cundall's monogram on the title page or verso, although the imprint is of Sampson Low alone. It can be assumed that these books were totally conceived by Cundall but that he could not afford to finance them; he would have taken his proposals to the publisher and, if they were accepted, would have been paid to produce them—what today is called "packaging." But Cundall continued, from time to time, to publish over his own name. How these books were financed and distributed is not known, although some may have been subsidized by their authors. In 1852 Cundall had an office at 168 New Bond Street and became increasingly involved in photography. In the 1850s his photographic business traded as Cundall,

Howlett and Company (his partner, Robert Howlett, took the famous photograph of I. K. Brunel chewing his cigar in front of the launching chains of the *Great Eastern* and the photograph from which W. P. Frith painted *Derby Day*); then as Cundall, Howlett and Downes; then Cundall, Downes and Company; and by 1866 as Cundall and Fleming. Cundall, Downes and Company were appointed Photographers to the Queen and had studios in Kensington and three other towns. In 1856 the queen instructed Cundall and Howlett to take photographs at Woolwich of soldiers newly returned from the Crimean War. Some memorable images of clay-pipe-smoking Highlanders were taken by Cundall himself.

Although Cundall seems to have been overoptimistic as a businessman, many of the books he planned and designed were successful and were reprinted many times: for example, *Sabbath Bells Chimed by the Poets* (1856), the first book with illustrations (by Birket Foster) printed in full color by Edmund Evans; and *A Book of Favourite Modern Ballads* (1860), also printed by Evans. In the first edition of *A Book of Favourite Modern Ballads* the illustrations, by various artists, were printed in black and a tint, and decorations by Albert Warren were printed in gold on every page; in later editions all the illustrations were printed from wood in six or eight colors.

In 1862 Cundall was appointed superintendent of the *Illustrated Catalogue* of the International Exhibition held that year in London. Published in four volumes totaling approximately three thousand pages, the work required five printers in England, with contributions by two others and also by the Imperial Printing-Office in Vienna and the Printer to the Court of Prussia. In 1866 Cundall was appointed to a post in the South Kensington Museum (now the Victoria and Albert), where he was involved in some of the earliest systematic photographing of works of art. In 1871 he was sent to Bayeux, France, to obtain permission to make the first full-sized photographic reproduction of the Bayeux Tapestry. He was successful in his mission, and the photographer E. Dossetter completed the project the following year. The negatives, twelve inches by twelve inches, and a set of prints colored by hand by students of the Art School (now the Royal College of Art) are still in the Victoria and Albert Museum.

Cundall continued writing and editing in his later years. He was responsible for a series of books which were among the first to be illustrated by photographs, mostly taken by his own firm; the photographs had to be pasted down on the pages, since photographic printing plates did not become commercially feasible until the 1880s.

Cundall seems to have been a gentle and modest man, whose achievement, perhaps because so much of it was "behind the scenes," went largely unrecognized for a long time. He died on 10 January 1895, survived by his second wife and six of the seven children of his first marriage.

**References:**
Austin Dobson, *Little Passion of Albert Dürer* (London: Bell, 1894);

Ruari McLean, *Joseph Cundall: A Victorian Publisher* (Pinner, U.K.: Private Libraries Association, 1976).

*—Ruari McLean*

# Daniel Press

*(Frome: 1845-1856; Oxford: 1874-1919)*

The work of the Daniel Press was so clearly the expression of one man that it has been called a personal press rather than a private press. Although its publications were known to only a small circle until after the mid 1890s, when the work of the Kelmscott Press brought attention to private press publications in general, the Daniel Press is an important link between earlier printing and the aesthetics that William Morris and the private press movement sought to revive.

Charles Henry Olive Daniel, known as Henry, was born on 30 September 1836 at Wareham, Dorset, but grew up at the Frome, Somerset, where his father was vicar of Trinity Church. He began to print in 1845, a few months after his ninth birthday, using type from the one font at his disposal, inking it with his thumb, and making the impression on paper by hand with the help of his younger brother George. By the following year their father had provided a small press, probably one of Cowper's Parlour Printing Presses, sold by Holtzapffel and Company, London, in 1846 for one pound, fourteen shillings plain and two pounds, two shillings "japanned and finished in the best manner."

In July 1850 the family acquired a miniature Albion press, capable of fine work. In all, Henry, George, and two younger brothers, W. E. and W. N. A. Daniel, are known to have printed 11 books or pamphlets and about 520 minor pieces at Frome. The minor pieces consisted of single-sheet items, mostly parish activities notices, programs, and invitations, as well as more per-

*Charles Henry Olive Daniel, in 1904 (unfinished portrait by C. Furse; Worcester College)*

sonal items such as bookplates. Henry Daniel's 1852 printing of *Sir Richard's Daughter: A Christmas Tale of the Olden Time*, by W. C. Cruttwell, is quite similar to the later Daniel Press books, being small and square, with large margins and blue paper wrappers. Even in these early years his typographic style was similar to that of the Tudor printers—especially to editions of Tudor poetry, such as the first edition of Edmund Spenser's *Amoretti and Epithalamion*, printed by Peter Short for William Ponsonby in 1595. The most substantial publication of this early period was the 108-page *Sonnets* (1856) by C. J. Cruttwell, an uncle of the printers.

In 1854 Henry Daniel entered Worcester College, Oxford; he graduated in 1858. From 1859 until 1863 he was classical lecturer at King's College, London. Returning to Oxford in 1863, Daniel took a fellowship at Worcester College. In 1874, returning from a visit to Frome, he brought the miniature Albion and type to Oxford. The first production of what can be considered the second phase of the press was an eighty-two-page pamphlet, *Notes from a Catalog of Pamphlets in Worcester College Library*. Daniel printed twenty-five copies and distributed them to friends toward the end of the year. Unsatisfied with this production, he began a continuation of the project using an improved layout but soon abandoned it.

Daniel found a solution to his typographical problems in 1876 with the help of Professor Bartholomew Price, secretary to the Delegates of the Oxford University Press, who arranged for Daniel to buy some Fell type. This type was made from the punches and matrices that had been purchased in 1666 by Dr. John Fell, Bishop of Oxford, for the Sheldonian Press (later the Clarendon or Oxford University Press). The Fell types were hardly ever used in the eighteenth century and by the 1870s were virtually forgotten. Daniel used the Fell types for every subsequent production of his press.

The first use of the Fell types at the Daniel Press was in 1876, when Daniel printed fifty copies of *A New Sermon of the Newest Fashion*, an anonymous satire written about 1643. For this book he used the Fell small pica roman that was to become his favorite type. In addition, Daniel used the Fell small pica italic, an English black letter, and a double pica italic, as well as type ornaments from the original Fell purchase or from even older matrixes owned by the university. After 1877 Daniel used handmade papers, including those of Van Gelder, Whatman, and Alton Mill.

In 1878 Daniel married his cousin, Emily Olive, and moved from his college rooms to Worcester House in Worcester Street. The press was not used again until 1880, when Daniel printed an edition of Erasmus's *Colloquia* that was described by Walter Pater as "the most exquisite specimen of printing that I have ever seen." The most celebrated of all the Daniel Press books appeared in October of the following year: *The Garland of Rachel*, a compilation of poems written by friends of the Daniels in honor of the first birthday of their daughter, Rachel. The eighteen contributors included Robert Bridges, Charles Lutwidge Dodgson (signed "Lewis Carroll"), Austin Dobson, Edmund Gosse, Andrew Lang, and Daniel himself. Only thirty-six copies were printed, with one for each contributor bound in vellum over beveled boards with gold stamping. In addition to handsome use of the Fell types, the volume also contained ornamental red initial letters drawn by Mrs. Daniel and two ornamental bands, designed and engraved on wood by Alfred Parsons. It also contained the first appearance of the press's device, representing Daniel in the lion's den, designed by Parsons and Edwin Austin Abbey.

During the winter of 1881-1882 Daniel purchased a full-size "Hopkinson's Improved" Albion press, made by John and Jeremiah Barrett in 1835. The first work printed on this press was his *Hymni ecclesiae* (1882). It was followed by an Elizabethan translation of Theocritus's *Six Jdillia* (1883), printed in 100 copies. This was the first Daniel Press book to be offered for sale—for twelve shillings—and the first for which a prospectus was issued. From then until 1903 the press produced 52 books and at least 145 minor pieces. Among these were many first editions of Robert Bridges's poetry, including *Prometheus the Firegiver* (1883), printed in 100 copies and sold for ten shillings, and five books of his *Shorter Poems* (1893-1894), printed in 150 copies and offered as one volume for twenty-five shillings. As a volume, the *Shorter Poems* constitute the most substantial publication of the Daniel Press.

As with the early Daniel Press, the Oxford Daniel Press was a family affair, and many items were printed for local occasions or causes. In 1885, shortly after Rachel's fifth birthday, there appeared an edition of twelve of William Blake's *Songs*, "edited and printed" by Rachel and her younger sister, Ruth, and sent to twenty-eight of their friends for Christmas. In 1889, at age eight, Rachel printed about twelve copies of Blake's *The Lamb* on her own, and helped with many of the other works of the press. In 1891 the press published 100 copies of a small book of Robert

Herrick's poems, *Herrick, His Flowers*, to benefit St. Thomas's Orphanage. A short doggerel poem was set as a kind of prospectus, using the formal black letter of the Fell type. Presumably written by Dr. Daniel, it runs in part: " . . . To make an end / Buy Herricks page / And so be-friend / The Orphanage / You must lay down / To fill our till / A good Half-crown / Or more at will." A proof copy of this poem exits with an extra verse: "You munch Your lunch We work Like Turk." As Colin Franklin has pointed out, this verse must have been added by the Misses Daniel and left for their father to find in proofreading. In 1894 Mrs. Daniel printed 200 copies of John Milton's *Ode on the Morning of Christ's Nativity*, and sold half of the run for two shillings, sixpence to benefit St. Thomas's Orphanage; the other half sold for five shillings. In addition to drawing initial letters in many of the press's books, Mrs. Daniel also bound some of them, generally in limp vellum. For example, *The Muses Gardin for Delights or The Fift Booke of Ayres, Onely for the Lute, the Base-Vyoll and the Voice, Composed by Robert Jones* (1901), printed in 130 copies, was available in wrappers for ten shillings or "bound by Mrs. Daniel in limp Classic Vellum with leather ties" for a pound.

Daniel printed the work of his friends, as well as texts from the Tudor period. In addition to that of Bridges, he printed poetry by Laurence Binyon, F. W. Bourdillion, Sara Coleridge, Richard Watson Dixon, Thomas Herbert Warren, and Margaret L. Woods, all young, unestablished poets of the day. In many cases, their works first appeared in Daniel Press publications. When selecting earlier material, Daniel often chose texts that were known to exist in only one copy. *A New Sermon of the Newest Fashion* was printed from a seventeenth-century manuscript owned by the Worcester College Library; *Sixe Jdillia* had been printed in Oxford in 1588, but the only known copy was owned by the Bodleian Library; and *The Muses Gardin* (1610) was also known in only one surviving printed copy, owned by Lord Ellesmere. A trade edition of 350 copies of *The Muses Gardin* was published by B. H. Blackwell later in 1901, following the appearance of the Daniel Press edition.

A pirated edition of *The Garland of Rachel* appeared in 1902, reprinted by Thomas B. Mosher of Portland, Maine. In addition to reproducing the full text, complete with engravings and device, Mosher included a long preface in which he discussed the importance of the Daniel Press. He also incorporated H. R. Plomer's account of the Daniel Press that had appeared in the *Library* for September 1900 and a checklist of fifty-one Daniel Press works owned by Henry W. Poor of New York. Mosher wrote: "Among private presses of the Nineteenth, which happily survive and bid fair to continue well into the Twentieth century, The Daniel Press of Oxford stands highest in the order of literary merit; its books are concerned with literature to a larger extent than can be safely said of the output of any other private press in England or America." This edition of 450 copies of *The Garland of Rachel*, and Mosher's subsequent reprinting of other Daniel Press books, did much to publicize the work of the press throughout the United States.

After he was elected provost of Worcester College in 1903, Daniel decided to close the press. He printed only one more work before his death, a run of 140 copies of an evening service used in the college for the 1906 Gaudy; the title page says the work was printed by "a man and the Misses Daniel." After Daniel's death, on 6 September 1919, two items that he had left unfinished in 1903 were completed, and the 1835 Albion was given to the Bodleian Library. There it was used to print *The Daniel Press: Memorials of C. H. O. Daniel with a Bibliography of the Press, 1845-1919* (1921), a quarto book set in Fell types. An edition of five hundred regular copies sold for one guinea, and sixty large-paper copies, illustrated with a few specimens of Daniel Press printings, for two guineas. It was published by Worcester College and included a memoir by Sir Herbert Warren, president of Magdalen College, and a full bibliography of the press compiled by Falconer Madan. Including the two books finished after Daniel's death, the Daniel Press at Oxford printed 58 books and 145 minor pieces such as notices, invitations, prospectuses, fragments of projected books, menus, and proofs.

The work of the Daniel Press can be seen as one of the first attempts to raise the standard of Victorian printing in England, and it also influenced American printing. In 1947 Holbrook Jackson wrote, "The restoration of design in printing . . . was inspired, not by the professional printer, but by two scholarly amateurs of printing," Henry Daniel and William Morris. Daniel's 1876 revival of the excellent seventeenth-century Fell types led to the revival of Nicholas Jenson's fifteenth-century types by Emery Walker and Morris in 1890. In December 1894 C. H. St. John Hornby began using Fell type to print the first Ashendene Press book, *The Journal of Joseph Hornby*, finished in February 1895. The Clarendon Press did not revive the Fell type until 1896, when it was used in E. G. Duff's *Early English Printing*.

**References:**

*The Daniel Press: Memorials of C. H. O. Daniel with a Bibliography of the Press, 1845-1919* (Oxford: Printed on the Daniel Press, 1921);

Colin Franklin, *The Private Presses* (London: Studio Vista, 1969), pp. 19-34;

H. R. Plomer, "Some Private Presses of the Nineteenth Century," *Library*, new series 1 (September 1900): 407-428;

Will Ransom, *Private Presses and Their Books* (New York: Bowker, 1929), pp. 61-70.

*—Jennifer B. Lee*

# John Dicks
*(London: 1848-1909)*
## John Dicks Press, Limited
*(London: 1909-1929)*

Not much is known about John Dicks, one of the most prolific publishers of cheap literature and popular periodicals in the nineteenth century, nor about the details of his publishing concern. No photograph of him seems to survive; there is no bibliography of his firm's publications. The survival in libraries of books that bear his imprint is haphazard, and his several series of cheap reprints of English classics are almost everywhere incomplete. Because of his policy of repeatedly republishing his works, the initial publication dates of many of his series are uncertain. Nonetheless, he remains one of the most important forces in the increase of cheap reading material for the masses. As his obituary indicated, his publishing concern was "a marvel in cheap and good literature."

Dicks's career and the expansion of his publishing business were initially tied up with the fortunes of G. W. M. Reynolds, whom the *Bookseller* called in 1868 the "most popular writer in England" in the nineteenth century. Early in his career Reynolds had several bankruptcies, but his association with Dicks, beginning in 1848, turned him into a wealthy man. In turn, Reynolds's novels and periodicals, which provided the bulk of Dicks's list throughout most of the mid nineteenth century, made a fortune for Dicks.

John Thomas Dicks was born in London in 1818; he entered the printing trade in 1832 and was employed at the queen's printing office and other government offices. In 1841 he became the chief assistant to P. P. Thomas, who was in the business of publishing, printing, and stereotyping in Warwick Square. In 1848 Dicks went into business with Reynolds, who had been editing the *London Journal* for George Stiff but had quarreled with Stiff. Dicks took over the publication of *Reynolds's Miscellany* and also began a new fictional series, *The Mysteries of the Court of London* (1849-1856), by Reynolds. He established his office at Wellington Street North, Strand.

For the next ten years Dicks published Reynolds's periodicals and novels. In addition to *Reynolds's Miscellany*, he was also the publisher of *Reynolds's Political Instructor* (1849-1850), the precursor of the successful *Reynolds's Weekly Newspaper*. He was the publisher of Reynolds's massive, eight-volume work *The Mysteries of the Court of London* (1849-1856) and of some thirty other works. Reynolds's wife, Susannah Reynolds, also had works published by Dicks.

In 1852, at the first reported "Annual Dinner of Persons in Mr. Reynolds's Employment," Reynolds toasted Dicks as his "managing and confidential clerk" (*Reynolds's Weekly Newspaper*, 18 July 1852); in 1857 he gave Dicks a tea service val-

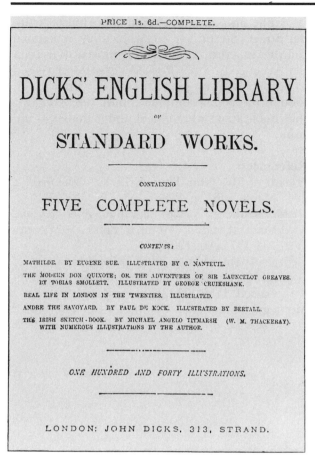

PRICE 1s. 6d.—COMPLETE.

# DICKS' ENGLISH LIBRARY

OF

## STANDARD WORKS.

CONTAINING

## FIVE COMPLETE NOVELS.

CONTENTS:

MATHILDE. BY EUGENE SUE. ILLUSTRATED BY C. NANTEUIL.

THE MODERN DON QUIXOTE; OR, THE ADVENTURES OF SIR LAUNCELOT GREAVES. BY TOBIAS SMOLLETT. ILLUSTRATED BY GEORGE CRUIKSHANK.

REAL LIFE IN LONDON IN THE 'TWENTIES. ILLUSTRATED.

ANDRE THE SAVOYARD. BY PAUL DE KOCK. ILLUSTRATED BY BERTALL.

THE IRISH SKETCH-BOOK. BY MICHAEL ANGELO TITMARSH (W. M. THACKERAY). WITH NUMEROUS ILLUSTRATIONS BY THE AUTHOR.

ONE HUNDRED AND FORTY ILLUSTRATIONS.

LONDON: JOHN DICKS, 313, STRAND.

*Cover for a volume in a series begun by the Dicks firm in 1884. By salvaging remainder sheets from unsold monthly parts of novels the firm was able to offer inexpensive fiction.*

ued at fifty-five pounds. In 1863, "after having for so many years maintained the most friendly relations as employer and employed, it was only natural that such a connection should be consolidated by a partnership," as Reynolds put it at the annual dinner. For a "splendid annuity," according to Montague Summers, Dicks bought Reynolds's copyrights and the right to use Reynolds's name.

In the 1860s Dicks's publishing house began to expand dramatically by reprinting novels, plays, "classics," and miscellaneous material rather than originating new works. Dicks moved his office to 313 Strand. According to Montague Summers, during the latter half of the century the firm was "one of the largest and busiest printing and publishing offices in England."

In 1860 Dicks began one of his most popular series of cheap reprints, Dicks's Penny Standard Plays; they were published at a rate of one play per week for more than twenty years and two a week from 1882. More than a thousand were published altogether, and many of the popu-

lar melodramas, farces, and comedies of the nineteenth century exist only in a Dicks imprint. In 1866 Dicks began Dicks's Shakespeare (individual plays for a penny, thirty-seven plays in one volume for a shilling); in 1868 Reynolds announced at the annual dinner that 150,000 copies of the penny Shakespeare had been sold. Another popular series begun at about this time was Dicks's Waverley Novels (thirty-two volumes at threepence each). Yet another was Dicks's English Classics, which included the works of Shakespeare, Lord Byron, Alexander Pope, Oliver Goldsmith, Robert Burns, John Milton, William Cowper, and William Wordsworth for one shilling in stiff paper covers or two shillings in cloth. Many of these books were illustrated, and nearly all contained a memoir and a portrait. They were printed in small type, three columns to the page.

In 1869, probably because of its reputation as a radical and sensational periodical, Dicks merged *Reynolds's Miscellany* into *Bow Bells*, a popular family magazine that he had begun in 1862 "to cultivate a taste for beauty and goodness in humanity." *Bow Bells* increased its circulation steadily; it became *Bow Bells Weekly* in 1888 and continued until 1897. Also in 1869 he began the series Dicks's English Novels (sixpence a volume), which eventually included 243 titles, including reprints of novels from writers as diverse as William Harrison Ainsworth, G. P. R. James, Charles Dickens, Edward Bulwer-Lytton, Theodore Hook, Paul de Kock, and, of course, Reynolds.

Though Dicks stopped attending the annual festivities of the "Messrs. Reynolds and Dicks Establishment" in 1870, his involvement in the various enterprises continued. He even added a few more. A new journal, *Reynolds's Builder's Trade Circular*, began in 1876 becoming *Building World* in 1877. Under that name the journal continued until 1926. The *Boy's Halfpenny Journal* started in 1878, became *Boy's Herald* in 1879, and continued for another six years.

The wide variety of other publications under the Dicks imprint included sheet music; illustrations and prints, including William Hogarth's works and Francis Wheatley's *London Cries*; chromolithographs, at sixpence, "for framing," including works by Sir Edwin Landseer and portraits of politicians. According to Summers, novels published separately included Johnson's *Rasselas*, Bernardin de Saint-Pierre's *Paul and Virginia* and John Polidori's *The Vampyre*.

Dicks retired in the late 1870s and moved to a villa, St. Valentine, in Menton, France. His two sons, Henry and John Thomas, managed the firm; apparently, however, he maintained some connection with the firm. In his autobiography (1895) George Augustus Sala recalls: "Mr. Dicks' appetite for novelettes was insatiable, and whenever I wanted cash I had only to scribble for a few hours, take the copy over to Mentone and receive from the hands of my friendly publisher a crisp ten-pound note and two louis and a half in gold. Was not this, practically speaking, alchemy?"

In 1880 the firm began the series Dicks's Standard Operas, at half a crown per volume. Dicks died on 4 February 1881. In 1884 the firm began a new series, Dicks's English Library of Standard Works. Dicks's English Library of Standard Works, New Series, began in late 1896; priced at sixpence a volume, it included reprints of works by Byron, Tom Hood, Percy Bysshe Shelley, Dickens, Charlotte Brontë, Elizabeth Cleghorn Gaskell, Sir Walter Scott, Alexandre Dumas, and Eugene Sue, as well as works by Ainsworth, Bulwer-Lytton, Arthur Conan Doyle, and Frederick Marryatt.

The firm moved to Effingham House, Arundel Street, Strand, in 1905. In 1909 it became John Dicks Press, Limited, and moved to 8 Temple Avenue. In 1929 *Reynolds's Newspaper* ceased to be published by John Dicks Press, Limited, although the paper continued until 1963. No further publications were issued under the Dicks imprint.

**References:**
"Death of Mr. John Thomas Dicks," *Bow Bells*, 2 March 1881, p. 224;
Victor Neuberg, *Popular Literature: A History and Guide* (London: Woburn Press, 1977), pp. 174-177, 186, 190;
George Augustus Sala, *The Life and Adventures of George Augustus Sala*, 2 volumes (London: Cassell, 1895), II; 367;
Montague Summers, "John Dicks, Publisher," *Times Literary Supplement*, 7 November 1942, p. 552.

*—Anne Humpherys*

# William Dugdale
## *(London: circa 1820-1868)*

The firm of William Dugdale gained notoriety in the early Victorian period as, in the words of Henry Spencer Ashbee, "one of the most prolific publishers of filthy books." Dugdale began as a radical pressman, but by 1830 he was considered a professional in the hard-core pornographic trade.

The son of a Stockport tailor and bookseller, educated in a Quaker school, Dugdale learned weaving and tailoring before migrating to London in 1818. He first worked as a freelance writer, contributing to James Watson's *Shamrock, Thistle and Rose* and doing other hackwork for various printing firms. His preface to a revised edition of Voltaire's *A Philosophical Dictionary* (1843) expresses his resentment of the professional dependence that this kind of work imposed. Early records of Dugdale's activities in London also reflect his association with radical populist organizations. The British Home Office spy records of 1818 to 1830 note his attendance at the radical Unitarian chapel of Robert Wedderburn and describe him as "a very active incendiary of Profligate and Deistical principles." He was also implicated in the 1819 Cato Street conspiracy.

Many of Dugdale's publications reflect the radical populist roots from which he sprang. Procriminal, antiestablishment sentiments are evident in his collection of songs and bawdy ballads, *The Coal Hole Companion* (several series), as well as in his periodical, the *Exquisite: A Collection of Tales, Histories and Essays . . . Amorous Adventures, Piquants Jests and Spicey Sayings* (1842-1844). A later publication, *The Nunnery Tales; or, Cruising under False Colours: A Tale of Love and Lust* (1866), reflects the anticlericalism that was a common theme in populist literature.

Not all of Dugdale's publications were an outgrowth of political radicalism, however. Dugdale prided himself on being an erotic philosopher, and he linked his pornographic publications to the libertine tradition that extended back to the ancient Greeks. He promoted a scholarly image of himself in the preface to a pirated edition of Lord Byron's *Don Juan* (1823), where he is described as a litterateur and a philosopher of love.

*Illustration from an 1844 issue of the* Exquisite, *published by William Dugdale under the pseudonym H. Smith*

Dugdale maintained this tradition of scholarship by employing some talented and well-educated hack writers, including John Davenport, an Orientalist and linguist; James Campbell, a multilingual bibliographer of erotica; and his close friend Edward Sellon, an atheist, epicurean, anthropologist, and suicide. Iain McCalman observes that although men like Dugdale may have tried to use scholarship to dignify their profession, they were nevertheless "cut off from their radical milieu when they became known as hardcore pornographers."

Dugdale may have tried to legitimize the content of his work, but his publishing methods were inescapably corrupt. He produced translated French works under new titles and pseudonyms, often lengthening the titles to add detail and spice. He was reputed to have divided texts in two, rewritten beginning and ending sections, and published both as new works. He published new editions and scores of plagiarisms of the great classic of English libertinism, John Cleland's *Memoirs of a Woman of Pleasure* (1748-1749), and was one of many publishers to reintroduce John Wilkes's obscene 1763 parody *An Essay on Woman* to nineteenth-century audiences. He published various translations and adaptations from French authors, such as the Marquis de Sade, Nicolas Edme Restif de la Bretonne, and Andréa de Nerciat, some of which were reexported to Paris. Dugdale is also responsible for one of the first publications of *Don Leon* (1866), a detailed account of the sexual aberrations of Byron's failed marriage that was mistakenly attributed to that author. Steven Marcus describes Dugdale as "a master of the racket of reprinting," though he also occasionally wrote his own material.

Dugdale came under frequent attack from the Society for the Suppression of Vice. His first publication to be declared obscene was *Yokel's Preceptor; or, More Sprees in London!* (1855), a guide through London's underworld; subsequent pornographic material covered a wide range of subjects in fiction, poetry, and prints. He evaded the police by publishing at different locations, including 23 Russell Court, Drury Lane; 3 and 44 Wych Street; and 5, 16, and 37 Holywell Street. He also adopted a series of aliases, including Turner, Smith, Henry Young, and Brown. By the time Lord Campbell's Obscene Publications Act of 1857 became law Dugdale had sustained many raids on his premises by the Vice Society and had served at least nine prison sentences. He died on 11 November 1868 in the Clerkenwell House of Correction; only then did his firm come to an end.

Dugdale's influence on England's cultural life is considerable, though difficult to measure. The radical populist literature that he published in the form of songs and miscellany, along with his various legal defenses, place him among those nineteenth-century English radicals who were involved in the struggle for press freedom. His influence on certain talented writers is easier to identify. After working for Dugdale, the Chartist author Thomas Frost turned to writing crime stories and scurrilous novels. Dugdale also probably influenced G. W. M. Reynolds while the latter was working as a hack journalist in the 1830s. Toward the end of the century Dugdale's works were republished by Edward Avery and Charles Carrington; they may have influenced A. C. Swinburne, Aubrey Beardsley, and Oscar Wilde and his set. British soldiers entertained themselves by reading Edward Sellon's *The New Lady's Tickler* (1866) as late as World War I.

**References:**

Edward J. Bristow, *Vice and Vigilance: Purity Movements in Britain since 1700* (Dublin: Gill & Macmillan, 1977), pp. 45-46;

Pisanus Fraxi (Henry Spencer Ashbee), *Index librorum prohibitorum: Being Notes Bio-Biblio-Icono-Graphical and Critical, on Curious and Uncommon Books* (London: Privately printed, 1877); republished as *The Encyclopedia of Erotic Literature* (New York: Documentary Books, 1962);

Patrick Kearny, *The Private Case: An Annotated Bibliography of the Private Case Erotica Collection in the British Library* (London: Landesman, 1981);

Steven Marcus, *The Other Victorians: A Study of Sexuality and Pornography in Mid-Nineteenth Century England* (New York: Basic Books, 1966);

Iain McCalman, *Radical Underworld: Prophets, Revolutionaries and Pornographers in London, 1795-1840* (Cambridge: Cambridge University Press, 1988);

McCalman, "Unrespectable Radicalism: Infidels and Pornography in Early Nineteenth-Century London," *Past and Present*, 104 (August 1984): 74-110;

Donald Thomas, *A Long Time Burning: The History of Literary Censorship in England* (New York: Praeger, 1969).

                                                              —*Marilyn D. Button*

# Frederick Startridge Ellis
*(London: 1868-1872; 1884-1885)*
## Ellis and White
*(London: 1872-1884)*

Frederick Startridge Ellis made his reputation first as an outstanding bookseller; next as the publisher of works by his friends William Morris, Algernon Charles Swinburne, and Dante Gabriel Rossetti; and finally as an author and editor. Born on 7 June 1830, he was the sixth son of Joseph Ellis, proprietor of the Star and Garter Hotel on Richmond Hill, London. Little attention was paid to his education; but an early love of books led him to make the most of the time he spent during his teens in Paris and Frankfurt, where he gained a knowledge of French, German, and Latin that was to be of great use in his professions. He returned in 1846 to serve an apprenticeship in London with Edward Lumley, a Chancery Lane bookseller, and afterward worked as an assistant with C. J. Stewart, a well-known bookseller in King William Street. From Stewart he gained most of his knowledge of books, and in 1860 he set up on his own as a bookseller at 33 King Street in Covent Garden.

Dealing mainly in manuscripts and rare books, he was soon recognized as a most discriminating buyer with an original turn of mind. In 1863 he was appointed to buy prints, drawings, and manuscripts for the British Museum; while acting for this institution he also built up his own stock. His great rival in the auction rooms was the bookseller Bernard Quaritch, but the two men maintained warm personal relations.

Ellis made his debut as a publisher with Morris's *The Earthly Paradise* (1868-1870). This work appeared over Ellis's imprint from his bookshop address in King Street, as did two more distinguished works: *Poems* (1870), by Rossetti, and *An Ode on the Proclamation of the French Republic* (1870), by Swinburne.

In 1872 Ellis took over premises at 29 New Bond Street, where bookselling had been carried on since 1728, and took David White into partnership. Among the clients Ellis served as bookseller were nearly all the leading collectors of his day. For Lord Ashburnham he bought a vellum copy of the Gutenberg Bible, and he also made important purchases for the earl of Crawford, Robert

*Frederick Startridge Ellis, circa 1895*

Hoe, John Jacob Astor, and Sir Thomas Brooke. Soon after moving to New Bond Street he made a journey which at that period was almost unprecedented for a London bookseller, traveling to the United States with some rare items. There he made the rounds of American bibliophiles, with such success that he returned a few years later.

Ellis made his shop an informal meeting place for several prominent later Victorians, among them William Ewart Gladstone, Alfred Tennyson, John Ruskin, and Swinburne, who had introduced Ellis to Morris in 1864. From 1874 to 1884 Ellis held jointly with Morris the lease of Kelmscott Manor in Gloucestershire, where they spent weekends. Five more works by Morris were published between 1875 and 1882 over the imprint Ellis and White. White retired in 1884.

In 1885 incipient tuberculosis forced Ellis to retire from bookselling and publishing. His rare stock was sold by Sothebys for sixteen thousand pounds, and he went to live in the milder climate of Torquay in Devonshire.

Retirement in his mid fifties gave Ellis time to tackle several ambitious literary tasks. He had already edited some important catalogues, such as that of the Henry Huth Library in five volumes (1880) and *Descriptive Catalogue of a Collection of Drawings and Etchings by Charles Meryon, Formed by the Rev. J. J. Heywood* (1880); and he had compiled *The Hours of Albert of Brandenburg* (1883), which had been published over the imprint of Ellis and White. In retirement he compiled for the Shelley Society *An Alphabetical Table of Contents to Shelley's Poetical Works* (1888). Six years went into compiling *A Lexical Concordance to the Poetical Works of P. B. Shelley: An Attempt to Classify Every Word Found Therein According to Its Signification* (1892). By the time it was published Ellis had become deeply involved in editing and reading texts for the Kelmscott Press, which Morris had set up near his London home, Kelmscott House. Twenty-two of its fifty-three publications name him as editor, reviser, or overseer of the text, and he read many other Kelmscott books in proof, including the monumental *Works of Geoffrey Chaucer* (1896). Completion of that work on 26 June 1896 almost coincided with the death of Morris on 3 October. Ellis and Sydney Cockerell acted as trustees of Morris's estate, clearing up work in hand at the time Morris died and carrying through the more important undertakings he had begun. Many scholars now consider that Kelmscott texts fall short of modern editorial standards; but they fulfilled the shared aim of Morris and Ellis in providing readable texts of broad literary appeal, rather than textual accuracy.

Ellis died on 26 February 1901. He was remembered by his contemporaries as a man of the highest integrity, tall and handsome with genial manners, warmhearted and good-natured, though inclined at times to be impetuous.

**References:**

William S. Peterson, *A Bibliography of the Kelmscott Press* (Oxford: Clarendon Press, 1984);

George Smith and Frank Benger, *The Oldest London Bookshop: A History of 200 Years* (London: Ellis, 1928).

**Papers:**

Frederick Startridge Ellis's papers are at the University of California, Los Angeles.

*—John Dreyfus*

# Eyre and Spottiswoode
### (London: 1812-1989)
# William Strahan
### (London: 1739-1812)

Until the company disappeared in the flurry of mergers and takeovers of publishing houses in the 1980s, Eyre and Spottiswoode could trace its ancestry to William Strahan in the eighteenth century. Strahan was born in 1715 in Edinburgh; after completing his apprenticeship to a printer he moved to London, was soon made a freeman of the Stationers' Company, and by 1739 had set up his own printing business. He quickly made a name for himself as a printer and acquired the most prestigious contracts, such as the printing of the first edition of Dr. Samuel Johnson's dictionary (1755). Besides his contract printing work, Strahan was often involved more directly in publication. For example, he had a share with Andrew Millar in publishing many of David Hume's works, and with Millar or other booksellers in publishing Johnson's *Rasselas* (1759) and *A Journey to the Western Islands of Scotland* (1775), Adam Smith's *Wealth of Nations* (1776), and the first volume of Edward Gibbon's *The History of the Decline and Fall of the Roman Empire* (1776).

By mid century Strahan's business was quite secure, and in 1766 he strengthened his position still further. The office of royal printer, which had descended from the earlier post of royal stationer, was not just an empty title but carried with it some lucrative privileges—for example, the exclusive right to print all acts of Parliament and the Authorised Version of the Bible. It was possible for the royal printer to sell his privileges, or a share in them, and even to buy and sell them in advance. In this way John Baskett owned the title and privileges of King's Printer for a period of thirty years, beginning on 21 January 1770, even though Baskett died in 1742. Before his death Baskett sold this thirty-year patent to John Eyre in 1724. Eyre's son Charles was not a printer, and when he inherited the patent from his father he needed a practical printer to do the work. Strahan heard of Charles Eyre's predicament, saw an opportunity for himself, and in 1766 bought a one-third share from Eyre for five thousand pounds.

*Andrew Strahan, who took over his father's business in 1785 (painting by William Owen; from Richard Austen-Leigh,* The Story of a Printing House, *1912)*

When Strahan died in 1785, his son Andrew succeeded to the business. Andrew Strahan had no children; but his sister, Margaret Penelope, had married John Spottiswoode, and their two sons, Andrew and Robert, joined their Uncle Andrew and began to learn the business. A separate company, Eyre and Spottiswoode, was founded about 1812. Andrew Strahan gave his nephews full control in 1819. Robert Spottiswoode died in 1832, leaving the business in the hands of his brother, Andrew. Andrew Spottiswoode had two sons, William and George Andrew, and when he retired in 1855 the company was divided between them. William took charge of Eyre and Spottiswoode, which included the publishing house and the office of royal printer; George Andrew Spottiswoode continued purely as a printer, without any publishing interests.

William Spottiswoode was one of the most gifted men of his day. Besides his roles as publisher and royal printer, he was an eminent mathematician and scientist whose academic work alone would have been a sufficient career for most people. He wrote and lectured frequently, particularly on mathematics and physics, was president of the mathematics section of the British Association, and was president of the Royal Society from 1878 until his death in 1883. He was also an accomplished linguist with a mastery of several European and Oriental languages.

In 1866 William and George Andrew took the initiative in establishing a school for the apprentices employed in all the family businesses. Some idea of the scale of the Spottiswoode operations can be gathered from the report that three hundred students attended in the first year.

In the 1870s Eyre and Spottiswoode was at the forefront of events. Since the 1850s there had been a dispute in the book trade concerning the sale of new books to the public at discount prices. The booksellers were divided on the issue, and, while most of the publishers were opposed to discount selling, by 1870 there was still no consensus nor any agreed plan of action. Then Eyre and Spottiswoode declared that it would no longer deal with booksellers who sold below the recommended retail price. By the turn of the century this strategy had become the main sanction behind the publishers' "terms and conditions of supply of net books," and this document formed the basis of the present-day Net Book Agreement.

William's son, William Hugh, joined the board of Eyre and Spottiswoode in 1885 and later became chairman. He died in 1915. It would have been difficult to rival his father in his range of interests, but William Hugh did not confine himself to printing and publishing. He was a director of Broadwood, a piano-manufacturing company; a director of the Royal Academy of Music; and a manager of the Royal Institution of Great Britain. Although there had been outstanding publishing successes in the early days under William and Andrew Strahan, in later generations the company began to rely on reprints from its back list. Printing was always an important and secure part of the business, and it appears to have been too easy to forgo the risks of publishing for the safety and guaranteed income of the

printing department. In time, printing became the company's main concern and ceased to be regarded as a separate business which could provide a cushion for the occasional and inevitable publishing losses.

At the beginning of the twentieth century a new company was formed: Eyre and Spottiswoode (Bible Warehouse) Limited, which included the Bible and prayer book division of Thomas Nelson. The main company was still privately owned by members of the Eyre and Spottiswoode families, but in 1908 it was decided to change to a limited liability company. In 1920 Thomas Nelson withdrew from the Bible Warehouse. Over the next few years attempts to revive publishing ended in failure.

In June 1928 Douglas Jerrold became a director and the managing editor. As an editor for Benn Brothers since 1923 he, along with Victor Gollancz, had helped that firm move from publishing trade journals, mainly for the chemical and gas industries, to become a respected trade publisher with a turnover of a quarter of a million pounds. When he moved to Eyre and Spottiswoode, Jerrold brought some of his authors with him; thus Eyre and Spottiswoode published Hugh Kingsmill's *An Anthology of Invective and Abuse* (1930) and Charles Petrie's *George Canning* (1930). Jerrold also discovered many new authors for Eyre and Spottiswoode.

By 1932 Eyre and Spottiswoode had a well-balanced catalogue with literary novels and crime stories in the fiction sections and historical, political, legal, and religious works and books about country pursuits in the nonfiction sections. This spread of subjects was to remain the general pattern of Eyre and Spottiswoode lists for many years. Two authors whose works were published by the firm in the early years were Wyndham Lewis, with *The Emperor of the West* (1932), and J. B. Morton ("Beachcomber"), with *1933 and Still Going Strong* (1932) and *Sobieski, King of Poland* (1932). Both authors remained with the firm in later years.

In 1934 Eyre and Spottiswoode published *Winter in Moscow*, Malcolm Muggeridge's account of his experiences as the Moscow correspondent for the *Manchester Guardian*, which contained his critical views on Russian communism. The book became notorious and antagonized many of Muggeridge's left-wing friends. It was to have been followed in the same year by *Picture Palace*, which, although a work of fiction, was obviously based on incidents involving the *Manchester Guard-*

*Andrew Spottiswoode, who gained full control of Eyre and Spottiswoode in 1832 (painting by Thomas Phillips, R.A.; from Richard Austen-Leigh,* The Story of a Printing House, *1912)*

*ian* when Muggeridge was working for the paper between 1930 and 1932. *Picture Palace* had been printed and bound, and review copies had been dispatched, when it was learned that the *Manchester Guardian* had applied for an injunction and was prepared to sue for libel. There was an out-of-court settlement, the book was withdrawn, and all stocks at Eyre and Spottiswoode were destroyed. The only copies to survive were the few which had been sent out for review. Extracts appeared in the *New Statesman* in 1972, but it was not until 1987 that the full text was published by Weidenfeld and Nicolson.

During this time Jerrold was keeping himself at the center of the world of letters in other ways besides his work at Eyre and Spottiswoode: he founded the *English Review* in 1930 and edited it until 1936. The two occupations complemented each other as new authors came to the publisher via the *English Review*. (Jerrold edited the periodical again, under the title *New English Review*, from 1945 to 1950.)

By the outbreak of World War II the company had clearly reestablished itself as an important publisher. Then, on the night of 29 Decem-

ber 1940, its office at 6 Middle New Street was destroyed in a German air raid. Eyre and Spottiswoode was not the only casualty; the raid wiped out a large part of the London publishing industry. Ever since the year 1500 publishing had been concentrated around St. Paul's Cathedral, and since the nineteenth century Paternoster Row and the surrounding streets had been where the most important publishers had established themselves. Paternoster Row almost disappeared in the bombing. Eyre and Spottiswoode, however, survived better than most, partly because it owned several properties in London that had been acquired gradually over its long history, but mainly because of the prompt action of Douglas Jerrold. He arrived for work by taxi on the morning of 30 December, saw his office in flames, drove straight to the office of another publisher, Thornton Butterworth, and offered the managing director ten thousand pounds for the business. The offer was accepted on the spot. This new base enabled Eyre and Spottiswoode to continue trading almost without a break and to recover from its losses quickly.

Jerrold was a Roman Catholic convert; the Crosthwaite-Eyres, descendants of John Eyre, and other directors of the firm were also Catholic. In 1939 Jerrold and an organization known as the Eyre Trust bought the Catholic publishing firm of Burns, Oates and Company, which had been founded in the 1830s. Burns, Oates was publisher to the Holy See and had always been committed to Catholic publishing, and when Jerrold became chairman this policy was unchanged. The firm's output was almost completely nonfiction works on Catholic doctrine, history, or biography. In 1943 Jerrold and Christopher Hollis formed Hollis and Carter as a subsidiary of Burns, Oates. The Hollis and Carter publications were similar to those of Burns, Oates, with more emphasis on contemporary Catholic issues and about half the list devoted to children's literature. Several Eyre and Spottiswoode authors became Hollis and Carter authors—for example, Denys James Watkins-Pitchford (B. B.) with *Brendon Chase* (1944); Petrie, with *Diplomatic History, 1713-1933* (1946); and Morton, with *Here and Now* (1947). In 1948 Jerrold and the Eyre Trust sold their interest in Burns, Oates and Hollis and Carter to the Burns family.

The firm of E. and F. Spon was acquired by Eyre and Spottiswoode in 1944. Founded in 1834, E. and F. Spon had always specialized in works on science and technology, fields which had not been represented in Eyre and Spottiswoode lists. The Spon imprint remained separate, and the organization was managed independently.

Perhaps the most illustrious name connected with Eyre and Spottiswoode was Graham Greene, another Roman Catholic convert, who was a codirector with Jerrold from 1944 to 1948. Muggeridge described the two men at this time in his *The Infernal Grove* (1973): "At the Eyre and Spottiswoode office in Bedford Street, he [Graham Greene] sat in a room with Douglas Jerrold.... It would be difficult to imagine two more strangely assorted human beings; both Catholic converts, certainly, but Jerrold induced thereby to move to the extreme Right, as a supporter of General Franco, and Greene to move ever further Leftwards as a fervent advocate of Catholic-Marxist dialogue." It was Greene's idea to bring out a collected English translation of François Mauriac's works (1946-1970), and he persuaded Muggeridge to act as mediator in the negotiations. Mauriac and his publishers agreed, and in later years Mauriac's English translations continued to be published by Eyre and Spottiswoode.

The inclusion of a French author in the catalogue was not out of character, because from the earliest years under Jerrold the works of non-British authors had been published. For example, the Indian novelist R. K. Narayan appeared with *The English Teacher* (1945) and *Mr. Sampath* (1949). Furthermore, an occasional British author who dealt with life outside the capital was included. For example, Welshman Emyr Humphreys was published regularly from 1946, as was Sid Chaplin from the early 1960s. In the 1960s it became commonplace for a publisher to bring out "regional" novels about working-class life or life in a British colony on the point of independence, but in the 1940s such works were rare.

Americans, however, formed the largest group of overseas representatives. Almost as soon as Jerrold arrived at Eyre and Spottiswoode he began to publish the work of Frances Parkinson Keyes (yet another Roman Catholic convert), beginning with *Christian Marlowe's Daughter* (1934), published the previous year in the United States as *Senator Marlowe's Daughter*. *Honor Bright* appeared in 1936, and it was not long before Keyes was having new titles published simultaneously in the United States and by Eyre and Spottiswoode in Britain. Works by Robert Penn Warren also made regular appearances in the

list, with *Night Rider* (1940) and *At Heaven's Gate* (1943) being the earliest. American authors continued to be a strong feature in the lists over the years.

After World War II the important new contributors included Mervyn Peake, especially his *Titus Groan* (1946), *Gormenghast* (1950), and *Titus Alone* (1959) and Ivy Compton-Burnett, with *A Family and a Fortune* (1959). Antonia White, Anthony West, and Paul Scott also began to appear at this time. The catalogue still contained a section of books about the countryside, with new works by A. G. Street in evidence, although history continued to be the main nonfiction subject. There were also publications which presented original historical evidence, including *The Private Papers of Douglas Haig, 1914-1919* (1952), edited by Robert Black. The catalogue had always included small sections for poetry, in which at this time John Heath Stubbs began to be featured, and for children's books, in which for many years the work of B. B.—including *The Little Grey Men* (1942) and *Down the Bright Stream* (1948)—had appeared. Peake, too, had some titles in the children's list, including *Letters from a Lost Uncle* (1948).

Maurice Temple Smith, an editor who had moved from the subsidiary E. and F. Spon, was responsible for a wide range of successful biographies and novels. It was he who added John Braine to the catalogue, beginning with *Room at the Top*, the first regional novel to receive worldwide recognition, in 1957. Temple Smith left to form his own publishing company in the late 1960s.

In May 1957 negotiations were completed for a merger of Eyre and Spottiswoode, Methuen, and Chapman and Hall. In June of the following year a parent company, Associated Book Publishers, was formed, within which the three original imprints operated separately except that the production and marketing departments were centralized. Charles Friend, who had been with Eyre and Spottiswoode almost as long as Jerrold, became sales director of Associated Book Publishers. In 1959 Jerrold retired, and Sir Oliver Crosthwaite-Eyre became chairman of Eyre and Spottiswoode.

An incident occurred in 1961 which had its origins in the 1760s, when William Strahan became a shareholder in the office of King's Printer. The Strahans and the Spottiswoodes had kept their hold on the office and its privileges: the original arrangement had expired in 1799 but had been renewed for thirty years and renewed again in 1830 for a further thirty years. In 1860 the House of Commons had allowed the patent to remain with Eyre and Spottiswoode "during her Majesty's will and pleasure." There had been only one further renewal, in 1901, after the death of Queen Victoria. In 1961 a new translation of the Bible, the New English Bible, was being prepared, and the New Testament was ready. The combined presses of Oxford and Cambridge universities had obtained the copyright from a committee of the churches, and publication was about to begin. At this point Eyre and Spottiswoode, by virtue of its position as Queen's Printer and the accompanying right to print Bibles, claimed that it should be allowed to join with the Oxford and Cambridge university presses in the publication. To bring matters to a head, Eyre and Spottiswoode published the Gospel of St. John from the new translation. The two universities immediately served a writ for infringement of copyright and applied for an injunction to prevent Eyre and Spottiswoode from publishing anything further from the new translation. In July 1963 the judgment went against Eyre and Spottiswoode: it was decided that the privilege of the Queen's Printer to print Bibles extended only to the Authorised Version.

The list of important American authors continued to grow; new works included Bernard Malamud's *The Assistant* (1959) and *The Magic Barrel* (1960), Thomas Berger's *Reinhart in Love* (1963), and J. P. Donleavy's *The Beastly Beatitudes of Balthazar B* (1969). Another non-British author was the Australian Patrick White, whose *Aunt's Story* appeared in 1958. Poetry was represented by Iain Crichton Smith's *Thistles and Roses* (1961) and John Lehmann's *Collected Poems, 1930-1963* (1963). A significant critical work, Martin Esslin's *Theatre of the Absurd*, was published in 1962. An outstanding work in history was Hugh Thomas's *The Spanish Civil War* (1961).

In 1968 it was decided to rearrange the subject coverage of the three imprints that made up Associated Book Publishers. All the scientific titles moved to Chapman and Hall, Methuen took the remaining academic titles, and Eyre and Spottiswoode became the general publisher. The new general publishing division was known as Methuen, Eyre and Spottiswoode until 1972, when its name was changed to Eyre Methuen. In 1982 the name of the general publishing division became simply Methuen. Associated Book Publishers was sold to International Thomson in 1987

and then to Octopus in January 1988. The Eyre and Spottiswoode name had been retained as the imprint for a small number of theological works and for the office of Queen's Printer, but it disappeared at the end of 1989 when these interests were sold to Cambridge University Press.

From the days of William Strahan until the bombing in 1940 the company had owned premises in New Street near St. Paul's Cathedral, but from the late nineteenth century the publishing office had a bewildering array of addresses. From 1898 to 1929 the main office was on East Harding Street; from 1903 to 1906 there were additional offices at 33 Paternoster Row and 13 Paternoster Square, from 1906 to 1922 at 12 and 13 Paternoster Square, from 1910 to 1922 at 2 Victoria Street, and from 1922 to 1929 at 27 Victoria Street. From 1930 to 1934 the main office was at 6 Great New Street, from 1934 to 1940 at 6 Middle New Street (merely a street name change); from 1936 to 1940 additional offices were located at 14-16 Bedford Street. In 1940, after the blitz, a temporary office was occupied at 98-99 Fetter Lane. From 1940 to 1952 the firm was at 14-16 Bedford Street, from 1952 to 1958 at 15 Bedford Street, from 1958 to 1966 at 22 Henrietta Street, from 1966 to 1967 at 167 Fleet Street, and after 1967 at 11 New Fetter Lane.

Eyre and Spottiswoode had a long, varied, and influential history. The company was often at the center of affairs in the book trade, such as the move to educate apprentices and the events leading to the Net Book Agreement in the nineteenth century. The company was also a leader on at least two other occasions. The first was at the beginning, under William Strahan, when publishing as a separate occupation was still struggling to break away from bookselling. Strahan's friendships with Johnson, Hume, Gibbon, Benjamin Franklin, and his other authors was not a one-way affair; these friends actively sought his advice, and Strahan undoubtedly helped to shape their work. The second period of leadership was in the mid twentieth century, when British insularity was opened up to writing from the Commonwealth, from America, and from British authors outside the literary establishment.

**References:**

R. A. Austen-Leigh, *The Story of a Printing House*, second edition (London: Eyre & Spottiswoode, 1912);

J. A. Cochrane, *Dr. Johnson's Printer: The Life of William Strahan* (London: Routledge & Kegan Paul, 1964);

Maureen Duffy, *A Thousand Capricious Chances: A History of the Methuen List 1889-1989* (London: Methuen, 1989);

Douglas Jerrold, *Georgian Adventure* (London: Collins, 1937);

Malcolm Muggeridge, *The Infernal Grove*, volume 2 of *Chronicles of Wasted Time* (London: Collins, 1973).

**Papers:**

There is a large archive of Strahan's papers in the British Library which is available on microform.

*—John R. Turner*

# Samuel French, Limited
*(London: 1893-    )*
## T. H. Lacy
*(London: 1830-1872)*
## Samuel French
*(London: 1872-1893)*

See also the Samuel French entry in *DLB 49: American Literary Publishing Houses, 1638-1899.*

Samuel French, Limited is the oldest and largest publisher and supplier of theatrical plays in the world. Calling itself "The House for Plays," Samuel French has provided amateurs and professionals alike with scripts, performing rights, and advice in Great Britain, the United States, and many other countries around the world.

The founder of the firm was Thomas Hailes Lacy, an actor who started his theatrical career in 1828 at the Olympic Theatre in London in William Dimond's *The Foundling of the Forest* (1809), which he would republish in 1867. He opened his publishing business at 11 Wellington Street, which became No. 17 when the street numbers were changed. In the beginning he acquired titles by buying up plates from earlier publishers, such as Oxberry, Dunscombe's Acting Edition of the British Theatre, and Webster's Acting National Drama. He also became the proprietor of John Cumberland's British Theatre (399 plays in forty-eight volumes) and Cumberland's Minor Theatre (152 plays in sixteen volumes).

In 1833 an act of Parliament, the so-called Bulwer-Lytton's Act, gave the author of a play exclusive rights over any performance, provided the play had been published. This measure was a great incentive for authors to have their plays published as soon as possible and no doubt boosted Lacy's early business. The Theatre Regulation Act of 1843 put an end to the monopoly on the spoken drama in London held by the Drury Lane and Covent Garden theaters. This act caused a rapid development of smaller theaters in the 1850s and 1860s, which greatly increased the demand for plays. Lacy employed or encouraged many aspiring playwrights and may have supplied plots and characters for new works himself to keep up with the demand for original works.

Lacy left the stage in 1849 to devote himself full-time to publishing. In 1873 he began to publish Lacy's Acting Editions of Plays, which eventually ran to 1,485 pieces in ninety-nine volumes. Among the titles included in the collection were *I've Eaten My Friend, Tooth-ache* and *Wanted, 1000*

*The founder of the firm that became Samuel French, Limited*

*Milliners*, none of them dated. Lacy was the author of eight plays, including the drama *The Pickwickians* (1850) and the farce *A Silent Woman* (1851).

The history of the acting edition can be traced to the early nineteenth century, when the term was applied to a version of a play marked with stage business and directions from performances at the Theatres Royal. It was based on the prompt copy of a production and contained all the details of the setting, the handling of the props, and the movement of the actors. In its modern form, the acting edition of a script contains only the barest of stage directions, a simple plan of the sets and lights, and perhaps a list of the props.

In addition to the many plays carried by T. H. Lacy, Theatrical Bookseller, the store was also well stocked with "Shakesperiana; Theatrical Biography and Criticism; Controversial works for and against the Stage; History of Theatres, London, Irish, Scottish, and Provincial—Their Architecture and Topography; Play-bills in Great Variety: Portraits, Autographs, Costumes & Music," all "for ready money only," as described on the title page of his 1854 catalogue. Lacy also published *The Amateur's Handbook and Guide to Home*

*and Drawing Room Theatricals: How to Get Them Up and How to Act in Them. By W. J. Sorrell. To Which Is Added How to "Get Up" Theatricals in a Country House, by Captain Sock Buskin. And a Supplement Containing A List of Suitable Plays* (1869). This booklet, in updated form, was still available as late as the 1920s. As a result of the rapid growth of his business, Lacy was forced to move in 1859 to a larger building at 89, Strand.

In the same year a successful theatrical publisher from the United States named Samuel French visited London. He soon began to do business with Lacy, each acting as the other's agent across the ocean. French had begun publishing plays in 1854, and by 1856 he was advertising that he had a hundred thousand plays on hand at his premises at 151 Nassau Street in New York City. Among his titles were the first edition of George L. Aiken's *Uncle Tom's Cabin* (1858) and Dion Boucicault's *The Poor of New York* (1857). In 1872 French left the business to his son Thomas Henry French and moved to London permanently.

Lacy found himself ready to retire that same year, and with no family members interested in taking over his business, he turned it over to French. The contract, dated 19 March ety, which attempted to undercut his commission rates without providing the same level of service.

Lacy, French, and Hogg attempted to provide the most complete service available to the amateur thespian. In 1860 Lacy had published more than four hundred plates of dramatic, national, and historical costumes, which were still on sale as late as 1946. French offered paper scenery that was printed in four colors and came in sheets two yards wide, ready for mounting on canvas. There was a special high-ceilinged room in the basement of the bookshop in which scenery was displayed and sold until 1940.

Another service provided by French was theatrical makeup. In 1877 French published *How to "Make-Up": A Practical Guide*, by Haresfoot and Rouge (a pseudonym for an unknown author), which was followed by other books on the same topic. The firm sold makeup supplies until 1963, when that end of the business was transferred to Charles H. Fox.

The firm had a great advantage over other publishers because Samuel French was in London and his son Thomas Henry was in New York. The father was able to secure the American performing rights to English and Continental scripts, from which the son was able to profit in the United States. There was much transferring of scripts back and forth between New York and London in the 1890s; but the traffic soon became uneven, with Thomas Henry French ordering greater quantities of books and neglecting to pay for them. In 1893 the London branch became a limited company.

Hogg built up strong friendships with many of the firm's authors, and the company's fund of goodwill was largely based on his personal contacts. As French's health deteriorated, Hogg took on more and more of the burden of running the firm. In 1898 French died, leaving the business entirely in Hogg's hands.

In 1900 the Strand was widened, and No. 89 was torn down. Hogg moved the bookshop to 26 Southampton Street. The company's offices were next door at No. 27, which had been the home of the great actor David Garrick nearly a century earlier. The atmosphere of French's Theatre Bookshop became more that of a reading room or library than a bookstore. Members of theatrical companies could browse for as long as they wanted in quiet surroundings with ample seating and several tables. Staff members were on hand to assist and advise on any matter relating to the theater. The bookshop carried not

*Samuel French in 1851, three years before he began publishing plays in New York. He bought Lacy's business in 1871.*

1872, shows that French paid five thousand pounds for the business, with three thousand pounds payable immediately and five hundred pounds to be paid each 1 July for the next four years. On 1 August of the following year, Lacy died.

Two years after taking over Lacy's firm, French hired a young man named Wentworth Hogg as manager. Hogg compiled the first *Guide to Selecting Plays* (1882), a catalogue that gave a complete description of each play the firm controlled. Arranged according to the requirements of the company (number of male and female characters, and so forth), the guide, which sold for a shilling, proved invaluable to amateur theater groups. In the 1890s Hogg began to put more emphasis on the amateur performing-group business, while not ignoring the professionals. Hogg also collected all performing fees for playwrights whose works were published by the firm. At one point he fought with the Dramatic Authors' Soci-

*Building in the Strand where the Lacy and then the French firm remained from 1859 until 1900*

tle branch in London." Information, publishing and performing rights, and stock continued to be passed frequently across the Atlantic, but the relationship between the firms became more business-like. Under Edwards's leadership the New York firm began to publish more contemporary American plays, relying less on the European dramas and farces that had dominated both branches.

In the early 1920s Hogg retired and left his son Cyril in charge of the business. In 1936 Cyril Hogg championed authors' rights in the case of *Jennings v. Stephens*, which established that under the Copyright Act of 1911 a performance of a play is considered "public" and subject to the payment of royalties unless it is considered "domestic" in the strictest definition of the term; neither the charging of admission nor the size or nature of the audience is a consideration. The case established a basic code of practice that has protected authors' rights ever since.

By 1950 Cyril Hogg had consolidated several agencies that were ancillary to the play publishing industry: the costumers B. J. Simmons and Charles H. Fox; the armorer and jeweler Robert White; Fashion Hire, which supplied modern-day costumes; hat and cap makers, A. and L. Corne; and Stage Scenery, which rented sets to amateur theater groups. Only Charles H. Fox and Robert White are still operating, with Fox remaining the foremost outlet for makeup supplies and costume rentals in Great Britain, and White specializing in stage jewelry, armor, and replicas of the Crown Jewels.

Cyril Hogg died in 1964 and was succeeded by his son Anthony; Harold F. Dyer became managing director, after having been in charge of the company's musical plays. In 1975 Dyer retired, and the British and American firms merged once again, under the direction of Thomas R. Edwards's grandson, M. Abbott Van Nostrand, who had been chairman of Samuel French, Incorporated, since 1952.

The twentieth century brought many challenges to the play publishing business, the most significant being the introduction of television. "It really hurt for a few years, but the market came back when the novelty of tv. wore off," recalled Van Nostrand (*Variety*, 21 May 1980).

Samuel French has published the works of all the important playwrights and continues to dominate the field of stock and amateur rights licensing in the United States and Britain. The current catalogue lists nearly four thousand plays, from Shakespearean classics and Oscar Wilde's

only plays but also books on all theatrical subjects, including scenery, lighting, costumes, and makeup.

In 1902 Thomas Henry French died, and the New York end of the business was taken over by a partnership headed by Thomas R. Edwards. Though the business had become two financially independent operations, they would still refer to each other as "the New York branch" and "the lit-

*The Importance of Being Earnest* (1903) to Neil Simon's *Barefoot in the Park* (1964) and *The Odd Couple* (1965) to *Amadeus* (1980, by Peter Shatter). M. Abbott Van Nostrand remains the chairman of Samuel French, Incorporated; the managing director of Samuel French, Limited is John Laurence Hughes. In addition to New York and London, the company has offices in Hollywood, Toronto, and Sydney. Authorized agents of Samuel French, Limited work from offices in Dublin; Brookvale, Australia; Wellington, New Zealand; Valletta, Malta; Johannesburg; Singapore; Nai-robi; and Harare, Zimbabwe. Samuel French, Limited moved in 1983 from Southampton Street to 52 Fitzroy Street.

**References:**

*French's: The House for Plays* (London: Butler & Tanner, 1937);

*Truly Yours: One Hundred and Fifty Years of Publishing and Service to the Theatre* (London: French, 1980).

—*Marilouise Michel*

# Hodder and Stoughton, Limited
*(London: 1919-     )*
## Hodder and Stoughton
*(London: 1868-1919)*

Matthew Henry Hodder, who came from a Nonconformist background, served an apprenticeship with the house of Jackson and Walford, publishers to the Congregational Union; he bought a one-third share in this firm in 1861. Thomas Wilberforce Stoughton was the son of the Dissenter John Stoughton, D.D., and had received a wider education than Hodder before being apprenticed to the publisher James Nisbet and Company. When Hodder had the chance to buy out his retiring partners, Jackson and Walford, he found in Stoughton a partner with the money and reli-gious connections he sought to start a new house. The firm of Hodder and Stoughton was founded in June 1868 at 17 Paternoster Row, London.

Hodder and Stoughton's first list was announced in the *Publishers' Circular* on 1 July 1868. The five titles included *Jesus Christ: His Times, Life and Work*, second edition, by E. de Pressense; A. Raleigh's *Christianity and Modern Progress*, second edition; and C. Tischendorff's *The Origin of the Four Gospels*, translated from the German. In their first year the partners published educational books; children's stories; translations from French, German, and Swedish; and travelers' tales, including two by Hodder's brother, Edwin. Many of their titles were taken over from Jackson, Walford and Hodder: David C. and Alexander M. Bell's *Bell's Standard Elocutionist* sold more than 250,000 copies, and Ann Taylor's *Hymns for Infant Minds* had reached its forty-seventh edition when it was taken over by Hodder and Stoughton. Such established titles gave the new firm's salesmen entrée into bookshops; the salesmen included T. Fisher Unwin, who had been with Jackson and Walford and remained with Hodder and Stoughton until he founded his own house in 1882. The partners themselves regularly traveled, Hodder in the north of England and Stoughton in Scotland; on their journeys they listened to sermons and acquired such authors as Dr. Joseph Parker, the third edition of whose *Ecce Deus* the firm published in 1868.

The finances of the partnership began at equality, with each partner's capital consisting of stock valued at £1,861.9.1, lease at £356.5.0, goodwill at £950, cash £500, and cash from Jackson, Walford and Hodder of £826.7.4. In 1870 there was a profit of £1,484; but in 1871 there was a loss of £260 after the firm paid £500 in damages in a libel suit brought by George Augustus Sala. Stoughton regularly put more money into the firm and took out less cash than Hodder, so that by 1876 Hodder's capital account amounted to £4,860.14.4 and Stoughton's to £8,543.2.10. During this period the best annual profit was £2,162.

Profits came mainly from new books and reprinted titles, but the partners also published several magazines. They had taken over from Jackson, Walford and Hodder some Congregational Union journals, including the *British Quarterly Review*. They launched the *Expositor* in 1875, with the Reverend Samuel Cox as editor; this journal was aimed at Christians of Nonconformist and Episcopalian backgrounds and printed articles by biblical scholars. In the 1870s and 1880s the young partners published several substantial theological works involving high production costs for translation or for Hebrew and Greek typesetting. These works signaled their commitment to rigorous biblical scholarship but were risky publishing ventures.

The American connection was important in the early development of the house. Hodder made his first voyage to the United States in 1869 and during an energetic visit called on Charles Scribner, George Putnam, and other pub-

lishers, establishing business connections and securing orders in New York and other major eastern cities of the United States and Canada. In 1871 and 1873 he extended his American traveling, reaching west to St. Louis and south to Nashville. He traveled to America every other year until 1899.

Stoughton's influence is apparent in the staff, which was recruited from his home mission. In 1873 Cuthbert Huckvale and Joseph Apted joined the firm; each remained for more than fifty years, Huckvale in the countinghouse and Apted as confidential clerk. They brought into the firm other workers with the same strict and loyal standards and were responsible for training Stoughton's sons and Hodder's grandsons when they came into the business.

The ambitious publishing program of the house was sustained by luck as well as by successful traveling. The murder of President James A. Garfield in 1881 turned Hodder's recent purchase of William Thayer's biography of Garfield, *From Log Cabin to White House* (1881), into a bestseller which sold seventy-nine thousand copies in a year. It reached its fortieth edition in 1893.

Cox's tenure of the editorial chair of the *Expositor* was terminated in 1884 when his theological position became intolerable to the partners and to some of the subscribers. The partners were in negotiation with the Reverend William Robertson Nicoll about a new series, the Clerical Library. This young minister of the Free Church of Scotland in Kelso already had a reputation as a religious journalist and preacher, and on Cox's departure Nicoll was offered the editorship of the *Expositor*. His subsequent influence on the firm was profound. The scholarly level of contributions to the *Expositor* rose, and he proposed an ambitious series of fifty volumes of biblical criticism, *The Expositor's Bible* (1887-1896), of which he wrote the first volume and which included George Adam Smith's seminal *Isaiah* (1889). The latter achieved sales which supported the costs of the series, which ultimately ran to forty-eight volumes. Nicoll also persuaded the partners to found a new journal, the *British Weekly*, which began publication in November 1886; it reached a circulation of one hundred thousand within the decade. Nicoll included a literary section as well as religious news, and for Hodder and Stoughton the *British Weekly* was the route to the publication of fiction. The first Annie S. Swan novel was serialized in 1887. In the same year Nicoll recruited J. M. Barrie, then a journalist in

*Matthew Henry Hodder and Thomas Wilberforce Stoughton, who bought out the publishers Jackson and Walford to start their own company in June 1868*

London, to write for the periodical; his articles were published in book form by Hodder and Stoughton as *Auld Licht Idylls* (1888) and *When a Man's Single* (1888). The Scottish connection was strong in fiction as well as in theology: the firm published the work of the Kailyard writer, the Reverend John Watson, who wrote under the pseudonym Ian Maclaren and whose *Beside the Bonnie Brier Bush* (1894) and *The Days of Auld Lang Syne* (1895) each reached sales of more than one million copies.

Nicoll persuaded the partners to undertake further ventures in magazine publication: the *Bookman* was begun in 1891 and *Woman at Home*, with Swan as editor, in 1893. These successes were followed in 1895 by a general-interest magazine; it was titled *Success*, but it failed. Hodder and Stoughton did not again attempt a mass circulation magazine.

Hodder had a daughter but no sons. In 1894 J. Ernest Hodder-Williams, his eldest grandson, joined the firm; J. E. H. W., as he signed himself, came under Nicoll's tutelage. In 1896 John and Cecil Stoughton, sons of T. W. Stoughton, and Robert Percy Hodder-Williams, Hodder's second grandson, also came into the firm. In 1898

Nicoll agreed to edit the *British Weekly* for another seven years. Jane Stoddart of Kelso, who had joined the staff in 1886, was the subeditor of the magazine.

In the 1890s the theological list was strengthened by several successful works: Henry Drummond's *The Greatest Thing in the World* (1890), of which millions of copies have been sold, was added to his 1883 success, *The Natural Law in the Spiritual World*, which sold seventy thousand copies in five years; Sir George Adam Smith's *The Life of Henry Drummond* (1899) reached sales of sixteen thousand in ten months. The firm also published Smith's *Historical Geography of the Holy Land* (1894) and Sir William Ramsay's *St. Paul the Traveller and Roman Citizen* (1895). The partners' evangelical convictions were evident in the publication of missionary biographies such as *John G. Paton, Missionary to the New Hebrides: An Autobiography* (1889) and J. W. Harrison's *A. M. Mackay* (1890). Undistinguished moral tales for children gave way to tales of adventure such as those by W. H. G. Kingston. Novels for women readers in the style of Swan continued, but the fiction list acquired some zest with the publication of Ellen T. Fowler's *Concerning Isabel Carnaby* (1898), which was reviewed as the "novel of the season" and sold forty thousand copies in nine months. Hodder and Stoughton published the first book to take advantage of the queen's Diamond Jubilee: *The Personal Life of Queen Victoria* (1896), by Mrs. Sarah Tooley. Extension into the history of English literature and language, which developed from the *Bookman* and was contemporary with the establishment of university departments of English, was marred by Nicoll's entanglement with the literary forger Thomas J. Wise. Two volumes of a projected ten-volume series, Literary Anecdotes of the 19th Century, edited by Nicoll and Wise, were published in 1895 and 1896 before the series ceased—possibly because Nicoll discovered that most of the anecdotes were false. When Nicoll learned of unpublished Brontë letters which Wise supposedly could obtain, he planned a Hodder and Stoughton Brontë edition; this project also came to naught.

In the 1890s J. E. H. W. worked in the advertising department of the firm's five periodicals; he introduced the company's first typewriting machine. In 1901 he traveled to America in Hodder's place and brought back the first bestselling novel from the United States, *Mrs. Wiggs of the Cabbage Patch* (1902), by Alice Hegan Rice. In 1902 he was taken into partnership. His opportunity to direct editorial policy arose not only from his formal status but from Nicoll's turning to national politics with the *British Weekly* as his grandstand; the magazine's opposition to the 1902 Education Act had shown it to be the acknowledged voice of Nonconformity. Hodder and Stoughton was recognized as a specialist publisher of religious works, and this distinction continued in the new century with works by the Scottish theologians John Oman and James Moffatt and works from America and Europe. John Stoughton translated from the German the work of Rudolf Schmid and Adolf Deissmann. The fiction list remained conservative, constrained by the founders' abhorrence of fiction characteristic of Dissent. In 1906, however, the firm published *The Saint*, the first of three liberal-Catholic novels by Antonio Fogazzaro; *The Saint* sold more than twenty thousand copies. J. E. H. W. broke new ground with a profitable series of art books with original work by Arthur Rackham, Edmund Dulac, Hugh Thompson, and Heath Robinson.

In 1906, on J. E. H. W.'s initiative, Hodder and Stoughton entered into a joint venture with Oxford University Press (O.U.P.), neighbors at the firm's new premises in St. Paul's House, War-wick Square. J. E. H. W.'s opposite number at O.U.P. was Sir Humphrey Milford. The venture enabled O.U.P. to enter the field of popular children's books and Hodder and Stoughton to get into educational publishing. Herbert Ely and Charles James L'Estrange were appointed editors. In the end, losses on educational books exceeded profits on children's books. The two houses also undertook joint medical publications, with Dr. J. Keogh Morphy as editor and Robert E. Sare as manager. The joint ventures were housed in Falcon Square off Aldersgate Street. In the early 1900s John Stoughton left the firm; Cecil Stoughton and Robert Percy Hodder-Williams became partners in 1908. Putting into effect the sales lessons learned from O.U.P., William S. Smart expanded the export sales. In 1908 Hodder and Stoughton came to a five-year agreement for O.U.P. to represent the firm in Australia and New Zealand on a commission basis. In the same year E. A. Roker toured England and brought home 180 new accounts; in 1910 he established the first provincial sales office in Leicester. In 1908 the George H. Doran Company was founded in New York, with Hodder and Stoughton holding a one-third stake and J. E. H. W. as vice-president. The new firm became the American publisher for the British house.

In 1910, with the agreement of the senate of the University of London, Hodder and Stoughton joined with the printers Richard Clay and Sons as shareholders in a new company, University of London Press, Limited (U.L.P.). Each firm agreed to subscribe up to fifteen thousand pounds. J. E. H. W. hoped to see a scholarly press bearing the name of his alma mater; Clay would do the university's printing, and Hodder and Stoughton would build the publishing side. But in 1916 the university, dissatisfied with the charges for printing, set up an inquiry. At this time the press had a cumulative loss of twenty-eight hundred pounds. Although no fault was found, the university resumed control of its own printing, and Clay's shareholding was taken over by Hazell, Watson and Viney. An editorial board was established, consisting of Professor S. L. Loney, Ernest and Percy Hodder-Williams, and John Crowlesmith of Hazell, Watson and Viney. The first manager, F. Brown, was succeeded on his death in 1915 by Stanley Murrell.

Between 1902, when J. E. H. W. became a partner, and 1911, the year of Matthew Hodder's death, the firm's lists were strengthened by the addition of works by A. T. Quiller Couch, A. E. W. Mason, Winston S. Churchill, Zane Grey, Ramsay MacDonald, Gene Stratton Porter, and E. Phillips Oppenheim. *Broken Earthenware* (1909), by Harold Begbie of the Salvation Army, sold more than one million copies. Robert E. Peary's *The North Pole* (1910) began a continuing specialty in books of adventure and challenge. *Where's Master?* (1910), by J. E. H. W., a book about King Edward VII's dog written in forty-eight hours hard upon the king's death, sold more than one hundred thousand copies in a few weeks. An illustrated edition of Barrie's *Peter Pan and Wendy*, the last book read for the firm by Matthew Hodder, was published for the Christmas trade of 1911. In 1912 Arnold Bennett's *The Old Wives' Tale* (1908), Baroness Orczy's *The Scarlet Pimpernel* (1905), and Jean Webster's *Daddy Long-Legs* (1913) were added to Hodder and Stoughton's list by purchase of the rights. That year the firm published Rose Macaulay's *The Lee Shore*, which won the Bookman Novel Prize. The year 1913 was distinguished by the publication of Moffatt's *The New Testament: A New Translation*.

Until the outbreak of war in 1914 export markets in Australia, Canada, and South Africa were nursed and developed. In 1913 the O.U.P. agency in Australia was replaced by Hodder and Stoughton's own representative; the same year a Canadian Company was founded with Charles Musson as managing director and Percy Hodder-Williams as president. The Warwick Colonial Library of reprints was directed at these markets. Smart, who had resigned after a row with Apted, returned to represent the firm in Australia and New Zealand in 1921.

As war drew closer Hodder and Stoughton were in an uncommon position among publishers in that Nicoll was close to the Cabinet and used the *British Weekly* in the Liberal cause, synthesizing the historic pacifism of Nonconformity with commitment to a righteous war. Profits from charity books under royal patronage, such as *Princess Mary's Gift Book* (1914), which sold six hundred thousand copies in two years, went to the war effort. For such publications there were special allowances of paper, but shortage of paper was a source of anxiety to the firm during the war. The wartime appetite for poetry was met by *The Collected Poetry* (1913) of Francis Thompson; a deluxe edition of *For the Fallen* (1917), by Laurence Binyon; and G. A. Studdart Kennedy's *Rough Rhymes of a Padré* (1918). Novels by John Buchan, Ian Hay, and Sapper (Herman Cyril McNeile)

*The Reverend William Robertson Nicoll, 1897 (photograph by H. S. Mendelssohn). After his appointment as editor of the* Expositor *in January 1885, Nicoll had a major influence on Hodder and Stoughton's publishing decisions for more than three decades.*

were popular with readers in search of distraction. J. E. H. W. devoted himself particularly to the Red Cross; with E. C. H. Vivian he wrote *The Way of the Red Cross* (1915), and during Red Cross Week in 1916 threepence out of each shilling spent by buyers of Hodder and Stoughton books went to the charity.

In May 1917 T. W. Stoughton died, and J. E. H. W. became the senior partner. During Stoughton's lifetime J. E. H. W. had refrained from disturbing the original partnership arrangement, even though it had become inappropriate as a legal and financial vehicle for a twentieth-century publisher; but after Stoughton's death Hodder and Stoughton was incorporated as a limited company, with J. E. H. W. as chairman and Cecil Stoughton and Percy Hodder-Williams as directors.

The Joint Medical Publications partnership with O.U.P. was renewed for seven years from 1 April 1916, with Sare as manager. At the same date Ely and L'Estrange's school texts and juveniles were sold to O.U.P. for £19,481, under the conditions that Hodder and Stoughton not publish any new juvenile or elementary school texts before 1 July 1924 except with 50 percent participation by O.U.P. and that the American market for Ely and L'Estrange's children's books was reserved to George Doran of New York until 1924.

Peacetime brought increased business; sales in 1920 were double those in 1914, mainly owing to the two-shilling "yellow-jacket" novels. J. E. H. W., who was knighted in 1919, sought new authors and titles for the series through literary agents, especially A. P. Watt and Son. George Doran sent advice about American works, and Laurence Pollinger of Curtis Brown handled the contracts in London. In 1919 *Rudyard Kipling's Verse 1885-1918* and Carola Oman's *The Menin Road and Other Poems* were published. In 1920 *The New Jerusalem*, by G. K. Chesterton; *The Old Grey Homestead*, by Frances Parkinson Keyes; and, in the Hodder and Stoughton tradition of real-life adventure books, Sir Wilfred Grenfell's *A Labrador Doctor* were added to the list. "Bubble" Books containing phonograph records were launched in 1920 and sold in record shops. In 1921 Edgar Wallace joined the Hodder and Stoughton list with *The Law of the Four Just Men*. A. S. M. Hutchinson's *If Winter Comes* (1921) sold more than one hundred thousand copies within twelve months.

In 1920 Hodder and Stoughton bought the major shareholding in Wakley and Son, thereby becoming proprietors of the *Lancet*. J. E. H. W. transferred 50 percent of the shares to O.U.P. for £9,098, and the *Lancet* thus came under the same arrangements as the other joint ventures. In 1923 O.U.P. acquired the stock and interest in the joint-venture medical books; Hodder and Stoughton became sole proprietor of Wakley and Son and the *Lancet*, giving O.U.P. a guarantee to refrain from publishing medical books, except for *Lancet* extras, for five years. The *Lancet* was edited from 1908 to 1938 by Sir Squire Sprigge.

Not all of the decisions taken by J. E. H. W. in the 1920s had satisfactory outcomes. In 1922 he entered into partnership with the University Press of Liverpool to publish specialist academic works; the partnership was ended in 1928. A technical list was begun with the Hodder and Stoughton imprint which might have been better

managed under the University of London Press imprint. In 1924 he bought the *Boot and Shoe Trade Journal*, which was sold at a loss the following year. On the other hand, the idea of crossword puzzle books, which Roker brought back from America, proved successful from first publication in 1924 until the daily newspaper puzzles stole the market.

In 1921 Nicoll was knighted; he was seventy, and successors had to be found. Arthur Hird, a Primitive Methodist minister, was appointed in 1922 as religious book adviser. In 1923 St. John Adcock was appointed editor of the *Bookman*, the Reverend J. M. E. Ross editor of the *British Weekly*, and Moffatt editor of the *Expositor*. A change in the partnership was made necessary in 1923 by Cecil Stoughton's decision to resign; his role in the business had been mainly confined to London sales rather than policymaking. J. E. H. W. and Percy Hodder-Williams invited the one male member of the two families who was of suitable age, and who might possibly give up his own career, to join the firm. This was Ralph Hodder-Williams, their youngest brother and an associate professor of history at the University of Toronto. He answered the call and moved to London in August 1923. His history of his regiment, *Princess Patricia's Canadian Light Infantry*, was published by Hodder and Stoughton in 1923.

In the mid 1920s Hodder and Stoughton yellow-jackets dominated the bookshops, and more than a hundred novels were added annually to the firm's fiction list. The circulating libraries, led by W. H. Smith, Boots, and Harrods, placed the largest orders for the books of Hutchinson, A. E. W. Mason, John Buchan, Sapper, and O. Douglas (pseudonym of Anna Buchan). During this decade some authors, including Macaulay and Phyllis Bottome, left Hodder and Stoughton to escape the stigma of popularity in a yellow-jacket. Cecil Roberts's first novel for Hodder and Stoughton was *Little Mrs. Manington*, published in 1926 when he had already received critical recognition; with Hodder and Stoughton he achieved best-seller status. Whereas the firm's fiction list was inclusive of all the popular genres—romance, western, thriller, and detective story—publisher and public shared the understanding that the list excluded any improper or immoral work. On such grounds J. E. H. W. refused to take Michael Arlen's *The Green Hat* (1924), a successful Doran title. Doran's lists were conforming less and less to the strict standards of Hodder and Stoughton, and in 1924 the connection was severed. Doran's purchase of the Hodder and Stoughton stake in his company returned 400 percent to the English firm on its 1908 capital investment. In 1924 J. E. H. W. sold, for little profit, the company's subsidiary in Canada to Musson and his family.

Such transactions left J. E. H. W. in possession of the cash needed to attract to Hodder and Stoughton the works of men well known to the public, including Lord Rosebery's *Miscellanies* (1921), Earl Grey of Fallodon's *Twenty-five Years* (1925), Sir Oliver Lodge's *Ether and Reality* (1925), and Lord Birkenhead's *Law, Life and Letters* (1927). Religious books of the 1920s included Moffatt's *The Old Testament: A New Translation* (1924) and *The Complete Moffatt Bible* (1926). Arthur Mee edited *The Children's Bible* (1924). University of London Press produced several long-staying works: *Modern Developments in Educational Practice* (1922), by Sir John Adams, and *The Young Delinquent*, by Sir Cyril Burt (1925), were in print for more than fifty years. Dr. P. B. Ballard introduced his theory of objective testing in *The New Examiner* (1923). His *Fundamental Arithmetic* (1926) and *Fundamental English* (1926) achieved larger sales than any other primary U.L.P. textbook; *Fundamental English* remained in print until 1981.

In 1926 Huckvale resigned as company secretary and was succeeded by R. J. Davis. Ross died and was succeeded as editor of the *British Weekly* by Dr. John A. Hutton. Thomas Wakley and Son Limited was renamed The Lancet Limited.

On 8 April 1927 J. E. H. W. died at the age of fifty. His entire property was left to his second wife, Lilian. Since the founding of the firm, control of decisions and ownership of invested capital had been inseparable, and incorporation had not changed this practice. When J. E. H. W.'s shares were left to his widow, the surviving partners moved to regain the old pattern. Private holdings in The Lancet Limited were bought by Hodder and Stoughton, Limited; Percy Hodder-Williams bought Lady Hodder-Williams's debentures. Percy's equity was then eighty thousand shares and Ralph's seventy thousand.

The brothers were assisted by Davis, who extended the duties of company secretary beyond those performed by Huckvale to include responsibility for finance and investment policy. Roker exercised a similar authority in trade matters. Advertising, wrappers, and list were controlled by Fred Austin, in consultation with Percy Hodder-Wil-

*J. Ernest Hodder-Williams, who joined the firm in 1894 and became a partner in 1902*

liams. George Staples, a successful salesman, also had ready access to the elder partner. Hird acted as scout for all kinds of books and contributed a necessary dynamism to the new regime.

During the next few years Hodder and Stoughton lists were characterized by retention of authors and exploitation of steady sellers rather than by acquisition of new writers. The fiction list was strengthened by Patricia Wentworth's first "Miss Silver" novel, *Grey Mask* (1928); *The Galaxy*, by Susan Ertz (1929); and especially by the new writer Leslie Charteris, whose *Getaway* was published in 1932. *The Ship of Truth* (1930), by Lettice Cooper, won the one-thousand-pound religious novel prize. A substantial body of biblical criticism was published, including the Reverend David Smith's *The Disciples' Commentary on the Gospels* (1928-1932) and, in the Moffatt Commentary series, Dr. C. H. Dodd's *The Epistle of Paul to the Romans* (1932). Religious titles came from diverse theological backgrounds and included *Christian Ethics and Modern Problems* (1930), by Dean Inge; Hugh Redwood's book on the Salvation Army, *God in the Slums* (1930), which sold 250,000 in the first year; and A. J. Russell's *For Sinners Only* (1932), which was an Oxford Group best-seller.

In 1934 the Oxford Group Movement, which held the allegiance of Paul Hodder-Williams, was given publicity in a special number of the *British Weekly*, with a consequent increase in sales of the periodical. *Straight and Crooked Thinking* (1930), by Dr. R. H. Thouless, became a classic. The policy of publishing prestige books continued with Philip Guedalla's biography of the Duke of Wellington (1931). U.L.P. extended the list of textbooks with Dr. F. W. Tickner's The Headway Histories (1928) and Elsie Knight's Golden Nature Readers (1931).

In 1929 Sare died, and F. G. H. Holt took over management of the *Lancet*. Hugh Ross Williamson became editor of the *Bookman* in 1930 on the death of Adcock; circulation fell in spite of injections of contemporary literary criticism, and the journal was sold in 1935. When Moffatt could no longer edit the *Expositor*, it ceased publication. The *British Weekly*, although its voice was muted by political division within the Liberal party and by the weakness of Nonconformity and the Church of Scotland in public affairs, was still profitable; continuity was assured by Stoddart, who moved from subeditor to editor.

In 1931 Paul Hodder-Williams and John Attenborough, nephews of Percy and Ralph Hodder-Williams, were taken into the firm. Sales were declining except in educational textbooks; bookshop sales dropped from £637,770 in 1928 to £289,375 in 1939. The two-shilling yellow-jackets were hard hit by the Depression, especially in Australia. The effect of the Depression was exacerbated by the publishing policies and personal habits of Percy and Ralph Hodder-Williams: retiring in nature, they did not mix with other publishers, travel to America, nor call on booksellers; moral constraints inhibited the publishers' readers and literary agents on whom they relied, and a sense of propriety carried beyond measure resulted in lost opportunities. Other, young houses took the lead, but it was particularly Allen Lane's sixpenny Penguins which in 1935 cut the market away from Hodder and Stoughton's two-shilling books.

In 1932 Hird died and Leonard Cutts took over his work. Apted also died in 1932. The two great-grandsons of Matthew Hodder were moved into Apted's old office and given the responsibility of sorting typescripts and getting printers' estimates by way of informal training. In 1935 they were made directors, but they were not thereupon made privy to the firm's accounts. Paul

Hodder-Williams became more involved with the *British Weekly* and the religious books, and John Attenborough with the fiction and general list. In 1934 Attenborough was given the task of building up a technical list to be published under the imprint of a newly formed subsidiary, the English Universities Press (E.U.P.). In consultation with Henry Brown of U.L.P. and Dr. F. H. Spencer, a retired senior inspector of the national Board of Education, several works were commissioned which remained in print for decades. In 1937 there was a list of twenty-eight books, but the ten thousand pounds allocated for production was exhausted. Attenborough proposed that to achieve quick sales, E.U.P. should publish *The Motor Manual* and other books associated with the Temple Press technical magazines; this solution proved successful. At the same time Percy Hodder-Williams proposed resurrecting a series of self-education books originally planned by Sir John Adams. Titles and wrappers were brought up to date, and in 1939 the series, first marketed as Steeplejacks but soon known by Cutts's subtitle Teach Yourself, was launched. A two-shilling series of reprinted nonfiction works, including Hugh Ruttledge's *Everest 1933* (1934), began well but was quashed by the war.

To combat the falling book sales of the 1930s Percy Hodder-Williams created a variety of promotional schemes. Hodder and Stoughton was a part-promoter with a New York publisher of a four-thousand-pound first-novel prize, which was awarded to Janet Beith for *No Second Spring* (1933). In 1935 Hodder-Williams offered a prize for the "autobiography of an unknown man"; it was won by Igor Schwezoff for *Borzoi* (1935), which became Hodder and Stoughton's first Book Society choice. George V's Silver Jubilee and the coronation of George VI were seized as opportunities for royal books, which found a market as commemorative gifts to schoolchildren. Roker sold special editions of old illustrated books exclusively to Boots. *The Scarlet Pimpernel* was heavily promoted to take advantage of the 1935 film. Editorial policy remained conservative; Leslie Weatherhead's *Psychology and Life* (1934) met the public temper and sold well. U.L.P. published the best-selling *Writing and Writing Patterns* (1935), by Marion Richardson, and Hodder and Stoughton took the lead as a publisher of mountaineering books. The fiction list was weakened by the deaths of Edgar Wallace in 1934 and of Sapper in 1937. A. E. W. Mason, although passing threescore and ten, was a Book Society choice in 1938 for his *Königsmark*. Novelists enlisted in the 1930s included D. L. Murray with *Trumpeter Sound* (1933) and Eric Ambler with *The Dark Frontier* (1936). James Hilton's *Goodbye Mr. Chips* (1934) came to the firm as a result of Cutts's search for a long short story for the *British Weekly*.

Staples urged that the commonwealth countries be visited to develop the markets. The first journey, by Davis and Staples in 1937, was occasioned by the death of C. H. Lamb, the firm's representative in South Africa; on this visit they engaged Howard B. Timmins as agent on commission. During World War II he would organize the production of Hodder and Stoughton books in South Africa. The visit of Davis and Staples to Australia in 1938-1939 was treated as an intrusion by Smart, who had traveled Australia for Hodder and Stoughton since 1921. Returning through India they investigated but found no opening for Hodder and Stoughton.

In 1939 Percy and Ralph Hodder-Williams prepared the firm for war. They rented St. Hugh's School in Bickley, Kent; arranged with Hazell, Watson and Viney for accommodation in Aylesbury, Buckinghamshire; and prepared for evacuation from the city. Paul Hodder-Williams and John Attenborough volunteered for military service; when war came about half the staff enlisted, leaving sixty-six men and eighteen women to carry on at Bickley (editorial and accounts), Aylesbury (warehouse), and Warwick Square (London sales). On the day after war was declared Hodder and Stoughton began publishing from Bickley. On New Year's Eve 1940 most of the publishing center of London was destroyed by an air raid, but the fire was stopped just short of Warwick Square; Little Paul's House was saved and St. Paul's House only partly damaged. The building which housed U.L.P. was demolished and the London book stock ruined by water. In May 1941 part of St. Paul's House was destroyed by a bomb. In June 1944 St. Hugh's School was destroyed by a flying bomb. Staff who had worked at the school were moved back to Little Paul's House or to Sevenoaks, Kent. U.L.P. was housed at Malham House in Bickley.

During the war Cutts carried the chief editorial responsibility, and Davis was, in effect, managing director. In 1939 Loney died and was succeeded as chairman of U.L.P. by Percy Hodder-Williams. In the same year the firm also lost J. H. Wharmby, who had started as north of England salesman in 1912 and had easily fulfilled his promise to double sales there.

After the move to Bickley one book which occupied the attention of the firm was *The Queen's Book of the Red Cross* (1939), conceived after the fashion of the charity books published during World War I. Again, paper rationing was a constant problem: the quota was set by the government and the Publishers' Association at 37 1/2 percent of normal consumption. All yellow-jacket stock was sold out, and authors accepted the publisher's promise to reprint their works after the war. Most of the paper quota was used for new books, a policy which brought forward several less-well-known writers. The Hodder-Williams brothers based their wartime publishing policy on ethical considerations and the national interest, and pursued it to their own financial detriment. Paper supplies above quota were available for books which were in the national interest, and extra rations were obtained for the Temple Press aeroplane spotters' manuals; the Teach Yourself titles, of which there were forty-eight in print at the end of the war compared with eighteen when war began; and the educational titles of U.L.P. Educational books rose from 30 percent to 40 percent of the firm's book sales during the war. In 1938 the Brockhampton Book Company was founded in Leicester, with Roker as manager, to reduce surplus stocks of theological works; it was renamed Brockhampton Press in 1940. That year Roker, who had long held an interest in children's book publishing, used paper offcuts from the local printing of color magazines to produce cartoon booklets and engaged Enid Blyton to write the texts; print runs for her "Mary Mouse" books, which began in 1942, reached two hundred thousand. In the same year Hodder and Stoughton published the first of her "Famous Five" books, and also the first of W. E. Johns's "Biggles" books to come to the firm. In this way the firm regained a portion of the children's book market which it had left in 1916. In 1945 sales of the Brockhampton Press were £62,843.

Attenborough and Paul Hodder-Williams returned from the war in autumn 1945. In March 1946 space suitable for warehousing and shipping was purchased in Brockley, making Hodder and Stoughton one of the first publishers to move these operations out of central London except in war. In May 1946 the directors returned to St. Paul's House. Attenborough was put in charge of home and export sales, advertising, and reviews; Paul Hodder-Williams was given responsibility for production. In 1946 the *British Weekly* was sold; Hutton, the editor for twenty years, was failing, and the journal was in decline. In 1947 Hodder and Stoughton invested in the new paperback company Pan Books, in association with Collins, Macmillan, and Heinemann. Ralph Hodder-Williams joined the Pan board.

On 31 March 1947 Percy Hodder-Williams retired, aged sixty-seven, after twenty-one years as chairman. Ralph Hodder-Williams, fifty-seven, succeeded him. At the same time Staples was promoted to senior salesman for London and export, Sare to advertising manager, and Ewart Wharmby to manager of the Brockhampton Press. The *Lancet* was the only journal still owned by Hodder and Stoughton; Sir Theodore Fox had taken over the editorship in 1944. At the U.L.P. Henry Brown succeeded Murrell as manager and proposed expansion into the markets of West and East Africa, the West Indies, and Southeast Asia. The promise made to authors at the beginning of the war to give priority to reprinting their works caused the loss of some new works, notably H. F. M. Prescott's *Man on a Donkey*, which was published by Eyre and Spottiswoode in 1953.

In 1948 Davis learned that two decades earlier an agreement had been reached between Percy and Ralph Hodder-Williams which gave the latter the option of purchasing the whole of the former's shareholdings over a ten-year period following Percy's retirement or death. No changes had been made to the share register since the redistribution in 1927 when J. E. H. W. left his holding to his widow, except for the 2,000 shares registered in the names of the two nephews. This arrangement left the futures of Paul Hodder-Williams and Attenborough uncertain; furthermore, when estate duties came to be levied on Ralph Hodder-Williams's holdings, the firm would have to be sold. Davis's representations to Ralph Hodder-Williams on behalf of the nephews were readily accepted; with more reluctance, he agreed that the company should be restructured. The chairman sold his nephews 17,500 shares each; Percy Hodder-Williams bought back some of his shares; some of the firm's printers bought shares; and Lady Hodder-Williams became a major shareholder. Thus in 1948 there were twenty-two shareholders of Hodder and Stoughton, of whom only three were directors. Confidence returned on the adoption of the plan, and the end of paper rationing

in March 1949 brought a mood of optimism to publishing.

In 1947 Ralph Hodder-Williams was elected president of the Publishers' Association. The achievements of his presidency included establishing better relations with the Booksellers Association, giving effective evidence to the Monopolies Commission, and helping to bring the United States to sign the Universal Copyright Convention.

The Hodder and Stoughton list recovered strength and reputation in the late 1940s and early 1950s: Richard Mason's *The Wind Cannot Read* (1946) was a Book Society choice and was translated into ten languages; Carola Oman's *Nelson* (1947) won the *Sunday Times* one-thousand-pound award; Elizabeth Goudge's *Herb of Grace* (1948) was a Literary Guild choice in the United States; Neil Paterson's *Behold, Thy Daughter* (1950) was also a Book Society choice. High sales figures were achieved by Sir Francis de Guingand's *Operation Victory* (1947), Sir Donald Bradman's *Farewell to Cricket* (1950), P. R. Reid's *The Colditz Story* (1952), Thomas B. Costain's *The Silver Chalice* (1953), and Ernest K. Gann's *The High and the Mighty* (1953). Elizabeth Cadell, Hermina Black, and Jerrard Tickell joined the Hodder and Stoughton fiction list. The tradition of religious publishing continued: Archbishop Cyril Garbett's *The Claims of the Church of England* (1947) was followed in 1949 by J. G. Lockhart's life of Cosmo Gordon Lang and in 1950 by the final volume of the Moffatt commentaries, *Thessalonians*. *Psychology, Religion and Healing* (1951), by Weatherhead, and David Mace's *Marriage: The Art of Lasting Happiness* (1952) met the public interest in practical psychology. *The Practice of Evangelism* (1951), by Canon Bryan Green, accorded with the commitment of the founders as well as the contemporary phenomenon of missions. U.L.P. published Goudge's *The Little White Horse* (1946), which won the Carnegie Medal, and George A. Carr's *Reading for Meaning* (1948-1952), which was accepted against the advice of the educational advisers and sold more than one million copies. E.U.P. brought out its first secondary school publication, *Concise General Science* (1949), by W. A. J. Musson and R. D. Reid; sales exceeded 170,000 copies. After a lapse of thirty years personal links with American publishers were renewed in 1952 by Attenborough and his wife, who traveled to the United States by sea and returned with four bestsellers.

Hodder and Stoughton counts 1953 as its annus mirabilis. This was the year of the coronation of Elizabeth II and of the first successful ascent of Everest. Richard Dimbleby's *Elizabeth, Our Queen* followed the precedent of royal family books which John Buchan and Arthur Mee had written for Hodder and Stoughton in the 1930s. Hodder and Stoughton had sponsored two unsuccessful expeditions on Everest in 1933 and 1936 and had established a reputation as a publisher of Everest books. The contract to publish the account of Col. Sir John Hunt's expedition was negotiated with the Royal Geographical Society's sponsoring committee against keen competition from other publishers. Extraordinary efforts were made to publish it in time for the Christmas trade; the text was written in a month. The first edition of *The Ascent of Everest* sold out before publication day, 14 November; 329,000 copies of the original edition and 310,000 book club copies were sold. Translation rights were sold in twenty-six countries, and there were also school readers, a children's version, and a paperback.

To strengthen Hodder and Stoughton's position in export markets, directors traveled frequently to America, and profitable two-way traffic in book rights resulted. The Musson Book Company in Canada was not active, but Timmins was a vigorous agent in South Africa. Smart was difficult to deal with, and in 1960 management of the Hodder companies in Australia was handed to Sare. An independent agency had been established in New Zealand in 1950, and a New Zealand list was started in 1967. Educational publishing was the strongest sector of the export drive; the value of U.L.P. educational sales increased fourfold between 1946 and 1961. Several resident overseas educational representatives were appointed, and L. M. H. Timmermans traveled Africa, India, and Southeast Asia between 1948 and 1953. Dame Dorothy Brock joined the board of U.L.P. in 1951; she was the first woman director and first nonexecutive director of the firm.

E.U.P. ceased to publish the Temple Press manuals in 1948. From 1947 the Teach Yourself series was promoted by an annual "Teach Yourself Fortnight"; 325 titles were in print in 1961. By 1961 E.U.P. and U.L.P. sales together amounted to more than half the business of Hodder and Stoughton. A resident editor, Olive Jones, was appointed for the Brockhampton Press in 1954. By 1961 sales were three times the best recorded by Roker.

Sales of the parent company doubled between 1945 and 1961. It was holding its place in fiction and in religious and educational publishing but not in the field of cheap reprints, partly because of the promise to authors to restore prewar titles but also because the contract with Pan Books transferred paperback rights in Hodder and Stoughton's most successful books to Pan. In 1950 the former ninepenny yellow-jacket series was resurrected at two shillings; it was withdrawn after two years. In 1956 another unsuccessful attack was made on the paperback market, with current authors and in the popular "Penguin" size; it was planned by Toby Hodder-Williams, who had joined the firm in 1950 and had just been made a director.

In 1959 a holding company, Matthew Hodder Limited, was formed; the publishing enterprises were reconstituted as wholly owned subsidiaries. Davis joined the board of Matthew Hodder Limited, and Cutts became a director of Hodder and Stoughton. At the end of the year Wharmby, Foster, Timmermans, and Tyas were made directors of their respective companies. Attenborough became chairman of E.U.P. and Paul Hodder-Williams chairman of Brockhampton Press. In April 1960 Ralph Hodder-Williams resigned as chairman of Hodder and Stoughton and was succeeded by Paul Hodder-Williams; Attenborough became deputy chairman and took editorial responsibility for the Hodder and Stoughton list. The author and critic Peter Green was appointed consultant editor with special responsibility for fiction and general lists. Robin Denniston, manager of the Faith Press, joined the firm with responsibility for religious books and the Teach Yourself series and in 1961 was placed in charge of publicity and subleases of book rights. Elsie Herron was appointed senior resident editor in 1960. In 1960 Philip Attenborough was recalled from New Zealand to become export manager. Mark Hodder-Williams, elder son of Paul, joined the firm in 1961. Michael Attenborough, younger son of John, joined in 1962 expecting to be the first in a new graduate training scheme; in fact, he traveled the West Country because of the sudden illness of J. C. Bryant. Davis retired from the position of company secretary in 1964 after fifty-six years with the firm. In 1964 Toby Hodder-Williams relinquished his responsibilities because of chronic ill health.

In 1960 a new company, Hodder Publications Limited, was established with responsibility for invoicing, shipping, and booksellers' payments. Office space for Hodder Publications was extended in 1967 by the purchase of premises in Sydenham.

In 1963 the new St. Paul's House on the Warwick Lane site was completed. With ninety thousand pounds from the sale of the Hodder and Stoughton interest in Pan Books, the directors decided to demolish the old St. Paul's House, and rebuild and extend the new one along the south of Warwick Square. In 1965 editorial and production units were housed in the one building.

At a 1961 company conference John Attenborough presented a paper on contemporary publishing in which the optimum number of books marketable annually through trade sales was set at eighty novels, thirty general books, twenty religious books, and ten to twenty others, including juveniles. The rising importance of book clubs and paperback subleases was recognized, and the separation of paperback editorial and sales became accepted policy. From this conference dates the firm's chessmen symbol, each of the four pieces representing a publishing arm of the group. In 1964 a second company conference set three objectives: to develop paperbacks; to bring together all children's books at the Brockhampton Press; and to acquire a list of household reference manuals. The first of the latter was *The Reader's Digest Great World Atlas* (1962), a "marketed book" (sold directly to individuals by mail). The Langenscheidt dictionaries, Fodor Guides, and Drive books followed. Marketed books soon amounted to 20 percent of Hodder and Stoughton's hardback sales. The reputation of the Brockhampton Press rose in 1969 with the publication of the *Asterix* cartoon books.

Green left in 1963, having brought Gavin Lyall to Hodder and Stoughton. Denniston was responsible for Anthony Sampson's *Anatomy of Britain* (1962), which achieved prepublication orders of thirty thousand; he was also responsible for the implementation of editorial policy set at the 1961 and 1964 conferences and for lifting the caliber of the fiction list, especially through the acquisition of John le Carré. When John Attenborough became president of the Publishers' Association in 1965, Denniston was given responsibility, under the chairman, for the editorial policy of Hodder and Stoughton.

In 1967 two crises overseas had to be resolved. In Canada, after the death of Musson, the company bearing the Hodder and Stoughton name had come near bankruptcy and was bought by the directors in London for a nominal sum of $1.00; there was a loss of £250,000 when the company was sold in 1967. In Singapore the Donald Moore agency was near insolvency; Moore resigned and the three managers in Singapore, Tokyo, and Hong Kong, who were given equity in the renamed Educational Associates Limited, succeeded in trading out of debt. John Attenborough became chairman of the new Asian company. In the politically turbulent postwar decades Hodder and Stoughton's operations in African countries were repeatedly in hazard.

The centenary of Hodder and Stoughton in 1968 was celebrated as "One hundred years of Christian publishing" with an exhibition of religious books in Stationers' Hall, lectures, and a conference. Edward England, who had joined Hodder and Stoughton in 1966 and had revived the list of religious books across the theological spectrum, started a line of Christian paperbacks in 1969. In 1969 Cutts retired after forty-seven years with the firm. The religious list had been his particular responsibility either directly or indirectly through the editors he brought to the firm. He had also played the role of tutor to new recruits.

In 1968 Urwick, Orr and Partners, management consultants, proposed, and the directors accepted, three structural changes: amalgamation of U.L.P. and E.U.P., leaving Teach Yourself books as a separate unit; welding of the hardback sales force into a single division; and the appointment of a group personnel director. The management committee then consisted of Michael Attenborough (paperbacks), Philip Attenborough (group sales and marketed books), Denniston (hard-cover trade books), Mark Hodder-Williams (group computer and warehouse), Timmermans (educational division), Tyas (group personnel), Wharmby (children's books); R. J. Fowles (accounts) and Henry Jones (property and share register) were joint secretaries. In 1971 the board of the parent company consisted of these individuals. The firm was thriving, and sixty thousand pounds of stock was offered to senior employees. In 1972 a four-and-a-half-acre site was bought at Dunton Green, Kent, which would accommodate all warehousing and much of the staff.

In the 1960s and 1970s the export market received vigorous attention; limits were placed on overseas investment, and personnel were selected with care. This market, like the group's diverse lists, depended on efficient computerized warehousing, shipping, and invoicing. Whereas between 1961 and 1974 book sales increased from less than two million to more than eight million pounds, correction to the value of the pound in 1927 showed that sales did not increase beyond the level of 1928 until 1953. From 1953 sales remained steady until the benefits of Coronet and Knight paperbacks were felt in 1966.

In 1973 Denniston left to become deputy chairman at Weidenfeld and Nicolson; his work was taken over by Michael Attenborough, who had built Hodder Paperbacks into a dominant share of the market and a major contributor to the group's profits, especially through a 1966 link with the American house of Fawcett and the Coronet and Knight paperbacks. His target of one million pounds in sales by 1972 was exceeded. In 1973 Herron retired after thirty-four years' service; Eric Major arrived from Collins to take responsibility for editorial publicity. At the end of 1973 John Attenborough retired. In 1974 Paul Hodder-Williams retired and was succeeded as chairman by Philip Attenborough. In 1975 the publishing companies of the Matthew Hodder Group adopted the original Hodder and Stoughton imprint.

During the chairmanship of Philip Attenborough profits have been affected by fluctuations in sterling and other currencies, and educational markets have been weakened at home by public sector cuts. A rail strike in 1979 affected production. Discussions were opened with overseas printers in several countries with a view to reducing costs. In 1979 Richard Morris was appointed to develop a corporate plan for the 1980s and beyond. In 1980-1981 forty-six jobs were eliminated. In 1976 Hodder and Stoughton had formally recognized the National Union of Journalists as the representative of much its staff. Teleordering by booksellers, which the company had promoted, was operational in 1979. Editorial, publicity, and rights sections moved from St. Paul's House to 47 Bedford Square in 1976, and additional space was subsequently taken on short leases in Great Russell Street and 24 Bedford Square. In 1985 a long lease was taken on 46 Bedford Square. The Dunton Green building was enlarged in 1984. In South Africa Hodder and Stoughton joined forces with the young publisher Jonathon Ball and moved from Cape Town to Johannesburg in 1980; sales and distribution, except for educational books, were merged with the Macmillan Company in 1985. Hudahuda Limited was established in Nigeria in 1981. In 1982 an

Irish sales office was set up in Dublin. In 1983 an agreement was signed with an agent in the Middle East to carry the firm's books.

In 1981 a contract was signed with American Express to offer cardholders a book-a-month program consisting of a luxurious reissue of titles illustrated by Dulac, Rackham, and others before World War I. In 1982 Hodder and Stoughton sold Commodore computers with a teaching manual at a special price, and the first line of children's videocassettes was produced. In 1983 the firm began copublishing with John Murray. The first sales of educational and games software were made in 1984 and 1985. Film, television, and radio tie-ins were used in promotions; in 1985 Saatchi and Saatchi was appointed to handle advertising of selected titles.

In 1979 Hodder and Stoughton joined forces with Dargaud Éditeurs as Hodder Dargaud Limited to publish the *Asterix* books. In 1980 the firm bought into Simon and Schuster's Silhouette romances, but when the American company sold its share four years later Hodder and Stoughton backed out. In 1981 the New English Library imprint was acquired from the Times Mirror Company of Los Angeles. Dormac Incorporated, a special education publisher based in Oregon, was acquired in 1985.

Religious publishing, no longer confined to Nonconformist Christianity, has been notable for the 1978 hardback and paperback editions of the New International Bible and the award of one of the three contracts for the Alternative Service Book for the Church of England in 1980. England, the religious books editor, resigned in 1980. General publishing has benefited from the Book Marketing Council's campaign to sell practical, as opposed to literary, books. Medical and scholarly works and some poetry books are now published under the imprint of Edward Arnold.

In the 1970s and 1980s Hodder and Stoughton books won several international prizes, including the Booker Prize, and recorded good figures in various best-seller lists. The fiction list was particularly strong with Jeffery Archer, James Herbert, Thomas Kenneally, Stephen King, John le Carré, William McIlvanney, Harold Robbins, and Fay Weldon.

In 1986 sales reached more than forty-five million pounds. Philip Attenborough continues as executive chairman; the deputy chairman is Mark Hodder-Williams.

**References:**

John Attenborough, *A Living Memory: Hodder and Stoughton Publishers 1868-1975* (London: Hodder & Stoughton, 1975);

Edward England, *An Unfading Vision* (London: Hodder & Stoughton, 1981).

—*Dorothy W. Collin*

# Hurst and Blackett
## *(London: 1853-1954)*

In January 1853 Henry Colburn, the "Prince of Puffers," sold his publishing business to his junior partner, Daniel Hurst, and Henry Blackett; Blackett apparently put up the cash. The business at 13 Great Marlborough Street, London, was in good running order, so Hurst and Blackett continued Colburn's policies and sharp business practice. They took over his former authors, among them Mrs. Frances Trollope and Mrs. Anne Marsh, and translators such as Mary Howitt, and they continued to publish E. Lodge's *Peerage and Baronetage of the British Empire* until 1912. Hurst and Blackett also followed the Colburn tradition of cheap editions of standard classics and contemporary novels, including works that had originally appeared in magazines such as *Household Words, All the Year Round, Cassell's, Fraser's, Macmillan's,* and *Temple Bar.*

Mrs. Trollope's final four works were published by the new firm, including the melodramatic *The Young Heiress* (1853) and *The Life and Adventures of a Clever Woman* (1854). Her son Anthony, who had two novels published by Colburn, took *The Three Clerks* (1858) to Hurst and Blackett; but as no one was in the office except a foreman, Trollope went to Richard Bentley. Two of his later novels were published by Hurst and Blackett, however. Alexander Macmillan purchased the copyright of *Sir Harry Hotspur*

*of Humblethwaite* for £750 to begin in the January 1870 issue of *Macmillan's Magazine,* but he sold the book publication rights to Hurst and Blackett. Hurst and Blackett intended to publish the one-volume work in two short volumes, because readers enjoyed getting through volumes quickly; the move would also increase the firm's profit on the book. When Trollope complained, Blackett explained to Macmillan that almost half the book was already in type, and that it was the same length as the firm's last two-volume novel. In the end, however, the novel was published in one volume. The firm also published *Ralph the Heir* (1870-1871) in nineteen monthly parts.

Hurst and Blackett worked with other publishing firms by sharing renowned authors; thus they managed to publish works by many of the most popular and some well-respected authors of the mid-Victorian period—Dinah Maria Craik, Georgiana Craik, Elizabeth Gaskell, Julia Kavanagh, Anne Marsh, Margaret Oliphant, Mrs. S. C. Hall, James Grant, and George MacDonald—albeit rarely their best works.

As one of the less substantial houses—along with William Tinsley, T. C. Newby, and Saunders and Otley—Hurst and Blackett was most anxious to be on the lists of Mudie's and W. H. Smith's subscription libraries. This meant that the company needed a steady supply of three-deckers suitable for the library audience. Of the twenty-eight publishers of novels in London in 1866, Hurst and Blackett published the most, twenty-eight; the nearest competitor was T. C. Newby with twenty-three, followed by Chapman and Hall and Tinsley with twenty each.

Not all were selected by the libraries; George Edward Mudie was ever cautious about what he circulated. The anonymous *Walter Blake's Heroine* (1866), for example, had to be withdrawn by Hurst and Blackett because of ultrasensational scenes. In 1868 Mortimer Collins's autobiographical *Sweet Anne Page* was withdrawn from circulation, reappearing some years later in a one-volume form. It described a boy witnessing a tickling match between two young women as they disrobed for the night; it also contained love scenes unsuitable for the libraries. The firm, however, published nine of Collins's subsequent works, and after his death it brought out his wife Frances's *A Broken Lily* (1882).

From the beginning Hurst and Blackett published primarily women's novels, focusing initially on domestic fiction and then on popular romantic melodrama and sensational fiction. Emily Jolly, whose stories appeared in the *Cornhill* and *Macmillan's*, had nine books published by Hurst and Blackett, including *Bond and Free* (1860), *Pearl* (1868), and *Safely Married* (1874). Julia Kavanagh had five three-deckers published by the firm, which also brought out Ouida's *A House Party* (1887). The firm also produced a few children's books by E. Nesbit, Mrs. Molesworth, and Netta Syrett.

Caroline Norton sold her sensational novel *Old Sir Douglas* (1868) to Hurst and Blackett, which resold it to Macmillan for publication in his magazine without her knowledge. The firm had earlier published Mrs. Norton's *Lost and Saved* (1863), causing a stir because the heroine closely resembled the author and because the novel allowed a titled murderess to continue to live in prosperity.

In 1859 Wilkie Collins, who later became famous for sensational fiction, had a collection of short fiction published by Hurst and Blackett under the title *The Queen of Hearts*. Most of the stories had appeared in Charles Dickens's magazine *Household Words*; Dickens had rejected one of the stories because it dealt with hereditary insanity, but it had appeared in *Fraser's*.

William Hepworth Dixon, editor of the *Athenaeum* from 1853 to 1869, had eleven works, mostly historical, published by Hurst and Blackett. The firm may have welcomed his books at least partly because they were guaranteed a review in his magazine. Dixon was also valuable because he had built his reputation on a series for the *Daily News* attacking immorality in popular literature; thus he set a tone that was to provide sanction for the firm's more sensational novels. Hurst and Blackett similarly worked with Henry Fothergill Chorley, John Cordy Jeaffreson, and Geraldine Jewsbury, all *Athenaeum* reviewers of the novels of the week, and with Dr. John Doran, who briefly edited the periodical. Jewsbury, who became a reader for Hurst and Blackett in 1860, had two novels published by the firm—*Constance Herbert* (1855) and *Right or Wrong* (1859)—in which she spoke frankly about matrimony. Later in the century Adeline Sergeant, a reader for Bentley, had nineteen novels published by Hurst and Blackett. Other writers with connections to rival houses whose books were published by Hurst and Blackett include Edmund Downey, an assistant to Tinsley; James Payn, a former editor of *Chambers's Journal*; and Dinah Maria Craik, whose husband, George Lillie Craik, was a partner of Macmillan from 1865 to 1905.

A novel with many positive reviews was likely to find an enduring place in Mudie's catalogues; for example, Dinah Maria Craik's *A Noble Life* (1866) was reviewed in the *British Quarterly Review, Examiner, Reader, John Bull, Spectator, Athenaeum, London Review, Queen*, and *Press*, and remained in Mudie's catalogue until 1914, as did Margaret Oliphant's *Madonna Mary* (1867), which was noticed in the *British Quarterly Review, Saturday Review, Spectator, Athenaeum*, and *London Review*. Mark Lemon's *Falkner Lyle* (1866) was reviewed in the *Examiner, Reader, Saturday Review, Athenaeum*, and *London Review*, thus ensuring its place in Mudie's catalogue until 1876.

In 1866 the "Recent Novels" column in the *London Quarterly Review* featured Frederick William Robinson's *Beyond the Church* alongside works by George Eliot, Charles Kingsley, and Wilkie Collins. In 1894 Robinson was included by Jerome K. Jerome along with twenty-one other authors—including Mary Elizabeth Braddon, H. Rider Haggard, and James Payn—in *My First Book*, published by Chatto and Windus. In his reminiscence Robinson recalls his first visit in 1853 to the premises of Messrs. Hurst and Blackett, where, he was told by an acquaintance, about seven novels a day came in and most went back. Robinson received a standard letter of polite refusal for his first work, but

Hurst and Blackett accepted his second novel, *The House of Elmore* (1855). The firm published a total of thirty-seven works by Robinson.

To avoid saturating the market, to hide identity or sex, or to branch out into different subjects, Hurst and Blackett authors often used two or more names: Arthur Applin was really Julian Swift, Charles Barry was Charles Bryson, Ada Cambridge was Mrs. G. F. Cross, Catherine Clark was Mrs. Evelyn Uniacke, Geoffrey Coffin was Van Wyck Mason, G. Colmore was Mrs. Baillie Weaver, Edna Lyall was Ada Ellen Bayly, Iota was Mrs. Mannington Caffyn, Violet Fane was Lady Currie, Robert Orr Chipperfield was David Fox, Douglas Grant was Isabel Ostrander, E. W. Savi was Elizabeth Grey, A Prison Matron was F. W. Robinson, Fiona MacLeod was William Sharp, Silverpen was Eliza Meteyard, Sam Slick was Thomas Chandler Haliburton, and Sarah Tytler was really Henrietta Keddie. The most colorful were Ouida, whose real name was Marie Louise de la Ramée, and Achmed Abdullah, who was actually the son of Grand Duke Nicholas Romanoff and Princess N. Durani of Russia. There were also works by "A Clergyman's Daughter" (1859), "A Contemporary" (1860), and "A Clergyman" (1864). "An English Lady" wrote *Six Years in Russia* (1859), and Mrs. Cashel Hoey, who wrote many of the novels attributed to Edmund Yates, had six published under her own name by Hurst and Blackett.

An outstanding and enduring success for Hurst and Blackett was *John Halifax, Gentleman* (1856) by Dinah Maria Craik. Ten of her twenty novels were published by the firm, including *A Life for a Life* (1859), her favorite. Henrietta Keddie, who had two novels published by the firm, paid tribute to her (quoted by Alleyn Lyell Reade [1915]): "Mrs. Craik was a good business woman, while it may be in part explanatory of her successful arrangements for her books that the household could wait for the terms which she believed herself entitled to. She got what was held to be a good price. . . . She received two thousand pounds for the copyright of one of her stories." Mrs. Oliphant, who introduced her to Blackett at his request, complained in 1886 that Hurst and Blackett admitted to paying Mrs. Craik "£1,500 merely I think for the reprint of a book called Hannah [1872], a very objectionable book, the worst of all hers, I think, in two volumes." Only one of Mrs. Oliphant's novels—*The Perpetual Curate*, published by Blackwell in 1864—had earned that much. She also jealously

reported in her autobiography (1898) that Blackett "turned pale at Miss Mulock's sturdy, businesslike stand for her money."

Mrs. Oliphant, who began with Colburn, had novels published throughout the 1850s by Hurst and Blackett. Because she was so prolific, she had three principal publishers, who adjusted dates of publication so that new works by her would not appear simultaneously. *Zaidee*, however, published in 1856 by Blackwood's, suffered from competition with her *Lilliesleaf* (1855), brought out by Hurst and Blackett—who, she explained to John Blackwood, had always waited "at least six months after [a manuscript] is in their hands." She advised Hurst and Blackett about books—for example, she and Dinah Maria Craik strongly recommended publishing George MacDonald's *David Elginbrod* (1863). Hurst and Blackett published thirty-three books by Mrs. Oliphant, including *The Life of Edward Irving* (1862), *Salem Chapel* (1863), and *Phoebe Junior* (1876). She dedicated her novel *Agnes* (1866) to Mrs. Blackett and lived near the Blacketts in Ealing from 1861 to 1863. She did not hold Blackett in high regard, however; she wrote to Blackwood in 1861 that "He is no genius . . . . Blackett . . . is not exactly what you understand by a gentleman."

Mrs. Oliphant's relations were strained with Blackett's sons, who took over the firm after Blackett's death on 7 March 1870 and Hurst's on 6 July 1871. She wrote Blackwood, "I was offended by the manner of the eldest, an underbred and uneducated young man, whom I have been very kind to all his life but whom I should now prefer to have no further dealings with." She had only six new books published by the firm from 1883 until her death in 1897, but she could not afford to sever relations with the company completely. A Hurst and Blackett reprint of her 1883 novel *It Was a Lover and His Lass* appeared as late as 1951.

Mrs. Oliphant did contribute the opening essay, "The Sisters Brontë," to *Women Novelists of Queen Victoria's Reign: A Book of Appreciations* (1897), a special volume brought out by Hurst and Blackett in honor of the Queen's Diamond Jubilee. The book featured living women novelists who had had books published by the firm writing about deceased women writers. The eight featured writers who had never had books published by the firm tended to fare badly. Eliza Lynn Linton, who had had only one novel—*Through the Long Night* (1888-1889)—published by Hurst and Blackett, made acerbic remarks about George Eliot that provided some sensation. Mrs. Oliphant dismissed Anne Brontë and was critical of Emily Brontë, but found mitigating circumstances to explain Charlotte Brontë's perceived lapses from propriety. Clearly, Hurst and Blackett's volume, with its authors' names imprinted in gold under the title on the cover, was designed as a marketing tool. Although Bentley and Chatto and Windus brought out similar works, only Hurst and Blackett sought to present its book as a volume of serious criticism.

While Hurst and Blackett specialized in novels by women, it also published works by popular Victorian male novelists. In addition to fourteen works by MacDonald, the firm published novels by Haggard, Robert Smith Surtees, and Charles Lever. James Hannay's *Eustace Conyers* (1855) was typical of his work—lively writing about naval life and lore with excess theorizing and an awkward, improbable plot—yet it was well received. The company published two novels by Joseph Sheridan Le Fanu, including the last to appear in his lifetime, *Willing to Die* (1873). There were three adventures for boys by Mayne Reid, including *Oceola the Seminole* (1859), with an Indian hero and an independent woman, and *The Maroon* (1862), set in Jamaica and containing Reid's most scathing denunciation of slavery as well as violent and even implicitly sexual scenes.

Hurst and Blackett also published travel books with such titles as *Lake Ngami; or, Explorations and Discoveries during Four Years Wandering in the Wilds of South Western Africa* (1856), by Karl Johan Andersson; *Passages in the Life of a Soldier* (1857), by Lt. Col. Sir James Alexander; and *Italy under Victor Emanuel: A Personal Narrative* (1862), by Count Carlo Arrivabene. The firm published many biographies, including *The Life of St. Teresa* (1865) by Archbishop Henry Manning, and three works by Cardinal Nicholas Wiseman on science and art, religion, and Shakespeare.

As the firm moved into the twentieth century it published a smattering of critical works on literature and art, such as William Michael Rossetti's edition of *Præraphaelite Diaries and Letters* (1900). The list always found a place for military memoirs, including Capt. Nikolai Klado's *The Russian Navy in the Russo-Japanese War* (1905) and Maj. Gen. Sir John Frederick Maurice's four-volume *History of the War in South Africa* (1906-1910).

In the 1920s the Hurst and Blackett list was broadened to include books by celebrities from the world of entertainment, such as Charlie Chaplin's *My Wonderful Visit* (1922), Rudolph Valentino's *Day Dreams* (1924), Will Rogers's *The Illiterate Digest* (1925), Marie Dressler's *My Own Story* (1935), and Sonja Henie's *Wings on My Feet* (1947). Hurst and Blackett attempted to capitalize on public interest in royalty by publishing Crown Prince William of Germany's *My War Experiences* (1922) and Prince Christopher of Greece's *Memoirs* (1938). Works on American politics included *The True Story of Woodrow Wilson* (1924), by David Lawrence, Wilson's former student; Samuel Gompers's autobiography (1925); and *Cordell Hull: A Biography* (1942), by Harold Hinton of the *New York Times*.

The firm published the first two novels of Nicholas Monsarrat, *Think of Tomorrow* (1934) and *At First Sight* (1935). It also published two translations of Adolf Hitler's *Mein Kampf* (1924) as *My Struggle*. The first, in 1933, was abridged to remove the violent passages; in 1939 there was a new translation of the unabridged work that was reprinted several times during World War II. Cherry Kearton, who was head of the firm at the time, had brought the rights with him when he came to Hurst and Blackett from the foreign department of Curtis Brown. In the same vein, the firm published *Germany's Hitler* (1934), by Heinz A. Heinz; *My Part in Germany's Fight* (1935), by Joseph Goebbels; *My Autobiography* (1937), by Benito Mussolini; and *Hermann Goering: The Man and His Work* (1939), by Erich Gritzbach, as well as *Japan Must Fight Britain* (1936) and *The Next World War* (1937), both by Lt. Comdr. Tota Ishimaru. Ironically, the company's offices were destroyed by German bombers in the war. The firm did not publish only pro-Axis works, however. Taid O'Conroy's *The Menace of Japan* (1933) and Gerhard Schacher's *Germany Pushes South-East* (1937) and *Germany Pushes West* (1939) gave timely warnings of the expansionist designs of those countries. Hurst and Blackett also published a biography of Chiang Kai-shek (1938), by Hollington Tong, as well as Madame Chiang's *China in Peace and War* (1940).

During its final decade the firm, which had been purchased in the 1920s by the Hutchinson publishing company, produced works by only forty-seven undistinguished authors, most of them fiction. Few were noticed by reviewers. The last books bearing the Hurst and Blackett imprint were produced in 1954. The valuable properties, such as Hitler's *My Struggle*, continue to appear under the Hutchinson imprint.

**References:**

James J. Barnes and Patience P. Barnes, *Hitler's "Mein Kampf" in Britain and America: A Publishing History 1930-39* (Cambridge & New York: Cambridge University Press, 1980);

Vineta and Robert A. Colby, *The Equivocal Virtue: Mrs. Oliphant and the Literary Marketplace* (New York: Archon Books, 1966);

Monica Correa Fryckstedt, *On the Brink: English Novels of 1866* (Uppsala: Almqvist & Wicksell, 1989);

Robert Lusty, *Bound to Be Read* (London: Cape, 1975);

Alleyn Lyell Reade, *The Mellards and Their Descendants, Including the Bibbys of Liverpool, with Memoirs of Dinah Maria Mulock and Thomas Mellard Reade* (London: Privately printed, 1915);

R. H. Super, *The Chronicler of Barsetshire: A Life of Anthony Trollope* (Ann Arbor: University of Michigan Press, 1988);

J. A. Sutherland, "Henry Colburn Publisher," *Publishing History*, 19 (1986): 59-84;

Sutherland, *Victorian Novelists and Publishers* (Chicago: University of Chicago Press, 1976);

R. C. Terry, *Victorian Popular Fiction 1860-80* (Atlantic Highlands, N.J.: Humanities Press, 1983; London: Macmillan, 1983);

George J. Worth, *James Hannay: His Life and Works* (Lawrence: University of Kansas Publications, 1964).

—B. Q. Schmidt

# Jarrold and Sons

*(Norwich: 1823-1847; Norwich and London, 1847-1916; Norwich: 1916-1941, 1952-1975)*

## Jarrold's Publishers (London) Limited

*(London: 1916-    )*

## Jarrold and Son

*(Norwich: 1942-1951)*

## Jarrold Colour Publications

*(Norwich: 1975-      )*

In 1810 John Jarrold, the younger son of a grocer and the grandson of Colchester cloth merchants, established at his son John's farm at Dallinghoo, Suffolk, a printing press which produced cheap tracts, elementary schoolbooks, and small volumes on natural history. In 1814 John II abandoned farming when farm prices collapsed after the Napoleonic war. He opened a printing establishment at Woodbridge in partnership with his brother-in-law, Benjamin Smith, who had learned printing at Brightly's of Bungay. They operated under the names of Smith and Jarrold and Smith and Company until the dissolution of the partnership in 1821.

In 1823 John II moved his press to 3 Cockey Lane (later renamed London Street), Norwich, where he, his wife, and their four sons went into business under the name of Jarrold and Sons, dealing in stationery and patent medicines as well as printing and publishing. Jarrold and Sons prospered and in 1840 moved to larger quarters in London Street. Expansion slowed

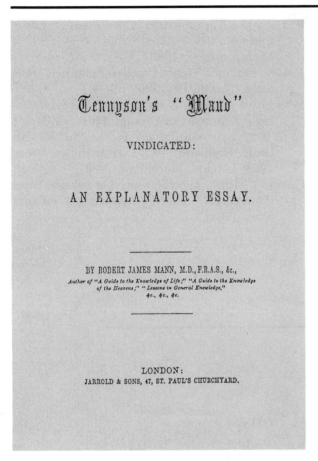

*Title page for the only work of literary criticism (1856) by one of the popular-science writers whose books brought success to Jarrold and Sons*

after the retirement of John II in 1844. In 1845 the *Norfolk News* was started, with Thomas Jarrold one of the proprietors. The newspaper was printed by Jarrold and Sons from 1853 to 1858.

By 1847 the publishing wing of the firm had achieved great success with a series of textbooks. E. C. Brewer, best known for his *Dictionary of Phrase and Fable* (1870), published by Cassell, had most of his large output published by Jarrold and Sons. His *Theology in Science* (1860) discussed geology, physical geography, ethnology, philology, and "the plurality of worlds" in the light of Darwinian theory. In a similar vein was his *Guide to Christian Evidences* (1874). Brewer also wrote many popular catechism-style history and science textbooks, the best-selling of these being *Guide to Scientific Knowledge of Things Familiar* (1847). This book reached its twelfth edition in 1848 and its fifty-fourth in 1850, with more than two hundred thousand copies sold.

Another notable science popularizer was Robert James Mann, whose work on astronomy, chemistry, physiology, and health were published by Jarrold and Sons. A former doctor, Mann wrote *A Guide to the Knowledge of Life* (1855). His one foray into literary criticism was *Tennyson's "Maude" Vindicated* (1856). Another popular author of the time was Agnes Strickland, whose *Historical Tales of Illustrious British Children* was published by Jarrold and Sons in 1859.

In 1847 the firm opened a London office, where educational books became something of a specialty. The office's address was 47 St. Paul's Churchyard from 1847 to 1862, with some 1,848 works being published at 7 Wine Court, Fleet Street. From 1862 to 1872 the branch was at 12 Paternoster Row. By 1872 the office was advertising its books with the slogan "for workers and thinkers." In 1873 it moved to 3 Paternoster Buildings.

New printing works were built in Little London Street, Norwich, around 1860. The Norwich branch at this time was undertaking the series Norwich Household Tracts for the People, sixty of which were published by 1864. The most popular work in the series seems to have been *Love a Reality Not a Romance: Household Truths for Working Men* (1860). The authorship of some of the tracts, including this one, has been attributed to Samuel Jarrold, one of the partners in the firm. Another prolific contributor to the series was Hannah Elizabeth Jarrold, the second wife of Thomas Jarrold. By 1900 Jarrold and Sons had a long tradition of printing temperance literature, the most important being the series Temperance Tracts, published around that date, and the journal *Temperance Monthly Visitor*, founded in 1856 and edited by Mrs. Jarrold until her death in 1917. Map- and chartmaking were also something of a specialty of the firm.

Jarrold and Sons' most important literary associations centered around the Sewell family. The firm published the phenomenally popular works of the Quaker poet Mary Sewell for many years. Her best-known poem, *Mother's Last Words* (1860), sold 1,088,000 copies (420,000 of the cheap version alone by 1865), and its subsequent companion piece, *Our Father's Care* (1867), sold 776,000. Sewell's *Patience Hart's Experiences in Service* (1862) sold more than 30,000 copies in five large editions. *Children of Summerbrook* (1859), a tale in verse, sold 63,000 by 1865, and *Homely Ballads for the Working Man's Fireside* (1858) sold 40,000 copies by 1889. The firm's advertising slogan in the 1860s, "for the cottage and hall," was certainly justified in light of Sewell's sales figures.

The best-selling novel ever published by Jarrold and Sons was written by the invalid daughter of Mary Sewell. On first publication Anna Sewell's *Black Beauty: The Autobiography of a Horse* (1877) seemed about to sink into immediate obscurity; only 100 copies were taken by the London booksellers. The firm had great faith in the book's potential, however, and advertised it relentlessly, with such success that by 1894 100,000 copies had been sold in the United Kingdom, and by 1923 it was the sixth best-seller of any book in the world. The American Society for the Prevention of Cruelty to Animals circulated six million copies in North America alone.

In 1893 the London branch moved to 10 and 11 Warwick Lane. In 1894 it began publishing the Jarrold's Ever Welcome Series of Toy Books, well-illustrated instructional tales for children that were printed in Bavaria.

In 1902 a private company was formed to acquire the Norwich branch; the London branch was continued as a private firm by W. and T. Jarrold. Starting in 1908 the London firm published Jarrold's Popular Penny Stories. After 1908 the firm moved to the forefront in the development of photolithography. In 1916 the London firm was formed into a private limited company and renamed Jarrold's Publishers (London) Limited, under the directorship of W. Jarrold, T. Jarrold, E. Benn, and C. Hughes; the latter two directors were connected with the firm of Benn Brothers. During World War I the publishing of books slowed greatly, but the firm survived by manufacturing stationery for the armed forces and for export. After the war normal operations resumed. In 1921 a branch was opened at Cambridge, joining earlier branches at Cromer, Cowgate, Sheringham, Lowestoft, and Yarmouth.

Jarrold's Publishers (London) Limited was sold to Hutchinson and Company in 1921. Hutchinson assigned its more ephemeral general books, as well as the Jay Library and a monthly series of thrillers and murder mysteries, to the Jarrold imprint.

Jarrold and Sons of Norwich never abandoned its general printing business, running it alongside its publishing concern. By 1939 the firm was producing two million books a year and a million labels per day for the canning trades. At the outbreak of World War II Jarrold and Sons made a largely unsuccessful bid to enter the munitions industry, although it did produce several thousand bomb parts. By 1941 the staff of printing workers had been reduced by nearly 50 percent, to 225. In that same year the Yarmouth works were destroyed by German bombs.

After the London blitz, which destroyed large quantities of books, Jarrold's special expertise in photolithographic reproduction came into heavy demand. The firm also produced handbooks as well as millions of paybooks for the armed forces; it has been claimed that every individual in the British forces and most American airmen carried at least one piece of Jarrold printing. By the end of the war the firm employed more than six hundred employees.

Now at Barrack Street in Norwich, Jarrold continues to emphasize lithography and color processes, as reflected in the firm's current name, Jarrold Colour Publications. Its primary product is guidebooks and travel books, although it does much work in colored brochures and catalogues.

**References:**
*History of Jarrold & Sons, 1823-1943* (Norwich: Jarrold, 1948);

*The House of Jarrolds, 1823-1923* (Norwich: Jarrold, 1924);

*Jarrold 1770-1970: A Book of East Anglian Prints and Documents* (Norwich: Jarrold, 1970);

Michael Joseph, *The Commercial Side of Literature* (London: Hutchinson, 1925).

*—S. D. Mumm*

# William Kidd
## (London: 1830-1859)

Born in 1803, William Kidd was apprenticed at an early age to the London booksellers and publishers Baldwin, Cradock and Joy. In 1830 he began his own bookselling and publishing firm at 6 Old Bond Street. His business depended heavily on inexpensive illustrated guides in pocket formats published and republished throughout the 1830s with slight changes in title and in the information included. These guidebooks were apparently most successful. Kidd did publish more substantial and historically significant works, however. One of these was *Four Years' Residence in the West Indies* (1830), by Frederick William Naylor Bayley, later the first editor of the *Illustrated London News*. This book went through at least three editions and was highly praised by reviewers. Kidd also published in 1830 a collection of short works, *The Dominie's Legacy*, by the promising Scottish writer Andrew Picken. In April 1830 Kidd published *Derwentwater: A Tale of 1715*, by the historical novelist Edward Duros.

It was at this time that Kidd began his commercially rewarding but stormy relationship with Robert Cruikshank, the older but less successful brother of the illustrator George Cruikshank. Robert Cruikshank drew almost all the illustrations for Kidd's works, and Kidd often gave preeminence in his advertisements to Cruikshank's illustrations rather than to the books' texts.

In 1832 Kidd moved to 228 Regent Street. While at this address Kidd copublished many works with James Gilbert of 51 Paternoster Row. At least two numbers of the shilling *Comic Magazine*, edited by Gilbert Abbott à Beckett with illustrations by Robert Seymour, appeared for April and May 1832 as a cheap competitor to Thomas Hood's *Comic Annual*.

It was while he was at Regent Street that signs first appeared of Kidd's willingness to capitalize on controversy to increase sales. He drew attention in an advertisement to an alleged imitation of a deluxe edition of John Bunyan's *Pilgrim's Progress* (1832) that he and Gilbert had published, and he warned buyers of the importance of purchasing the genuine edition with illustrations engraved by G. W. Bonner. At Regent Street he also published a satirical work by Nicholas Michell, *Living Poets and Poetesses* (1832), and exacerbated through his advertisements the controversy caused by the book's contents.

By May 1833 Kidd had moved to 14 Chandos Street, West Strand. There may have been some dispute about ownership of some of the properties published jointly with Gilbert; in at least one case Gilbert included in his imprint "successor to William Kidd," while Kidd issued an advertisement in June 1833 with a "Correct List" of his Picturesque Pocket Companions series.

Around this time Kidd realized that he could increase sales tremendously by failing to specify which of the Cruikshank brothers was in his employ. This was a distinction he had been careful to make earlier, particularly since George had completed one project for him—the illustrations for the novel *The Gentleman in Black* (1830), by James Forbes Dalton. But by December 1833 Kidd stopped specifying which brother he meant. When Kidd published volume 1 of *Cruikshank at Home* in March 1834 a bitter quarrel developed between the brothers over this inadequate identification, and George included a disclaimer of his association with Kidd in the April 1834 installment of *My Sketch Book*, published by Charles Tilt. Kidd responded in the 5 April *Spectator* with a thoroughly deceptive advertisement that again failed to mention any Christian names; it referred only to a dispute between the "Older" and the "younger brother," thus playing on the public's erroneous idea that the better-known George was the older. On 12 April the editors of the *Spectator* blamed Robert himself for intentional deception of the public. On 19 April the magazine published Robert's letter to the editor attributing all responsibility for the fraud to Kidd. In the next week's issue Kidd fired back. On 5 May the *Spectator* summarized but refused to publish Robert's rejoinder and declared its pages off limits to the combatants in the future. Throughout the quarrel Kidd continued blithely to refer only to "Cruikshank"; reprinted the correspondence in advertisements in other journals, such as the *Athenaeum*; and generally drew as much attention to the quarrel as possible while publishing volume 2

*Cartoon by George Cruikshank that concluded his six-month quarrel with William Kidd*

of *Cruikshank at Home* on 5 April and volume 3 in early May. George Cruikshank's last salvo in the fight was fired in part 5 of *My Sketch Book* (August 1834), when he included a vignette depicting himself as a modern-day St. Dunstan (whose church spire presided over Fleet Street) pulling Kidd's nose with a pair of tongs.

Kidd quit using the Cruikshanks in his advertisements shortly thereafter; from then on he publicized the works under the names of the engravers, such as Bonner and Slader, rather than under the names of the artists. He also published some of the plates that were to have made up volume 4 of *Cruikshank at Home*, in combination with some plates by Seymour, as *The Odd Volume, or Book of Variety* (1835). Kidd again drew attention to the earlier dispute in a note in the book and in advertisements.

Twenty-four numbers of *Kidd's London Journal* appeared between May and October 1835. In December 1835 and January 1836 works such as *Kidd's Practical Hints for the Use of Young Carvers*

(1835), *The Book of the Heart* (1835), and *Kidd's Art of Fashionable Cookery* (1836), were advertised as "Published for W. Kidd by W. Ingham."

By early 1837 Kidd had reestablished himself at 7 Tavistock Street, where he would remain as a bookseller until 1859. His publishing ventures became more and more sporadic, and he allowed others to publish the articles he wrote about his developing career as a naturalist, as well as his popular lectures, such as "Genial Gossip" and "Happiness Made Comparatively Easy." In 1837 he published some numbers of the *Idler; and Breakfast-Table Companion*, a journal about fashionable doings in the city, the arts, and drama, and from 1852 to 1854 he published *Kidd's Own Journal for Intercommunications on Natural History, Popular Science, and Things in General*.

In 1859 he sold his business. He devoted the remaining years of his life to a career as a naturalist, creating an aviary in Hammersmith and writing extensively about birds. He got along well with animals and reportedly proved his ownership of a stolen dog to the Bow Street magistrate by having the animal perform remarkable tricks in court. The aviary burned several years before Kidd's death, causing him such distress that he was never willing to rebuild it or to replace the pets to which he had become attached. He died, survived by his wife, on 7 January 1867.

**Reference:**

"Mr. William Kidd" [obituary], *Gentleman's Magazine*, new series, 3 (February 1867): 247.

*—Logan D. Browning, Jr.*

# Charles Knight and Company
*(London: 1836-1909)*
## Charles Knight
*(London: 1822-1836)*
## Charles Knight and Company Limited
*(London: 1909-circa 1970)*
## Charles Knight Publishing
*(London: circa 1970-   )*

The self-educated man of letters Charles Knight established himself as a London publisher at the end of 1822. By the time he ceased active involvement in the business in the mid 1850s, contemporaries would acknowledge his publishing house to be one of the most important pioneering endeavors in the popularization of literature and learning. Knight himself would achieve wide personal acclaim for his unflagging efforts to advance education. His professional life is characterized in Henry Curwen's *History of Booksellers* (1873) as "earnest in its purpose of spreading cheap literature far and wide, brave in difficulty, [and] utterly unmindful of self-gain in the work planned out and done."

Knight's interest and experience in printing and publishing can be traced to his boyhood. His father, also Charles Knight, was a printer, bookseller, and publisher in Windsor, where his son was born on 15 March 1791. In 1805, when the latter was only fourteen, the elder Knight took him on as an apprentice. During the seven years of his indentures the young Charles learned to appreciate quality printing and publishing; meanwhile,

to compensate for the premature termination of his formal education, he assiduously made use of his father's stock of books, thus gaining a sound working knowledge of fine literature. In 1810, as part of his program of self-education, he was among the founding members of a reading society in Windsor.

In 1812, his apprenticeship behind him, Knight entered a stage of his career in which he would divide his activities between London and Windsor. He first worked briefly for two London newspapers, the *Globe* and the *British Press*. Then, in August, he became joint proprietor with his father of the weekly *Windsor and Eton Express*; he would continue as its editor until the paper met with financial trouble and passed into other hands in 1827. It was during his time with the *Express* that Knight initially confronted the difficulties imposed on publishers and readers alike by stamp, advertising, and paper duties. He would set down some of his thoughts on such taxation in *The Struggles of a Book against Excessive Taxation* (1850).

*Charles Knight*

Knight's concern with the taxes on knowledge stemmed from his developing interest in the popularization of literature and other forms of high culture. In the issue of the *Express* for 11 December 1819 he aired his views on the need for "cheap publications" of good quality to be made readily available to the mass of the population. This early venture into what Curwen describes as "the dimly descried regions of popular literature" provided Knight with the central motivation of his publishing career: the desire to make knowledge accessible to all those whose schooling and economic means were limited. He next expressed his desire to further the cause of reading and education in "Diffusion of Useful Knowledge," an editorial in one of the last numbers of the *Plain Englishman* (1820-1823), a periodical which Knight coedited with man of letters, painter, Royal Society fellow, and Greenwich Hospital commissioner Edward Hawke Locker. The *Plain Englishman* dispensed its "useful knowledge" in the form of original discussions of religion, literature, and political economy, as well as excerpts from the works of well-known writers. In 1820 Knight also became part proprietor of the *Guardian*, a London weekly newspaper combining literature and politics. After two years of involvement with this enterprise he sold his interest and set up on his own.

One of the first works to be published from the premises of "Charles Knight, Pall-Mall East," was a literary periodical, *Knight's Quarterly Magazine* (June 1823 - November 1824). Edited by Walter Blunt and Winthrop Macworth Praed, the magazine included stories, poetry, reviews, and articles by such young literary men as H. N. Coleridge and Thomas Babington Macaulay, and by their older contemporary Thomas de Quincey. Other early Knight publications were André Vieussieux's *Italy and the Italians* (1824) and John Milton's *Treatise on Christian Doctrine* (1825).

The next few years were not successful ones for the new business. The *Quarterly Magazine* failed after only six numbers. At the end of 1825 Knight planned a "National Library" which would consist of one hundred or so volumes on science, history, art, and literature. This project came to nothing, as did the *Brazen Head*, a weekly satirical and humorous journal which, in Curwen's words, "fell upon the public like a leaden lump" and ceased publication after only four issues. The year of this periodical's debut and demise—1826—was unpropitious generally for those in the publishing trade. Knight held on to his failing business as long as possible; then, as so many small publishers had to do, he placed his affairs in the hands of a trustee. The *Windsor and Eton Express* and all the copyrights and property associated with the London business were sold in the spring of 1827, leaving Knight virtually penniless.

For the next twelve months or so he engaged in independent literary work. Then, in March 1828, he became part proprietor of the *London Magazine*. The following month, in an article in this publication entitled "Education of the People," he gave fullest expression to his belief that "knowledge is power" and ought to be made "the common possession of every class of mankind." Popular literature and education, he felt sure, had the potential both for directing "the mass of the population" to the "pure gratifications of the understanding" and for instilling widespread awareness of "the duties to themselves and to society" incumbent upon all "rational and responsible beings."

Knight's views had already brought him to the attention of members of the Society for the Diffusion of Useful Knowledge (S.D.U.K.). Under the chairmanship of Lord Brougham the society had been formed in 1826 to counteract worker unrest and the disruptive influence of the radical press by providing working people with in-

*Robert Seymour's cartoon attacking the Society for the Diffusion of Useful Knowledge. Charles Knight is pictured twice—at the far left with ass's ears, where he is cutting out material to use in the society's publications, and at the right administering portions of useful knowledge to John Bull while draining money from his pocket (from MacLean's Monthly Sheet of Caricatures, October 1830).*

expensive, educational, morally improving, and politically innocuous reading material. Knight's involvement with the S.D.U.K. began in July 1827 when he became superintendent of its publications, a position which involved reading manuscripts, deciding on their suitability for publication, and editing and proofreading them. The following year his duties expanded to include touring Britain to help found local S.D.U.K. committees and to encourage booksellers to stock the society's publications. With the assistance of salesmen he established and maintained a distribution network which ultimately extended as far north as Edinburgh, down to the south coast of England, and to outlets in Ireland, Wales, Germany, and the United States.

It was also in 1828 that Knight reestablished himself as a publisher, this time at 13 Pall Mall East—only a few doors away from his original premises. In the same year he became one of the

S.D.U.K.'s two principal publishers; the other was Baldwin and Cradock. In the prior year that firm had brought out the first number of the society's *British Almanac*, but starting in 1828 and for more than forty years following, it would be a Knight publication. Recollecting its early days in his *History of Booksellers*, Curwen praises the *British Almanac* as "a wonderful change for the better after the 'Poor Robins' and 'Old Moores' of the past."

Knight's next major endeavor for the society was the series Library of Entertaining Knowledge, which commenced in March 1829 and ran until 1838. Baldwin and Cradock had been producing a similar series, the Library of Useful Knowledge, since 1827; but some S.D.U.K. members felt that its volumes were rather too heavy going for their intended working-class readership and proposed a new library which offered learning in lighter and more "amusing form." Comprising works such as Robert Mudie's *A Description and History of Vegetable Substances* (1829) and James Rennie's *Domestic Habits of Birds* (1833), Knight's series is hardly entertaining by present-day standards. In its own time, however, it enjoyed a fair success among working people and others eager for information to which they had not previously had ready access. In his *The Old Printer and the Modern Press* (1854), Knight would proudly count the Library of Entertaining Knowledge among such other leaders of the first "great movement in Popular Literature" as Archibald Constable's Miscellany and John Murray's Family Library. It was Knight who bore the costs and risks for the Library of Entertaining Knowledge and subsequent series that he produced on the society's behalf. He incurred losses with what must have been disconcerting frequency, and some of these were substantial. One such case was the Penny Cyclopaedia (1833-1846), whose net loss at the end of its run would amount to well over thirty thousand pounds.

In addition to the Penny Cyclopaedia, which first appeared in penny weekly parts, then in monthly parts at one shilling, sixpence, the 1830s saw the appearance of three other series and two periodicals which Knight brought out under the auspices of the S.D.U.K.: the Working Man's Companion (1831-1832), the Gallery of Portraits (1833-1837), the Library for the Young (1835-1840), the *Quarterly Journal of Education* (1831-1835), and the *Penny Magazine* (1832-1845). Two of the four volumes of the Working Man's Companion series were written by Knight: *The Results of Machinery* and *The Rights of Industry*, both published in 1831, reveal their author as one who was, for his time, an enlightened champion of workingmen's rights.

Of all the publications which Knight produced under the nominal sponsorship of the S.D.U.K., the most influential was the weekly illustrated miscellany, the *Penny Magazine*. As the introduction to the first issue (31 March 1832) made clear, the magazine primarily addressed itself to a working-class readership, promising to "enlarge the range of observation, to add to the store of facts, to awaken the reason, and to lead the imagination into agreeable and innocent trains of thought. . . ." Each issue offered detailed articles and skillfully executed wood engravings treating a range of subjects—art and architecture, science and technology, history and biography, travel, topography, and natural history. Among the magazine's contributing authors and artists were William Hone; the travelogue writer John Kitto; the art critics Allan Cunningham and Anna Jameson; the editor of *Blackwood's Magazine*, Thomas Pringle; the historian and man of letters George Lillie Craik; the engravers William Harvey and John Jackson; and the draughtsman F. W. Fairholt. As the only widely affordable periodical of its kind, the *Penny Magazine* enjoyed tremendous popularity among both the middle and the working classes. In its first three years it maintained a weekly circulation of two hundred thousand—and, with the custom of the day being to share any one issue among several individuals, this figure likely implies a regular readership of a million or more. Knight would later judge this innovative miscellany to be one of the proudest achievements of his publishing career; in the second volume of his autobiography, *Passages of a Working Life* (1864), he recalls the *Penny Magazine* as "the most successful experiment in popular literature that England had seen."

In 1833 Knight moved to 22 Ludgate Street, where he produced some of his most popular and best-remembered publications. These works were brought out strictly under his own name; they were unconnected with the S.D.U.K. and must have offset the losses sustained on the society's behalf. Among the most commercially successful of such publications were three works that were published in parts: the *Pictorial Bible* (1836-1838), edited by Kitto; an illustrated edition of the works of Shakespeare (1838-1841), principally edited by Knight; and the *Pictorial History of England* (1837-1844), written by Craik and other knowledgeable contributors. The history long remained "unbeatable for domestic use"—such at least was the claim made for it in the 1892 edition of the *Dictionary of National Biography*.

By the end of the 1830s illustrated publishing had become what Knight would describe in his memoirs as "a marked feature of my business." He was among the first publishers to apply the steam-powered press and the process of stereotyping to the cost-efficient mass reproduction of imagery. His first important venture in illustrated publishing was the *Penny Magazine*, which had from its outset provided a generous number of large, high-quality wood engravings at a low price for the public and a profit for the publisher. Having thus satisfied himself as to the commercial viability of pictorial works, Knight continued to produce the majority of his publications with illustrations. Not only did he lead the way in the use of wood engraving but he was also in the vanguard of publishers who included color lithographs in atlases and books on art. It is small wonder that in recollecting his working life Knight would later claim credit for the popularization of both the concept and the word *pictorial*. "I felt rather daring," he wrote, "in the employment of a term which the dictionaries pronounced as 'not in use.'" All of Knight's publications were printed by the firm of William Clowes, later William Clowes and Sons. In 1836 one of Clowes's sons married Knight's daughter; in 1841 he saved his father-in-law from the threat of bankruptcy.

In the 1840s Knight continued his policy of producing well-illustrated, interesting, and informative reading matter for a wide general market. His significant publications during this decade included *London* (1841-1844), in weekly parts; the *Pictorial Museum of Animated Nature* (1844); *The Pictorial Gallery of the Arts* (1847), in two volumes; and *The Land We Live In* (1847-1850). For the latter work, much of which he wrote himself, Knight had traveled all over the country gathering material. On completion, the work ran to four volumes of descriptions and pictures of notable English monuments and sights.

Knight's most ambitious project of the 1840s was a series which began in 1844 as the Weekly Volumes; in 1846 it became the monthly Shilling Volumes. Continuing until 1849, the series ran to 186 volumes and covered a broad spectrum of subject matter that included history, biography, fine arts, geography, and theology. Works of general literature totaled 16 volumes; original fiction, 6; and literary criticism, 13. The first volume was a biography written by Knight: *William Caxton, the First English Printer* (1844). Among the other volumes were Harriet Martineau's *Feats on the Fiord* (1844), Charles Lamb's *Tales from Shakespeare* (1844), Craik's *Sketches of the History of Literature and Learning in England* (1844-1845) and *Bacon: His Writing and His Philosophy* (1846-1847), and John Saunders's condensation of Geoffrey Chaucer's *The Canterbury Tales* (1845-1847). Knight had originally conceived the volumes as a means by which those lacking substantial education and income might create communal libraries by pooling their money. The series was at best a modest success: sales averaged just 5,000 copies per title, with perhaps 20 volumes achieving sales of 10,000 copies each. As Knight was aware, he was faced with the formidable competition of peri-

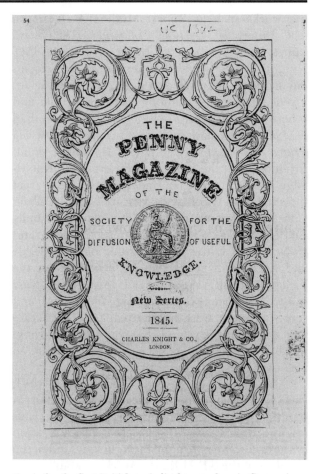

*Cover for the first British periodical to reach a six-figure circulation. Competition from imitators began eroding its profits around 1840 and caused its demise in 1845.*

odical fiction and railway novels, both of which were as cheap as or cheaper than the Shilling Volumes and, for most readers, more entertaining.

Competition also brought about the demise of the *Penny Magazine* in 1845. Its market share had been increasingly eroded since about 1840 by the penny journals, gazettes, and papers that had begun to proliferate in the field of popular publishing. In January 1846 Knight published a new version under the title *Knight's Penny Magazine*, a signal of its independence from S.D.U.K. sponsorship. This project survived for only six months. The year 1846 also witnessed the suspension of the society's operations. For several years prior to its disbanding, Knight had been progressively curtailing his activities on its behalf to devote more time to his own literary endeavors—for example, his *William Shakespeare: A Biography* (1843), the life of Caxton, and *Half-Hours with the Best Authors* (1847-1848).

In 1848 the firm moved to 90 Fleet Street. Knight began gradually withdrawing from active participation in the business; the day-to-day management he left to others, among them his son Barry Charles Henry Knight, who was by this time a partner in what since 1836 had been known as Charles Knight and Company. Knight continued to supervise the publication of certain works in which he had a particular interest, such as *History of England during the Thirty Years' Peace, 1815-1846* (1851); he had written the first sixteen chapters, and Harriet Martineau had completed the rest. Around the same time Knight became intrigued by the publishing possibilities afforded by the Great Exhibition and its popular appeal; in response to the widespread enthusiasm for exhibitions and the industrial arts he brought out *Knight's Cyclopedia of the Industry of All Nations* (1851) and one or two other such publications. He was also concerned with catering to the expanding information needs of a newly mobile, train-traveling, sightseeing populace. *The Land We Live In* had been conceived for such a market, as were *Pictorial Half-Hours of London Topography* (1850) and the *Excursion Train Companion* (1851). These works were among the last of his ventures as a publisher. He retired in 1855, leaving the business in the hands of his son.

No longer active in publishing, Knight channeled his energies into writing and editing; over the next decade or so he produced the *English Cyclopedia* (1856-1862); *Popular History of England* (1856-1862), in monthly parts; an abridgment of this work, *School History of England* (1865); three volumes of memoirs, *Passages of a Working Life*; and *Half-Hours with the Best Letter Writers and Autobiographers* (1867-1868). In the same year that the latter title appeared, failing eyesight put an end to his career as a writer and editor. His entry in the *Dictionary of National Biography* records that "he had to be led by a friend" at the dinner given on 1 October 1867 for another of his friends, Charles Dickens. Knight died on 9 March 1873—as Curwen puts it, "full of years and of honours." In anticipating much that would be accomplished later in the century by firms such as Cassell and Company, his contribution to publishing had been forward-looking and enlightened. The benevolence and constancy with which he dedicated himself to popularizing literature and imagery had been such that his many literary friends agreed with affectionate humor that he could have no more appropriate epitaph than the two telling words "Good Knight."

After the death of its founder, Charles Knight and Company concentrated on what had

once been merely a sideline: government publications. This aspect of the business dated back to 1835, when Knight was appointed publisher to the Poor Law Commission. In the early 1850s, as his retirement drew near, the firm had shifted from principally general to mainly official publishing. By the 1860s its list included only a few titles of popular interest, such as a monthly part-publication of John Foxe's *History of Protestant Martyrs* (1861), and the *British Almanac*, which passed to the Stationers Company in 1869. Even the books that Knight himself had written during this period had gone to other publishers—Bradbury and Evans, John Murray, and George Routledge and Sons.

In the 1870s and 1880s Charles Knight and Company continued its policy of government publishing—remuneratively, it would seem, for the firm not only maintained premises in Fleet Street but also in Harp Alley from 1874 to 1877 and in Salisbury Square from 1878 to 1884. Barry Knight died in 1884. From that date until well into the twentieth century the firm survived as a publisher of handbooks, guides, and manuals which it produced for local authorities on behalf of the Poor Law Commission, the Ministry of Health, and the Local Government Board. From the mid 1880s to the early 1900s it continued the practice of dividing operations among several locations: the old Fleet Street offices; Bridewell Place from 1885; and the Belle Sauvage Yard, which it shared with Cassell and Company from 1899.

In 1909 what had begun as a sole proprietorship, then expanded to a partnership, was incorporated as Charles Knight and Company Limited, with new headquarters in Tooley Street, southeast London. The company maintained its independence until it was acquired by Ernest Benn Limited in about 1970. It is presently a subsidiary of Tolley Publishing, specialists in business law, taxation, and accounting, and remains a member of the Benn Group, which has itself been part of A. and C. Black plc since 1984. Now known as Charles Knight Publishing, the firm is located in Tolley House, Addiscombe Road, Croydon, where it continues to specialize in legal works on local government, as well as publications on various technical subjects and the offshore oil and construction industries. The original association between the name Charles Knight and a tradition of literary and pictorial publishing has been perpetuated in recent years by other publishers' reprint and facsimile editions of such works as Knight's 1844 biography of Caxton (London: Lund Humphries, 1976) and his 1851 *Pictorial Half-Hours of London Topography* (Clifden, Ireland: Boethius, 1984).

**References:**

P. Anderson, "Pictures for the People: Knight's *Penny Magazine*, an Early Venture into Popular Art Education," *Studies in Art Education*, 28 (Spring 1987): 133-140;

Scott Bennett, "Revolutions in Thought: Serial Publication and the Mass Market for Reading," in *The Victorian Periodical Press: Samplings and Soundings*, edited by Joanne Shattock and Michael Wolff (Leicester & Toronto: University Presses, 1982), pp. 225-257;

W. A. Chatto, "History of Wood-Engraving," *Illustrated London News*, 22 June 1844, pp. 405-406;

Alice A. Clowes, *Charles Knight: A Sketch* (London: Bentley, 1892);

William Clowes, *Family Business, 1803-1953* (London: Clowes, 1953);

Henry Curwen, *A History of Booksellers* (London: Chatto & Windus, 1873), pp. 251-266;

"Illustrated Books," *Quarterly Review*, 74 ( June 1844): 168-199;

Mason Jackson, *The Pictorial Press* (London: Hurst & Blackett, 1885), pp. 276-282;

William F. Kennedy, "Lord Brougham, Charles Knight, and *The Rights of Industry*," *Economica*, new series 29 (February 1962): 58-71;

Charles Knight, "Diffusion of Useful Knowledge," *Plain Englishman*, 3 (1823): 277;

Knight, "Education of the People," *London Magazine*, third series 1 (April 1828): 1-13;

Knight, *The Old Printer and the Modern Press* (London: Murray, 1854);

Knight, *Passages of a Working Life*, 3 volumes (London: Bradbury & Evans, 1864);

Charles C. F. Morbey, *Charles Knight: An Appreciation and Bibliography of the Work of a Great Victorian Publisher* (Birmingham: Birmingham Polytechnic Department of Librarianship, 1979);

Janet Percival, *The Society for the Diffusion of Useful Knowledge, 1826-1848: A Handlist of the Society's Correspondence and Papers* (London: University College Library Occasional Publications No. 5, 1978);

Harold Smith, *The Society for the Diffusion of Useful Knowledge, 1826-1846: A Social and Bibliographical Evaluation* (Halifax, Nova Scotia: Dalhousie University Libraries Occasional Paper No. 8, 1972);

Geoffrey Wakeman, *Victorian Book Illustration* (Newton Abbot: David & Charles, 1973).

**Papers:**

Records of Charles Knight and Company were destroyed by bombing in 1941. Information on the firm's history between 1828 and 1846 can be gleaned from the correspondence, letter books, and publication committee and penny publication subcommittee minutes of the Society for the Diffusion of Useful Knowledge in the University College Library, London. Knight catalogues from the nineteenth century are in the Bodleian Library's John Johnson archive at Oxford and in the Knight Collection of the Department of Librarianship, Birmingham Polytechnic. Additional information may exist in the archives of Knight's printers, William Clowes and Sons. Ledgers dating from 1822 are in the company's offices at Beccles, Suffolk; other records are in the Suffolk County Record Office.

　　　　　　　　　　　　　—*Patricia J. Anderson*

# Leadenhall Press
*(London: 1892-1905)*
## Field and Tuer
*(London: 1863-1892)*

The Leadenhall Press was a small late-Victorian publishing house distinguished for its high-quality, decoratively produced publications. These works included abridgments of literary classics, facsimile editions of children's stories, a small amount of new fiction, and an array of nonfiction covering such subjects as popular history and antiquarianism, music, sport, and travel. Many were printed in antique type and are now collectors' items.

The firm's wide-ranging list reflected the many and diverse interests of Andrew White Tuer, the man most closely associated with the press throughout its operation. Tuer was not only a publisher but also a stationer, author, editor, antiquarian, and inventor. Born in Sunderland on 24 December 1838, he moved to London in the mid 1850s; in 1862, after studying medicine and working briefly in a city merchant office, he established himself as a wholesale stationer at 136 The Minories. In the following year he entered into partnership with the stationer and printer Abraham Field; the firm traded under the name Field and Tuer. In 1868 it moved to 50 Leadenhall Street, with adjoining works at 6, 7, and 8 Sugar Loaf Court.

Throughout the 1860s and into the 1870s the partnership operated principally as stationers, diverging occasionally into printing. Its first venture into publishing was the *Paper and Printing Trades Journal*, launched in December 1872 and edited by Tuer. It was not until 1879 that the first book to bear the Field and Tuer imprint appeared, and it was at this time that the firm became a small publishing house with an arm still devoted to the stationery trade. That first book was

*Andrew White Tuer, circa 1890*

Tuer's *Luxurious Bathing*, a treatise with etchings of river- and seascapes. It was initially published in a limited edition of twenty-five copies printed on "Japanese paper" and bound in vellum. Such a format was typical of the kind of uniquely designed book that would become the hallmark of the firm.

Field's role in the business is not clear. Perhaps, once the firm entered publishing, he handled the stationery side while Tuer managed the new venture; it is also possible that Field was never anything other than a silent partner or financial backer. In any case, Tuer was the most active partner. He invented a paper paste called Stickphast, which contributed much to the profits of the business; he also designed a useful writing tablet, "The Authors' Hairless Paper Pad," and formulated an ink powder for home mixing. In addition to editing the journal he also wrote, edited, or compiled other works which appeared as Field and Tuer publications. Among these were *The Printers' International Specimen Exchange* (1880-1898); *Bartolozzi and his Works* (1882), in two volumes; and *Old London Street Cries and the Cries of Today* (1885), which sold seventy-six thousand copies.

The 1880s and the first few years of the 1890s were the most prolific period in the firm's history, during which it published well over half of the 317 books it would ultimately bring out. Among the firm's output during this time were three early archaeological works by Flinders Petrie; Jerome K. Jerome's first and second books, *On the Stage—and Off* (1885) and *The Idle Thoughts of an Idle Fellow* (1886). Jerome's books generally sold well, as did a work by Max O'Rell (the pseudonym of an expatriate Frenchman, Paul Blouet), whose observations of the English national character, *John Bull and His Island* (1883), would sell two hundred thousand copies by 1898. During the 1880s the firm brought out several series, including the Oblong Shilling-Series (1884) and Ye Leadenhall Presse Pamphlets (1884), as well as the Sixteen Penny Series (1886-1888), whose "Gleanings from the Classics" included abridgments of Samuel Richardson's *Sir Charles Grandison* (1886), James Thomson's *The Seasons* (1886), and Laurence Sterne's *Tristram Shandy* (1888), all illustrated with the original copperplates.

Field died in 1891, and early in the following year the firm incorporated as a limited liability company under the name Leadenhall Press. The firm's imprint had previously read "Field and Tuer, The Leadenhall Press, E.C."; but from the date of its incorporation the firm dropped "Field and Tuer" and used the "Leadenhall Press" designation exclusively. Tuer became the major shareholder and managing director and would maintain the latter position until his death. After its incorporation the firm significantly decreased the quantity of its publications—in 1893 it published only fourteen books, a number which declined further to the decade low of three titles in 1897. Among the works to carry the Leadenhall Press imprint were Jerome's *Novel Notes* (1893); Tuer's *The History of the Horn-Book* (1896); and, compiled in the main from works in Tuer's own library, two sets of facsimile editions of children's literature: the eight-volume *Pages and Pictures from Forgotten Children's Books* (1898-1899) and *Stories from Old-Fashioned Children's Books* (1899-1900), also in eight volumes. The reasons for this drop in output are not clear, but the most likely explanation is Tuer's failing health; he died on 24 February 1900. The firm continued to manufacture Stickphast, a product which survived under at least one other owner until about 1960. But without its moving spirit the publishing end of the business did not long continue, and in 1905 the Leadenhall Press ceased operations.

The Leadenhall Press owed much of its reputation to the quality and generosity of the illustrations that enhanced many of its publications. Accordingly, with the exception of Jerome and a few others, it is not the firm's authors but its illustrators who are primarily remembered today. The best known of their number were Edward Burne-Jones, James McNeill Whistler, Charles Keene, and Henry S. Tuke. Others who enjoyed a measure of prominence in their own time were Joseph Crawhall, Phil May, and the lesser-known William Luker, Jr., who contributed illustrations for such topographical publications as William J. Loftie's *London City* (1891) and Percy Fitzgerald's *London City Suburbs* (1893).

**References:**

"A. W. Tuer" [obituary], *Illustrated London News*, 10 March 1900, p. 324;

J. P. Bury, "A. W. Tuer and the Leadenhall Press," *Book Collector*, 36 (Summer 1987): 225-243.

*—Patricia J. Anderson*

# Edward Lloyd
## (London: 1833-1923)

Edward Lloyd has been called—and rightly so—"the father of the cheap press." He founded a publishing empire based on cheap fiction (the "penny dreadfuls" or "penny bloods") for the newly literate populace and popular periodicals for an emerging mass market. He was also among the first to introduce the new techniques of printing, advertising, and distribution necessary for the mass production of all varieties of cheap publications.

His career and that of his firm fall into two separate phases. The first, the publishing of hundreds of volumes of original if undistinguished cheap fiction, made him rich. The second, the publishing of the enormously successful Sunday paper *Lloyd's Weekly Newspaper*, made him respectable.

As the number of cheap newspapers declined in the 1830s due to the Stamp Tax, the demand for fiction—which was not taxed—increased. Lloyd's penny fiction filled this widespread desire. At the same time, the steady supply of sensational tales helped to increase literacy and in turn to intensify the demand for more cheap reading material. From the beginning Lloyd tried to fill the need for reading matter with cheap periodicals as well as cheap books, but it was not until midcentury, after various changes in the laws, that he was able to do so at a price the lower classes could afford.

Lloyd was born on 16 February 1815 at Thornton Heath, Surrey, where his father was a farmer. The family moved to London when Lloyd was still young. In the city he studied at a Mechanics' Institute, where he learned stenography. While still "quite a boy," according to the *Dictionary of National Biography*, he opened a shop on Curtain Road, Shoreditch, where he sold books and newspapers and began his publishing career. His first publication was *Lloyd's Stenography* in 1833; both the use of his name in the title and his energy and sharpness in writing, publishing, and selling it to the bookshops himself are early signs of the self-promotion and shrewd business sense that led to his eventual success.

Following the publication of his book on stenography, Lloyd turned to one of the oldest and

*Edward Lloyd*

most persistent types of popular book, the "true crime" narrative, publishing *A History of Pirates of All Nations* (1836-1837), *Lives of the Most Notorious Highwaymen* (1836-1837), and *Calendar of Horrors* (1836). He also published that year seven numbers of *Lloyd's Political Jokes: Being a Series of Caricatures of Passing Events, Designed by the Most Eminent Artists of the Present*, of which no copies have survived.

But Lloyd's real success in book publishing was in the area of penny fiction—that is, gothic or historical or domestic romances in penny parts. Between 1836 and 1856 Lloyd published some two hundred titles. These "penny bloods" grew out of the eighteenth-century popular literature of broadsides, chapbooks, and Newgate calendars, as well as the popular stage. They mostly depicted seduction, murder, robbery, and assault, with the villainous upper classes routed and the innocent workers victorious. But however much blood and near-disaster the books contained, Lloyd allowed nothing prurient. A random selection of titles gives a sense of the typical "penny blood": Malcolm J. Errym's *Susan Hopley; or, the Trials and Vicissitudes of a Servant Girl* (1842) and George Dibdin Pitt's *The Wreck of the Heart; or, The Story of Agnes Primrose* (1842); Thomas Peckett Prest's *The Maniac Father; or, The Victim of Seduction* (1842); Robert Huish's *The Nun of Gnadenzell* (1846); Prest's *Helen Porter; or, A Wife's Tragedy and a Sister's Trials* (1847).

The bibliographic details of this mass of penny serialized fiction, both that published by Lloyd and that published by others, are scarce. Even the twentieth-century *Bibliography of Edward Lloyd's Penny Bloods* (1945) was privately printed in just two hundred copies. Some of the most popular novels survive in specialized libraries, and reminiscences of the period sometimes give titles of others. But much of the information about these cheap novels and tales appears to be lost.

In his early days, Lloyd published from a variety of locations—Curtain Road, Shoreditch; Wych Street, Strand; Broad Street, Holborn. Finally, in 1843 he located his offices at 12 Salisbury Square—in the house where, he liked to point out, Samuel Richardson wrote *Pamela* (1740-1742) and Oliver Goldsmith once worked as a printer's reader.

Lloyd's first great successes in the area of popular publishing were his plagiarisms of works by Charles Dickens: *The Sketch Book* (1836), in eleven penny numbers with seventeen woodcuts; *The Penny Pickwick* (1837); *Pickwick in America* (1842); *Nicholas Nickelbery* (1838); *Life and Adventures of Oliver Twiss* (1839); and *Mister Humphries Clock* (1840), all by Prest under the pseudonym "Bos." Writing perhaps half of Lloyd's penny bloods, Prest was one of his most prolific and most successful authors. In addition to the plagiarisms of Dickens, Prest also produced the best-seller *Ela the Outcast; or, The Gipsy of Rosemary Dell* (1839).

Another prolific writer for Lloyd was James Malcolm Rymer, who used the pseudonym Malcolm J. Errym but was known as "Ada the Betrayed" after the domestic romance that was his most popular work: *Ada the Betrayed; or, The Murder at the Old Smithy* (1842). Prest and Rymer were periodically credited with the same works. According to Thomas Catling, a later editor for Lloyd, Rymer had "ten different stories running serially at one period," the best-known of which

were the gothic romance *The Black Monk; or, The Secret of the Grey Turret* (1844) and the 868-page forerunner to Bram Stoker's *Dracula* (1897), *Varney the Vampire; or, The Feast of Blood* (1847), which has also been attributed to Prest.

Other popular writers who wrote one or more novels for Lloyd included John Frederick Smith, with the historical romance *The Chronicles of Stanfield Hall* (circa 1840); Thomas Frost, with *Sixteen String Jack* (1845); and Mrs. Elizabeth Caroline Grey, who won Lloyd's one-hundred-guinea prize for a gothic thriller in 1847 with *Ordeal by Touch*. More obscure writers included Harry Hazel, Faucit Saville, Mrs. M. L. Sweetser, B. Barker, and Ellen T.

All these authors were paid ten shillings per number; Lloyd provided them with specially lined paper that, covered with average-sized writing, would constitute a one-penny issue. Each number consisted of eight pages of small type, approximately five thousand words. If Lloyd was uncertain of a particular author's abilities, he apparently gave the manuscript to a machine boy (a boy who tended the printing presses) to read; if the boy pronounced that it would do, the story was published. A few works were published in large size, but most were in a uniform demy octavo (8 3/4 inches by 5 5/8 inches); the earlier titles were in a single column and the later in double. Most were illustrated by at least one engraving.

In 1847 alone Lloyd published about thirty-eight new works of fiction. In addition to their exciting subjects and familiar forms, these works were popular because of their illustrations, which tended to be of various sensational scenes. But, unlike the illustrations in such popular journals as *Reynolds's Miscellany*, they were not salacious. Their quality may be indicated by an experience that George Augustus Sala, who as a young man worked as an illustrator for Lloyd, recounted in his autobiography: Lloyd returned a drawing to him, saying "the eyes must be larger, and there must be more blood—much more blood."

Lloyd's publications during the 1840s and 1850s included more than the "penny bloods." He also published penny songbooks, cookery books, self-help treatises, dictionaries, atlases, encyclopedias, handbooks, volumes of natural history, and a wide variety of miscellaneous collections and reprints.

In the mid 1850s, however, Lloyd's book publishing decreased. He had other interests. Lloyd recalled later to Joseph R. Hatton that as early as

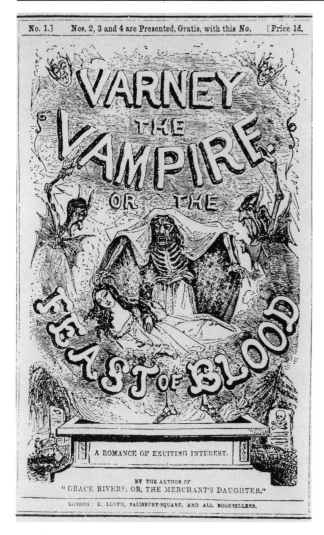

No. 1.]    Nos. 2, 3 and 4 are Presented, Gratis, with this No.    [Price 1d.

VARNEY THE VAMPIRE OR THE FEAST OF BLOOD

A ROMANCE OF EXCITING INTEREST.

BY THE AUTHOR OF
" GRACE RIVERS; OR, THE MERCHANT'S DAUGHTER."

LONDON : E. LLOYD, SALISBURY-SQUARE, AND ALL BOOKSELLERS.

*Cover for one of the "penny dreadfuls" on which Lloyd built*
*his publishing empire*

1829 "he was strongly imbued with Liberal opinions, and with the idea of starting a 'free and independent newspaper' for their advocacy." He started his first newspaper as early as 1836 but was forced to close it quickly when it became impossible to avoid the Stamp Tax. Newspapers were required to purchase a stamp for each copy of the paper, a tax designed to make newspapers too expensive for the lower classes. Though the tax was reduced in 1836, it was more rigorously enforced, resulting in a steady decline in the number of cheap newspapers.

Lloyd's newspaper publishing career really began in 1840 when he inaugurated *Lloyd's Penny Sunday Times and People's Police Gazette*, a combination of fiction—much of it plagiarized from other writers—and fictionalized police reports. This mix may have originated as a way to avoid the Stamp Tax, since the fictional content of the journal kept it from being a "newspaper," but the formula combining fiction, domestic news spiced with crime, and other sensational reports would make Lloyd's ultimate success as a publisher. It was for this journal that Prest seems to have invented the legend of Sweeney Todd, the demon barber of Fleet Street, in "The String of Pearls," which was published in thirty-seven installments in *Lloyd's Penny Sunday Times* in 1846-1847.

In 1842 Lloyd started what was to be the most long-lasting of all his publications. In the beginning it was called *Lloyd's Illustrated London Newspaper* and was intended to compete with the *Illustrated London News*—most of Lloyd's early periodicals intended to compete with other popular journals by undercutting their prices. After seven weeks he ran a "news" story about an escaped lion and was immediately threatened with prosecution if he did not pay the Stamp Tax. Lloyd decided to take a serious financial gamble and make the paper a "real" newspaper, one with news and without illustrations. He paid the Stamp Tax (fourpence per copy) and raised the price to twopence, which he figured was just in the range of the mass readership. This price was a boon to the lower-middle-class readers, women, and skilled and semiskilled workers who made up his audience; but it did not please the news agents whose profits were cut since they sold their copies at the same price, and they boycotted *Lloyd's Weekly London Newspaper*. In response, Lloyd developed his own distribution system and embarked on a vigorous advertising campaign; he was notorious throughout his career for his aggressive advertising. Lloyd's most daring advertising scheme was to stamp copper coins with his advertisements and to pay part of his workers' wages with these coins to insure their general circulation. He was only stopped when the *Times* called attention to the practice (incidentally providing Lloyd with even more publicity) and Parliament passed a law making it an offense to deface the coin of the realm.

Not surprisingly, the early days of the newspaper were financially uncertain. Thomas Frost, a prolific writer of working-class fiction and an active Chartist, reported, "Mr. Lloyd told me that repeatedly he found himself, at the end of the week, in the position of not knowing where the money would come from to bring out the next number. The profits from the sale of a large run of tales, with gardening and other practical handbooks, proved the main source of revenue." But

*An American-made Hoe Web-Fed Rotary Press, of the kind Lloyd introduced into England in 1871*

the newspaper was very popular, selling thirty-two thousand copies a week in the first year of its existence, and this popularity insured its financial success. The obvious demand for cheap periodicals led Lloyd to publish several others, including *Lloyd's Penny Atlas and Weekly Register of Novel Entertainment* (1843-1845), *Lloyd's Penny Weekly Miscellany of Romance and General Interest* (1843-1846), and *Lloyd's Monthly Volume of Amusing and Instructive Literature* (1845-1847).

The title of *Lloyd's Illustrated London Newspaper* changed in 1843 to *Lloyd's Weekly London Newspaper* and in 1849 to *Lloyd's Weekly Newspaper*. A Mr. Ball was the first editor, followed by Walter Carpenter. In 1852, in a bid for respectability, Lloyd offered the editorship at a salary of one thousand pounds a year to Douglas Jerrold, a well-known playwright, journalist, and editor, and a friend of Dickens, William Makepeace Thackeray, and Henry Mayhew. Under Jerrold's editorship the newspaper gained credibility and prestige. When Jerrold died in 1857, his son Blanchard Jerrold became editor. Horace Mayhew, brother of Henry, who had written theatrical notices for the paper, succeeded Blanchard Jerrold, and Catling became editor in the late 1860s. All of these middle-class editors who served under Lloyd during the second half of the nineteenth century spoke of him with respect

and admiration. Indeed, Lloyd seems to have been a genuinely friendly and likable man.

Around 1847 Lloyd had been among the first to introduce Hoe rotary printers to enable rapid printing, some 5,000 copies an hour. In 1853 the circulation of *Lloyd's Weekly Newspaper* was about 90,000. After the repeal of the Stamp Tax in 1855 circulation jumped, and Lloyd introduced new modifications to enable even faster and larger printing runs. By 1861 circulation had risen to 170,000; Lloyd returned the price to the original penny, and the circulation rose to 350,000 in two years. In the 1860s Lloyd introduced the first great web machine, which could print two sheets of the newspaper from a single reel of paper. In 1879 circulation was at 612,902. Another modification near the end of the century allowed the firm to produce on each of seven different machines 55,000 thirty-two-page papers an hour. Circulation continued to increase, and in 1896 *Lloyd's Weekly Newspaper* became the first British paper to sell a million copies.

It was not just the price that made the journal popular; Lloyd had a good sense of what the mass readership wanted. Although it was liberal, the newspaper more or less supported the status quo; and it concentrated on British affairs rather than international ones. As *Mitchell's Newspaper*

*Press Directory* said in 1851: "It is peculiarly the poor man's paper, and endeavours, of course, to embrace as many articles of intelligence and as much under each head, as it can contrive to compress together; giving prominence to police reports, and similar matters of *popular* interest. At the same time, its contents are far more creditable, and comprise far more of a light and literary character, than might be conceived. Certainly it presents an immense mass of matter for the money; with a little of everything, and a good deal of many things; so that even if its readers saw no other paper, they would not be much behind the rest of the world as to news."

Lloyd completely abandoned the publishing of fiction; it is said that he sent agents around to buy up the old stocks of his "penny bloods" and destroy them. In 1876 he bought a daily newspaper, the *Clerkenwell News*, which he renamed the *Daily Chronicle* and turned into a paper of liberal policies. The first editor was R. W. Boyle. The same year Lloyd began the *Poet's Magazine*.

At this time Lloyd found he was having difficulty getting enough paper for his increasing sales. When he found out that esparto grass could be used to make paper he leased one hundred thousand acres in Algeria to insure a supply of the grass; imported it through his own dock at Bow; and made paper from it in his own factory, the Paper Mills at Sittingbourne, Kent.

Lloyd died in 1890, leaving an estate of more than five hundred thousand pounds to his four sons and stipulating in his will that the two newspapers should always have liberal policies. He was buried in Highgate Cemetery. His son Frank became the managing director of the newspapers. The *Poet's Weekly*, which had gone through a variety of name and format changes, finally emerged as *Lloyd's Magazine* in 1895; it ceased publication in 1900. Robert Donald became editor of *Lloyd's Weekly* in 1904; by 1914 he was also editor of the *Daily Chronicle* and managing director of United Newspapers Limited, the subsidiary that owned the two properties. In 1918 Frank Lloyd sold the *Daily Chronicle*, and *Lloyd's Weekly Newspaper* became *Lloyd's Sunday News*.

After World War I Donald and Lloyd returned to the activities of the early days of the company by publishing several series of cheap books, such as Lloyd's Boys' Adventure Series (1921-1922), Lloyd's Detective Stories (1921), Lloyd's ABC of Careers for Girls (1922), and Lloyd's Sports Library (1922). In 1923 the newspaper dropped the name *Lloyd's*. Though the *Sunday News* continued to be published by United Newspapers, a public company, until 1931, the loss of *Lloyd's* in its name marked the effective end of the Lloyd publishing house.

**References:**

Virginia Berridge, "Popular Journalism and Working Class Attitudes, 1852-86: A Study of *Reynolds's Newspaper*, *Lloyd's Weekly Newspaper*, and the *Weekly Times*," Ph.D dissertation, University of London, 1976;

H. R. Fox Bourne, *English Newspapers: Chapters in the History of Journalism*, 2 volumes (London: Chatto & Windus, 1887), I: 120-123, II: 346-347;

Thomas Catling, *My Life's Pilgrimage* (London: Murray, 1911);

Thomas Frost, *Forty Years' Recollections: Literary and Political* (London: Low, 1880);

Joseph R. Hatton, *Journalistic London* (London: Low, 1882);

P. R. Hoggart, "Edward Lloyd, 'The Father of the Cheap Press,'" *Dickensian*, 80 (Spring 1984): 33-38;

Louis James, *Fiction for the Working Man* (London: Oxford University Press, 1963);

J. Medcraft, *Bibliography of Lloyd's Penny Bloods* (Dundee, Scotland: Privately printed, 1945);

W. Roberts, "Lloyd's Penny Bloods," *Book Collector's Quarterly*, 17 (April-June 1935): 1-16;

George Augustus Sala, *The Life and Adventures of George Augustus Sala: Written by Himself*, second edition, 2 volumes (London: Cassell, 1895), I: 172.

*—Anne Humpherys*

# Macmillan and Company
*(Cambridge: 1850-1857; Cambridge and London: 1857-1863; London: 1863-1990)*
## D. and A. Macmillan
*(London: 1843-1845)*
## Macmillan, Barclay and Macmillan
*(Cambridge: 1845-1850)*
## Macmillan Publishers Limited
*(London: 1990-    )*

See also the Macmillan Company entry in *DLB 49: American Literary Publishing Houses, 1638-1899.*

After three years as a bookseller's assistant at Mr. Johnson's shop in Cambridge, where he earned thirty pounds per year, Daniel Macmillan moved to London in 1836 to continue in the same trade at the Messrs. Seeleys' in Fleet Street. His brother Alexander joined him there in 1839. The brothers, largely self-taught, worked at self-improvement by reading the works of Percy Bysshe Shelley, Thomas Carlyle, and other contemporary authors as well as pamphlets by Alexander Scott; the latter brought them into correspondence with Julius Charles Hare and his friend Frederick Denison Maurice. Hare, the archdeacon of Lewes, was destined to become the young men's benefactor.

During the autumn and winter of 1842 the Macmillans began to plan for a bookshop and publishing house of their own at 57 Aldersgate Street, which they occupied in February 1843. Daniel Macmillan was thirty years old; Alexander was twenty-five. Their first two titles were published that year: *The Philosophy of Training*, by A. R. Craig, and *The Three Questions: What am I? Whence Came I? Whither Do I Go?*, by William Haig Miller, published for the Religious Tract Society. The Craig book was concerned with training teachers for the wealthier classes; the Miller book took an affirmative view of life, quoting

*Daniel Macmillan (painting by Lowes Dickinson; from Frank Arthur Mumby,* Publishing and Bookselling, *1931)*

from John Gibson Lockhart's *Memoirs of the Life of Sir Walter Scott, bart* (1837-1838): "Is the grave, then, the last sleep? Ah, no! It is the last and final awakening." These first publications reflected the Macmillan philosophy of business, which was influenced by their devout belief in God and their deep interest in education. Their success, as a 1943 article in *Publisher's Weekly* put it, was a product of "a unique combination of a sound business training and an almost religious sense of the duties and responsibilities of their profession."

In 1843 the Macmillans acquired the bookselling business of a Mr. Newby at 17 Trinity Street, Cambridge, assisted by a loan of five hundred pounds from Archdeacon Hare. Daniel set up shop there while Alexander carried on in London. This arrangement proved unfeasible, however, and by year's end both brothers were established in Cambridge.

In 1845 the Macmillans had the opportunity to buy a bookselling business established in Cambridge in the eighteenth century; in addition to the prestige involved, the shop at 1 Trinity Street was a corner house and much better situated. To acquire it from its owner, Thomas Stevenson, the Macmillans needed six thousand pounds. They temporarily sacrificed their independence by taking into partnership a Mr. Barclay, a wholesale druggist with no experience in books, in return for his investment. The firm became Macmillan, Barclay, and Macmillan until 1850; then Barclay retired, and it became Macmillan and Company.

During its first ten years the firm engaged in careful, conservative growth. Between 1843 and 1852 it published only 131 titles, never as many as two dozen in one year. It was a serious list, addressing such subjects as Christianity, education, classical literature, science, and mathematics. There were educational guides and companions, syllabi for courses at Cambridge, and several handbooks, such as *A Short and Easy Course of Algebra* (1850) for junior classes, J. H. Boardman's *Arithmetic: Rules and Reasons* (1850), and *Arithmetical Examples* (1851). There were also indexes of manuscript collections in Cambridge libraries, a volume of Tennyson verses set to music (1842), and several collections of sermons and sonnets on the death of the duke of Wellington (1852). More unusual were two books of verse by women: *Hours of Reflection* (1845), by Ellen Taylor Hudson, and *Sketches of Character* (1849), by Anna H. Potts. There were several attempts at

publishing periodicals: the *Cambridge Mathematical Journal* (1846), the *Journal of Classical and Sacred Philology* (1854), and *Academica: An Occasional Journal* (1858), none of them successful. In 1852, of the 131 titles so far published, 75, or three-fifths, were either by Cambridge scholars or about Cambridge affairs.

The shop at 1 Trinity Street rapidly became a sort of social center for Cambridge dons and undergraduates. Daniel was known to the townspeople from his earlier three-year residence there, and others were attracted to the shop by the hardworking and congenial brothers. Thus, according to company historian Charles Morgan, Macmillan built on the "resources of the University and an upper room at Number One became a common-room where young men or old men assembled to discuss books or God or social reform—but chiefly, it would appear, God—before going into four o'clock hall."

Having become relatively successful, the brothers felt themselves in a position to marry. On 4 September 1850 Daniel married Frances Orridge, daughter of a chemist and magistrate of Cambridge. The Macmillans had four children: Frederick Orridge, Maurice Crawford, Katherine, and Arthur. In August 1851 Alexander married Caroline Brimley, eldest sister of his friend George Brimley, librarian of Trinity College, by whom he had five children: Malcolm Kingsley, George Augustin, William Alexander, Margaret, and Olive.

The Macmillans believed devoutly in God; and in Maurice, the Christian Socialist, who was introduced to them by Archdeacon Hare, they found their "Prophet," as Alexander regularly referred to him. Believing in him more strongly, perhaps, than posterity would support, they readily published his works, which were profuse. He first appeared in their catalogue in 1844 as the author of the introduction to a reprint of Bernard Mandeville's *Fable of the Bees* (1714), which was published for the sole purpose of giving opportunity for his pen; and again in 1845 with a public letter of thirty-one pages, *The New Statute and Mr. Ward*. There were three offerings each year from Maurice in 1853 and in 1854, and fifteen in 1855. The Macmillans believed in the importance of his message, yet they were far from fools where business was concerned; Maurice brought with him many of the other Cambridge scholars who combined slowly but steadily to build a quietly profitable list. But chiefly he brought to them the Reverend Charles Kingsley,

*Portrait by Sir Hubert von Herkomer, R.A., 1887 (from Charles L. Graves,* Life and Letters of Alexander Macmillan, *1910)*

a former pupil of Maurice's who was then rector of Eversley, a village in Hampshire.

Kingsley first appeared on the Macmillan list in 1850, with the pseudonym "Parson Lot" attached to a thirty-six-page pamphlet, *Cheap Clothes and Nasty*, dealing with the scandal of sweatshop tailoring. Next the firm published *Phaethon; or, Loose Thoughts for Loose Thinkers* (1852), with a third edition in 1858; it was one of the Company's early strong sellers. In 1854 Macmillan and Company published his four lectures delivered at the Philosophical Institution in Edinburgh, *Alexandria And Her Schools. Glaucus; or, The Wonders of the Shore* appeared in May 1855 and was reprinted ten times by 1887. Clearly, Kingsley was a good author for a young firm to have.

The company's first venture into fiction, Kingsley's *Westward Ho!* (1855), proved to be a huge success both artistically and commercially. Kingsley had been cogitating for some time on an Elizabethan romance that would employ the idea of "muscular Christianity" to deliver a tonic to his readers and embolden them to fight bravely for the extinction of evil in Victorian society. As it happened, this pugnacious novel coincided with the country's dismay over the mismanagement of the Crimean War. It became, to all intents and purposes, a war propaganda novel, as well as one of the most remarkable best-sellers of the century. For Macmillan it signaled a major change of direction as the firm turned increasingly to fiction. *Westward Ho!* was followed on Macmillan's list by many other works from Kingsley's pen, including the equally popular *The Water-Babies* (1863), again with innumerable editions and reprints. Kingsley's brother Henry, a novelist, also became a Macmillan author, with nine titles between 1859 and 1873.

Macmillan's second popular best-seller was directly influenced by the success of the muscular-Christianity theories of *Westward Ho!* In September 1856 Thomas Hughes wrote to Alexander proposing a novel based on a boy's experiences at Rugby during Headmaster Thomas Arnold's time. In a jovial mood, Hughes remarked, "I've always told you, I'm going to make your fortune." The Macmillans agreed to publish *Tom Brown's School Days* and began to print the early parts even before the work was finished. It was published anonymously in April 1857; by the end of the year eleven thousand copies had been sold, an astonishing number for a time when the usual first printing was not more than fifteen hundred copies. There was a *sixth* edition by 1858. Hughes did, indeed, become enormously profitable for Macmillan, as well as for himself.

Meanwhile, calamity had struck the Macmillan family with the death of Daniel on 27 June 1857 of tuberculosis, which he had fought since 1831. The younger brother took in Daniel's family as his own.

As early as 1852 Daniel had felt the need for a London office. With his characteristic caution he had postponed action, although he was also deterred in part by cash-flow difficulties. After Daniel's death, Alexander felt in a position to act on the idea. A nephew, Robert Bowes, employed by the firm since 1846, was installed at 23 Henrietta Street in Covent Garden; the headquarters of the firm remained in Cambridge.

The basic character of the firm had been established by this time: cautious, careful about money, choosing books "to last," and scrupulously fair with authors. Alexander Macmillan transplanted these successful publishing practices to the larger London market. A congenial man,

*The Christian Socialist writer Frederick Denison Maurice, many of whose works were published by Macmillan (engraving by F. Holl, after a portrait by Lowes Dickinson)*

he came to town every Thursday and in adjoining rooms entertained his authors, prospective authors, and friends in what came to be known as the "Tobacco Parliaments." Men gathered to smoke, take tea and spirits, and talk about the theories of Charles Darwin and other topics of the day, much in the manner of the upper rooms at 1 Trinity Street. Macmillan recognized that successful publishing was an intensely personal affair, and he attracted such leading literary figures to these gatherings as Alfred Tennyson, Herbert Spencer, Thomas Henry Huxley, Francis Turner Palgrave, Coventry Patmore, Maurice, Charles Kingsley, and Hughes.

Beginning in 1858 Macmillan books appeared with either of two imprints: "Cambridge: Macmillan and Co." or "Cambridge: Macmillan and Co. and 23 Henrietta Street, Covent Garden." Of the forty-three titles published that year, thirteen bore both locations. By the following year all had switched to the double address. There also were small, subtle, but unmistakable changes in the character of the Macmillan list. Books on religion, education, university affairs,

mathematics, and sermons still predominated, but also appearing in 1859 were H. Lushington's *The Italian War, 1848-9, and the Last Italian Poet*, David Masson's *Sketches of the British Novelists— Their Style* and *The Life of John Milton*, James Clerk Maxwell's *Essay On the Stability of the Motion of Saturn's Rings*, Margaret Oliphant's *Agnes Hopetoun's Schools and Holidays: The Experiences of a Little Girl*, the anonymous *Out of the Depths: The Story of a Woman's Life*, and Hughes's *The Scouring of the White Horse; or, The Long Vacation Ramble of a London Clerk*.

After much discussion over a period of years at the Macmillan Thursday evenings, Alexander Macmillan decided to join the trend among major publishing houses of the late 1850s and early 1860s and found a monthly shilling magazine. He chose Masson to be the editor, and the first issue of *Macmillan's Magazine* appeared on 1 November 1859. It contained articles by Masson, Hughes, George Wilson, F. G. Stephens, Franklin Lushington, and J. M. Ludlow. Its birth was celebrated at a dinner party at Henrietta Street that evening.

Over its forty-eight-year life its pages were host to many serials: Hughes's *Tom Brown at Oxford* (November 1859-July 1861), Henry Kingsley's *Ravenshoe* ( January 1861-July 1862), Charles Kingsley's *The Water-Babies* (August 1862-March 1863), Oliphant's *A Son of the Soil* (November 1863-April 1865), R. D. Blackmore's *Craddock Nowell* (May 1865-August 1866), Charlotte Mary Yonge's *The Dove in the Eagle's Nest* (May 1865-December 1865), Anthony Trollope's *Sir Harry Hotspur of Humblethwaite* (May 1870-December 1870), William Black's *Strange Adventures of a Phaeton* ( January 1872-November 1872), Annie Keary's *Castle Daly* (February 1874-July 1875), Henry James's *The Portrait of a Lady* (October 1880-October 1881), and Thomas Hardy's *The Woodlanders* (May 1886-February 1887). Many of the early and faithful members of the Macmillan "family" appeared in the magazine, including Dinah Maria Craik, Maurice, and Palgrave; Frances Power Cobbe, Harriet Martineau, and Octavia Hill represented women's interests; Mrs. Oliphant, Patmore, Caroline Norton, and Matthew Arnold were all frequent contributors. From the mid 1870s to the early 1890s Walter Pater was a consistent contributor, and the names W. W. Skeat and William Hale White ("Mark Rutherford") cropped up from time to time. Masson was succeeded as editor by George Grove in

1868; John Morley was the editor from 1883 to 1885, and Mowbray Morris from 1885 to 1900.

Between 1860 and 1872 Macmillan and Company, under Alexander's guidance, established itself as one of the premier publishing houses in London. It never forsook its commitment to religious, educational, and scientific works, nor its loyalty to Maurice, Kingsley, Archbishop Hare, and the intellectual community of Cambridge. But the list became more eclectic and diversified, and it moved with events of the time.

Perhaps one of the greatest accomplishments of 1861 was Palgrave's *The Golden Treasury of the Best Songs and Lyrical Poems in the English Language*. He was attempting a national anthology of verse, something that had not been done before. Macmillan was immediately supportive of the project, but with typical caution he initially printed only two thousand copies. He must have been astonished at the public interest in the book: there were twenty-three reprints by 1888. Reflecting the prejudices of his age, Palgrave's selections—or rather his omissions—may seem odd to modern eyes; he urged that "passion, colour and originality cannot atone for serious imperfections in clearness, unity and truth." Thus he rejected the work of William Blake, John Donne, and Emily Brontë, and cut back sharply selections from Samuel Taylor Coleridge, Henry Vaughan, Richard Crashaw, and George Herbert.

Palgrave's book inaugurated the Golden Treasury series, which by 1889 amounted to forty-four titles. These included Roundell Palmer's *Book of Praise* (1862), William Alligham's *Ballad Book* (1864), Younge's *Book of Golden Deeds of All Times* (1864), the *Book of Thoughts* (1865), and Yonge's *Book of Worthies Gathered from Old Histories* (1869). More enduring volumes in the series were Patmore's *Children's Garland* (1862), M. C. Aitken's *Scottish Song* (1874), Matthew Arnold's selections from William Wordsworth (1879) and Lord Byron (1881), and T. H. Ward's *The English Poets* (1880). Other books by Palgrave included *Songs and Sonnets by William Shakespeare* (1865), *Essays on Art* (1866), *Hymns* (1867), *Lyrical Poems* (1871), and *Chrysomela* (1877), a selection of the lyrics of Robert Herrick.

As he approached mid life, Macmillan entered his period of greatest productivity. He was personally involved, as always, with supervising and building the firm's list. He also followed American affairs and Anglo-American relations with keen interest, and supported the Northern cause during the Civil War. He was deeply trou-

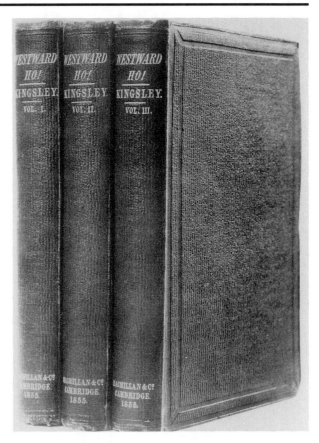

*Charles Kingsley's "three-decker" novel, published in 1855, was Macmillan's first venture into fiction*

bled by failure to resolve the problems of international copyright. He took over the early works of Charles Kingsley, Maurice, Archbishop Trench, and Yonge from their defunct publisher, John W. Parker. In 1863 Macmillan and Company moved its headquarters from Cambridge to 16 Bedford Street, London; Bowes, the faithful nephew, was sent back to Cambridge to manage the bookselling. Macmillan took a house in Upper Tooting, which he named Knapdale; it was large enough to consolidate his double family and to accommodate the entertaining he envisioned in the years ahead.

Ironically for a man whose business had risen from his Cambridge connections, Macmillan became publisher to the University of Oxford in 1863. He held the post until 1880, when a change in business conditions brought about a friendly parting. He was given an honorary M.A. degree in recognition of his services.

In 1864 Macmillan inaugurated what was to become one of the firm's most enduring ventures: *The Statesman's Year Book*, edited by Frederick Martin, a statistical, genealogical, and historic account of the states and sovereigns of the civilized world. To this day it is an invaluable reference. It was edited by Martin until 1883, by Sir John Scott-Keltie from 1883 to 1926, by Mortimer Epstein from 1927 to 1946, by S. H. Steinberg from 1946 to 1969, by John Paxton from 1969 to 1989, and by Brian Hunter since 1990.

In 1865 Macmillan appointed George Lillie Craik to assist him with administrative matters; Craik remained with the firm until 1905. In artistic matters Macmillan assembled a team of trusted advisers, among them John Morley, George Grove, and Norman Lockyer. Among the ideas he helped to originate or suggest were Allingham's *Ballad Book*; Mark Lemon's *Jest Book* (1864); Mrs. C. F. Alexander's *Sunday Book of Poetry* (1864), a selection of verse for children's Sunday reading; and Alexander Smith's edition of the works of Robert Burns (1865). He initiated textbooks for elementary schools on botany, geology, and chemistry. He supported publication in 1863 of a biography of Blake, then a neglected poet, by Alexander Gilchrist.

The first Macmillan books for children appeared in 1860 with Georgina M. Craik's *My First Journal; A Book for the Young* and Dinah Maria Craik's *Our Year: A Child's Book in Prose and Verse*. There was a novel by Westland Marston, *A Lady in Her Own Right* (1860); and more novels in 1861: May Beverley's *The Moor Cottage*, Oliver Wendell Holmes's *Elsie Venner*, and Hughes's *Tom Brown at Oxford*. In 1862 there were Arthur Hugh Clough's *Poems with a Memoir*, Christina Rossetti's *Goblin Market and Other Poems*, and Norton's *The Lady of La Garaye*. J. E. Cairnes's *The Slave Power* (1863) was an important attempt to explain the real issues in the American Civil War. The first Macmillan book by Matthew Arnold, *A French Eton*, appeared in 1864, followed by *Essays in Criticism* in 1865. In the latter year the firm also brought out Lewis Carroll's *Alice's Adventures in Wonderland. Through the Looking-Glass, and What Alice Found There* appeared in 1872.

Macmillan and Company was quite early in recognizing the work of writers who would be leaders in the women's movement in the 1860s and 1870s. The firm published Sophia Jex-Blake's *A Visit to Some American Schools and Colleges* (1867); Josephine Butler's *The Education and Employment of Women* (1868); Harriet Martineau's *Biographical Sketches* (1869) and *A Letter to the Deaf* (1869); *Woman's Work and Woman's Culture* (1869), edited by Butler; and Millicent Garrett Fawcett's *Political*

*Economy for Beginners* (1870). In 1870 Lady Mary Anne Barker's *Station Life in New Zealand* was a surprise best-seller, going through four editions between 1870 and 1883.

A splendid scholarly edition of *The Works of William Shakespeare*, eventually to reach nine volumes, began to appear in 1863. Volume 1 was edited by W. G. Clark, the public orator in Cambridge, and John Glover, librarian of Trinity College; subsequent volumes were edited by Clark and W. Aldis Wright, Glover's successor as librarian. Uncommon care was taken with the text, which was based on the superb collection of early quartos lodged at Trinity, and the work came to be known as *The Cambridge Shakespeare*. From this project emerged Macmillan's second important series, first envisioned by Alexander Macmillan: *The Globe Shakespeare* (1864) used the same material as *The Cambridge Shakespeare* but was priced and designed for popular consumption. Writing to James MacLehose, head of the Glasgow firm that printed many Macmillan books, Alexander suggested a venture of fifty thousand copies, to be sold for three shillings, sixpence: "You see it would be immeasurably the cheapest, most beautiful and handy book that has appeared of *any kind*, except the *Bible*."

Thus was born the Macmillan Globe Library: scholarly annotated editions of the works of major literary artists, attractively produced and popularly priced. The Globe books were of a peculiar size, called the Globe octavo. The library concerned itself mainly with the works of poets, including Robert Burns (1868), Oliver Goldsmith (1869), Alexander Pope (1869), Edmund Spenser (1869), William Cowper (1870), John Dryden (1870), Virgil (1871), Horace (1873), and Milton (1877).

In 1865 Alexander Macmillan projected a series of children's books, to be published in monthly parts under the general title the Sunday Library for Household Reading. It was to start with the topography and history of the Bible lands. He invited first Charlotte Yonge and later Frances Martin to edit it; both were readers of educational and devotional books for the firm. The series included *Pupils of St. John the Divine* (1868), by Yonge; *Pioneers and Founders: England's Antiphon* (1868), by George Macdonald; *Nations Around* (1870), by Keary; and titles by Charles Kingsley, Hughes, Archdeacon Frederic William Farrar, and Mrs. Oliphant.

In 1867, after a visit to the United States, Macmillan concluded that an American branch

*John Morley, who served the Macmillan firm for more than fifty years as a reader, adviser, and editor. It was Morley who, in 1877, proposed the English Men of Letters series (an 1881 chalk drawing by Frederick Sandys; from F. W. Hirst,* Early Life and Letters of John Morley, *1927)*

of the firm would be desirable. True to his nature, he began in a small way by sending an agent, George Brett, to New York in 1869 with books to sell. By 1990 there would be branches not only in the United States but also in Toronto, Melbourne, Bombay, Calcutta, Madras, Auckland, Delhi, Dublin, Gaborone, Hamburg, Harare, Hong Kong, Johannesburg, Kuala Lumpur, Lagos, Manzini, Mexico City, Nairobi, Singapore, and Tokyo.

In 1871 Macmillan's wife died after an extended illness. In the fall of 1872 he married Emma Pignatel, and he later fathered two more children: Mary and John Victor. Although he maintained an active interest in Macmillan and Company through the 1870s, much of his energy went to diversifying control of the business and ensuring its smooth transfer to the next generation.

In its early years the firm had attempted to publish some specialized scholarly journals, including the *Cambridge Mathematical Journal* (1846) and the *Journal of Classical and Sacred Philosophy* (1854-1859). The *Journal of Anatomy and Physiology* was published by Macmillan and Company from 1866 until 1885, after which it was published elsewhere. The *Journal of the East Indian Association* was launched in 1867, followed in 1868 by the *Journal of Philology* and *Practitioner: A Monthly Journal of Therapeutics*.

At the urging of Norman Lockyer, a well-known astronomer and spectroscopist and one of the firm's "family" of authors, Alexander Macmillan founded an illustrated weekly scientific journal in 1869; *Nature* is still a respected international scientific publication. Other journals of this type had failed: the *Natural History Review* in 1865 and the *Reader* after a few issues in 1867. It required courage on Macmillan's part and also the financial security of a large publishing house, which could afford to wait for success, to undertake this venture. Indeed, the firm had to wait for several decades before *Nature* became profitable.

The journal's purpose was to forge links between scientists and the general community, to battle ignorant suspicion and prejudice, and to provide a forum in which scientists could discuss current scientific issues. It was a risky venture because weekly publication required a lot of copy and a large readership; but Macmillan sensed that lay interest in science was growing. Also, the journal was supported from the start by such leading scientists as Thomas Huxley, Charles Darwin, John Tyndale, and Henry Enfield Roscoe.

Lockyer (later Sir Norman) was the first editor, serving until 1919. His successor was Sir Richard Gregory, who was also a scientific publisher and science adviser to Macmillan and Company. L. J. F. Brimble and A. J. V. Gale shared the editorship from 1938 to 1962, and Brimble served alone from 1962 to 1965. John Maddox has been editor since 1965, except for 1973 to 1980, when Dai Davies was editor. In recent years the focus has become much more international: since 1972 *Nature* has been printed simultaneously in Britain, the United States, Japan, and the People's Republic of China.

Macmillan and Company also published the *Journal of Physiology* from 1878 to 1880, *Brain* from 1878 to 1974, the *Economic Journal* from 1891 to 1970, and *Philosophy* from 1934 to 1971. In 1990 the firm published more than twenty learned journals, mainly in the field of medicine, in addition to *Nature*; they included *Nursing Times, Health Science Journal, Therapy, Bio-Technology, Social Work Today, Diagnostics,* and the *Stock Exchange Year Book.*

Macmillan and Company ventured into popular publishing with the *English Illustrated Magazine*, which it maintained for ten years despite disappointing sales. The first issue appeared in October 1883, featuring such leading illustrators as Hugh Thomson, A. D. McCormick, Herbert Railton, Joseph Pennell, and Walter Crane. The magazine's contributors were drawn from *Macmillan's Magazine* and would come to include Henry James, George Meredith, Algernon Swinburne, Robert Louis Stevenson, and Rudyard Kipling. It was edited first by J. Comyns Carr and later by Sir Clement Kinloch-Cooke.

Macmillan and Company consolidated its position as a major London publishing house during the 1870s with several important events. In 1874 the firm published J. R. Green's *Short History of the English People*, a volume of 847 pages designed as a school manual or a handbook for universities. Green intended the work to be strictly a history of England's political, social, religious, and intellectual growth, as opposed to a chronicle of its wars and conquests. This approach caught the imagination of English readers, and the book sold thirty-five thousand copies in eighteen months. It was reprinted, with corrections, fifteen times in the next twelve years. Another version was expanded to four volumes (1877-1880). A second edition of the one-volume version (1887) was also reprinted; it was printed in parts in 1889, with analysis by C. W. A. Tait. Macmillan and Company originally offered Green an outright payment of £350, with an additional £100 after the sale of two thousand copies; when the firm's executives realized how popular the work was to be they voluntarily rewrote the contract, substituting a royalty agreement which would prove much more lucrative for the author. This success led to a position for Green as editor of two new series, Literary Primers and Historical Primers, which ran to seven and eleven titles, respectively.

In 1877 Henry James suggested that Macmillan and Company publish a volume of his essays, *French Poets and Novelists.* It appeared in February 1878, followed by *The Europeans* in September. Although James was never a profitable author for Macmillan and Company the firm published

*A 1903 advertisement for one of Macmillan's most successful series*

most of his subsequent books up to 1899, as well as the definitive New York editions of his novels.

Also in 1877 John Morley proposed what was to become a distinguished, influential, and highly successful series: the English Men of Letters. It required a skillful man, with broad contacts in the intellectual world, to match successfully each subject with his author. Five volumes inaugurated the series in 1878: *Gibbon*, by James Cotter Morison; *Goldsmith*, by William Black; *Johnson*, by Leslie Stephen; *Scott*, by Richard H. Hutton; and *Shelley*, by John Addington Symonds. Nine volumes followed in 1879: *Burke*, by John Morley; *Burns*, by John Campbell Shairp; *Chaucer*, by A. W. Ward; *Defoe*, by William Minto; *Hume*, by Thomas Henry Huxley; *Milton*, by Mark Pattison; *Southey*, by Edward Dowden; *Thackeray*, by Anthony Trollope; and *Hawthorne*, by Henry James. In 1880 there were *Spenser*, by R. W. Church; *Bunyan*, by James Anthony

Froude; *Byron*, by John Nichol; *Cowper*, by Goldwin Smith; and *Pope*, by Stephen. Four volumes appeared in 1881: *Wordsworth*, by F. W. H. Myers; *De Quincey*, by David Masson; *Dryden*, by George Saintsbury; and *Landor*, by Sidney Colvin. There were seven in 1882: *Dickens*, by Ward; *Gray*, by Edmund Gosse; *Lamb*, by Alfred Ainger; *Sterne*, by H. D. Traill; *Swift*, by Stephen; *Bentley*, by Richard Jebb; and *Macaulay*, by J. Cotter Morison. Thereafter, the series comprised *Fielding* (1883), by Austin Dobson; *Sheridan* (1883), by Mrs. Oliphant; *Addison* (1884), by W. J. Courthope; *Bacon* (1884), by Richard William Church; *Coleridge* (1884), by Traill; *Sir Philip Sidney* (1886), by Symonds; *Keats* (1887), by Colvin; *Locke* (1888), by J. H. Fowler; and *Thomas Carlyle* (1892), by Nichol. The books were written by good scholars, were suitable for either the general reader or as a starting point for specialists, were well produced, and were sold at an affordable price. Positioned between the official three-volume Victorian "Life," so often commissioned by grieving relatives, and the "definitive" biographies of modern times, they provided reliable interpretive scholarship for the general reader and remained standard texts for many years.

Another important and enduring project was executed by George Grove, musicologist, director of the Royal College of Music, and editor of *Macmillan's Magazine*. In 1874 he began work on his great *Dictionary of Music and Musicians*, which appeared in four volumes between 1879 and 1889. A second edition, in five volumes, was edited by J. A. Fuller Maitland (1904-1910); the third, also in five volumes, by H. C. Colles, (1927); the fourth, also by Colles in five volumes with a supplement (1940); the fifth, by Eric Blom, in nine volumes (1954), with a supplementary volume (1961). The sixth edition (1980), edited by Stanley Sadie in twenty volumes, was completely rewritten and reestablished *Grove* as the world's leading work of reference in its field. The title was changed to *The New Grove Dictionary of Music and Musicians*, and by 1990 it had been reprinted nine times. This edition has spawned a group of ancillary volumes: *The New Grove Dictionary of Musical Instruments* (1984) in three volumes, edited by Sadie; *The New Grove Dictionary of American Music* (1986) in four volumes, edited by Sadie and H. Wiley Hitchcock; *The New Grove Dictionary of Jazz* (1988) in two volumes, edited by Barry Kernfeld and Sadie; and *The Grove Concise Dictionary of Music* (1988), edited by Sadie.

In the 1870s control of the firm gradually shifted from Alexander to the next generation of Macmillans. Receptions at Bedford Street continued in the tradition of the Tobacco Parliaments, but the names of those attending, such as Trollope, James, and Oscar Wilde, attest to changing times. In the catalogue there were still the Kingsleys, Hughes, Richard Chenevix Trench (archbishop of Dublin and author of some forty theological and poetical books and pamphlets on the Macmillan lists), the sermons and the devotional material. But theology began to play a less dominant part on the list, which was becoming occupied with three themes of more modern interest: education (in the wake of the Education Act of 1870); science, which was to claim the public mind so insistently in the last quarter of the nineteenth century; and the romance of empire, travel, and faraway places.

Among the younger men of the Macmillan family, Daniel's son Frederick knew the business well. He had learned retail bookselling with his cousin, Bowes, in Cambridge, where he also observed printing at the university press. He entered the firm in 1876 and worked in various departments at the Bedford Street offices, and also traveled for the firm, selling books in the provinces. He was then dispatched to America, where he made valuable contacts among American authors; he also brought back an American bride, Georgiana Warrin, who survived him until 1943.

Maurice, Daniel's other son, was graduated from Christ's College, Cambridge—the only one of the cousins to attend a university—and taught classes at St. Paul's before entering the firm in 1883. He toured extensively in Australia and India in 1884-1885, also with an American bride, Helen Artie Belles. His interests were scholarship, the classics, the British Empire, and the Far East. He was quick to sense the opportunity for business expansion overseas which would be so important to the second Macmillan generation. George, Alexander's son, entered the firm in 1874. He served as honorary secretary of the Hellenic society off and on for forty years and was for many years chairman of Stainer and Bell, music publishers. From his varied interests came many important books in archaeology, classical art, history, and literature, including the *Journal of Hellenic Studies* (1880), and perhaps his greatest triumph, Arthur Evans's *The Palace of Minos* (1921-1935). During the 1870s William Jack was a partner and adviser on mathematical subjects until he accepted a chair of mathematics at the University of Glasgow in 1879.

*First page of report by Macmillan reader J. C. Squire, strongly recommending the publication of Margaret Mitchell's* Gone with the Wind *in 1936 (auctioned by Sotheby's 19 July 1990)*

In 1873 Macmillan and Company published Pater's *Studies in the History of the Renaissance*; in 1874 it published Lady Barker's *First Lessons in the Principles of Cooking* and R. Jardine's *Elements of Psychology*, followed by Rhoda and Agnes Garrett's *Suggestions for House Decoration* (1876). Such titles testify to the increasing diversity in the firm's list. Texts, readers, and primers proliferated after 1874; and there were many titles on teaching algebra, anatomy and physiology, arithmetic, astronomy, calculus, chemistry, and classics. G. E. Fasnacht was something of a legend with his teaching companions, textbooks, and readers for French and German. C. Colbeck edited Foreign School Classics, which ran to twenty-one titles, and A. Geikie produced geology and geography primers and sketches. The first book by a member of the Macmillan family was *First Latin Grammar* (1879), by Maurice Macmillan, published while he was assistant master in St. Paul's School; it fulfilled the firm's goal of publishing "books that last" when it went through three reprints by 1886. Also in 1879 appeared *Studies in Fermentation*, by Louis Pasteur.

*John Inglesant* (1881), by Joseph Henry Shorthouse, which had been privately printed by the author after repeated rejection by publishers, came to Alexander Macmillan through Mrs. Humphry Ward. He read and accepted it, possibly influenced by its portrayal of the religious and historical interests revived by the Oxford Movement and the Pre-Raphaelites. Surprising the publisher, it was a best-seller, running through five editions by March 1882, including a Globe edition in two volumes.

George Saintsbury, the noted literary critic, first came to Macmillan and Company as a contributor to T. H. Ward's four-volume anthology *The English Poets* (1880). He remained partly because of his affection for Frederick Macmillan. The firm next published his book on Dryden in 1881; it was reprinted as part of the English Men of Letters series in 1888. In 1887 Macmillan and Company published his influential *History of Elizabethan Literature*.

The American expatriate F. Marion Crawford was a vastly popular author but not a particularly profitable one because of the hard bargains he drove with Frederick Macmillan over royalties. Between 1882 and 1909 he entrusted all but three of his forty novels to Macmillan, including *Zoroaster* (1885), *A Tale of a Lonely Parish* (1886), *Sant' Ilario* (1889), and *Don Orsino* (1892).

Several important textbooks were added to the Macmillan list: Henry Sidgwick's *Principles of Political Economy* (1883); James Fitzjames Stephen's *A Digest of the Criminal Law: Crimes and Punishment* (1883-1887); and *A Text-Book of Pathological Anatomy and Pathogenesis*, by Ernst Ziegler and D. MacAlister (1883-1887).

Lord Tennyson, long a friend of Alexander's and a guest at his Tobacco Parliaments and receptions, had remained aloof from the "Macmillan family" of authors, evidently for financial reasons. Instead he signed a series of five-year contracts with such houses as H. S. King, Alexander Strahan, and Kegan Paul. He finally came to Alexander in 1884, as both men were nearing the ends of their careers. The poet drove a hard bargain, insisting on a guarantee of four thousand pounds plus any additional royalties earned beyond that sum.

Thomas Hardy's early books had been rejected by Macmillan and Company, but he supplied *The Woodlanders* as a long serial to *Macmillan's Magazine* in 1886; it was published in three volumes in 1887 and followed by *Wessex Tales* (1888). In 1886 Macmillan secured *The Mayor of Casterbridge* for its Colonial Library. Late in 1893 the firm contracted to add a dozen Hardy titles, including *Tess of the D'Urbervilles* (published by Osgood, McIlvaine in 1891), which had earlier been rejected by Macmillan. After the turn of the century Hardy transferred all his books to Macmillan and Company. *The Dynasts*, a vast work in prose and blank verse, was published in three parts (1904, 1906, 1908). Hardy continued to send manuscripts to the firm for another twenty years.

The Colonial Library was developed to serve the reading needs of India and the other colonies. It was also designed to make use of standard works and popular fiction on the Macmillan list, or other works whose copyrights the firm could acquire cheaply. It was launched in 1886 with thirty-four titles, which included works by Crawford, Mrs. Oliphant, Yonge, Hardy, Lady Barker, Ralph Waldo Emerson, and Hugh Conway.

As the 1880s reached their close Alexander Macmillan was less and less involved with the firm. He was devastated by the death of his son Malcolm, who disappeared on an outing on Mount Olympus in 1889. By 1890 his successors were ready for their responsibilities. Frederick supervised general business matters, fiction, poetry, art, and American ties; Maurice presided over

India, education, the classics, and foreign expansion; George was in charge of Greek literature, archaeology, and music. The boundaries of responsibility were fluid, however, and any of them might supervise a book he thought promising in any field. They developed a working relationship as smoothly efficient as the partnership between the founding brothers, Daniel and Alexander, had been. At Alexander's death in 1896 Macmillan became a limited company, with Frederick as its first chairman.

In early November 1889 George received a letter from a young Cambridge anthropologist, James G. Frazer, proposing a book to be called *The Golden Bough*. George and his reader, Morley, recognized the work at once as an important contribution to social anthropology; it was immediately accepted, initiating a long relationship between author and publisher. The first two volumes appeared in May 1890. Although sales were slow, the book progressed through several editions until it was completed in twelve volumes in 1915 (they were followed by *Aftermath: A Supplement* in 1937). In 1922 an abridged one-volume edition caught the public's attention and at once made it an influential book. Macmillan and Company also published Frazer's translations, with commentaries, of *Pausanias* (1898) and the *Fasti* (1929) of Ovid. *The Golden Bough* drew to the firm other books on anthropology, myth, and comparative religious studies, such as Edvard Westermarck's *History of Human Marriage* (1891) and *Marriage Ceremonies in Morocco* (1914), Arthur Evans's *The Mycenaean Tree and Pillar Cult* (1901), and W. W. Skeat and C. O. Blagden's *Pagan Races of the Malay Peninsula* (1906). Frazer's wife, Lilly, edited several French schoolbooks for Macmillan. The Frazer correspondence with the firm, from both husband and wife, runs to several thousand items from 1884 to 1940.

A colonial flavor was added to the list by Alexander Browne, a police magistrate in New South Wales who wrote under the pseudonym Rolf Boldrewood. His novel *Robbery under Arms*, an Australian classic, had been published by Remington and Company in 1888, but Macmillan secured it for the Colonial Library in 1889. The firm published two of his three-deckers, *Miner's Right* and *A Colonial Reformer*, in 1890.

It might be argued that Macmillan and its readers failed to keep pace with new developments in fiction during the years 1890 to 1914; the firm rejected H. G. Wells's *Ann Veronica* (1909) and *The New Machiavelli* (1910), as well as

work by George Bernard Shaw, Arnold Bennett, and Somerset Maugham. Wells perhaps summed up the situation: "I don't think you advertise well and I think you're out of touch with the contemporary movement in literature.... On the other hand, you are solid and sound and sane." The firm did publish his *Twelve Stories and a Dream* (1903), *The Food of the Gods and How It Came to Earth* (1904), *Kipps* (1905), *In the Days of the Comet* (1906), *Tono-Bungay* (1909), *Marriage* (1912), *The Passionate Friends* (1913), *The Wife of Sir Isaac Harman* (1914), *The World Set Free* (1914), and *The Research Magnificent* (1915). It also published Maurice Hewlett's *The Forest Lovers*, a romantic novel of the Middle Ages and a best-seller of 1898. The list included American novelists such as Winston Churchill and Gertrude Atherton, as well as Owen Wister's *The Virginian* (1902).

Kipling came to the firm through *Macmillan's Magazine*, which published eight of his pieces between December 1889 and January 1893, beginning with "The Incarnation of Krishna Mulvaney." In 1890 Macmillan and Company brought out *Plain Tales from the Hills*, and the firm henceforth was the principal publisher of Kipling's prose works. His popularity gave rise to innumerable collected editions—"Uniform," "Pocket," "De luxe," "School," and so forth— limited only by the publisher's inventiveness.

Frederick Macmillan contributed to the publishing profession by leading the campaign for the Net Book Agreement and by taking an active part in the *Times* "Book War." For many years it had been the custom for booksellers to sell their wares not at the price fixed by the publishers but at a discount fixed by individual sellers, which resulted in cutthroat competition. Macmillan began his campaign to reform this practice with a letter to the *Bookseller* on 6 March 1890. He suggested two classes of books: "net," where prices were fixed by the publisher, and "subject," to be discounted at the booksellers' discretion. The proposal provoked much discussion in the trade. He then took the lead in putting theory into practice in July 1890 by publishing an important book, *Principles of Economics*, by Alfred Marshall, on the net principle, claiming "if a book is good enough, a bookseller cannot afford to be without it." Differences of opinion in the trade were so keen, however, that it was not until January 1899 that the Publishers' Association was able to send to the Associated Booksellers a proposal acceptable to all.

In 1905 the *Times* offered its annual subscribers membership in the new Times Book Club, which would serve as a lending library. The *Times* was soon selling, as "used," books that had been borrowed only once or twice and appeared to be new, and was setting its own prices, thus subverting the Net Book Agreement. After a bitter struggle between publishers and the *Times*, matters were resolved in May 1908 when ownership of the newspaper changed hands. Lord Northcliffe, the new owner, secretly visited Frederick Macmillan to ask his assistance in putting an end to the Book War. It was not until fall, however, that the book club capitulated to the Net Book Agreement. Macmillan served as president of the Publishers' Association from 1900 to 1902 and again from 1911 to 1913. He was knighted in 1909.

In 1897 Macmillan and Company occupied a new building, designed especially for publishing purposes, in St. Martin's Street, between Leicester Square and the National Gallery. In 1898 the firm purchased Richard Bentley and Son, of 8 New Burlington Street, a flourishing publishing business whose proprietor wished to retire. The price of eight thousand pounds brought sufficient unwanted stock; steel- and copperplates by George Cruikshank, John Tenniel, and George Du Maurier; and portraits to be sold to finance the purchase. What remained represented a significant addition to the Macmillan list, including R. H. D. Barham's *Ingoldsby Legends* (1840-1846) and *Life and Remains of Theodore Hook* (1849), Theodore Mommsen's *History of Rome* (1862-1875), Frederick Courtney Selous's *Hunter's Wanderings in Africa* (1881), Edward Fitzgerald's *Letters to Fanny Kemble* (1895), and Harold Fielding-Hall's *The Soul of a People* (1898). There was a generous collection of female novelists: Mrs. W. K. Clifford, Mrs. Annie Edwardes, Rhoda Broughton, Helen Mathers, Mary Cholmondeley, Jessie Fothergill, Florence Montgomery, Rosa N. Carey, and Mrs. Henry Wood. Male novelists were represented by Anthony Trollope, Joseph Sheridan Le Fanu, and Marcus Clarke. Two periodicals came with the purchase: the *Argosy* and *Temple Bar*.

This was an era that saw steady expansion of Macmillan's presence in India and the Far East. The Text-Books for Indian Schools series, begun by Alexander Macmillan in 1875, was expanded under the direction of Maurice. Suitable books from the regular list were sent out; some were specially planned for India but manufactured in London and shipped; and Macmillan also published abroad. Branches were established in Bombay in 1901, in Calcutta in 1907, and in Madras in 1913, and there were agencies in Bangalore, Colombo, and Rangoon.

Maurice Macmillan supervised the educational division, which became one of the largest and most profitable branches of the business. A less remunerative success was Morley's *Life of Gladstone* (1903): the book sold 25,041 copies in the first year, but the profits went to the Gladstone family, who published it on commission.

Joining Macmillan around the turn of the century were the Irish writers Sidney Royse Lysaght, with *Poems of the Unknown Way* (1901) and *Horizons and Landmarks* (1911), and Stephen Gwynn, who wrote *Old Knowledge* (1901), *John Maxwell's Marriage* (1903), *The Masters of English Literature* (1904), and *Robert Emmet* (1909). Rabindranath Tagore, the eminent Bengali poet, critic, essayist, and author of short fiction, also joined the Macmillan list early in the twentieth century. His free-verse re-creations of his Bengali poems modeled on a medieval Indian devotional lyric, *Gitanjali: Song Offerings* (1913), won the Nobel Prize for Literature, the first ever awarded to an Asian.

There was a new English Men of Letters series, this time under the editorship of J. C. Squire. The twenty-five titles were *Matthew Arnold* (1902), by Herbert Paul; *George Eliot* (1902), by Leslie Stephen; *William Hazlitt* (1902), by Augustine Birrell; *Samuel Richardson* (1902), by Austin Dobson; *John Ruskin* (1902), by Frederic Harrison; *Tennyson* (1902), by Alfred Lyall; *Jeremy Taylor* (1903), by Edmund Gosse; *Fanny Burney* (1903), by Dobson; *Crabbe* (1903), by Alfred Ainger; *Robert Browning* (1903), by G. K. Chesterton; *Maria Edgeworth* (1904), by Emily Lawless; *Hobbes* (1904), by Stephen; *Rossetti* (1904), by Arthur C. Benson; *Sidney Smith* (1904), by George W. E. Russell; *Adam Smith* (1904), by Francis W. Hirst; *Sir Thomas Browne* (1905), by Gosse; *Edward Fitzgerald* (1905), by Benson; *Andrew Marvell* (1905), by Birrell; *Thomas Moore* (1905), by Stephen Gwynn; *Jeremy Taylor* (1905), by Gosse; *Walter Pater* (1906), by Benson; *Shakespeare* (1907), by Walter Alexander Raleigh; *James Thomson* (1908), by G. C. Macaulay; *Jane Austen* (1913), by F. Warre Cornish; and *Ben Jonson* (1919), by G. Gregory Smith.

World War I did not disrupt Macmillan's publishing schedule. Some volumes dealing with wartime subjects did appear, such as Wister's *The Pentecost of Calamity* (1915), F. S. Oliver's *Ordeal by*

Battle (1915), Mabel Dearmer's *Letters from a Field Hospital* (1915), Winston S. Churchill's *The Fighting Line* (1916), and Edith Wharton's *The Marne* (1918); and Kipling offered *France at War, The New Army in Training*, and *Fringes of the Fleet*, all in 1915. In general, however, it was business as usual, with the inauguration in 1918 of the Blue Guide travel books. There were novels by Algernon Blackwood, Maurice Hewlett, and Wells, as well as Henry Clay's *Economics: An Introduction for the General Reader* (1916), Morley's *Recollections* (1917), Edmund Gosse's *Life of Algernon Charles Swinburne* (1917), and Saintsbury's *History of the French Novel* (1917-1919). Macmillan's theological list continued strong during wartime with such titles as William Temple's *Studies in the Spirit and Truth of Christianity* (1914), J. R. Illingworth's *The Gospel Miracles* (1915), H. B. Swete's *The Holy Catholic Church* (1915), and Hensley Henson's *Christian Liberty* (1918). There were also important scholarly works, such as P. M. Sykes's *History of Persia* (1915); *New System of Gynaecology*, by Thomas Watts Eden and C. H. J. Lockyer (1917); and Frazer's *Folk-Lore in the Old Testament* (1918).

On the literary side there were two collections of Hardy's poetry, *Satires of Circumstance* (1914) and *Moments of Vision and Miscellaneous Verses* (1917), and a two-volume edition of Wilfred Scawen Blunt's *Poetical Works* (1914). Most significant, however, was a change in the principal reader, from Morley to Charles Whibley, who was more open to modern trends in imaginative literature. Young Irish poets began to find their way onto the list, precursors to a whole group of literary artists who would bring fresh blood to Macmillan. "AE" (George William Russell), a leading figure in the Irish literary renaissance, gave Macmillan *Gods of War* (1915), *Candle of Vision* (1918), *Voices of the Stones* (1925), *Vale and Other Poems* (1931), *The House of the Titans and Other Poems* (1934), and *Selected Poems* (1935). He was assiduous in recommending his younger colleagues, such as James Stephens. Macmillan published Stephens's first novel, *The Charwoman's Daughter* (1912), as well as his *The Crock of Gold* (1912), *The Demi-Gods* (1914), *Songs from the Clay* (1915), and *Adventures of Seumas Beg* (1915). Ralph Hodgson's *Poems* (1917) contained one of his most ambitious works, "A Song of Honour," and established his reputation.

Although AE was the first to recruit young Irish colleagues for the list, once William Butler Yeats was secured they came in a torrent. Yeats himself was slow to be accepted by Macmillan se-

nior readers Mowbray Morris and John Morley. In a 1900 reader's report Morris wrote: "I should be sorry to think that work so unreal, unhuman and insecure would be found to have any permanent value." Morley concurred, writing: "The work does not please the ear, nor kindle the imagination." By 1916, however, company thinking had changed: that year Yeats's *Responsibilities and Other Poems* and *Reveries over Childhood* were published and thirteen volumes of previous work were transferred to the firm, where he remained until his death in 1939. *The Poems of W. B. Yeats* (1949) and *The Collected Plays of W. B. Yeats* (1952) were delayed by World War II, but Yeats had supervised the revision of the works before his death.

Padraic Colum came to Macmillan in 1916 with *The King of Ireland's Son*, and in the ensuing ten years had fifteen titles published by the firm. In 1925 the firm published two Sean O'Casey plays, *Juno and the Paycock* and *The Shadow of a Gunman*, in one volume. From then on, Macmillan and Company published all of O'Casey's plays; *The Flying Wasp* (1937), a collection of his articles on the theater; six volumes of his autobiography between 1939 and 1963; and two editions of his collected plays (1949, 1951). The firm published Alice Stopford Green's *History of the Irish State to 1914* (1925). Eimar O'Duffy's satire *King Goshawk and the Birds* (1926) showed enough promise to make his death two years later a sad loss. Similarly, F. R. Higgins's *The Dark Breed* (1927) and *The Gap of Brightness* (1940) indicated great potential, only to be cut off by his premature death in 1941. Esme Stuart Lennox Robinson, who served Dublin's Abbey Theatre for nearly fifty years as manager, director, and playwright, had his *Plays* published in 1928. Katharine Tynan's *Collected Poems* appeared in 1930, as did George Shiels's *Two Irish Plays*; he remained on the list for the next fifteen years. Frank O'Connor (pseudonym for Michael O'Donovan) brought out his first book of short stories, *Guests of the Nation*, in 1931, and many other collections after that. John Eglinton (pseudonym for William Kirkpatrick Magee) produced *Irish Literary Portraits* (1935) and *Memoir of A.E.* (1937). Paul Vincent Carroll, an important Irish playwright, had his *Shadow and Substance* published by Macmillan and Company in 1938. Joseph Hone's biography *W. B. Yeats* appeared in 1942.

The novelist Hugh Walpole came to Macmillan in 1918. Although some critics felt he wrote too much, too fast, *The Herries Chronicle*—a historical sequence set in Cumberland, consisting of *Rogue Herries* (1930), *Judith Paris* (1931), *The Fortress* (1932), and *Vanessa* (1933)—was hugely successful with the public. *Judith Paris* marked the fourteenth novel Walpole had delivered to Macmillan in fourteen years, and sold twenty thousand copies in a fortnight.

William Edward Frank Macmillan, George's son, joined the board in 1911. Maurice's son Daniel De Mendi Macmillan also joined the board in 1911, and was chairman from 1936 to 1965. His brother (Maurice) Harold Macmillan (later earl of Stockton) entered the firm in 1920 as a director and continued except when serving as a government minister; he was deputy chairman from 1936 to 1940, from 1945 to 1951, and from 1963 until he succeeded his brother Daniel as chairman in 1965. William was a good classical scholar, a musician, a historian, and a director of Stainer and Bell; Daniel, who was a classical scholar, continued development of the Indian branch and the educational lists and supervised the continuity of the firm's publications. Others involved in the firm's direction included Thomas Mark, who joined Macmillan in 1913 as secretary to the board and became a director in 1944. Horatio Lovat Dickson served on the board from 1941 to 1964.

The postwar world proved not to be in the mood for collected or limited editions. The only real success was the Mellstock Hardy (1919-1920) in thirty-seven volumes. Otherwise, Morley's fifteen-volume collected works (1921) found an unresponsive public; of W. E. Henley's five volumes of collected works (1921) only the *Poems* sold; and the works of Henry James in thirty-five volumes (1922-1933) failed. This lack of response says something about the democratization of the reading public: a broader segment of society was buying books, but not for decorative purposes.

The market for history and science, however, was still strong. John Fortescue's *The Correspondence of George III* (1927) was successful, as was *The Greville Memoirs* (1938), edited by Lytton Strachey and Roger Fulford; J. L. Garvin brought out his *Life of Joseph Chamberlain* (1932-1969); Emily Anderson edited *The Letters of Mozart and his Family* (1938). Macmillan's strong economics list was enhanced by John Maynard Keynes's *The Economic Consequences of the Peace* (1919), considered by many to be the outstanding book of that year, as well as Alfred Marshall's *Industry and Trade* (1919) and Arthur C. Pigou's *Economics of Welfare* (1920). The Great English Churchmen, a series begun and concluded in 1927, included studies of Thomas Arnold, St. Thomas of Canterbury, Thomas Cranmer, Archibishop Laud, and John Wesley.

In the 1920s and 1930s Macmillan and Company set about updating its language texts with the Modern French series and the Modern German series. The Modern Classics series was introduced as an addition to Elementary Classics. Responding to contemporary concerns with teaching "methodology," E. J. S. Lay wrote Macmillan's *Teaching in Practice for Infant Schools: Projects and Pictures* (1934-1937). The first volume was a complete teaching scheme for infant schools; later volumes covered primary and secondary syllabi. The work was a big seller for about thirty years.

During the 1930s Macmillan was constantly on the lookout for promising new fiction writers. The next popular novelist after Walpole was Mazo de la Roche, who brought the firm *Whiteoakes* in 1929. Her earlier *Jalna* (1927) had originally been published by Little, Brown but was transferred to Macmillan in 1929. These two titles served to inaugurate the popular Whiteoak series, which proved to be similar in public appeal to the Herries series. In the late 1920s and early 1930s Macmillan also acquired E. M. Delafield, Richard Crompton, Edward Shanks, John Collier, Edward Thompson, A. G. Macdonell, and Naomi Royde Smith. In 1933 the firm had a runaway best-seller with James Hilton's *Lost Horizon*. He had previously produced half a dozen unsuccessful novels, and Macmillan accepted this one with reservations, but it was an immediate success on both sides of the Atlantic and in 1934 was awarded the Hawthornden Prize. At that time Hilton became a fiction reader for Macmillan.

Osbert Sitwell became a Macmillan author with *Penny Foolish* (1935), a volume of essays. The firm also published a volume of lectures, *Trio* (1938), by Edith, Osbert, and Sacheverell Sitwell, as well as Osbert's monumental autobiography in five volumes: *Left Hand, Right Hand!* (1945), *The Scarlet Tree* (1946), *Great Morning* (1948), *Laughter in the Next Room* (1949), and *Noble Essences* (1950). The firm published Edith Sitwell's *Street Songs* (1942), *Green Song* (1944), *Song of the Cold* (1945), and *Canticle of the Rose* (1949). She remained a Macmillan author for most of her life.

Two noted names from America were added to the list: Pearl Buck, a Nobel Prize winner, in 1940 with *Other Gods*; and Margaret Mitchell, with *Gone with the Wind* (1936). Exercising typical Macmillan caution, the firm printed only 3,000 copies of Mitchell's Pulitzer Prize-winning novel; soon that became 30,000. Ultimately, 100,000-copy printings were required. Well-known poets, such as Sturge Moore, Edward Shanks, and Edmund Blunden, came to Macmillan in the late 1930s and early 1940s after establishing themselves elsewhere.

The year 1936 was notable for the deaths of the three senior partners: George on 3 March, Maurice on 30 March, and Sir Frederick on 1 June. Once again, the family had planned so carefully for transfer of power that there was no confusion or interruption in the work of the firm. Daniel and Harold became the central figures, while William retired.

Economics and politics continued to command an important place on the Macmillan list. E. H. Carr wrote *International Relations since the Peace Treaties* (1937) and *The Twenty Years' Crisis, 1919-1939* (1939). His *Conditions of Peace* (1942) was a foreshadowing of things to come. Marshall, Pigou, and Keynes were the mainstays in economics. Keynes, who also served as an economics reader for the firm, wrote *General Theory of Employment, Interest, and Money* (1936) and *How to Pay for the War* (1940). He also edited the *Economic Journal* for the firm from 1912 to 1945. Keynes attracted to Macmillan other leading economists, including G. D. H. Cole, George Peel, Norman Crump, Paul Einzig, Colin Clark, Sir Cecil Kisch, Lord Stamp, Lionel Robbins, and Joan Robinson.

When war was declared in September 1939 many publishing houses made hasty arrangements to move out of London, where they hoped to avoid bombing. Harold Macmillan made the decision to stay put; the building at St. Martin's Street was strong and well built, with a deep basement that was fitted up as a bomb shelter. Gas masks were issued, drills were held, supplies were stockpiled. It withstood the worst the Germans could offer; no one was injured at Macmillan throughout the war.

Publishing continued, although paper rationing was a problem. Arthur Bryant's *Unfinished Victory* (1940) was an analysis of the problems of dealing with Germany; Storm Jameson's novel *Europe to Let* (1940) dealt with the fate of Europe; A. G. Macdonell's *Crew of the Anaconda* (1940) was a wartime thriller. In collaboration with Oxford University Press, and at the instigation of Lovat Dickson, Macmillan produced a new edition of Louise and Aylmer Maude's translation of Leo Tol-

stoy's *War and Peace* (1942) just as Germany was attacking Russia and the British public was sympathetic to the Soviets. The classic sold ninety-two thousand copies in the first year and continued to be a good seller for another twenty years. The Scottish novelist Eric Linklater offered his autobiography, *The Man on My Back* (1941). The young Richard Hillary, already desperately disfigured in the war and destined soon to die in air combat, brought a memorable account of war in the air, *The Last Enemy* (1942). Escape literature was also popular during wartime: Rebecca West's *Black Lamb and Grey Falcon*, an account of a journey through Yugoslavia, was published in two volumes in 1940, despite the severe paper shortage. Romney Sidgwick's *Letters from George III to Lord Bute* (1939), Sir Percy Sykes's *History of Afghanistan* (1940), Sir Aurel Stein's *Old Routes of Western Iran* (1940), a two-volume edition of the *Journals of Dorothy Wordsworth* (1941), Lord Ponsonby's memoir of his father, *Henry Ponsonby* (1942), and C. M. Bowra's *Heritage of Symbolism* (1943) all demonstrated that readers wanted books that had nothing to do with the war.

To commemorate its centenary Macmillan commissioned a history, *The House of Macmillan*, by Charles Morgan. The firm also offered two prizes of five hundred pounds each, one for a novel and one for a piece of nonfiction. The winners were *Desert Episode* (1945), by George Greenfield, and *Lower Deck* (1945), by John Davies.

After the war publishers faced many problems with continuing paper restrictions; Macmillan had more than three thousand titles that were out of print. Schoolbooks and university texts received first priority. Other important scholarly texts, such as *The Golden Bough*, and nearly one hundred other titles, classics in their fields, also claimed attention. The firm also had responsibilities to living authors, to the estates of those who had died, and especially to those who earned their livings from their royalties. Most authors retained their own copyrights and gave the publisher the "license to publish," with the usually unwritten understanding that if the book was allowed to go out of print the author had the right to place it elsewhere. The goodwill that Macmillan had always fostered with its authors served it well in a time of crisis. Winston Churchill had been one of Macmillan's authors since 1906, when the firm published his biography of his father, *Lord Randolph Churchill*. In the late 1940s he was preparing his war memoirs; the publisher had to decide whether its responsibility was to him, and to itself for an enormously important and potentially profitable work, or to those who trusted the firm to keep the faith. In the end, Macmillan let Churchill go to Cassell, which was willing to invest an enormous share of its paper ration in him. Macmillan used its supplies for those who depended on the firm to get their books back in print.

In peacetime Macmillan added more series in the educational field. There was the Casebook series for undergraduates, which provided surveys of criticism on dozens of authors. The Companion series provided background material for the general reader on major authors such as Wordsworth, Tennyson, George Eliot, D. H. Lawrence, the Brontës, Jane Austen, T. S. Eliot, Hardy, and others. The Master series provided textbooks for direct sale to pupils rather than to the schools. There were schemes for teaching infants to read, such as the Gay Way and the New Way. The biggest series was the Macmillan Crime Fiction series, in which forty to fifty titles were published each year.

In 1965 the firm moved its editorial offices to Little Essex Street, just off the Strand, later augmented by additional quarters in nearby Stockton House. Its supply, distribution, accounting, and archival facilities were moved to Basingstoke. Harold Macmillan was followed as chairman by Maurice Macmillan in 1974, Michael Hamilton in 1984, and Lord Macmillan of Ovendon (Alexander Macmillan, who succeeded his grandfather as earl of Stockton) in 1985.

A sampling from the list of Macmillan authors since the 1960s reads like a "Who's Who" of scholars, historians, poets, fiction writers, and critics: R. G. D. Allen, Edward Blishen, E. R. Boyce, Roger Buliard, David Butler, Charles Carrington, Charles Causley, Robert Conquest, William Cooper, Edward Crankshaw, Elizabeth David, Leon Edel, Dorothy Emmet, David Garnett, Catherine Gavin, Rumer Godden, John S. Goodall, Margaret Gowing, Rupert Hart-Davis, Jack Harvey, F. A. Hayek, Shirley Hazzard, Lillian Hellman, Paul Horgan, Alistair Horne, A. Norman Jeffares, Frank Knight, R. H. Bruce Lockhart, E. T. Nevin, John Julius Norwich, Graham Oakley, Frank O'Connor, John Pearson, F. B. Pinion, Ronald Ridout, E. A. G. Robinson, A. L. Rowse, Robert Skidelsky, Muriel Spark, Jean Stubbs, A. J. P. Taylor, R. S. Thomas, Geoffrey Trease, Hugh Trevor-Roper, Barbara Tuchman, Frank Tuohy, Vercors, John Wain, and Edmund Wilson.

Macmillan had first published R. H. Inglis Palgrave's *Dictionary of Political Economy* from 1891 to 1899. In 1987 the firm published *The New Palgrave: A Dictionary of Economics*, in four volumes, edited by John Eatwell, Murray Milgate, and Peter Newman; the work is the definitive reference in economics today.

As the original Macmillan list of two books represented the founders' interests in education and theology, so today's list reflects the complexity of the modern world. Macmillan is today a vast company, with as many as twenty-one separate catalogues. It is a leading publisher of reference works in all fields: its 1989 *Reference Catalogue* has seventeen sections, including "Microcomputing and Information Technology," "Biotechnology," "Physical and Earth Sciences," "Life Sciences and Medicine," "Social Sciences and Education," "Business," "Finance," "Economics," "History," and "Literature and Languages." The *Macmillan Literary Annuals* gives scope not afforded by the average journal for lengthy articles on important writers. *Macmillan Literary Companions* answers questions about major authors. *British Archives* (1982) is a helpful guide to manuscript collections throughout the United Kingdom. The *Continuum Dictionary of Women's Biography* (1989), edited by Jennifer S. Uglow, is an indispensable reference for women's studies.

In 1980 the firm published *The Macmillan Encyclopedia*, the first such work to be compiled with the aid of computer technology. In his foreword, Harold Macmillan noted with pride: "In 1877 my great-uncle Alexander Macmillan published Autenrieth's *Homeric Dictionary*. This standard work of reference is still available. . . ." *The Macmillan Encyclopedia*, Macmillan concluded, aimed to achieve equal endurance by addressing the same vital ideas that had always dominated the Macmillan list, "ideas which we need to understand in order to appreciate the intellectual currents of our time."

In March 1990 the new Macmillan chairman, Nicholas Byam Shaw, announced a corporate restructuring to form three separate entities. The Macmillan Press Limited represents educational, professional, and reference book publishing divisions, and includes as its United Kingdom subsidiaries Macmillan Education Limited, Macmillan Academic and Professional Limited (previously named the Macmillan Press), and Modern English Publications Limited. Adrian Soar was named managing director of the Macmillan Press Limited. Pan Macmillan Limited represents the adult and children's trade books publishing divisions, including Pan Books Limited, Macmillan London Limited, and Sidgwick and Jackson Limited. Alan Gordon Walker is managing director of Pan Macmillan Limited. Macmillan Magazines Limited, the magazine publishing division, includes among its titles *Nature, Nursing Times, Health Service Journal, Therapy, Bio/Technology, Social Work Today*, and *Diagnostics*. The managing director is Raymond Barker. Shaw is executive chairman of the three companies and chairman and managing director of the holding company, Macmillan Publishers Limited.

**References:**

Richard Altick, *The English Common Reader: A Social History of the Mass Reading Public, 1800-1900* (Chicago: University of Chicago Press, 1957);

Altick, "Nineteenth Century English Best-Sellers: A Further List," *Studies in Bibliography*, 22 (1969); 197-206;

Altick, "Nineteenth Century English Best-Sellers: A Third List," *Studies in Bibliography*, 39 (1986): 235-241;

Phillip V. Blake-Hill, "The Macmillan Archive," *British Museum Quarterly*, 36 (Autumn 1972): 74-80;

Horatio Lovat Dickson, *The House of Words* (New York: Atheneum, 1963);

Ruth D. Edwards, *Harold Macmillan: My Life in Pictures* (London: Macmillan, 1983);

John Collins Francis, "Macmillan's Magazine," *Notes and Queries*, eleventh series, 1 (10 February 1910): 141-142;

Charles L. Graves, *The Life and Letters of Alexander Macmillan* (London: Macmillan, 1910);

Graves, *The Life and Letters of Sir George Grove* (New York: Macmillan, 1903);

June Steffensen Hagen, *Tennyson and His Publishers* (University Park: Pennsylvania State University Press, 1979);

F. W. Hirst, *Early Life and Letters of John Morley*, 2 volumes (London: Macmillan, 1927);

Thomas Hughes, *Memoir of Daniel Macmillan* (London: Macmillan, 1882);

Frederick Macmillan, *The Net Book Agreement 1899 and the Book War 1906-1908: Two Chapters in the History of Publishing* (Glasgow: Printed for the author, 1924);

George Macmillan, ed., *Letters of Alexander Macmillan* (London: Macmillan, 1908);

Charles Morgan, *The House of Macmillan, 1843-1943* (London: Macmillan, 1944);

"One Hundred Years of Macmillan History," *Publisher's Weekly*, 144 (9 October 1943): 1430-1438;

J. W. Robertson Scott, *The Life and Death of a Newspaper* (London: Methuen, 1952);

"Story of the Macmillan Company," *Book Production Magazine*, 78 (December 1963): 26-29;

Arthur Waugh, *A Hundred Years of Publishing* (London: Chapman & Hall, 1930).

**Papers:**

Archives of Macmillan and Company papers are held by the British Library and by the University of Reading.

—*Rosemary T. VanArsdel*

# John Macrone
## (London: 1835-1837)

John Macrone's career as an independent publisher was brief; it lasted a mere three years before influenza killed him at twenty-eight. But Macrone was Charles Dickens's first publisher; he launched William Harrison Ainsworth as a best-selling author; and he teamed both Ainsworth and Dickens with George Cruikshank, thus setting up the most fruitful liaisons of novelist and illustrator in the century. As one of his near misses, Macrone considered the young William Makepeace Thackeray as an illustrator for Ainsworth's *Crichton* (1837), which wound up being published by Richard Bentley, and he commissioned Thackeray's first book.

The basic facts of Macrone's life can be pieced together from asides in letters and memoirs and a fairly substantial recollection by George Augustus Sala. Born in 1809, he was either a Scot, an Irishman, an Italian ("Macirone"), or, most probably, a Manxman. Sala recalls Macrone as a "handsome and intelligent young man," who won the heart of Sala's aunt Sophia, borrowed five hundred pounds from her—which apparently went to purchase Dickens's *Sketches by Boz* (1836)—and then caddishly married another woman.

Macrone came to London in the early 1830s and entered into partnership with James Cochrane of 11 Waterloo Place around 1833. Cochrane, who had been an assistant of Henry Colburn's, passed on to his junior partner a sense of the value of aggressive advertising and of the primacy of the three-volume novel. More important, Cochrane specialized in illustrated books and had brought out between 1831 and 1833 the Novelist's Library, edited by Thomas Roscoe and featuring works by Henry Fielding and Oliver Goldsmith illustrated by Cruikshank.

Macrone broke with Cochrane in late 1834. In January 1835 he set up as "a young and spirited publisher" at 3 St. James's Street. Macrone modeled himself on Bentley and Colburn; like them he specialized in novels, the bulk of which were three-decker, quick-turnover library fodder, and relied on lavish advertisement and loud publicity to bring in business. He was not a patient

*Engraved title page for the second series of the sketches that launched Charles Dickens's career and earned substantial profits for his publisher*

publisher, and his lack of long-term planning eventually led to his downfall.

Macrone's debut was proclaimed in advertisements of mid January 1835. He offered a "Standard National" edition of the works of John Milton, to be published in six volumes, edited by Sir Egerton Brydges and embellished with "imaginative vignettes" by J. M. W. Turner. The first volume was announced for April; as was to be

196

Macrone's publishing hallmark, subscribers were kept waiting until May for delivery. Macrone gave the American gossip columnist Nathaniel Parker Willis a hefty £250 for his *Pencillings by the Way*; it came out, in three volumes, in November 1835.

Macrone came by Ainsworth at second hand. Bentley had published the three-volume edition of *Rookwood* in April 1834; the novel was immensely popular. Risking his limited capital, Macrone purchased the copyright and brought out his three-volume "third" edition of *Rookwood* in 1835. More imaginatively, Macrone commissioned a one-volume "fourth" edition. Borrowing from Roscoe's Novelist's Library, this edition would have twelve illustrations by Cruikshank, attractive green binding, and, as a frontispiece, a "Fraserian"-style portrait of the debonair author by Daniel Maclise. The text would be spruced up with an introduction and a few extra ballads by Ainsworth, and the whole handsome package would be marketed at fifteen shillings. The partnering of a major illustrator with a living novelist was momentous. Macrone went on to combine Dickens and Cruikshank in *Sketches by Boz*, enhancing and enriching Dickens's journalism as effectively as he enhanced Ainsworth's fiction.

In mid or late 1835 Ainsworth introduced Dickens to Macrone. The two young men and their wives got on extremely well. The result was *Sketches by Boz*; what Macrone added to the original newspaper and magazine articles was Cruikshank. In February 1836 appeared two volumes of the first series of sketches, "richly illustrated" with sixteen full-page etchings by Cruikshank.

Hastily scraped together, Macrone's list in 1836 was around twenty titles, mixing a preponderance of fiction with nonfiction and pictorial books. The biggest names on Macrone's list after Dickens and Ainsworth were two novelists: W. H. Maxwell, the veteran of Waterloo; and the similarly passé Leitch Ritchie. Macrone's list was, however, lengthy enough to put him in the first division of three-volume producers, a considerable achievement in the publisher's second year of trading. And, as Ainsworth immodestly put it in a letter to the publisher, Macrone had one great card in his hand—namely, Ainsworth.

The illustrated "fourth" edition of *Rookwood* came out in May 1836 (having been announced for January). It was a hit with the public and gave Ainsworth's career a boost. In June an agreement was made for *Crichton*, and Ainsworth was given (or promised) £350, the highest single pay-

ment Macrone had hitherto ventured. The new novel was to be published first as a three-decker, with a second edition illustrated by Thackeray or John Franklin. Later in June Macrone and Ainsworth made a further contract for a highwayman tale, "Claude Du Val." Macrone was clearly riding high in the summer of 1836. July saw the publication of Benjamin Disraeli's *Letters of Runnymede*. In August Macrone apparently went to Paris to negotiate with Victor Hugo. He also had an agreement with Thomas Moore in prospect. And, at the most ambitious phase of their relationship, in November 1836, Ainsworth and Macrone planned to bring out a one-shilling monthly serial, "The Lions of London," illustrated by John Leech and Cruikshank.

Meanwhile, the runaway success of *Sketches by Boz* had not been foreseen, to judge by the scale of payments given. Dickens had received £100 for each of the two editions of the first series and £150 for the second series, to be published at Christmas 1836 in one volume, with twelve etchings by Cruikshank. With the success of the project, Dickens felt underpaid. An agreement for a novel, "Gabriel Vardon," was made by letter on 9 May 1836, with copy to be delivered in November. Macrone never saw the novel. Dickens allowed himself to be sucked into a morass of agreements with other publishers, following the unprecedented success of *The Posthumous Papers of the Pickwick Club* (1836-1837), published by Chapman and Hall. Accordingly, on 17 August 1836 he simplified his obligations by transferring the Vardon project to Bentley. Macrone was angry at what he reasonably felt to be breach of contract. As was his usual and eventually disastrous practice, he continued to advertise the unwritten and alienated work as "in the course of publication." By early 1837 Macrone and Dickens were not on speaking terms, and lawsuits were threatened. But a compromise was reached: Macrone canceled the Vardon contract, and Dickens surrendered his ever more valuable *Sketches by Boz* copyrights for £100 in January 1837. After publishing a third edition of the first series of sketches in February, Macrone sold the copyrights, together with his stock in hand, to Chapman and Hall for £2,250 in June. It was the biggest single coup of his publishing career, but it was forced on him by financial distress.

Macrone was disastrously in debt—to the tune of five thousand pounds. It seems most likely that his involvement with the chronically ailing radical quarterly, the *Westminster Review*, was

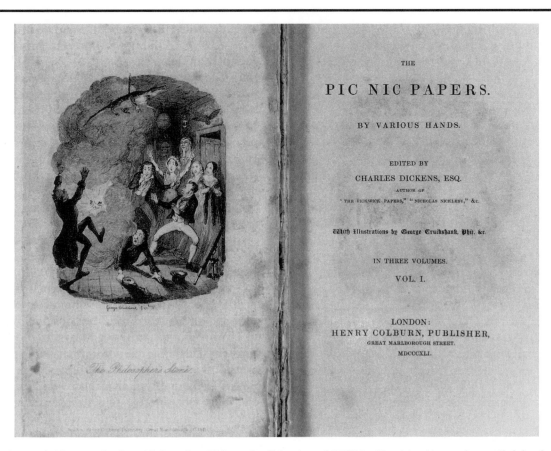

*Frontispiece and title page for the anthology that Dickens, Cruikshank, and William Harrison Ainsworth compiled for the benefit of Macrone's widow and children*

the reason. Until July 1835 the magazine was printed and published by Hansard in conjunction with Simpkin and Marshall; from July 1835 to January 1836 it was published under the partnership name of Macrone and Hansard, and after that solely by Macrone. It merged with its rival to become the *London and Westminster Review* in April 1836, and the price went up to a massive six shillings. Macrone was not the proprietor, but there would have been considerable expense involved in the launching of the remodeled journal. Furthermore, Macrone had started up his business too precipitously. He had failed to win subscriptions from the London and provincial circulating libraries because he had not been established long enough to build up goodwill or a reputation for reliability. For the same reason, his authors were, on the whole, second-raters. And his disagreement with Dickens left a gaping hole in his operations. Although he came out well enough financially from the quarrel, his credit was fatally injured.

Thus, the new year of 1837 found Macrone desperate for cash. He sold his one remaining val-

uable property, *Crichton*, to Bentley; Macrone received £1,000 and Ainsworth £150. For his £1,150 Bentley purchased the copyright and printed stock of *Crichton* and the option on Ainsworth's next work—the highwayman novel "Claude Du Val," which became the sensationally successful *Jack Sheppard* (1839). Bentley's *Crichton* appeared in February 1837, to good reviews. In April the *London and Westminster Review* was sold to Henry Hooper.

Macrone had another future winner in his last list of new books for 1837. At the bottom he mentions a forthcoming title by Thackeray— "Rambles and Sketches in Old and New Paris." *The Paris Sketch Book*, as it was to be retitled, eventually emerged in July 1840. After being considered as a possible illustrator for *Crichton*, Thackeray had offered Macrone the "1st Edition of a book in 2 volumes, with 20 drawings entitled Rambles & Sketches in old and new Paris," in January 1837. When Macrone died, apparently after a short illness, in September 1837, his business was taken over by Hugh Cunningham; Cunningham was evidently Macrone's partner or assistant. In

1838 Cunningham moved to 1 St. Martin's Place. Whether out of reticence or as a graceful gesture, Cunningham used Macrone's name as publisher of *The Paris Sketch Book* and allowed Thackeray's *The Second Funeral of Napoleon*, published in December 1840, to be similarly attributed in reviews and advertisements. This resuscitation of the dead publisher has caused perplexity among Thackeray's biographers and bibliographers.

Macrone's family was left penniless. Dickens, Ainsworth, and Cruikshank provided £450 for them with a charitable anthology, *The Pic Nic Papers* (1839). In a generous though surely untruthful eulogy, Dickens claimed that the young publisher had died "when his prospects were brightest and the difficulties of his enterprise were nearly overcome." Dickens probably meant that Bentley's, Chapman and Hall's, and Hooper's purchases had allowed Macrone to clear some of his debt. But he had sold his seed corn, and it is hard to conceive of a bright future for the house had its head survived. Others were luckier. Chapman and Hall, which had come close to bankruptcy with *The Pickwick Papers*, went on to make a fortune with Dickens. Bentley reaped a rich reward from his *Miscellany*, which founded itself on the partnerships of Dickens and Ainsworth with Cruikshank that Macrone had pioneered. "The Lions of London" was transmuted eventually into Ainsworth's greatest success in fiction, *The Tower of London* (1840). And after doing this novel with Bentley, Ainsworth returned to Cunningham (who was by this time doing business as Cunningham and Mortimer) to bring out the most successful of his collaborations with Cruikshank, *The Miser's Daughter* (1842). All these, and Thackeray too, could have been Macrone's had things gone more his way. As it is, he remains a great might-have-been of early Victorian publishing.

**References:**

Stewart Marsh Ellis, *William Harrison Ainsworth and His Friends*, 2 volumes (London: Lane, 1910);

Madeleine House and Graham Storey, eds., *The Letters of Charles Dickens*, volume 1 (Oxford: Clarendon Press, 1965);

Gordon N. Ray, ed., *The Letters and Papers of William Makepeace Thackeray*, 4 volumes (Cambridge, Mass.: Harvard University Press, 1945-1946);

George Augustus Sala, *The Life and Adventures of G. A. Sala*, 2 volumes (New York: Scribners, 1895);

John Sutherland, "John Macrone Publisher," *Dickens Studies Annual*, 13 (1984): 243-259.

*—John Sutherland*

# John Maxwell
*(London: circa 1843-1879)*
# J. and R. Maxwell
*(London: 1879-1889)*

"A big, burly, florid-faced loud-spoken Irishman, far from unkindly by disposition," as Harriet Jay characterizes him, John Maxwell came to London around 1839 from Limerick to superintend the publication of the collected works of the Irish poet Gerald Griffin. He completed this task in a year or two. By age twenty-five Maxwell was, according to his son W. B. Maxwell, "a publisher of enterprising methods and beginning to do well. . . . He bought old periodicals, he started new ones. He published all kinds of books, chiefly bringing them out through different publishing houses and not often with his own imprint. At thirty-five he was really a force in Fleet Street."

Maxwell was primarily an "entrepreneur of periodicals" appealing to a wide range of literary tastes: from the *Halfpenny Journal* and *Welcome Guest* for the working classes to *Temple Bar* and *Belgravia* for affluent readers. Many of the contributors to his magazines—and the editors he chose for them, including George Augustus Sala, Edmund Yates, Percy Fitzgerald, and Mary Elizabeth Braddon—were considered "bohemian." He made his most significant contribution to literature as the husband, agent, and publisher of Braddon, who was author of some eighty historical and sensation novels.

Maxwell's first wife, Mary Anne Crowley Maxwell, was in a mental institution when he met Braddon in 1860 or 1861. Braddon and Maxwell lived together for fourteen years before his first wife died, and had five children: Gerald (later a novelist), Francis, William (or W. B., also a novelist), Edward, and Rose. They also raised the five children from his first marriage, including Jack (John, Jr.) and Robert, to whom Maxwell later turned over the publishing firm. Maxwell and Braddon were married in 1874. Braddon's biog-

rapher, Robert Lee Wolff, says that Maxwell "seems to have promised [Braddon] that she would be the editor of *The Welcome Guest* and then reneged."

Maxwell had bought the *Welcome Guest* from Henry Vizetelly in 1859. He published it first as a penny, then as a twopenny weekly. The magazine was edited by Robert Brough, who died in 1860, then by Sala, and then by Robert Buchanan; the Christmas editions were edited by Yates. An essay by Braddon, "London on Four Feet," and her first published story, "My First Happy Christmas," appeared in the magazine, and Yates and Buchanan both bragged of having "discovered" Braddon. Other important works that ran serially in the magazine include Sala's *Twice round the Clock* (1858-1859), which was published in book form in 1859 by Houlston and Wright; *Under a Cloud* (1859), by Frederick and James Greenwood, published in book form by Guildford in 1860; and "Looking Back" (1859), by Frederick Greenwood alone.

The last issue of the *Welcome Guest* (14 August 1861) proclaimed that "The tradesman's wife, the hard-working girl, and the shopboy want a stronger class of fiction for their halfpenny than we ever cared to give them at twopence." Maxwell met that demand on 1 July 1861 with the *Halfpenny Journal: A Weekly Magazine for All Who Can Read*. It specialized in lurid fiction; before it ceased publication in June 1865 Braddon supplied seven or eight anonymous novels to the magazine.

Maxwell almost inadvertently launched Braddon's career as a novelist when, at his request, she began writing *Lady Audley's Secret* for serialization in his more respectable sixpenny weekly, *Robin Goodfellow*. Braddon wrote the first installment of the novel overnight, and the rest

*John Maxwell and his family circa 1872. Seated with him on the bench are Mary Elizabeth Braddon and their daughter Rosie. Three of their other children—Will, Gerald, and Fanny—are seated on the ground in front of them. Standing behind the bench are John, Jr., and Polly, two of Maxwell's five children by his wife, who was living in an Irish insane asylum. After her death in 1874, Maxwell married Braddon.*

in less than two weeks. *Robin Goodfellow*, edited by Dr. Charles Mackay, failed in September 1861 after only thirteen issues; but Braddon finished her novel, which was published serially in Ward and Lock's *Sixpenny Magazine* and then (1862) in three volumes by Tinsley Brothers. It was, with Mrs. Henry Wood's *East Lynne* (1861), one of the two top English best-sellers of the nineteenth century.

*Town Talk*, which Maxwell founded in 1858, was significant mainly because of one of its articles. Yates, its editor, described it as "a quiet harmless little paper, with a political cartoon drawn by Watts Phillips, who also contributed its politics and heavy literature. It contained a portion of a serial story, a set of verses . . . and a certain amount of scissors-work; all the rest of the original matter was mine." One of Yates's first contribu-

tions to any of Maxwell's magazines was a portrait of William Makepeace Thackeray that he wrote to fill space in an early issue of *Town Talk*. Deeply offended, Thackeray pressed the Garrick Club to expel Yates. Dickens and others defended Yates on the basis of his youth and inexperience, but he was eventually dismissed from the club. *Town Talk* seems to have been bought in 1878 by Adolphus Rosenberg, who added the subtitle *A Journal for Society at Large* and transformed it into a scandalous weekly edited by "Paul Pry."

In the 1860s Maxwell published, in addition to his periodicals, a series of humorous essays by Sala, *Breakfast in Bed; or, Philosophy between the Sheets: A Series of Indigestible Discourses* (1863). He also republished Braddon's novels *Henry Dunbar* (1864), *The Doctor's Wife* (1864), *Only a Clod* (1865), and *Sir Jasper's Tenant* (1865).

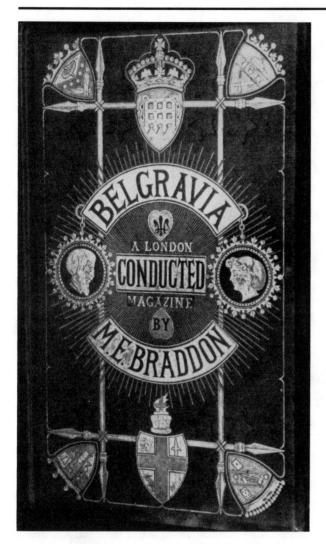

*Cover for the first bound volume of the successful magazine published by Maxwell and edited by Braddon from 1866 to 1876*

In 1871 Braddon bought Lichfield House in Richmond, and the large family settled in there. In the same year she settled a debt Maxwell owed Ward, Lock and Tyler by allowing that firm—a collaborator turned competitor—to publish nine of her novels. Maxwell—and later his sons Jack and Robert—published thirty-three of her tremendously popular novels from 1871 through 1886.

The magazines *Temple Bar: A London Magazine for Town and Country Readers* and *Belgravia: A London Magazine* were significant and lasting publishing successes for Maxwell. He published *Temple Bar* from 1860 through 1862 with Sala as editor, then sold the magazine to Sala. Sala chose purple as the color for its cover and selected as its motto a statement Sala himself wrote and attributed to Dr. Johnson: " 'Sir,' said Dr. Johnson,

'Let us take a walk down Fleet Street.' " Sala chose Yates as his subeditor. Both *Temple Bar* and the *St. James Magazine*, which Maxwell launched in 1861, supplied light reading for the middle classes. In 1861 Maxwell apparently tried to persuade Anthony Trollope to be the editor of *Temple Bar*, with Yates as a subeditor, but Trollope refused. Sala's *The Seven Sons of Mammon* was serialized in the magazine in 1861; Braddon's successful novel *Aurora Floyd* appeared there in 1862.

*Belgravia: A London Magazine* was published by Maxwell from 1866 to 1876, then sold to Chatto and Windus. This monthly shilling magazine, edited by Braddon, appealed to middle-class female readers by serializing sensation novels, many of them by Braddon herself. Sala, W. S. Gilbert, and Joseph Sheridan Le Fanu were also contributors; the art critic R. Folkstone Williams reviewed exhibitions and discussed the business of buying and selling artwork. The magazine also contained biographies, travel accounts, light essays, and poetry.

The *Mistletoe Bough* was a Christmas publication founded by Braddon after the sale of *Belgravia*; the *Belgravia* Christmas annual had always been particularly lucrative. The publication was edited by Braddon until 1887 and then by her son W. B. Maxwell. Braddon published several of her own contributions in it, including the short novels *Flower and Weed* (1882) and *Under the Red Flag* (1883).

Maxwell was a successful, prosperous publisher. The firm became J. and R. Maxwell in 1879, when Maxwell passed the directorship to his sons Jack and Robert. He continued to serve as Braddon's agent. J. and R. Maxwell ceased to exist when Jack Maxwell died in 1889. After a long illness, John Maxwell died in 1895 at his country home at Annesley Bank; Braddon died in 1915.

**References:**

Winifred Hughes, *The Maniac in the Cellar: Sensation Novels of the 1860s* (Princeton: Princeton University Press, 1980);

Harriet Jay, *Robert Buchanan: Some Account of His Life, His Life's Work, and His Literary Friendships* (New York: AMS Reprint, 1970);

W. B. Maxwell, *Time Gathered: Autobiography* (New York: Appleton-Century, 1938);

Joanne Shattock and Michael Wolff, eds., *The Victorian Periodical Press: Samplings and Soundings*

(Toronto: University of Toronto Press/
Leicester University Press, 1982);

Ralph Straus, *Sala: The Portrait of an Eminent Victorian* (London: Constable, 1942);

Robert Lee Wolff, *Sensational Victorian: The Life and Fiction of Mary Elizabeth Braddon* (New York: Garland, 1979);

Edmund Yates, *Edmund Yates: His Recollections and Experiences* (London: Bentley, 1884).

*—Elizabeth J. Deis*

# McGlashan and Gill
*(Dublin: 1856-1876)*
## M. H. Gill and Son
*(Dublin: 1876-1903)*
## M. H. Gill and Son Limited
*(Dublin: 1903-1979)*
## Gill and Macmillan
*(Dublin: 1968-    )*

The firm of McGlashan and Gill was founded in 1856 when Michael Henry Gill, one of the capital's best-known printers, bought out one of the city's biggest bookselling and publishing houses, that of James McGlashan at 50 Upper Sackville Street (now O'Connell Street).

McGlashan was a Scot; some sources say he worked for Blackwoods, the Edinburgh publishers. He arrived in Dublin around 1830. In that year he was on the committee of the Dublin Booksellers' Society, which would indicate that he was well-to-do when he came to Ireland, and not a simple journeyman. He continued to serve on the committee throughout his career in Dublin, as secretary in 1835 and 1846. Between 1830 and 1846 he was in partnership with William Curry, Jr., at 9 Upper Sackville Street. A shrewd businessman, he spotted the potential of the fledgling *Dublin University Magazine* and bought it six months after its launch in January 1833, with the intention of making it the Irish *Blackwood's* or *Fraser's*. The magazine was founded as a bastion against all the reforms of the day and built up a strong circulation among Dublin's Protestant Ascendancy. Isaac Butt, a conservative lawyer and politician, was editor from August 1834 until McGlashan himself took over in December 1838. As editor and proprietor of the magazine he redirected its interests and in doing so made a fundamental contribution to the rising spirit of Irish national literature. He held the post of editor until he persuaded the novelist Charles Lever to take on the role in April 1842.

Lever's voluminous correspondence is the source of much of what is known about McGlashan. "Jemmie" McGlashan emerges from the letters as a sociable character, fond of conversation over a good dinner with his friends, and especially fond of the bottle. But he was also an astute and often ruthless businessman; in Lever's terms, "a devil of a screw . . . [who] will fight to the last for low terms" but also "the very ablest man in his walk."

McGlashan dissolved the partnership with Curry in 1846, establishing his publishing and bookselling business at 21 D'Olier Street. He took the *Dublin University Magazine* with him and continued to publish the works of some of the authors that appeared in it. He also brought out a broad range of general publications. His catalogue for December 1847 includes works on history, classics, science, literature, religion, and politics and is particularly strong in agriculture and horticulture. In 1850 he moved to 50 Upper Sackville Street.

Shortly afterward Lever began to see the first signs of McGlashan's failing mental health—tetchiness and failure to answer letters. By July

*Contents page from an issue of the magazine James McGlashan bought in 1833 and published until 1855, when mounting debts forced him to sell it*

1855 the symptoms were alarming, and McGlashan called a meeting of his creditors. Initially it was thought that he would only be able to pay seven or eight shillings to the pound. McGlashan was obviously held in high esteem by his creditors, however, and efforts to have him declared bankrupt were vigorously resisted. Indeed, it was agreed that an annuity of two hundred pounds should be afforded him. It was little consolation to McGlashan. In September he wrote to Lever: "I am utterly ruined in health and fortune; they have given me a pittance to live on, but have taken away the Magazine and all that I care to live for." By October he had returned to Edinburgh, where he lived on in a deranged state until his death on 4 March 1858.

At a meeting of McGlashan's London creditors on 24 November 1855 it was decided to sell the *Dublin University Magazine* to its London distrib-

utors, Hurst and Blackett, for £750. The meeting also accepted Gill's offer of £250 for copyrights, steel plates, woodcuts, and stock of the magazine and £500 for fixtures and fittings, lease, copyrights and goodwill. (Some sources say Gill paid £2,966; the higher figure would appear to be more realistic.) These agreements were ratified by the Dublin creditors and took effect on 1 January 1856. In taking over one of the foremost publishing and bookselling businesses in Dublin Gill wisely decided to retain McGlashan's name, calling the firm McGlashan and Gill.

Gill had been born in Dublin in 1794, the son of Henry Gill, a woollen draper of Skinner's Row. In 1813 he was apprenticed to Graisberry and Campbell, printers at 10 Back Lane. Since 1807 the firm had been printers to Dublin University. In 1827 Gill was appointed manager of the firm. Ruth Graisberry inherited the business around this time, and on 1 March Gill entered into partnership with her. In 1837 he paid £362 for a half share in her printing equipment and agreed on an annuity of £100 for her goodwill. Although they had been in partnership for over a decade, it was only in 1841-1842 that the names Graisberry and Gill appeared jointly on any imprints. On 7 September 1842, following Graisberry's death, Gill was appointed university printer by the board of Trinity College. This was a surprising choice, as Gill was a Roman Catholic and Trinity was staunchly Protestant. He obviously had proved his worth over the years, and the college must have felt that it could not lose such a competent printer.

Like McGlashan, Gill was an astute businessman. He had extensive investments outside the book trade, notably in property and in the provisions trade. He expanded his publishing interests in 1846 through the purchase of the copyrights of John Cumming, who had recently been declared bankrupt. The purchase of McGlashan's business in 1856 was a logical step in the growth of his book trade interests.

Gill was scrupulous in his business dealings, which prompted Thomas Hodgson of London to write to him in 1856: "It is an unbounded satisfaction to hear you so well spoken of by all. . . . This cash and quick settlement of yours will act like a charm. . . . It is a new epoch in the wholesale trade of Ireland." Hodgson's prediction proved correct, and in succeeding years McGlashan and Gill did business with all the major London and Edinburgh publishers and established contacts in North America and Australia.

McGlashan had used a variety of printers, the University Press among them, for his publications. But after Gill took over the business the majority of McGlashan and Gill's publications were printed at Trinity's Printing House. When Gill resigned as university printer in mid 1874 his personal printing equipment was transferred to Moore Lane, behind the Sackville Street premises.

The name of the firm was changed to M. H. Gill and Son in 1876, presumably when Gill's eldest son, Henry Joseph, was taken into partnership. The father died on 20 March 1879 and is buried in the family plot in Glasnevin Cemetery. Under Henry Gill's guidance nationalist and Catholic literature came to dominate the firm's lists. This trend was followed by succeeding generations of the Gill family. Schoolbooks became another staple of the firm's output. Among the books published by the company were Ulick J. Bourke's *Early Lessons; or, Self-Instruction in Irish* (1876) and Charles Russell's *"New Views on Ireland"; or, Irish Land, Grievances, Remedies* (1880).

The firm was incorporated as M. H. Gill and Son Limited in 1903, the year Henry Joseph Gill died. Among the works to appear under the Gill imprint in the twentieth century were James MacCaffrey's *History of the Catholic Church from the Renaissance to the French Revolution* (1915); *Poems of James Clarence Mangan (Many Hitherto Uncollected)* (1922), edited by D. J. O'Donoghue; Ailbe Luddy's *The Cistercian Nuns: A Brief Sketch of the History of the Order from Its Foundation to the Present Day* (1931); and John K. Casey's *The Rising of the Moon and Other Ballads, Songs, and Legends* (1933). The firm continued to print its own publications until 1965, when it was decided to concentrate on publishing and bookselling; the Dublin University Press bought some of the printing plant. In 1968 a partnership was formed with the Macmillan publishing company, and the publishing interests of M. H. Gill and Son Limited were transferred to the new company, Gill and Macmillan. The retail bookselling business continued to trade out of 50 Upper O'Connell Street until 1979, when it was decided to cease retail bookselling and to concentrate on publishing. The business continues as Gill and Macmillan in Inchicore, an inner suburb of Dublin. The present managing director is Michael Gill, great-great-grandson of Michael Henry Gill.

**References:**

Edmund Downey, ed., *Charles Lever: His Life in His Letters*, volume 1 (Edinburgh: Blackwood, 1906);

"A Dublin Firm of Long Standing," *Irish Monthly*, 34 (1906): 564-567;

William John Fitzpatrick, *The Life of Charles Lever*, 2 volumes (London: Chapman & Hall, 1879);

"The Late Mr. M. H. Gill," *Irish Monthly*, 7 (1879): 223-224;

Thomas Wall, *The Sign of Doctor Hay's Head* (Dublin: Gill, 1958).

**Papers:**

Most of Michael Henry Gill's papers were destroyed in a fire at 50 Upper O'Connell Street in 1979. What remains is in Trinity College Library, Dublin. The papers include J. J. O'Kelly's "The House of Gill," an unpublished typescript prepared for the centenary of the firm in 1956.

*—Vincent Kinane and Michael Gill*

# Middle Hill Press

*(Middle Hill, Worcestershire: 1822-1872)*

Sir Thomas Phillipps of Middle Hill, Worcestershire, was an obsessive bibliophile who amassed a collection of nearly sixty thousand historical and literary manuscripts and fifty thousand printed books. He became interested in printing as a means of preserving and circulating copies of early manuscripts and publishing catalogues of his rapidly growing library. His particular interests were in English and Welsh history, local history, topography, and genealogy.

Phillipps's earliest publications were printed by John Agg of Evesham. Following a legal dispute between the two men, however, Phillipps determined to set up his own private press. In 1822 he purchased a printing press, and in August of that year he acquired the services of Adolphus Brightley, a printer from London, who set up an office in the nearby town of Broadway.

From the moment of its creation the Middle Hill Press was beset with financial difficulties, caused largely by Phillipps's excessive expenditure on book collecting. Brightley, in common with all his successors, was poorly and erratically paid for his work and was expected to economize on printing costs. The press was essentially a two-man operation: Phillipps selected and edited the texts for Brightley to set and print. But Phillipps was neither judicious nor accurate as an editor; consequently, much of the output of the press was trivial in subject matter and poorly edited and corrected. From 1822 to 1844 the average size of a Middle Hill Press edition was about twenty-five copies; thereafter it increased to between fifty and one hundred. Phillipps distributed his publications to London booksellers on a sale-or-return basis. Because of their marginal interest, these works rarely sold more than a few copies.

The books printed for Phillipps during the 1820s were mainly of a topographical nature, including his editions of *Aubrey's Collections for Wilts.* (1821) and *Parochial Collections for the County of Oxford* (1825). Brightley was replaced in January 1826 by F. Crees, who remained in Phillipps's employment for only six months. Edwyn Offer, who had been an apprentice to Brightley, succeeded Crees, and he printed Phillipps's *Catalogue of the*

*Sir Thomas Phillips, 1860*

*Printed Books in the Library of Sir Thomas Phillipps Bart.* (1827) and *Visitatio Heraldica Comitatus Wiltoniae, A.D. 1623* (1828). Offer left Middle Hill in November 1829, and during the years that followed Phillipps employed several outside commercial printers.

In the autumn of 1824 Phillipps printed the first part of his *Catalogus Librorum Manuscriptorum in Bibliotheca D. Thomæ Phillipps, Bart.* Additions to the catalogue were printed sporadically over the next forty-seven years, both at Middle Hill and by outside firms such as Eyre and Spottiswoode. In its final form the catalogue listed 23,837 manuscripts. Although few complete copies exist, and in spite of its uneven quality and amateurish presswork, it remains the single most important work to have come out of the Middle Hill Press.

In 1834 Thomas Timbrell took over the job of printer at Middle Hill, and in that year he produced an edition of Richard Gough's *Human Na-*

*ture Displayed in the History of Myddle*. During this period Phillipps began a project to publish a continuation of Edward Bernard's great union catalogue of manuscripts in British libraries. In 1832 he published a catalogue of 163 manuscripts belonging to Samuel Butler, headmaster of Shrewsbury School, followed in 1837 by a catalogue of 47 manuscripts in the collection of Robert Curzon of Parham and a further 47 manuscripts belonging to Walter Sneyd of Cheverels in Hertfordshire.

Charles Gilmour succeeded Timbrell as printer in 1836 and printed Phillipps's editions of parish registers and visitations of Berkshire, Cambridgeshire, Oxfordshire, Somerset, and Sussex. He also printed pedigrees for Phillipps. In 1838 the second part of *Aubrey's Collections for Wilts.* was printed, followed in 1839 by an *Index to Cartularies Now or Formerly Existing, since the Dissolution of Monasteries* and *A Catalogue of Scientific Manuscripts in the Possession of J. O. Halliwell Esq. 1839*. Phillipps sought to suppress the latter publication in 1843 following the revelation that some of the manuscripts listed had been stolen from Trinity College, Cambridge.

Unable to make a decent living from the wages paid by his employer, Gilmour left the press in 1842. He was succeeded by J. Hunt from 1842 to 1843, Charles Henry Burt from 1846 to 1847, and George Bretherton from 1848 to 1851. In 1854 James Brumbley briefly worked at Middle Hill prior to the arrival of James Rogers. Rogers was taken on as printer at Middle Hill in 1854, and he remained in Phillipps's employment until the latter's death. He printed Phillipps's *Pedigrees from the Heraldic Visitation of Northumberland, 1815* (1858) and *Grants of Manors and Lands in Wales and England from James I to his son, Prince Charles* (1866). Phillipps also had printed, both at Middle Hill and in Cheltenham, where he moved in 1864, some vehemently anti-Catholic tracts and broadsides, including *On a Puseyite Parson* (1863) and *De Conquestu Angliae per Hispanos, Tempore Elizabethae Reginae 1588* (1869). The press continued in operation until Phillipps's death on 6 February 1872.

**References:**

A. N. L. Munby, *Phillipps studies*, 5 volumes (Cambridge: Cambridge University Press, 1951-1960);

Munby and Nicholas Barker, *Portrait of an Obsession* (London: Constable, 1967).

*—Robin Francis*

# William Milner
*(Halifax: 1834-1850)*
## Milner and Sowerby
*(Halifax: 1850-1883)*
## Milner and Company
*(Halifax: 1883-1913)*

Born in Halifax, Yorkshire, in 1803, William Milner was apprenticed to a printer, and in the early 1830s he set up his own printing business. By 1834 he had turned to publishing.

Milner was a shrewd businessman whose philosophy was summed up in the phrase "small profits and quick returns." It was on this basis that he built up one of the most successful publishing ventures of the Victorian period. The success was attributable to Milner's ability to provide cheap, strongly bound, serious books of various kinds for the rising number of working class and artisan readers who sought to "better themselves" through works of literature, instruction, religion, wholesome amusement, and, occasionally, exhortation. There were contemporaries publishing cheap books for a rising readership, among them William Nicholson of Wakefield, J. S. Pratt of Stokesley, and Thomas Allman of London, all of whom had extensive lists; but to judge by the quantity of titles and series, Milner was the leader. Milner, like Nicholson and Pratt, found it necessary to establish offices in London, the center of the book trade.

In his early days Milner stumped the country with a stock of books, sometimes taking stalls at country fairs. He would also travel to an important center such as Bristol, Glasgow, or Norwich, where he would rent a shop for a week or so and sell his wares, sometimes by auction. As his premises in Halifax expanded and more titles were published, his selling methods became more orthodox. The firm's products could then be purchased from booksellers, or could be ordered from the publisher with one penny in the shilling being charged for postage and packing.

Milner married a Mrs. Sowerby, a widow with two sons who were involved in the family firm. When he died in 1850 it continued to flourish under the imprint of Milner and Sowerby until, in 1883, it became a limited company trading as Milner and Company.

The firm often bound its catalogues in at the back of its books; in the 1880s (it is impossible to be more precise because after 1867 none of the firm's output seems to have been dated) a catalogue emphasized more than half a century of achievement and it was claimed that Milner's publications were circulated all over the world, wherever English was spoken. "The especial features of our Publications," according to the catalogue, "are their cheapness, completeness and durability."

There were books of all kinds, with prices ranging from a penny for a paperbound *Guide to the Art of Conjuring* to two shillings and sixpence for birthday books in ornate gilt bindings with beveled boards. Fiction could be had for a shilling a volume bound in cloth, and sometimes with more elaborate bindings which would cost sixpence or a shilling more. Novels were by contemporary British writers and popular American authors; there were reprints of "Gothic novels," some of which had been published by the Minerva Press in the 1790s; the collected works of many poets were readily available, the poetry of Robert Burns being a particularly strong seller; and there were religious books, temperance reciters, dream books, juvenile storybooks, dictionaries, cookbooks, manuals of instruction and etiquette, and home medicine. Much of the fiction was organized into "libraries" and series; the best known and largest was the Cottage Library, 32mo books which were well printed and stoutly bound in cloth with a variety of decorations for one shilling each. This "library" exemplified the firm's practice of republishing standard works at a rock-bottom price which can have left no margin for copyright fees or royalties to authors. The series was apparently discontinued in 1883.

Most Milner books were bound in cloth, with variations in quality and style. Use was made of gilt lettering and ornaments, and to a great extent the Milner books reflected the changes in the decoration of publishers' cloth throughout the book trade over the second half of the nineteenth century.

Milner and Company went into liquidation in 1913. Its demise was brought about by a failure to respond to changing patterns of popular taste, by increased competition from publishers of cheap books, and by the rise of the weekly periodical and the pictorial newspaper.

**References:**
D. Bridge, "William Milner: Printer and Bookseller," *Courier* (Halifax), 24 and 31 January and 7 and 14 February 1970;

H. E. Wroot, "Literature: An Old Halifax Publisher," *Yorkshire Observer*, 20 January 1917;

Wroot, "A Pioneer in Cheap Literature," *Bookman*, 11 (March 1897): 169-175.

—*Victor Neuburg*

# A. R. Mowbray and Company, Limited
*(Oxford and London: 1903-    )*
## A. R. Mowbray
*(Oxford: 1858-1873; Oxford and London: 1873-1903)*

From its first publication in 1873, the firm of A. R. Mowbray has played a major role in diffusing the teaching of the Anglo-Catholic revival or Oxford movement. To this day Mowbray's list bears evidence of its roots, even as it has become more ecumenical.

Alfred Russell Mowbray was born in 1824. A native of Leicester, he attended St. Mark's Teacher Training College in London and by twenty-one was both a schoolmaster and an enthusiastic High Churchman. At the New Church School in Bingham, Nottinghamshire, he met and married a fellow teacher, Susan Thomas. He also painted a window in the church there; his in-terest in ecclesiastical art would manifest itself in his decorations for the Anglican missal.

Mowbray felt called as a missionary and wished to work under Bishop George Selwyn in New Zealand, but while visiting Oxford to take leave of friends he was persuaded that his work lay in England. The Reverend Thomas Chamberlain, vicar of St. Thomas Church, wanted him to present the full faith of the church in a style comprehensible to Oxford bargemen and their families. Mowbray taught for some years on the Boatmen's Floating Chapel, a barge used as a classroom for poor children by day and for their parents at night. Through the Oxford Churchman's

Union he met many of the leading High Churchmen in the diocese.

Mowbray saw the need for a bookshop that would serve as a center for the distribution of tracts and other religious publications. In 1858 he leased a shop at 2 Cornmarket in Oxford, where he sold religious books, prints, and cards. For a time he maintained a photography studio to support his growing family. As Canon William Ernest Purcell writes in *The Mowbray Story* (1983): "From the first it was plain to those who knew him that to Mowbray these enterprises were more than business. They were the outcome of his deep religious convictions. Always he was a man for whom his secular calling was really a part of his religious life. . . ."

In 1867 Mowbray moved to larger quarters at 116 St. Aldgate's, where he set up a small printing works for leaflets and tracts. He also acquired a London agent, his old friend John Masters, who ran The Church Bookseller in New Bond Street. Increased sales soon necessitated a separate London outlet, and in 1873 Mowbray's younger son, Edwin, was put in charge of the firm's first branch at 20 Warwick Lane, Paternoster Row.

In 1873 Mowbray began his career as a publisher with his own *The Deformation and Reformation*. Its two parts, "The House of God" and "The Holy Table," present through his drawings and text the degraded state of English churches before the Anglo-Catholic revival. *The Handy Book of Illustrations and Suggestions for Christian Memorials* appeared in the same year.

Mowbray died in Oxford on 17 December 1875 at the age of fifty-one. Under the direction of his widow the firm attracted authors in sympathy with its aims who remained loyal to it for years. One of the chief was Augustine David Crake, whose instruction manual for confirmation, *The Sevenfold Gift*, first appeared in 1889. Among his enormous output were books of devotions for girls and boys and religiously centered historical novels of the sort Charlotte Yonge had made popular. *The Last Abbott of Glastonbury: A Tale of the Dissolution of the Monasteries* (1884) and *The Doomed City; or, The Last Days of Durocina: A Tale of the Anglo Saxon Conquest* (1885) are representative.

Another Mowbray author was Vernon Staley, who wrote on ceremonial and theology. His *Catholic Religion* taught the doctrines and practices of Anglo-Catholicism and remained in print from 1893 to 1960. Revised and updated, it was re-published in 1983 to mark the sesquicentennial of the Oxford movement. Mowbray also published several editions of Staley's *Ceremonials of the English Church* (1899) as well as his *The Liturgical Year: An Explanation of the Origin, History and Significance of the Festival Days and Fasting Days* (1907).

In 1877 the firm opened a small warehouse at 64-65 Farringdon Street in London which was expanded in 1894 into a bookshop and ecclesiastical furnishings department. Edwin Mowbray was then in charge of the business, but in October 1897 he died from a gas leak in his home. Susan Mowbray, sixty-eight, took control for the second time. Thomas William Squires, who had joined the firm in 1876, was general manager. The firm still functioned as a family business, with the apprentices indentured to Mrs. Mowbray for seven years and bound to abstain from gambling or visiting public houses. Along with required attendance at Sunday services, these restraints shaped devoted, long-term employees. Edward Cordrey, for example, was apprenticed in 1898 and ended sixty years with the firm at its centenary in 1958.

A fire at the firm's Oxford printing works in New Inn Yard destroyed both machinery and records in February 1902, but the business was able to recover. In May 1903 the firm was incorporated as A. R. Mowbray and Company, Limited. Alfred Judges, editor of the *Surrey Comet*, was recruited as chairman.

Judges took two initiatives almost immediately. The *Gospeller* (1868-1908), a four-page parish paper inaugurated by Alfred Mowbray, had been redesigned in 1883 as a thirty-two-page magazine to which local churches added some pages of their own. Believing that a new vehicle was needed, Judges created the *Sign*. The name was supplied by Miss G. M. Ireland Blackburne, who served as literary assistant for many years. According to contemporary advertisements, the *Sign* was established to supply a parish magazine which was to be "thoroughly popular in character, definite in its Church teaching." The first issue, for January 1905, sold 116,000 copies; by 1909 more than 700,000 copies were sold each month. Bulk rates and gift copies to each parish that subscribed kept the price low. As the circulation grew, the type continued to be set at the New Inn Yard works, but the actual printing was shared with Oxford University Press.

Judges's second initiative was a series of biographies of nineteenth-century English churchmen, under the general editorship of George W. E. Russell. As undersecretary of state in the

Home Department he had written the report *Cab Service in the Metropolis* (1895), an unsparing view of the abuses endured by both men and horses. He was president of the Liberal Churchman's Union and regarded himself as a radical and social reformer. Yet the biographies he chose to write for the series, *Henry Parry Liddon* (1905) and *Dr. Pusey* (1907), are sympathetic portrayals of the socially conservative leaders of the Anglo-Catholic revival.

Another series was The Churchman's Penny Library, with Judges as general editor. The series included brief treatments of historical, liturgical, and mission themes, such as *The Ornaments Rubric* (1907), by the artist F. C. Eeles.

In 1908 the prospering firm celebrated its first half century with a river excursion for its staff of more than one hundred and undertook publication of *The Churchman's Yearbook and Encyclopedia* (generally known as *Mowbray's Annual*). The first issue claimed that the annual had a broader appeal than that of *The Official Year Book of the Church of England* as *Mowbray's Annual* sought to serve the entire Anglican communion and provided information on social topics such as Christian socialism and orphan homes. The annual did not survive the Depression; the last issue appeared in 1932.

In 1904 the firm moved to expanded quarters at 34 Great Castle Street, Oxford Circus; but in 1909 a long lease became available at nearby and even more attractive premises, 28 Margaret Street. No more appropriate location could have been chosen. Margaret Street was the site of the Church of All Saints, the cornerstone of which had been laid in 1849 by Dr. Pusey; its services displayed the fullness of the Anglo-Catholic tradition. Soon a clerical tailor shop was added in a showroom next door to the bookstore to "supply at reasonable prices Cassocks and Surplices *made under fair and healthy conditions of labour*." Patterns and "self-measurement" forms were available by mail, thus bringing the standards of Mowbray's tailoring to the most obscure parish priest.

At Oxford the printing works and church furnishings section continued to grow. The latter was dedicated to the tenets of the "Prayer Book Catholics"—that the interiors of English churches should be restored as nearly as possible to their appearance during the reign of Edward VI, when Archbishop Thomas Cranmer had supervised the publication of the Book of Common Prayer. The Reverend Percy Dearmer was a leader in this national movement; his *Arts of the Church* was published by Mowbray in thirteen parts between 1908 and 1915. The firm made altar tables and litany desks, as well as portable altars and fittings for private chapels and oratories.

As William Morris's firm had raised the standard of color and workmanship in ecclesiastical stained glass during the late Victorian period, Mowbray, under the leadership of Squires, raised them for church vestments and ornaments in the early twentieth century. In 1913 the Warham Guild was established at 72 Margaret Street for the making of all "ornaments of the Church and of the Ministers thereof." The Mowbray firm acted as manager, and some of the work was carried out at the works in New Inn Yard "under the directions of ecclesiologists and artists of repute."

World War I brought strains as personnel were drafted and the Mowbrays' two aging daughters gave up their posts. Frank Bryant succeeded Marion Mowbray as secretary; and on the death of Alfred Judges, Gordon Crosse became publishing director and editor of the *Sign*. If postwar disillusion and doubt affected the sale of the firm's books, the grim work of carrying out commissions for war memorials to be placed in churches helped the ecclesiastical design works to prosper. Christmas card sales grew, as did those of the *Sign*.

In 1921 Mowbray published Kenneth Macmorran's *A Handbook for Churchwardens and Church Councillors*, which has been revised many times and remained continuously in print. Crosse's collection *Everyman's Book of Sacred Verse* appeared in 1923. The poems of Henry Ernest Hardy, who used the pseudonym Father Andrew, enjoyed a wide audience in the quarter century before 1950. *Love's Argument* (1922) and *The Divine Compassion* (1930) sold well, and he maintained his audience even after his death in 1946: *The Wisdom of Father Andrew* appeared in 1949 and *The Romance of Redemption* in 1954.

In 1927 the Convocation of Bishops approved a revision of the Book of Common Prayer, which used the text of 1662 but allowed alternative versions of some of the sacraments and additional prayers. It was twice rejected by the House of Commons, but although it was unauthorized, the revision passed into general use. The period of uncertainty hurt Mowbray's bookshop sales of both versions and of manuals based on the old prayer book.

Interest in ceremonial and ecclesiastically correct furniture remained evident in the firm's

# MOWBRAYS

## Church Woodwork
## Metalwork and Needlework

Information on all classes of Church Woodwork, Metalwork and Needlework, and illustrations of work done, may be obtained by post from any of Mowbrays' shops.

Mowbrays' craftsmen at Oxford undertake Church wood-carving and joinery of all kinds, under expert supervision.

## A. R. MOWBRAY & Co. Limited

28 MARGARET STREET, OXFORD CIRCUS
LONDON, W.1

9 HIGH STREET, OXFORD    5 ALBION PLACE, LEEDS, 1

39 CANNON STREET, BIRMINGHAM, 2

44 BRAZENNOSE STREET, MANCHESTER, 2

*Advertisement included in* The Problem of England's Historic Churches: Eleventh Report of the Central Council for the Care of Churches, *published by Mowbray in 1951*

publication of the Alcuin Society Tracts in the 1920s. Named for the Anglo-Saxon theologian and educational reformer who served Charlemagne, the society promoted the study of the history of the Book of Common Prayer and of ceremonial and ornament.

With the death of Squires in 1933 F. J. R. Cox became director in charge, while Gordon Crosse served as chairman. Until his retirement in 1957 Bryant, as managing director, played a vital role in British publishing through his work in developing the Book Tokens scheme in the 1930s and his "Mr. Omnium" column in the *Bookseller*.

Wallace Harold Elliott, canon and precentor of St. Paul's Cathedral, was a popular radio preacher, and Mowbray published collections of

his addresses between 1932 and 1942. *The Sunny Side of Life* (1927) and *Be of Good Cheer: Broadcast Talks in Peace and War* (1940) are representative.

World War II saw a rise in book and greeting card sales, and the postwar era brought a group of new faces to the firm. Ronald Cox and Arthur J. Bryant were appointed directors in 1950, the year in which Crosse resigned. Bryant took over the *Sign* and recruited the Reverend William E. Purcell, editor of the *Canterbury Diocesan News*, to assist him. Purcell became the firm's historian and the author of some Mowbray titles on Anglican spirituality.

The firm's centenary in 1958 brought congratulatory messages from the archbishops of Canterbury and York, but inflation and the secular spirit of the 1960s led to changes in Mowbray's activities. A New Zealander, John Gormansway, was brought in to develop the shops, and in 1969 the completely renovated Margaret Street bookshop reopened as a general trade shop with strong religious and theological sections. While the dean of St. Paul's presided over the opening, the new secular emphasis was highlighted by autographing sessions which included authors as varied as Spike Mulligan and Harold Wilson. Mowbray ceased publishing greeting cards in 1969. In the same year the Society for Promoting Christian Knowledge took over the publication of the confirmation and baptism cards and church notices that had given the shops much of their original character. The 1960s were years of theological instability and shifting values, and Mowbray's backlist, which had always been a steady source of income, suffered. The continuing revision of the Book of Common Prayer affected the sales of altar and service books once again. The *Sign* became the *Sign and the Window* in April 1972. The directors' desire to expand the range of books published resulted in the recruitment of Richard Mulkern, an editor with the Advisory Council for the Churches Ministry, in 1975. Books on sex education, clergy stress, and ecology began to appear.

In the 1970s and 1980s new series were launched that reaffirmed the relevance of the Christian, and sometimes specifically Anglican, approach to modern life. Kenneth Cragg's *The Christian and Other Religions* (1977) was a representative title in the Library of Theology. The modest prefatory note to this series, by the Reverend Michael Perry, says that all the contributors are Anglicans "confident that theirs is a particular expression of the universal faith which still merits serious consideration." Richard Harries, the bishop of London, contributed *Christianity and War* (1986) to the Christian Studies series. *Church Music in a Changing World* (1984) by Lionel Dakers was published in the Popular Christian Paperbacks series, and the Religious Reprints series republished works of popular theology of the preceding half century. The board of directors remained all male but included a Baptist and a Roman Catholic. Mowbray's continued importance in the sphere of religious publishing was affirmed when it shared the imprint of the Alternative Service Book of 1980 with Oxford and Cambridge University presses.

In November 1988 the directors sold the firm to the Pentos Group, which in turn sold the

publishing end of the business to Cassell. A new imprint, Geoffrey Chapman Mowbray, was launched in 1990 with a reprint of Brian Martin's biography of Cardinal John Henry Newman to mark the centenary of Newman's death. Cistercian and Orthodox titles are also published by Mowbray.

The firm's address is Artillery House, Artillery Row, London SW1P 1RT.

**Reference:**

William Ernest Purcell, *The Mowbray Story* (London & Oxford: Mowbray, 1983).

—*Barbara J. Dunlap*

# Edward Moxon
### *(London: 1830-1868)*
## Edward Moxon, Son, and Company
### *(London: 1869-1877)*

Edward Moxon inaugurated his publishing firm in August 1830 with the publication of Charles Lamb's *Album Verses*. The firm soon became known as one that specialized in verse, and it would be a key publisher of major Romantic and Victorian poets and essayists. Henry Curwen's assessment is still apt: "it remained for Edward Moxon to identify his name with all the best poetry of the period in which he lived, to a greater extent than any previous bookseller at any time whatsoever."

Born in Wakefield in 1801, Moxon was the eldest of the nine children of Ann and Michael Moxon; the latter was a woolen worker. Moxon attended the charity school in Wakefield and was later apprenticed to a local bookseller named

Smith. He went to London in 1817, and within four years he joined the firm of Longmans. In 1828 he left Longmans to join Hurst, Chance, and Company.

One impetus for his eventual specialty of publishing poetry was Moxon's own aspiration to be a poet. Longmans published his first book, *The Prospect and Other Poems*, in 1826; Hurst, Chance published his second, *Christmas: A Poem*, in 1829. A two-volume edition of his sonnets was published privately in 1830 and 1835 and reprinted in one volume in 1837 and 1843.

In 1830 Moxon borrowed five hundred pounds from the wealthy poet Samuel Rogers, set up shop at 64 New Bond Street, and published Lamb's book. Lamb had introduced Moxon to Rogers about six years earlier.

In April 1831 Moxon launched the *Englishman's Magazine*; its brief but illustrious run ended the following October. The Irish poet William Kennedy and the Scottish novelist Leitch Ritchie served as editors. Hurst, Chance published the first four numbers, but starting in August Moxon published the magazine himself.

Moxon was sympathetic to the British Romantics. Like most publishers, he had his cautious moments, inspired by the need to stay in business, but he was genuinely interested in discovering good poetry by new writers. Among the new poets the *Englishman's Magazine* presented was Alfred Tennyson, whose sonnet "Check every outflash . . ." appeared in the August issue. The *Englishman's Magazine* included poems and essays by Lamb, Arthur Hallam, Leigh Hunt, John Clare, Charles Cowden Clarke, and John Forster, friend and eventual biographer of Charles Dickens. In 1832 Moxon and Forster founded the *Reflector*, which lasted three issues. (This magazine should not be confused with the *Reflector* that Leigh and John Hunt edited and published from 1811 to 1812.)

In 1832 Moxon also published Tennyson's *Poems*, Allan Cunningham's *Maid of Elvar*, and Barry Cornwall's *English Songs and Other Small Poems*. The next year Moxon published Lamb's *The Last Essays of Elia*. In January 1833 the firm moved to 44 Dover Street, a more fashionable district. Moxon made the new shop so inviting to browsers that Leigh Hunt once remarked that Moxon was more of a "secreter" of books than a publisher of them. The firm continued to give its printing business to Bradbury and Evans, which would print all but one of Moxon's books. On 30 July 1833 Moxon married Lamb's adopted daughter, Emma Isola. Lamb died in 1834, leaving his books to Moxon, who published a collection of Lamb's prose in 1836 and a collection of his prose and poetry in 1840.

Perhaps Moxon's most important publishing relationship was that with William Wordsworth, a volume of whose poems Moxon published in 1831. Moxon published Wordsworth's works until the latter's death in 1850, including a six-volume edition of his poems in 1836 and 1837 and an edition of 415 sonnets in 1838.

Moxon's working relationship with Wordsworth is emblematic of the way he did business. According to Mary Moorman, Wordsworth "was on affectionate terms with his publisher, Edward Moxon, frequently staying with him on his visits to London. . . . Moxon readily executed small com-

missions for him." The errands included taking Wordsworth's dentures to a dentist for repair. Moxon also agreed to Wordsworth's costly desire to have his poems published in unbroken stanzas with wide margins, particularly in *The Poems of William Wordsworth* (1845).

Moxon was close to Tennyson as well. After *Poems*, Moxon personally oversaw the publication of five more Tennyson volumes, ending with *Maud, and Other Poems* (1855); his firm would publish three additional books, *Idylls of the King* (1859), *Enoch Arden, etc.* (1864), and *The Holy Grail and Other Poems* (1869). June Steffensen Hagen has observed that during the 1840s, when Tennyson suffered from depression, Moxon "acted as a tonic for Tennyson's spirits almost as much as did the watercures." Indeed, after Hallam's death in 1833 Moxon and Edward Fitz-Gerald offered much of the emotional support and literary advice that Hallam had provided Tennyson.

With the publication of *In Memoriam* in 1850, the publishing arrangement between Moxon and Tennyson changed. Moxon's typical practice was to pay publication and advertising costs, recoup those costs, and thereafter share profits with the author. For *In Memoriam* Tennyson received an advance of three hundred pounds but gave Moxon an additional five percent of sales above the usual one-third percentage that Moxon received. Hagen claims that Tennyson gave up some profit in order to exert more control over the production of the book, specifically to order a trial run of fifteen hundred copies to ascertain reviewers' responses. Critics praised the book but predicted low sales. They were wrong: *In Memoriam* sold so well for several years that Tennyson was able to live comfortably on its sales. *Maud, and Other Poems* did not fare as well with reviewers, but Moxon, according to Hagen, "passed along praise to Tennyson whenever he could" to try to bolster his spirits.

On 23 June 1841 Moxon was tried for "blasphemous libel" in connection with his publication of *Queen Mab* in a one-volume edition of Percy Bysshe Shelley's poems (1839). The same poem had appeared in a four-volume edition earlier in the year, but Mary Shelley had edited out the atheistic passages that were likely to offend readers. The trial came about chiefly because the radical newspaper publisher Henry Hetherington, who had also been indicted for libel, attempted to prevent his own trial—or at least affect his eventual sentencing—by bringing another publisher into

*My dear Mr Moxon*

*By this time I hope you have rec'd the packet of Lamb's letters — To speak frankly — I am scarcely at ease in my own mind at having given them up; it appears that L. destroyed all the letters that he rec'd from his friends, except one or two. If it may not be inferred from this, that he would not have been sorry if his own had met with the same fate, the fact, if it be a fact, at least seems to imply, that he cared little or nothing about their being preserved. Nor am I at a moment satisfied, that he would have approved of the publication which you are preparing*

*In his case I could not have got over the objection I feel to publishing private letters, had it not been the habit of his mind to throw itself off in an unpremeditated way. His letters may often be considered as the growth of the same tree that produced the better Essays of Elia. For my own part, I do most earnestly wish that not a single letter I ever wrote should survive me. & I shall endeavour to make it known to all my correspondents, whether accidental or regular, that such is my wish & farther, that I sh'd deem a breach of the laws of social intercourse, as I wish them to be maintained, between me & my friends &*

the fray. The single witness for the prosecution at Moxon's trial was one Thomas Holt, whom Hetherington had persuaded to buy a copy of Shelley's poetry at Moxon's establishment. The trial of Moxon, therefore, was something of a test case set up not by the government but by another potential defendant.

Thomas Noon Talfourd defended Moxon, arguing that an entire book cannot be indicted because of excerpts taken out of context. He asserted that Shelley himself had expressed doubts about the views suggested in *Queen Mab*, and that such ideas should be seen as one element in the growth of an intellectual's mind. He also claimed that if Moxon were convicted, the publishers of Henry Fielding, Samuel Richardson, John Milton, Edward Gibbon, Lord Byron, and dozens of other writers would be vulnerable as well.

Despite the eloquence and passion of Talfourd's defense, Moxon was rapidly found guilty by the jury. A sentence was never imposed, however; the prosecution was more concerned with establishing a precedent than with punishing Moxon, particularly since all parties were aware of Hetherington's role in the proceedings. Similar trials of Hetherington and others followed. Thereafter, judges no longer admonished juries to convict out of "Christian duty," and Parliament removed cases of blasphemous libel from the jurisdiction of local magistrates. Moxon's editions of Shelley's poems for many years thereafter printed *Queen Mab* without the offending passages.

In 1848 a man calling himself Icodad George Gordon Byron, who claimed he was Byron's son, let it be known that he had a thousand Byron letters and the poet's Ravenna journal of 1822. Byron's half sister, Augusta Leigh, disputed the authenticity of the letters and journal. In the same year a woman who turned out to be Gordon Byron's wife brought other letters to the bookseller W. White. In turn White offered them to John Murray, who published Byron's works, and Moxon, who published Shelley's. Murray bought the Byron letters directly from White; Moxon purchased the Shelley letters at a Sotheby's auction in 1851.

The man claiming to be Byron's son was probably the infamous forger who also referred to himself as "De Gibler." Moxon published the letters, with an introduction by Robert Browning, in 1852. After publication Sir Francis Palgrave wrote Moxon to tell him that one of the "letters" was a copy of an article he had written for the *Quarterly Review*. Alarmed, Moxon had handwriting experts analyze the letters and postal workers examine the postmarks. When he discovered that the letters were forgeries, he stopped publication and called in the copies he had sent to booksellers.

In 1848 Murray refused to publish Harriet Martineau's *Eastern Life Present and Past*. In a letter to her he called the manuscript "a work of infidel tendency, having the obvious aim of deprecating the authority and invalidating the veracity of the Bible." Moxon published the book that year, and the reviewers blasted it for its unorthodox religious views. Despite his experience with *Queen Mab*, Moxon committed himself to a book he believed in and immersed his firm in a classic Victorian religious controversy. Later Martineau offered *Letters on the Laws of Man's Nature and Development* to Moxon, saying that "we had rather that you publish the book than any other, but shall not urge it upon you." John Chapman published the book in 1851, and while it is not clear why Moxon declined to publish it, Martineau's letter reveals the extent to which Moxon had acquired a reputation as a leading liberal publisher.

The personal relationship Moxon established with most of his authors at one point involved him in a dispute between his brother William and Leigh Hunt. In 1835 Hunt borrowed money three times from William Moxon, a solicitor. In 1836, after Hunt had not repaid the loans, William served him with a writ, threatening to arrest him. The ensuing legal skirmish involved Edward Moxon; the publisher Charles Knight; Talfourd; Lord Holland, a cabinet member; and John Bowring, a member of Parliament. At the end of it all Hunt did not go to jail, did pay the debt, and even received a government pension. For Moxon the incident was embarrassing and time-consuming.

In 1851 Moxon was involved in a struggle that affected the publishing industry at large. Booksellers had been increasingly distancing themselves from publishers, acting as independent professionals. One symptom of this change in the industry was the practice of "underselling"—selling large numbers of books, particularly in America, well below the suggested retail price.

Moxon did not advocate underselling, but he did support the right of booksellers to sell books they had purchased at any price they saw fit. The controversy led to the dissolution of the Booksellers' Association, which had tried to enforce regulations against underselling. Moxon was on the committee that recommended dissolution, and he helped draft resolutions that supported free trade.

Moxon's most important contribution to scholarly publishing was probably Richard Monckton Milnes's *Life, Letters, and Literary Remains of John Keats* (1848). Scholars have ascertained that Moxon made useful editorial notes to the first edition which improved the accuracy of reprinted Keats letters in the second edition of 1867.

Moxon began suffering from lung ailments as early as the 1840s. Nonetheless, he remained active in his business through 1857, when he was working on volumes of poetry by Tennyson and Dante Gabriel Rossetti. In April 1858 he prepared a will, and he died on 2 June at his home in Putney Heath. He was buried in Wimbledon churchyard.

Bradbury and Evans managed the firm from 1858 to 1864 on behalf of Emma Moxon and her son, Arthur. In 1864 J. Bertrand Payne, who had worked at the firm for several years, became manager. He owned stock in the firm until he surrendered his interest to the Moxons in 1869 for eleven thousand pounds. During Payne's tenure the firm published works by Algernon Charles Swinburne and also brought out an inexpensive series of books by such poets as John Milton, Alexander Pope, Robert Burns, Wordsworth, Byron, Shelley, Keats, Sir Walter Scott, Samuel Taylor Coleridge, and Thomas Moore. By 1869 Tennyson and Swinburne had transferred their business to other firms. The personal tension between Payne and Tennyson was considerable because of what Tennyson referred to as Payne's "abrasive business tactics," a sharp contrast to Moxon's manner. In 1869 the firm changed its name to Edward Moxon, Son, and Company.

In 1871 Ward, Lock and Tyler purchased the stock and copyrights from Mrs. Moxon. Ward, Lock and Tyler used the name Edward Moxon, Son, and Company until 1877, when the imprint disappeared. Arthur Moxon established his own firm in Paternoster Row in 1878.

In preferring to publish poetry, Moxon was to a degree old-fashioned, because poetry was becoming less profitable to publish. He was not blind to the changing trends, however, and one important innovation he helped introduce was the one-volume collection of poetry that readers of limited means could afford. Thus Moxon main-

tained the profitability of poetry while he enhanced the careers of several poets and, for a time, kept the reading of poetry alive in the lower middle class. Some of these one-volume collections are regarded today as fine examples of the art of Victorian bookbinding.

In his dealings with authors Moxon was something of a transition figure. "Publishing giants" such as Murray had supplanted the patrons of earlier centuries and wielded enormous power in determining reading tastes and shaping careers. While Moxon was not without power and influence, he tended to create relationships with authors that were based not on power but on mutual respect and a common desire to publish excellent literature—some of which would offend the popular taste. Moxon was by no means a radical firebrand, but neither was he resistant to radical ideas, as his interest in Shelley and Martineau demonstrates. He was often cautious and pragmatic, but he represented an important publishing "bridge" between the Romantic and Victorian eras.

**References:**

Betty T. Bennett, ed., *The Letters of Mary Wollstonecraft Shelley*, volume 2 (Baltimore: Johns Hopkins University Press, 1983);

Edmund Blunden, *Leigh Hunt* (London: Cobden-Sanderson, 1930);

David Cheney, "Leigh Hunt Sued for Debt by a Friend," *Books At Iowa*, 27 (November 1977): 30-56;

Winifred F. Courtney, "*The Englishman's Magazine*," in *British Literary Magazines*, volume 3: *The Romantic Age, 1789-1836*, edited by Alvin Sullivan (Westport & London: Greenwood Press, 1984), pp. 144-150;

Henry Curwen, *A History of Booksellers, Old and New* (London: Chatto & Windus, 1873);

June Steffensen Hagen, *Tennyson and His Publishers* (University Park & London: Pennsylvania State University Press, 1979);

Timothy J. Lulofs and Hans Ostrom, *Leigh Hunt: A Reference Guide* (Boston: G. K. Hall, 1985);

Ruari McLean, *Victorian Publisher's Bookbindings in Cloth and Leather* (Berkeley & Los Angeles: University of California Press, 1973);

Harold G. Merriam, *Edward Moxon: Publisher of Poets*, Columbia University Studies in English, no. 137 (New York: Columbia University Press, 1939);

Mary Moorman, *William Wordsworth: A Biography. The Later Years, 1803-1850* (London: Oxford University Press, 1965);

Valerie Kossen Pichanik, *Harriet Martineau: The Woman and Her Work 1802-76* (Ann Arbor: University of Michigan Press, 1980);

T. N. Talfourd, "Speech for the Publisher of Shelley," *Monthly Review*, 155 (August 1841): 545-552;

Jack Welch, "The Leigh Hunt-William Moxon Dispute of 1836," *West Virginia University Philological Papers*, 18 (September 1971): 30-41;

Newman I. White, "Literature and the Law of Libel: Shelley and the Radicals of 1840-1842," *Studies in Philology*, 22 (January 1925): 34-47;

E. G. Wilson, "Moxon and the First Two Editions of Milnes's Biography of Keats," *Harvard Library Bulletin*, 5 (1951): 125-129.

**Papers:**

Moxon materials are held mainly in the Wordsworth correspondence in the Huntington Library, San Marino, California; the British Library; and the Morgan Library, New York. Complete runs of the *Englishman's Magazine* are held by Harvard University Library, the Newberry Library, the Library of Congress, and the British Library.

*—Hans Ostrom*

# Thomas Nelson and Sons
*(Edinburgh: 1858-1962; London: 1962-    )*
## Thomas Nelson
*(Edinburgh: 1818-1858)*

See also the Thomas Nelson and Sons entry in *DLB 49: American Literary Publishing Houses, 1638-1899*.

Thomas Neilson was born near Bannockburn, Scotland, in 1780; he left the family farm for London in 1796 to undertake an apprenticeship as a bookseller. He returned to Edinburgh in 1798 to begin business as a secondhand bookseller in a small, half-timbered shop with its trading booth opening onto the street at the head of the West Bow, near St. Giles' Cathedral. His experience of the demand for secondhand books showed him that there was a ready market for cheap editions of standard, noncopyright works. In 1818 he began publishing in monthly parts well-known religious texts, such as John Bunyan's *Pilgrim's Progress* and John Howie's *Scots Worthies*, and what became the Nelson hallmark: popular reprints of classics such as Daniel Defoe's *Robinson Crusoe* and Oliver Goldsmith's *The Vicar of Wakefield* and *Essays*. In 1818 the company name, and that of its founder, was changed from Neilson to Nelson to accommodate a frequent misspelling on checks. Nelson made a joke of it: "Like the naval hero of the same name, I have had to sacrifice an 'i' in a good cause."

The emphasis from the beginning was on price—the books had to be inexpensive to be accessible to a new reading public of the skilled working classes—and Nelson employed the still uncommon process of stereotyping to reduce production costs over a large print run. To circumvent the hostility of a book trade that saw its profit margins reduced, he found alternative outlets: direct sales at fairs, at markets, or in vacant shops rented for the purpose. Nelson established the publishing holy trinity of wide distribution, mass production, and low costs. The list expanded until in 1829 he employed a "bagman"—James Macdonald, the first publisher's representative—to hawk the Nelson wares around Scotland and the north of England. The experiment seems not to have been successful initially, with orders coming from only one Aberdeen bookseller. But the business generally flourished, and outlets were found throughout the smaller towns of Scotland. Nelson's early publications reflected the strict religious outlook of his family. John A. H. Dempster views the early history of Thomas Nelson and Sons as conforming to a fairly common early-nineteenth-century model: the founder of the publishing house is motivated by an evangelical zeal to spread the Word of God and commences general, secular publishing only as an adjunct to this purpose, either to create an element of cross-subsidy or to increase his profile among booksellers and public. Succeeding generations inherit the prosperous business but none, or only a diluted form, of the religious motivation. The religious output of the firm decreases but remains as a steady income generator on the back list. Persuasive though this analysis is, it perhaps ignores another strong motive in Thomas Nelson which was passed on to his heirs and even shared by those who came into the company from outside the family: the urge to spread learning and knowledge through good, cheap books across a wider section of the population than had previously enjoyed it. This is the evangelism of the educator, of the democrat who wishes to see all people participating in the community of the learned. It is the mission which lay behind the story of Thomas Nelson and Sons until after World War II.

Nelson's sons William and Thomas entered the family business in 1835 and 1839, respectively. William had to give up his studies at Edinburgh University to help his ill father run the firm, while Thomas remained at the high school in Edinburgh only until he reached his sev-

enteenth birthday. William concentrated on the marketing side, Thomas on editing and production. In his early days with the firm, William attempted to reduce stock holdings by rebinding some of the reprints in a more attractive cloth finish and took to the road to sell them. The repackaging was successful, particularly when it was coupled with an increased discount, and booksellers who had earlier perhaps turned up their noses at the Nelson list subscribed eagerly. William went as far as Liverpool on his first sales expedition and gathered many subscriptions. In 1844 Thomas established a London branch of the firm at 35 Paternoster Row, where his father had served his apprenticeship.

The firm continued to deal only in reprints until 1845, when a new printing house was built at Hope Park in Edinburgh. Then the company began to publish original stories of adventure and travel for young people—"moral books," as they were called—as well as educational titles generally. The former were suitable as Sunday school, church, or school prizes for children: their contents were elevating and wholesome; the books were attractively presented in accordance with the firm's high standards; their price did not strain the purses of church committees or school boards.

In 1850 Thomas perfected a rotary press, a model of which was demonstrated at the Great Exhibition the following year; but because he refused to patent his invention, little fame and no fortune resulted from the many imitations that were built by competitors. A continuous web of paper fed cylinders holding curved stereotype plates, passing the printed paper under a serrated knife for cutting into sheets. This machine was the parent of all newspaper presses until well into the twentieth century. (In 1914 the original press was exhibited at a Leipzig trade fair and on the outbreak of war was interned until its return, intact, in 1919.) Thomas's obituary in the *Bookseller* stressed the high production values of the Nelsons' books: "they were better printed, better illustrated and more tastefully bound than any other books of their class, and for years enjoyed the distinction of being conspicuously the best cheap books to which the public had access."

In 1854 Thomas established at William's suggestion a branch of Thomas Nelson at 42 Bleecker Street in New York, the first branch of a British publishing house ever to be established in the United States. It was to prove a sound investment for reasons not altogether to do with publish-

*The rotary printing press invented by Thomas Nelson the Younger in 1850*

ing, as William's obituary in the *Bookseller* explained: "When the Civil War broke out in America the Nelsons were steadfast in the support of the Northern cause, and, in spite of an overwhelming current of public opinion at home, they held to their convictions. This resolution was chiefly due to Mr. Thomas Nelson, who allowed himself to be guided by the wise counsels of Mr. George H. Stuart, a Philadelphian merchant. Every dollar that could be spared was invested in American bonds during a time when gold commanded almost three times its value in currency. The firm reaped an enormous harvest from their investments in American securities, besides doing an immense trade in English books of which, in spite of restrictive tariffs, they were for years the largest importers."

The work of R. M. Ballantyne, whose *Snowflakes and Sunbeams; or, The Young Fur-Traders* (1856) was written at the suggestion of William Nelson out of Ballantyne's experiences with the Hudson's Bay Company, fit well into the cate-

gory of "moral books." Ballantyne was a profoundly religious man, believing that he had a mission to use his gift for writing for young people under "guidance from God." According to his biographer Eric Quayle, he "seemed more interested in redeeming souls than in adding acres to the Queen's empire." Harriet Beecher Stowe, an outstanding example of the moral, humane Nelson author, was another of the more prominent writers, while artists such as Sir Edwin Henry Landseer and David Scott were among the illustrators. William Nelson discovered in his European travels such artists as Jules Mangin and H. Giacomelli, whose detailed engravings demonstrated the draftsman's skill at its highest. Less well remembered figures, important in their time, were Charlotte Maria Tucker, who used the pseudonym "A.L.O.E." (A Lady of England), and Evelyn Everett-Green. The former was, like Ballantyne, possessed of a Christian mission in her writing. In 1858 the firm changed its name to Thomas Nelson and Sons.

Copyrights of the works the firm published were on acceptance of manuscript, the author receiving no other payment or royalty. Ballantyne protested against such exploitation by taking the only course of action open to him, removal of future titles to another publisher. Quayle quotes him as calling William "a mean old codger." He certainly felt that he had been the victim of sharp practice when he set the popularity of the works published by Thomas Nelson and Sons against the—to his mind—paltry sums he had received for their copyrights: fifty pounds for *Snowflakes and Sunbeams*, sixty pounds for *Ungava* (1857) and for *The Coral Island* (1858), rising to seventy-five pounds for *Martin Rattler* (1858). Ballantyne further claimed that the original, spoken agreement for *Snowflakes and Sunbeams* had promised an additional ten pounds in royalties for every five hundred copies sold after exhaustion of the original, conservative print run of fifteen hundred. The Nelsons denied everything but offered extra payments if Ballantyne would assign to the firm all rights to future editions of the works already published. He declined, and when in 1860 the Nelsons refused to allow him to retain copyright in a new work, he left. This episode reflects a lack of commercial foresight on the part of the Nelsons. The publisher with whom Ballantyne eventually signed, James Nisbet, agreed initially to a royalty of forty pounds per thousand copies sold, and Ballantyne retained copyright. In his lifetime Ballantyne wrote some eighty stories; such fecundity would have been worth a concession or two. In 1865 he asked, rather naively, if the Nelsons would sell back to him the copyrights of the titles already published so that he could consolidate all his works under one imprint and have them published in a cheap edition. Quayle quotes from a letter in which Ballantyne discusses his proposal: "I have hopes in regard to this. It would be a graceful thing for Nelson to do, as a *friend*, to let me have them cheap, and as a *publisher* he might think he had got a good enough return for the small sums he gave me for them. Besides, they cannot be of *much* value to him now, I should think." But the books were still best-sellers for Nelson, and Ballantyne saw not a penny more.

Thomas Nelson, Sr., died in 1861, after a period of invalidism; by then he had turned over total responsibility for the firm to his sons. William visited the American branch on several occasions; on a transcontinental tour in 1870 he narrowly missed falling into the hands of raiding Sioux. A third brother, Peter, who had managed the London branch of the firm but had never become a partner, died in 1871.

A fire devastated Hope Park in 1878, causing damage estimated between one hundred thousand pounds and two hundred thousand pounds, only some of which was covered by insurance. William Nelson wrote: "Never did fire do its work more speedily or more thoroughly. It broke out about three o'clock in the morning, and in little more than an hour the whole building was in flames. I was aroused about a quarter past four, and hurried as fast as I could to the scene; but I found when I arrived that the roof all around had fallen in, and that flames were bursting forth from all the windows in the very front of the building. The fire broke out somewhere in the back part of it; there was a strong east wind blowing at the time, and this fanned the flames and made them rush along the various flats, as they successively caught fire with extraordinary rapidity. Not a book or sheet of paper was saved."

Within two months Thomas Nelson and Sons was back in operation, albeit on a limited scale. Within two years the production works moved to a new site at Parkside, near Arthur's Seat. The calamity had brought the benefit of investment in a new plant, from which a flood of reprints, schoolbooks, prize books, and religious books poured—all at inexpensive prices.

The various Education Acts after 1870 stimulated a tremendous demand for learning materi-

als. Thomas Nelson and Sons responded with the Royal Readers series, which sold in vast quantities throughout the British Empire; it was followed by the Royal School series, which eventually included seventy titles. The company corresponded with educationalists; it maintained contacts with school boards, at home and abroad, seeking always to answer particular needs; and the products of rivals such as Blackie and Arnold were monitored. Between 1878 and 1881 educational books represented 25 percent (187 titles) of the firm's output but yielded 88 percent of its profits. Moreover, these figures conceal the disproportionate contribution made to that profit by just six books, the Royal Readers: 51 percent of all educational profit came from these key titles alone. The situation can be described in an even more dramatic fashion: from 1878 to 1881, 0.8 percent of the total output of the company provided 45 percent of its profits. Thomas Nelson and Sons published the first school atlases, and Thomas is credited with the introduction into these books of lines of latitude and longitude and of the scale in English miles. (He bought a controlling interest in John Bartholomew and Company, the cartographical and geographical specialists, not long before his death.) From these precedents, books on all subjects flowed from the Nelson presses to satisfy the need for good, cheap educational material.

From 1878 to 1881 fiction represented 40 percent (299 titles) of the books produced, but only 10 percent of the profits. Books by certain authors, such as Ballantyne, were much more profitable than the norm; 53 percent of the profit for fiction was derived from 17 percent of the titles. The conclusion must be that the greater proportion of the fiction published by Nelson made very little money.

A final "first" set by Thomas was his experiments with coated paper, partly made by hand, for use with halftone blocks. William died in 1887 and Thomas in 1892. A form of trusteeship operated until the latter's two sons, Thomas III (Tommy) and Ian, were old enough to take over the business: a Canadian cousin, George Brown, acted as regent.

Even when he was dying, in 1893, Ballantyne failed to wring any concessions out of the new generation then at the helm of the firm. That generation also came into conflict with Everett-Green, not over the financial but the moral aspects of her work; editorial objections included her portrayal of kissing. Again, the publisher made no concessions.

Brown continued as a partner in the company after Tommy and Ian Nelson took over; he revolutionized the accounting side of the business through the introduction of an up-to-date American system. Tommy, born in 1877, carried on the family tradition of innovation in mass publishing. The name of Thomas Nelson and Sons appeared over branches in France and Germany, and reprint series of foreign-language books increased, including an edition of the works of Victor Hugo. The American Thomas Nelson and Sons remained a branch until 1903, when it became a New York corporation wholly owned by the parent British company.

From the turn of the century many of the firm's fiction books were grouped into various popular libraries, all in a standard size of 6.5 by 4.25 inches. The New Century Library included titles by Charles Dickens, William Makepeace Thackeray, and Sir Walter Scott, "handy for the pocket or knapsack, and especially suitable for railway reading." The Sixpenny Classics, which later became the Nelson Classics, began in 1903 as a reprint series of noncopyright works and eventually consisted of more than four hundred volumes. The Nelson Library, selling at sevenpence, offered from 1907 reprints of copyright works in red and gold cloth bindings; new titles appeared each fortnight.

Friendship from their days at Oxford led to Tommy bringing John Buchan—author, politician, and later, as Lord Tweedsmuir, governor-general of Canada—into the firm as literary adviser in late 1906. For some years Buchan was largely responsible for editorial policy. He was inspired by the same principles that had been Nelson's from its earliest days: place good books within the means of as many people as possible. To this end he negotiated with publishers and authors to bring the titles he wanted to the firm. Buchan brought into the Classics fold works by William James, Joseph Conrad, and H. G. Wells. To undertake these and other series, a new factory was built in 1907 capable of producing 200,000 books a week. The Shilling Library provided further titles of general literature, while several foreign series catered for languages other than English. Janet Adam Smith recounts in *John Buchan and His World* (1979) that Wells wished that the reprint of his *A Modern Utopia* (1904) "should be sold in bulk to Boy Scouts; when told it would be far above their heads, he retorted

that Boy Scouts were always growing up, and that they would be likely to read a book that had somehow been identified with their movement." By no means all of the titles Buchan chose were so edifying: authors such as E. F. Benson, W. W. Jacobs, Anthony Hope, E. C. Bentley, and Erskine Childers rubbed spines with the literary lions. Only a limited number of new works were published; one outstanding example was the Nelsons' biography of Edward VII, which was on sale in an edition of 120,000 copies within three days of his death in 1910. Another, in 1912, was the biography of Gen. William Booth, founder of the Salvation Army. He died on a Tuesday evening; the book went on sale in Edinburgh on Thursday afternoon, and 50,000 copies were dispatched to England on Friday morning. Nelson also published some of Buchan's own best-known books, including *Prester John* (1910) and *The Marquis of Montrose* (1913).

Among the firm's educational works, *Highroads of History* (1907), *Highroads of Literature* (1911), and *Highroads of Geography* (1911) were to remain on the company's back list for more than forty years. Thomas Nelson and Sons was also active in the periodical field. From 1895 the *Practical Teacher* appeared under its imprint. This, like many of the firm's other periodicals, carried a high proportion of advertising for titles published by Nelson. The most successful of the periodicals was the *Children's Paper*, which Nelson published from 1855 until 1925. Buchan took charge of a weekly published by Nelson, the *Scottish Review*, and attempted to slough off its dour, worthy image as a house journal of the United Free Church and make it the center of a new Edinburgh-based Enlightenment. In this goal Buchan was pursuing a similar policy to that envisaged by Brown and the Nelsons when they had bought the magazine. A consensus existed on the need for a periodical which would cover Scottish political, literary, and social matters, and efforts were made to drum up subscribers. But despite his own industry—each week he contributed a London letter and an article or long review—Buchan could not sustain the necessary sales, even at a mere penny a copy, to keep it afloat. The magazine closed at the end of 1908.

The North American branches expanded, with a Toronto branch opening in 1914. In *Memory Hold-the-Door* (1940), his autobiography, Buchan wrote of that period in the firm's history: "We were a progressive concern, and in our standardized Edinburgh factories we began the publication of cheap books in many tongues. On the eve of the war we must have been one of the largest businesses of the kind in the world, issuing cheap editions of every kind of literature not only in English, but in French, German, Magyar and Spanish, and being about to start in Russian."

Buchan became a director of Nelson in 1915, when it became a limited company. The book which was to bring Buchan lasting popular success, *The Thirty-Nine Steps* (1915), is dedicated "To Thomas Arthur Nelson, Lothian and Border Horse. My dear Tommy, you and I have long cherished an affection for that elementary type of tale which the Americans call the 'dime novel' and which we know as the 'shocker'—the romance where the incidents defy the probabilities, and march just inside the borders of the possible. During an illness last winter I exhausted my store of these aids to cheerfulness, and was driven to write one for myself. This little volume is the result, and I should like to put your name on it, in memory of our long friendship, in these days when the wildest fictions are so much less improbable than the facts."

The need to be doing something (he was writing *The Thirty-Nine Steps*, but to his mind that did not count) preoccupied Buchan in the early months of World War I. He was also anxious that the denial of foreign markets, the loss of manpower, and the general exigencies of wartime should not lead to the decline of the firm. He proposed a history of the war to be published in monthly parts, and the idea was readily accepted by his colleagues. When his original suggestion for the author, Hilaire Belloc, declined to undertake the task, one may imagine that there was only the minimum of reluctance on Buchan's part to accept what he would have regarded as a challenge to his talents. Each issue, of about fifty thousand words, was seized on by a public eager for clear, authoritative accounts of the war. It was published from 1915 to 1919 and represents a staggering feat of stamina and consistency. Over the same period another Nelson author, Edward Parrott, produced *The Children's Story of the War*, which was also published in installments.

After the death of Tommy Nelson at the Battle of Arras in 1917, Ian took over as head of the firm. In the interwar period, Nelson expanded its educational list; the takeover in 1915 of the publishing house of T. C. and E. C. Jack, with its strengths in children's titles, had consolidated the direction to which the company was to commit itself. Buchan brought in Sir Henry Newbolt, with whom he had worked in the Ministry of Information during the war, to act as editorial adviser in the educational field. Various series, such as the Nelson School Classics, were inaugurated. In part in response to Newbolt's 1921 report on the teaching of English in schools in England and Wales, Nelson produced in 1922 The Teaching of English series, which eventually ran to some two hundred titles, under the editorship of Newbolt and Richard Wilson. The latter also introduced a new type of school reader in *Reading for Action* (1935) and *Read and Remember* (1940-1941). A further series, The Teaching of History, also grew out of Buchan and Nesbolt's collaboration. Buchan left the firm in 1929. Ian Nelson remained head of the firm until his death in 1958.

In the post-1945 period educational books became all-important to the company, and the tradition of cheap reprints died. Overseas markets for textbooks were nurtured; the links Nelson had with the Empire were reinforced in the new Commonwealth, especially East and West Africa and the West Indies. In 1949 the Canadian branch became an independent company; in 1960 an Australian firm was established; in 1962 the South African branch was registered as a distinct company; a Nigerian company was set up in 1961; a Kenyan company followed in 1963. As early as 1887, a reader had been produced in the Nyanja language of what was then Nyasaland, now Malawi, and sixty years later Nelson was publishing a wide range of textbooks in Kiswahili, Yoruba, Ewe, Twi, and Ga. Specialist schoolbooks such as West Indian histories and Malayan arithmetics illustrated the company's determination to retain its hold on a growing but sensitive market.

In 1962 Thomas Nelson and Sons merged into the Thomson Organization, run by Roy (later Lord) Thomson, in an effort to sustain its educational publishing interests on a global scale. The production plant remained in Edinburgh while the editorial offices moved to London. The firm also began to seek competitive quotations for production work from printers in Britain and, more frequently, abroad. The printing division of Nelsons was sold to Morrison and Gibb in 1968; the Parkside works, at one time the glory of the firm, were razed to make way for the headquarters of an insurance company. In 1969 the American company was sold to Royal Publishers Incorporated of Nashville, Tennessee, which retained the name Thomas Nelson and Sons.

During the 1960s Thomas Nelson and Sons made a brief foray out of educational publishing into coffee-table books, the sort of highly illustrated book that is the backbone of the remainder merchant's list. The lesson was learned. After the mid 1970s Nelson specialized in schoolbook publishing and concentrated on its export markets, particularly in the Caribbean. In 1980 new premises, Nelson House, were opened at Walton-on-Thames, and the company began to look beyond print to computer software and video as suitable vehicles for its educational material. What was left of its academic list was transferred to Van Nostrand Reinhold (UK), which Thomson took over in 1982. In 1983 the colophon of Thomas Nelson's Edinburgh shop was dropped. Thomas Nelson and Sons has become a niche imprint within the International Thomson group.

**References:**

John Buchan, *Memory Hold-the-Door* (London: Hodder & Stoughton, 1940);

John A. H. Dempster, "Thomas Nelson & Sons in the Late Nineteenth Century: A Study in Motivation," *Publishing History*, 13 (1983): 41-87; 14 (1983): 5-63;

Eric Quayle, *Ballantyne the Brave* (London: Hart-Davis, 1967);

Janet Adam Smith, *John Buchan and His World* (London: Thames & Hudson, 1979);

*Thomas Nelson & Sons: Two Centuries of Success* (Walton-on-Thames: Nelson, 1987);

Sir Daniel Wilson, *William Nelson: A Memoir* (Edinburgh: Privately printed, 1889);

John T. Winterich, "The American Thomas Nelson & Sons Celebrates Its First 100 Years," *Publishers' Weekly*, 166 (30 October 1954): 1786-1791.

—*Alistair McCleery*

# Thomas Cautley Newby

## (London: circa 1840-1879)

Thomas Cautley Newby has earned notoriety as the less-than-honorable publisher of first novels by Emily and Anne Brontë—*Wuthering Heights* and *Agnes Grey*, respectively—in 1847. Born around 1798, Newby began as a printer and publisher of novels and miscellaneous works about 1840. In 1843 he had offices at 65 Mortimer Street, Cavendish Square, moving to 72 Mortimer Street a year later and to 30 Welbeck Street, Cavendish Square, in 1849. Biographers and editors of the three Brontë sisters record Newby's practice of agreeing to publish books by unknown writers and then failing to live up to the terms of the contract. For example, he asked the two younger Brontë sisters for an advance of fifty pounds, his standing price for first books by young authors, to cover costs of production but held on to their corrected proofs for several months. Then Charlotte Brontë's novel *Jane Eyre* (1847) was published by Smith, Elder and attracted wide critical attention. Newby quickly published the other Brontë novels, but with such a multitude of errors in spelling and punctuation that Charlotte, who had been responsible for sending the works to Newby, decried them as "mortifying to a degree." Moreover, to insure that he would not lose money on the venture, Newby printed only 250 copies of each novel instead of the 350 he had promised. He then implied in his advertising that all three novels were by the same author. Some months later, when Anne Brontë offered Newby her second novel, *The Tenant of Wildfell Hall* (1848), he made a deal for an American edition by insinuating that it was a new work by the author of *Jane Eyre*. Charlotte Brontë's friend and fellow novelist, Mrs. Elizabeth Gaskell, told Smith, Elder that she intended to warn unsuspecting writers about Newby; in her 1857 biography of her friend she called him a "mean publisher" fit to be "gibbeted." The publisher Richard Bentley once said that he would talk to Newby only in the presence of a witness.

In 1847, the year he published the first Brontë novels, Newby also published Anthony Trollope's first novel, *The Macdermots of Ballycloran*, after holding off for two years (Irish novels, he told Trollope, were not selling). Trollope's

*Newby's edition of Anne Brontë's second novel (1848). Newby sold the American publication rights to it by implying that the book was the work of Charlotte Brontë, whose* Jane Eyre *(1847) had been far more successful than her sister Anne's 1847 novel,* Agnes Grey *(auctioned by Sotheby's, 30 April 1990).*

mother, the successful writer Mrs. Frances Trollope, had encouraged Newby to publish her son's work, and in his advertising Newby gave the impression that the book was hers. As in the case of the Brontës, Newby printed fewer than the number of copies agreed upon, and Trollope earned nothing for the novel. By advertising only briefly and then being unwilling to hold on to stock until the work caught on, Newby allowed first novels of unknown writers such as Trollope to fail prematurely. Eliza Lynn Linton, later an enormously popular Victorian novelist, also lost money on her first novel, *Azeth, the Egyptian*, which was published by Newby in 1847.

Charlotte Riddell got nothing from Newby for her first published novel *Zuriel's Grandchild* (1855), but went on to achieve fame. In 1864 Riddell's sensation novel *George Geith of Fen Court* became a best-seller, and during the 1860s and 1870s she was one of the dozen most popular English women writers; she lampooned Newby in *A Struggle for Fame*, published by Bentley in 1883. Newby evidently did not have the discernment—or sufficient working capital—to encourage promising but immature talent.

Grander figures in the literary world looked down on Newby. Bentley's publisher's reader, Geraldine Jewsbury, advised Bentley against taking inferior work that was merely "good enough for Newby." Yet, in spite of his poor reputation within the publishing trade and his niggardly ways, Newby repeatedly received manuscripts from several authors, especially women. He published five three-volume novels by Hannah D. Burdon (afterwards Mrs. Wolfensberger) from 1840 to 1847, five three-volume novels and two collections of charades for acting by Ellen Pickering from 1842 to 1844, nine two- and three-volume novels and two shorter works by Elizabeth Caroline Grey from 1843 to 1854, no fewer than nineteen two- and three-volume novels by Mrs. Robert Mackenzie Daniel from 1843 to 1871, six mostly three-volume novels by Laura Jewry from 1846 to 1853, and five three-volume novels by Sophia Crawford from 1850 to 1857.

Historical romance figured prominently in Newby's list. Louis Alexis Chamerovzow's *Chronicles of the Bastille* (1845), originally published by Newby in twenty monthly parts, went into a fifth edition. Chamerovzow then produced *The Embassy; or, A Key to a Mystery Romance* (1846), *Philip of Lutetia* (1848), and *Man of Destiny* (1860). Additional works by Chamerovzow illustrate Newby's free-wheeling range of publications: *The New Zealand Question and the Rights of Aborigines* (1848) and *The Industrial Exhibition of 1851; Being a Few Observations upon the General Advantages Which May Be Expected to Arise from It* (1851). The remarkably prolific George Payne Rainsford James, who is said to have written more than a hundred novels, had fifteen works published by Newby between 1849 and 1858, including *Dark Scenes of History* (1849) and *Ticonderoga; or, The Black Eagle* (1854), written after James served as consul to Massachusetts. Newby published twelve sea romances and a set of short stories by F. Claudius

Armstrong from 1854 to 1868; second editions of Armstrong's romances came out under other publishers.

On occasion Newby veered close to plagiarism in his use of titles or pseudonyms. William North's *Anti-Conigsby; or, The New Generation Grown Old: A Novel, by an Embryo M.P.* (1844) was a satire on Benjamin Disraeli's popular novel *Coningsby; or, The New Generation*, which was published by Henry Colburn in 1844 as part of Disraeli's plan to launch his political ideas. *The Impostor; or, Born without a Conscience: By the Author of "Anti-Coningsby"* (1845) capitalizes even more flagrantly on the spin-off. In 1857 Newby caused a violent literary quarrel when he printed Julia Kavanagh's name on the title page as editor of her far-less-talented father Morgan Peter Kavanagh's novel *The Hobbies*, which was called by the *Athenaeum* "an insult to the public." In 1859 Newby angered George Eliot by publishing a work called *Adam Bede, Junior* and implying that it was a sequel to her *Adam Bede*, which had been published that year by Blackwood. Heatedly, Eliot wrote to the *Times* on 30 November, pointing out that she was "not the first writer who has had to suffer from this publisher's method of trading." Undaunted, Newby replied in the *Times* on 5 December that he had had no disagreement with the two Brontës, and that "long after the publication of *Jane Eyre*, Miss Anne Brontë brought me a work ... which I published in due course"—again pointing to Anne as the author of her sister's work.

Newby no doubt also hoped for second-hand publicity when he published seven novels by Frank Trollope from 1865 to 1872. Anthony Trollope, unceremoniously dumped by Newby in 1847, had by then reached a peak of popularity with his Barsetshire series and the first of his Palliser novels. The works of Anthony's mother and his brother, Thomas Adolphus Trollope, also enjoyed wide popularity at this time.

Although Newby specialized in novels, well over a third of the works he published were nonfiction. A selection of titles in the category of history and biography reveals the lure of famous political, literary, and classical names: *The Age of Pitt and Fox* (1846), by Daniel Owen Madden; *Eastern Europe, and the Emperor Nicholas* (1846) and *The Past and Future of Hungary* (1852), both by Charles Frederick Henningsen; *The Prisoner of Ham: Authentic Details of the Captivity and Escape of Prince Napoleon Louis* (1846), by Frédéric T. Briffault; *Rizzio: or, Scenes in Europe during the Six-*

*teenth Century* (1849), by William Henry Ireland; *History of Alexander the First* (1858), by Ivan Golovin; and *Mexico under Maximillian* (1871), by John Jennings Kendall. Nonpolitical memoirs included *Anecdotes of Actors* (1844), by Mrs. Anne Mathews; *Evenings of a Working Man* (1844), by John A. Overs with a preface by Charles Dickens; and *The Literary Life and Correspondence of the Countess Blessington* (1855), by Richard Robert Madden. In the category of travel and adventure Newby published *Scenes and Adventures in Affghanistan* [*sic*] (1842), by Sgt. Maj. William Taylor, Fourth Light Dragoons; *Algeria, Past and Present* (1844), by John Harcourt Blofield; *Egypt under Mehemet Ali* (1845), by the inveterate traveler Prince Hermann Pückler-Muskau; *Sixteen Years in the West Indies* (1845), by Lt. Col. Henry Capadose; *Days and Nights in the East* (1845), by Matilda Plumley; *Analogies and Contrasts; or, Comparative Sketches of France and England* (1848), by Henningsen; *From Babylon to Jerusalem* (1851) and *From Jerusalem* (1852), by Countess Ida Maria Hahn-Hahn; *History of the City and County of Cork* (1861), by Charles Bernard Gibson; and *Recollections of Central America and the West Coast of Africa* (1869), by Mrs. Henry Grant Foote. Still other works describe "rambles," "rides," and "wanderings" through the continent of Europe.

Newby evidently had a better sense of timely nonfiction than of first novels: *Seven Years' Service on the Slave Coast of Western Africa* (1850) and *California: Its Gold and Its Inhabitants* (1856), by former navy captain and colonial administrator Sir Henry Veel Huntley, reflected concern over the British campaign against slave traders and excitement over the California gold rush of 1849 to 1860. Newby then published four well-timed books by Kinahan Cornwallis—lawyer, traveler, writer, and editor of the New York *Knickerbocker* magazine: *New Eldorado; or, British Columbia* (1858) and *A Panorama of the New World* (1859) reflected the mania for immigration to British Columbia after gold was discovered there; *Two Journeys to Japan, 1856-7* (1859) tapped the new interest in Japan following its first commercial treaties with Western nations in 1858; *Wreck and Ruin; or, Modern Society* (1859) coincided with Charles Darwin's *On the Origin of Species by Means of Natural Selection*.

Mostly aimed at lower-middle-class readers eager for practical information were *Hints to a Soldier on Service* (1845), by William Hamilton Max-

well; the anonymous *Hints on the Nature and Management of Duns* (1845); and *Hints on Husband Catching; Manual for Marriageable Misses* (1846); and nine or ten short guides for sportsmen by Charles Bindley (pseudonym, Harry Hieover) from 1853 to 1861, such as *Hints to Horsemen: Shewing How to Make Money by Horses* (1860). Another guide, *Hints on Agriculture*, by "Cecil" (pseudonym of Cornelius Tongue), came out in 1858. Books on India included *Indian Railways, and their Probable Results* (1848), by Sir William Patrick Andrew, and *Indian Religions; or, Results of the Mysterious Buddhism* (1858), by Hargrave Jennings. *The Night Side of Nature; or, Ghosts and Ghost Seers* (1848), by the popular novelist and translator Mrs. Catherine Crowe, was republished at least twelve times in English and once in German, mostly by other houses; Crowe also wrote *Spiritualism, and the Age We Live In* (1859) and *Ghosts and Family Legends* (1859). *Supernatural Illusions* (1851), by Peter James Begbie, was meant for the same readership. For music lovers Newby published *History of the Modern Music of Western Europe* (1848), by Rafael Georg Kiesewetter; for specialists he published *Antiquarian and Architectural Yearbook* (circa 1831-1855) and *The Isthmus of Darien in 1852: Journal of the Expedition of Inquiry for the Junction of the Atlantic and Pacific Oceans* (1853), by Lionel Gisborne. In spite of these varied subjects and titles, however, Newby continued to lean heavily on minor works of fiction until the closing of his business in 1879. He died in 1882.

**References:**

J. A. V. Chapple and Arthur Pollard, eds., *The Letters of Mrs. Gaskell* (Manchester, U.K.: Manchester University Press, 1966);

Nigel Cross, *The Common Writer: Life in Nineteenth-Century Grub Street* (Cambridge: Cambridge University Press, 1985);

Winifred Gérin, *Emily Brontë: A Biography* (Oxford: Clarendon Press, 1971);

N. John Hall, ed., *The Letters of Anthony Trollope* (Stanford: Stanford University Press, 1983);

J. A. Sutherland, *Victorian Novelists and Publishers* (Chicago: University of Chicago Press, 1976);

Thomas James Wise, ed., *The Brontës: Their Lives, Friendships and Correspondence*, 4 volumes (Oxford: Shakespeare Head Press, 1932).

*—Elisabeth Sanders Arbuckle*

# David Nutt
## (London: 1829-1916)

The firm of David Nutt had a long and varied history, spanning more than eight decades. Its importance lies in its international links, especially with Germany; in the strong connection it maintained between publishing and bookselling; and in the personal imprint put on its list by the father and son who ran it for so long.

David Nutt was born in London on 3 April 1810. He was educated at the Merchant Taylors' School and was employed for several years as a clerk by a large mercantile firm in London. Edward Moberly, the senior partner in that firm, encouraged Nutt to enter into bookselling and introduced him to Adolph Asher, a bibliographer and, later, founder of the house of Asher and Company of Berlin. Asher had found it necessary to leave St. Petersburg for political reasons and needed an agent in London to dispose of his large stock of valuable books. Nutt accepted the commission. His start in business is variously reported as 1829 and 1833, and even between 1833 and 1836 his bookselling activities at 90 Bartholomew Close occupied only a portion of his time.

Finding it increasingly difficult to maintain both his position with Moberly and his bookselling for Asher, in 1837 Nutt resigned from the mercantile firm, set up a bookshop at 158 Fleet Street, and commenced publishing as well as bookselling. His first recorded publication was J. G. Tiarks's *Sacred German Poetry* (1838). The general character of the firm's list can be seen in its 1838 *Catalogue of Modern Foreign Books*, which includes thirty-two closely printed pages of German, French, Italian, Classical, and Oriental titles. The firm moved to 270-271 Strand in 1850.

Many rare books passed through Nutt's shop into the libraries of Cambridge and Oxford universities and into the collections of the British Museum, Lord Spencer, Thomas Grenville, and others. His bibliographical and antiquarian bent came out in his catalogues. In 1856 he printed a seven-hundred-page octavo *Catalogue of Modern, Hebrew and Syriac Books Illustrative of Church and General History*, which was cited as an authority by Jacques-Charles Brunet in his *Manuel du Libraire, et de l'Amateur des Livres* (1860-1865) and by Jo-

*Alfred Trübner Nutt, who took over his father's firm in 1878*

hann G. T. Graesse in his *Tresor des Livres Rares* (1859-1869). In 1857 he printed a *Catalogue of Theological Books in Foreign Languages*.

Concurrent with these activities as collector, bookseller, and bibliographer, Nutt expanded the publishing side of his trade from foreign to educational texts. The firm gained a sterling reputation as a publisher of religious and educational books. This reputation garnered for Nutt in 1844, on the recommendation of Dr. George Moberly, the headmaster, the business of Winchester College. The Winchester business was conducted in partnership with Joseph Wells at the Wells Bookshop in College Street.

Nutt's early educational books include many conversational grammars, of which the Method Gaspey-Otto-Sauer and the Modern Linguist series are noteworthy. Also heavily represented in

Nutt's lists are such respected nineteenth-century educational authors as Henry Weston Eve, Marius Deshumbert, Henry Cadwallader Adams, and Anton Bartel. The large number of German volumes in his lists is probably accounted for by Nutt's association with Asher and by his partnership after 1851 with Nicholas Trübner. Religious, antiquarian, and literary texts account for about half of the firm's other publications; of especial interest are the scholarly works of John Allen Giles and of Salomon Caesar Malan.

Little is known about the firm's leadership after Nutt's death on 28 November 1863, but in 1878 his son, Alfred Trübner Nutt, born on 22 November 1856, took charge after serving three years' apprenticeship in Leipzig, Berlin, and Paris. Under Alfred Nutt's supervision the firm grew considerably, and the publishing department developed new interests, especially in folklore and antiquities. The more well-known collections he published include The Waifs and Strays of the Celtic Tradition (1889-1895), unedited Scottish Gaelic texts; The Northern Library (1895-1899), old Icelandic texts; The Tudor Translations (1892-1909), sixteenth-century prose; The Grimm Library (1894-1908); and Nutt's Juvenile Library (1910). Nutt also published new works by such authors as W. E. Henley, Andrew Lang, Joseph Jacobs, and Jessie Laidlay Weston. In 1890 the firm moved to 57-59 Long Acre, "At the Sign of the Phoenix."

Nutt promoted the growing interest in folklore and the Celtic languages. In 1883 he founded the *Folk-Lore Journal*, which he published beginning in 1890. He helped to establish the Folk-Lore Society in 1878, the English Goethe Society in 1886, and the Irish Texts Society in 1898. He also wrote and published significant scholarly works on the legend of the Holy Grail and the Celtic doctrine of rebirth.

After Alfred Nutt's death on 23 May 1910 his wife, M. L. Nutt, undertook the leadership of the firm, which she moved to Grape Street, New Oxford Street, in 1912. Like her husband, she promoted new authors, publishing Robert Frost's first two volumes of poetry—*A Boy's Will* (1913) and *North of Boston* (1914). Financial difficulties forced her to sell the business in 1916 to Simpkin, Marshall, Hamilton, Kent, and Company, Limited.

**Reference:**

"Mr. David Nutt [obituary]," *Gentleman's Magazine*, 216 (January 1864): 126.

—*Crys Armbrust*

# J. H. Parker

*(Oxford: 1832-1856)*
## John Henry and James Parker
*(Oxford: 1856-1866)*
## James Parker and Company
*(Oxford: 1866-1900)*

John Henry Parker, publisher, bookseller, and prolific writer on architecture and archaeology, was born on 1 March 1806. He was the son of John Parker, a London merchant, and the nephew of the eminent Oxford publisher and bookseller Joseph Parker, who was himself the nephew of Sackville Parker, the Oxford bookseller praised by Dr. Samuel Johnson in 1784 for marrying his maid. After attending Dr. Horne's school at the Manor House, Chiswick, Parker worked for his uncle as an apprentice before succeeding him in 1832 as a bookseller and publisher.

The business Parker inherited was a most lucrative one: Uncle Joseph had been a Bible printer since 1790 and a partner in the Oxford University Press since 1810. Parker took over all of his uncle's duties but one: he was not admitted to the Bible partnership. Before long Parker established a reputation as the foremost publisher of Tractarian or Oxford Movement works.

Parker's first brush with the Oxford Movement came in 1834 when John Henry Newman tried in vain to get him to sell the controversial *Tracts for the Times*, which, since the previous year, had been printed by private subscription and distributed free. By July 1835 it seems that Parker had relented, for Newman was sending copies of individual tracts to him to be "done up in a volume . . . in order to save the expence of new Editions." Newman felt that "they were more likely to sell in this way than separately" and furthermore would make "a permanent historical document." The sales of this first collected volume were so high that Parker eagerly brought out further collections of tracts, which were even more successful. By January 1839 the tracts were selling faster than they could be printed. In 1841 Parker brought out a reprint of the complete series to date, comprising five volumes and priced at two pounds, while continuing to sell unsold numbers of the original pamphlets. Rarely had re-

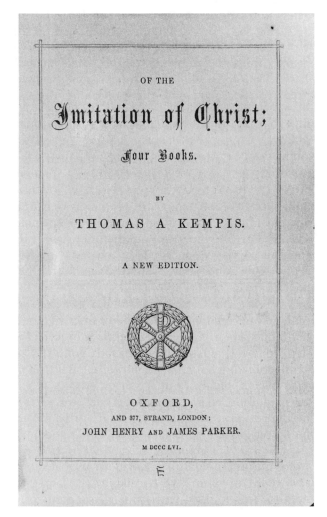

*Title page for one of the books published during the year in which James Parker became a partner in his father's firm*

ligious controversy been so lucrative. Newman's winning over of an initially reluctant Parker had proved profitable to them both, but Parker needed no inducements to publish Newman's own uncontroversial *Parochial Sermons* (1834). "If they are as good to read as they are to hear, they ought to be very popular anywhere," he wrote in

December 1833, before buying an eighth share in them. They proved so popular that Parker's request in 1843 for his share to be increased to a quarter was politely declined by Newman. Uncle Joseph's decision in 1837 to bring out two anonymous and seemingly unremarkable volumes of pious verse by John Keble, an obscure thirty-five-year-old don, proved to be a fortunate one for his nephew. As Keble's central role in the Tractarian movement became more apparent there were repeated calls for fresh editions of his seminal work, and it was Parker who reaped the rewards. By 1841 *The Christian Year* had passed through twenty-two editions, and in that year Parker brought out a luxurious Library Edition at three times the standard price. Two years later he offered the author one thousand pounds for the copyright but received no response.

E. B. Pusey was another Parker author. He sold his carriage and horses and Mrs. Pusey her jewelry to help finance a Library of the Fathers that was begun by Parker in 1835.

In March 1841 Parker launched the Library of Anglo-Catholic Theology, thereby popularizing a recently coined term. Six volumes were published, one a year. A collection of Bishop Andrewes's sermons began the series. Three months later appeared the first volume of *Catena Aurea* (1841-1845), a commentary by St. Thomas Aquinas on the four Gospels, edited by Newman, Keble, and Pusey.

Besides Tractarian literature Parker published a variety of other, more conventional, theological works, but most if not all seem to have had a High Church flavor. Little is known of Parker's own religious bent, but the editorial that appears in volume 2 of his *Penny Post*, a weekly started in January 1851 from the London office at 377 Strand which he had opened in 1849, is revealing. The magazine had been established "to make, under God, the Church to triumph in the working man's home . . . and to vindicate the position of the English church against the assumptions of Popery, and the virulence of Dissent." It later flourished under Parker's son James until 1896. There was also a *Twopenny Post* ( January-December 1854), which was run along similar lines. Far less successful was the *National Miscellany*, an attractive shilling monthly which, although edited by the Reverend J. Armistead, aimed to supply "high-principled and high-toned literature of a secular kind," such as articles on the Pre-Raphaelites and on Railway Literature. It

ran from 1853 to 1855 before being merged with Ward and Lock's *Illustrated Magazine*.

Parker also brought out important historical monographs, such as Joshua Sprigge's *England's Recovery: History of Sir Thomas Fairfax's Army* (1854), a steady stream of grammars and other textbooks, and improving literature. Parker was an active representative of the Booksellers' Association and was called to give evidence to Lord Campbell early in 1852 on the issue of booksellers' discounts; at the same time he was indulging in a lengthy debate on this question in the *Times*.

Parker realized a personal ambition in 1856 with the purchase, from John Bowyer Nicholls and his son, of the *Gentleman's Magazine*, which he edited himself until ill health forced him to sell it in 1865.

Parker devoted much of his leisure to the study of architectural history and archaeology and throughout his life was a prodigious writer and lecturer in these burgeoning fields. He numbered architects such as G. E. Street and Gilbert Scott, both fellow ecclesiologists, among his friends, and through his active membership in groups such as the Oxford Architectural Society, the British and American Archeological Society of Rome, and the Société française d'archaeologie he met and corresponded with most of the leading lights in those fields and published some of their work. His *Glossary of Terms Used in Grecian, Roman, Italian and Gothic Architecture* (1836), published in London by Charles Tilt, was one of his earliest ventures in this field and sold well, reaching four editions by 1845. From its first appearance it became a vade mecum for students of architecture—representing as it did good value (eighteen-hundred illustrations in the three-volume 1861 edition at one pound, ten shillings) and a fair degree of reliability. By 1900 it had progressed to a tenth edition. Parker's *Introduction to Gothic Architecture* (1849) sold less well, possibly because it was written not so much for "architects as for their employers, the gentry and clergy of England." Parker was the Oxford agent for the *Ecclesiologist* while it was the house journal of the Cambridge Camden Society from 1841 to 1843; when the society cut its ties with the magazine so did Parker. Criticism in the *Ecclesiologist* of his role as publisher and writer on architecture dates from this severance. He was slapped down frequently, but most notably in 1844, when he was attacked for making a volume of inferior designs for model churches appear uniform with the "accredited works" of the Oxford Architectural Society. Five years later a similar accusation was made. In 1845 the printing quality of the woodcuts in his *Glossary*, most of which were by the highly rated Orlando Jewitt, was criticized, as were the drawings themselves. The *Ecclesiologist* also found Parker's architectural judgments in his popular *Handbook for Visitors to Oxford* (1847) unsound and his account of the university as an institution "facetious." One contention of the *Ecclesiologist*—that much of Parker's publishing output in ecclesiology was mere antiquarianism, lacking in a spiritual dimension—seems to have a grain of truth. Parker was a zealous and diligent antiquary and archaeologist, not a theologian nor even an evangelist.

Bad publicity did not dampen Parker's rage for the antique. By 1861 his architecture/archaeology list was impressive. The folios of working drawings for model churches, which the *Ecclesiologist* had panned, had grown to nine, and one was in a second edition. As agent to the Oxford Architectural Society, Parker sold the society's sixpenny sheets of South Midlands church furnishings. There were architectural histories of English cathedrals, shilling manuals on Gothic sculpture, the classic work by Viollet-le-Duc on medieval military architecture, and monographs on medieval stained glass, church plate, armor, brasses, and sepulchral slabs. Parker also published the *Archaeological Journal*, beginning in 1844, and the annual proceedings of the Archaeological Institute, whose congresses he regularly attended. Also available at this time was Parker's four-volume edition of Hudson Turner's *Some Account of Domestic Architecture in England, from the Conquest to the End of the Thirteenth Century* (1851-1859). In recognition of his contribution to antiquarianism Oxford University awarded him an honorary M.A. on 27 June 1867. By this time he was engaged in excavations among the ruins of Rome. In 1866 Parker had handed over the running of the business to his son James, who had been an active partner since early 1856, and the firm became James Parker and Company.

Freed from the trammels of profit and loss Parker was able to devote the rest of his life to antiquarian pursuits. In 1870 he was appointed the first keeper of the Ashmolean Museum, having the previous year endowed the keepership with a sum yielding £250 a year. In 1871 he was nominated a Companion of the Bath (civil division) on the recommendation of Prime Minister William Gladstone. He died at his home in Turl Street on 31 January 1884. James Parker and Company continued to specialize in archaeology and architectural history until it went out of business in 1900.

**References:**

James J. Barnes, *The Free Trade in Books* (Oxford: Oxford University Press, 1964), pp. 54-56, 58, 63, 73, 74n;

Raymond Chapman, *Faith and Revolt* (London: Weidenfeld & Nicolson, 1970);

Geoffrey Faber, *Oxford Apostles* (London: Faber & Faber, 1974);

Septimus Rivington, *The Publishing House of Rivington* (London: Rivington, 1919), pp. 113-114, 117, 156;

Peter Sutcliffe, *The Oxford University Press: An Informal History* (Oxford: Oxford University Press, 1978), pp. 9, 16.

—*R. M. Healey*

# John W. Parker
### (London: 1832-1843)
# John W. Parker and Sons
### (London: 1843-1848)
# John W. Parker and Son
### (London: 1848-1860)
# Parker, Son, and Bourn
### (London: 1860-1863)

Born in 1792, John William Parker, the son of a navy man, began working for the London printer William Clowes in childhood and was formally apprenticed to him at age fourteen. On completing that apprenticeship in 1813 he remained with Clowes as an accountant.

Operating in Northumberland Court, the Strand, Clowes had a small but innovative business; he was among the first printers in London to use a steam-driven press. When a lawsuit brought against him successfully argued that the machine was a nuisance, Clowes was forced to move his facilities to Duke Street, leasing space and equipment from Augustus Applegarth, the inventor of the steam press. Parker was placed in charge of the business, which succeeded so well that he was able to establish a separate printing press of his own nearby.

Parker's reputation for sound management soon reached the University of Cambridge Press, which had been doing poorly in recent years as compared with its counterpart at Oxford. In 1828 the Syndics applied for advice to Clowes, who sent Parker to Cambridge to inspect the facilities there. Parker's perception of their problems and suggestions for improvement so impressed the Syndics that Clowes was appointed superintendent of the press in February 1829, with the understanding that he would take care of the press's affairs in London while the actual superintendence at Cambridge would be left to Parker. The latter introduced superior methods of bookkeeping, bought new types and hydraulic presses, installed a heating system, and established in 1832 a depository for the sale of Cambridge Bibles and prayer books at his home in the Strand. By 1852 the Cambridge plant would include eight presses, seventy composing frames, and several subsidiary machines, and would employ about one hundred men and boys.

Parker had hoped to enter into partnership with Clowes. When family arrangements precluded this possibility, he left in 1832 and established his own business under his own name at 445 West Strand. Besides retaining his Cambridge assignment, he was immediately appointed as an official publisher of the Society for Promoting Christian Knowledge (SPCK). The books given him to print were mostly "improving" works on grammar, composition, reading, arithmetic, geography, history, nature, and religion, with some titles intended for children. Under SPCK auspices Parked inaugurated the *Saturday Magazine* in July 1832. Costing only a penny per copy, it was intended to counteract cheap, licentious publications directed toward the poorer classes. An entertaining and sometimes useful compendium of facts, the *Saturday Magazine* lasted until 1845; it was then replaced by *Parker's London Magazine*, which died after two issues. Similarly unsuccessful was Parker's *Magazine of Popular Science, and Journal of the Useful Arts* (1836-1837).

*Cover for an issue of the one-penny magazine Parker founded in 1832 hoping to provide a moral, useful, and entertaining alternative to the sensational periodicals that other publishers aimed at the lower class*

On 15 November 1836 Parker was elected official printer to the University of Cambridge following the retirement of John Smith. He held the post until 1854 at a salary of four hundred pounds per year. Much of the business he did for Cambridge consisted of Bibles, Testaments, and editions of the Book of Common Prayer, all of which he made available at greatly reduced prices. The Bible Society at Cambridge originally objected to such cheap editions, but the quality and popularity of Parker's works eventually changed their minds. A Bible that cost two shillings and fivepence in 1830, for example, was available for only one shilling and tenpence in 1850; a prayer book costing six and a halfpence in 1830 could be had for two and a halfpence in 1850. Much of this reduction in price was attributed to improved machinery and better manage-

ment. At William IV's request, Parker also designed and published the "King's Bible," with red rules all around. Though William IV died in 1837 before the project was completed, Queen Victoria received a special copy on vellum; published in various forms and sizes, the "King's Bible" was a great success.

Parker's concern for the availability of books to lower-income households made him one of the leading figures in the free-trade controversy of 1852. In May of that year he solicited, compiled, edited, and published *The Opinions of Certain Authors on the Publishing Question*, dealing with whether "underselling" (retail sales of books below the established price) was desirable. One hundred authors, including Thomas Carlyle, Wilkie Collins, Charles Darwin, Charles Dickens, William Gladstone, Leigh Hunt, Charles Kingsley, G. H. Lewes, John Stuart Mill, Alfred Tennyson, and William Whewell, almost unanimously thought it was. By midyear all restrictions were removed, and half a century of free trade and reduced prices began.

In 1843 John William Parker, Jr., born in 1820 and educated at King's College, Cambridge, joined his father's firm—which became John W. Parker and Sons—as general manager. Within a few years both his mother and brother were dead. In 1848 his father married Ellen Maria Mantell, the daughter of the well-known geological writer Gideon Mantell. The firm's name was changed to John W. Parker and Son.

Under the management of Parker Junior, John W. Parker and Son became a major bastion within the London publishing establishment of liberal Christianity, and eventually of Christian Socialism. One major expression of the new trend was a significantly redirected *Fraser's Magazine for Town and Country*, which had been founded by James Fraser in 1830. Parker Junior became editor in July 1847. Under Parker, *Fraser's* was deeply concerned with the social utility of the Church of England and the condition of English society. As Parker explained in the issue for January 1849, he had undertaken "to bolster up no faction, to pin our faith to no man, nor any set of men, to support to the best of our ability the established institutions of the country; and deal with every public measure, as it came before us, strictly according to its merits." It was often his policy to publish contributions critical of previous contributions, so that openness of debate was preserved. His major authors included F. D. Maurice, Charles Kingsley, Mill, Lewes, Carlyle, John Ruskin, and Tennyson.

On 6 May 1848 John W. Parker and Son published the first issue of *Politics for the People*, a monthly journal of sixteen pages intended for lower- and middle-class readers. Its appearance marked the beginning of the Christian Socialist movement. The journal's position was that the exploitation of the lower classes by supposedly Christian capitalists was fundamentally contradictory. It ceased publication in July, due to a lack of subscriber support; Parker Senior disliked losing money. The Christian Socialists then founded a night school for working people in Little Ormond Yard on 21 September, with Parker Junior among its voluntary teachers. The school succeeded, becoming a precursor of the Working Men's College.

Kingsley is today the best known of the Christian Socialist writers associated with the Parkers. During July 1848, just as *Politics for the People* was expiring, the first installment of Kingsley's *Yeast*, a high-minded examination of current social, economic, and religious problems in England, appeared in *Fraser's*, running to completion that December despite some canceled subscriptions. Ever cautious about money, Parker Senior turned down Kingsley's second and more effective novel, *Alton Locke*, which exposed the misery of the working classes. It was published in August 1850 by Chapman and Hall, having been recommended to them by Carlyle. When *Alton Locke* succeeded, Parker agreed to publish *Yeast* in book form. It appeared in March 1851 under the pseudonym "Parson Lot." Thereafter, Parker and Son published several titles by Kingsley, including *The Message of the Church to Labouring Men* (1851); *Hypatia* (1853), reprinted from *Fraser's*; *Andromeda and Other Poems* (1858); and *Miscellanies* (1859).

Other members of Parker's circle included Richard Chenevix Trench, with *Sacred Latin Poetry* (1849), *On the Lessons in Proverbs* (1853), and *English Past and Present* (1855); Sir Arthur Helps, who wrote *Companions of My Solitude* (1851; Parker edition, 1854), *Friends in Council* (1857), *The Spanish Conquest in America* (1855-1861), and *Organization in Daily Life* (1862); and Maurice, with many religious publications, such as *On Right and Wrong Methods of Supporting Protestantism* (1848), opposing censorship at Oxford, and *The Lord's Prayer* (1851). Whewell had several of his major works published by Parker, including *History of the Inductive Sciences* (1837), *The Philosophy of the Inductive Sciences* (1840), *Of a Liberal Education in Gen-*

*eral* (1845-1852), and a three-volume translation of Hugo Grotius on international law (1854). Mill contributed his most distinguished works: *Essays on Some Unsettled Questions of Political Economy* (1844); *Principles of Political Economy* (1848); *On Liberty* (1859); *Thoughts on Parliamentary Reform* (1859); *Considerations on Representative Government* (1861); and *Utilitarianism* (1863), originally published in *Fraser's* in 1861. Henry Thomas Buckle contributed essays to *Fraser's*, as well as his great *History of Civilization in England* (1857-1861).

John W. Parker and Son published none of the major Victorian novels except Kingsley's. The firm's notorious nonfiction book was *Essays and Reviews* (1860), in which seven contributors, all but one of them clergy, argued that traditional Christianity must accept the so-called Higher Criticism of the Bible and the implications of modern natural science, particularly geology. A petition condemning the book was signed by every Anglican bishop in Great Britain. In a petition to the Archbishop of Canterbury, some ten thousand clergymen chastised the book and its authors, two of whom were suspended from their clerical duties until reinstated by the Privy Council.

In the midst of this controversy John W. Parker, Jr., died on 9 November 1860. His father had just taken a longtime employee, William Butler Bourn, into partnership, the firm becoming Parker, Son, and Bourn. It lasted only three years under that name, being sold to Longmans in 1863 for twenty thousand pounds. Thus the first volume (1858) of the second edition of Buckle's *History* was published by Parker and the second (1864) by Longmans. Algernon Charles Swinburne's *Dead Love* (1862), however, was *not* published in 1864 by J. W. Parker and Son; this printing is a later forgery. Following the sale of his firm, Parker entered into partnership with Thomas Richard Harrison as printers in St. Martin's Lane. Their arrangement continued until Parker's death at his home near Farnham, Surrey, on 18 May 1870.

**References:**

James J. Barnes, *Free Trade in Books: A Study of the London Book Trade Since 1800* (Oxford: Clarendon Press, 1964);

Robert Bowes, *Biographical Notes on the University Printers* (Cambridge: Cambridge University Press, 1886);

Henry Curwen, *A History of Booksellers, the Old and the New* (London: Chatto & Windus, 1873), pp. 317-324;

Sydney Castle Roberts, *The Evolution of Cambridge Publishing* (Cambridge: Cambridge University Press, 1956);

Roberts, *A History of the Cambridge University Press* (Cambridge: Cambridge University Press, 1921).

—Dennis R. Dean

# S. W. Partridge and Company
*(London: 1867-1939)*

## Partridge and Oakey
*(London: 1848-1853)*

## Partridge, Oakey and Company
*(London: 1853-1855)*

## Partridge and Company
*(London: 1855-1860)*

## Samuel Wm. Partridge
*(London: 1860-1867)*

The Partridge imprint existed for nearly a hundred years, from the late 1840s until 1939. In 1848 Samuel William Partridge and Daniel Francis Oakey formed a partnership at 34 Paternoster Row, moving in 1852 to 70 Edgware Road.

As a young man Partridge had taken the pledge against drink, and it was in relation to antidrink campaigns of the 1850s that he first came to be known. The *Band of Hope Review* (1851-1937) was published by Partridge almost from its first issue. The success of his magazines and annuals (by the end of the century he had ten) gave him the capital to engage in medium-scale publishing—in 1904 he had nearly six hundred titles in print. These magazines were long-lived: after most of the great publishers had given up their popular magazines Partridge was still publishing the *Infants' Magazine* (1866-1930s), the *British Workman* (1855-1921), the *Family Friend* (1849-1867; 1870-1921), and the *Juvenile Instructor and Companion* (1850-1893; then as the *Young People* 1899-1907). They had a high moral tone but were entertaining with good stories, information, and above all a high standard of illustration. The *Infants' Magazine* was the best produced of the many magazines; it is now much collected

for its attractive pictures, many of them showing ordinary children doing the kinds of things children loved to do—a rare phenomenon in British publishing, compared to the German publishing scene at the same time.

Partridge and Oakey added "and Company" to their names in 1853. In 1854 they moved back to 34 Paternoster Row. In 1855 the partnership was ended, and Partridge and Company continued at the same address. From 1860 to 1867 Partridge traded as Samuel Wm. Partridge, and after 1867 as S. W. Partridge and Company.

Partridge was an important publisher of books designed as a reward for Sunday school attendance, and later as school prizes. Partridge's reward books were adventure stories and school stories, many of them forming long series. They were lavishly produced, with attractive cloth covers, much gold ink, and colored illustrations. They were meant to go on a special bookshelf in an ordinary home which may have had few other books. Partridge charged for this lavishness: Mary Botham Howitt's *Our Four-Footed Friends* (1867), with fifty engravings, was available in cloth with a medallion on the cover at five shillings or with extra gilt at seven shillings, sixpence—a high price for a children's book.

*Cover, illustrated by Robert Barnes, for one of Partridge's annual publications*

One of the most attractive of Victorian alphabets was Partridge's *The Mother's Picture Alphabet* (1862), with twenty-seven finely engraved plates. It was available in boards with illustrated paper covers at five shillings; in cloth with red edges at seven shillings, sixpence; and in "cloth elegant" at ten shillings, sixpence. It had a dedication to Queen Victoria and was intended for the drawing rooms of the rich as well as for the poorer classes. Thus Partridge was able to cover a wide market with the same book in different packagings.

Because a friend told him that no well-illustrated books existed for children in Damascus or Beirut, Partridge produced in 1870 an Arabic edition of his annual *The Children's Friend* (1861-1899) with a beautiful colored medallion depicting the sultan on the cover. Like most Victo-

rian publishers, Partridge bought illustrations from abroad, mostly from Germany. *Child-Land* (1873) has nearly two hundred pictures by Oscar Pletsch and L. Richter. His favorite illustrator was Harrison Weir, perhaps the best Victorian illustrator of animals. Partridge published long series of books on the love of animals, animal adventures, and kindness to animals. The *Band of Hope Review* was both a monthly illustrated paper and an annual for animal lovers.

In 1912 S. W. Partridge and Company had magnificent new premises built at 21-22 Old Bailey in the City of London. By the 1920s Partridge was publishing books by such authors as Bessie Marchant, Percy Francis Westerman, Tom Bevan, and Elsie J. Oxenham. Lady Cynthia Asquith's *Flying Carpet* (1925) and *Treasure Ship* (1926) and Rose Fyleman's *Round the Mulberry Bush* (1928) included contributions by Thomas Hardy, Hilaire Belloc, Walter de la Mare, James M. Barrie, John Galsworthy, Hugh Lofting, E. V. Knox, and Eleanor Farjeon.

Even with such authors, however, Partridge could not survive the depression of the 1930s, and on 12 May 1930 the receiver sold the goodwill, name, stock, and annuals to A. and C. Black for six thousand pounds. The firm continued to exist as a subsidiary of Black at 4, 5, and 6 Soho Square. Black sold off some of the list, including some evangelical and psychological titles. During the nineteenth century publishers often copublished works with other publishers, and it took Black a long time to determine exactly what rights it had acquired. Black announced that it would continue most of the annuals; the *Infants' Magazine* and *Partridges' Children's Annual* were sold at two shillings, sixpence each. But by this time annuals were being replaced by so-called Bumper Books, printed on thick cardlike paper. Partridge ceased to be an imprint used by A. and C. Black in 1939.

**Reference:**

W. Francis Aitken, *Some Memories of the Row* (London: Partridge, 1912).

*—Peter Stockham*

# Kegan Paul, Trench, Trübner and Company Limited
*(London: 1889-1912)*
## H. S. King and Company
*(London: 1871-1877)*
## C. Kegan Paul and Company
*(London: 1877-1881)*
## Kegan Paul, Trench and Company
*(London: 1881-1888)*

Kegan Paul, Trench, Trübner and Company Limited—known in the trade in the 1890s as "the long firm" because of its unwieldy name—emerged from the publishing business of Henry S. King, which came under the control of Charles Kegan Paul, expanded by partnership to include Alfred Trench, and later absorbed the firm of Nicholas Trübner. When the business disappeared into that of Routledge and Sons, the Kegan Paul imprint remained. Between 1851 and 1912 the component companies, separately and together, published a wide variety of books by literary, scientific, and scholarly authors. They also published books in prestigious collections and brought out some distinguished journals.

Henry Samuel King was born in 1817 in Brighton. Although his grandfather had been a banker, his father lost the family fortune, leaving King to earn his own living from the age of thirteen. Self-educated, he started a bookselling business at Brighton with his brother. In 1850 he married Ellen Blakeway, whose sister Elizabeth married George Smith. Because of this alliance, in 1853 King joined the London firm of Smith, Elder and Company as a partner, taking a quarter share of the business and becoming a skilled editor. The firm's trade was not confined to publishing; it also engaged in banking and acted as East India and Colonial agents. The partners were famously incompatible: one of their employees remembered how they met once a week to discuss business matters only, bowing stiffly to each other. The family connection was dissolved in 1860 with the death of Ellen Blakeway King.

Smith, meanwhile, was establishing the *Pall Mall Gazette* (1865-1921), and King, who disapproved of the new paper's Liberal politics, exercised his option to require that Smith buy out his interest in it.

When his partnership agreement with Smith, Elder came to an end in 1868, King retained the firm's premises at 65 Cornhill and the Indian agency but agreed not to engage in publishing for a period of three years. When the time was up he published Stopford Brooke's *Freedom in the Church of England* (1871). King was described by Charles Kegan Paul in terms of his "great urbanity to all who were first introduced to him, unwearied attention to business, a large power of generalisation combined with extraordinary attention to details, an almost unexampled memory, and an iron will."

King's most important contribution to publishing was his sponsorship of the International Scientific Series, which was initiated in 1871 when Edward L. Youmans came to London on behalf of D. Appleton and Company of New York to promote among "English men of science" the idea of "an elegant and valuable library of popular science, fresh in treatment, attractive in form, strong in character, moderate in price, and indispensable to all who care for the acquisition of solid and serviceable knowledge." Once he had the support of the scientists, Youmans looked for a London publisher who would be willing to work with Appleton. Describing King as "a wide-awake, whole-hearted fellow," Youmans offered him the opportunity to bring out this prestigious series. King signed copublishing agreements with Appleton and with firms in Europe, with each publisher committed to paying fair remuneration to the scientific authors involved. The series included John Tyndall's *The Forms of Water* (1872), Walter Bagehot's *Physics and Politics* (1872), Herbert Spencer's *The Study of Sociology* (1873), and Henry Maudsley's *Responsibility in Mental Disease* (1874), as well as books by prominent American, French, Italian, and German scientists.

King was Tennyson's publisher for five years. The poet laureate's contract with Alexander Strahan, whose business had failed, expired in January 1874. King offered generous terms: five thousand pounds per year for publication of previous works, and a commission of only five percent for himself on new works. Small wonder that Tennyson's son Hallam, reflecting on his father's relationship with publishers, observed that "With none of the publishers into whose hands circumstances had thrown my father, was the connection so uninterruptedly pleasant as with Messrs. Macmillan, unless perhaps that with Mr. Henry King." The relationship was pleasant but not particularly profitable, since the poet wrote only two new books, *Queen Mary* (1875) and *Harold* (1876), during his years with King; and both were plays, which were less popular than his lyric poetry. King published three new collections of Tennyson's poetry: the Cabinet Edition (1874-1877) appeared in twelve volumes at two shillings, sixpence per volume, with illustrations by Julia Margaret Cameron and a portrait of the author. The Author's Edition (1875-1877) included portraits and numbered six volumes, while the Imperial Library (1877) comprised seven volumes. Tennyson called the Imperial Library a "very handsome issue of my Poems," but complained to King that some important revisions had not been incorporated.

Tennyson remained on friendly terms with King but came into conflict with the publisher's manager, Charles Kegan Paul, over the latter's aggressive approach to the marketing of books. When Tennyson refused to permit the firm to advertise the existence of additional lines to a poem in the Cabinet Edition, lines that would create a much wider audience for the works, Paul asked him to remember "that the success of literature has two sides, and that the trade element is an important one, nor if rightly considered is it, I think, a wholly prosaic one." The author won the dispute; he also prevented the publication of illustrations that portrayed his private life, and of an

*Charles Kegan Paul*

edition of his poems with unauthorized annotations. On these occasions King intervened between the diffident author and the enterprising manager. The latter, when he took over the business, was to secure only one more five-year contract with the poet laureate before losing him to Macmillan.

In 1876 King established the journal *Nineteenth Century* under the editorship of John Thomas Knowles, the founder of the Metaphysical Society. The *Nineteenth Century* published some of the most innovative and controversial literature of its day, including exchanges about the effect of scientific method and biblical criticism on traditional Christian values. These articles, moreover, were written by the leaders of church and state and of the scientific and literary worlds: Cardinal Henry Edward Manning, William Ewart Gladstone, Thomas Henry Huxley, and Tennyson were contributors.

Paul had been manager and publisher's reader for King for several years when he purchased the company in October 1877. King was ill; he died the next year. Then fifty years of age, Paul had been an Anglican priest and a master at Eton; his theological views had become more and more unorthodox (he would die a

Roman Catholic), and he had finally left his living in Dorsetshire to come to London. In 1876 H. S. King and Company had brought out Paul's best-known work, *William Godwin: His Friends and Contemporaries*. In his *Memories* (1899), in which he referred only briefly to his career in the book trade, Paul reflected that publishing "is not by any means the ready road to wealth that many people think it, and that it is very inexpedient for any one without a large capital and considerable literary skill to enter such a business. Supposing, however, any one to have the capital and the literary skill, I can imagine no more interesting work." Paul's own "literary skill" was highly regarded. He always distinguished between the "clever and the clever-*ish*," and he regarded splitting an infinitive, or writing "Bravo" to a woman, as "hopelessly illiterate." He was also an accomplished translator, a skill that stood him in good stead in judging the translations he commissioned, including those of European contributions to the International Scientific Series.

Paul paid Robert Louis Stevenson twenty pounds for *An Inland Voyage* (1878); only 485 copies were sold in the first year. The next year the firm refused to bring out "Latter-Day Arabian Nights"—which was eventually published as *New Arabian Nights* (1882) by Chatto and Windus—"on account of their preposterous character." But the published *Travels with a Donkey in the Cevennes* (1879). Two years later there was a collection of essays, *Virginibus Puerisque* (1881), but Stevenson wrote, "I only got £20 for Virg. Puer. I could take Paul by the beard and knock his head against the wall."

Other books published by the firm included the works of George William Cox, a first cousin and a school friend of Paul's, who wrote historical works of a popular character. His *Manual of Mythology* and *The Mythology of the Aryan Nations*, which had been published by Longmans in 1867 and 1870, respectively, were republished by Kegan Paul in 1878. Sir Richard and Lady Isabel Burton both wrote for the firm; the latter was the author of *The Inner Life of Syria, Palestine, and the Holy Land* (1875), a traveler's guide. In January 1879 the firm took over the publication of the *New Quarterly Magazine*, and Paul served as editor as well as publisher. Before it came to an end in April 1880 Paul attracted authors such as Edmund Gosse, Thomas Hardy, and Stevenson; some of the contributors to the magazine would later bring their books to the firm. There were several poets on the list: Aubrey de Vere, Sir Henry

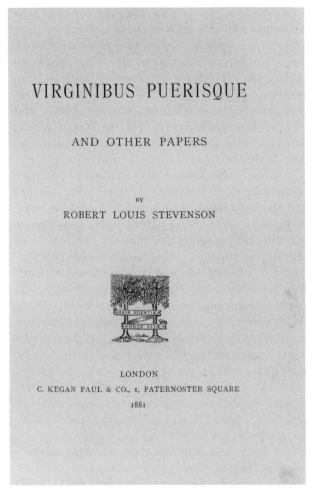

VIRGINIBUS PUERISQUE

AND OTHER PAPERS

BY

ROBERT LOUIS STEVENSON

LONDON

C. KEGAN PAUL & CO., 1, PATERNOSTER SQUARE

1881

*Title page for the collection of essays for which Stevenson received only twenty pounds. In a letter, the author wrote: "I could take Paul by the beard and knock his head against the wall."*

Taylor, Archbishop Trench, Andrew Lang, Frederick Locker, and Austin Dobson, as well as Paul's favorite, Wilfrid Blunt. Gosse and Dobson were personal friends, who traveled abroad with Paul. Paul also brought out the work of William Barnes, a lyric poet who worked in the dialect of Dorset, and of Robert Stephen Hawker, whom Paul described as "the Cornish High Church poet."

Along with these lesser poets, Paul continued for a further five years to publish the work of the laureate. Paul's combative relationship with the Tennyson family had already been established by the time he took over from King, despite the fact that he had taught Hallam Tennyson, by then his father's business manager, as a child in Dorsetshire. There is some evidence that Paul believed that authors should not be able to live entirely by their pens, a notion that was dramatically controverted by Tennyson's career. Nor did he like the man personally, thinking him a poseur, in contrast to the "absolute simplicity" of Robert Browning. Although both Alfred and Hallam Tennyson regarded Paul as "mean and tricky" in business dealings, they were reluctant to change publishers. A detailed and restrictive contract was hammered out during 1878, to run from 1879 to 1883. The guaranteed payment for previous works was reduced, and new books were to come out at the publishers' expense, not the author's, with a five percent commission to Tennyson. The agreement, however, explicitly prohibited the sort of clever marketing scheme that Paul had envisioned when he planned an unauthorized "Annotated Edition." Under this contract, it was Paul's company that first published Tennyson's works in one volume: more than 100,000 copies of the Crown Edition (1878) were sold in three variant bindings, from the six-shilling "Plain" through the seven shilling, and sixpence "Gilt" to the "Roxburgh" at eight shillings, sixpence. When the contract expired, Tennyson signed an agreement with the more congenial Alexander Macmillan. In Paul's judgment, the poet was "a thorough man of business, and our final parting at the end of one of our periods of agreement was that we, as publishers, and he, as author, took a different view of his pecuniary value."

Paul was more enthusiastic about Hardy; the two Dorsetshire natives were close friends. Paul was important to Hardy both as a reviewer, offering praise and attesting to the authenticity of Hardy's regional descriptions, and as an editor. He published Hardy's short stories in the *New Quarterly Magazine* in 1879 and 1880, and the firm brought out cheap editions of *A Pair of Blue Eyes* (1877) and *The Return of the Native* (1879).

Although George Meredith's books were chiefly published by Chapman and Hall, for whom he served as publisher's reader for many years, he had two novels published by C. Kegan Paul and Company. The firm published the second English edition of *The Ordeal of Richard Feverel* in 1878 and *The Egoist* in 1879-1880. Paul paid £450 for the copyright of the latter, then infuriated Meredith by selling the serial rights to the *Glasgow Herald*: "The diplomatic Kegan has dealt me a stroke," Meredith told a friend. "I wrote to him in my incredulous astonishment." But Paul was apparently never much impressed by Meredith's innovative style. "To understand

George Meredith," he remarked, "it is perhaps necessary to belong to a somewhat esoteric circle who can enter into a literature which will probably increase as time brings a wider education."

Paul took Alfred Trench into partnership in 1881. Trench was the son of the Anglican archbishop of Dublin, Richard Chenevix Trench. Besides his financial contribution to the firm, Trench brought to it the right to publish his father's books of poetry, exegetical works on the parables and miracles, and contributions to philology. The younger Trench gradually became an active partner. Not much is known about his literary judgment, except for one story that he told on himself when interviewed by F. A. Mumby for a history of the company (1934). After the firm had supported Robert Louis Stevenson for his first few unpopular books, Trench allowed himself to be outbid for the copyright of all Stevenson's works—on the eve of publication of *Treasure Island* (1883). When Trench declined *Familiar Studies of Men and Books* (1882), Chatto and Windus acquired it, along with the first refusal on new works, for £100, and paid an additional £100 to Paul and Trench for the rights to Stevenson's earlier books. In 1884 Kegan Paul, Trench and Company's ledgers were still showing a loss of £180 on the three early titles. The creator of Dr. Jekyll and Mr. Hyde characterized the duality of his publisher this way: "Oh, yes. Kegan is an excellent fellow, but Paul is a publisher."

Paul was a literary entrepreneur who delighted in outbidding others and taking risks on concepts that captured his imagination. One such was *The Journals of Major-Gen. C. G. Gordon* (1885). When Paul heard that the journals of the fallen hero Charles George Gordon had been recovered after the battle of Khartoum, he applied to the general's brother, Sir Henry Gordon, for the right of publication. In competition with several other publishers, Paul made a rough estimate of the cost and offered five thousand guineas. The editorial and production costs amounted to seven thousand pounds, and there were lengthy delays. The popular excitement over Gordon had declined by the time the book came out, and it was a long time before there was any profit on it.

While most of the firm's books were undistinguished in type, paper, and binding, Kegan Paul and Trench made an exception with their Parchment Library, a series of editions of the classics begun in 1880. One of the books in the series was Geoffrey Chaucer's *Canterbury Tales: The Pro-*

*1880 advertisement for several editions of the poet laureate's
works. Paul inherited Tennyson from his predecessor, Henry
S. King, but Paul and Tennyson did not get along. In 1883
Tennyson moved to the Macmillan firm.*

logue (1886), edited by Alfred William Pollard, a
young man on the staff of the department of
printed books at the British Museum. Pollard observed that "the pleasant form" of the Parchment
Library (the books came in parchment or cloth
bindings for six shillings and vellum for seven shillings, sixpence) "had greatly increased the publishers' reputation for pretty books." An intimate
friend of Paul despite the difference in their
ages, Pollard was establishing a distinguished career in bibliography and rare-book librarianship.
In 1893-1894 he edited for the firm the series
"Books about Books," including his own *Early Illustrated Books* (1893). Pollard observed that "The series started at the height of a craze for large
paper copies, and the sale before publication of

150 sets of these secured its financial success." Encouraged by this experience, Pollard persuaded
his friend Paul to sponsor *Bibliographica: A Magazine of Bibliography* (1895-1897), published in
twelve quarterly parts. In 1899 Sir J. Y. W.
MacAlister founded the *Library*, the journal of
the Bibliographical Society published by Kegan
Paul, Trench and Company; Pollard was a contributor and became coeditor in 1904.

The company's premises in Paternoster
Square, including several warehouses containing
sheets and bound books, were destroyed by a fire
in April 1883. The firm recovered from this disaster, however, bringing out the Gordon journals
in 1885 and in 1886 sponsoring a best-seller in
*The Silence of Dean Maitland* by "Maxwell Gray,"
whose real name was Mary Gleed Tuttiett.

In 1889 the firm was merged with that of
Nicholas Trübner, the "prince of oriental publishers." Trübner was born in 1817 in Heidelberg,
where he studied languages and began his working life as apprentice to the university bookseller.
He later worked for a bookseller in Frankfurt.
Like King, Trübner continued his education
while learning to deal in books. Trübner's employer did business with the Longman publishing
firm, and William Longman brought Trübner to
London in 1843 as his foreign corresponding
clerk. Eight years later Trübner started his own
business on Ludgate Hill. He soon established a
reputation for publishing oriental literature,
works in philology and philosophy, and American literature. He wrote and published *Bibliographical Guide to American Literature* (1855) and traveled several times to the United States. He edited
and completed the work of Hermann E. Ludewig
of New York, who died before he finished *The Literature of American Aboriginal Languages* (1857),
and also produced *A Catalogue of the Dictionaries
and Grammars of the Principal Languages and Dia-
lects of the World* (1872). Trübner published on commission four of the novels of Charles Reade between 1858 and 1861, and *The Breitmann Ballads*
(1871) of the American writer Charles Godfrey
Leland. Trübner, however, seldom competed
with his fellow publishers for novels or belles-
lettres. One of them, William Heinemann, told
Mumby: "Nicholas Trübner was the friend and adviser of all who were engaged in the study of Oriental literature. His firm during this period has
been the intermediary between Europe and the
East. His agents are scattered all over the globe,
and they send from the remotest parts the literary productions of every people of the world to

London. Here they are catalogued and carefully described, and *Trübner's Record* makes them widely known among librarians and scholars." *Trübner's American and Oriental Literary Record* (1865-1891) was a "register of important works" widely used by scholars of the eastern languages.

In 1878 he launched Trübner's Oriental Series, edited by the linguist E. Reinhold Rost. The first book was E. W. West's edition of *Essays on the Sacred Language, Writings and Religion of the Parsis* (1878), by Martin Haug, and the sixth was John Dowson's *Classical Dictionary of Hindu Mythology and Religion, Geography, History and Literature* (1879). The series was encouraged and supported by the India Office Library, where Rost worked from 1869 to 1893.

Trübner also published the English and Foreign Philosophical Library, which included *Enigmas of Life* (1872-1879), by William R. Greg. Through Greg, who was controller of the government Stationery Office, Trübner became the supplier of reference books and periodicals to government bureaus. Trübner combined his oriental interests with the contemporary popular market when he published Edwin Arnold's *The Light of Asia* in 1879. This book of Indian lore in blank verse was frequently reprinted as well as translated into several languages.

Samuel Butler is perhaps the best known of Trübner's authors today. After his *Erewhon* (1872) was rejected by Chapman and Hall, Butler sent it to Trübner and Company. The firm returned the manuscript unread, saying "they supposed it was something to do with the Contagious Diseases Act." When that mistake was rectified the firm agreed to publish it anonymously on a commission basis. Trübner and Company initially agreed to share the costs of production of *Life and Habit* (1878), but the publisher, according to the author, "insulted me so grossly that I offered to pay for the whole myself and take it away at once." Butler departed briefly to David Bogue, then returned to an apologetic Trübner. He stayed until the amalgamation with Kegan Paul, Trench and Company, when he moved to Longmans.

Trübner, who also handled the publishing, delivery, and agency for government departments and learned societies in England, Australia, America, Denmark, and Sweden, died in 1884. His widow continued the business until 1889, when she sold it to Horatio William Bottomley.

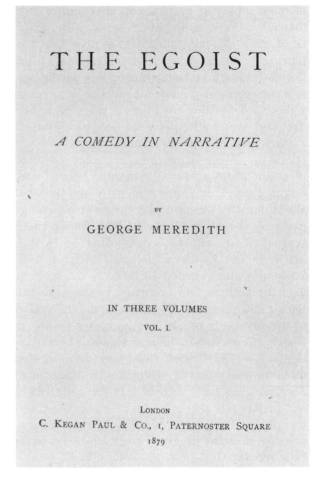

THE EGOIST

*A COMEDY IN NARRATIVE*

BY

GEORGE MEREDITH

IN THREE VOLUMES
VOL. I.

LONDON
C. KEGAN PAUL & CO., 1, PATERNOSTER SQUARE
1879

*Title page for the first volume of the novel for which Paul sold the serialization rights to a Glasgow newspaper, infuriating Meredith*

Born in 1860, Bottomley had begun as a printer in 1884 with the *Hackney Hansard*, a suburban weekly, which soon expanded to other local "Hansards." In 1888 he was managing director of Macrae, Curtice and Company, Limited, which secured the contract for publishing the parliamentary debates. With the new income, Bottomley purchased several other printing and publishing firms, and by April 1889 they were operating under the umbrella of the Hansard Publishing Union in Great Queen Street; Paul was on the board of directors. In Bottomley's words, "the Union aimed at being a combination of every department of the printing and publishing trades. The object was to give newspaper printers and others the opportunity of securing the benefit of a cooperative organization dealing with every detail of newspaper and book production, from the growing of the wood from which the pulp for making paper is obtained to the distribution and sale of the finished periodical or book—with the intermediate supply of every technical requisite, commercial, literary and artistic." Begun with a capital of £500,000, the company at its peak "was employing about a third of the members of the London Society of Compositors; was paying several thousands of pounds per week in wages; had a thousand printing machines at work night and day; and produced every week over two hundred . . . newspapers and other publications."

Two of the firms that Bottomley gathered up in this extraordinary "publishing Union" were Kegan Paul, Trench and Company and Trübner and Company. A third was the firm of George Redway, a small publisher in York Street which specialized in esoteric books such as Arthur Machen's *The Anatomy of Tobacco* (1884). In 1889 Bottomley amalgamated all three as Kegan Paul, Trench, Trübner and Company Limited. Trench fell ill and resigned about this time. The offices of the firm were moved to Paternoster House, in Charing Cross Road, when the Hansard Union collapsed in 1891. The firm was reconstituted under its own board of directors, with Paul as manager, and was quite successful in the early 1890s; but profits fell abruptly in 1895, and the directors resigned. The same year Paul was seriously injured in a traffic accident, from which he never fully recovered.

A new board of directors was established, chaired by J. E. Smids and made up of shareholders who hoped to protect their investment. They engaged a manager, Spencer Blackett, who in turn employed Arthur Waugh as literary adviser. Neither of them shared Paul's sensitivity to literary excellence or Trübner's to scholarly standards. Blackett was the son of a publisher, but he had started out in a military career and continued to wear his Hussar uniform when he entered the London book trade as a publisher of sensational novels and shilling shockers, then left it to try his luck at other businesses. Waugh remembered him as a "genial figure" and "a man of smart appearance and fascinating address." Blackett "had the business experience which comes from having been disillusioned once or twice; and he was blessed with overflowing energy. . . . But he would never have claimed to know much about literature." Blackett and Waugh embarked on a policy of producing more popular books for the firm. They felt impeded by the fact that members of their board of directors were businesspeople, none of whom had any experience in the book trade. Paul, who had re-

tired in 1899, died in 1902. That same year Waugh moved to Chapman and Hall.

Little is known about the vicissitudes suffered by the firm in the early years of the twentieth century. It continued to reprint popular books for which it held the copyright and to add new volumes to some of its series. But it was no longer taking risks on unknown talents such as Hardy, Stevenson, and Meredith had been in the 1870s. In 1912 it was incorporated with Routledge and Sons, which retained the Kegan Paul imprint for many years.

**References:**

*The Archives of Kegan Paul, Trench, Trübner and Henry S. King 1858-1912* (Bishop's Stortford: Chadwyck-Healey, 1974);

Horatio Bottomley, *Bottomley's Book* (London: Odhams, 1909);

Michael Collie, *George Meredith: A Bibliography* (Toronto: University of Toronto Press, 1974);

Gillian Furlong, comp., *The Archives of Routledge & Kegan Paul Ltd. (1853-1973) Publishers* (London: University College London Library, 1978);

June Steffensen Hagen, *Tennyson and His Publishers* (London: Macmillan, 1979);

Sandy Merrick, *Index of Authors and Titles of Kegan Paul, Trench, Trübner & Henry S. King 1858-1912* (Bishop's Stortford: Chadwyck-Healey, 1974);

Michael Millgate, *Thomas Hardy: A Biography* (Oxford: Oxford University Press, 1982);

Frank Arthur Mumby, *The House of Routledge 1834-1934, with a History of Kegan Paul, Trench, Trübner and Other Associated Firms* (London: Routledge, 1934);

Charles Kegan Paul, *Memories* (London: Kegan Paul, Trench, Trübner, 1899; reprinted, Hamden, Conn.: Archon Books, 1971);

A. W. Pollard and Gwendolen Murphy, *A Select Bibliography of the Writings of Alfred W. Pollard* (Oxford: Oxford University Press, 1938);

Patricia Thomas Srebrnik, *Alexander Strahan Victorian Publisher* (Ann Arbor: University of Michigan Press, 1986);

Roger G. Swearingen, *The Prose Writings of Robert Louis Stevenson* (London: Macmillan, 1980);

Hallam Tennyson, *Alfred Lord Tennyson: A Memoir*, 2 volumes (New York & London: Macmillan, 1897), II: 383;

Arthur Waugh, *One Man's Road* (London: Chapman & Hall, 1931).

**Papers:**
The archives of Kegan Paul, Trench, Trübner and its component firms are held at University College London, and have been published on microfilm by Chadwyck-Healey, Limited.

—*Leslie Howsam*

# William Pickering
*(London: 1820-1853)*
## Basil Montagu Pickering
*(London: 1858-1878)*

William Pickering's achievements in the early nineteenth century are well known: the introduction of cloth binding, leading to the wider availability of books at lower prices; improvements in book design; and the production of important new editions of both standard and neglected works, particularly of the older English literature. In a period when the function of the publisher was beginning to separate from that of the bookseller, and publishers themselves were beginning to specialize, he provided a link between the old and the new.

Pickering was born on 2 April 1796 of obscure parentage. In 1810 he was apprenticed to J. and A. Arch, Quaker booksellers of 61 Cornhill, London. In January 1818 he moved to Longmans and later the same year to John Cuthill of 4 Middle Row, Holborn. In July 1819 he married Mary Ann Gubbins, by whom he had three daughters and a son. In June 1820 he set up his own bookshop at 31 Lincoln's Inn Fields and began to specialize in the antiquarian trade. Close to other bookshops, to the publishers of Paternoster Row, to the British Museum, and to the Inns of Court, Pickering's shop was accessible to the trade as well as to potential authors and customers. There he met the barrister Basil Montagu, whose works he later published and after whom he named his son.

Among his fellow apprentices had been John Joseph Thornthwaite, who provided the capital to set him up in business; borrowing from friends or relatives was the typical practice of the period. This financial connection lasted for twenty-five years, during which Pickering was dependent on Thornthwaite for credit, usually through the medium of bills of exchange.

Pickering's publishing began immediately with Gilbert Burnet's *Lives of Sir Matthew Hale and John, Earl of Rochester* (1820). The miniature Diamond Classics were made possible by his acquaintance with the printer Charles Corrall, who had the small diamond type. They were dedicated to Earl Spencer and intended as an advertisement to mark Pickering's entry on the scene. The series included Latin classics, such as the works of Horace (1820) and Virgil (1821); Italian classics, including Torquato Tasso's *Gerusalemme liberata* (1822) and Dante's *La Divina Commedia* (1823); and the works of major English authors, such as Shakespeare's *Plays and Poems* (1825) and John Milton's *Paradise Lost* (1828). The Burnet book and Richard Baxter's *Poetical Fragments* (1821) were an indication of the direction his publishing was to take and of his early interest in book design. The Baxter title page, with its tapering layout and arabesque ornament, was a pointer to his future style. In 1824, to accommodate a larger stock, he moved to 57 Chancery Lane.

The publication in 1822 of Geoffrey Chaucer's *The Canterbury Tales* had given Pickering the idea for a Masters of English Poesy series. A prospectus was issued, and although it was not implemented, the complete works of Shakespeare and Edmund Spenser were published in 1825, followed by those of Milton in 1826. All had a joint imprint with Talboys and Wheeler of Oxford, and a wreath device on the title pages. The year 1825 saw the beginning of the important reprints in the Oxford English Classics series, with the works of Samuel Johnson and William Robert-

son. These were followed by *The History of England* (1826-1827), by David Hume and Tobias Smollett, and Edward Gibbon's *The History of the Decline and Fall of the Roman Empire* (1828). Pickering had also put out a prospectus for the Italian Classic Poets, but only one publication eventually materialized, the *Orlando Innamorato di Bojardo* and *Orlando Furioso di Ariosto*, edited in nine volumes by Antonio Panizzi from 1830-1834. Pickering performed a service to historical research when *The Privy Purse Expenses of King Henry VIII* appeared in 1827, followed by other Royal Household books. *A Journal by One of the Suite of Thomas Beckington* was published in 1828; the editor, Sir Harris Nicolas, had tried six other publishers without success.

Probably Pickering's major innovation was his introduction in 1825 of dyed cotton cloth to cover the boards, with a printed paper title label. Thereby Pickering provided for the first time a cheap, serviceable, and standardized publisher's binding, with the books so bound selling at fixed prices both wholesale and retail. Some booksellers undercut the publisher's retail price, and Pickering was accused by the Booksellers' Association of supporting the "undersellers." This controversy led to his being denied the right to buy new books at wholesale prices. In 1832, in reply, he wrote two pamphlets: *Booksellers' Monopoly* and *Cases Showing the Arbitrary and Oppressive Conduct of the Committee of Booksellers*, alleging that the real reason he had been singled out was his publication of cheaper but superior editions of standard works in competition with the "trade" editions, for which many publishers shared costs and profits. The issue was resolved in 1833 when he brought out the first of the profitable Bridgewater Treatises, Thomas Chalmers's *On the Adaptation of External Nature to the Moral and Intellectual Constitution of Man*, and only allowed other booksellers to have the work when the ban was lifted. He later supported the booksellers' committee against those who wanted free trade in books.

Pickering's publications of the 1820s were not aimed at the growing literate public, as were the publishing projects of Charles Knight, but at the older select market of aristocracy, middle class, and clergy, characterized by wealth and scholarship. He brought out small editions at relatively high prices, often with even more expensive copies on large paper. The limits of this market were apparent when he wrote to Sir Jospeh Hunter in connection with the publication of *The Hallamshire Glossary* (1829): "In the course of nine years publishing I have never had the good fortune to reprint more than two works, which is a small proportion to 100." In 1828 he entered the field of popular gift books with *The Bijou* and *The Carcanet*; *The Bijou* was an annual which lasted only until 1830.

Thereafter he concentrated on the series which, more than any other, made him famous, The Aldine Edition of the British Poets. Starting with Robert Burns in 1830 and ending with Chaucer in 1845, this set of fifty-three volumes, priced at five shillings in cloth or ten shillings, sixpence in morocco, is a lasting monument both textually and in design. He tried without success to induce Sir Walter Scott to contribute an introductory companion volume, but did secure the editorial skills of Nicolas, John Mitford, and Alexander Dyce. For the second edition of Burns in 1839 he advertised for and secured two hundred original manuscripts and letters. The series was timed to coincide with the appearance of the new edition of Scott's *Waverley Novels* (1829-1833), the monthly *Murray's Family Library* (1829-1836), and Dionisius Lardner's *The Cabinet Cyclopaedia* (1830-1836). Although, being poetry and in small editions of fifteen hundred copies, they were not as profitable as fiction or "improving" works, they achieved good sales and were reprinted. After Pickering's death they were taken over by Bell and Daldy and continued in print for much of the century.

The title pages were decorated with the dolphin-and-anchor device, with the motto "Aldi Discip. Anglus," based on the device used by the sixteenth-century Venetian printer Aldus Manutius. Pickering had first used it in 1828 in J. W. Brown's *The Life of Leonardo da Vinci* and subsequently developed many different versions. In later years he also used other devices, such as the pike and ring—a pun on his name—and a heraldic shield with his initials. This revival of the device was an aspect of his desire to reproduce or reinterpret the past in his publishing. He was assisted and encouraged by Charles Whittingham the Younger, whom he had met in 1829 and who became his chief printer.

Pickering's concern with fine reprints was closely linked with his antiquarian bookselling business: the select public which provided the customers for most of his publications tended to be the same which collected antiquarian books. He had developed his interest in such books from an early age and was influenced by Thomas Frognall Dibdin, whose *Bibliomania* (1811) and *Bibliographical Decameron* (1817) were published dur-

ing his apprenticeship. From the financial point of view, the importance of the bookselling was greater than that of the publishing. He devoted much time to it and attended sales almost daily. By the time he published his 1834 catalogue he had accumulated a considerable stock, including incunabula, Aldine press books, and early Bibles. It also included many finely bound copies of his own publications, showing his pride in them as a continuation of the fine printing of the past. Much of the stock consisted of earlier editions of standard English works and literary manuscripts, providing an essential publisher's archive. By the time of his death he had accumulated an enormous stock which took five sales to auction off.

Pickering's book buying developed into book collecting, and he formed his own private library, including a collection on his leisure pastime of angling. A particular favorite was Izaak Walton, and he searched throughout his life for anything connected with him. This enthusiasm led in 1836 to the publication of a fine illustrated edition of *The Compleat Angler*, which the editor, Nicolas, said was as much the work of the publisher as his own. At six guineas for two volumes it was expensive and unprofitable, a case of enthusiasm outrunning commercial prudence.

During the 1830s and 1840s Pickering's publishing career reached its peak. He joined the Surtees Society, concerned with publishing manuscripts relating to Northumbria; with J. B. Nichols and Son and Laing and Forbes of Edinburgh he was copublisher of the Society's volumes from 1834 to 1845. Other local history undertakings were S. Hibbert-Ware's *History of the Foundations in Manchester* (1834), copublished with Thomas Agnew and Joseph Zanetti, and George Poulson's *The History and Antiquities of the Seigniory of Holderness* (1840-1841), with Robert Brown of Hull. In 1834 he became part proprietor with J. B. Nichols of the new series of the *Gentleman's Magazine*, again reflecting his antiquarian tendencies as well as providing publicity for his publications.

The most important contemporary literary author published by Pickering was Samuel Taylor Coleridge, whose *Poetical Works* came out in 1828, followed by further editions in 1829 and 1834. During the next two decades most of the new editions of Coleridge's other works appeared under the Pickering imprint. *Aids to Reflection* came out in 1836, followed by *The Literary Remains* (1836-1838), *The Friend* (1837), *On the Constitution of Church and State* (1839), *Biographia Literaria*

*William Pickering (left) with the printer Charles Whittingham the Younger (engraving after a drawing by Frank Dadd from an oil painting by Charlotte Whittingham)*

(1847), and *Essays on His Own Times* (1850). The first edition of *Confessions of an Enquiring Spirit* appeared in 1840. Conflict later arose with the poet's family over the terms of publication, whereby the publisher was taking half the profits under the commission method. In 1851 Edward Moxon bought the whole stock and publication rights for £831, and Pickering's twenty-three-year connection with Coleridge was broken.

Among his favorite authors for reprinting were such seventeenth-century divines as George Herbert, Thomas Fuller, Jeremy Taylor, and Richard Sibbes. A complete edition of Herbert's works was published for the first time in 1835-1836, followed by corrected and augmented editions in 1838-1841 and 1844-1848. The care he took in their preparation is illustrated in his correspondence with his friend Philip Bliss, registrar of Oxford University, who supplied much information on sources and earlier editions. This series of letters is the only substantial correspondence of Pickering's to survive. These works illustrate Pickering's interest in theology. He supported the traditions of the established church, and some of his publications reflect the controver-

sies in the era of the Oxford Movement. In 1837, as the principal publisher, he launched the *Church of England Quarterly Review*, although his association with it lasted only two years. He had a close relationship with the High Churchman William Maskell, for whom he published *The Ancient Liturgy of the Church of England* (1844) and *Monumenta Ritualia Ecclesiae Anglicanae* (1846-1847), as well as controversial pamphlets in 1850. Tracts by William Dodsworth and Theodora Crane also appeared under his imprint.

Pickering did on occasion publish "useful" and educational works. Such were Charles Richardson's *A New Dictionary of the English Language* (1836-1837), Isaac Cory's *A Practical Treatise on Accounts* (1839), Frank Howard's *The Science of Drawing* (1839-1840), and Arthur Bowes's *Practical Synopsis of English History* (1845). From 1843 to 1853 he published a series of twenty-two volumes, Small Books on Great Subjects, mostly written anonymously by Caroline Frances Cornwallis.

As well as publishing Coleridge, Pickering in the latter part of his career also published works by other notable contemporary authors. In 1836 the second edition of Thomas Malthus's *Prin-*

ciples of Political Economy appeared, and 1839 saw the first appearance of that popular poem of the Victorian era, P. J. Bailey's *Festus*. Aubrey de Vere's *A Song of Faith, Devout Exercises and Sonnets* came out in 1842. Other first editions included the early works of Edward FitzGerald: *Euphranor* (1851), *Polonius* (1852), and his translation of *Six Dramas of Calderon* (1853). Coventry Patmore's *Tamerton Church Tower and Other Poems* was published the same year. In 1851, two years after the poet's death, he published the first collected edition of Thomas Lovell Beddoes.

The bookselling business had grown in these later years, and in 1842 he had moved to 177 Piccadilly. He had become a major supplier to the British Museum and the Bodleian Library. From 1846 he was, with Lilly and Rodd, the main source of antiquarian books to the museum, and the principal English bookseller supplying early Americana. In 1849, on the death of Rodd, he became the museum's auction agent. On the publishing side, he made developments in book design which evoked the spirit as well as the material of the past. Titles were sometimes framed by an engraved monumental design in the Renaissance style, as in the editions of Herbert. There was an increased use of ornaments and decorated initial letters derived from older designs and engraved by Mary Byfield. Pickering and Whittingham revived Caslon old-face type, which was confined at first to title and half-title pages as in Fuller's *History of the Holy War* (1840) and later extended to the whole text, as in Herbert's *The Temple* (1844). The works of the popular essayist Arthur Helps, such as the fourth edition of *Essays Written in the Intervals of Business*, published in 1848, are typical examples of the "antique" style he had evolved.

The year 1844 saw the appearance of the set of six *Books of Common Prayer*, magnificently printed in Caslon old English type with title pages and ornaments in facsimile of the original editions of 1559 to 1662. With a printing bill of £1,243 and priced at eighteen guineas the set, these were costly productions, as were the superbly illustrated, hand-colored works of Henry Shaw, such as *Dresses and Decorations of the Middle Ages* (1843). They may have contributed to the financial crisis which overtook Pickering in 1845, adding to the effects of the depression of 1842. His vulnerable position was revealed when he received a claim for £17,795, alleged to be the balance of an account from 1825 to 1845. It was easy to run up debts when bills of exchange were

continually renewed, but there was also evidence of sharp practice by Thornthwaite. Rather than having a sale of stock and settling out of court, Pickering allowed the matter to go before Chancery and then to arbitration. After eight years of litigation an award of £11,345 in Thornthwaite's favor was made on 5 May 1853. On 9 May Pickering went bankrupt. Appeals were made on his behalf by the assignee and other creditors, but he had mislaid vital documents from earlier years which he ought to have put before the arbitrator. After much expense the final appeal was rejected on 22 April 1854. The anxiety had affected his health, and five days later he died at Turnham Green, aged fifty-eight. He was buried at Kensal Green cemetery. Friends raised an appeal for his daughters, and creditors were paid in full after the sale of his stock. Few of his business records have survived.

His reputation lived on at home and in America, where collector/dealers such as Henry Stevens and William F. Fowle included a high proportion of his publications in their libraries. They are much sought after today. In 1858 his son, Basil Montagu Pickering, revived the business at 196 Piccadilly and published some notable books, including the works of John Henry Newman. He died on 8 February 1878, his wife and children having predeceased him, and the firm became extinct.

Andrew Chatto purchased the stock of Basil Montagu Pickering in 1878 and established the firm of Pickering and Chatto, which became one of the world's leading antiquarian booksellers. The William Pickering imprint has been revived by Pickering and Chatto with the Pickering Masters, a series of first complete editions beginning with the works of Charles Babbage and Thomas Malthus (1986) and Charles Darwin (1986-1987).

**References:**

Geoffrey Keynes, *William Pickering, Publisher: A Memoir and a Check-list of His Publications*, revised edition (London: Galahad Press, 1969);

James M. McDonnell, "William Pickering, 1796-1854, Antiquarian Bookseller, Publisher and Book Designer: A Study in the Early Nineteenth Century Book Trade," Ph.D. thesis, Polytechnic of North London, 1983;

A. N. L. Munby, "The Sales of William Pickering's Publications," *Book Collector*, 21, no. 1 (1972): 33-39;

Philip Sperling, "Looking for Mr Pickering," in *A Miscellany for Bibliophiles*, edited by H. George Fletcher (New York: Grastorf & Lang, 1979), pp. 159-187;

Gerrish Thurber, "Aldus in England," *Publishers' Weekly*, 137 (6 April 1940): 1413-1418;

Arthur Warren, *The Charles Whittinghams, Printers* (New York: Grolier Club, 1896);

Bernard Warrington, "The Bankruptcy of William Pickering in 1853," *Publishing History*, 27 (1990): 5-25;

Warrington, "William Pickering and the Book Trade in the Early Nineteenth Century," *Bul-letin of the John Rylands University Library of Manchester*, 68, no. 1 (1985): 247-266;

Warrington, "William Pickering, Bookseller and Book Collector," *Bulletin of the John Rylands University Library of Manchester*, 71, no. 1 (1989): 121-138;

Warrington, "William Pickering, His Authors and Interests: A Publisher and the Literary Scene in the Early Nineteenth Century," *Bulletin of the John Rylands University Library of Manchester*, 69, no. 2 (1987): 572-628.

—*Bernard Warrington*

# G. P. Putnam's Sons
### (London: 1883[?]-1916)
## Wiley and Putnam
### (London: 1838-1848)
## G. P. Putnam's Sons Limited
### (London: 1916-1929)
## Putnam and Company Limited
### (London: 1930-1986)

See also the George Palmer Putnam entries in *DLB 3: Antebellum Writers in New York and the South* and *DLB 79: American Magazine Journalists, 1850-1900*, and the G. P. Putnam's Sons entry in *DLB 49: American Literary Publishing Houses, 1638-1899*.

The first American publishing house to open a branch office in London was Wiley and Putnam. In August 1838 the firm announced to the English book trade that it was in business at 67 Paternoster Row, where customers could secure the latest in American periodicals and books.

The manager of the new shop was George Palmer Putnam. Born in Brunswick, Maine, on 7 February 1814, he was the fourth child of Henry and Catherine Putnam. The family's financial troubles led Putnam's mother to open her own school, where he received his early education. At the age of eleven he became an apprentice to his uncle, a carpet merchant in Boston. In 1829 he went to New York City and secured employment as an errand boy and shop assistant for George W. Bleeker, a bookseller and stationer. He earned twenty-five dollars per year plus room and board and used his evenings to educate himself by reading prodigiously. This activity paid off several years later when he became a clerk for Jonathan Leavitt, the leading New York publisher of books on theology and religion, who may have been induced to hire him because of his accomplishment of compiling, at odd moments, an index to world history. This work appeared in 1832 as *Chronology*, under the joint imprint of Leavitt and his brother-in-law, Daniel Appleton. The initial one thousand copies sold quickly, and many revised and retitled impressions followed; it remained in print for nearly a century. Besides introducing Putnam as an author, his work for Leavitt gave him valuable book trade experience; enough, in fact, that from 1834 to 1836 he edited the first American trade journal, a monthly titled the *Booksellers' Advertiser and Monthly Register of New Publications*.

By 1836 Putnam had saved $150, with which he purchased a junior partnership in the firm of John Wiley and Charles Long. Soon he found himself taking an eight-month trip to Europe to scout for books which could either be imported or reprinted for the American market. From his travels Putnam became convinced that he and Wiley should open their own branch in London so that they could preempt other American publishers from acquiring advance copies of the latest British publications. A London outlet would also permit them to sell their own books directly to the London trade. Putnam later characterized these plans as "a Yankee barter of our fresh young literature for the maturer and slower production of the fatherland." Putnam opened the branch on Paternoster Row in 1838.

Establishing Wiley and Putnam in London was not easy because many British people echoed Sidney Smith's quip: who reads an American book? Nonetheless, the American author and politician Charles Sumner encouraged Putnam to persevere: "I think it highly important that you should employ all proper means to make your establishment known as the Depot of American books, so that the complaint need not be made, which I heard so often in London, 'nobody knows where to purchase American books.'"

Putnam discovered that the British were abysmally ignorant of the United States, so he compiled and published a volume titled *American Facts*. Appearing in 1845 under the imprint of Wiley and Putnam, the book pointed out that British publishers had reprinted at least 382 American publications between 1833 and 1842; many more reprints came out disguised as British in origin. Supporting the contention that English readers fancied American books, a United States congressional committee later estimated that at least 600 American works had appeared in England before 1838.

*George Palmer Putnam*

The only possibility of promoting most American books in the London market was to price them so low that they undercut comparable British volumes. This was the principle that presumably guided Wiley and Putnam in establishing a new series called the Library of Choice Reading, edited by Evert Duyckinck. The Library of Choice Reading, with its low price and uniform binding, and comprising comparatively recent works rather than old remainders, entered the London scene as something of a novelty. In November 1845, however, Putnam reported to Duyckinck that "the plan has found an imitator and a bold one, even in old-fashioned benighted London." David Bogue had inaugurated his European Library at the disconcertingly low price of three shillings, sixpence—"Cheaper even than ours," Putnam admitted, going on to say: "Our 'library' has already given the hint to three or four similar ones here, one of them called by the same Library of Choice Reading. Bogue's Library is imitated to a T by H. G. Bohn, and there is an uncivil war between Fleet Street and York Street as well as on the Thames." The fifty-volume Library of Choice Reading included works by John Keats, Leigh Hunt, Thomas Love Peacock, Thomas Carlyle, Thomas Hood, Charles Lamb, William Hazlitt, Samuel Taylor Coleridge, Alexander William Kinglake, Eliot Warburton, and William Beckford. Occasionally Wiley and Putnam paid a British author for the early sheets of a forthcoming book, but more often the firm pirated works for its library series, just as British firms did with American writers. In addition Wiley and Putnam published the Library of American Books (1845-1848), which included volumes by Nathaniel Hawthorne, Bayard Taylor, William Gilmore Simms, and Judge James Hall.

In early 1841 Putnam returned to New York, and on 13 March he married Victorine Haven, a sixteen-year-old pupil of his mother's. They returned to London that autumn, initially settling in St. John's Wood and later in Mornington Road. Their house became a gathering place for both British and American literati. The future publisher and heir, George Haven Putnam, was born on 2 April 1844. He later recalled: "My father had a taste which might almost be called a genius, for hospitality. The income was at this time very limited, and the entertainment that could be afforded to guests must have been modest. My father believed, however, that the right kind of people would enjoy the privilege of being together and of coming to know his wife, and the little cottage seemed to have had a considerable number of guests from week to week."

Putnam represented his firm in London from 1838 to 1847. It was characteristic of the economically uncertain times that premises were relocated often. In 1839 the office was moved from 67 to 35 Paternoster Row, and it remained there until the latter part of 1841, when it moved to nearby 7 Amen Corner, Stationers' Hall Court, where it continued until 1845. For the next two years Putnam called his larger quarters at 6 Waterloo Place, Regent Street, the "American Literary Agency," because one room was allocated as a reading room and reception area for visitors from America. In the spring of 1847 Wiley and Putnam moved back to the City at 12 Paternoster Row.

That summer Putnam and his family sailed for America. He had become bored spending the bulk of his time in London selecting books for shipment to New York, and it was becoming clear that he and Wiley held quite different ideas about the future of their business. Putnam was much more interested in cultivating literary talent and promoting the publication of new works, whereas Wiley viewed the enterprise primarily in terms of bookselling and reprinting foreign works.

During his nine years overseas Putnam's accomplishments were many. He made the acquaintance of many British authors and publishers; he helped introduce to the American reading public many British books which might otherwise have been slow to reach American shores; and he made the British reading public significantly more aware of what the United States could offer by way of literature. On both sides of the Atlantic he promoted international copyright, and he impressed many British authors and publishers by treating them fairly. Among those he reimbursed for the right to reprint their works in America were Elizabeth Barrett Browning, Carlyle, and Fredrika Bremer.

Putnam severed his connection with Wiley in 1848 and opened his own publishing and bookselling offices at 155 Broadway. He continued to specialize in importing British books, as indicated by the letterhead on his stationery in 1851: "G. P. Putnam, American and Foreign Bookselling and Purchasing Agent for the Trade and Public Institutions." He made periodic trips to London, and in a form letter he assured his customers that "my new arrangements in Europe are such as to enable me, at any time, to execute orders for foreign books generally, with much greater expedition than has been usual heretofore." Putnam chose his words to give the impression that he had opened a branch office at 49 Bow Lane, Cheapside. This address was actually the location of the bookseller and publisher Thomas Delf, the first of several agents who would handle Putnam's commissions during the ensuing years.

Realizing that the Philadelphia firm of Carey, Lea and Blanchard had allowed many of Washington Irving's works to go out of print, Putnam proposed to the author a uniform and revised edition using new stereotype plates. The volumes began appearing in 1848 and rekindled interest in Irving, as Putnam had hoped. Stereos manufactured in America were well regarded in London, and John Murray purchased a duplicate set for the British market.

Putnam enjoyed remarkable success in the early 1850s. James Fenimore Cooper gave him an exclusive three-year contract to republish six books, including *The Spy* (1849), *The Pilot* (1849), and *The Red Rover* (1850). The year 1850 witnessed the publication of Elizabeth Wetherell's tremendously popular book *The Wide, Wide World*, written under the pseudonym Susan Bogert Warner. As business improved, Putnam fulfilled a long-held dream of having his own periodical, *Putnam's Monthly: A Magazine of Literature, Science, and Art* (1853-1857), in which he eschewed reprints of foreign articles and published only original contributions from Americans.

In 1854 Putnam moved his offices to 10 Park Place. By September of that year he sensed that he had assumed too many obligations, and he was forced to retrench quite suddenly. Much of his stock and plates had to be sold at auction, and although he received seventy thousand dollars, he had to part with editions of works by Oliver Goldsmith, Andrew Jackson Downing, Austin Henry Layard, Thomas Hood, Bremer, and many others. Then came the painful task of notifying his authors. Typical was his letter of June 1855 to Bremer, apologizing for the small payment he was able to make on authorized editions of her works in America due to the competition of a pirated reprint by Harper and Brothers.

In 1856 Putnam was beset by even worse news. The firm's accountant was discovered to have embezzled the company's funds; bills came due which could not be paid, requiring more plates and stock to be sacrificed, including his prized set of Irving's works. The financial panic of 1857 inflicted yet more damage. Only Irving's generosity in purchasing at auction the stereotypes of his own books, and then commissioning Putnam to use them, saved his publisher from immediate collapse. When the Civil War started Putnam was virtually out of business. In 1862 he placed his remaining stock in the hands of others and took a job as a federal tax collector.

His son George Haven studied at Göttingen University until he reached the age of eighteen; he then came to the United States and enrolled in the 176th New York Volunteers. Promoted to major, he was captured by the Confederates and was released on the condition that he terminate his active service.

After the war George Palmer Putnam was relieved of his government post. With his oldest son able to help him in the financial and sales aspects of the publishing business, he resumed trade in March 1866 as G. P. Putnam and Son. Soon George Haven Putnam visited England to renew the ties his father had established a quarter century before. The date the firm opened a

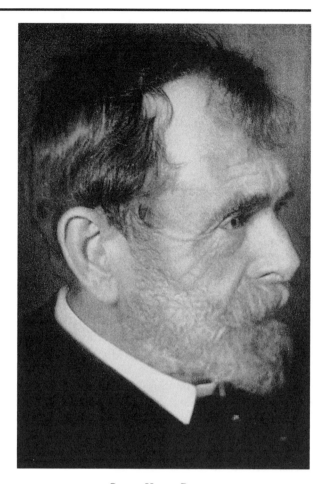

*George Haven Putnam*

London branch is unclear; although the younger Putnam later suggested that an office had existed as early as 1870, London street guides and advertisements do not indicate any premises until 1883, when 25 Henrietta Street, Covent Garden, is listed as the address. By this time two more sons had joined the firm: John Bishop Putnam in 1871 and Irving Putnam the following year. On 20 December 1872 their father died, and the name of the business was modified to G. P. Putnam's Sons.

Editions of Irving kept rolling off the presses, including a new set called the Knickerbocker Edition. Fiction was somewhat exceptional, however, since the firm concentrated on history, biography, and technology. In 1874 John Bishop Putnam organized a printing plant and bindery in New Rochelle, about fifteen miles from New York City. The plant was incorporated in 1889 as the Knickerbocker Press and thenceforth printed all of Putnam's works.

Little is known of the London branch until the early twentieth century, except for its several changes of location. Street directories for 1886 to 1891 place Putnam's at 27 King William Street, Strand; 24 Bedford Street, Strand, remained the firm's London premises until 1936.

Between 1906 and 1953 the name of Constant Huntington was inextricably linked with Putnam's of London. Born in Boston in 1876, he attended St. Paul's School in Concord, New Hampshire, and graduated from Harvard University in 1899. He began graduate study in medicine at Harvard, then switched to engineering at the Massachusetts Institute of Technology. When this profession failed to satisfy him he called on his distant relatives, the Putnams, who gave him a job in New York. In 1906 he was sent to London to manage the firm's branch office. He worked there at first in comparative obscurity, sending finely bound editions of British classics to the New York office and occasionally originating a volume. His first business coup was the promotion of Florence L. Barclay's *The Rosary* (1909), a highly sentimental tale of a blind man and the woman who cares for him. Huntington shrewdly sent a copy to Queen Alexandra, who let it be known that it was the best book she had read all year. This recommendation circulated among Huntington's aristocratic friends, and soon a brisk demand was created.

Huntington's wife, the former Gladys Parrish, was an heiress from the United States, and the two of them gained entry into high society and literary circles where they met well-connected British aristocrats and members of the intelligentsia such as Henry James. These associations may have accounted for another of Huntington's coups: securing an option from the publisher William Heinemann on all of John Galsworthy's writings for the American market. In 1916 the London office became a private company, G. P. Putnam's Sons Limited, and Huntington became chairman.

At the end of World War I Huntington agreed to publish the significant but highly controversial work of Marie Charlotte Carmichael Stopes. Stopes was already known within the scientific community as a paleobotanist before she digressed to write treatises on sex and marriage. The annulment of her marriage in 1916 on grounds of nonconsummation strengthened her conviction that most couples were woefully ignorant about sexual matters. In 1918 she married Humphrey Verdon-Roe; with his encouragement she completed *Married Love*, which was published by Fifield later that same year and in a revised edi-

tion by Putnam in 1919. The controversial work proved to be a huge success, eventually being translated into thirteen languages.

Both supporters and critics noted that Stopes's first book contained little about contraception, so she wrote a sequel, *Wise Parenthood*, which was published by Fifield in 1918; Huntington rushed a revised and enlarged edition into print before the end of 1919. This extended pamphlet sold a half million copies within the decade. In 1921 Stopes and her husband founded the Mothers' Clinic for Constructive Birth Control, the first of its kind in Britain; this institution, in turn, helped promote her publications, all of which carry the G. P. Putnam's Sons imprint: *Radiant Motherhood* (1920), *Truth about Venereal Disease* (1921), *Our Ostriches: A Play of Modern Life in Three Acts* (1923), *Mother, How Was I Born?* (1924), *The Human Body* (1926), *Sex and the Young* (1926), *Enduring Passion* (1928), *Change of Life in Men and Women* (1936), and *Your Baby's First Year* (1939). Some of these books were banned in one or more American states, and both the author and the publisher were cited for obscenity and libel. Litigation and the air of scandal served sales well. Huntington admitted that Stopes was an extraordinarily difficult person, but he relished the publicity that resulted from publishing her books.

Alongside the success of Stopes's volumes, the years following World War I brought a marked increase in the number and variety of books initiated and published by Putnam's London branch. These included *The Cambridge History of American Literature* (1917-1921), Wilfred Ewart's *The Way of Revelation* (1921), and Leopold Hamilton Myers's *The Orissers* (1923), *The Clio* (1925), and *Strange Glory* (1936). One of Putnam's more prolific authors was Leslie Poles Hartley, with *Night Fears, and Other Stories* (1924), *Simonetta Perkins* (1925), *The Shrimp and the Anemone* (1944), *The Sixth Heaven* (1946), and *Eustace and Hilda* (1947). For juvenile readers there were the popular tales of Henry Williamson: *The Peregrine's Saga* (1923), *The Old Stag* (1926), and *Tarka the Otter* (1927).

Huntington had made many useful contacts with publishers on the Continent, and in 1929 he sought permission to publish a foreign novel in Britain. The work he proposed was *Im Westen nichts Neues* (1929), by the German author Erich Maria Remarque. The New York office, thinking that the market was not only saturated with war stories but also that the public would not take

*Bust of Constant Huntington, chairman of the London Putnam's from 1916 until 1953*

kindly to an antiwar story written from the German perspective, declined Huntington's proposal. Nevertheless, he arranged for a translation to be done; the result, *All Quiet on the Western Front* (1929), took the British by storm. (In the United States the translation was published the same year by Little, Brown.)

It may have been this achievement that induced Huntington to approach George Haven Putnam about purchasing a controlling interest in the London office. Perhaps the Wall Street crash, combined with continued poor sales in New York, paved the way for the acceptance of Huntington's offer. In any case, during the course of 1929-1930 Huntington acquired 55 percent of the shares of the privately held London company and changed its name to Putnam and Company Limited.

Many publishers on both sides of the Atlantic fell on hard times during the Great Depression, but the 1930s afforded Huntington prestige and profitability. In 1930 he gambled on a brief and eccentric tale about a builder of outdoor privies called *The Specialist*. For some reason the pub-

lic found this story, written by Charles Sale, delightfully naughty, and it sold one million copies in Britain over a twenty-five-year span.

Huntington took another sort of risk on Francesco Fausto Nitti's *Escape* in 1930. This time the London and New York houses cooperated on the publication, and well before the book appeared it attracted considerable attention. The author, the nephew of the former Italian prime minister, described how he and others had been rescued from a Fascist prison. The Italian dictator Benito Mussolini strongly denied Nitti's version of events and issued death threats against George Haven Putnam.

During the 1930s Huntington forged business relationships with major British and foreign authors which lasted well after World War II. One of these authors was Robert Hamilton Bruce Lockhart, a Scotsman who found himself in Russia at the outbreak of the revolution in 1917 and who was one of a very few Westerners who remained on reasonably good terms with the Bolsheviks. In 1932 he recounted his experiences in *Memoirs of a British Agent*. Lockhart's subsequent titles with Putnam included *Retreat from Glory* (1934), *My Scottish Youth* (1937), *Guns or Butter* (1938), *Comes the Reckoning* (1947), *The Marines Were There* (1950), *Jan Masaryk* (1956), *Friends, Foes, and Foreigners* (1957), and *Giants Cast Long Shadows* (1960).

Karen Blixen, using either the pen name Isak Dinesen or her own, first came to Putnam in 1934 with *Seven Gothic Tales*. Her best-known work, *Out of Africa*, appeared in 1937, followed by *Winter's Tales* in 1942, *The Angelic Avengers* in 1946, and *Last Tales* in 1957.

Less well known today but popular in their time were books by Hans Fallada. The first to appear was *Little Man, What Now?* (1933), followed by *Who Once Eats out of the Tin Bowl* (1934), *Once We Had a Child* (1935), *Sparrow Farm* (1937), *Wolf among Wolves* (1938), *Iron Gustav* (1940), and *The Drinker* (1952).

Another foreign author whom Huntington introduced to the English reading public was Italo Svevo. His *Confessions of Zeno* came out in 1930, followed in 1932 by *As a Man Grows Older*. From within the depths of Joseph Stalin's Russia Huntington discovered Mikhail Aleksandrovich Sholokhov, whose work first appeared in London with Putnam's publication of *And Quiet Flows the Don* (1934). In succeeding years Putnam published his *Virgin Soil Upturned* (1935), *The Don Flows Home to the Sea* (1940), *Harvest on the Don*

(1960), *Tales from the Don* (1961), and *One Man's Destiny* (1966).

Putnam distinguished itself with books on music and the arts, including Cyril W. Beaumont's *The Complete Book of Ballets* (1937); Ernest Newman's *Opera Nights* (1943), *Wagner Nights* (1950), and *More Opera Nights* (1954); and Mark Lubbock's *Complete Book of Light Opera* (1962).

One reason that Putnam and Company Limited did well during the war was its acquisition of one or two smaller firms, such as Nattali and Maurice in 1931. Its increased size qualified it for a more generous allocation of paper, thereby allowing production of larger editions of new works and reprints.

Continuing interest in the recent global conflict and the subsequent reconstruction of Europe provided ample scope for Putnam's postwar lists. Typical examples were Robert Aron's *The Vichy Regime, 1940-44* (1958), *De Gaulle before Paris* (1962), and *De Gaulle Triumphant* (1964). The novels of Martyn Goff were also characteristic of these years: *The Plaster Fabric* (1957), *A Season with Mammon* (1958), *A Sort of Peace* (1960), *The Youngest Director* (1961), and *Red on the Door* (1962). Occasionally there was something more provocative, such as Dylan Thomas's *Adventures in the Skin Trade* (1955). C. Day Lewis ventured into children's literature with *The Otterbury Incident* (1948). Reprints of back-list books also appeared regularly during the 1940s and 1950s, including those of Stopes, Remarque, Blixen, and Sholokhov.

In 1936 the firm relocated at 42 Great Russell Street. John Huntington, Constant's nephew, joined the firm in 1945. In 1951 Constant Huntington hired Roger Lubbock, an experienced journalist, to replace James MacGibbon as an editor for the firm. During the next few years Constant Huntington was inclined to favor traditional and tested ways, while Lubbock wished to be more innovative. The result was a classic conflict between the experience of age and the challenge of youth. Tensions mounted until 1953, when, in a fit of exasperation, Huntington offered to retire if Lubbock would purchase a controlling interest in the firm. With the support of the poet and author John Pudney, who later became a literary adviser to the firm, Lubbock accepted the challenge.

Huntington disappeared from the publishing scene without ceremony and with scarcely a farewell to his colleagues. He lived until December 1962, and his obituary in the *Times* captured

*Dust jacket for the 1929 antiwar novel that Huntington published against the advice of the New York office. The work became a best-seller.*

his essence: "Constant Huntington was one of the very last of the individual publishers.... [He] was a soldierly-looking, strikingly handsome man, patrician in taste, radical in outlook; his qualities were consistently reflected in the books he published."

Under Lubbock's leadership Putnam inaugurated a series of books on the history of aviation. Begun as individual volumes, it evolved into what is still known as Putnam Aeronautical Books. Among the early titles were *Aircraft of the Royal Air Force, 1918-1957* (1957) and *British Naval Aircraft* (1958), by Owen Thetford. In 1961 it seemed desirable to have a specialist editor for this series, and the firm hired the free-lance services of John Stroud. He oversaw the publication of *Bristol Aircraft since 1910* (1964) and *Shorts Aircraft since 1900* (1967), by C. H. Barnes; and *Boeing Aircraft since 1916* (1966), by Peter M. Bowers. By the early 1980s the list numbered sixty volumes, including aircraft company histories, biographies, and autobiographies.

The firm acquired the prestigious list of books from the Cambridge publishing house of Bowes and Bowes in 1956. By 1962, however, Putnam and Company Limited suffered from declining profits and a shortage of investment capital. Mergers were becoming more common in the British book trade, and the Bodley Head Group, with Max Reinhardt as managing director, took over Putnam. Already in the group were the imprints of Werner Laurie, Hollis and Carter, and the Nonesuch Library. The buyout, concluded in July, meant that the Bodley Head acquired not only Lubbock's 55 percent of Putnam's privately held shares but also the remaining shares held by Putnam's of New York.

To finance this merger Reinhardt approached the merchant bank of Henry Ansbacher and Company, whose managing director, L. A. Hart, was also a Bodley Head director. Hart was given a seat on the newly organized Putnam and Company Limited's board, while Lubbock was retained as managing director and Reinhardt became Putnam's new chairman. The Putnam board of directors then included John Huntington, J. B. Blackley, John Ryder, and J. R. Hews (Bodley Head's secretary and chief accountant). Pudney remained as literary adviser. The Putnam office, still located at Great Russell Street, was granted substantial editorial autonomy.

On the surface the match was good, with each publisher's lists complementing the others'. But the marriage of convenience lasted only about a year. In March 1963 Pudney resigned, and Lubbock and Reinhardt, who had been on good terms before the merger, encountered growing disagreements about policy. Later that year the Bodley Head found itself short of cash, due in part to having made an advance to Charlie Chaplin for an autobiography which was slow to materialize. Extreme economies were mandated, including the almost total absorption of Putnam's into the Bodley Head Group. Lubbock was offered a directorship on the group's board, but without any editorial independence he preferred to resign. The once proud Putnam firm then consisted only of John Huntington and his secretary, who occupied a modest office first in Earlham Street and then in Bow Street, dealing primarily with Putnam books still in print. Stroud continued as editor of the aeronautical list.

The Bodley Head had acquired eight hundred Putnam titles, but only a handful remained in print. In 1986 William R. Blackmore of Conway Maritime Press, 24 Bride Lane, approached the Bodley Head about purchasing the remaining Putnam books. The Bodley Head retained a few current Putnam works of a general character and sold Conway twenty-one volumes of the aviation series. Since Conway had acquired a nautical list from Macmillan the previous year and had hired Stroud as aeronautical editor, the firm was in a good position to specialize.

The Putnam imprint survives as a part of Conway Maritime Press, which publishes high-quality books. This result is consistent with the Putnam image: the office in London had never been large, but it prided itself on quality and prestige.

**References:**

J. W. Lambert and Michael Ratcliffe, *The Bodley Head, 1887-1987* (London: Bodley Head, 1987);

"Putnam Celebrates 100th Year," *Publishers' Weekly*, 134 (2 July 1938): 29-33;

George H. Putnam, *George Palmer Putnam: A Memoir* (New York: Putnam's, 1912);

Putnam, *A Memoir of George Palmer Putnam*, 2 volumes (New York: Privately printed, 1903);

Putnam, *Memoirs of a Publisher, 1865-1915* (New York: Putnam's, 1915);

George P. Putnam, "Rough Notes of Thirty Years in the Trade," *American Publishers' Circular*, 1 (1 August 1863): 242-245; (15 August 1863): 258-259, 290-292;

Putnam, *Wide Margins: A Publisher's Autobiography* (New York: Harcourt, Brace, 1942);

"Sketches of the Publishers: George P. Putnam," *Round Table*, 3 (10 February 1866): 90-91;

Edith M. Stern, "G. P. Putnam's Sons," *Saturday Review of Literature*, 24 (17 May 1941): 12-13;

John Wiley and Sons, *Wiley: One Hundred and Seventy-Five Years of Publishing* (New York: Wiley, 1982).

**Papers:**

Putnam's business records are in the Archives of British Publishers at the University of Reading. Letters are in the manuscript department of the New York Public Library.

*—James J. Barnes and Patience P. Barnes*

# Joseph Rickerby

*(London: circa 1831-1850)*

A fairly undistinguished early Victorian printer-publisher, Joseph Rickerby occupies a small niche in the annals of literature as the first publisher of Martin Tupper's *Proverbial Philosophy* (1838). The work went on to earn its author considerable wealth and fame, but today it is almost totally forgotten; when remembered at all, it is generally considered the foremost expression of a peculiarly middle-class Victorian moral code.

Little is known of Rickerby's early career as a master printer. He was certainly operating from premises at 3 Sherbourn Lane, a narrow thoroughfare off King William Street in the heart of the City of London, from 1831 until at least December 1833. That month *Bent's Monthly Literary Advertiser* announced that the first volume of a series of "Standard Theological Works of England" would appear on the first day of the new year. Entitled the Sacred Classics and "uniform in size with Dr. Lardner's cyclopaedia," the series would appear at a rate of one volume per month priced at three shillings, sixpence and would form "the cheapest series of works ever offered to the public." Authors represented would include Thomas à Kempis, John Donne, Isaac Barrow, John Wesley, John Locke, and Isaac Watts. The series was launched with Jeremy Taylor's *A Discourse of the Liberty of Prophesying*. Rickerby's aim was "that he who purchases at present the cheapest of ephemeral publications, may for the same money, possess himself of works which cannot fail to afford him guidance and support in the highest exercises of his faculties, and under every vicissitude of life."

The series editors were the Reverends Richard Cattermole and Henry Stebbing, verse writers and booksellers' hacks; it is possible that Stebbing's two-volume *History of the Christian Church* (1833) in Dionysius Lardner's Cabinet Cyclopaedia (1830-1850) got him noticed by Rickerby. Both editors subsequently became members of Rickerby's select band of writers. At the same time that Stebbing and Cattermole were engaged on their project, Robert Southey was telling the publisher Edward Moxon of his plans for an outline of Christian philosophy in twelve volumes. Moxon, who had brought out Cattermole's poetic tragedies, wrote back warning him of the rival scheme, and Southey abandoned his plans. Publishers were found in London, Edinburgh, Dublin, Oxford, and Cambridge. The Sacred Classics evidently proved popular; Rickerby displayed extracts from favorable reviews in his advertisements. By January 1836 the price of each volume had increased to four shillings, sixpence, and the original editors had been joined by Southey, George Croly, and Henry Pye Smith, all of whom had provided introductory essays. By the following September the series was complete at thirty volumes.

By this time Rickerby had embarked on another ambitious project. On 1 February 1836 he had launched the series Masterpieces of English Prose Literature with an edition of John Milton's prose writings, including *Areopagitica* and *An Outline of a Perfect Commonwealth*. There were to be editions of works by Francis Bacon, Sir Thomas More, the earl of Clarendon, Jonathan Swift, David Hume, Edmund Burke, Sir Joshua Reynolds, Adam Smith, and Payne Knight. The introductions and notes were to be provided by James Augustus St. John, an astonishingly versatile miscellaneous writer who had left school at sixteen to join the staff of a radical Plymouth newspaper, had cofounded the *Weekly Review* at twenty-six, and had recorded his travels alone in Egypt and Nubia in *Egypt and Mohammed Ali* (1834). One of his sons also became a Rickerby author. Rickerby had by this time assembled an intimate circle of contributors who were willing to supply him with further contacts; for instance, Richard Cattermole's brother George, a book illustrator, was asked to provide a design for the portrait of Milton in the debut volume of Masterpieces of English Prose Literature. The series never progressed beyond six volumes.

Rickerby began publishing on his own account around November 1837. From 1838 until 1850 directories list him as working from 15 Sherbourn Lane, an address that had been occupied by the master printer William Graves from 1820 to 1831.

To celebrate his new role as printer-publisher Rickerby launched five new editions, four

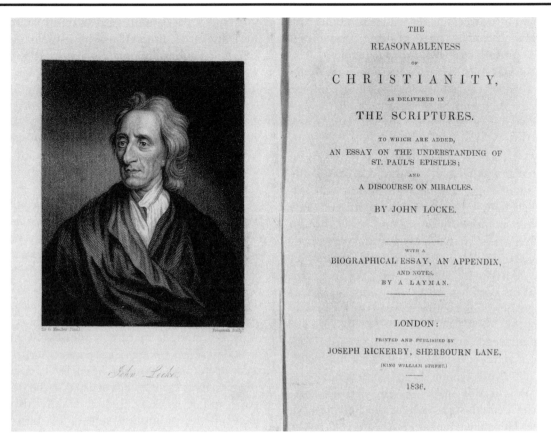

THE
REASONABLENESS
OF
CHRISTIANITY,
AS DELIVERED IN
THE SCRIPTURES.
TO WHICH ARE ADDED,
AN ESSAY ON THE UNDERSTANDING OF
ST. PAUL'S EPISTLES;
AND
A DISCOURSE ON MIRACLES.

BY JOHN LOCKE.

WITH A
BIOGRAPHICAL ESSAY, AN APPENDIX,
AND NOTES,
BY A LAYMAN.

LONDON:
PRINTED AND PUBLISHED BY
JOSEPH RICKERBY, SHERBOURN LANE,
(KING WILLIAM STREET.)

1836.

*Frontispiece and title page for a volume in Joseph Rickerby's thirty-volume series* Sacred Classics, *published from 1834 to 1836*

of them familiar works. There was a single-volume Greek Testament at a guinea; yet another *Pilgrim's Progress* (1838)—John Bunyan had been omitted from the Sacred Classics library—this time including biblical chapter and verse; and a republication in twenty monthly volumes of Hume and Tobias Smollett's *History of England* (1838-1839), brought up-to-date by Henry Stebbing, who also supplied an introduction and notes. These volumes, Rickerby suggested, might be awarded each month by indulgent fathers as gift books to their sons. There was also a miniature edition of Watts's *Lyric Poems*, with a memoir by Southey. The star item was Richard Cattermole's account of the Raphael Cartoons (1837), with steel engravings by Charles Warren, available in a large-paper as well as a standard edition; Rickerby even advertised India proof impressions of the plates at a guinea. Art publishing, even at this modest scale, was a bold departure for Rickerby, but the reviews were generally favorable; the *Atlas* praised the quality of the engravings.

Sales of his two major series of classics were evidently so steady that by the end of 1837, out

of the total of thirty-six volumes published, only eight were being advertised for sale. But even better times were ahead. Martin Farquhar Tupper, a failed barrister and inveterate versifier, whose previous slim volumes had been largely ignored, was one of Henry Stebbing's parishioners. In August 1837 Stebbing had called on Tupper and, learning of his literary ambitions, promised to get something from him into the *Athenaeum*, which he had once edited. Tupper found some versified proverbial advice on matrimony that he had prepared many years before for his wife but insisted on expanding it to make a book. By the end of ten weeks he had completed his task, and Stebbing gave him Rickerby's name. Thus, according to his own account, Tupper, "card in hand and manuscript in pocket ... ascended the dingy staircase" of the publisher's office. Rickerby found Tupper's manuscript sufficiently intriguing to publish it at his own risk on a profit-sharing basis. *Proverbial Philosophy: A Book of Thoughts and Arguments, Originally Treated*, appeared on 24 January 1838. Its reception was mixed. The *Atlas* considered it "one of the most original and curious products of our time." St. John, in spite of being one of

Rickerby's authors, had reservations about the work. His *Sunday Times* review condemned Tupper's underlying Toryism but praised the book's essential spiritual tendency. The hostile *Athenaeum* review caused a long-lasting coolness between Tupper and Stebbing, although the latter denied any responsibility for the magazine's stance. Tupper himself was well pleased with Rickerby's efforts. In his autobiography (1886) he recalls that the publisher "produced a beautifully printed small folio volume with ornamental initials" which had since become "very scarce." The first edition is indeed a handsome book, though not much more so than any typical Rickerby product at this time. The printer prided himself on his craft: "All Works Published by J. Rickerby are printed at his Establishment, and under his immediate superintendence," he boasted in his advertisements.

An enlarged second edition of *Proverbial Philosophy* at a reduced price appeared the following October. A third edition failed to sell, and the greater part of this stock was shipped by Rickerby to the United States, where the Philadelphia publisher Herman Hooker was offering it for sale in 1842. The following year Tupper granted Hooker sole rights to publish *Proverbial Philosophy* in the United States, and the work quickly established itself there as standard middle-class family reading matter. Meanwhile, Rickerby had published other works by Tupper: *An Ode on the Coronation of Her Majesty, Queen Victoria, June 28, 1838* (1838); *Geraldine, a Sequel to Coleridge's Christabel: With Other Poems* (1838); and *A Modern Pyramid* (1839), a bizarre compilation of sonnets and essays on seventy historical characters. John Murray had rejected the latter work, but Rickerby brought it out after Tupper's mother paid the publication expenses as a birthday present for her son. Little interest was aroused by these productions. In 1841 Tupper, evidently disappointed at Rickerby's handling of the third edition of his bestseller, left him for Hatchard; a fourth edition of *Proverbial Philosophy* sold well under the new publisher.

Rickerby's 1839 list contained translations by Jonathan Duncan from French historical works by Felix Bodin, together with other works by Duncan on French history and his controversial *Religions of Profane Antiquity* (1838). There were biographies of Archbishop Sharp and Thomas Clarkson; a book on birds by St. John's son Percy; a five-act play, *Joan of Arc*, by Mrs. Jane Alice Sargant; and a *Grammar of Law*. Fiction was generally of the "improving" kind, and verse—for instance, Lady Emmeline Stuart Wortley's three-volume *Queen Berengaria's Courtesy* (1838)—was insipid.

Getting one novel from Agnes Strickland, the first volume of whose *Lives of the Queens of England* (1840-1848), written with her sister Elizabeth, had been so well received, was a minor coup for Rickerby; but *Alda: The British Captive* (1841) was essentially a potboiler and sold badly. Rickerby may have had high hopes also for *The Parlour Table Book* (1841), whose editor, Robert Aris Willmott, a mature student at Cambridge, was described by the *Gentleman's Magazine* as "a man of genius." Around April 1841 Rickerby appears to have stopped advertising in the trade journals, and it is likely that at about this time he gave up the publishing side of his business and concentrated on printing. There is evidence that Arthur Hall Virtue and Company bought up the unsold stock of Sacred Classics in the mid or late 1840s together with other Rickerby stock.

Rickerby died on 28 December 1850. The executor of his estate was his daughter, Mary Susannah, who within two years was printing under her own name at her late father's address. The business subsequently moved to Cannon Street, then to Walbrook. Mary Rickerby continued as a printer at 4a Walbrook until 1900.

**References:**

Derek Hudson, *Martin Tupper: His Rise and Fall* (London: Constable, 1949), pp. 23-27, 30, 59;

Una Pope-Hennessy, *Agnes Strickland* (London: Chatto & Windus, 1940), p. 103;

Martin F. Tupper, *My Life as an Author* (London: Low, Marston, Searle & Rivington, 1886), p. 113.

—*R. M. Healey*

# George Routledge and Sons
*(London: 1865-1889)*
# George Routledge
*(London: 1836-1848)*
# Routledge and Warne
*(London: 1848-1851)*
# Routledge and Company
*(London: 1851-1858)*
# Routledge, Warne and Routledge
*(London: 1858-1865)*
# George Routledge and Sons Limited
*(London: 1889-1947)*
# Routledge and Kegan Paul
*(London: 1947-1986)*
# Routledge
*(London: 1986-   )*

Born on 23 September 1812 in Brampton, Cumberland, George Routledge was fifteen when he was apprenticed to Charles Thurman, a Carlisle bookseller. After six years he asked Thurman to release him prematurely from his contract, and upon gaining his freedom he hastened to London to seek employment. He was hired as a shop assistant by the large publishing and wholesale firm of Baldwin, Craddock and Joy at 47 Paternoster Row. His new employers clearly thought well of him, as they increased his salary from sixty pounds to eighty pounds during the next three years and placed him in charge of the binding department. In 1836 the company's sales began to flag, and Routledge decided to venture out on his own.

To assist him in his newly acquired shop at 11 Ryder's Court, Leicester Square, he hired a promising fifteen-year-old, William Henry Warne, whose older sister, Maria Elizabeth, he married within the year. Apparently unable to support a wife on his income from selling books, he took on a full-time job at the Tithe Office in Somerset House, leaving Warne in charge of the bookshop.

With Warne managing the shop by day, Routledge could work evenings building his stock of publications, adding a line of stationery, and from time to time writing a book himself. In 1836 he wrote *The Beauties of Gilsland* to celebrate a spa near his native Brampton. The venture was a failure, but it taught him to be more patient before rushing into print.

In 1840 he shared publication costs with Baldwin, Craddock and Joy of a reprint of Maria Edgeworth's novel *Harry and Lucy*, but he soon realized that selling remainders from other firms was even more lucrative than sharing the cost of new works. The markup was minimal, but the volume of trade yielded big dividends, a lesson

Routledge learned early and which he practiced assiduously the rest of his life.

In 1843 Routledge combined his working and living premises at 36 Soho Square. At the same time he expanded his business by making frequent trips to booksellers in the North. In 1846 he published a series of pirated volumes that had immediate appeal and proved highly successful for many years: *Biblical Commentaries*, by an American, the Reverend Albert Barnes.

In 1848 Warne became a partner in the firm, and its name became Routledge and Warne. Three years later William's young brother, Frederick, was hired, and it was renamed Routledge and Company.

By the late 1840s publishers such as Bentley, Longmans, Murray, and Chapman and Hall had fewer remainders for Routledge to acquire because they no longer unloaded their slow-moving stock onto others but republished the works in cheaper editions themselves. Nevertheless, Routledge and a few others, such as Henry Bohn and David Bogue, were convinced that there were a great many readers who were unwilling or unable to spend even five or six shillings for a book, so they persisted in finding ways to attract customers with volumes costing just one shilling or eighteen pence.

Since the copyright of foreign works, especially American, was doubtful at best, Routledge considered these to be ideal additional sources of current literature. In the summer of 1848 he started the Railway Library, the first volume of which was *The Pilot*, by James Fenimore Cooper. Soon other volumes, mostly written by Americans, appeared at unprecedentedly low prices; seven of the first ten were by Cooper. As the series caught on, out-of-copyright British fiction began to appear. Eventually Routledge bargained with authors for permission to reprint their older works, and Jane Austen, G. P. R. James, W. Harrison Ainsworth, Frederick Marryat, and Benjamin Disraeli agreed.

When he inaugurated the Railway Library, Routledge could hardly have imagined the extent of its success. In 1848 W. H. Smith's first railway bookstall opened in Euston Station, and other outlets soon sprouted in stations throughout the country. As demand for titles in the series grew, Smith placed a standing order for one thousand copies of each new volume, ushering in the era of mass marketing.

In the years that followed Routledge published several library series: Routledge's Ameri-

*Cover for a "yellowback" novel: Richardson's seven-volume* Clarissa *(1747-1748), abridged by Mrs. Humphry Ward to one volume for Routledge's Railway Library*

can Poets, Routledge's Books for the Country, British Poets, Routledge's Cheap Series, Routledge's Standard Novels, Routledge's Popular Library, and Routledge's Useful Library. The Railway Library was the most successful, comprising nearly thirteen hundred titles when it concluded at the end of the century.

In February 1850 Bohn introduced his Shilling Series with Ralph Waldo Emerson's essay *Representative Men*. Routledge recognized the potential appeal of this book and, without qualms, included it in his new Popular Library series. Bohn retaliated by printing Washington Irving's *Life of Mahomet* (1851), which Routledge had already announced, signaling open warfare between the two pirates. Neither was deterred by warnings from John Murray and Richard Bentley that their copyrights in these works were being infringed flagrantly. Murray and Bentley decided to take legal recourse and began gathering evidence by sending clerks to bookshops to purchase the disputed reprints. In August 1850 Murray applied to the Court of Chancery for an injunction to stop the pirates; but the court ruled that there were too many disputed facts in the case, so the abuse continued.

While the case was pending in a Court of Queen's Bench, a similar copyright infringement case involving two music publishers, *Boosey v. Jefferys*, was being heard by a Court of Error. The court ruled in favor of Boosey, declaring that a foreigner could secure a valid copyright in England provided that the work appeared there first. After this judgment was handed down, Routledge immediately settled with Murray and Bentley out of court, agreeing to refrain from reprinting the works in question, to destroy the stereotype plates, to turn over existing stock, and to cover Murray's legal costs.

In 1852 an unprecedented number of uncopyrighted reprints of Harriet Beecher Stowe's *Uncle Tom's Cabin* appeared. Twenty British firms published the novel in forty different editions, and Routledge printed versions ranging in price from sixpence to six shillings. He sold more than half a million copies, a publishing record.

Routledge did well with books by other American authors also. Most were piracies, but a few writers received compensation for permitting early access to their works. The race to reprint and flood the market with copies before the competition could enter the field was constant. For example, Routledge secured an advance copy of *Queechy* (1852), by Susan Warner (pseudonym of Elizabeth Wetherell), on a Monday morning; by keeping the presses going night and day he produced 20,000 copies, which were bound and rushed into the hands of booksellers in one week. Eventually 100,000 copies were sold.

The year 1852 was memorable for Routledge not only because of the publication of *Uncle Tom's Cabin* but also because he acquired larger business premises at 2 Farringdon Street. His recognition that continuing prosperity could not rest entirely on American reprints forced him to undertake in December 1853 what many regarded as a foolhardy speculation in contemporary English novels. He arranged with Sir Edward Bulwer-Lytton for the inclusion of nineteen of his novels in the Railway Library for a period of ten years. For this concession Routledge offered Bulwer-Lytton twenty thousand pounds. Until then only major firms such as Longmans

had dealt in such large sums. Routledge was gambling heavily on reviving the novelist's popularity through quantity sales, and the strategy worked. Each year thereafter Routledge and Bulwer-Lytton renewed their agreement, with an increment of one thousand pounds.

In 1854 the *Boosey* decision was reversed by the House of Lords. Prior or simultaneous publication was declared insufficient to ensure copyright; only if a foreign author *resided* in Britain while his or her work was being published would copyright be secure. The decision touched off a renewed scramble for popular American titles and conferred upon Routledge a competitive advantage, since he had specialized in cheap American reprints for many years and could acquire easily almost anything he wanted. Bentley, on the other hand, realized that he would be deprived of a thousand pounds a year from his American list.

The repercussions within the book trade were felt by both authors and publishers. For example, the books of William Hickling Prescott, which had been published by Bentley, were suddenly pirated by Routledge, forcing Bentley to lower his prices. Prescott had played these two publishers off against each other, raising the bidding to £1,000 per volume for advance sheets of his projected five-volume work about Philip II of Spain; but once the 1854 copyright decision went into effect, Routledge and Bentley reduced their offers to £500 and £125 per volume, respectively. *History of the Reign of Philip II* was published in three volumes by Bentley from 1855 to 1859 and by Routledge from 1856 to 1866. Prescott had to accept the same reduction for his two volumes on Charles V (1857). Outbid, Bentley sold all his interest in Prescott to Routledge for £2,600. Routledge's transition from piratical reprinter to Prescott's authorized London publisher may appear bizarre, but it was by no means unique in the Victorian book trade.

In 1854 Routledge opened a branch office in New York City in order to have better access to new American works as well as to distribute his own publications in the United States. On one of his trips to America he persuaded Henry Wadsworth Longfellow to allow his poem *Evangeline* (1856) to be used in an illustrated edition with drawings by Sir John Gilbert and woodcuts by the Dalziel brothers. The idea proved so successful that it became the model for Routledge's future Christmas gift books. Routledge's output of American works included *Routledge's American Hand-Book and Tourist's Guide*

*Cover for the Routledge republication in one volume of Disraeli's 1845 three-volume novel*

(1854), William Edward Baxter's *America and the Americans* (1855), a collected set of George Bancroft's *History of the United States* (1860-1861), and John Lothrop Motley's *Rise of the Dutch Republic* (1861).

Routledge's wife, the mother of his eight children, died in 1855. Three years later he married Mary Grace Bell, with whom he had two more children. Also in 1858 Robert Warne Routledge became a partner in his father's firm at the age of twenty-one, and its name was altered to Routledge, Warne and Routledge. The following year William Warne died.

On the death of Sir Robert Peel in 1850 the firm had rushed into print a hastily prepared biography. Two years later the Duke of Wellington had been similarly honored. Routledge had collected the wartime newspaper dispatches of William Howard Russell into a book titled *History of the Crimean War* (1855), which sold twenty thousand copies. He did the same with Russell's account of the Indian Mutiny of 1857, which was published as *My Diary in India* (1859).

Routledge introduced *Every Boy's Magazine* in January 1862. Initially edited by Routledge's son Edmund, it was intended to raise the tone of children's periodicals without sacrificing their appeal. It flourished for twenty-eight years and was imitated, although less successfully, by *Every Girl's Annual* (1878-1888).

In the 1850s and 1860s Routledge was in the vanguard of those exploiting the illustrated publications genre. He commissioned the four Dalziel brothers and other engravers to decorate a series of volumes, including the works of Shakespeare and books on natural history and rural delights. In 1859, when Edward Moxon's deluxe and costly illustrated edition of Alfred Tennyson's poems was languishing in bookshops, Routledge purchased the remainders and made an agreement with the author to reduce the selling price; the rest of the books were then quickly sold. He promoted collaboration between the artist Walter Crane and the color printer Edmund Evans, resulting in Crane's colorful pictures appearing in children's stories and poetry and in "yellowbacks" in bookshops and railway stalls.

In 1864 the firm's premises in Farringdon Street were taken for railway expansion, and new premises were opened at 7 Broadway, Ludgate Hill. In 1865 Edmund Routledge came into the partnership. The name of the firm then became George Routledge and Sons, which may have precipitated the departure of Frederick Warne.

In 1854 Routledge and others had freely reprinted Maria Cummins's first novel, *The Lamplighter*, and Routledge had sold more than 100,000 copies in two months. When her second novel, *Haunted Hearts*, made its appearance in 1864, Routledge did not hesitate to reprint it. In 1868, Sampson Low, the authorized London publisher, objected, claiming that the book was entitled to copyright protection because Cummins had been residing temporarily in Canada when the book appeared. Routledge challenged this interpretation, but the House of Lords agreed with Low, declaring that a foreigner could indeed secure a valid copyright if temporarily resident within the British Empire at the time of publication. As before, Routledge moved quickly to take advantage of the new provision in the law: he persuaded Longfellow to remain in England after receiving an honorary degree from Cambridge Uni-

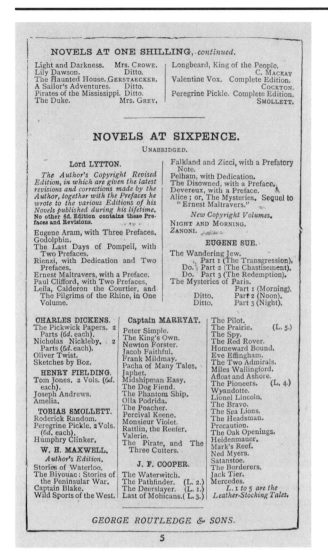

NOVELS AT ONE SHILLING, *continued*.

Light and Darkness. Mrs. CROWE.
Lily Dawson. Ditto.
The Haunted House. GERSTAECKER.
A Sailor's Adventures. Ditto.
Pirates of the Mississippi. Ditto.
The Duke. Mrs. GREY.

Longbeard, King of the People.
C. MACKAY.
Valentine Vox. Complete Edition.
COCKTON.
Peregrine Pickle. Complete Edition.
SMOLLETT.

### NOVELS AT SIXPENCE.
UNABRIDGED.

**Lord LYTTON.**

*The Author's Copyright Revised Edition, in which are given the latest revisions and corrections made by the Author, together with the Prefaces he wrote to the various Editions of his Novels published during his lifetime. No other 6d. Edition contains these Prefaces and Revisions.*

Eugene Aram, with Three Prefaces.
Godolphin.
The Last Days of Pompeii, with Two Prefaces.
Rienzi, with Dedication and Two Prefaces.
Ernest Maltravers, with a Preface.
Paul Clifford, with Two Prefaces.
Leila, Calderon the Courtier, and The Pilgrims of the Rhine, in One Volume.

Falkland and Zicci, with a Prefatory Note.
Pelham, with Dedication.
The Disowned, with a Preface.
Devereux, with a Preface.
Alice ; or, The Mysteries. Sequel to "Ernest Maltravers."
*New Copyright Volumes.*
NIGHT AND MORNING.
ZANONI.

**EUGENE SUE.**

The Wandering Jew.
Part 1 (The Transgression).
Do. Part 2 (The Chastisement).
Do. Part 3 (The Redemption).
The Mysteries of Paris.
Part 1 (Morning).
Ditto. Part 2 (Noon).
Ditto. Part 3 (Night).

**CHARLES DICKENS.**
The Pickwick Papers. 2 Parts (6d. each).
Nicholas Nickleby. 2 Parts (6d. each).
Oliver Twist.
Sketches by Boz.
**HENRY FIELDING.**
Tom Jones. 2 Vols. (6d. each).
Joseph Andrews.
Amelia.
**TOBIAS SMOLLETT.**
Roderick Random.
Peregrine Pickle. 2 Vols. (6d. each).
Humphry Clinker.
**W. H. MAXWELL.**
*Author's Edition.*
Stories of Waterloo.
The Bivouac ; Stories of the Peninsular War.
Captain Blake.
Wild Sports of the West.

**Captain MARRYAT.**
Peter Simple.
The King's Own.
Newton Forster.
Jacob Faithful.
Frank Mildmay.
Pacha of Many Tales.
Japhet.
Midshipman Easy.
The Dog Fiend.
The Phantom Ship.
Olla Podrida.
The Poacher.
Percival Keene.
Monsieur Violet.
Rattlin, the Reefer.
Valerie.
The Pirate, and The Three Cutters.

**J. F. COOPER.**
The Waterwitch.
The Pathfinder. (L. 2.)
The Deerslayer. (L. 1.)
Last of Mohicans.( L. 3.)

The Pilot.
The Prairie. (L. 5.)
The Spy.
The Red Rover.
Homeward Bound.
Eve Effingham.
The Two Admirals.
Miles Wallingford.
Afloat and Ashore.
The Pioneers. (L. 4.)
Wyandotte.
Lionel Lincoln.
The Bravo.
The Sea Lions.
The Headsman.
Precaution.
The Oak Openings.
Heidenmauer.
Mark's Reef.
Ned Myers.
Satanstoe.
The Borderers.
Jack Tier.
Mercedes.
*L. 1 to 5 are the Leather-Stocking Tales.*

*GEORGE ROUTLEDGE & SONS.*

5

*An endpaper advertisement for some of the novels in Routledge's various series*

versity so that his *New England Tragedies* (1868) could be published in London before appearing in America. As an inducement Routledge offered him a thousand pounds.

During the 1870s Routledge discovered the talents of younger artists such as Randolph Caldecott and Kate Greenaway; the latter's *Under the Window*, a book of nonsense verse with her own illustrations, became an overnight sensation when it appeared in 1879. The same success was accorded her *Almanack* for 1883, of which Routledge sold 100,000 copies; the *Almanack* was published annually until 1895.

As long as George Routledge was actively involved in the operations of the firm it never strayed far from the formula that had made his

fortune: cheap reprints. In 1878 he acquired and reprinted the entire stock of Chapman and Hall's two-shilling edition of the works of Charles Dickens. In 1883 he inaugurated Morley's Universal Library, well-printed volumes of four hundred pages representing the classics of many nations and epochs. Priced at one shilling, they were a far more serious and weighty foray into cheap literature than he had made thus far. Edited by Henry Morley, the series continued until 1888.

Toward the end of the 1880s the firm's founder began to spend more and more time in his beloved Cumberland and less running the business. While still coming to the office regularly, he increasingly enjoyed the role of a country squire, adding land to his estate and serving alternately as a justice of the peace, deputy lieutenant, and high sheriff. In 1887 he retired amid congratulatory banquets and tributes. Fifty years in trade had resulted in a total output of about five thousand titles, an average of two volumes each week. On 12 December 1888 he died in the house at 50 Russell Square in London where he and his family had lived for many years. He left an estate worth more than eighty thousand pounds in addition to extensive real estate holdings. His sons Robert and Edmund succeeded to the business.

The following year the firm became a limited liability company and moved its premises to Broadway House, 68-74 Carter Lane. As often happens, the second generation lacked the ambition and the ruthlessness of the founder and allowed the business to slide along well-worn grooves, rarely experimenting with new or original publications. In 1892, however, they initiated a popular reprint series based on Sir John Lubbock's list of the "Hundred Best Books," publishing one handsome volume every fortnight until the set was complete in 1896. Since no one with literary pretensions agreed with the selections on Lubbock's list, controversy generated effective publicity and advertising. This success encouraged the two Routledge sons to authorize for themselves annual salaries of ten thousand pounds each, and in 1899 the firm had to declare bankruptcy. The older son, Robert, resigned, intending to establish himself as a literary agent; but he died in July. His brother Edmund died the following September.

Rudderless and in receivership, George Routledge and Sons Limited was adrift until 1902, when it attracted the attention of several investors. Chief among them was Arthur E.

Franklin, a partner in the merchant banking firm of A. Keyser and Company. Literary by inclination but lacking experience in publishing, Franklin recruited an impressive board of directors for a revived George Routledge and Sons Limited. One of these was William Swan Sonnenschein, who had owned his own publishing house, Swan Sonnenschein and Company, from the age of twenty-three. At the turn of the century he had been forced to retire and had sold most of his copyrights to George Allen. Another investor with publishing experience was the thirty-year-old Laurie Magnus, son the educational authority Philip Magnus; Laurie Magnus had worked in the educational department of John Murray. Magnus and Sonnenschein became joint managing directors, with Franklin as chairman of the board. The fourth director was Sir William Crookes, a chemist and psychic researcher.

With this infusion of new capital and energy, the firm began to expand. In 1903 it purchased the remaining stock and copyrights of the John C. Nimmo Company, a publisher of fine texts and bindings since 1879. In 1911 it took over the management of Kegan Paul, Trench, Trübner Limited. The two companies were run separately, with separate boards and accounts, until 1947. Its control of Kegan Paul enabled Routledge to expand its offerings in fields such as science, technology, and literature and to cover the full range of publications from the cheapest and most ephemeral to the scholarly and highly sophisticated.

Among the key individuals guiding the firm prior to World War I was Franklin's son Cecil, who came to Routledge as an apprentice in 1906 and was made third joint managing director in 1912. He provided continuity for both the Routledge and the Kegan Paul operations until well after World War II.

World War I caused considerable dislocation to the Routledge and Kegan Paul firms. Staff was in short supply, as was paper. The stereotype plates of many cheap series were melted down and contributed to the war effort. Ironically, at the same time there was a huge demand by the armed services for inexpensive reprints. Accumulated stock disappeared and could not be replaced.

Like many other commodities, the price of books rose considerably after the war due to the need to manufacture new plates, hire staff, and replenish stock. Changes in procedure and personnel were inevitable, and one of the most signifi-

*Edmund Evans, the unrivaled color engraver-printer of the nineteenth century, who produced his first cover for a Routledge "yellowback" in 1854*

cant was the arrival in 1921 of C. K. Ogden, a socialist and pacifist bookseller from Cambridge. After he joined the editorial staff several new series were inaugurated, starting in 1922 with the International Library of Psychology, Philosophy and Scientific Method. G. E. Moore's *Philosophical Studies* became volume 1 with *The Misuse of Mind* (1922), by Karin Stephen, as volume 2. Ludwig Wittgenstein's *Tractatus Logico-Philosophicus* (1922) eventually enjoyed a towering reputation among philosophers. All of the books in the series were published under the Kegan Paul imprint; they numbered about 120 in the mid 1930s and 150 at the time of Ogden's death in 1957.

The year 1923 introduced a provocative series of pamphlets called To-day and To-morrow, costing only twelve and a half pence each. The initial volume was *Daedalus; or, Science and the Future*, by J. B. S. Haldane; the second was a rejoinder by Bertrand Russell called *Icarus; or, The Future of Science* (1924). Subsequent titles included Anthony Ludovici's *Lysistrata; or, Woman's*

*Future and Future Woman* (1924), Basil H. Liddell Hart's *Paris; or, The Future of War* (1925), and John C. F. Fuller's *Pegasus; or, Problems of Transport* (1926). This series also carried the Kegan Paul imprint and by the mid 1930s had grown to one hundred titles. Another series, begun by Ogden in 1924, was History of Civilization. It included works of history, anthropology, archaeology, and sociology with a worldwide perspective.

Ogden's distinctive contribution to publishing history was later noted by Frederic J. Warburg: "The value of Ogden to Kegan Paul was immense. He put them among the most important publishers of the day in the wide fields of psychology, theoretical and practical philosophy, ethics, psycho-pathology, educational theory, and scientific method." Lord Zuckerman added: "Ogden, as has been said by many, had a superhuman capacity for absorbing information and ideas, and I suppose that he read everything for whose publications he became the middleman. I used to feel that what was not widely appreciated was how splendid a midwife he was to unsuspecting authors who were mildly pregnant with ideas which could develop into a book."

The postwar years brought changes in management. Crookes died in 1919. Warburg, a former artillery officer and Oxford graduate, joined Routledge in 1923; in 1929 he was made joint managing director with Cecil Franklin. Sonnenschein died in January 1931, and Laurie Magnus in April 1933. That summer Arthur Franklin retired as chairman and was replaced by Major General Sir Frederick Maurice, who was well known as president of the British Legion and principal of East London College.

As in other sectors of the economy, the early 1930s proved a time of hardship in the book trade. Not only did the Great Depression take its toll on George Routledge and Son but a difference in personal style divided Warburg and Franklin. The former was younger and inclined to be more experimental, while the latter had grown cautious. Warburg expressed his frustration with the firm's old-fashioned ways: "The 'pony-and-trap' period of English publishing, virtually unchanged for fifty years or more, had been superceded by the 'automobile' epoch. Chief among the internal combustion engines was Victor Gollancz, with a very high horsepower. With the foundation of his firm in 1928, the revolution may be said to have begun. Then we saw the shape of things to come. Instead of the dignified advertisement list of twenty titles

*Cover for a novel by the American author Maria Cummins, republished without permission or compensation in 1854 by Routledge's Railway Library. Such legal "piracy" was common at the time because of the absence of Anglo-American copyright.*

set out primly in a modest space, there was the double or triple column, with the title of one book screaming across it in letters three inches high ... [Gollancz's] competitors did not lag far behind. Hutchinson, Hodder and Heinemann, Cassell, Chatto, and Constable, beat the big drum in an ever more shattering tattoo. Amid all the clatter, how could the quiet whisper of a Routledge advertisement, the gentle nudge of a Routledge promotion, be heard or felt by an over-stimulated public?" For his part, Franklin was content to continue exploiting traditional markets for books such as *Heaton's Ready Reckoner*, *The Ideal Cookery Book*, and Hoyle's *Games*; he felt that Warburg often promoted unsalable books. In 1934 the younger partner departed and bought the firm of Martin Secker, converting it into Secker and Warburg. He was replaced as a director by Thomas Murray Ragg, who was formerly with

Putnam and Company Limited. Another recruit from Putnam's was John G. Carter, who became sales manager.

When George Routledge and Sons finally decided to try some of the newer business practices being adopted in the trade, it began by engaging the well-known author and prolific novelist Georges Simenon, creator of Inspector Jules Maigret. But Simenon had been counting on at least six of his books appearing each year, whereas Routledge published only two or three; the misunderstanding led to a parting of the ways in 1954. Despite such efforts to become more competitive, Routledge's balance sheet between 1929 and 1944 never showed a profit.

The Second World War, like the First, stimulated production and sales as long as a large enough paper quota could be obtained. Responding to Gollancz's Left Book Club, Routledge introduced its own Labour series in 1939. Balancing this political slant, Karl Popper's *The Open Society and Its Enemies* appeared in 1945.

The year 1945 was Routledge's first profitable year since the onset of the depression. The firm was able to pay a dividend to its shareholders, and with a steadily improving financial outlook it was decided that the time had come to merge formally with Kegan Paul and cease to maintain two offices and imprints. Thus, in 1947 the firm became Routledge and Kegan Paul, retaining its headquarters at 68-74 Carter Lane. Franklin continued as chairman and was joined in 1949 by his son Norman.

In postwar Europe and America there was a surge in demand for university-level books when veterans resumed their educations. Routledge and Kegan Paul, with its strong tradition of publishing works in the social and behavior sciences, took a commanding lead in these areas. Paperbacks were generally accepted by this time, and beginning in 1958 more and more Routledge titles appeared in this form.

Cecil Franklin's death in 1961 brought Carter to the chairmanship; his demise in 1966 thrust Norman Franklin into the position. His first major decision dealt with the need for more spacious quarters because the business had far outgrown its premises in Carter Lane. A new warehouse at Henley-on-Thames was paid for by taking the company public. Shares were issued in 1967, allowing for the removal of half a million volumes from Carter Lane to Henley in 1968.

Financial problems persisted, however, and in 1969 the firm again found itself short of cash.

This time it turned to the American publisher Crowell, Collier and Macmillan, which acquired £350,000 of convertible loan stock, equivalent to a twenty-five percent share of the company, and one seat on the Routledge board of directors. The plan allowed for the reacquisition of shares as Routledge's financial position improved, and this occurred in 1974.

One of the results of this cooperation was the recognition that the American market was too important for Routledge and Kegan Paul not to have a branch office in the United States: among other things, American higher education was emphasizing the social sciences. After exploring the scene personally, Norman Franklin decided to make 9 Park Street in Boston the entrepôt for Routledge and Kegan Paul publications. Subsequent foreign sales figured so prominently in the balance sheet that a Routledge and Kegan Paul representative was designated for Australia in 1980. Later the American office moved to 25 West 35th Street, New York.

The 1970s witnessed a revival of several Ogden-style ventures: a new International Library of Philosophy, edited by A. J. Ayer, and the republication of old standbys such as Eric Partridge's *Dictionary of Slang*, which reached its eighth edition in 1984. Routledge and Kegan Paul even boasted a best-seller in 1979: Stephen Pile's *Book of Heroic Failures*. That same year profits began to slide. The company had spent heavily to computerize itself in 1974; and in 1976 the rent at Carter Lane had increased tenfold, forcing a move of the editorial offices to 39 Store Street in Bloomsbury.

Efforts to improve the firm's financial position in the early 1980s centered on innovation. Since seventy percent of its output was already in paperback form, it introduced a lower-priced line called ARK Paperbacks. This line was followed by Arkana Books, which featured all aspects of the "mind, body and spirit." In 1983 Pandora, an imprint dealing with women's issues, was launched under the leadership of Philippa Brewster. In spite of these measures Routledge and Kegan Paul's deficit for 1983-1984 was £119,000, reflecting the rising cost of book production and declining sales. Outside members were added to the board of directors, Philip Sturrock was appointed new managing director, and stringent economies were imposed. These steps produced a profit of £400,000 for the 1984-1985 financial year, which made the firm a tempting "takeover" target. In April 1985 the publishing conglomer-

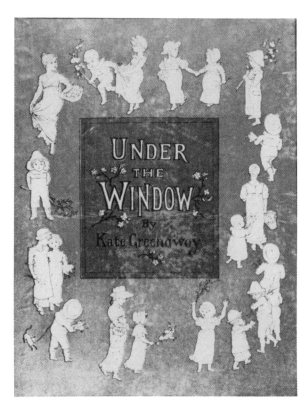

*The illustrator Kate Greenaway (top), her hugely successful 1879 book of nonsense verse (bottom left), and some of her almanacs (bottom right)*

ate Associated Book Publishers (ABP) acquired Routledge and Kegan Paul.

Associated Book Publishers had begun in 1954 as a scheme to merge publishing houses of different types and traditions to achieve efficiencies of warehousing, marketing, and sales. By the 1980s ABP comprised an impressive and varied group: Methuen was known for its educational and general trade books; Chapman and Hall for academic selections; Tavistock for sociology; and Sweet and Maxwell for law. The conglomerate also included Stevens and Company, Spon, and W. Green. Within about a year of acquiring Routledge and Kegan Paul, Associated Book Publishers found itself short of cash. In a reorganization it sold the Routledge imprint to the Thompson newspaper empire. Kegan Paul survived as a partly owned subsidiary of ABP, run by Peter Hopkins, publishing books mainly on Arabian subjects for the Middle Eastern market.

Routledge has retained a strong reputation for academic publishing. Its linguistics list includes titles formerly associated with Routledge and Kegan Paul, Croom Helm, and Methuen. It continues to publish significant research and textbooks in ancient history, literature, and philosophy, as well as books of broader appeal in archaeology. Since 1988 Routledge has published and distributed books on social work and social policy, including media, culture, film, gender studies, politics, international business, marketing, industrial relations, management information systems, and economics. Separate lists represent the behavioral sciences, geography, development studies, the Middle East, and general literature. Thus, it is no idle boast that "Routledge is now one of the largest international academic publishers and this status has brought significant power in the market place."

Routledge moved its editorial offices to 14 Leicester Square in 1984 and to 11 New Fetter Lane in 1986. Its chairman, Franklin, retired in 1988 at the age of sixty.

**References:**

James J. Barnes, *Authors, Publishers and Politicians: The Quest for an Anglo-American Copyright Agreement, 1815-54* (London: Routledge & Kegan Paul, 1974);

P. Sargant Florence, ed., *C. K. Ogden: A Collective Memoir* (London: Elek, 1977);

Norman Franklin, *150 Years of British Publishing: Routledge & Kegan Paul* (London: Routledge & Kegan Paul, 1985);

Gillian Furlong, comp., *The Archives of Routledge & Kegan Paul Ltd., 1853-1973* (London: University College Library, 1978);

Frank A. Mumby, *The House of Routledge & Sons Ltd., 1834-1934* (London: Routledge, 1934);

Fredric Warburg, *An Occupation for Gentlemen* (Boston: Houghton Mifflin, 1959).

*—James J. Barnes and Patience P. Barnes*

# Saunders and Otley
## (London: 1826-1859)
# Saunders and Otley and Company
## (London: 1859-1871)

Saunders and Otley, "Public library and booksellers," 50 Conduit Street, Hanover Square, was in the second rank of Victorian publishers. Although well over half the firm's books were nonfiction, drama, or poetry, it published novels by such popular writers as Edward Bulwer, Frederick Marryat, and G. P. R. James. William Saunders and his partner Edward John Otley bought the Conduit Street library from Henry Colburn in 1824. They published their first five books in 1826, followed by four in 1827. Respected, if somewhat cautious businessmen, by 1829 they were publishing works such as *Hungarian Tales*, by the popular "silver fork" novelist Mrs. Catherine Gore, followed by her *Polish Tales* in 1833. In 1835-1836 they published four editions of a newly edited eight-volume *Life and Works* of the poet William Cowper. In 1836 they were responsible for an early experiment in publishing a novellike work in cheap (two shillings, sixpence) numbers: Bulwer's *Pilgrims of the Rhine* (first published in 1834)—a travel book with digressive tales on the order of Charles Dickens's *Pickwick Papers* (published by Chapman and Hall in 1836-1837).

A previous venture with Bulwer-Lytton had been *A Letter to a Late Cabinet Minister on the Present Crisis* (1834), which sold ninety thousand copies in at least six editions, some by other publishers. In 1835 Saunders and Otley published Bulwer's historical romance *Rienzi*. His popularity in the 1830s may be judged by his *Athens: Its Rise and Fall* (1837): Saunders and Otley published the first and nineteenth (1887) editions. The eighteen titles Saunders and Otley ultimately published for Bulwer included fiction, nonfiction, drama, and poetry. The firm's ten-volume edition of Bulwer works appeared in 1840. Bulwer may also have been responsible for Saunders and Otley's publication of Lady Blessington's novel *Two Friends* (1835), followed by her *Victims of Society* (1837).

After Bulwer, the highly respected Mrs. Anna Jameson appears most frequently on Saunders and Otley's lists for the 1830s and 1840s. Her *Characteristics of Women* (1832) was reprinted at least seven times by 1858. Between 1834 and 1844 the firm published eight or nine of her works on art, travel, and women's lives. Among the latter were the second (1834) and third (1840) editions of *Memoirs of Celebrated Female Sovereigns*, *Winter Studies and Summer Rambles in Canada* (1838), and *Companion to Private Picture Galleries* (1844).

In 1834 Harriet Martineau helped her friend Anne Caldwell Marsh get *The Two Old Men's Tales*, the hit of the season, published by Saunders and Otley. Martineau had become a celebrity in 1832-1834 with her *Illustrations of Political Economy*, published by Charles Fox. She had then sailed off to tour the United States for two years, and when she returned to London, Saunders was one of three publishers who arrived on her doorstep to ask for a book on America. Martineau liked Saunders, but he at first declined to offer her terms. Martineau tells the episode in her *Autobiography* (1877): "So I sat strenuously looking into the fire,—Mr. Saunders no less strenuously looking at me, till it was all I could do to keep my countenance. . . . he at last opened his lips. 'What would you think, Ma'am, of £900 for the first edition? . . . Including twenty-five copies of the work, and all proceeds of the sale in America over and above expenses.' " Martineau was satisfied with those terms for *Society in America* (1837). For a sequel, *Retrospect of Western Travel* (1838), Saunders offered her £600 plus twenty-five copies. Martineau's high reputation warranted outright purchase of the copyright to her books, with all British proceeds going to Saunders and Otley. Martineau later objected to Saunders's request for notes to her critic friends asking for favorable reviews, but she continued to think well of the firm.

Saunders and Otley set up a New York office at 45 Ann Street under the management of William Saunders's son Frederick in 1836. The object of the branch was to publish American editions under the Saunders and Otley imprint before they could be pirated by American publish-

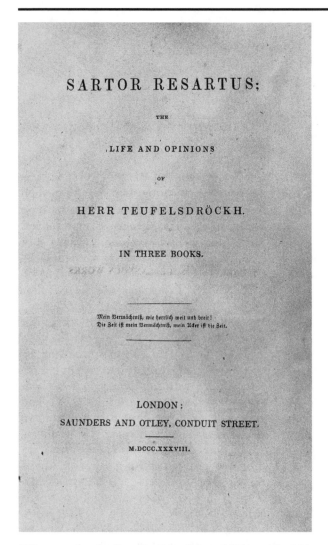

SARTOR RESARTUS;

THE

LIFE AND OPINIONS

OF

HERR TEUFELSDRÖCKH.

IN THREE BOOKS.

Mein Vermächtniß, wie herrlich weit und breit!
Die Zeit ist mein Vermächtniß, mein Acker ist die Zeit.

LONDON:
SAUNDERS AND OTLEY, CONDUIT STREET.

M.DCCC.XXXVIII.

*Title page for the first English edition of Thomas Carlyle's philosophical satire. Carlyle was not happy with the appearance of the book or with Saunders and Otley's distribution of it.*

ers. From his bookshop—which became a meeting place for such distinguished American authors as N. P. Willis, Theodore Fay, George Morris, Edgar Allan Poe, and William Cullen Bryant—Frederick Saunders launched the first organized movement for an international copyright. On 6 June 1836 an announcement in the *New York Evening Post* stated that Saunders and Otley would deliver its new books in New York at the same time as in London. Advertisements referred to Saunders and Otley as the "only authorized publishers" of its books. In the first test case, Harper and Brothers pirated Saunders and Otley's *Memoirs* (1836) of Prince Lucien Bonaparte. When Frederick Saunders protested publicly, Harper defied him, claiming the right to publish cheaper books. In a similar case, Saunders and Otley published James Grant's *The Great*

*Metropolis* in January 1837 at £1.50. Before Saunders and Otley could market Grant's work in the United States the American publisher T. Foster put out a pirated edition, with added notes, at fifty cents.

A petition for an international copyright law, prepared by Martineau and Saunders and Otley and signed by fifty-six authors (including Robert Southey, Thomas Moore, and Samuel Rogers) was presented by Henry Clay to the United States Congress on 2 February 1837. This petition, as well as at least six others (one conveyed by Dickens), and appeals by American authors headed by Washington Irving, George Bancroft, and Bryant failed to bring about an international copyright law owing to the recalcitrance of American publishers. Frederick Saunders's expenses during the campaign for international copyright were supplied by the London firm, which finally abandoned its New York branch office. Frederick Saunders then continued as an independent bookseller and publisher.

In 1838 Thomas Carlyle made a "half-profits" deal with Saunders and Otley to publish five hundred copies of *Sartor Resartus*. The book came out on 21 July, advertising Carlyle's miscellaneous works to follow. Carlyle described this first English edition of *Sartor Resartus* in book form as "one of the shabbiest . . . printed by Clowes in the cheap fashion my Conduit St men are used to." Carlyle admitted, however, that Saunders and Otley "comport themselves with vast civility" and were "more reputable" than Fraser, his original publisher. In the event, Saunders and Otley did not bring out Carlyle's miscellaneous works, and he soon complained about their failure to distribute copies of *Sartor Resartus* to Edinburgh. In 1840 Saunders and Otley offered Carlyle fifty pounds for an edition of 750 copies of his review articles. The offer was not accepted, and by February 1841 Carlyle was referring to Saunders and Otley as "Blockheads" for threatening him over rights to a second edition of *Sartor Resartus*.

Saunders and Otley brought out a half-dozen or more titles each by the well-known writers Marryat and James. After reprinting Marryat's popular *Peter Simple* in 1833, the firm published *Jacob Faithful* (1834) and *Mr. Midshipman Easy* (1836), as well as *The Floral Telegraph: A New Mode of Communication by Floral Signals, with Plates* (1836). The commercial worth of Marryat's books is evident from Saunders and Otley's payment of twelve hundred pounds for *Mr. Midshipman Easy* and from the firm's later sale of his copyrights. For Bentley's Standard Novels series, Saunders and Otley at first asked five hundred pounds for each Marryat title they controlled. After negotiating with Otley, however, Bentley's chief clerk got seven of Marryat's titles for fifteen hundred pounds.

Like Marryat, James was a former military man who turned to writing. Influenced by Sir Walter Scott, he wrote popular histories and historical romances. Of James's seven titles Saunders and Otley published, two show the partners' interest in promoting useful and informative works: *On the Educational Institutions of Germany* (1835) and *A Brief History of the United States Boundary Question* (1839).

While the popular American poet and journalist Willis was working in London, Saunders and Otley brought out two of his books: *Melanie, Lord Ivon and His Daughters, and other Poems* (1835) and *Inklings of Adventure* (1836) a collection of articles written under the pseudonym Philip Slingsby. Willis also contributed to Saunders and Otley's *Metropolitan Magazine* under the same pseudonym.

Perhaps owing to their conservatism, Saunders and Otley often ended by publishing only one or two works by the better-known writers of fiction, drama, poetry, or nonfiction with whom they had dealings; the multiple titles by Marryat, James, Bulwer-Lytton, and Jameson are exceptions. In addition to the two novels by Lady Blessington, they published just single works by Leticia Elizabeth Landon (L. E. L.): *Vow of the Peacock, and Other Poems* (1835); William Hazlitt: *Literary Remains* (1836); H. F. Chorley: *Memorials of Mrs. Hemans* (1836); and Mary Shelley: *Falkner* (1837). By the well-known Lady Charlotte Bury they published *Suspirum Sanctorum; or, Holy Breathings* (1826) and *Family Records; or, The Two Sisters* (1841); and by Mrs. Catherine Crowe: *Susan Hopley* (1841) and *Men and Women; or, Manorial Rights* (1844). Saunders and Otley published two blank-verse tragedies by R. H. Horne: *The Death of Marlowe* (1837) and *Gregory VII* (1840).

From 1832 to 1847 Saunders and Otley published the *Metropolitan Magazine: A Monthly Journal of Literature, Science & the Fine Arts*, which featured nautical fiction. Marryat was the magazine's editor and proprietor from 1832 to 1836; Saunders and Otley bought his interest for £1,050 in 1836. In an 1839 advertisement for the magazine, Saunders and Otley claimed that it had published "all the Popular Novels of Captain Marryat, as well as many productions of the first

*Elaborate binding for an 1837 edition of the sea novels of Frederick Marryat ( from Michael Sadleir's 1937 Sandars lectures, "Aspects of the Victorian Novel," Publishing History, 5 [1979]: 7-47)*

writers of the day. . . . Articles in Prose and Verse by Thomas Campbell, Esq., and Thomas Moore, Esq., Papers by Sir Charles and Lady Morgan [and] a vast variety of Original Articles, Critical Notices, Reviews, Papers on the Fine Arts, Literature, The Drama, &c. &c."

The 1839 advertisement appeared in *The Author's Printing and Publishing Assistant*. Aimed at beginning authors, the slender volume explains the process of printing; preparation and calculation of manuscripts; choice of paper, type, and binding; illustrations; publishing; and advertising. It also explains the typographical marks used for corrections. Saunders and Otley must have hoped to encourage authors to send them their manuscripts; thirty-six pages are devoted to advertising their books. The list includes nine works by Bulwer-Lytton, seven by Marryat, four by Mrs. Jameson, two by Martineau, and four by James Grant; memoirs by Lord Burghley, the Marquis de Lafayette, Prince Lucien Bonaparte, Lord Herbert of Cherbury, Sir Kennelme Digby, and Lord Liverpool; fourteen works of travel; William Hazlitt's *Remains* (1836); the third edition of

Alexis De Tocqueville's *Democracy in America* (1838), translated by Henry Reeve; Friedrich von Schlegel's *Philosophy of History* (1835), translated by J. H. Robertson; *The Naval Service; or, Officer's Manual* (1836), by Capt. W. N. Glascock; *The Poetry of Life* (1835), by Sarah Stickney; *Citation and Examination of William Shakespeare for Deer Stealing* (1834) and *Pericles and Aspasia* (1836), by Walter Savage Landor; and *The Ancient Ballad of Chevy Chase* (1836). Popular books on flowers and birds include *Floral Emblems* (1825), by Henry Philips; *The Language of Flowers* (1834), revised by F. Shoberl; *The Book of Flowers* (1836), by Sarah Hale; and *The Language of Birds* (1837), by Mrs. George Spratt (1837). Included under "History, Philosophy, &c." are *Sartor Resartus* and works on the peerage, on beekeeping, on the factory system, and on English history. Of the total 164 books, novels represent less than one-half; history, biography, philosophy, and other nonfiction about one-fourth; poetry and drama one-eighth; and travel literature one-eighth.

On 4 May 1852 Dickens, Herbert Spencer, the publisher Charles Knight, Saunders, and others met at the home of the publisher John Chapman to discuss the system of protected profits being enforced by the London Booksellers' Association. Saunders supported those in favor of protection from unfair competition. Knight, however, moved that fixed prices kept books too high-priced, to the injury of authors, and that publishers should not fix retail prices. Saunders's view did not prevail, but he was listened to with respect.

The firm attempted to meet the demand for a guide to expanding interests in world affairs with *Saunders, Otley & Co.'s Oriental Budget: Literary, General, and Commercial, for India, Australia, China and the Colonies* (December 1859 - October 1861), followed by *Literary Budget for England, India, China, Australia and the Colonies* (November 1861-June 1862) and *Saunders, Otley and Morgan's Oriental Budget, etc.* (September 1863). The firm also published *Saunders, Otley & Co.'s Shilling Pocket Overland Guide to India, Australia, etc.* (1861) and *Saunders, Otley and Morgan's British Army Review* (November 1863).

Saunders and Otley published works for both rising and established middle-class readers. Early examples of the latter, for career naval officers, are *New System of Signals* (1828), by Rear Adm. Henry Raper, and *The Nautical Steam Engine Explained* (1839), by Sir Robert Spencer Robinson. Typical of the former are *The Print Collector: Introduction to the Knowledge of Prints* (1844), by Joseph Maberly, and *Plans for Gentlemen's Libraries, with Remarks on their Formation and Arrangement* (1845).

Otley died in 1857. In 1859 the firm—renamed Saunders and Otley and Company—moved to 66 Brook Street. Saunders died in 1861. The firm continued under Arthur Robins and George Edward Hudson, who dissolved their partnership on 6 July 1863. In 1868 the firm moved to 7 Brook Street. It closed in 1871. In its last years of active publishing Saunders and Otley and Company continued to bring out works in roughly the same proportions as in the 1839 listing: well under one-half were fiction; the other major categories were history and biography, travel, poetry and drama, and a variety of books and pamphlets on currently popular religious, political, and other topics.

**References:**

Arno L. Bader, "Frederick Saunders and the Early History of the International Copyright Movement in America," *Literary Quarterly*, 8 (1938): 25-34;

Royal A. Gettmann, *A Victorian Publisher: A Study of the Bentley Papers* (Cambridge: Cambridge University Press, 1960);

Harriet Martineau, *Harriet Martineau's Autobiography, with Memorials by Maria Weston Chapman* (London: Smith, Elder, 1877);

Michael Sadleir, "Aspects of the Victorian Novel," *Publishing History*, 5 (1979): 7-47;

Sadleir, *The Strange Life of Lady Blessington* (New York: Farrar, Straus, 1947);

Frederick Saunders, "A Reminiscence in Copyright History," *Publishers' Weekly*, 33 (June 1888): 988;

J. A. Sutherland, *Victorian Novelists and Publishers* (Chicago: University of Chicago Press, 1976);

Clara Thomas, *Love and Work Enough: The Life of Anna Jameson* (Toronto: University of Toronto Press, 1967);

Oliver Warner, *Captain Marryat: A Rediscovery* (London: Constable, 1953).

*—Elisabeth Sanders Arbuckle*

# Simms and M'Intyre

*(Belfast: 1820-1842; Belfast and London: 1842-1858; Belfast: 1858-1870)*

The genealogy of the firm of Simms and M'Intyre, which played a major part in revolutionizing the cheap publishing of quality fiction, goes back to 1797, when the offices of the radical Belfast newspaper *Northern Star* were raided by the militia and the premises wrecked. Two journeymen, David Simms and John Doherty, purchased what was still usable and set up a press of their own. They ran a printing, publishing, and bookselling business, publishing a variety of books, pamphlets, and ephemera from several addresses until the partnership was dissolved in November 1803. Doherty took the printing business; Simms initially continued the bookselling and stationery side, though he soon acquired a press of his own.

In December 1806 Simms took another partner, George L. M'Intyre, late of the Belfast bookselling and circulating library firm of I. Warrin. They printed a wide variety of material but had a strong emphasis on schoolbooks. Their emergence as fully fledged publishers came in 1820 with the publication of the first volumes of their first literary series in a uniform binding, printed for them by another Belfast printer. By 1821 there were about twenty-five books in this series, all reprints in small format with paper-covered boards, ranging in price from sixpence-halfpenny to four shillings and fourpence. For the next decade or so they concentrated on the lucrative schoolbook market, building up a reliable stable of authors, such as James Thomson, who wrote mathematical and geographical works. They were also the official Belfast agents for the best-selling little books produced by the Kildare Place Society of Dublin.

The 1830s saw Simms and M'Intyre's second uniform reprint series, this one aimed at a popular audience. It consisted of novels such as Oliver Goldsmith's *The Vicar of Wakefield* and such older material as *The Seven Champions of Christendom*, and was published in direct competition to almost identical series produced by Joseph Smyth of Belfast and C. M. Warren of Dublin. The Simms and M'Intyre series, like the others, was priced at sixpence and bound in flimsy paper covers representing almost the last manifestation of the old chapbook tradition

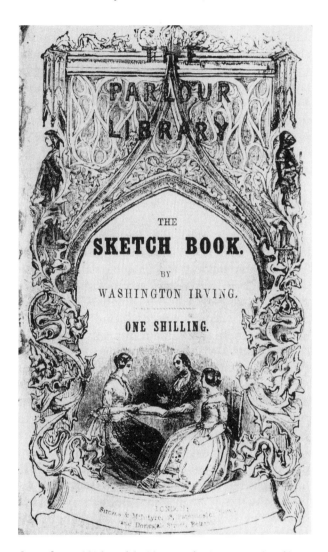

*Cover for an 1850 work in Simms and M'Intyre's series of inexpensive but high-quality novels. The Parlour Library was published by the firm from 1847 until 1853.*

brought partly up to date. The firm printed and published the Holy Bible (Douai version) in 1839.

M'Intyre died in October 1834 and Simms in December 1841. They were succeeded by their sons, James M'Intyre and John Simms. In 1841 the firm made what was apparently its first commercial contact with England, printing a dictionary for William Milner of Halifax (a firm that was also of importance in mass cheap publishing). In 1842, for the first time, Simms and M'Intyre published a book under a London imprint, with Belfast firmly in second place: Sir Walter Scott's *Rokeby*.

Thus, by February 1846 Simms and M'Intyre had a London imprint; a large printing capacity; a long experience of printing, publishing, and bookselling; and a history which included cheap series. It was therefore no mere provincial firm of schoolbook printers which in that month launched volume 1 of the Parlour Novelist series, John and Michael Banim's *Tales by the O'Hara Family: Part 1*. There were altogether fourteen works in this series. They were published at the rate of one a month and priced at two shillings and sixpence, and consisted of reprints and some original translations of foreign novels. The bindings were of plum-colored, horizontally fine-ribbed cloth.

In March 1847 the Parlour Library was launched. This series, described by the firm as "one of the boldest speculations that has ever been made in the history of bookselling," consisted of roughly monthly volumes, bound in green glazed paper, priced at one shilling and including both new and reprint fiction. It commenced with the first edition of William Carleton's *The Black Prophet*. Number eleven was the first edition of Carleton's *The Emigrants of Aghadarra* (1848), and number twenty-four the first edition of his *The Tithe Proctor* (1849). In 1849 Simms and M'Intyre purchased, with much fanfare, the copyrights of the extremely popular novelist G. P. R. James. By October 1853 the firm had published 101 volumes in the series, mostly reprints. At this point it sold the series to its London agent, Thomas Hodgson, and Simms and M'Intyre's connection with the series that heralded the advent of the really cheap high-quality novel ceased. The Parlour Library continued to be published by a variety of London publishers until the 1870s.

During the Simms and M'Intyre era there were several small associated series: the Parlour Library of Instruction (1849), the Parlour Book Case (1852), and Books for the People (1852). The last consisted of reprinted portions of Parlour Library volumes, priced at sixpence.

After 1853 the firm continued to print and publish schoolbooks. James M'Intyre severed his connection with it, but the name remained the same. The London imprint was retained until 1858, after which the firm again published only from Belfast. By this time it had left the address, 26 Donegall Street, where it was to be found during its heyday, and was publishing from a variety of addresses. Its schoolbooks generally bore the names of Longmans and Company and Simkin and Company of London in the imprint, as did its last volume, published in 1870. In the late 1850s John Simms seems to have handed over his interest in the firm to a relative, Robert Simms. He ended his days in 1911 as a handkerchief manufacturer in Banbridge, County Down.

**References:**

J. R. R. Adams, *The Printed Word and the Common Man: Popular Culture in Ulster 1700-1900* (Belfast: Institute of Irish Studies, 1987);

Adams, "Simms & M'Intyre: Creators of the Parlour Library," *Linen Hall Review*, 4 (Summer 1987): 12-14;

J. S. Crone, "The Parlour Library," *Irish Book Lover*, 2 (1911): 133-135;

Barbara Hayley, *A Bibliography of the Writings of William Carleton* (Gerrards Cross: Colin Smythe, 1985);

Michael Sadleir, *XIX Century Fiction: A Bibliographical Record Based on His Own Collection*, 2 volumes (London: Constable, 1951).

—*J. R. R. Adams*

# William Skeffington
*(Islington Green: 1844-1850; London: 1851-1876)*
## Skeffington and Southwell
*(London: 1850-1851)*
## Skeffington (William) and Son
*(London: 1876-1888)*
## Skeffington and Son
*(London: 1888-circa 1962)*

The House of Skeffington, which for over a century specialized in religious works, dates back to 1844, when William Skeffington began trading as a bookseller at 7 Islington Green, Middlesex. He was still at this address the following year, but from 1846 to 1850 is recorded as operating from Oddy's Row, Islington Green. In 1850 he moved to 192 Piccadilly, London, a smart address, and there, with a partner named Southwell, he began publishing religious books. These included Henry Hayman's *Dialogues of the Early Church* (1851), W. E. Heygate's *Pierre Poussin* (1851), and John Jackson's *Repentance* (1851). There was also an edition of J. P. Collier's *Dramatic Works and Life* (1850-1851), edited by T. Heywood, and Major Parlby's *Sketch of the Anglican Church in India* (1851).

Before long Southwell left, and until 1853 Skeffington published alone at the same address. In 1854 he moved to 163 Piccadilly. His son became a partner in 1876. In these years the Skeffington list continued to be dominated by religious or quasi-religious titles, although the publication in 1856 of a new edition of *Art of Preserv-*

*ing the Teeth*, by Josiah Saunders, constituted a bold departure. By the 1870s Skeffington had established a reputation as a major publisher of sermons. Sydney William Skeffington's *Sinless Sufferer* (1872), a collection of six sermons, reached a seventh edition by 1879 and a twelfth by 1882.

In 1888 Skeffington (William) and Son became Skeffington and Son—possibly indicating the death of William Skeffington and the accession as partner of his grandson. In the 1920s the firm was taken over by Hutchinson and Company, which kept the Skeffington imprint. Within Hutchinson, Skeffington kept its specialty in religion but also brought out Elliott O'Donnell's *Famous Curses* (1929), Paul Tabori's *The Real Hungary* (1939), and Victor Booth's *We Piano Teachers* (1946). The Skeffington imprint survived until the early 1960s.

**Reference:**
Robert Lusty, *Bound to Be Read* (London: Cape, 1975), pp. 58-59, 178.

—*R. M. Healey*

# W. H. Smith and Son

*(London: 1846-  )*
# W. H. Smith
*(London: 1828-1846)*

Though W. H. Smith and Son is best known for its shops selling newspapers, magazines, and stationery in railway terminals and high streets throughout Britain, its foresight in anticipating readers' demands changed publishing history. The firm was founded in 1792 by H. W. and Anna Smith, who began with a small newsagent's shop in Little Grosvenor Street, London. The business prospered and was passed down in 1816 to their sons Henry Edward and William Henry Smith, who also sold and bound books. In 1821 they opened a room in the Strand, where, for a small fee, patrons could read a variety of periodicals and books in peaceful surroundings. Henry Edward Smith left the business in 1828, and William Henry carried on alone. In 1846, four years after his son William Henry II joined the firm, it became W. H. Smith and Son.

Smith capitalized on a new source of customers by opening the first railway bookstall at Euston Station in 1848. Soon virtually every major railroad station was graced by one of the firm's bookstalls ministering, then as now, to travelers in search of light reading. Almost immediately, the firm became aware of a need for inexpensive, portable reading material: the conventional three-volume novel was too bulky and expensive for railway readers. Smith consequently bought up the copyrights of various popular "three-decker" novels and arranged for each to be published in one inexpensive, closely printed volume, normally bound in yellow covers.

These "yellowbacks," with their vividly illustrated covers and appealing size, were enormously popular, especially as they usually cost only two shillings apiece. The novels of Anthony Trollope and Charles Lever were the early mainstays of the series, and eventually it included all of Jane Austen's works except *Emma* (1816). Novels by Dinah Maria Mulock Craik, William Harrison Ainsworth, Oliver Wendell Holmes, Victor Hugo, Elizabeth Gaskell, Emily Eden, Joseph Sheridan Le Fanu, and Henry Kingsley also appeared

*W. H. Smith II*

in the series. Works by many less remembered authors, such as Lady Emily Ponsonby, Mrs. Edmund Jennings, and Percy Fitzgerald, were also offered.

W. H. Smith and Son was not formally the publisher of the Select Library of Fiction, as the series was called; if the firm branched into publishing it would incur the wrath of the publishers whose works it distributed. So the printing and binding were done by Chapman and Hall until the early 1860s, when Ward, Lock and Tyler took over the series. In years to come many other publishers, including Blackwood and Bentley, would publish works for Smith. Other publishers noticed the success of the Select Library of Fiction and began their own series of inexpensive novels, which were also offered at Smith's rail-

MESSRS W. H. SMITH AND SON'S PREMISES IN THE STRAND.

*Offices of W. H. Smith and Son in the Strand, London*

way bookstalls. Bentley's Railway Library and Routledge's Railway Library were started in 1848 and 1849, respectively, and in the early 1850s Longman's Traveller's Library and Murray's Railway Reading appeared. Despite publishing the Select Library of Fiction for W. H. Smith and Son, Chapman and Hall began its own Reading for Travellers series in 1852. Routledge's Cheap Series (1853), Smith, Elder and Company's Shilling Series of Standard Works of Fiction (1861), and Simpkin's Cheap Library (1861) offered light literature at the low price of one shilling to two shillings, sixpence a title. Such cut-rate merchandising pressured rival publishers to reduce the prices of their existing series in the 1840s and 1850s. In 1849, for example, the Society for the Diffusion of Useful Knowledge reduced the works in its Library of Entertaining Knowledge from four shillings, sixpence per volume to two shillings, threepence.

Smith's popularization of one-volume reprints had profound consequences for publishing. There was, of course, no reason to limit the sales of such profitable books to railway bookstalls; other booksellers began to stock them. They also appealed to customers of Smith's network of lending libraries, and to those of Charles Edward Mudie, whose huge purchasing orders were immensely significant in determining a nov-

el's popularity. Mudie's had long been able to charge novel borrowers three times, once for each volume of a three-decker, but the many new series of cheap reprints originally designed for railway travelers inspired publishers to follow up their release of each new three-decker with an inexpensive one-volume version, often shortly after the original publication. The three-deckers consequently became less and less profitable, and in 1894 Mudie's reluctantly agreed with Smith that the format was doomed.

W. H. Smith, Sr., retired in 1854; he died on 28 July 1855 at his country home in Bournemouth. W. H. Smith II carried on the business. The younger Smith, who was elected to Parliament in 1868, died in 1891. His son, W. H. Smith III, became head of the firm two years later. Charles Harry St. John Hornby was made a partner in 1894.

Smith formally announced itself as a publisher in 1908, when it bought the Arden Press in Leamington. Shortly thereafter, it also purchased the St. Catherine Press. The firm, always aware of the perils of competing with the publishers who supplied its bookstores, decided in 1911 to abjure publishing. The Arden Press, aside from printing miscellaneous periodicals and Smith's in-house pamphlets and handbooks, did fine printing and binding in the arts and crafts tradition,

*W. H. Smith and Son bookshop on the rue de Rivoli in Paris*

often for other publishers. The St. Catherine Press publishes, on commission, such works as the *Victoria County Histories* and *The Complete Peerage of England, Scotland, Ireland, Great Britain, and the United Kingdom.*

Though in 1928 it became a limited company, the firm remains a family business. In 1966 W. H. Smith and Son joined with Doubleday of New York to create Book Club Associates, which runs the Reprint Society and publishes and distributes cut-rate versions of new books for the members of a cookbook club and the Literary Guild.

**References:**

*The Story of W. H. Smith* (London: Privately printed, 1951);

Charles Wilson, *First with the News: The History of W. H. Smith 1792-1972* (London: Cape, 1985).

—*Anita Hemphill McCormick*

# Elliot Stock

## (London: 1859-1939)

In 1859 Elliot Stock, the son of a West End hosier and previously an apprentice in the bookseller's firm of Benjamin L. Green, 62 Paternoster Row, sold some family property and purchased the bookselling concern of a Mr. Heaton of 53 Paternoster Row. Later that year he bought his former master's business.

Stock originally specialized in nonsectarian religious works and periodicals, as had his predecessor, Green, who had published much of the material for the Sunday School movement. In 1866 Stock married the daughter of Samuel Bellin, a well-known engraver. This introduced him to a wider circle of artists and litterateurs and contributed to the expansion of the scope of his lists in the 1870s.

Among Stock's religious publications of this time was *The Biblical Museum*, in fifteen volumes, edited by James Comper Gray; it was first published from 1871 to 1881, with a new edition in 1898. Stock founded the *Baptist* in 1873 (it was absorbed into the *Baptist Times and Freeman* in 1910) and was financially interested in at least a dozen denominational magazines. A writing room, originally set aside at the Paternoster Row address for the use of ministers and clergymen of all denominations, gradually became a center for antiquarians and bibliophiles.

Stock's facsimile reprints of early first editions are still remembered today, especially his unauthorized 1897 reprint of the first edition of John Keble's *Christian Year* (1827), the poetic lodestone of the Oxford Movement. When Stock was sued successfully for infringement of copyright the book was withdrawn from circulation, and the value of the few copies left on the market soared. Other facsimile reprints included John Bunyan's *Pilgrim's Progress* (1875)—Stock's first such attempt; George Herbert's *The Temple* (1876); and Izaak Walton's *The Compleat Angler* (1876). Among the most popular were Thomas à Kempis's *The Imitation of Christ* (1879); Juliana Berners's *The Boke of Saint Albans* (1881); and *Cromwell's Soldier's Bible* (1895), a reprint of *The Souldiers Pocket Bible* (1643). To most of these works Stock added a specially commissioned preface. The firm published about twenty-five fac-

*Elliot Stock circa 1900*

similes of first editions or manuscripts in all; most were sixteenth- to eighteenth-century English books, but some were replicas of nineteenth-century works, such as Charles Dickens's *A Christmas Carol* (1890) and the Pre-Raphaelite journal, the *Germ* (1901), with an introduction by William Michael Rossetti. Stock's continuing interest in the Pre-Raphaelite movement is indicated by the number of works the firm published by members of the Pre-Raphaelite circle, including Hall Caine, William Bell Scott, William Sharp, Philip Bourke Marston, Francis Hueffer, and J. H. Ingram.

When publishing new works Stock preferred to use the joint-share method, with the author agreeing in advance to buy up all unsold copies, rather than outright purchase of copyright.

He was occasionally accused of deceit by disgruntled authors who believed that he deliberately overpriced their books, thus calculating on making his profit from the author rather than from the public. The typical edition size for a book of verse published by the firm in the 1880s was one thousand copies.

Elliot Stock's greatest success as a publisher was Augustine Birrell's *Obiter Dicta*, first published in 1884 and reprinted five times in 1885. The collection of literary essays received an appreciative review in the *Times* and became an instant hit. Stock also published the second series in 1887, a third edition in 1890, and two cheap editions in 1896. Another best-seller for the firm, on a less elevated plane, was *The Anglican Sister of Mercy*. The book was published anonymously but is usually attributed to Augusta Dill. It was originally published in 1869 as *Maude; or, The Anglican Sister of Mercy*; Stock published the revised edition in 1895 and a cheap edition in 1899. A thinly disguised attack on the Devonport Sisterhood, it contained a fictionalized and hostile portrait of the important and highly controversial Anglican churchwoman Priscilla Lydia Sellon. Stock himself made only one attempt at authorship: *The Publisher's Playground*, a book of verse published anonymously by Kegan Paul, Trench and Company in 1888 although its authorship was no secret, was well received. *The Gentleman's Magazine Library* (1883-1905), edited by George Lawrence Gomme in thirty volumes, provided "in a concise and tabulated form the chief contents of that magazine from 1731 to 1868."

Bibliographical ventures included the *Bibliographer* (1881-1884), edited by H. B. Wheatley. Wheatley was also the editor of Stock's Book-Lover's Library, a series of inexpensive handbooks which played an important role in the popularization of bibliography. The contributors included several well-known bibliographers, such as William Blades (Stock published his *The Enemies of Books* in an enlarged and revised edition in 1888), W. Carew Hazlitt, William Rovers, Gleeson White, and H. T. Wood. The *Bibliographer* was succeeded by *Book-Lore*, edited by William Azon and intended to be a popularization of bibliographical studies. In 1888 *Book-Lore* was succeeded by *The Bookworm: An Illustrated Treasury of Old-Time Literature* (1888-1894). Another journal launched by the firm was the *Antiquary* (1880-1915), originally edited by Edward Walford.

The most important of Stock's bibliographical periodicals was *Book Prices Current* (1886-1956), which recorded prices paid for rare books at sales and auctions. It was edited by J. Herbert Slater until his death in 1921. Another journal published for a time by Elliot Stock was the *London Quarterly Review* (1865-1875), edited by W. B. Pope, which Stock took over from Henry James Tresidder.

In 1908 Stock sold his business to Robert Scott, who retained the firm's original name until 1939. Stock, described by Stanley Morison as "a minor author and a major publisher," died in 1911. In a career lasting more than half a century, Stock published many works of enduring value. His firm's contribution to the study of bibliography was an important and lasting one.

**Reference:**
Sybille Pantazzi, "Elliot Stock," *Book Collector*, 20 (Spring 1971): 25-46.

*—S. D. Mumm*

# Strahan and Company
*(Edinburgh: 1858-1862; London: 1862-1873)*

# W. Isbister and Company
*(London: 1873-1874)*

# Daldy, Isbister and Company
*(London: 1874-1878)*

# Isbister and Company Limited
*(London: 1878-1904)*

# William Isbister Limited
*(London: 1878-1890)*

# Alexander Strahan
*(London: 1873-1874; 1882-1893)*

# Strahan and Company, Paternoster Row
*(London: 1875-1876)*

# Strahan and Company Limited
*(London: 1876-1882)*

# George Virtue
*(London: 1820-1855)*

# J. S. Virtue and Company
*(London: 1855-1875)*

# Virtue and Company Limited
*(London: 1875-1899)*

# H. Virtue and Company Limited
*(London: 1899-   )*

Alexander Strahan was a pioneer in several ways. Although he began his career as a religious publisher in Scotland, he contravened the conventions of the time by refusing to limit himself to the literature of a single denomination. He attempted also to bridge the gap between religious and secular publishing. After he moved from Edinburgh to London, Strahan had difficulty persuading readers and critics to regard him as anything other than a "Scottish Presbyterian" publisher. He was, however, deeply interested in the literature of Christian social reform. Politically, Strahan was committed to Gladstonian Liberalism.

At the peak of his career Strahan published essays by William Gladstone, fiction by Anthony Trollope, children's literature by George MacDonald, and poetry by Alfred Tennyson. He is most important, however, as the founder, publisher, and in large part the conductor of several of the most significant and innovative periodicals of the nineteenth century, including *Good Words, Good Words for the Young*, the *Sunday Magazine*, and the

*Contemporary Review.* Strahan believed that it was necessary to provide "the people" with inexpensive literature; thus he attempted to persuade the "chief authors" of the time to "descend to the magazines."

Strahan founded Strahan and Company in Edinburgh in 1858. He and his partner, William Isbister, had been apprentices together in the firm of Johnstone and Hunter, publishers to the Free Church of Scotland. Strahan assumed responsibility for most editorial decisions; Isbister was more concerned with the technicalities of print and paper. Their firm initially specialized in devotional works, evangelical tracts, and illustrated literature for children. Like many other British publishers, Strahan and Isbister also sold thousands of copies of pirated editions of works by well-known American authors: their early lists included *Life Thoughts* (1858), by Henry Ward Beecher; *The Autocrat of the Breakfast Table* (1859), by Oliver Wendell Holmes; and *The Rise of the Dutch Republic* (1859), by John Lothrop Motley.

Strahan and Company brought out its publications in a variety of formats: two-volume editions that cost ten shillings, sixpence; single volumes at two shillings for the "fine edition" and one shilling for the "cheap edition"; monthly shilling parts; and sixpenny tracts. Beecher's *Life Thoughts* was published in a two-shilling edition and in a special Christmas edition "on toned paper, with richly ornamented borders," which sold for seven shillings, sixpence. In 1859 Strahan and Isbister acquired a sixpenny monthly, *News of the Churches and Journal of Missions*, which had been established in 1854 by the firm of Johnstone and Hunter; in 1863 the name was changed to *Christian Work throughout the World*.

In February 1859 Strahan and Company published the first issue of the *Christian Guest: A Family Magazine for Leisure Hours and Sunday.* The *Christian Guest* was nominally edited by the Reverend Norman Macleod, a prominent member of the Church of Scotland who was also a favorite chaplain of Queen Victoria; in fact, Strahan did much of the editing himself. The magazine differed from other evangelical publications by including stories and poems and by publishing work signed by ministers of various denominations. The *Christian Guest* was also less expensive than its competitors: a monthly issue of forty-eight pages cost threepence; weekly numbers on poorer quality paper were a halfpenny.

*Alexander Strahan in 1878*

The *Christian Guest* ceased publication with the December 1859 issue. On 23 December Strahan and Company published the first number of *Good Words*, which was also advertised as being edited by Macleod. It sold thirty thousand copies at sixpence. Like the *Christian Guest*, *Good Words* published contributions signed by ministers of various denominations. Although in England the magazine was regarded as a periodical for Scottish Presbyterians, Macleod solicited contributions from Anglican clerics such as A. P. Stanley, Charles Kingsley, and Henry Alford. In addition to religious articles and serialized fiction, early issues of *Good Words* included articles on science, travel, and social problems, as well as woodcuts by W. Holman Hunt, Arthur Boyd Houghton, and J. E. Millais. Circulation climbed steadily, reaching seventy thousand in January 1862.

Strahan published in volume form the work of many contributors to *Good Words*. One of his best-selling titles was *Wee Davie* (1861), a pious and sentimental story by Macleod, which was attacked by some Presbyterian ministers for being insufficiently evangelical. Strahan published several more books by Macleod, including *The Gold Thread* (1861), a story for children, and the fictional *Reminiscences of a Highland Parish* (1867). Strahan's lists also featured half a dozen volumes of religious poetry and prose by Dora Greenwell and several volumes of prose and fiction by "Sarah Tytler" (Henrietta Keddie), including her highly successful historical novel *Citoyenne Jacqueline* (1865). Strahan sold tens of thousands of copies of the "popular edition" of *Recreations of a Country Parson* (first published in 1859) by "A.K.H.B." (Andrew Kennedy Hutchison Boyd). Like other reprints included in Strahan's Family Library, *Recreations of a Country Parson* sold for three shillings, sixpence. Strahan also published Boyd's *Graver Thoughts of a Country Parson* (1862, 1865, 1876) in three series.

In the spring of 1862 Strahan and Isbister moved their business from Edinburgh to Ludgate Hill, London. Strahan was well aware that *Good Words* must include as many contributions by English authors as possible to appeal to English readers. In 1862 he offered Trollope one thousand pounds to serialize his novel *Rachel Ray* in *Good Words*. But before serialization commenced, *Good Words* was attacked by the *Record*, the organ of Calvinists within the Church of England. The *Record* charged that *Good Words* was unfit reading for Christians because it published articles by non-Calvinists such as Stanley and Kingsley. The views of Macleod were also impugned.

Although many writers in the periodical press defended *Good Words*, Macleod was so alarmed that he insisted on returning to Trollope the manuscript of *Rachel Ray*, which included passages likely to offend strict Calvinists. (The novel was published in 1863 by Chapman and Hall.) Despite—or perhaps because of—the controversy, the circulation of *Good Words* continued to increase. The magazine was sold in the United States, Canada, and Europe, and missionaries distributed it throughout the British Empire. In 1864 Strahan claimed an average circulation of 160,000, which would have made *Good Words* the best-selling magazine in the English-speaking world.

The attack by the *Record* seems to have taught Strahan that the market for periodical literature consisted of a multitude of reading publics, which could be identified and to some extent created. In the case of *Good Words* he had attempted to amalgamate a variety of audiences: readers of fiction and readers of sermons, English readers and Scottish readers, Anglican readers and Nonconformist readers. In the mid 1860s, however, he launched three new periodicals, each intended for a different readership.

The *Sunday Magazine*, a sevenpenny monthly, appeared in October 1864. It was intended for Christians who regarded *Good Words* as too latitudinarian. The prospectus for *Good Words* had claimed that that magazine was fit reading for every day of the week; the prospectus for the *Sunday Magazine* said that the new periodical would provide reading appropriate for the Sabbath. The *Sunday Magazine* was nominally edited by Dr. Thomas Guthrie of the Free Church of Scotland, whose contributions to *Good Words* had been praised even by the *Record*. Again, however, it was Strahan who did much of the actual editing. Sales of the first few issues of the *Sunday Magazine* exceeded one hundred thousand before it settled down to an average of ninety thousand.

The *Argosy*, a sixpenny monthly, appeared in December 1865. Strahan explained in his reminiscences (1881) that this magazine was intended to include material deemed unsuitable even for *Good Words*. The first novel to be serialized, Charles Reade's *Griffith Gaunt* (published in book form by Chapman and Hall in 1866), was attacked by critics in New York and London for being an "indecent" delineation of the crime of bigamy. Reade kept the controversy alive by suing the New York magazine *Round Table* for libel; he eventually won his suit but was awarded only six cents. Despite the publicity, the *Argosy* did not sell enough copies to make a profit.

In 1866 Strahan established the periodical that he always regarded as his "most important literary enterprise." The *Contemporary Review* was a half-crown monthly that featured signed articles on theology, philosophy, literature, and social problems. It was intended as a progressive but Christian competitor to secular reviews such as the *Fortnightly Review*, which had been established in 1865. Strahan believed that the *Contemporary Review* would have a much better chance of success if it were edited by an Anglican; his choice was Alford, the dean of Canterbury. During Alford's editorship, which continued until 1870, many of the contributors were Anglican ministers.

Strahan's book list also expanded rapidly in the mid 1860s. Devotional works continued to be a staple: the firm's advertisements featured prose and poetry by well-known clerics such as Alford, Guthrie, Macleod, W. E. Boardman, Horace

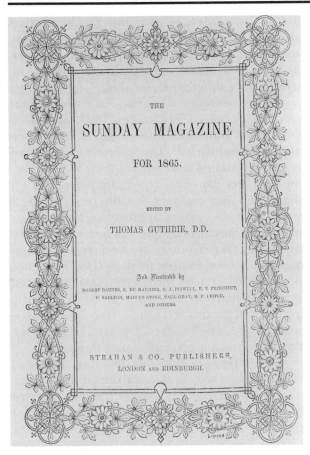

*Cover for the periodical Strahan published from 1864 to 1872 as a vehicle for social reform and to "bring the Bible into relation to common life"*

Bushnell, E. H. Plumptre, and C. J. Vaughan. The firm published such highly successful children's books as *Lilliput Levee* (1864), by "Matthew Browne" (W. B. Rands); *Stories Told to a Child* (1865) and *Mopsa the Fairy* (1869), by Jean Ingelow; and *Madame How and Lady Why* (1870), by Kingsley. Other publications of note included *Essays on Woman's Work* (1865), by Bessie Rayner Parkes, and *The Higher Education of Women* (1866), by Emily Davies.

The Strahan imprint also began to appear regularly on the work of highly regarded secular authors such as Alexander Smith, William Gilbert, and Robert Buchanan. Smith was already known for his *Poems* (1853) and *City Poems* (1857) when Strahan published his first volume of essays, *Dreamthorp* (1863). Strahan also published Smith's nonfiction *A Summer in Skye* (1865) and his novel *Alfred Hagart's Household* (1866). Gilbert was a physician who took a specialist's interest in the treatment of the mentally ill and in charity administration. Remembered today as the father of W. S. Gilbert, he won a literary reputation as the

author of *Shirley Hall Asylum* (1863), a novel about monomania. Strahan published half a dozen titles by Gilbert, including *De Profundis* (1864), a novel about life in the slums, and *Dr. Austin's Guest* (1866), a sequel to *Shirley Hall Asylum*. Strahan published Buchanan's *Idyls and Legends of Inverburn* (1865) and *London Poems* (1866). The latter volume, which made Buchanan's name, included narrative poems and dramatic monologues that described in realistic detail the lives of the London poor. It was followed by the mystical *Book of Orm* (1870). Buchanan and Strahan worked out an agreement whereby every month Buchanan supplied Strahan's periodicals with a certain amount of copy—verse, fiction, or essays. The October 1871 issue of the *Contemporary Review* included "The Fleshly School of Poetry," Buchanan's notorious attack on A. C. Swinburne and the Pre-Raphaelites; a revised and expanded version was published by Strahan in volume form in 1872.

The move to London, the establishment of the new periodicals, and the expansion of the general publishing list were expensive undertakings. In the 1860s Strahan and Company became more and more deeply indebted to its stationer, Spalding and Hodge, and to its printer, J. S. Virtue and Company. It was not uncommon in the nineteenth century for stationers, printers, and publishers to form business alliances and invest in each other's firms. Thomas S. Spalding, the head of Spalding and Hodge, had invested in the London publishing firm of Bell and Daldy. In the mid 1860s Bell and Daldy was expanding so rapidly that it was having difficulty distributing its publications. It was perhaps at the urging of Spalding that in 1867 Strahan and Company became the distributor on commission of Bell and Daldy publications.

The Virtue firm was descended from a bookshop opened by George Virtue on Ivy Lane, Paternoster Row, in the early 1820s. Virtue had soon become a publisher of popular fiction, devotional literature, and illustrated art and travel books. He was one of the booksellers who invested in Pierce Egan's *Life in London* (1821), which appeared in shilling pamphlets illustrated by George and J. R. Cruikshank. Some of Virtue's most important publications were written by W. Beattie and illustrated by William Henry Bartlett; they include *Switzerland* (1836), *Scotland* (1838), and *The Danube: Its History and Scenery* (1844). In 1849 Virtue purchased the *Art Union*, founded in 1839, which he renamed the *Art Jour-*

*nal*. In 1851 he established a printing business for the production of his many art books. In 1855 his son James Sprent Virtue took over the printing business and the original bookshop; together these enterprises became known as J. S. Virtue and Company. In 1862 James Sprent Virtue and his older brother George Henry Virtue established the publishing firm of Virtue Brothers and Company. In 1866 George Henry Virtue died and Virtue Brothers ceased to exist. James Sprent Virtue tried unsuccessfully to sell the assets of the publishing firm.

By 1866 Strahan and Company owed J. S. Virtue and Company and Spalding and Hodge a total of twenty-five thousand pounds. One drain on Strahan's resources was the *Argosy*. The *Argosy* might have been made profitable if Strahan had been prepared to capitalize on the "sensational" reputation it had achieved as a result of the controversy over *Griffith Gaunt*. But when Reade's novel was concluded in the November 1866 issue, Strahan chose to begin serialization of *Robert Falconer*, by George MacDonald, whose work was beginning to appear regularly on Strahan's general publishing list. Soon critics were complaining that *Robert Falconer* was "too Scotch and too theological for general appreciation."

At about this time Virtue was looking for a magazine to purchase; he had already arranged for Trollope to be the editor. Virtue considered buying the *Argosy*, a transaction that would have reduced Strahan's debt to him. He decided instead, however, to establish a new shilling periodical. The inaugural issue of *Saint Pauls Magazine* appeared in October 1867. It included the first installment of Trollope's novel *Phineas Finn, the Irish Member*, illustrated by J. E. Millais. In the same month Strahan sold the *Argosy* to Mrs. Henry Wood. She raised the price of the magazine to one shilling and transformed it into a vehicle for her own "sensational" fiction.

Strahan continued to expand his list of periodicals. *Good Words for the Young*, a sixpenny monthly, appeared in November 1868. It featured the fiction of MacDonald, who was its editor from 1869 to 1873. MacDonald's "faerie-allegory," *At the Back of the North Wind*, was the first serial; it ran from November 1868 to October 1870 and was published by Strahan in volume form in 1871. It was followed by *Ranald Bannerman's Boyhood* from November 1869 to October 1870 (book version, 1871) and *The Princess and the Goblin* from November 1870 to June 1871 (book version, 1872).

In 1869 Virtue decided to sell *Saint Pauls Magazine*, which had failed to achieve a circulation much over ten thousand; he was also determined to dispose of the copyrights of the defunct firm of Virtue Brothers. In the spring he transferred the magazine and many of the copyrights to Strahan and Company. As Strahan and Company was already in debt to Virtue, all he gained by this transaction was a greater financial interest in Strahan's business. Strahan gained many new titles, including three by Trollope: *Phineas Finn*, which had been serialized in *Saint Pauls Magazine* from 1867 to 1869 and published by Virtue in two volumes in 1869; *He Knew He Was Right*, published by Virtue in sixpenny numbers and monthly parts in 1868-1869 and by Strahan in two volumes in 1869; and *Ralph the Heir*, published as a "Supplement" to *Saint Pauls Magazine* in 1870-1871 and by Strahan in three volumes in 1871. Strahan also acquired novels by Frank E. Smedley and by Emma Jane Worboise which were so popular that they had remained in print since the 1850s.

In the late 1860s and early 1870s, however, Strahan aspired to publish the major literature of his time. He republished from the periodicals Gladstone's *On "Ecce Homo"* (1868); Trollope's *Lotta Schmidt, and Other Stories* (1867) and *An Editor's Tales* (1870); and MacDonald's *Works of Fancy and Imagination* (1871).

Strahan was unsuccessful in his attempts to purchase *The Ring and the Book* (1868-1869) from Robert Browning. His diligent pursuit of Tennyson did pay off, however. Strahan offered the poet laureate four thousand pounds per annum for the right to republish his earlier poetry; Strahan and Company was to deduct a commission of five percent on the proceeds from new works. Tennyson signed a five-year contract making the firm his exclusive publisher as of 15 January 1869. The Strahan imprint appeared on *Idylls of the King* (1869), *The Holy Grail and Other Poems* (1870), and *Gareth and Lynette* (1872). Thirty-one thousand copies of *Idylls of the King* were ordered prior to the date of publication; prepublication orders for *The Holy Grail and Other Poems* may have totaled forty thousand. Strahan also published the first collected edition of Tennyson's works, the ten-volume "Miniature Edition" (1870), which sold for two pounds, five shillings.

As a result of his dealings with Tennyson, Strahan came to know Tennyson's friend James Thomas Knowles. In 1869 Knowles established the Metaphysical Society, a discussion and debating group whose members included Tennyson, Alford, Stanley, Gladstone, J. R. Seeley, George Grove, James Martineau, R. H. Hutton, Walter Bagehot, H. E. Manning, W. G. Ward, T. H. Huxley, John Tyndall, and John Ruskin. In the late 1860s Knowles began to assist Alford in editing the *Contemporary Review*; his primary role was to secure contributions from members of the Metaphysical Society. In 1870, in the interests of economy, Trollope ceased to be editor of *Saint Pauls Magazine* and Alford resigned from the *Contemporary Review*. Strahan edited both the periodicals, assisted by Knowles in the case of the *Contemporary Review*.

Strahan and Company published two of the most sensationally successful titles of the early 1870s: *Ginx's Baby* (1870), by Edward Jenkins, and *The True History of Joshua Davidson* (1872), by Eliza Lynn Linton. Jenkins, a barrister and politician, was made famous by *Ginx's Baby*, a satire on religious sectarianism and urban charity administration that, according to the publisher, went through thirty-seven editions by 1877. In 1871 Strahan and Company republished from *Good Words* a series of investigative articles by Jenkins entitled *The Coolie*, which attacked bureaucracy and colonial exploitation in British Guiana. In 1872 Strahan published three more titles by Jenkins: *Little Hodge* was a short novel about the hardships of agricultural laborers, *Lord Bantom* was a two-volume novel attacking political pretensions, and *Barney Geoghegan* was a pamphlet-length satire on the Home Rule debate republished from *Saint Pauls Magazine*.

The first edition of *The True History of Joshua Davidson* was published anonymously. The novel imagined the rebirth of Jesus Christ in Victorian England; it included harsh criticisms of contemporary "Christian" morality, and it suggested that a contemporary Christ would have to be a communist. The book attracted great attention, and Linton's name appeared on the title page of the second edition. *The True History of Joshua Davidson* went through ten editions by 1890.

Despite these critical and popular successes, however, the financial situation of Strahan and Company continued to worsen. Virtue and Spalding believed that Strahan was too lavish in his payments to authors, especially Tennyson. In March 1872 they forced Strahan to resign. Spalding and Virtue became the owners and operators of the firm; Isbister served as their manager. *Good Words* and the *Sunday Magazine* re-

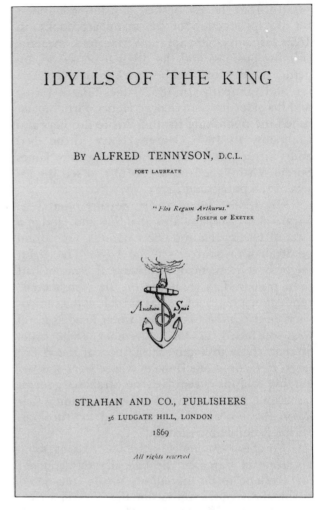

Title page for the volume that brought together the first eight idylls

mained with Virtue, Spalding, and Isbister; *Christian Work throughout the World* was sold to the Evangelical Alliance; Strahan took with him a portion of the general publishing list, as well as the *Contemporary Review*, *Saint Pauls Magazine*, and *Good Words for the Young*, which was retitled *Good Things for the Young*.

With the financial assistance of another publisher, Henry S. King, Strahan moved into offices on Paternoster Row. By the terms of his separation from Strahan and Company, Strahan was barred from using his own name until December 1873. Thus his periodicals were distributed by King, and King's imprint appeared on their title pages. King became half-owner with Strahan of a new penny weekly, the *Day of Rest*, launched in December 1872. King's imprint also began to appear on several titles originally published by Strahan and Company, including works by Buchanan and Jenkins. King was eager to become Swinburne's publisher; Swinburne refused to consider King's offer, however, because he did not wish to have the same publisher as Buchanan. In 1874, when Tennyson's contract with Strahan and Company expired, Strahan and Knowles assisted King in the negotiations that led to his becoming Tennyson's new publisher.

Late in 1873 the name of Strahan and Company was changed to W. Isbister and Company. The partnership of Bell and Daldy had been dissolved in 1870, and in 1874 F. R. Daldy joined the firm on Ludgate Hill, which was renamed Daldy, Isbister and Company. Daldy, Isbister and Company was one of several subsidiary companies managed by Virtue and Company Limited, which was incorporated in 1875 with Spalding as one of the major shareholders.

In 1878 the assets of Daldy, Isbister and Company were divided between two new corporate entities. Isbister and Company Limited acquired a long list of schoolbooks, including many published formerly by Virtue Brothers and then by Strahan and Company. William Isbister Limited continued to publish *Good Words* and the *Sunday Magazine*. Isbister was only a minor shareholder in the limited companies.

James Virtue and Company Limited was formed in 1879 to take over the *Art Journal* and other copyrights. Virtue's printing business remained highly successful; in the 1880s as many as four hundred people were employed in its printing works. The department for steel engravings and etchings, which housed forty presses, was thought to be the largest in the trade.

In December 1873 Strahan was once again able to use his own name, and his periodicals began to appear under the imprint "Alexander Strahan." So many prospective customers went looking for Strahan on Ludgate Hill, however, that in January 1875 he changed his imprint to "Strahan and Company, Paternoster Row." Strahan's publishing list was quite short. In 1875 he republished from the *Contemporary Review* Gladstone's *The Church of England and Ritualism*. He also published *The Devil's Chain* (1876), a three-volume temperance novel by Jenkins. A new author on his list was Emily Pfeiffer; her *Poems* (1876) combined religious sentiment with concern for the working poor, especially women.

One of Strahan's apprentices was G. Thompson Hutchinson, who eventually established his own publishing business. One of his employees was his brother-in-law, A. P. Watt, who began to develop a career of his own as an "Advertising Agent." Watt also assisted MacDonald in placing with other publishers manuscripts that Strahan could no longer afford to buy. In the 1880s and 1890s Watt amassed a fortune as one of the first professional literary agents.

In March 1874 *Saint Pauls Magazine* ceased publication. Strahan seems to have been interested in publishing less costly periodicals. In April 1874 he launched a penny weekly called the *Saturday Journal*, which promised "literature not written for any class, but for all classes alike." *The Peepshow*, a halfpenny weekly for children, also appeared in 1874; it included contributions by MacDonald, Buchanan, Ingelow, Greenwell, and William Allingham. At about this time Strahan purchased *Evening Hours*, a sixpenny monthly established in March 1871. Strahan persuaded Gladstone to contribute to *Evening Hours* the essay "Science and Art; Utility and Beauty."

Strahan financed these ventures by increasing his indebtedness to King and to McCorquodale and Company, his stationer and printer. At one point Strahan transferred a half interest in the periodicals to McCorquodale and Company; he sold another quarter interest to a new partner, Robert Mullan, who was the son of William Mullan, a printer and bookseller in Belfast. But in June 1876 George McCorquodale placed a receiver in the offices of Strahan and Company, claiming that Strahan owed McCorquodale and Company thirty-five thousand pounds. The partnership with Mullan was dissolved, and Mullan took as his share of the assets the copyrights to *Evening Hours* and to several books; these publications began to appear under the imprint of William Mullan and Son.

In late 1876 Strahan persuaded a group of evangelicals, headed by the wealthy Congregationalist manufacturer Samuel Hope Morley, to invest the money necessary to form Strahan and Company Limited. McCorquodale and Company became a major shareholder in the new company, which purchased the periodicals and hired Strahan to be its "Editorial Director."

Despite Strahan's financial difficulties, the *Contemporary Review* flourished during these years, achieving an average circulation of eight thousand. Its success was due in large part to the efforts of Knowles, who in 1873 signed a contract appointing him "joint Editor" with Strahan. It was at Knowles's request that Matthew Arnold contributed to the *Contemporary Review* the series of essays which were later published by Smith,

Elder as *God and the Bible* (1875). Knowles managed to coax several contributions from Gladstone, including three which boosted circulation by attracting widespread comment: "Ritualism and Ritual" (October 1874), "Is the Church of England Worth Preserving?" ( July 1875), and "The Courses of Religious Thought" ( June 1876). Knowles also continued to secure contributions from members of the Metaphysical Society, such as Cardinal Henry Edward Manning, Bagehot, Greg, Martineau, J. F. Stephen, and W. K. Clifford.

The evangelicals who established Strahan and Company Limited were, however, determined to dismiss Knowles and appoint Strahan sole editor of the *Contemporary Review*. They were deeply offended by Clifford's article "The Ethics of Belief," an attack on Christian faith that triggered tremendous controversy when it appeared in the *Contemporary Review* for January 1877. Knowles's departure from the *Contemporary Review* was also widely discussed in the periodical press. He immediately set about launching his own review: the first issue of the *Nineteenth Century*, which appeared in March 1877, included contributions from Tennyson, Gladstone, Manning, and Arnold.

Circulation of the *Contemporary Review* decreased as a result of the negative publicity and the loss of many of its famous contributors to Knowles's review. As editor of the *Contemporary Review*, Strahan was hampered by the fact that not enough capital had been invested in the new limited company. In its first year of operation the company was involved in expensive lawsuits initiated by King and Knowles. King's claims were dismissed, but Knowles was awarded damages of nearly fifteen hundred pounds. The new company made every attempt to economize. *Good Things for the Young* ceased publication in 1877; the *Peepshow* came to its end in 1879. Strahan and Company Limited continued to publish the *Day of Rest* and the *Contemporary Review*, but little money was available for advertisements or for payments to contributors.

Although the limited company had been founded primarily to publish the periodicals, it gradually built up a general publishing list. From 1879 to 1882 the firm published *Jobson's Enemies*, a new novel by Jenkins, in eight monthly parts. Many other titles on the company's list were reprints of books originally published by Strahan in the 1860s; these included volumes by Buchanan, Ingelow, Rands, Vaughan, and MacDonald. The company also advertised dozens of books for children. But few of these titles were actually available: the company was in such dire financial straits that in 1880 the board of directors pawned its stock of periodicals and books. Strahan was preoccupied in preparing an elaborate edition of *The Pilgrim's Progress* (1880) that included more than one hundred drawings by well-known artists such as Fred Barnard, William Small, E. G. Dalziel, John Ralston, and J. D. Linton. The engravings for this project were produced by the firm of Dalziel Brothers. The cheaper edition sold for 21 shillings; the "Edition de Luxe," printed on handmade paper, cost 105 shillings.

In 1881 the directors voted to dismiss Strahan and appoint Percy William Bunting editor of the *Contemporary Review*. Strahan was still disputing the board's legal right to take such a step when the company was declared bankrupt in April 1882. The *Day of Rest* and the *Contemporary Review* were sold to Isbister and Company Limited. The *Day of Rest* was merged into the *Sunday Magazine*; the *Contemporary Review* continued to appear, edited by Bunting.

After the collapse of the limited company Strahan opened an office in Covent Garden and published a score of titles under the imprint "Alexander Strahan." Most were reprints; they included several works by MacDonald. Strahan seems not to have published any new titles after 1884. The London Post Office Directory of 1893 is the last to include him on its list of publishers.

In 1883 Isbister was replaced as manager of Isbister and Company Limited and William Isbister Limited, but the two companies continued to operate under his name. In 1890 William Isbister Limited was merged into Isbister and Company Limited; this company was purchased by Isaac Pitman and Sons Limited in 1904.

When James Sprent Virtue died in 1892, he was succeeded as head of the family business by his son Herbert. Toward the end of the century the business was reorganized, becoming H. Virtue and Company Limited. In 1923 Herbert's son Guy joined the firm. Although no longer a printing business, H. Virtue and Company Limited survives to this day, publishing books and selling them through salesmen directly to the general public. The company is managed by Guy's son Michael Virtue.

*Good Words* and the *Sunday Magazine* were sold by Isbister and Company Limited to the Amalgamated Press in 1905. The *Sunday Magazine* ceased publication at that time; *Good Words* survived as a tabloid-sized weekly until 1910. The *Contemporary Review* was sold to Columbus Company Limited in 1900 and was edited by Bunting until his death in 1911. It is still published.

**References:**

Edward Bell, *George Bell Publisher: A Brief Memoir* (London: Privately printed, 1924);

Alan Willard Brown, *The Metaphysical Society: Victorian Minds in Crisis, 1869-1880* (New York: Columbia University Press, 1947);

B. F. Maidment, "Victorian Publishing and Social Criticism: The Case of Edward Jenkins," *Publishing History*, 11 (1982): 42-71;

Patricia Thomas Srebrnik, *Alexander Strahan: Victorian Publisher* (Ann Arbor: University of Michigan Press, 1986);

Srebrnik, "Trollope, James Virtue, and *Saint Pauls Magazine*," *Nineteenth Century Fiction*, 37 (December 1982): 443-463;

Alexander Strahan, "Charles Knight, Publisher," *Good Words*, 8 (September 1867): 615-621;

Strahan, "Twenty Years of a Publisher's Life. Giving Reminiscences of Well-Known Writers," *Day of Rest*, new series 3 (1881).

—*Patricia Thomas Srebrnik*

# Swan Sonnenschein Limited
*(London: 1895-1911)*
## Swan Sonnenschein and Allen
*(London: 1878-1881)*
## Swan Sonnenschein, Lowrey and Company
*(London: 1881-1888)*
## Swan Sonnenschein and Company
*(London: 1888-1895)*

The Swan Sonnenschein firm published works by Karl Marx, George Bernard Shaw, George Meredith, J. M. Barrie, Henry James, George Moore, and Edward Carpenter. Essentially, however, Swan Sonnenschein's reputation was based on its various series of handbooks, principally in philosophy and social science.

Born on 5 May 1855, William Swan Sonnenschein had been intended by his parents for the medical profession. But he found operations and dissections unpalatable, and so he was apprenticed instead to the publishers and book importers Williams and Norgate of 14 Henrietta Street, Covent Garden, London. This firm was well known as a clearinghouse for continental literature, especially German. It also published the *Theological Review* and works by Herbert Spencer and Thomas Henry Huxley, and it began the Home University Library. During these years Sonnenschein acquired a lifelong fascination with

*William Swan Stallybrass ( formerly William Swan Son-nenschein) in 1927*

contemporary European thought as well as the catholic interests that were to lead him to include on his own lists works various in style, ideology, and genre.

Swan Sonnenschein and Allen began its life in 1878 in offices at 15 Paternoster Square, close by Smithfield Market. Sonnenschein had entered into partnership with a young businessman, J. Archibald Allen, who stayed with the firm until 1881. The firm's first catalogue reflected Sonnenschein's family and business background. Adolf Sonnenschein, the publisher's father, ran a school in Highbury and was a respected figure in educational circles. His "Model Lessons" textbooks were well known, and in 1880 he transferred many of his educational works from older houses to swell his son's list. His book *The New Science and Art of Arithmetic*, coauthored with Henry A. Nesbitt, was published in 1899.

Other works that Sonnenschein published showed his interest in European writing and scholarly work. There was an edition of Wilhelm Müller's life of Count Moltke (1880) and a translation by Sonnenschein's uncle, James S. Stallybrass, of the first volume of Jacob Grimm's *Teutonic Mythology* (1883). The only concession to lighter reading was an assortment of illustrated gift books. It was also during these years that Swan Sonnenschein established a close connection with the Froebbel Society; the firm published books by leading figures in the movement such as Alexander B. Hanschmann's *The Kindergarten System* (1897), which was still selling well in the 1950s.

Finally, the early lists of the company were swelled by Sonnenschein's own contributions. Under the pen name W. S. W. Anson he edited an English adaptation of Wilhelm Wägner's tales of the old Norsemen, *Asgard and the Gods* (1880). It was followed by a version of another work by Wägner, *Epics and Romances of the Middle Ages* (1883). Sonnenschein also wrote and published stories for children (1883, 1884), a selection of Elizabethan lyrics (1905), and books of Shakespearean quotations (1909). All those who met Sonnenschein commented that his achievements were founded upon his fanaticism for work; the future publisher Frederic Warburg, who worked for Sonnenschein after the latter moved to George Routledge and Sons, said: "First to arrive at the office at 9 a.m., last to leave at 5:30 p.m., he took home with him . . . manuscripts on which he would labour that evening. A product of the Victorian age, work was his pleasure and enlightenment his gospel."

His willingness to undertake selfless labor to advance scholarship is nowhere better seen than in his compilation *The Best Books* (1887-1935). This work had been announced in Swan Sonnenschein's list for several years; when nothing was forthcoming from the author who had proposed it, the publisher undertook it himself. It was, according to its subtitle, *A Reader's Guide to the Choice of the Best Available Books (about 25,000) in Every Department of Science, Art, and Literature, with the Dates of the First and Last Editions, and the Price, Size and Publisher's Name of Each Book: A Contribution towards Classified Bibliography*. The project was begun in 1881, and the first volume appeared in 1887. It was not completed until a week before its author died at the end of January 1931. It was published in quarto and bound in boards, eventually consisting of five large volumes plus an index compiled by his daughter.

Shaw was the first of the unknown authors, later to be famous, who came to the attention of

Swan Sonnenschein. Although their business relationship was never harmonious, the publisher appears to have been willing to negotiate with a difficult client because of his conviction that here was "the brightest brain I have come across." Shaw wrote to Swan Sonnenschein on 16 February 1885 offering the firm his novel *An Unsocial Socialist*. The book had already been rejected by Kegan, Paul, Trench and Company, Chatto and Windus, and by John Morley of Macmillan, as being "too clever" for the general public. Shaw had then sent the novel to J. L. Loynes, one of the editors of *To-Day*, a socialist monthly magazine, who recommended it for serialization. It had appeared in this form between March and December 1884. As Shaw said, "That took me into print and started me." Swan Sonnenschein agreed to publish the work, but the contract the firm offered produced a three-week-long correspondence with Shaw over the copyright of the book. Upon examining Swan Sonnenschein's standard contract, Shaw discovered that he would have to assign his copyright in the novel to the publisher indefinitely. He refused to do so, offering only to lease the rights for five years, subject to renewal. Shaw justified his position by reference to what he saw as imminent developments in the world of publishing, which would "so diminish the costs of printing that the value of copyrights which are genuine monopolies will be greatly increased." Swan Sonnenschein capitulated on 21 March 1885, suggesting as a compromise a seven years' lease at 10 percent royalty, renewable for a like period at the firm's option at 20 percent. The book was published in 1887.

*An Unsocial Socialist* was an extraordinary book for Swan Sonnenschein to have published in the 1880s. As Shaw later remarked, it was "the first English novel written under the influence of Karl Marx, with a hero whose character and opinions forecast those of Lenin."

Another dispute between Sonnenschein and Shaw that occurred at the same time as the one over copyright reveals the publisher's refusal to negotiate about work that he judged to be of negligible worth. In 1879 Swan Sonnenschein had started a journal called *Time: A Monthly Miscellany of Interesting and Amusing Literature*. In March 1885 Shaw contributed a story, "The Miraculous Revenge," and a review of Michael Davitt's *Leaves from a Prison Diary*. There ensued a wrangle over how much this work was worth. Sonnenschein considered that the story was only "make-up matter" and that the review had been paid for by Shaw's re-

tention of the book discussed. The dispute over the amount of payment continued for months. This time it was Shaw who failed to have his way, for he only ever received three of the nine guineas he claimed.

In 1886 Swan Sonnenschein published Marx's *Capital*, translated into English by Samuel Moore and Edward Aveling, edited by Frederick Engels, and containing most of Marx's final revisions. The work had been available in German since 1867, and the theories advocated in it, according to Engels's preface, had been "constantly referred to, attacked and defended, interpreted and misinterpreted, in the periodical press and the current literature of both England and America." As Shaw's novel had shown, and as Engels noted in his preface, Marx's ideas were already exercising "a powerful influence upon the socialist movement which is spreading in the ranks of [cultured] people no less than in those of the working class." Certainly sales confirmed the interest in Marx's ideas. A month after its appearance only fifty copies were left of the first edition, and the second was in preparation. Engels, no doubt jaundiced by the year's editorial work he had spent on "this incubus," commented acidly that "the ass of a publisher . . . had no notion what he had got hold of" and was "quite surprised" that the book was doing so well.

There were others, however, who were convinced that Swan Sonnenschein was establishing itself as a publisher of radical works. This suspicion was fueled by its continuing to publish works by Carpenter, the homosexual poet who argued that sex was the paramount issue of civilization. *England's Ideal*, which revealed the influence of Marx and John Ruskin, appeared in 1887; *Civilisation: Its Cause and Cure*, which had a wide circulation in England and abroad, was published in 1889. Finally, *Towards Democracy*, which Carpenter described as the kernel of his work, was transferred to Swan Sonnenschein and Company in 1905 with the fourth and final part added to it by the author. It had originally been published in Manchester at Carpenter's expense in 1883 and had fallen flat. It was published in London in 1892 by T. Fisher Unwin, just at the time of Oscar Wilde's trial for homosexuality. Narrowly escaping the creditors of its next publisher (1896), the bankrupt Labour Press, it arrived at the offices of Swan Sonnenschein, who agreed to sell it on a commission basis. Sales of the book increased from 100 to 150 per annum in 1902 to between 800 and 900 in 1910.

Sonnenschein's dealings with Carpenter after the publication of Marx and Shaw kept alive the notion that he was a radical; in fact, his lists reveal a willingness to publish authoritative books from any political standpoint. His son described his political position as "a generous conservatism," and Engels, in his dealings with the publisher, found nothing more sympathetic than a commitment to publish what he deemed to be a worthy contribution to social, political, and economic debate. What is impressive about his firm is the eclecticism of its interests.

In contrast, for example, to Marx, Shaw, and Carpenter, there was the Imperial Parliament series (1885-1909), edited by Sydney C. Buxton, who was governor general of South Africa from 1914 to 1920 and became Earl Buxton in 1920. These were shilling volumes, written by members of Parliament, discussing the rights and responsibilities of citizens. During these same years Swan Sonnenschein began a series with which its name was always to be associated: the Library of Philosophy (1890-1911), edited by John H. Muirhead. Sonnenschein was himself greatly interested in philosophical thought; he was a member of the Ethical Society and published its literature—always at a loss. Nor was there much financial return from the Library of Philosophy. Sonnenschein's motivation seems to have been an idealistic wish to rescue English philosophy from its insularity and give it a worthier place "in the realm of international thought"; he hoped, in this way, to build "those bridges which are so hard to build from the political side." Volumes were published on aesthetics, utilitarianism, political economy, and psychology.

Another long-running series was the Social Science series. Published at first at two shillings, sixpence, "to place it within everybody's reach," it included David George Ritchie's *Darwinism and Politics* (1889) and Sir Charles Stewart Loch's *Charity Organization* (1890). The series ran from the 1880s well into the twentieth century, receiving many accolades from reviewers. The *Literary World* observed that "There is a certain impartiality about the attractive and well-printed volumes. . . . There is no editor and no common design. . . . The system adopted appears to be to select men known to have a claim to speak with more or less authority upon the shortcomings of civilisation, and to allow each to propound the views which commend themselves most strongly to his mind without reference to the possible flat

contradiction which may be forthcoming at the hands of the next contributor."

Other books that were to earn a distinguished reputation, such as F. H. Bradley's *Appearance and Reality* (1893) and Sir Paul Vinogradoff's *The Growth of the Manor* (1905), were published by Swan Sonnenschein. Perhaps the most fitting comment on this aspect of the publisher's work was made in a letter to the *Times* by Muirhead when William Swan Stallybrass died: "Little as I know of the history of publication, I doubt whether idealism of this kind has been common in it; but it was characteristic of the man, and I have ventured to think worthy of record in the attempt to do justice to his courageous life as a publisher and writer."

Swan Sonnenschein could not set off these scholarly publications against a lucrative list of popular fiction. The house was associated with none of the better-known names of the 1890s, such as Thomas Hardy or Rudyard Kipling. In fiction its only notable success was in the 1880s, when the three-decker novel was still in vogue and it published *Lord and Lady Piccadilly* (1888), by the earl of Desart. J. M. Barrie came to the firm with *Better Dead* (1888), a collection of articles that had appeared in the *St. James's Gazette* and were a spoof on W. H. Mallock's *Is Life Worth Living?* (1879). Blackwood's and Kegan Paul had already rejected Barrie's work, and Swan Sonnenschein would only arrange for it to be published at the author's expense. It was published as a shilling shocker, with a paper cover by William Mitchell showing a silk-hatted individual lurking at a street corner, knife in hand, as two hapless pedestrians approached. The author never recouped the money he had advanced to publish the book. After this experience, Barrie submitted his work to Hodder and Stoughton.

George Moore, the infamous author of *A Modern Lover* (published by Tinsley in 1883), was also temporarily associated with Swan Sonnenschein. The stories in *Parnell and His Island* (1887) still showed the influence of the Naturalist school. In 1888 came *Confessions of a Young Man*, parts of which had already appeared in Swan Sonnenschein's magazine, *Time*. The book sold well; the flamboyant rejection in it of Moore's former master, Emile Zola, and the principles which had until then guided Moore's own work provided a talking point in literary circles. Although Moore offered more of his work to *Time*, it was not deemed suitable for a family journal; thus this author's connection with Swan Sonnenschein also ceased.

*Time* was discontinued in 1891. Another of the firm's journals, the *Contemporary Pulpit*, was folded in December 1893. It had run for ten years, having started in January 1884. At a time when competition in the periodical press was particularly fierce Swan Sonnenschein had little success; its only other involvement was to publish the *Universal Review*, edited by Harry Quilter. The firm had no financial interest in this journal, which began in May 1888 and ceased in December 1890. Henry James, who at this time was not well known, appeared in the issues of July and August 1888 with "The Lesson of the Master." In October 1889 George Meredith's poem "Jump-to-Glory Jane," with its scathing comments about religious belief in England, appeared in the *Universal Review*. In spite of contributions such as these, the journal failed; priced at two shillings, sixpence, it was expensive at a time when monthlies were on the wane, and its advertising revenue proved to be inadequate to sustain it.

In 1895 Swan Sonnenschein became a limited liability company. The founder had a series of partners: Allen had been followed by Charles Le Bas and Francis Lowrey, but the longest relationship was with Col. P. H. Dalbaic, who had joined the firm in 1891 on his retirement from the army. He played an active role in the company, taking responsibility for the dictionaries of quotations it produced and originating in 1904 the Special Campaign series, to which leading military critics contributed.

In 1902 William Swan Sonnenschein left his own firm to become the senior managing director of the newly reconstructed George Routledge and Sons. The only reasons contemporary commentators could find for this move was "lust for work" and the challenge of reviving an ailing business. Dalbaic and Herbert Wigram took over the management of Swan Sonnenschein Limited. For a few years the founder of the firm maintained his association with it, but developments at Routledge led him to break with Swan Sonnenschein in 1906.

By the first decade of the twentieth century publishers were finding that the margins within which competition drove them to work made

their profits negligible. This was particularly true of the firm of Swan Sonnenschein Limited, which seemed to have lost initiative with the departure of the founder, and its annual profits in these years were no more than fourteen thousand pounds. Although Dalbaic resisted, in 1911 the company was merged with George Allen and Company Limited. The arrangement left the new firm weak and short of cash. There was a brief period of receivership in 1913, from which the firm was rescued by Stanley Unwin; the new firm of George Allen and Unwin emerged in 1914.

When George Allen and Unwin moved shortly thereafter to premises in Museum Street, Unwin recalled in his memoirs (1960), a "solicitor colleague . . . authorized the pulping, with much unwanted junk, of all the Swan Sonnenschein correspondence." William Swan Stallybrass—he had dropped the German "Sonnenschein" and adopted his mother's maiden name in 1917, during World War I—later commented in a letter to Shaw: "It is almost painful to contemplate the amount the Bolsheviks would have paid for those Karl Marx-Engels letters." Although the records and the imprint disappeared, the list of scholarly works that Swan Sonnenschein Limited had published remains, and it reveals its founder's ability to recognize works that were to have a crucial importance in the intellectual history of the twentieth century. Stallybrass died on 31 January 1931.

**References:**

Michael Holroyd, *Bernard Shaw, 1856-1898: The Search for Love* (London: Chatto & Windus, 1988);

Dan H. Laurence, ed., *Bernard Shaw: Collected Letters 1874-1897* (London: Reinhardt, 1965);

Frank Arthur Mumby, *The House of Routledge 1834-1934* (London: Routledge, 1934);

Mumby and Frances H. S. Stallybrass, *From William Swan Sonnenschein to George Allen & Unwin Ltd.* (London: Allen & Unwin, 1955);

Sir Stanley Unwin, *The Truth about a Publisher: An Autobiographical Record* (New York: Macmillan, 1960);

Frederic Warburg, *An Occupation for Gentlemen* (London: Hutchinson, 1959).

*—Ann Parry*

# Charles Tilt
## (London: 1826-1840)
# Tilt and Bogue
## (London: 1840-1843)

Charles Tilt conducted a tremendously profitable business as a London publisher and bookseller at 86 Fleet Street, at the corner of St. Bride's Passage or Avenue. The earliest work known to bear the Tilt imprint is *Head-Pieces and Tail-Pieces* (1826), by Leitch Ritchie, published pseudonymously as "By a Travelling Artist." The financial success of Tilt's firm derived mostly from the sale of richly illustrated books published in a variety of formats to suit all classes of book buyers. Tilt published gift books, annuals, almanacs (including one which fit neatly into the top of a man's hat), travel books, editions of the classics (Tilt's Miniature Classics came with a satin or rosewood cabinet with a glass door and lock), and a wide variety of children's literature.

Tilt sometimes worked in association with other publishers, publishing works with Charles Whittingham at the Chiswick Press and with William Kidd of Old Bond Street. One notable solo production was a series of illustrations for Sir Walter Scott's Waverley novels, engraved by William and Edward Finden (1830). Another popular enterprise was *Finden's Gallery of the Graces* (1832-1834), a collection of engraved female heads taken from paintings by such artists as Sir Edwin Landseer and Henry-Bernard Chalon. One of the children's books he published was by Mrs. Charlotte Reynolds, the mother of the poet John Hamilton Reynolds and mother-in-law of the poet and humorist Thomas Hood; she used the nom de plume "Mrs. Hamerton" for *Mrs. Leslie and Her Grandchildren* (1827). Tilt is said to have virtually cornered the early market for lithography by importing at low cost sheets of lavish designs from the Continent. Much of his successful marketing was attributed to the expansive side windows of his Fleet Street shop, which provided an effective display area for his wares.

His two most successful and notable collaborations were with Hood and George Cruikshank. Tilt's association with Hood probably began in 1827: Hood helped arrange the publication of his mother-in-law's work that year, and in November Tilt published the second volume of *Hood's Whims and Oddities*. In September 1829 Tilt published Hood's *The Epping Hunt*, with illustrations by Cruikshank, and in November 1831 he published an edition of his *Dream of Eugene Aram*. Hurst, Chance and Company published Hood's *Comic Annual* for 1830, but Hood split with that firm, and from 1831 to 1834 Tilt published the widely imitated and popular work. In 1833 Hood quarreled bitterly with Tilt, probably about the proposed novel *Tylney Hall*, which was finally published by Alfred Head Baily in late 1834. Though Tilt proceeded with the *Comic Annual* for 1834 (published in November 1833), the relationship ended. Hood, who feuded with several other publishers throughout the remaining twelve years of his life, seems always to have believed that Tilt treated him villainously.

In 1833 Cruikshank began a serious business relationship with Tilt, which seems to have been initiated by Cruikshank's regular publisher at the time, the ailing James Robins of Ivy Lane. Tilt had already published Cruikshank's illustrations in an edition of William Cowper's *The Diverting History of John Gilpin* (1827) and his illustrations for Hood's *The Epping Hunt*. But in 1833 Tilt published "for the artist" the first number of Cruikshank's nine-part *My Sketch Book* (1833-1836). In 1834, possibly as a replacement for Hood's *Comic Annual*, the two men also began the *Comic Almanack* (1834-1852). The printer and publisher James Henry Vizetelly, who became, under the pseudonym "Rigdum Funnidos," the almanac's first editor until his death four years later, may have been the originator of the project, though other sources attribute the idea to Tilt himself. For the next twenty-five years Tilt and his successors were Cruikshank's primary publishers, particularly for projects, such as *My Sketch Book*, that Cruikshank wanted to control completely.

William Makepeace Thackeray contributed some pieces to the *Comic Almanack* for 1839. He complained to Tilt's associate George Wright that he was to have been paid twenty guineas, not twenty pounds, for "Stubbs's Calendar; or, The Fatal Boots." "Such rich men as you and Mr. Tilt

*Illustration from George Cruikshank's* Comic Almanack *for 1835, depicting Charles Tilt's Fleet Street premises*

must not rob me of my shillings," the struggling writer admonished.

At about the same time Tilt published *The Loving Ballad of Lord Bateman* (1839), illustrated by Cruikshank. Most scholars now agree that the work was almost certainly written by Charles Dickens; it was long associated with Thackeray, who may have contributed some of the bogus scholarly apparatus to the book. The title page punningly lists a fictional copublisher, "Mustapha Syried [must-have-as-a-read], Constantinople," along with "Charles Tilt, Fleet Street."

Tilt had nearly become Dickens's first publisher. For much of 1833 he published the *Monthly Magazine*, but in October he sold the enterprise to J. B. Holland for three hundred pounds. Dickens's first published sketch, "A Dinner at Poplar Walk," appeared in the December number of the magazine.

When *The Pickwick Papers* was being published in monthly parts in 1836 and 1837, Tilt advised Chapman and Hall to send large numbers of copies of the work to provincial booksellers on a sale-or-return basis. Though the idea was not immediately successful (1,450 of the 1,500 copies were returned), the practice was used with much success in later years. Tilt advertised heavily in

the *Pickwick Advertiser*, a supplement that began to appear with the novel's fourth number.

Among Tilt's clerks was David Bogue, whose shrewdness and reliability appealed to him. Bogue had worked for Tilt since he came to London from Edinburgh in 1836. One night Tilt kept Bogue late for a stocktaking and then explained to his surprised employee his plan to hand over the firm to him after a trial partnership, and to allow Bogue generous terms for repayment of the capital advanced.

For 1841 Tilt and Bogue published an extensive list that included Cruikshank's new periodical, the *Omnibus* (May 1841 - January 1842). As with *My Sketch Book*, Cruikshank retained control of all details involving publication and marketing; on the cover "Messrs. Tilt & Bogue" were listed as "Conductors" of the vehicle and "86, Fleet Street" was given as the "Booking Office." Edited by Laman Blanchard, the periodical included contributions from Frederick Marryat, Horace Mayhew, and Thackeray.

By 1843 Tilt and Bogue had become simply "David Bogue" or "D. Bogue." Tilt began a life of travel, philanthropy, and leisure but occasionally invested in publishing ventures. After a tour of the Middle East he wrote an account of his experiences, *The Boat and the Caravan: A Family Tour through Egypt and Syria*. Published by Bogue in 1847, it went through several editions and was translated into German. Bogue died on 19 November 1856 at forty-five, leaving a wife and five children. Tilt, who no doubt still had a large investment in the firm, became involved in the settlement of the estate. He nagged Cruikshank and others about repayment of advances and sold off copyrights to Macmillan and Company. By 1860 the firm W. Kent and Company was including in its imprint "Late D. Bogue." Before the estate was completely settled, Tilt himself died on 28 September 1861.

**References:**

John Clubbe, *Victorian Forerunner: The Later Career of Thomas Hood* (Durham, N.C.: Duke University Press, 1968);

"Deaths," *Gentleman's Magazine*, new series 40 (December 1861): 691-692;

"Deaths," *Times* (London), 1 October 1861, p. 1;

Madeline House and Graham Storey, eds., *The Letters of Charles Dickens*, volumes 1-2 (Oxford: Clarendon Press, 1965-1969);

Malcolm Macleod, "Tilt Family," *Notes and Queries*, third series 1 (18 January 1862): 4-5;

Peter F. Morgan, ed., *The Letters of Thomas Hood*, Department of English Studies and Texts 18 (Toronto & Buffalo: University of Toronto Press, 1973);

Gordon N. Ray, ed., *The Letters and Private Papers of William Makepeace Thackeray*, 4 volumes (Cambridge, Mass.: Harvard University Press, 1945);

Henry Vizetelly, *Glances Back through Seventy Years: Autobiographical and Other Reminiscences*, 2 volumes (London: Kegan Paul, Trench, Trübner, 1893), I: 102-111.

                                —*Logan D. Browning, Jr.*

# Tinsley Brothers

*(London: 1858-1892)*

William and Edward Tinsley, the sons of a gamekeeper, were born in Hertfordshire in 1831 and 1833, respectively. Their father, by William's account, was not bookish, but Mrs. Tinsley could read and write better than most women of her class and acted as scribe for her village neighbors. The boys evidently went to the local dame's school. Throughout life William retained his country accent and imperfect grammar. Thomas Hardy once told him that he was an architect by profession and received the reply, "Damned if that isn't what I thought you wos." George Moore described William Tinsley as coming into the Gaiety bar, his favorite drinking place, carrying a bag "containing fish for the family and a manuscript novel." By their professional colleagues both brothers were generally thought to be ignorant and vulgar fellows, somewhat out of their station in life.

Edward, although the younger, left home for London before his brother—probably around 1849. He was employed in the engineering shop of the South Western Railway. William walked to London in 1852 with two shillings in his pocket. He found lodgings in Notting Hill and did odd jobs. He was exposed to working-class radical writing during this period and evidently read quite widely in a self-improving way.

Edward, meanwhile, was fretting at his railway work. He loved the theater, and the late nights made early rising difficult. He began to hang around publishers' offices, where he found more congenial employment. Edward Tinsley and Company is listed at 310 Strand as early as 1850. At some point—some accounts say 1854— the brothers set up together in the book trade in Holywell Street; in 1858 their partnership was formalized by legal agreement. Confusingly, William Tinsley alone is recorded as trading at 314 Strand in 1860-1861, which—if true—suggests that their business arrangements were volatile. In 1862 the brothers established themselves at 18 Catherine Street, the Strand, a location they were to keep for twenty-four years. (In 1873 it was renumbered 80.)

It is unclear what the Tinsley brothers did in the book trade before 1862. Some accounts

*Caricature of William Tinsley by F. Waddy*

say that Edward was a secondhand bookseller. An advertisement appeared in January 1860 for a newspaper, the *Leader and Saturday Analyst*, addressed from 18 Catherine Street, but without the Tinsleys' name mentioned; presumably they were distributing printed material on an agency basis. The *Dictionary of National Biography* says that they published the *New Quarterly Review* from 1854 to 1859. The best clue to their early activities is the description they give of themselves in their 1862 advertisements: "Tinsley Brothers, Library Depôt, 18 Catherine Street." At the same period they published the monthly *Library Circular of New and Second-hand Books*. It would seem that they acted as middlemen, selling job lots of volumes discarded by the large London libraries for sale to smaller and regional libraries. This connection with libraries—particularly the London leviathans of the trade—was to be crucial in the Tinsleys' later evolution.

Both Tinsleys had a reputation for conviviality. They consorted with journalists in neighboring Strand and Fleet Street public houses. Their first books reflect this "bohemian" connection—a flavor that was to persist in their list. Their earliest discoverable title is a reprint of *The Night Side of London*, by the journalist James Ritchie, in 1860. Their first successes, however, were with two "sensation" novels written by Fleet Street journalists: George Augustus Sala's *Seven Sons of Mammon* (1861) and W. B. Jerrold's *Two Lives* (1862). Sala was a notable catch, and no fewer than three of his works embellish the Tinsleys' advertisements in May 1862.

The connection with Fleet Street established the Tinsleys as publishers, but it was the connection with lending libraries that made them a dominant force in the book trade. Charles Edward Mudie, who had started his circulating library in 1842, was phenomenally successful by the late 1850s. In 1860 he moved into magnificent new premises in New Oxford Street. His success inspired competition. In 1858 W. H. Smith and Son proposed partnership, using its railway bookstalls as outlets for book lending; Mudie declined the offer. Smith went ahead with its own library, which by the early 1860s was another huge success. In the face of Mudie's growth, a consortium of rival London lending libraries was formed in 1858 as The United Libraries. Most momentously, in August 1862 the Library Company Limited was set up at 25 Pall Mall. This ambitious venture undercut Mudie's one-guinea, one-volume, one-year subscription by charging ten shillings, sixpence.

Mudie responded with a spending war that went on for five years. Lavish advertising and extravagant purchases of the "books of the day" were the means by which Mudie intended to beggar his rivals; they, too, were forced into extravagant buying. With their library connections, the Tinsleys were well placed to take advantage of the buying spree. And they had a huge stroke of luck when, through John Maxwell (another Fleet Street contact), they acquired the copyright of Mary Elizabeth Braddon's *Lady Audley's Secret*. This story of bigamy and murder had made no great stir as a magazine serial for Maxwell. But when released as a three-decker by Tinsley Brothers in October 1862, it became an overnight best-

seller. The libraries bought the work by the ton. The Tinsleys made so much money from this one novel that Edward built himself a house at Putney which he called Audley Lodge.

The Tinsleys had paid £250 for Braddon's copyright. With the infusion of capital it brought, they could go on their own buying spree, poaching authors from other publishers. They could also take chances on unknown authors. Informality and openhandedness were to be their style. The firm advanced £500 to G. A. Lawrence for a novel in the early 1860s. Lawrence promptly went off to Homburg, where he lost his advance at the card tables in less than a week. He received another loan from Tinsley Brothers, came home, and wrote his novel in short order. All the Tinsleys' energy went into commissioning. There was no editorial department in their firm; it was routine for novelists to send their manuscripts directly to the printer without the publisher even seeing them. Moore describes the Tinsley office as a permanent shambles: "There was a long counter, and the way to be published by Mr. Tinsley was to straddle on the counter and play with a black cat." Most of the work of the office was done by an Irishman behind the counter, "who for three pounds a week edited the magazine, read the manuscripts, looked after the printer and binder, kept the accounts and entertained the visitors." The one production detail to which the Tinsleys gave close attention was binding: the libraries demanded luxurious designs and materials. Tinsley boards—especially on three-deckers—were distinctively colorful and ornamental.

In their heyday Tinsley Brothers published (and in some cases "made") most of the kings and queens of the circulating libraries: Braddon, Ouida, Mrs. Riddell, Joseph Sheridan Le Fanu, Joseph Hatton, Rosa N. Carey, Justin McCarthy, Rosa M. Praed, Walter Besant and James Rice, William Harrison Ainsworth, Mrs. Henry Wood, B. L. Farjeon, Edmund Yates, Henry Kingsley, Annie Thomas, Eliza Lynn Linton, Percy Fitzgerald, Rhoda Broughton, Jean Ingelow, Margaret Oliphant, Lawrence, Florence Marryat, Mortimer Collins, Wilkie Collins, Annie Edwards, James Payn, and Amelia B. Edwards. Publishing in the quantity it did, the firm by 1867 had an impressive back list which it reprinted in six-shilling (eventually two-shilling) form for the "railway reader." Fiction was overwhelmingly Tinsley Brothers' main line of goods, although the firm also published some interesting reportage, such

FORM OF REQUIRING ENTRY OF PROPRIETORSHIP.

I, *Mary Elizabeth Braddon 26 Mecklenburg...* do hereby certify, That I am the Proprietor of the Copyright of a Book, intituled *Lady Audley's Secret* ; and I hereby require you to make entry in the Register Book of the Stationers' Company of my Proprietorship of such Copyright, according to the particulars underwritten.

| Title of Book. | Name of Publisher, and Place of Publication. | Name and Place of Abode of the Proprietor of the Copyright. | Date of First Publication. |
|---|---|---|---|
| *Lady Audley's Secret* | *Tinsley Bro* | *18 Catherine St Strand* | *Oct 1st 1862* |

Dated this *21* day of *Nov* .18*62*

Witness, *Kitrick LBorough*

N.B. *Office Hours from Ten to Four*

(Signed) *Mary Elizabeth Braddon.*

[NUMBER 67]

*Mary Elizabeth Braddon's application for copyright for her novel* Lady Audley's Secret *(auctioned by American Art Association/ Anderson Galleries, sale number 4283, 9 December 1936)*

as Sala's *My Diary in America* (1865). The firm also had a strong sideline in fiction for young readers, with authors such as G. Manville Fenn and G. A. Henty. Some "literary" novelists—notably Hardy, George Meredith, William Black, Richard Jefferies, and Moore—got their start with Tinsley. And the firm published one indisputably great novel, Wilkie Collins's *The Moonstone* (1868). But if there is one commodity that sums up the activities of Tinsley Brothers, it is the sumptuously bound, fatuous, three-volume novel.

The Tinsleys' golden period was relatively short-lived. The library war cooled down with the failure of the Library Company Limited in 1865, and sales dropped. Other publishers imitated the Tinsley formula, and in many cases they were better businessmen. Having gotten three best-sellers out of Braddon in a year, the Tinsleys lost her to Maxwell, her common-law husband. Mrs. Wood, with whom they replaced

Braddon, also went her own way. The Tinsleys' handling of other authors, such as Ouida, seems to have been tactless; and even those who remained loyal, like Mrs. Riddell, seem to have despised them. The greatest disaster for the firm was Edward Tinsley's sudden death in September 1866. All commentators agree that he was the abler of the brothers. Without him, William Tinsley's prospects were bleak.

After Edward's death the firm remained Tinsley Brothers, but its luster rapidly faded. In 1867, with much fanfare, William started *Tinsley's Magazine*, with Edmund Yates as editor. Modeled on the *Cornhill*, the magazine was illustrated and cost one shilling. The early issues serialized a first novel by Britain's most famous journalist, William H. Russell, for which Tinsley paid thirteen hundred pounds. Despite all these efforts, the magazine was a failure. Nevertheless, William kept it going, editing it himself after Yates left for better things in 1869.

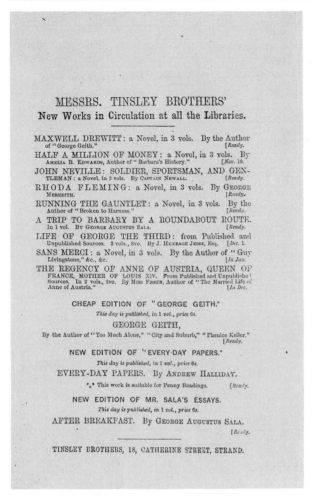

MESSRS. TINSLEY BROTHERS'
New Works in Circulation at all the Libraries.

MAXWELL DREWITT: a Novel, in 3 vols. By the Author of "George Geith."                                   [Ready.
HALF A MILLION OF MONEY: a Novel, in 3 vols. By Amelia B. Edwards, Author of "Barbara's History."        [Nov. 10.
JOHN NEVILLE: SOLDIER, SPORTSMAN, AND GEN-TLEMAN: a Novel, in 2 vols. By Captain Newall.                 [Ready.
RHODA FLEMING: a Novel, in 3 vols. By George Meredith.                                                   [Ready.
RUNNING THE GAUNTLET: a Novel, in 3 vols. By the Author of "Broken to Harness."                          [Ready.
A TRIP TO BARBARY BY A ROUNDABOUT ROUTE. In 1 vol. By George Augustus Sala.                              [Ready.
LIFE OF GEORGE THE THIRD: from Published and Unpublished Sources. 3 vols., 8vo. By J. Heneage Jesse, Esq. [Dec. 1.
SANS MERCI: a Novel, in 3 vols. By the Author of "Guy Livingstone," &c., &c.                             [In Jan.
THE REGENCY OF ANNE OF AUSTRIA, QUEEN OF FRANCE, MOTHER OF LOUIS XIV. From Published and Unpublished Sources. In 2 vols., 8vo. By Miss Freer, Author of "The Married Life of Anne of Austria."                                         [In Dec.

CHEAP EDITION OF "GEORGE GEITH."
This day is published, in 1 vol., price 6s.
GEORGE GEITH,
By the Author of "Too Much Alone," "City and Suburb," "Phemie Keller."
[Ready.

NEW EDITION OF "EVERY-DAY PAPERS."
This day is published, in 1 vol., price 6s.
EVERY-DAY PAPERS. By Andrew Halliday.
*.* This work is suitable for Penny Readings.       [Ready.

NEW EDITION OF MR. SALA'S ESSAYS.
This day is published, in 1 vol., price 6s.
AFTER BREAKFAST. By George Augustus Sala.
[Ready.

TINSLEY BROTHERS, 18, CATHERINE STREET, STRAND.

*1866 advertisement*

The Tinsley list shows a clear decline after 1868, although it still had some high points. In 1871-1872, for example, the firm put out Mrs. Oliphant's *Squire Arden* (1871), Lawrence's *Anteros* (1871), B. L. Farjeon's *Joshua Marvel* (1871) and *Blade o' Grass* (1872), James Grant's *Under the Red Dragon* (1872), Mortimer Collins's *Two Plunges for a Pearl* (1872), Anthony Trollope's *The Golden Lion of Granpere* (1872), Besant and Rice's *Ready Money Mortiboy* (1872), Hardy's *Under the Greenwood Tree* (1872), William Harrison Ainsworth's *Boscobel* (1872), and Yates's *The Yellow Flag* (1872). For readability, if nothing else, this selection would have been hard to beat.

A major confusion in charting the Tinsleys' history arises in 1872, with the arrival of Samuel Tinsley on the scene. With his office in 10 Southampton Street, just off the Strand, Samuel Tinsley began publishing books exactly like Tinsley Brothers' but by an inferior class of author. In the early 1870s, Samuel Tinsley's leading

novelist was Rosa Mackenzie Kettle, a distinct second-rater. As the decade progressed, however, Samuel Tinsley thrived and eventually overtook the languishing William. In 1878 Samuel Tinsley poached William's best-selling author, Florence Marryat. Samuel Tinsley sold out in 1881 to F. V. White, who also specialized in three-deckers for the library market. Tinsley (as William himself proudly notes) is an uncommon name, and one assumes that Samuel must have been a brother or cousin of William. Whether he conducted his business as a friendly disciple or a hostile rival is unknown.

Several forces drove William Tinsley to the wall in the 1870s, not the least of which was the strength of the competition. In addition to the mysterious Samuel there were Ward and Downey (Edmund Downey had been one of William Tinsley's employees), Henry S. King, Sampson Low, Chapman and Hall, and Richard Bentley and Son. Most aggressive was Chatto and Windus, which bought up everything in sight in the second half of the decade—including the journal *Belgravia*, which brilliantly outshone *Tinsley's*. Ouida, Wilkie Collins, Hardy, and Besant and Rice all gravitated to Chatto and Windus's list. By 1877 Tinsley's "star" author was the veteran hack Ainsworth, who turned in his stale historical romances at one hundred pounds apiece. In 1877 Tinsley launched a sixpenny humor magazine called *Mirth*, which failed within a year.

Tinsley Brothers went bankrupt in 1878 with losses of around thirty-three thousand pounds. In his *Random Recollections of an Old Publisher* (1900) Tinsley blames loyalty to his magazine for the crash. Other commentators suggest that he wildly overprinted works such as Grant's *The Newspaper Press*, the first two volumes of which were published by Tinsley in 1871, the third being taken over by Routledge in 1872. Moore, who only knew the publisher late in life, ascribed his calamities to unbusinesslike habits: "he conducted his business as he dressed himself, sloppily; a dear kind soul, quite witless and quite *h*-less. From long habit he would make a feeble attempt to drive a bargain, but was duped generally."

It seems that after 1878 Tinsley was allowed to continue publishing under the supervision of trustees. The quality of his postbankruptcy lists is generally dire, featuring such desperate descriptions as "*Cynthia*, A new novel by a new writer" (1881). Nevertheless, the occasional interesting novelist turns up, such as Theo Gift, William

*"Yellowback" cover for the 1871 republication of Rhoda Broughton's first novel, originally published in three volumes by Tinsley Brothers in 1867*

Westall, Bithia M. Croker, "Rita" (Mrs. Desmond Humphreys), and Percy Fitzgerald. The magazine suspended publication from June 1887 to January 1888. The magazine passed out of his hands; since 1874 it had been unillustrated and its contents were wholly undistinguished. It was devastatingly reviewed by the *Athenaeum* in June 1889: "The new series of *Tinsley's Magazine* is issued at 6*d*. This first number can only be described as amazingly bad." The journal suspended publication again in January 1892. It was sold off by its new owners and had a brief afterlife as the *Novel Review, with Which Is Incorporated "Tinsley's Magazine,"* before expiring in December 1892.

During his last years William was supported by Lily Tinsley, who is presumed to be his daughter. In the early 1880s Lily (sometimes called Laura) wrote three-volume novels for the libraries, serials for the magazine, and edited *Lily Tinsley's Annual*. This volume, in December 1888, seems to have been one of the last published by the firm. In 1886 the firm is listed at 80 Catherine Street; in 1888 it is listed at 25 Bury Street, where it remained until 1892.

In 1900 William Tinsley published his garrulous but not particularly informative *Random Recollections of an Old Publisher*. Reviews were dismissive and generally unaffectionate. He died on 1 May 1902.

**References:**

Guinevere L. Griest, *Mudie's Circulating Library* (Bloomington: Indiana University Press, 1970);

Florence E. Hardy, *The Life of Thomas Hardy*, 2 volumes (London: Macmillan, 1933);

George Moore, *Confessions of a Young Man* (London: Heinemann, 1888);

George Augustus Sala, *The Life and Adventures of George Augustus Sala: Written by Himself*, second edition, 2 volumes (New York: Scribners, 1895);

Sue Thomas, *Tinsley's Magazine (The Novel Review)*, Victorian Fiction Research Guides 7 (Queensland, Australia: Department of English, University of Queensland, 1989);

William Tinsley, *Random Recollections of an Old Publisher*, 2 volumes (London: Simpkin, Marshall, Hamilton, Kent, 1900);

Edmund Yates, *Fifty Years of London Life* (New York: Harper, 1885).

*—John Sutherland*

# T. Fisher Unwin
*(London: 1882-1926)*

Thomas Fisher Unwin was born in 1848 into a family of printers and publishers. His father, Jacob Unwin, was the founder of Gresham Press, which published books by Dr. Thomas Binney and other Congregational divines. His mother, Isobel Hall Unwin, was a member of the Miller family, which had published the *Cheap Magazine* (1813-1814). One branch of the family included the printing firm Unwin Brothers, which printed the wrappers for periodicals such as *Tit-Bits* and the *Strand*.

After working for Jackson, Walford and Hodder, the forerunners of Hodder and Stoughton, in 1882 Unwin started his own business in Holborn Viaduct, London, by buying the small publishing house of Marshall Japp and Company for one thousand pounds. He moved to 11 Paternoster Building in 1882.

Unwin was part of a new generation of publishers who took on young writers at the start of their careers. Such risks did not reap financial benefits: profits averaged six hundred to seven hundred pounds until the turn of the century. The firm moved to 1 Adelphi Terrace in 1905. By 1912 the profits had grown to six thousand pounds, and in 1920 the business became a limited company. Unwin was generous to unknown

writers, but he did not provide them increased benefits as they became famous and demanded more compensation. Thus, authors often left Unwin after achieving success. The risk of taking on unknown or unprofitable writers was balanced by the publication of extremely popular and lucrative titles.

The firm published books on the publishing trade, including the second edition of *The Literary History of the Adelphi and Its Neighbourhood* (1908), by Austin Brererton; T. H. S. Escott's *Masters of English Journalism* (1911); and William J. Couper's *The Millers of Haddington, Dunbar and Dunfermline: A Record of Scottish Bookselling* (1914), on Unwin's mother's family. E. T. Raymond's *Uncensored Celebrities* (1918) and *Portraits of the Nineties* (1921) attacked the new journalism for its commercialism.

Unwin specialized in series, producing twenty-eight by 1917. These included the Autonym Library; the Independent Novels series, which published *A Phantom from the East* (1892), by Pierre Loti; the Welsh Library; the Idle Hour series; the Children's Library; and the Literary History series. The First Novel series began in 1902 with *Wistons*, by Ellen Cobden, Unwin's sister-in-law; it also included Dorothy L. Sayers's *Whose Body?* (1923). The New Irish Library was copub-

*Sketch of T. Fisher Unwin by his office manager, 1918 (Cambridge University Library)*

lished with the Dublin firm of Sealy, Bryers and Walker.

Unwin took over the Mermaid series of Jacobean and Restoration plays in 1887 when its publisher, Henry Vizetelly, was arrested for publishing works by Emile Zola and Guy de Maupassant. The series consisted of scholarly editions edited by literary figures and included *Beaumont and Fletcher* (1887), edited by John St. Loe Strachey; *James Shirley* (1888), with an introduction by Edmund Gosse; *Nero and Other Plays* (1888), edited by Herbert P. Horne, Havelock Ellis, Arthur Symons, and A. Wilson Verity; *John Ford* (1888), edited by Ellis; *Thomas Middleton* (1890), with an introduction by Algernon Charles Swinburne; *Thomas Heywood* (1890), edited by Verity; *William Congreve* (1892), edited by Alexander Ewald; *Philip Massinger* (1893), edited by Symons; *Webster

*and Tourneur* (1893), edited by John Addington Symonds; *William Wycherley* (1893), edited by W. C. Ward; *Ben Jonson* (1893), edited by Brinsley Nicholson; *Thomas Otway* (1893), edited by Roden Noel; *Richard Steele* (1894), edited by G. A. Aitken; *Christopher Marlowe* (1897), edited by Ellis with an introduction by Symonds; *Robert Greene* (1909), edited by Thomas Dickinson; *Thomas Shadwell* (1920), edited by George Saintsburg; and *George Farquhar* (1920), edited by William Archer. Some of those books had been published by Vizetelly and were republished by Unwin.

Unwin also published the Story of the Nations Library, to which many distinguished historians contributed. This series reflected Unwin's interests in foreign writers, liberalism, free trade, international affairs, and the persecution of minorities, as well as his wife's interests in abolition and woman's suffrage. Included in this series were Zenaïde Alexeïevna Ragozin's studies of Chaldea (1886); Assyria (1887); Media, Babylon, and Persia (1889); and India (1895).

One of the most successful series was the fifty-six-volume Pseudonym Library of paperbound books with introductions by well-known authors. "John Oliver Hobbes" (Mrs. Pearl Craigie) contributed many novels, story collections, and plays: *Some Emotions and a Moral* (1891), *The Sinner's Comedy* (1892), *A Study in Temptations* (1893), *A Bundle of Life* (1893), *The Tales of John Oliver Hobbes* (1895), *The Herb Moon* (1896), *The School for Saints* (1897), *The Gods, Some Mortals and Lord Wickenham* (1897), *The Ambassador: A Comedy in Four Acts* (1898), *Robert Orange* (1900), *The Wisdom of the Wise: A Comedy in Three Acts* (1901), *Love and the Soul Hunters* (1902), *Tales about Temperaments* (1902), *Imperial India: Letters from the East* (1903), *The Vineyard* (1904), and *The Flute of Pan* (1905).

Other books by popular writers included John Buchan's first novel, *Sir Quixote of the Moors* (1895); Robert Buchanan's *Effie Hetherington* (1896) and *A Marriage by Capture* (1896); R. B. Cunninghame Graham's travel book *The Ipané* (1899); and Norman Douglas's *Unprofessional Tales* (1901). Henry de Vere Stacpoole wrote *The Doctor* (1899), *The Bourgeois* (1901), *The Lady-Killer* (1902), *Fanny Lambert* (1906), *The Crimson Azaleas* (1907), *Patsy* (1908), the best-selling *The Blue Lagoon* (1908), *Garryowen* (1909), *The Pools of Silence* (1909), and *The Vulture's Prey* (1909). Arminus Vambéry's autobiography was extremely popular as *Arminus Vambéry: His Life and Adventures* (1886) for boys. He also wrote *Hungary in Ancient, Medieval and Modern Times* (1886) in the Story of

*Edward Garnett, Unwin's principal manuscript reader, in 1895*

Nations series. Samuel Rutherford Crockett was the author of the popular *The Stickit Minister* (1893), one of the Kailyard School of romantic Scottish tales. Other Crockett novels published by Unwin were, *The Lilac Sunbonnet* (1894), *Mad Sir Uchtred of the Hills* (1894), and *The Grey Man* (1896).

Ethel May Dell's best-selling *The Way of the Eagle* (1912) was selected from a competition for young writers organized by Unwin and was heavily revised by the firm's talented staff. Advertised as "the novel with an ugly hero," it went through twenty-seven printings between 1912 and 1915. The firm's printing order books record 250,000 cheap reprints of the novel during World War I. Dell had a four-novel contract negotiated for the firm by Stanley Unwin, T. Fisher's nephew. Dell's fifth novel, *Greatheart* (1918), was taken on for terms more profitable to the author. The firm also published a volume of her stories, *The Safety Curtain, and Other Stories* (1919). When the popularity of her novels declined after 1914, the firm's profits fell sharply. At their peak her books accounted for half the firm's total sales. She left the firm after she and Unwin argued

over the number of free copies of her books she could have.

Other popular novels published by T. Fisher Unwin were Frederik Van Eeden's *The Deeps of Deliverance* (1902), one of the firm's best-selling novels, and the works of Victor L. Whitechurch: *The Canon in Residence* (1904), *The Locum Tenens* (1906), *Concerning Himself* (1909), *The Canon's Dilemma and Other Stories* (1909), *A Downland Corner* (1912), *Downland Echoes* (1924), *A Bishop out of Residence* (1924), *The Dean and Jecinora* (1926), and *Shot on the Downs* (1927). Edith Nesbit wrote many novels and children's books: *The Wouldbegoods* (1901), *Nine Unlikely Tales for Children* (1901), *New Treasure Seekers* (1904), *Man and Maid* (1906), *The Enchanted Castle* (1907), *The House of Arden* (1908), *The Phoenix and the Carpet* (1908), *Harding's Luck* (1923), *The Five of Us and Madeline* (1925), and *Wet Magic* (1926). Louis Becke had almost all of his South Seas adventure books published by Unwin: *By Reef and Palm* (1894); *The Ebbing of the Tide* (1896); *A First Fleet Family* (1896), written with Walter Jeffery; *The Mystery of the Laughlin Islands* (1896), with Jeffery; *His Native Wife* (1896); *Wild Life in Southern Seas* (1897); *The Mutineer* (1898); *Rodman the Boatsteerer* (1898); *Ridan the Devil* (1899); *Admiral Phillip* (1899), with Jeffery; *Edward Barry (South Sea Pearler)* (1900); *Tessa, the Trader's Wife* (1901); *Yorke the Adventurer* (1901); *The Strange Adventure of James Shervinton* (1902); *Breachley, Black Sheep* (1902); *Helen Adair* (1903); *Tom Gerrard* (1904); *Chinkie's Flat* (1904); *Under Tropic Skies* (1905); and *The Adventures of a Supercargo* (1905). Other writers who had books published by Unwin included Susan Ertz, a popular novelist of the 1920s, and William Henry Hudson. The firm published the complete works of Mark Rutherford, the pseudonym of William Hale White, in a uniform set; each volume sold for one shilling.

"Vernon Lee" (Violet Paget) wrote books on history and aesthetics for Unwin; she also wrote several novels for the firm: *Ottilie: An Eighteenth-Century Idyll* (1883), and *Penelope Branding* (1903). In 1887 and 1907 Unwin published new editions of Paget's successful *The Studies of the Eighteenth Century in Italy* which had first been published by Satchell in 1880.

Olive Schreiner, under the pseudonym "Ralph Iron," wrote the novella *Trooper Peter Halket of Mashonaland* (1897), for which Unwin paid her fifteen hundred pounds. The book accused Cecil Rhodes of the murder of envoys of the Matabele tribe in Africa. The frontispiece

Schreiner chose for the book was a photograph of Africans hanging from a tree (the same tree on which the Matabele envoys had been hanged), with Europeans casually standing by. The book cost Schreiner many friends, and she is alleged to have requested that on her tombstone be etched "She wrote *Peter Halket.*" For her first book with Unwin, the extremely popular *Dreams* (1890), which was reprinted twenty-two times (including twice in Dutch and four times in French), Havelock Ellis negotiated with Unwin on her behalf and read the proofs. *Woman and Labour* (1911), partly an outcome of work she had done with Ellis, was a feminist tract advocating professional careers for women. Her other works published by the firm included *Dream Life and Real Life* (1893) and *Stories, Dreams and Allegories* (1923). Unwin also published *The Political Situation in Cape Colony* (1896), by Schreiner and her husband, S. C. Cronwright-Schreiner.

Ouida (Marie Louise de la Ramée) was another popular Unwin writer. G. K. Chesterton wrote in a reader's report for the firm, "Though it is impossible not to smile at Ouida it is equally impossible not to read her." Among her books published by Unwin were *The Silver Christ and a Lemon Tree* (1894), *Toxin* (1895), *Le Selve and Other Tales* (1896), *An Altruist* (1897), *The Silver Christ* (1898), *The Waters of Edera* (1900), *Critical Studies* (1900), and *A Rainy June and Don Gesualdo* (1901). T. Fisher Unwin also published Elizabeth Lee's *Ouida: A Memoir* (1914).

Unwin's historical and political books included Wilfrid Scawen Blunt's *Atrocities of Justice under British Rule in Egypt* (1906), *Secret History of the English Occupation of Egypt* (1907), and *India Under Ripon* (1909). Wilfred Chesson and Brougham Villiers (pseudonym of Frederick John Shaw) wrote *Anglo-American Relations, 1861-1865* (1919). Pasquale Villari's works, translated by his wife Linda Mazini Villari, included *On Tuscan Hills and Venetian Waters* (1885), *Life and Times of Girolamo Savanarola* (1888), *The Life and Times of Niccolo Machiavelli* (1892), *The First Two Centuries of Florentine History* (1894-1895), and *Studies, Historical and Critical* (1907).

T. Fisher Unwin published works by some of the major literary figures at the end of the century. H. G. Wells's first book published by Unwin was his lecture to the Royal Institute, *The Discovery of the Future* (1902). *Ann Veronica* (1909), a novel about a modern woman and suffragist, created a scandal and was denounced from many pulpits. For that book Wells received the unusual

*Inscription to Garnett in a copy of Conrad's second book,* An Outcast of the Islands *(auctioned by American Art Association/Anderson Galleries, sale number 4004, 6 December 1932)*

sum of fifteen hundred pounds from the otherwise tightfisted Unwin. *Boon* (1915), published pseudonymously, included a barely disguised attack on Henry James and twenty-six illustrations by Wells. The novel was reprinted by Unwin in 1920, when Well acknowledged his authorship. Wells's last publications with Unwin were *The Year of Prophesying* and the *Atlantic Edition of the Complete Works of H. G. Wells,* both published in 1924. He also provided the introduction for *Friendly Russia* (1915), by Denis Garstin.

John Galsworthy's first book was published by Unwin, a collection of stories entitled *From the Four Winds* (1897). Five hundred copies were printed at the author's expense; Galsworthy eventually received ninepence per copy. The collection was part of the Pseudonym Library and published under the name of John Sinjohn. It received mostly favorable notices, many of which compared Galsworthy to Rudyard Kipling, but the volume did not sell out. Unwin rejected Galsworthy's second book, *Jocelyn*; the novel was published by Duckworth in 1898. Unwin's manuscript reader, Edward Garnett, had criticized Galsworthy as "a clubman."

Garnett had left school at sixteen; he had gone to work for the firm at ten shillings per week four years later, in 1887. Until his dismissal in 1899 he was one of Unwin's best readers. He spotted the genius of Joseph Conrad and was responsible for the publication of *Almayer's Folly* (1895), for which Conrad was paid about twenty pounds. Garnett's encouragement led to Conrad's second novel, *An Outcast of the Islands* (1896), for which he received fifty pounds. On Garnett's advice Conrad asked for one hundred pounds for *The Nigger of the "Narcissus"*; Unwin refused and offered fifty pounds, having lost money on Conrad's first two novels. *The Nigger of the "Narcissus"* was published by Heinemann in 1898. Unwin later published Conrad's *Tales of Unrest* (1898), *The Arrow of Gold* (1919), and *The Rover* (1923). The latter volume, published the year before Conrad's death, was very successful; the first edition went into several printings totaling forty thousand copies. Conrad received a 20 percent royalty. Unwin also acted as a broker between Conrad and *Blackwood's Edinburgh Magazine* for his short stories.

Garnett was responsible for thinking up several of Unwin's series of inexpensive books, including the Pseudonym series, and for inducing salesmen to put them on the stalls at railway stations. Garnett also had his own novels, *The Paradox Club* (1888) and *Light and Shadow* (1889), published by the firm.

When his *Liza of Lambeth* (1897) was published in Unwin's Adelphi Library series, Somerset Maugham was still a medical student. The novel was published at three shillings, sixpence instead of the usual six shillings, resulting in a royalty on five hundred copies of less than ten pounds. Unwin asked Maugham to write a second novel about the slums, but Maugham chose instead to write a historical novel, *The Making of a Saint* (1898), for which he received fifty pounds. Unwin rejected Maugham's autobiographical "The Artistic Temperament of Stephen Carey," an early version of *Of Human Bondage* (published by Heinemann in 1915), but published his *Orientations* (1899), a collection of seven short stories.

George Moore began having his works published by the firm in 1898; he switched to Heinemann in 1905. His pair of complementary novels *Evelyn Innes* (1898) went into several editions and sold more than ten thousand copies. He also wrote a play, *The Bending of the Bough*

(1900), and the novel *Sister Teresa* (1901). Moore's *The Untilled Field* (1903) was a collection of thirteen short stories. When Moore wanted to republish his complementary novels, Unwin, with whom Moore had quarreled, refused to relinquish the rights to the books and passed them on to Ernest Benn, the firm that later took over T. Fisher Unwin.

Unwin published Ford Madox Ford's first work, the fairy tale *The Brown Owl* (1891); Ford received ten pounds for the copyright of the book, which was published after some prodding by Ford's grandfather, the painter Ford Madox Brown. Ford's *The Shifting of the Fire* (1892) was published in the Independent Novels series.

Unwin published William Butler Yeats's *John Sherman and Dhoya* (1891) in the Pseudonym series, *The Countess Kathleen* (1892) in the Cameo series, *The Land of Heart's Desire* (1894), and *Poems* (1895). *Literary Ideals in Ireland* (1899) was coauthored by Yeats, John Eglinton, George William Russell (Æ), and William Larminie.

Unwin, a pro-Boer, outbid competitors to publish the memoirs (1902) of Paul Kruger, the president of the Transvaal. Unwin also supported the Aborigines Protection Society, publishing E. D. Morel's *Red Rubber* (1906), which denounced atrocities in the Congo. The firm published Karl Pearson's *The Ethic of Free Thought* (1888) and *The New University for London* (1892). The Reformer's Bookshelf series featured *The Political Writings of Richard Cobden* (1903) and George Jacob Holyoake's autobiography, *Bygones Worth Remembering* (1905). The Liberal critic J. M. Robertson wrote *Essays toward a Critical Method* (1889), *Britain versus Germany* (1917), *Neutrals and the War* (1917), *Shakespeare and Chapman* (1917), *The Economics of Progress* (1918), and *Bolingbroke and Walpole* (1919). Other political titles included John Morley's *Life of Richard Cobden*, which went through several editions from 1896 to 1920. The firm published the third edition of Edward Carpenter's controversial *Towards Democracy* (1892), but Unwin stopped distributing the work and broke his contract to publish Carpenter's *Love's Coming of Age* after a public controversy erupted over Carpenter's essay on homosexuality, "Homogenic Love," in 1894. (*Love's Coming of Age* was published by Swan Sonnenschein in 1903 and republished by Unwin in 1919.) Unwin's interest in free trade was reflected in the publication of *The Hungry Forties: Life under the Bread Tax from the Letters of Living Witnesses* (1904), which addressed the Tariff Reform controversy then rag-

Stanley Unwin, who worked at his uncle's firm from 1904
to 1912

ing. It was edited by Unwin's wife, Jane, a daughter of Richard Cobden, the free-trade advocate.

The range of T. Fisher Unwin's publications was vast, ranging from psychoanalysis to theosophy. The firm published one of the first of Sigmund Freud's books to appear in English, *Psychopathology of Everyday Life* (1914), translated by A. A. Brill, as well as *Wit and Its Relation to the Unconscious* (1916). At the other extreme, but consistent with Unwin's interest in freethinkers, was Annie Besant's *An Autobiography* (1893). Unwin's passion for mountaineering was reflected in the reception he organized in the old Hall of Clifford's Inn on 20 May 1894 to celebrate an exhibition of pictures of the Himalayas by Arthur David McCormick, the artist who accompanied Sir Martin Conway's 1892-1893 expedition to the Karakarams. Unwin published Conway's *Climber's Guide to the Central Pennine Alps* (1890), *Climbing and Exploration in the Karakaram-Himalaya* (1894), and *The Sport of Collecting* (1914). *How to Be Happy though Married* (1885), by the Reverend

Edward John Hardy, was published in six different styles, from a presentation edition in white vellum for seven shillings, sixpence to a modest sixpenny edition. The book sold for years. An extremely popular writer, Hardy had several books of sermons and advice published by Unwin: *Faint, Yet Pursuing and Other Sermons* (1888), *The Five Talents of Woman: A Book for Girls and Women* (1888), *The Business of Life: A Book for Everyone* (1891), *Doubt and Faith* (1899), *Mr. Thomas Atkins* (1900), *John Chinaman at Home* (1905), *How to Get Married* (1909), *How to Be Happy though Civil* (1909), *The Unvarying East* (1912), and *The British Soldier: His Courage and Humour* (1915). Unwin also published the autobiography of the artist William Simpson (1903) and Horace Hutchinson's *Portraits of the Eighties* (1920).

Several periodicals were among the firm's publications. *Cosmopolis: An International Monthly Review* (1896-1898) was created by its editor, F. Ortmans, to combat the rising nationalism that threatened European intellectual life. The journal appealed to a common cultural tradition and published short stories, drama, poetry, serial literature, and articles on politics (mostly radical or liberal) in English, French, and German. There were usually four or five signed pieces in each language in each issue. Among the contributors were Andrew Lang, Theodor Mommsen, Wilhelm Leibknecht, George Bernard Shaw, Charles Dilke, Max Muller, Robert Louis Stevenson, Somerset Maugham, Henry James, Yeats, George Gissing, Rudyard Kipling, George Meredith, Stéphane Mallarmé, Paul Bourget, Anatole France, William Archer, Israel Zangwill, Edward Dowden, Leo Tolstoy, and Edmund Gosse. Conrad's short story "An Outpost" appeared in June and July 1897. Other Pan-European periodicals published by Unwin were the *International Monthly Review*, the *Revue Bleue*, and the *Independent Review*.

Among those who worked for Unwin were Chesterton; A. D. Marks, later director of the Quality Press; T. Werner Laurie, later a publisher on his own; and Wilfrid Hugh Chesson, whose two-volume novel *Name This Child* (1894) was published by Unwin. Philip Lee Warner started in the firm with no pay for the first three months; he received ten guineas for the next year and thirty shillings a week after that, until he became a partner in Chatto and Windus in 1905.

An adventurous entrepreneur, Unwin was the only English-speaking publisher at the Leipzig Easter Book Fair. Along with George Bell and

Sons, he handled the colonial editions of publishers who chose to sell five hundred to one thousand copies of their new fiction in the form of unbound sheets at from tenpence to one shilling per copy, rather than carry on overseas business themselves. Unwin then bound the sheets for sale to colonial booksellers at one shilling, sixpence, in paper covers or in cloth at two shillings. The firm created Unwin's Library in an attempt to compete with the German publisher Tauchnitz by printing an extra two hundred copies and binding them for sale on the Continent at the equivalent price of one shilling, sixpence in francs or marks.

Unwin often acted as his authors' agent by placing short stories and novels for serialization and arranging for the publication of books in America, usually by the Appleton firm. The 10 percent commission Unwin received for these services often exacerbated his unpleasant relationships with his authors, who also complained about his hard bargaining and his predilection for small type and narrow margins. Holbrook Jackson, however, described Unwin as sympathetic to young modern writers and artists, as demonstrated by his employment of Aubrey Beardsley to advertise his books. Beardsley did posters for the Pseudonym Library, which used his "Girl and a Book Shop" as the cover of John Oliver Hobbes's *The Dream and the Business* (1906). A Beardsley poster in black and purple of a woman reading was used to advertise the Children's Library.

Unwin was also active in the Publishers Association, serving on a committee to consider jointly with the Associated Booksellers the possibility of reverting to a maximum allowable discount of twopence in the shilling. In 1919 he raised the question of repairing relations between the association and German and Austrian publishers. Unwin had had an excellent relationship with German booksellers until World War I.

Unwin was a founder of the Johnson Club and the National Liberal Club; the latter was a center for rising politicians, publishers, and literati. He organized evening parties at the National Liberal Club; according to his nephew, Stanley Unwin, he could be as pleasant in society as he was intimidating and harsh in the office.

Stanley Unwin worked at T. Fisher Unwin from 1904 to 1912 before founding his own firm, George Allen and Unwin, in 1914. He did a great deal of traveling to the Continent and the United States, was in charge of the sale of cheap edition rights (which assured the company's profits), and was instrumental in making many publishing and financial decisions. Early in his career he maintained close relations with booksellers at home and abroad for T. Fisher Unwin. Stanley Unwin introduced the Baedeker guides to T. Fisher Unwin and secured the agency for the sale of the Ordnance Survey Maps.

After 1912 the firm suffered a financial decline that was exacerbated by the book-trade strike of 1925 and the general strike of 1926. Unwin often bought the rights to books published by other houses, and had many such dealings with Grant Richards during the last twenty years of T. Fisher Unwin's existence. To the end T. Fisher Unwin specialized in Edwardian genres—memoirs, travel, adventure—but the firm published no textbooks, which might have increased profits. In 1926 Unwin retired to his Sussex home, and the firm merged with Ernest Benn Limited, an offshoot of Benn Brothers. George Allen and Unwin took over the Baedeker Guides. Unwin died in 1935.

## References:

Laurence Brander, *Somerset Maugham: A Guide* (Edinburgh: Oliver & Boyd, 1963);

S. C. Cronwright-Schreiner, ed., *The Letters of Olive Schreiner, 1876-1920* (Boston: Little, Brown, 1924);

Anthony Curtis, *The Pattern of Maugham* (New York: Taplinger, 1974);

Lovat Dickson, *H. G. Wells: His Turbulent Life and Times* (New York: Atheneum, 1969);

Ruth First and Ann Scott, *Olive Schreiner* (New York: Schocken, 1980);

Helmut E. Gerber, ed., *George Moore in Transition: Letters to T. Fisher Unwin and Lena Milman, 1894-1910* (Detroit: Wayne State University Press, 1968);

Edwin Gilcher, *A Bibliography of George Moore* (De Kalb: Northern Illinois University Press, 1970);

Peter Gunn, *Vernon Lee: Violet Paget, 1856-1935* (London & New York: Oxford University Press, 1964);

Carolyn G. Heilbrun, *The Garnett Family* (New York: Macmillan, 1961);

Joseph Hone, *The Life of George Moore* (New York: Macmillan, 1936);

Holbrook Jackson, *The Eighteen Nineties* (New York: Knopf, 1922);

Frederick R. Karl, and Lawrence Davies, eds., *The Collected Letters of Joseph Conrad*, 3 vol-

umes (New York: Cambridge University
Press, 1983-1988);

John Kelly, ed., *The Collected Letters of W. B. Yeats*,
volume 1: *1865-1895* (Oxford: Clarendon
Press, 1986; New York: Oxford University
Press, 1986);

Henry Maas, J. L. Duncan, and W. G. Good,
eds., *The Letters of Aubrey Beardsley* (Rutherford, N.J.: Fairleigh Dickinson University
Press, 1970);

Frank MacShane, *The Life and Work of Ford Madox
Ford* (New York: Horizon Press, 1965);

Harold V. Marrot, *The Life and Letters of John Galsworthy* (New York: Scribners, 1936);

J. Lewis May, *John Lane and the Nineties* (London:
Bodley Head, 1936);

Johannes Meintjes, *Olive Schreiner: Portrait of a
South African Woman* ( Johannesburg: Keart-
land, 1965);

Ted Morgan, *Maugham* (New York: Simon &
Schuster, 1980);

James G. Nelson, *The Early Nineties: A View from
the Bodley Head* (Cambridge: Harvard University Press, 1971);

Philip Unwin, *The Publishing Unwins* (London:
Heinemann, 1972);

Sir Stanley Unwin, *The Truth about a Publisher* (London: Allen and Unwin, 1960);

Allan Wade, *A Bibliography of the Writings of W. B.
Yeats*, second edition, revised (London: Hart-
Davis, 1958);

Frederic Whyte, *William Heinemann: A Memoir*
(Garden City, N.Y.: Doubleday, Doran,
1929).

*—Julie F. Codell*

# Victoria Press
*(London: 1860-1881)*

Fig. 2. *Victoria Regia* Device (⅞" × ⅝").

In November 1859 the Council of the National Association for the Promotion of Social Science appointed a committee to investigate new ave-
nues for the employment of women in light
industry. The committee, later subsumed into the
board of the Society for Promoting the Employment of Women, was made up of six men and
six women, including G. W. Hastings, Arthur
Kinnaird, Horace Mann, Anna Jameson, Bessie
Rayner Parkes, Adelaide Anne Procter, Jessie
Boucherett, Isa Craig, and Emily Faithfull. Several of the women on the committee were among
the Langham Place Group, who were already publishing the *English Woman's Journal*. After some consideration of fields as disparate as hairdressing,
watchmaking, and telegraphy, the committee de-

termined to support an experimental introduction of women to the less physically strenuous aspects of the printing trade. Bessie Parkes purchased a small press, and within several weeks
she and Faithfull learned the rudiments of printing from Austin Holyoake, a London printer.
Their experiment convinced them that, as
Faithfull commented, "any intelligent industrious
girl, under a proper apprenticeship, could earn
her living as a compositor." Hastings and
Faithfull purchased Parkes's press and the necessary type, machinery, and furniture for about six
thousand pounds, and on 25 March 1860
Faithfull opened a printing office at 9 Great
Coram Street, Russell Square, London, with a
group of young women as apprentice composi-

*Emily Faithfull, cofounder and proprietor of the Victoria Press*

tors. "Intelligent, respectable workmen" were hired to perform the strenuous labor of imposition and presswork. The printing office was named the Victoria Press after the queen.

By October 1860 Faithfull was overseeing sixteen apprentice women compositors, four of whom had learned something of printing in their fathers' shops. The apprentices paid ten pounds each as a premium for the first six months of their training (the Society for Promoting the Employment of Women paid the premiums for five of the first compositors). Faithfull altered the conventional male term of apprenticeship from seven years to four, and she reported that after the first six months the women were "paid by the piece, two-thirds of their earnings, according to the Compositors' Scale, (English prices), which is indeed higher payment than that of boy apprentices."

Public reaction to the notion of a press managed and staffed by women was mixed. As would be expected, readers of the radical *English Wo-*

*man's Journal* were enthusiastic, though one wrote to warn of potential hazards to women compositors' health. Male printers were angered by the admission of women to competition with them: one predicted that the women would "die off like birds in winter" under the hardships of the labor, and others argued that women, lacking "a mechanical mind," "have not sufficient intellect or education to become compositors." The queen's approbation, indicated by her permission to use her name and by her public congratulations, aided in attracting public regard. The press's initial orders came from the National Association for the Promotion of Social Science and the Langham Place Group. The Victoria Press printed all of the association's transactions, the *English Woman's Journal*, and a battery of pamphlets linked to the social and educational programs and interests of the two organizations. By the summer of 1861 the press was self-sustaining; had doubled its production; and was handling a weekly newspaper called the *Friend of the People*, the quarterly *Law Magazine*, and other legal, religious, and reformist miscellanea.

Faithfull then produced a showpiece to demonstrate the superlative skill of women printers and designers as well as the support the Victoria Press enjoyed from celebrated writers, male and female. This sumptuous volume, titled *The Victoria Regia* after the Amazonian water lily named for the queen, appeared in time for Christmas gift giving in December 1861 and sold out before the initial orders were filled. The queen was delighted; six months later, the great success of the volume prompted Faithfull's appointment as "Printer-in-Ordinary to the Queen." A second edition appeared in 1863.

The press produced two similarly impressive literary anthologies edited by Craig: *A Welcome: Original Contributions in Verse and Prose* (1863) was dedicated to Alexandra, the newly married Princess of Wales, and *Poems: An Offering to Lancashire* (1863) was published to benefit textile workers laid off because of the shortage of cotton imported from the war-torn American South. The *English Woman's Journal* ceased publication in 1863, and the Victoria Press published its successor, the *Victoria Magazine*, from 1863 to 1880. Faithfull carefully screened the material given to the women compositors; in 1867, for instance, she terminated a publishing contract on the grounds that the job contained material unsuitable for young women to read, much less set in type.

*The Victoria Press composing room*

In November 1862 the press supplemented its Great Coram Street office by setting up editorial offices at 14 Princes Street, Hanover Square, and purchasing for £950 a steam press at 83a Farringdon Street. The company was appraised in 1864 at £3,040 14s. 4d., at which time Faithfull noted, "My work in Great Coram Street is giving a profit, which I could show, only the books are badly kept, and the accounts in Farringdon Street, on which there is a loss, are mixed up with them."

At that time William Wilfred Head, a journeyman printer, became Faithfull's partner in the press for one thousand pounds. He succeeded her as proprietor of the Victoria Press printing office in August 1867, paying an additional fourteen hundred pounds; Faithfull retained her title as "Printer and Publisher in Ordinary to the Queen" and the Victoria Press imprint. Head's tenure as proprietor was a troubled one; he claimed to have had to defend himself "from the open attacks of Miss Faithfull in the morning journals." His pamphlet history of the Victoria Press (1869) drew negative comments from a reviewer in the January 1870 issue of the *Victoria Magazine*, who wondered why he knew so little of the press's ori-

gin. Head addressed a vitriolic seven-page response to the "editress" of the *Victoria*; at his request she published his letter verbatim in the February issue, adding some sarcastic clarifications and comments in notes. He seems to have left the business after this fracas.

Faithfull seems to have resumed her proprietorship, though she was deeply involved in a variety of women's causes during the 1870s. The Victoria Press had moved to 11, 12, and 13 Harp Alley in 1869; it moved to Praed Street in Paddington around 1878. In April 1881 the Victoria Press merged with the Queen Printing and Publishing Company and ceased to exist as a separate entity.

**References:**
"Employment for Women as Printers," *Victoria Magazine*, 14 ( January 1870): 261-263;
Emily Faithfull, "Preface," in *The Victoria Regia: A Volume of Original Contributions butions in Poetry and Prose*, edited by Adelaide Anne Procter (London: Emily Faithfull, Victoria Press, 1861), pp. v-viii;
Faithfull, "Victoria Press," *English Woman's Journal*, 6 (October 1860): 121-126;

Faithfull, "Women Compositors," *English Woman's Journal*, 8 (September 1861): 37-41;

William Fredeman, "Emily Faithfull and the Victoria Press: An Experiment in Sociological Bibliography," *Library*, fifth series 29 (June 1974): 139-164;

W. Wilfred Head, letter, *Victoria Magazine*, 14 (February 1870): 367-375;

Head, *The Victoria Press: Its History and Vindication*, with an *Account of the Movement for the Employment of Females in Printing* (London: Victoria Press, 1869);

James S. Stone, "More Light on Emily Faithfull and the Victoria Press," *Library*, fifth series 33 (March 1978): 63-67.

—*Lauren Pringle De La Vars*

# Vizetelly and Company
## (London: 1880-1889)

Henry Vizetelly was a leading wood engraver, journalist, and mass-market book publisher whose career illustrates how these three activities intersected in the second half of the nineteenth century. His work as a publisher led to his prosecution and imprisonment for printing the works of Emile Zola and other contemporary writers; the case is an important chapter in the struggle for freedom of expression in Victorian Britain.

Vizetelly was born in Bishopsgate, in the East End of London, on 30 July 1820. He was the son of James Henry Vizetelly, a well-known printer-engraver. At fifteen Vizetelly was apprenticed to two prominent London wood engravers: G. W. Bonner and then John Orrin Smith. Under Smith's supervision, Vizetelly did a woodcut for Charles Knight's edition of *The Thousand and One Nights* (1839-1841); he also made a set of engravings from drawings by Clarkson Stanfield for Frederick Marryat's sea novel *Poor Jack* (1840), which was published by Longman. Vizetelly also did hackwork for the *Weekly Chronicle* and other popular newspapers, which included sketching as well as engraving. He began to frequent the environs of Fleet Street and Covent Garden, where he became acquainted with many of the leading bohemian illustrators and writers of the time.

Vizetelly's father died in 1838, shortly after his printing firm, Vizetelly, Branston and Company, was dissolved. Three years later Henry Vizetelly and his older brother James, who had been a member of their father's firm, founded their own printing and engraving business, Vizetelly Brothers and Company. It was located in two adjacent London sites: 8 Peterborough Court and 135 Fleet Street. Henry was the more creative of the two, and under his prodding the company published several small books with its own imprint. But most of its work was done on commission for publishers such as David Bogue (who provided financial assistance to Vizetelly Brothers), John Murray, and Thomas Longman. Vizetelly Brothers did both wood engraving and letterpress printing, and Henry honed his skills

*Henry Vizetelly*

Vizetelly Brothers for Longman and described by one critic as "a triumph of letterpress colour printing."

Another success was *Country Year Book* (1846-1847), by Thomas Miller, a working-class poet; it was published in Chapman and Hall's Boys' Own Library series. Miller's popular stories and poems about rural life won him a large following in the 1840s. What made *Country Year Book* particularly noteworthy were the illustrations by Birket Foster, a prolific Victorian commercial artist whom Henry Vizetelly "discovered" at this time and with whom he maintained a close friendship for many years. *Country Year Book* also introduced into publishing a distinctive method of color printing developed by Vizetelly Brothers that replicated the translucent qualities of watercolor painting by means of wood block transparencies. It gave a distinctive look to the firm's work in a market that was becoming increasingly competitive.

During the 1840s Henry Vizetelly commenced an important friendship with Noel Humphreys, a writer and engraver who specialized in the burgeoning gift-book market. The best-known collaboration between Vizetelly Brothers and Humphreys was *A Record of the Black Prince* (1849), published by Longman. This illustrated antiquarian volume gained a large sale. Vizetelly also cultivated French contacts in the 1840s, initiating a lifelong publishing association with that country.

In the 1840s Vizetelly was a pioneer of weekly pictorial journalism, working to integrate elements of periodical and book production. His literary and artistic friends included William Makepeace Thackeray, Edmund Yates, Robert Brough, Kenny Meadows, Douglas Jerrold, Albert Smith, Gilbert à Beckett, Augustus Mayhew, George Augustus Sala, and Charles Bennett, some of whom helped him launch several important periodicals. He was a founder of the *Illustrated London News* in 1842 together with Herbert Ingram, who became its proprietor.

After severing his ties with Ingram as a result of a quarrel, Vizetelly commenced the *Pictorial Times*, a rival sixpenny weekly, in March 1843. This journal attracted a substantial group of talented artists, wood draftsmen ("black and white men"), and writers to its staff. Like the *Illustrated London News*, the *Pictorial Times* helped to make illustrated weekly journalism respectable by blurring the distinction between quality and popular newspapers. It combined some news coverage

in both areas. He became an adept writer and a fine sketch artist, engraver, and color printer.

Vizetelly Brothers did well financially and secured a solid reputation in London publishing circles. Its first great success, which inaugurated a long collaboration with John Murray, was the printing of a portion of *Ancient Spanish Ballads* (1842), translated by John Gibson Lockhart. This lavish gift book contained engravings of the Alhambra by John Orrin Smith. Vizetelly Brothers' complex engravings on tinted backgrounds with ornamental borders were highly praised. *Ancient Spanish Ballads* initiated a brief vogue for "Oriental" books, which included Louisa Stuart Costello's *The Rose Garden of Persia* (1845), done by with many pictures and amassed a huge circulation for a brief time. Vizetelly ended his association with the *Pictorial Times* in 1844. In March 1848 he launched the *Puppet-Show*, a penny comic periodical which ran for more than a year. It included "social sketches" by Gavarni, a leading French caricaturist. Vizetelly introduced his work to England in *Gavarni in London: Sketches of Life and Character* (1849), published by David Bogue, a book of tinted wood engravings with text by writers such as Albert Smith, Robert Brough, and Shirley Brooks.

In 1849 Vizetelly Brothers went into liquidation. Henry and James set up competing businesses: James at 8 Peterborough Court, Henry with greater success at 15-16 Gough Square, near Fleet Street. Most of the literary and artistic contacts nurtured by the brothers in the 1840s remained with Henry. His firm, known as Vizetelly (Henry), worked closely with previous contributors such as Noel Humphreys, Thackeray, and, particularly Foster. It did color printing primarily by chromolithography, a popular technique, in place of the wood blocks it had used in the 1840s. Among its greatest commercial and artistic successes as a set of illustrated volumes of the poems of Henry Wadsworth Longfellow (1850-1854) printed for Bogue and introducing *Evangeline* (1850), *Hyperion* (1853), and other of Longfellow's poems to an English audience. Several Christmas books written by Thackeray under the pseudonym "M. A. Titmarsh" were printed and engraved by Vizetelly (Henry), including *The Kickleburys on the Rhine* (1851) for Smith, Elder and Company. Vizetelly produced and edited for Bogue *Christmas with the Poets: A Collection of Songs, Carols, and Descriptive Verses* (1851), a lavish volume illustrated by Foster. He also printed Martin Tupper's *Proverbial Philosophy* (1854) for Thomas Hatchard; the book's tinted engravings added to its already huge popularity.

In 1852 Vizetelly helped produce the first English edition of Harriet Beecher Stowe's *Uncle Tom's Cabin*, which was published under the imprint of Clarke, Beeton, and Company. He printed under his own imprint Edgar Allan Poe's *Tales of Mystery, Imagination, and Humour; and Poems* (1852), which sold well and helped to establish Poe's literary reputation in England. He did engravings for several volumes by John Ruskin, including *Stones of Venice* (1851-1853) for Smith, Elder, though these were not to Ruskin's liking. Vizetelly also engaged in a vitriolic public dispute with Thomas Babington Macaulay, who de-

nounced his "sloppy" edition of a collection of his speeches in 1854 as a "gross fraud" and proceeded to bring out a version "corrected by himself."

Vizetelly made his most significant contribution to illustrated journalism in 1855, when he founded an even greater rival to the *Illustrated London News*, the *Illustrated Times*. The twopenny weekly found a winning formula in a combination of pictorial crime coverage and the public's fascination with Crimean War battles. The *Illustrated Times* was one of the first newspapers to give prominence to frontline sketch artists such as Julian Portch and "special correspondents" such as Vizetelly's younger brother Frank, who became a leading war reporter. In 1858 Vizetelly began the *Welcome Guest*, another illustrated twopenny weekly. Vizetelly, who ceased to print and edit it before the end of 1859, lost a large sum of money in trying to make it a success. It continued under other ownership until 1865.

Vizetelly terminated his printing and engraving company in 1861. He established two successive businesses in Gough Square, one of which—a partnership with Robert Loudan, a wood engraver—lasted four years. It did poorly, however, and had little impact on the publishing industry. In 1865 Vizetelly ceased to edit the *Illustrated Times*, which collapsed later that year. He then moved his family to Paris, where he became a special correspondent for the *Illustrated London News* at a substantial salary of eight hundred pounds per year. For the next fifteen years Vizetelly lived abroad, mostly in Paris but also in Berlin. He covered leading news stories such as the Paris Commune and the siege of Paris in 1870-1871 and the creation of the Three Emperors League in 1872. He also helped the British publishing world keep abreast of trends in Continental illustration and publishing. During these years abroad Vizetelly wrote several books, including *The Story of the Diamond Necklace* (Tinsley Brothers, 1867), a novel; *The Man with the Iron Mask* (Smith, Elder, 1870), a free translation of Marius Topin's popular work of fiction; and *Berlin under the New Empire* (Tinsley Brothers, 1879), a journalistic account of social and cultural life in imperial Germany. Vizetelly also became an authority on wines and wrote detailed studies of champagne, sherry, and port. In 1882 he wrote for Tinsley Brothers *Paris in Peril*, a history of the Paris Commune based on reports and sketches he had done for the *Illustrated London News*.

*Ernest Vizetelly, whose translations of the works of Emile Zola were among the books that led to Henry Vizetelly's imprisonment for "obscene libel"*

In 1877 Vizetelly returned to London, where in 1880 he established yet another firm, Vizetelly and Company, at 42 Catherine Street, Strand, with the help of his sons Frank and Arthur. Another son, Ernest, who later gained a reputation for his translations of Zola's novels, was marginally connected with the business.

Vizetelly and Company made a significant contribution to nineteenth-century publishing with its cheap editions of popular novels and its opposition to censorship. Vizetelly was not an ideological crusader, nor did he possess strong political convictions. His objective was simply to be able to sell books without hindrance and to earn a profit. Between 1880 and 1889 he published hundreds of volumes, which represented a curious blend of popular and "quality" works. Some of these books resulted in Vizetelly's being prosecuted. As a result, he gained a measure of fame but failed to achieve the financial security he desired.

Initially Vizetelly concentrated on the types of books he felt comfortable with from his years as a printer and a literary man-about-town. These included volumes by social satirists such as Sala and E. C. Grenville-Murray, both of whom he knew personally. He published Sala's profusely illustrated *America Revisited* (1882) and Murray's *Side-Lights on English Society: Sketches from Life, Social and Satirical* (1881) and *High Life in France under the Republic: Social and Satirical Sketches in Paris and the Provinces* (1885). Each of these books contained many engravings. Other works in this satirical genre were an anthology, *The Social Zoo* (1883-1884), which appeared in sixpenny monthly numbers and in volume form, and *Society Novelettes* (1885). These books contained comic fiction and essays by popular journalists such as Murray, F. C. Burnand, and Joseph Hatton, together with illustrations by caricaturists of the first rank such as Randolph Caldecott and Linley Sambourne. Satirical books appear to have earned little money for Vizetelly, probably because there was substantial competition from other publishers in this market. Equally disappointing was a series of books intended to tap the "low" end of the popular market. These cheap volumes ran the gamut from the humorous, such as *King Solomon's Wives; or The Phantom Mines* (1887), by "Hyder Ragged," to the crudely topical, such as R. C. Woodville's *Gordon and the Mahdi: An Illustrated Narrative of the War in the Soudan and the Death of General Gordon* (1885) and William S. Gregg's *Irish History for English Readers* (1886), advertised as "A Book for the Present Crisis."

In 1884 Vizetelly began to publish many novels, primarily Continental in origin. They appeared in several series and were intended to be commercially successful. Vizetelly's Popular French Novels, published simultaneously in paper and cloth editions, were recommended to prospective readers as "books that may be safely left lying about where the ladies of the family can pick them up and read them." They were bound in pink wrappers and featured lesser works by writers of solid reputation such as Prosper Mérimée, Alphonse Daudet, and George Sand. Sand's *The Tower of Percemont* and *Marianne* were published together in this series in 1881. All of Vizetelly's Popular French Novels were original translations, and in most instances they were the first English editions of the books.

Less "respectable" fiction was to be found in Vizetelly's Sixpenny Series of Amusing and Enter-

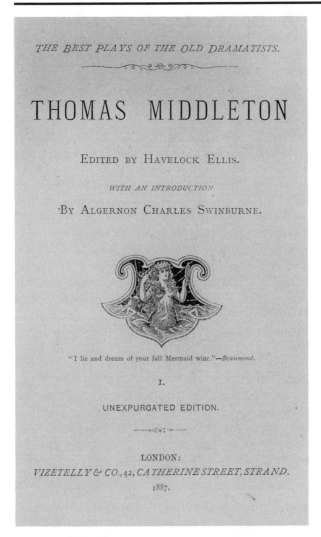

THE BEST PLAYS OF THE OLD DRAMATISTS.

# THOMAS MIDDLETON

EDITED BY HAVELOCK ELLIS.

WITH AN INTRODUCTION

BY ALGERNON CHARLES SWINBURNE.

"I lie and dream of your full Mermaid wine."—*Beaumont.*

I.

UNEXPURGATED EDITION.

LONDON:
VIZETELLY & CO., 42, CATHERINE STREET, STRAND.
1887.

*Title page for a volume in the Mermaid series of unexpurgated British plays. When Vizetelly and Company went out of business the series was taken over by the firm of T. Fisher Unwin.*

taining Books (1885-1887) and the Sensational Novels. The Sixpenny Series, bound in distinctive scarlet covers, included popular romances such as Auguste Vitu's *The Strange Phantasy of Dr. Trintzius* (1886), along with Thackeray's 1841 potboiler, *The Great Hoggarty Diamond* (1885). The Sensational Novels featured detective stories by the popular French writers Fortuné du Boisgobey and Emile Gaboriau, which were billed as "the favourite reading of Prince Bismarck." According to Ernest Vizetelly, both series made a lot of money for Vizetelly and Company while, predictably, coaxing into existence several cheap "unauthorized" reprints by competitors.

Vizetelly published several controversial novels in the series One Volume Novels (1884-1885), Boulevard Novels: Pictures of French Morals

and Manners (1885-1888), and Russian Novels (1884-1888). Many of the books on these lists had considerable literary merit. The One Volume Novels, by "English and Foreign Authors of Repute," were intended to destroy the conventional three-volume format of Victorian publishing, which kept the price of fiction high and preserved the dominance of the circulating libraries, Mudie's and W. H. Smith and Son. Vizetelly's friend George Moore was a leading opponent of this system, and two of his controversial early novels, *A Mummer's Wife* (1884) and *A Modern Lover* (1885), were featured in the One Volume Novels series. Vizetelly emphasized the realism of these books in his advertisements and compared them to the novels of Zola. Both Moore and Zola, Vizetelly maintained, were essaying a "photographic presentation" of aspects of modern life, some of which were admittedly seamy. Another volume in the series, Georges Ohnet's *Countess Sarah* (1884), was described by the translator as delineating "passion in its manifold phases" and dealing "with the movement and excitement rather than the tranquilities of life."

The Boulevard Novels were miscellaneous in nature. Several were inoffensive satires, including *Nana's Daughter: A Story of Parisian Life* (1885), by Alfred Sirven and Henri Leverdier. Others were of the popular "sensational" school, such as du Boisgobey's *A Mystery Still* (1886). Other novels in the Boulevard series were viewed as "dangerous" by segments of the public; among these works was Guy de Maupassant's *A Woman's Life* (1887).

The Russian Novels sold less well than the other two series and did not generate antipathy among the defenders of morality. But they were a landmark in Victorian book publishing. Of the twelve volumes in the series, five were by Fyodor Dostoyevski, including the first English translation of *Crime and Punishment* (1886); four by Leo Tolstoy, including cheap editions of *War and Peace* (1886) and *Anna Karenina* (1886); two by Nicolai Gogol; and one by Mikhail Lermontov.

These impressive lists earned for Vizetelly a passable income and some celebrity among the publishers of his time, but it was the Realistic series of Continental novels that gained him a permanent niche in publishing history. The Realistic novels were original translations into English, or, where American or British published translations already existed, were advertised as the first "unexpurgated" editions. Most were published in illustrated and cheap paper editions, which made them even more-controversial. The Realistic series included Gustave Flaubert's *Salambo: A Realistic Romance of Ancient Carthage* (1886) and *Madame Bovary* (1886), the latter in a "definitive" translation by Eleanor Marx Aveling; Alphonse Daudet's lesbian novel *Sappho* (1886), described by Vizetelly as a "deeply Interesting Story" that contained fifty pages more than any other edition; two delicate novels by Paul Bourget dealing with sensitive domestic subjects, *A Cruel Enigma* (1887) and *A Love Crime* (1887); and *Germinie Lacerteux* (1887) and *Renée Mauperin* (1887), controversial books by the brothers Eduourd and Jules Goncourt, translated into English for the first time.

It was the publication of Zola's novels that placed Vizetelly firmly on the literary map. Poor-quality American editions of some of Zola's works were circulating in London in the 1880s, as well as several French originals. Otherwise this author, whose works were achieving great popularity in Paris at the time, was unknown to English readers. Vizetelly began to publish Zola's novels in 1884 in the Realistic series. All of the seventeen novels he published were original translations. Ernest Vizetelly, who knew Zola personally, translated and edited several of the books, which were published in both a five-shilling and a six-shilling illustrated edition; some of the other novels sold for as little as sixpence. Vizetelly had negotiated the rights to the books with Zola or his assigns. Although they were advertised for the most part as "unabridged"—particularly *Nana* (1884) and *The Soil* (1888), the most controversial of them—emendations and alterations were inserted to soften their impact on an English audience. In Vizetelly's words, "a slight veil" was placed "over those passages to which particular exception was likely to be taken."

Nevertheless, in May 1888 an attack was commenced on Vizetelly in the House of Commons during a debate on "Corrupt Literature." Virtually every speaker demanded the suppression of the type of literature Vizetelly was publishing, with several singling him out as a "chief culprit." His Realistic novels were particularly condemned. In the words of the home secretary, they were calculated to reach "a lower depth of immorality than had ever before been known." The *Times* and other newspapers soon took up the campaign. In June a newly formed National Vigilance Association initiated a private prosecution against Vizetelly under the Obscene Publications Act of 1857. The Conservative government of

Lord Salisbury then took charge of the prosecution, and within six months Vizetelly was brought to trial twice for obscene libel. Maupassant's *A Woman's Life*, Bourget's *A Love Crime*, and passages from Zola's novels were selected for prosecution, with *The Soil* being the object of special denunciation.

At his first trial, in October 1888, Vizetelly initially pleaded not guilty to the charges; but midway through the trial, he unexpectedly entered a guilty plea. According to published reports at the time, he became convinced that the jury was going to convict him when it protested against the reading in court of "filthy" passages from Zola's novels. The judge sentenced Vizetelly to pay a fine of one hundred pounds and ordered him to put up recognizances for good behavior, but he was not imprisoned. The reason for this relative leniency, in light of the harsh things said about him in court, is that he gave an oral assurance that he would not publish further "objectionable" passages from Zola.

In the view of both the National Vigilance Association and the solicitor-general, Vizetelly proceeded to violate this undertaking when, early in 1889, he put out a catalogue announcing new publications of Zola's novels. His defense of this action was that he had made cuts and changes in the texts, thereby rendering Zola's "unclean" tendencies inoffensive. Once again Vizetelly was charged with obscene libel, and in May 1889 he was brought to trial a second time. He pleaded guilty and was sentenced to three months imprisonment in Holloway Gaol and to forfeiture of his earlier recognizances.

The two trials and imprisonment destroyed Vizetelly financially and physically. After the first trial booksellers had refused to handle the publications of Vizetelly and Company, and the firm had been closed in 1889 before the second trial even took place. Its assets were taken over by T. Fisher Unwin, which finished several projects the company had begun. These included the ambitious Mermaid series of unexpurgated dramas by British authors, under the general editorship of Havelock Ellis and with the participation of such leading scholars as George Saintsbury and Arthur W. Symons. Like many of the novels Vizetelly published, some of these plays were considered to "run counter to what is called modern taste" as a result of their "extreme realism." Vizetelly's health deteriorated in prison, although he was treated as a first-class misdemeanant. He was almost seventy years old when his incarceration began, and he suffered from several illnesses, including intestinal cancer. On his release in August 1889 he moved to Farnham, Surrey, where he took up poultry farming. He died there, in considerable poverty, on 1 January 1894.

Vizetelly's death was largely ignored by the press and his contemporaries, who tended to underestimate his achievements; nonetheless, these were considerable. He led the struggle to disseminate quality fiction cheaply and in unexpurgated form, and he was a central figure in the transition from quality to mass publishing during the middle and later decades of the nineteenth century.

**References:**

Rodney K. Engen, *Dictionary of Victorian Wood Engravers* (Cambridge: Chadwyck-Healey, 1985);

Marcus B. Huish, *Birket Foster: His Life and Work* (London: Virtue, 1890);

C. T. Courtney Lewis, *The Story of Picture Printing in England during the Nineteenth Century; or,* *Forty Years of Wood and Stone* (London: Low, Marston, 1928);

Ruari McLean, *Victorian Book Design and Colour Printing* (London: Faber & Faber, 1963);

George Augustus Sala, *The Life and Adventures of George Augustus Sala: Written by Himself*, second edition, 2 volumes (London: Cassell, 1895);

Donald Thomas, *A Long Time Burning: The History of Literary Censorship in England* (London: Routledge & Kegan Paul, 1969);

Ernest Alfred Vizetelly, *Emile Zola, Novelist and Reformer: An Account of His Life and Work* (London: Lane, 1904);

Henry Vizetelly, *Glances Back through Seventy Years: Autobiographical and Other Reminiscences*, 2 volumes (London: Kegan Paul, Trench, Trübner, 1893);

Geoffrey Wakeman, *Victorian Book Illustration: The Technical Revolution* (Newton Abbot, U.K.: David & Charles, 1973).

—*Joel H. Wiener*

# Ward, Lock and Company
### (London: 1873-1890)
# Ward and Lock
### (London: 1854-1865)
# Ward, Lock and Tyler
### (London: 1865-1873)
# Ward, Lock, Bowden and Company
### (London: 1890-1893)
# Ward, Lock and Bowden Limited
### (London: 1893-1897)
# Ward, Lock and Company Limited
### (London: 1897-1964)
# Ward Lock Limited
### (London: 1964-    )

The origins of the still-flourishing house of Ward Lock, one of the most successful Victorian publishers of cheap literature and educational and reference works, go back to 23 June 1854, with the signing of the articles of partnership between the thirty-five-year-old Ebenezer Ward and the twenty-two-year-old George Lock. Ward had learned the business of publishing with the firm of Henry G. Bohn but in 1854 was working as the bookshop manager at Herbert Ingram and Company, publisher of the National Illustrated Library series and other popular works. Lock, the son of a Dorchester farmer, had served an apprenticeship with a druggist in Salisbury and had come to London early in 1854 intending to pursue a career in the City. The two men were brought together by Lock's cousin Dixon Galpin, who had set up as a printer with George William Petter. Galpin was printing for Herbert Ingram, where he met Ward, who confessed a yearning to leave the company. Impressed by Ward's publishing acumen, Galpin introduced him to his newly arrived cousin, and before too long the firm of

Ward and Lock was launched with one thousand pounds advanced by Lock's father. According to the articles of partnership, each partner was "entitled to draw on account of his share . . . the sum of four pounds weekly," as well as one-half of the net profits. The business was located at 158 Fleet Street, premises formerly occupied by David Nutt, a leading seller of foreign books. Ward and Lock's printers were Petter and Galpin, who worked cheaply and on credit.

In its early years Ward and Lock concentrated mainly on cheap reprints of popular literature and reference works. Among the titles published in the firm's first full year were duodecimo editions (usually priced at one shilling or one shilling, sixpence) of recent or not-so-recent fiction, such as R. B. Kimball's *St. Leger Family; or Threads of Life* (1855) and John Mills's *Wheel of Life* (1859). But alongside these were books that appear to be new works by established authors—Cuthbert Bede's *Love's Provocations* (1855), for instance, and Watts Phillips's *Wild Tribes of London* (1855). There were also shilling accounts of the

*Ebenezer Ward (left) and George Lock*

Crimean campaign, then at its height; a *Political History of 1853-54* (1854); a reprint of P. T. Barnum's *Autobiography* (1855); and a pocket guide to the Liverpool and Cheshire coast (1878). In the more expensive category of reference works, few cost more than half a crown; for that price the *Practical Housewife* (1862) offered more than five thousand recipes and more than ten thousand references to other items of domestic economy.

Toward the end of its first year in business Ward and Lock benefited from the liquidation of the ailing Herbert Ingram and Company when Petter and Galpin acquired, for a little more than £830, either the whole, or a large part of, the firm's stock of publications, together with its copyrights, woodblocks, stereotype plates, and engravings. The printers shared the purchase price with Ward and Lock on profit-sharing terms from future sales. The schedules of this purchase are contained in a memorandum of agreement signed between the two firms on 10 January 1856. One of the works listed in these schedules is *Webster's Dictionary of the English Language* (1856), which Ward and Lock published at low prices and in several forms: the condensed version at half a crown; an *Illustrated Webster Spelling Book* (1862), colored or plain; a shilling pronouncing dictionary; and an *Il-lustrated Webster Reader* (1862). Cheap editions of works by established authors, such as Thomas Love Peacock, M. G. Lewis, Frances Trollope, Hans Christian Andersen, and William Roscoe, outnumbered the new publications in these early years, but Ward and Lock were also, it seems, concerned to make their list appear as happy a blend of the old and new as possible. New work by former contributors to *Punch*, then Britain's leading comic magazine, is especially well represented. Two books—Horace Mayhew's *Wonderful People* and Angus B. Reach's *Men of the Hour*, both of which appeared in 1856—are now exceptionally rare, as is *Christmas Cheer* (1856), the joint product of Reach, Albert Smith, and James Hannay, who worked together on the arch rival of *Punch*, the *Man in the Moon* (1847-1849). Ward and Lock also brought out *The Book of German Songs* (1856), by H. W. Dulcken. Dulcken was later to join Ward and Lock as an editor of high-quality illustrated books. In these fruitful early years relations between publisher and printer remained cordial, and an amalgamation of the two concerns seemed likely. The relationship ended in bitterness when Petter and Galpin bought the house of Cassell in 1859. Thus began a twenty-year-long rivalry between Ward and Lock and the firm of Cassell, Petter and Galpin.

In these years of rapid growth Ebenezer Ward and George Lock used no representatives but traveled the country personally, making valuable connections in the book trade and discovering at firsthand which publications were likely to yield a good profit. In 1861 John Henry Lock, George's younger brother, joined as an assistant. In that same year larger and better-situated premises were found at Amen Corner, Paternoster Row. The firm continued to prosper and added more original fiction to its list, including work by Charles Reade, Mary Elizabeth Braddon, and George Augustus Sala. Ward and Lock brought out Sala's *Make Your Game; or, The Adventures of the Stout Gentleman, the Slim Gentleman, and the Man with the Iron Chest: A Narrative of the Rhine and Thereabouts* (1860); it was followed by *The Ship Chandler and Other Tales* (1862) and *The Perfidy of Captain Slyboots and Other Tales* (1863), both Shilling Library productions. The multitalented Sala was also the first editor of Ward and Lock's *Temple Bar*, whose first number, for December 1860, sold thirty thousand copies. Another magazine, the *Family Friend*, acquired in 1855, was sold in 1861. Its contributors included Mary Howitt and Mrs. S. C. Hall.

The 1860s were a memorable decade in the history of English book illustration and binding, and Ward and Lock played a major role in both developments. The firm's *Holy Bible* (1861) was a lavish production, with a strong relief leather binding and brass edging and clasp, the whole designed by Owen Jones. *Beauties of Poetry and Art* (1865) contained color plates by Edmund Evans and had a binding possibly based on a manuscript Passionale, bound in the seventeenth century and owned by the Duc d'Orleans. But more significant perhaps than these contributions to the history of design was Ward and Lock's short but remarkable association with the Dalziel brothers, pioneers of the full-page wood engraving. In 1863 the brothers entered into a contract with Ward and Lock to produce a new series of fully illustrated standard works under the editorship of H. W. Dulcken. Production costs were to be shared by the two parties to the agreement, who were to participate equally in the profits "if there were any." Only two titles appeared in the series. The first, an edition of *The Arabian Nights' Entertainments*, which came out in weekly parts of eight pages each, commenced in October 1864 and ended about two years later. The first eighteen parts carried illustrations by seven artists, including such eminent figures as John Millais, George

*First offices of Ward and Lock at 158 Fleet Street, London*

Pinwell, and John Tenniel. In the remaining eighty-six parts most of the drawings are by A. B. Houghton and Thomas Dalziel, both mediocre artists. Thus, as Percy Muir, a historian of book illustration, has observed: "subscribers were secured by the splashing of familiar names in the early numbers, the remainder of the work being turned over to artists who could be more economically employed. . . ." The second Dalziel production, an illustrated edition of the works of Oliver Goldsmith containing a hundred drawings by Pinwell (for which he received thirty shillings a drawing), also came out in parts. But the first number of *The Vicar of Wakefield* appeared in the same week and at the same price as a rival edition from Cassell, Petter and Galpin. There ensued recriminations from both sides, from which Cassell, Petter and Galpin emerged the victor. That firm's illustrated series of the classics continued to flourish, whereas the Dalziel brothers, despite the press plaudits heaped on them, received little public response and were forced to abandon their scheme.

At about the time the Dalziel series was getting under way, new articles of partnership were drawn up between Ward and Lock. The document shows that in 1864 the credit balance of the firm just exceeded £13,279, of which £9,792 was allotted to Lock and £3,487 to Ward. A year later Charles T. Tyler, about whom little is known, was admitted as a partner for a premium of £1,250 and a capital investment of £3,000. During his eight years as partner the house of Ward, Lock and Tyler developed significantly. The firm brought out editions of the works of American authors, such as James Russell Lowell, Oliver Wendell Holmes, and Artemus Ward (Charles Farrar Browne), all with introductions by Sala. There was also a series of "select illustrated three-and-sixpenny volumes ... especially adapted for young people," which contained such titles as *Fifty Famous Women* (1864), along with juvenile classics.

There was also an important acquisition, perhaps the most valuable so far. In 1866 the successful publisher Samuel Orchart Beeton, who the year before had lost his wife Isabella, editor of *The Book of Household Management* (1861), found himself a licensee in bankruptcy of Ward, Lock and Tyler through the collapse of the Gurney bank. Impressed by his record as a publisher, the firm took him on as an editor at four hundred pounds a year and granted him one sixth of the profits as part of a deal in which he assigned to his new employers all his liabilities as well as his assets. The latter included such profitable periodicals as the *Boy's Own Magazine*, the *Englishwoman's Domestic Magazine*, and the *Englishwoman*, and bestsellers such as *The Book of Household Management*, *The Dictionary of Universal Biography* (1863), and the "All About It" books.

All went well until in 1872 Beeton (who was by then receiving a quarter share of the profits) published in his *Christmas Annual* "The Coming K—," a parody of Alfred Tennyson's *Idylls of the King* that poked fun at the Prince of Wales's amours. A sequel in book form, *The Siliad* (1874), which went further by ridiculing the queen, caused a furor among royalists. Ward, Lock and Tyler, alarmed at the bad publicity Beeton's verse had engendered, suppressed a second edition of "The Coming K—" and vetoed his proposed *Christmas Annual* for 1874, which was to be called "Jon Duan." Undeterred, Beeton arranged with another publisher, Weldon, to bring out "Jon Duan" as the genuine *Beeton's Christmas Annual* for 1874. Ward, Lock and Tyler, meanwhile, was planning to publish as its *Christmas Annual* a story entitled "The Fijiad," claiming that it was the work of Beeton. Rival advertisements appeared in the *Athenaeum* for 21 November 1874, after

which Ward, Lock and Tyler obtained an injunction to restrain Beeton from issuing advertisements under his own name. Beeton contested the writ and lost. He had broken his contract, and thus his association with Ward, Lock and Tyler was terminated.

Meanwhile, with the acquisition in 1871 of Edward Moxon, Son and Company, the firm had extended its interests in another and quite lucrative direction. Moxon, who had died in 1858, had since 1830 been a leading publisher of poetry, having published works by Charles Lamb (who was a close friend), Samuel Taylor Coleridge, Robert Southey, William Wordsworth, Walter Savage Landor, Samuel Rogers, Thomas Hood, Percy Bysshe Shelley, Coventry Patmore, Tennyson, and Robert Browning. Moxon had also published Lamb's *Last Essays of Elia* (1833); Thomas Talfourd's edition of the *Letters* (1837) and *Final Memorials* (1848) of Lamb; T. J. Hogg's *Life of Shelley* (1858); and *Recollections of the Last Days of Shelley and Byron* (1858), by E. J. Trelawny. Leigh Hunt was another Moxon author. After Moxon's death his firm, by then a trust administered by Bertrand Payne, continued to publish poetry, bringing out Algernon Charles Swinburne's *Atalanta in Calydon* (1865), although Payne withdrew Swinburne's *Poems and Ballads* (1866) from circulation. Under the terms of the 1871 agreement Ward, Lock and Tyler bought the whole Moxon stock and all copyrights, offering to pay creditors fifteen shillings on the pound and giving Mrs. Moxon "a large sum" together with an annuity of £250 and an additional sum to the family after her death. The acquisition of Moxon was a brilliant coup that established the firm as one of the foremost publishers of both classic and contemporary English literature—worthy to stand beside the likes of Longman, Macmillan, and John Murray.

With the departure of Tyler in 1873 Ward, Lock and Tyler became Ward, Lock and Company. By this time the company had increased its staff as well as its stock, and during the 1870s there were premises at 107 Dorset Street, off Baker Street. Before long lack of space demanded that specially built headquarters be constructed. The site chosen was Salisbury Square, a sequestered spot off Fleet Street, and in September 1878 Warwick House, a multistoried triangular building which had cost fourteen thousand pounds, was ready. A year after the move to Warwick House two new partners were brought in. James Bowden had started his publishing career

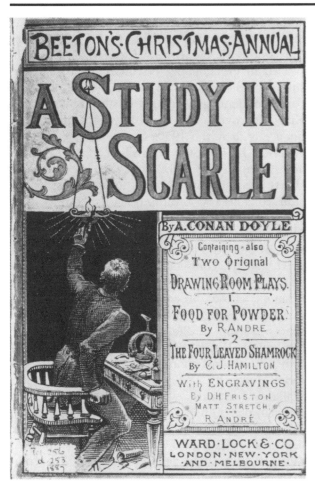

*Cover for the 1887 edition of* Beeton's Christmas Annual,
*containing the first Sherlock Holmes story*

with Beeton in 1865 and had followed his former employer to Amen Corner in 1869. Following Beeton's dismissal he had worked under Lock on the managerial and editorial side of the business, the financial side being supervised by Ward. The other new partner was George Lock's younger brother John, who had joined the firm as an assistant in 1861.

The purchase of William Tegg and Company in 1881 was another astute move. William Tegg's father, Thomas, the firm's founder, had gained notoriety and made a fortune out of cheap reprints of popular works, including William Hone's *Every-Day Book* (1826-1827) and *Table Book* (1860), whose stereotype plates he had acquired following the author's bankruptcy in 1828. William Tegg reprinted Hone's best-known works from these plates, properly repaired, in 1874, and thirteen years later their new owners tried them out—this time venturing on the original plan of publishing Hone's works in twenty-

seven monthly parts at sixpence each. In addition to the Hone plates and copyrights Ward, Lock and Company gained much "household" literature, "Peter Parley's" books for boys, and Clarke's Commentary, among other material. In 1882 a New York branch was opened. Two years later William Steele, a senior staff member, founded a branch in Melbourne, Australia. The 1880s also saw the installation of a book bindery on the top floor of Warwick House and the acquisition of the Botolph Printing Works. In 1885 six hundred titles were added to the company's list with the purchase of the Select Library of Fiction from W. H. Smith and Son. By the end of the decade Ward, Lock and Company was looked upon as a major force in the cheap-literature market.

A memorable chapter in the history of the company occurred in 1886. In September Arthur Conan Doyle sent his first Sherlock Holmes story, "A Study in Scarlet," to Warwick House; it had been rejected by three other publishers. Among the first to read it was the chief editor, Professor G. T. Bettany, who passed it on to his wife. The story was accepted on certain conditions: it would be held over for a year and full copyright would have to be sold to the publisher. Conan Doyle's request for a percentage of sales was flatly refused, and he ended up with a mere twenty-five pounds for the copyright. The tale eventually appeared in *Beeton's Christmas Annual* for 1887, which was published in November and was sold out before Christmas. Soon afterward the work was brought out in book form with new type, illustrations, and layout. Ward, Lock and Company made the most of its copyright, republishing the story in a variety of forms, mainly in very cheap editions. Conan Doyle never forgave the company for its meanness, for which James Bowden, who was then in charge of most of the magazines and annuals, must bear chief responsibility. The firm was never offered another work by Conan Doyle (although it did handle the Spanish translations of his works).

George Lock died in 1891. Ward had virtually retired in 1883, though he continued to take an interest in the firm until 1893; he died in 1902. After Lock's death the company was managed for two years by James Bowden and John Lock under the title of Ward, Lock, Bowden and Company. In 1893 it was converted into a limited company with the title of Ward, Lock and Bowden Limited. Bowden was managing director, and the board consisted of members of the Lock family—none of Ward's children wanted to join the business. Chairman of the board was George Lock, Jr., known for some reason as "Ernest," who had learned much during his three years with W. H. Smith and Son followed by thirteen years in the firm he now headed, including a considerable time as a sales representative. His aim, he later told an interviewer, was wholesomeness in publishing. Decadence in any form was anathema to him. "Ernest" was concerned with literature; the financial side of the business was the province of his uncle, John Lock, who was assisted by the first George Lock's second son, Robert Douglas Lock. Another son, Leslie Lock, entered the firm in the 1890s.

The last decade of the nineteenth century saw a rapid expansion of the company's diverse interests. The New York branch was quite active, and in Britain, Ward, Lock and Bowden Limited became the publisher of the English editions of American magazines such as *Lippincott's* and *Atlantic Monthly*. In Australia the Melbourne branch was distributing books across the antipodes and was encouraging native writers such as Ethel Turner and Mary Grant Bruce. A branch was also opened in Toronto. In 1894 the company's catalogue came to 170 pages. Warwick House was extended and a new warehouse built onto it. By this time the popular novels of Joseph Hocking and Guy Boothby were appearing, and G. T. Bettany's Minerva Library offered classic texts such as Johann Wolfgang von Goethe's *Faust* (1886), Charles Darwin's *Voyage in the Beagle* (1889), and Edgar Allan Poe's *Tales* (1890) as part of a thirty-eight-volume series that, at two shillings a volume, represented exceptional value.

Early in the 1890s the house was publishing twelve magazines and serials monthly. Most of the serials were of the "popular education" type and included *Universal Instructor* (1880-1884), *Illustrated History of the World* (1882-1884), and George B. Smith's *History of the English Parliament* (1894). Of the magazines the *Windsor Magazine: An Illustrated Monthly for Men and Women* broke important new ground. Launched in January 1895, it was primarily intended to entertain a new breed of middle-class reader. It was lighthearted, determinedly antiintellectual, proroyal, patriotic though not jingoistic, and above all, wholesome. It brought to the public works by Marie Corelli, Max Pemberton, Sabine Baring-Gould, Hall Caine, Rider Haggard, Bret Harte, William Dean Howells, Jack London, and Rudyard Kipling; later, Dornford Yates and Edgar Wallace wrote for it. Its first two editors were D. Williamson and A. Hutchinson, and it continued to appear until 1939. Another product of the 1890s were the Guides to the British Isles, which first appeared in green paper boards in 1896. The result of considerable field research by an army of correspondents and editors, this celebrated series aimed to cover every tourist spot of any consequence and by the 1950s had progressed to 136 volumes. In 1900 the acquisition of A. D. Innes and Company brought books on a variety of sports into the company's list together with historical romances by Anthony Hope and Stanley Weyman and the regional fiction of Eden Phillpotts.

In 1897 the long-serving James Bowden retired, and the company became Ward, Lock and Company Limited. It was by this time a family business whose directors were all members of the Lock family, which also controlled all the shares. As one of the country's leading publishing houses, Ward Lock began to steer a middlebrow course. In fiction it published in book form Rider Haggard's *Ayesha* (1905) and bought Edgar Wallace's *The Council of Justice* (1908) on a 15 percent royalty. Other Wallace stories followed. In children's literature the Wonder Book series, begun in 1905 with *The Wonder Book of Animals*, was a long-running popular success. The company suffered two major setbacks with the deaths of John Lock in 1904 and "Ernest" Lock two years later, but worse was to come. On 30 August 1911 Warwick House was destroyed by fire and much valuable stock lost. The new headquarters, completed in a little over a year, was considerably larger and had five stories. Following the death of Douglas Lock in 1926 the company was run by Wilfred and Leslie Lock for more than twenty-five years. Books on cookery (based on the Beeton model) and gardening were outstanding in this period, and new authors in the crime and detection field included Leslie Charteris. The early part of the century also brought a great expansion in the activities of the company's Commonwealth branches, particularly in Australasia. In 1940 the Luftwaffe bombed Warwick House, destroying the company's entire collection of file copies of its works extending back to the 1850s. Wilfred Lock died in 1945, his brother Leslie in 1952. From 1946 to 1954 Ward Lock operated from 6 Chancery Lane. Today it is based at 82 Gower Street. In 1964 the firm split in two with the establishment of the Ward Lock Educational Company Limited. The present Ward Lock Limited boasts a P. Lock as managing director. In

1989 it was acquired by Cassell plc. Although its list is still wide-ranging, it does not include either fiction or poetry.

**References:**

Richard Lancelyn Green and John Michael Gibson, *A Bibliography of A. Conan Doyle* (Oxford: Clarendon Press, 1983), pp. 10-11, 582-585;

Edward Liveing, *Adventure in Publishing: The House of Ward Lock, 1854-1954* (London: Ward, Lock, 1954);

Harold G. Merriam, *Edward Moxon, Publisher of Poets* (New York: Columbia University Press, 1939), pp. 194, 195;

Percival Muir, *Victorian Illustrated Books* (London: Batsford, 1971), pp. 17, 139-141, 160, 191, 229, 260;

Marion H. Spielmann, *The History of Punch* (London: Cassell, 1895; reprinted, New York: Greenwood Press, 1969), pp. 35, 154-156, 231, 238, 265, 306;

Ralph Straus, *Sala—The Portrait of an Eminent Victorian* (London: Constable, 1942), pp. 154-158, 168, 207.

—*R. M. Healey*

# Frederick Warne and Company
## *(London: 1865-1919)*
# Frederick Warne and Company, Limited
## *(London: 1919-  )*

See also the Frederick Warne and Company entry in *DLB 49: American Literary Publishing Houses, 1638-1899.*

Born in 1825, at age fourteen Frederick Warne joined his older brother William Henry Warne in working for the bookseller George Routledge. As Routledge expanded from bookselling into publishing, William (in 1848) and then Frederick (in 1851) became partners in the firm, which was renamed Routledge and Company in 1851 and Routledge, Warne and Routledge in 1858. When William died in 1859, Frederick continued as a partner with Routledge, Warne and Routledge. In 1865 Warne and his partners decided to dissolve their publishing house to form two independent firms—George Routledge and Sons and Frederick Warne and Company—and to divide the holdings between them. Frederick Warne and Company started business on 1 July 1865 at 15 Bedford Street, Covent Garden.

Warne was a family-run publishing house; Frederick Warne's three surviving sons—Harold, Fruing, and Norman—entered the business at the completion of their schooling. The company's device, a wing and horseshoe motif, is believed to have been based on the coat of arms of a branch of the Warne family.

An announcement of *Arabian Nights' Entertainment* in Warne's *Monthly List* for September 1865 reveals the firm's targeted audience and phi-

losophy of book selection: "Without the least destroying the imagery of any of the stories, or omit-
ting any of the tales or incidents, the Editor has
been able to expurgate entirely the parts that parents consider objectionable for their children to
read, and also to explain in short notes the origin
and peculiarities of most of the Oriental customs
and habits." Catering to the taste of the Victorian
family, the addition of the "short notes" made
works such as *Arabian Nights' Entertainment* educational; the "expurgation" of the "objectionable"
parts made them morally sound. Until his retirement in 1894 Frederick Warne sustained the
firm's policy of offering wholesome entertainment at popular prices: while the Crown Library
series at two shillings contained more than 60 volumes, the Notable Novels series at only sixpence
contained more than 150 volumes.

The period 1865 to 1894, and particularly
the 1880s, was a time of expansion for the firm.
Warne became British agents for *Scribner's Magazine* and the *Century Magazine*. In 1881 P. C.
Leadbeater accompanied Frederick Warne to
New York to open a branch office. The American branch focused primarily on children's
books; the British firm published dictionaries;
semireligious novels; and several literature series,
such as Warne's Star series and the Chandos Classic series. The Popular Tracts for Working and
Cottage Homes was a series of self-improvement
books; it suggests the didactic and instructional
tone of many of the firm's early publications.
Warne also developed an important specialization
in illustrated works of natural history. Noteworthy among the early titles are *Flowering Plants*
(1891), in four volumes, edited by Anne Pratt
and revised by Edward Step, and *The Royal Natural History* (1894-1896), in six volumes, edited by
Richard Lydekker, illustrated with seventy-two
color plates and more than sixteen hundred
wood engravings. The Lydekker work still com-
mands attention, in large part because of the
high quality of the illustrations.

In this period the firm also earned its reputation as a leading publisher of children's books.
Quickly expanding this part of the catalogue in response to the growing market, Warne launched
several popular series of books for children, including Warne's Large Picture Toy Books and
Aunt Louisa's Toy Books (named after Frederick
Warne's wife, Louisa Jane Fruing Warne). The
firm also published books by leading children's authors and illustrators, including Walter Crane,
Kate Greenaway, and Randolph Caldecott. Freder-

*Frederick Warne*

ick Warne and Company, like other children's
book publishers, was particularly interested in effective color printing and benefited from its association with Edmund Evans, an engraver noted for
improving color reproduction and the quality of illustration in general. Evans printed Crane's,
Caldecott's, and Greenaway's work for both Routledge and Warne.

Trained as an engraver, Crane produced a series of sixpenny toy books for Warne. His style
was more decorative than that of Caldecott,
whose work proved more popular. Beginning
with William Cowper's *John Gilpin's Ride* (1878),
Caldecott illustrated sixteen successful picture
books. Caldecott typically alternated between
lively brown ink drawings and color illustrations
of a lighter-toned palette than the brighter colors
of Crane. Whereas Crane tended to fill the entire page with decoration, Caldecott introduced
space into his designs. Greenaway, like Caldecott, was praised for delicate line drawings and
sparse backgrounds, but her colors were more
vivid than Caldecott's and closer to Crane's.

Greenaway's pictures influenced Victorian children's fashion. Warne gained distinction in children's literature because these works demonstrated an innovative interdependence of text and illustration.

Following Frederick Warne's retirement in 1894, the oldest son, Harold, took charge of the financial side of the business while the second oldest, Fruing, and the youngest, Norman, concentrated on book production. The talented children's illustrator Leslie Brooke began his association with Frederick Warne and Company in 1895, when he suggested that the firm publish an illustrated book of nursery rhymes. Edited by Andrew Lang, *The Nursery Rhyme Book* (1897) included black-and-white illustrations by Brooke and quickly established his professional reputation. Best known for his Johnny Crow series, initiated with *Johnny Crow's Garden* in 1903, Brooke's work was published exclusively by Warne until 1935, when he concluded the series. His work, blending a humorous narrative with lively pen-and-ink illustrations, reveals Brooke's understanding of animal character and anatomy. Warne also turned to Brooke to illustrate Edward Lear's *The Pelican Chorus* (1900) and *Jumbles and Other Nonsense* (1900). Brooke's acclaimed *Golden Goose Book* (1905) demonstrated his ability to blend creatively the natural and human worlds while still respecting animal anatomy.

The association of Frederick Warne and Company with Beatrix Potter had an unusual start. Warne was one of at least six publishers that politely declined the first version of *The Tale of Peter Rabbit*, based on a picture-letter of a playfully disobedient rabbit written to the ailing son of Potter's former governess. Potter used her own financial resources to have the book published privately in 1901. Reconsidering the book, Warne consulted with Brooke, who encouraged the brothers to publish it. Warne accepted the work conditionally and cautioned, "Of course we cannot tell whether the work is likely to run a second edition or not"; no doubt to its surprise, the company received orders for the entire first printing before actual publication on 2 October 1902.

Norman Warne's pointed suggestions and keen editorial eye turned the 1902 *Tale of Peter Rabbit* into a book that brings the author/illustrator fame today. Warne recommended that Potter trim her text and illustrations from the 1901 version. He marked with an *E* drawings and passages for possible excision, although the publisher left the decisions up to Potter. Warne also

advised Potter to color the illustrations throughout. Potter had originally chosen not to color the pictures, partly owing to the expense but mainly because she presumed "rabbit brown and green" to be "uninteresting" colors. In comparison with the black-and-white illustrations for the 1901 version, the color illustrations produced by Evans in 1902 with shades of greens, browns, and reds engage the reader. Moreover, Warne's criticism of her human figures, such as Mr. and Mrs. McGregor in *The Tale of Peter Rabbit*, ultimately nudged her in the direction of drawing animals, an area in which she excelled. Her only work after *The Tale of Peter Rabbit* featuring a human character, *The Tailor of Gloucester* (1902), was started before her association with the firm. The success of *The Tale of Peter Rabbit* led to a series of twenty-three picture books, concluding with *The Tale of Little Pig Robinson* in 1930.

Consistent with the policies established by Frederick Warne, the books were reasonably priced. At Potter's insistence, they were also small enough to fit into a child's hand; this notable innovation in marketing became associated with the firm. The series also gained distinction through the pictorial endpapers designed by Potter. With each new book, the hero or heroine of that tale appeared in the endpaper design alongside other familiar characters.

Potter's correspondence with the firm came to be handled almost exclusively by Norman Warne, and a romantic interest seems to have developed through the lengthy discussions of her work. Corresponding almost daily between the years 1902 and 1905, Warne and Potter discussed every aspect of her narratives and illustrations. The second version of *The Tailor of Gloucester*, under the Warne imprint, was better received than the first version, which, like *The Tale of Peter Rabbit*, she had initially printed privately. That success persuaded Potter to follow Warne's advice to rely on her own writing for her subsequent narratives rather than use popular rhymes and riddles.

Norman Warne was most actively involved in Potter's fifth book for the firm, *The Tale of Two Bad Mice* (1904). He sent her dollhouse food for the drawings of the mice raiding the dollhouse and photographed his niece's dollhouse because Potter's parents forbade her to travel to see it herself. Potter's biographer Margaret Lane has aptly called *The Tale of Two Bad Mice* "a collaboration between Norman and herself." They were engaged in 1905; one month later, Warne died suddenly.

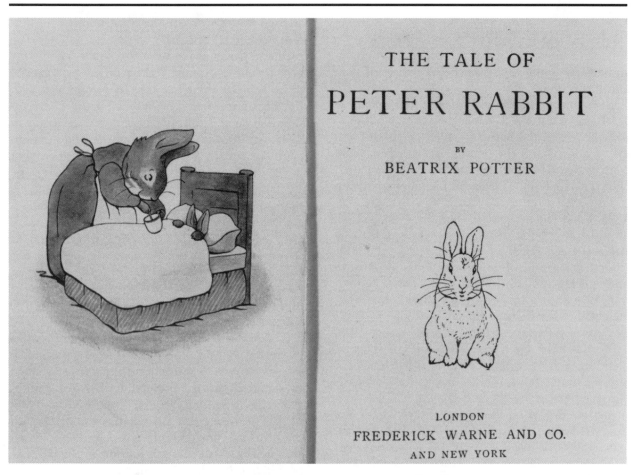

*Frontispiece and title page, illustrated by Potter, for the first of the Peter Rabbit books*

Potter continued her association with Frederick Warne and Company long after Norman Warne's death. Retreating to the Lake District, she wrote prolifically and added titles to the series yearly through 1913. The lake and woodland surroundings inspired many of her best tales under the Warne imprint, such as *The Tale of Jeremy Fisher* (1906), *The Tale of Tom Kitten* (1907), and *The Tale of Jemima Puddle-duck* (1908). Her illustrations followed Crane, Caldecott, and Greenaway in carefully integrating word and picture. Drawing from life, Potter, like Brooke, demonstrated in-depth knowledge of animal anatomy and behavior. She blended her years of scientific study of plant and animal life with a fanciful quality also found in Caldecott's drawings of animals in clothes. Her whimsical illustrations of the hedgehog in *The Tale of Mrs. Tiggy-Winkle* (1905) and the frog in *The Tale of Jeremy Fisher* reveal Potter's unusual ability to realize the charms of animal behavior.

Warne's juvenile section in the period 1895 to 1918 also included works of lesser known children's authors. The Reward Books series of adventure and school stories were decorated with vignetted blocking and gilt lettering on the binding cases. W. J. Gordon's lavishly illustrated *Our Home Railways* (1910) is still considered a classic of railway literature.

Prior to World War I, Warne regularly published standard literary anthologies for adult readers, as well as the works of Lord Byron, John Milton, Henry Wadsworth Longfellow, and William Shakespeare offered in a range of bindings. For example, the Landsdowne Pocket Edition entitled *Shakespeare* (1913) was available in four gilt bindings with casings ranging from simple half-white cloth to full calf-lined. The onset of the war, however, limited the elaborate styles and the variety of casings Warne could offer.

The reader and editor of Warne's Wayside and Woodland series was the well-known author and naturalist Edward Step. Step's own contributions, such as *Wayside and Woodland Blossoms* (1896), offered comprehensive discussions of nature subjects for the general reader, accompanied by his own photographs and drawings by his daughter, Mabel. Later additions to the series included Richard South's *Moths of the British Isles* (1908) and T. A. Coward's *Birds of the British Isles* (1920).

Still a small, private, family partnership in Edwardian times, the firm increased its efforts to sell books internationally. Frederick Warne Stephens, the founder's grandson, became the company's overseas representative. He visited Australia, New Zealand, and South Africa annually, the Far East and India occasionally. The staff during this period numbered forty-five to fifty, with only a few women. The firm maintained a personal, friendly atmosphere and a loyal staff, many of whom rejoined the firm after serving in World War I.

As a result of the war, rising production costs, and the uncertainty of the times, the firm had to modify some of its standards, notably its long commitment to low prices. In 1916 Harold Warne wrote to Potter to request her permission to raise the price of her books from one shilling to one shilling, threepence.

On 27 April 1917 Harold Warne was sentenced to eighteen months imprisonment for twenty thousand pounds in forgeries. He had redirected funds from the publishing house to support a separate enterprise, the Warne family fishing business in Jersey, which his mother had bequeathed to him. Harold, then fifty-six, never returned to the publishing business. Fruing Warne worked to reconstitute the publishing firm, which was fast approaching bankruptcy. He sold personal possessions, including his house, to stop the company's debtors from foreclosing. He also enlisted the aid of Potter, who had virtually stopped writing following her marriage to William Heelis in 1913. Although because of Harold Warne's mismanagement of funds she had not received any royalty payment for a lengthy period, at Fruing's request Potter agreed to continue her involvement while the company was being restructured. Warne went on to publish Potter's *Apply Dappley's Nursery Rhymes* (1917), a project Potter had initiated in consultation with Norman Warne in 1902 but had abandoned; *Tom Kitten's Painting Book* (1917), modeled after the format of *Peter Rabbit's Painting Book* (1911); and *The Tale of Johnny Town-Mouse* (1918).

The reconstituted company—Frederick Warne and Company, Limited—was registered on 25 May 1919. After nearly fifty-five years of operation, the family-run partnership was trans-

formed into an independent limited company maintaining family involvement yet operated by a board of directors. In 1920 Harry Wingfield was appointed chairman, and Fruing Warne was made managing director. Frederick Warne Stephens was appointed to the board in November 1923. The New York branch was incorporated as a separate company on 4 June 1920.

The great social unrest of the interwar years, climaxing in the General Strike of 1926, depressed the cash flow and dividends of the company. In the mid 1920s the warehouse staff went on strike; only a few of the warehousemen were retained when the strike was finally settled. In the 1920s the firm was also compelled to equip salesmen with automobiles to improve its competitiveness in the market.

Under Fruing Warne and Arthur L. Stephens, who succeeded him as managing director in June 1928, the catalogue retained a back list of old favorites and general publications, such as dictionaries and cookbooks. The company published a fine-arts series of English translations of monographs on famous Italian painters, such as Adolfo Venturi's *Michelangelo* (1928), translated by J. Redfern. It also produced many topographical books, such as W. G. Collingwood's *The Lake Counties* (1932), illustrated by A. Reginald Smith. The Wayside and Woodland series offered Edward Step's *Animal Life of the British Isles* (1921) and *Life of the Wayside and Woodland* (1922). T. A. Coward's three-volume *Birds of the British Isles and Their Nest Eggs* (1919-1926) was a useful reference work. Under Stephens's management, the company added many titles to the natural history section, such as the ambitious and generously illustrated *Standard Natural History* (1931), edited by W. P. Pycraft. During the mid 1930s the company introduced the Wayside Pocket Guides, one-volume abridgments of books in the Wayside and Woodland series. It launched the Observer's Pocket series in 1937, beginning with *The Observer's Book of British Birds*, compiled by S. Vere Benson, and *The Observer's Book of British Wild Flowers*, compiled by W. J. Stokoe.

Joining the production department in 1923, Richard Billington helped Warne compete in the growing market of annuals, then called "bumper books," for boys, girls, and toddlers. Annuals produced in the 1920s and 1930s under Billington's supervision include Warne's Pleasure Books, Happy Books, and Topall Books. Typical of the period, these rather bulky publications contained short stories, poems, anecdotes, and articles; boasting ample illustrations and bright covers to attract young readers, they sold for one shilling, sixpence to two shillings, sixpence. The 1930s also added to the juvenile section Potter's *The Tale of Little Pig Robinson* and Brooke's *Johnny Crow's New Garden* (1935), each work completing long-enduring series.

World War II severely affected the company just as it was beginning to expand under Stephens's management. Many members of the staff left the company to serve in the war. The scarcity of paper and printing plates affected Warne as it did other publishers of the period; a quota system during and just after the war ensured equal distribution of supplies among publishing firms. Warne's sheet stock was destroyed in an air raid on 29 December 1940; subsequently, an air raid shelter was constructed in the firm's basement.

Stephens retired as managing director in 1945 and was succeeded by Billington. Under Billington's management there were many changes in the staff and a steady increase in female employment. In September 1945 Warne acquired a small printing business, the Eden Press. In 1951 the firm purchased a small bindery, the Newdigate Press, in the village of Dorking, Surrey. Like Eden Press, Newdigate Press provided services for other firms in addition to its parent company, Warne. In 1956 new machinery was installed and a new warehouse built in Dorking; in 1958 the factory was enlarged and a second warehouse was completed. Following Billington's death in 1960, Cyril W. Stephens became managing director.

In the 1950s and 1960s Billington and then Stephens expanded the popular Observer's Pocket series into such subjects as music, ships, furniture, art, and architecture. Notable additions to the Wayside and Woodland series included John Clegg's *Freshwater Life of the British Isles* (1952), E. F. Linssen's *Beetles of the British Isles* (1959), and W. P. K. Findlay's *Wayside and Woodland Fungi* (1967). Findlay's work is illustrated with fifty-nine of Potter's watercolor studies of fungi, work she had completed prior to her career as a book illustrator. Many of the earlier titles, such as Step's *Life of the Wayside and Woodland*, were also revised and republished in the postwar period.

Aware that its financial and technical resources prohibited its venturing into cheaper, mass-produced picture books, Warne strove to maintain quality production of interesting stories and ideas. Thus, the children's book section in

the postwar years expanded to include the Jane Tompkins McConnell series of animal books, such as *The Black Bear Twins* (1954), and two series intended for very young children: the Prettimouse series and the Teddy Bear Coleman series. The company published several children's books illustrated by two skillful animal artists, K. Nixon and Inga Borg. Since Potter had bequeathed the copyrights to Frederick Warne and Company on her death in 1943, the firm continued to profit from her books. In 1952 it published an English edition of Potter's *The Fairy Caravan*, one of her few later works originally published not by Warne but by the Philadelphia firm of David McKay. Warne also published several of Potter's manuscripts posthumously, such as *The Tale of the Faithful Dove* (1955). Responding to a trend in the 1960s for instructional and informational as opposed to purely fictional books for children, Warne published I. O. Evans's *Inventors of the World* (1962) and Mary Cathcart Borer's *Women Who Made History* (1963).

Cyril Stephens managed the company until his death in 1981. David W. Bisacre became managing director and remained so during Warne's acquisition by Penguin Books in August 1983; he retired in February 1984, shortly before Warne was officially absorbed by Penguin. The last family member of the company, J. Barry Stephens, Cyril Stephens's son, left the firm in March 1984. Today Frederick Warne has neither a Warne nor a Stephens working for the company.

Frederick Warne and Company devoted a section of its catalogue to works on the life and art of Beatrix Potter following her death in 1943; Penguin Books has continued this division. In 1946 Warne published Margaret Lane's seminal biography *The Tale of Beatrix Potter*, which Lane revised in 1968, as well as her *The Magic Years of Beatrix Potter* (1978). In 1955 Leslie Linder's *The Art of Beatrix Potter* traced her development as a naturalist during the 1880s and 1890s and followed her career as a book illustrator; the book was revised in 1972. Warne also published Linder's *The Journal of Beatrix Potter* (1966), which was revised in 1989, and *A History of the Writings of Beatrix Potter* (1971). Other Warne books on Potter include the catalogue *Beatrix Potter: The V and A Collection* (1985), by Anne Stevenson Hobbs and Joyce Irene Whalley in cooperation with the Victoria and Albert Museum; *Beatrix Potter: Artist, Storyteller, and Countrywoman* (1986), by Judy Taylor; *Beatrix Potter: The Artist and Her World* (1987), by Taylor, Whalley, Hobbs, and Elizabeth M.

Battrick; *Beatrix Potter's Letters* (1989), edited by Taylor; and *Beatrix Potter's Art* (1990), by Hobbs. Warne published new editions of Potter's tales in 1987 using electronic scanning methods to create new transparencies of Potter's original watercolor illustrations.

## References:

Henry Brooke, *Leslie Brooke and Johnny Crow* (London: Warne, 1982);

"Frederick Warne [obituary]," *Times* (London), 15 November 1901, p. 4;

Arthur King and A. F. Stuart, *The House of Warne* (London: Warne, 1965);

Margaret Lane, *The Tale of Beatrix Potter*, revised edition (London: Warne, 1968);

Bob Sherman, "S. Pearson and Son [Penguin] to Buy Frederick Warne," *Publishers Weekly*, 224 (29 July 1983): 18;

Judy Taylor, *Beatrix Potter: Artist, Storyteller, and Countrywoman* (London: Warne, 1986), pp. 136-142;

"£20,000 Bill Forgeries," *Times* (London), 27 April 1917, p. 3.

*—Catherine Golden*

# Checklist for Further Reading

Ball, Douglas. *Victorian Publishers' Bindings*. London: Library Association, 1985.

Barnes, James J. *Authors, Publishers and Politicians: The Quest for an Anglo-American Copyright Agreement, 1815-1854*. London: Routledge & Kegan Paul, 1974.

Barnes. *Free Trade in Books: A Study of the London Book Trade since 1800*. Oxford: Clarendon Press, 1964.

Boase, F. *Modern English Biography*, 6 volumes and supplement. Truro, U.K.: Netherton & Worth, 1892-1921; reprinted, (London: Cass, 1965.

*Book Trade History Group Newsletter*, 1- (February 1986- ).

*Bookseller*, 1- (1858- ).

Briggs, Asa, ed. *Essays in the History of Publishing: In Celebration of the 250th Anniversary of the House of Longman 1724-1974*. London: Longman, 1974.

*British Book News*, 1- (March 1940- ).

Brown, Philip A. H. *London Publishers and Printers, c. 1800-1870*. London: British Library, 1961.

*Cassell's Directory of Publishing*. London: Cassell and the Publishers Association, 1960- ).

Cave, Roderick. *The Private Press*. London: Faber & Faber, 1971.

Clair, Colin. *A Chronology of Printing*. London: Cassell, 1969.

Clair. *A History of Printing in Britain*. London: Cassell, 1965.

Cross, Nigel. *The Common Writer: Life in Nineteenth-Century Grub Street*. Cambridge & New York: Cambridge University Press, 1985.

Cruse, Amy. *After the Victorians*. London: Allen & Unwin, 1938.

Cruse. *The Englishman and His Books in the Early Nineteenth Century*. London: Harrap, 1930.

Cruse. *The Victorians and Their Books*. London: Allen & Unwin, 1935.

Curwen, Henry. *A History of Booksellers, the Old and the New*. London: Chatto & Windus, 1873.

Curwen, Peter J. *The UK Publishing Industry*. Oxford & New York: Pergamon Press, 1981.

Eliot, Simon. "The Three-Decker Novel and its First Cheap Reprint, 1862-94," *Library*, 7 (March 1985): 38-53.

Engen, Rodney. *Dictionary of Victorian Engravers, Print Publishers and their Works*. Cambridge: Chadwyck-Healey, 1979.

Feather, John. *A History of British Publishing*. London & New York: Croom Helm, 1988.

Feltes, N. N. *Modes of Production of Victorian Novels*. Chicago: University of Chicago Press, 1986.

Flower, Desmond. *A Century of Best-Sellers, 1830-1930*. London: National Book Council, 1934.

Franklin, Colin. *The Private Presses*. London: Studio Vista, 1969.

Goldstrom, J. M. "The Correspondence between Lord John Russell and the Publishing Trade," *Publishing History*, 20 (1986): 5-59.

Gross, John. *The Rise and Fall of the Man of Letters: Aspects of English Literary Life since 1800*. London: Weidenfeld & Nicolson, 1969.

Haas, Sabine. "Victorian Poetry Anthologies: Their Role and Success in the Nineteenth-Century Book Market," *Publishing History*, 17 (1985): 51-64.

Hall, R. M. S. "Railway Publishing," *Publishing History*, 22 (1987): 43-72.

James, Louis. *Fiction for the Working Man, 1830-1850: A Study of the Literature Produced for the Working Classes in Early Victorian England*. London & New York: Oxford University Press, 1963.

Kingsford, R. J. L. *The Publishers Association, 1896-1946*. Cambridge: Cambridge University Press, 1970.

Knight, Charles. *Old Printer and the Modern Press*. London: Murray, 1854.

Knight. *Shadows of the Old Booksellers*. London: Bell & Daldy, 1865.

Lane, Michael. *Books and Publishers: Commerce against Culture in Postwar Britain*. Lexington, Mass.: Lexington Books, 1980.

McLean, Ruari. *Victorian Publishers' Book-Binding in Paper*. London: Fraser, 1983.

Mumby, Frank A. *Publishing and Bookselling*, fifth edition, revised by Ian Norrie. London: Cape, 1974.

Myers, Robin. *The British Book Trade from Caxton to the Present Day: A Bibliographical Guide*. London: Deutsch, 1973.

Myers, and Michael Harris, eds. *Author/Publisher Relations during the Eighteenth and Nineteenth Centuries*. Oxford: Oxford Polytechnic Press, 1983.

Myers and Harris, eds. *Development of the English Book Trade, 1700-1899*. Oxford: Oxford Polytechnic Press, 1981.

Neuburg, V. E. *Popular Literature*. Harmondsworth, U.K. & New York: Penguin, 1977.

Norrie, Ian. *Mumby's Publishing and Bookselling in the Twentieth Century*, sixth edition. London: Bell & Hyman, 1982.

Nowell-Smith, Simon. *International Copyright Law and the Publisher in the Reign of Queen Victoria*. Oxford: Clarendon Press, 1965.

Patten, Robert. *Charles Dickens and His Publishers*. Oxford: Clarendon Press, 1978.

Plant, Marjorie. *The English Book Trade: An Economic History of the Making and Sale of Books*, third edition. London: Allen & Unwin, 1974.

*Publishers' Circular*, 1-   (1837-   ).

*Publishers Weekly*, 1-   (18 January 1872-   ).

*Publishing History*, 1-   (1977-   ).

*Publishing News*, 1-   (1989-   ).

Sadleir, Michael. *XIX Century Fiction: A Bibliographical Record Based on His Own Collection*, 2 volumes. London: Constable, 1951; Berkeley: University of California Press, 1951.

Schmidt, Barbara Quinn. "Novelists, Publishers, and Fiction in Middle-Class Magazines: 1860-1880," *Victorian Periodicals Review*, 17 (Winter 1984): 142-153.

Shattock, Joanne. "Publishers' Archives." In *Victorian Periodicals: A Guide to Research*, edited by J. Don Vann and Rosemary VanArsdel. New York: Modern Language Association of America, 1989, pp. 32-44.

Steele, Robert. *The Revival of Printing: A Bibliographical Catalogue*. London: Macmillan and Philip Lee Warner, for the Medici Society, 1912.

Sutherland, John. "The British Book Trade and the Crash of 1826," *Library*, sixth series 9 ( June 1987): 148-161.

Sutherland. *Fiction and the Fiction Industry*. London: Athlone Press, 1978.

Sutherland. *Victorian Novelists and Publishers*. London: Athlone Press, 1976.

Tinsley, William. *Random Recollections of an Old Publisher*, 2 volumes. London: Simpkin, Marshall, Hamilton, Kent, 1900.

Todd, W. B., comp. *A Directory of Printers and Others in Allied Trades London and Vicinity, 1800-1840*. London: Printing Historical Society, 1972.

Tomkinson, G. S. *A Select Bibliography of the Principal Modern Presses, Public and Private, in Great Britain and Ireland*. London: First Edition Club, 1928.

Unwin, Sir Stanley. *The Truth about Publishing*, eighth edition, revised by Philip Unwin. London: Allen & Unwin, 1976.

*Victorian Periodicals Newsletter*, 1-11 (1968-1978).

*Victorian Periodicals Review*, 1-   (1979-   ).

Vizetelly, Henry. *Glances Back through Seventy Years*, 2 volumes. London: Kegan Paul, Trench, Trübner, 1893.

Watson, George, ed. *New Cambridge Bibliography of English Literature*, 5 volumes. Cambridge: Cambridge University Press, 1969-1977.

Waugh, Arthur. *A Hundred Years of Publishing: Being the Story of Chapman & Hall, Ltd.* London: Chapman & Hall, 1930, chapters 8, 16, and 17.

*Whitaker's Books in Print*. London: Whitaker, 1965-   .

*Whitaker's Cumulative Book List*. London: Whitaker, 1924-   .

Wilson, John Forbes. *A Few Personal Recollections by an Old Printer*. London: Privately printed, 1896.

*Writer's Handbook*. London: Macmillan, 1902-   .

*Writers' and Artists' Handbook*. London: Black, 1906-   .

# Contributors

J. R. R. Adams.................................................*Ulster Folk and Transport Museum*
Josef L. Altholz.................................................*University of Minnesota*
Patricia J. Anderson.................................................*Simon Fraser University*
Elisabeth Sanders Arbuckle.................................................*University of Puerto Rico*
Crys Armbrust.................................................*Columbia, South Carolina*
James J. Barnes.................................................*Wabash College*
Patience P. Barnes.................................................*Wabash College*
Logan D. Browning, Jr..................................*University of North Carolina at Chapel Hill*
Marilyn D. Button.................................................*Newark, Delaware*
Julie F. Codell.................................................*University of Montana*
Dorothy W. Collin.................................................*University of Western Australia*
Dennis R. Dean.................................................*University of Wisconsin—Parkside*
Elizabeth J. Deis.................................................*Hampden-Sydney College*
Lauren Pringle De La Vars.................................................*Saint Bonaventure University*
Diana Dixon.................................................*Loughborough University of Technology*
John Dreyfus.................................................*London*
Barbara J. Dunlap.................................................*New York*
Robin Francis.................................................*Victoria and Albert Museum*
Lowell T. Frye.................................................*Hampden-Sydney College*
Michael Gill.................................................*Gill and Macmillan*
Catherine Golden.................................................*Skidmore College*
R. M. Healey.................................................*University of London*
Leslie Howsam.................................................*University of Toronto*
Anne Humpherys.................................................*New York*
Vincent Kinane.................................................*Trinity College Library, Dublin*
Marjory Lang.................................................*Vancouver Community College*
Jennifer B. Lee.................................................*Brown University*
David Linton.................................................*Kent, England*
Brian E. Maidment.................................................*Manchester Polytechnic*
Alistair McCleery.................................................*Napier Polytechnic*
Anita Hemphill McCormick.................................*University of California, Los Angeles*
Ruari McLean.................................................*Carsaig, Scotland*
Marilouise Michel.................................................*Clarion University of Pennsylvania*
David B. Mock.................................................*Edison Community College*
S. D. Mumm.................................................*University of Sussex*
Victor Neuburg.................................................*London*
Hans Ostrom.................................................*University of Puget Sound*
Ann Parry.................................................*Staffordshire Polytechnic*
Jonathan Rose.................................................*Drew University*
B. Q. Schmidt.................................*Southern Illinois University at Edwardsville*
Beverly Schneller.................................................*Millersville University at Pennsylvania*
Patricia Thomas Srebrnik.................................................*University of Calgary*
Peter Stockham.................................................*The Staffs Bookshop*
John Sutherland.................................................*California Institute of Technology*
John R. Turner.................................................*University College of Wales*
Rosemary T. VanArsdel.................................................*University of Puget Sound*

J. Don Vann................................................................................*Denton, Texas*
William T. Walker ...............................*Philadelphia College of Pharmacy and Science*
Roger P. Wallins..................................................................*University of Idaho*
Bernard Warrington .......................................................*University of Manchester*
Joel H. Wiener .................................................................*City College of New York*

# Cumulative Index

*Dictionary of Literary Biography,* Volumes 1-106
*Dictionary of Literary Biography Yearbook,* 1980-1990
*Dictionary of Literary Biography Documentary Series,* Volumes 1-8

# Cumulative Index

**DLB** before number: *Dictionary of Literary Biography,* Volumes 1-106
**Y** before number: *Dictionary of Literary Biography Yearbook,* 1980-1990
**DS** before number: *Dictionary of Literary Biography Documentary Series,* Volumes 1-8

## A

# B

# C

## E

# H

# N

# O

# Q

## T

# Y

## Z